THE BUSINESS GUIDE
TO
INDIA

D1510963

THE BUSINESS GUIDE TO
INDIA

Edited by
Jitendra Kohli

Butterworth-Heinemann Asia,
an imprint of Reed Academic Publishing Asia,
a division of Reed Elsevier (Singapore) Pte Ltd
1 Temasek Avenue
#17-01 Millenia Tower
Singapore 039192

ISBN 981-00-7078-0

Cover design by Fred Rose
Typeset by Linographic Services Pte Ltd (10/12pt New Century Schoolbook)
Printed in Singapore by IPC

This book is dedicated to the United Nations

The UN's role in propagating the process of global thinking and initiating the process of creating a world order is invaluable. It is therefore appropriate that a book such as this, which encourages and facilitates interaction amongst nations, be dedicated to this august world body, the UNITED NATIONS.

Jitendra Kohli

ACKNOWLEDGEMENTS

My sincere thanks to the publishers and to all those whose dedication and support have enabled the production of *The Business Guide to India*. I wish to acknowledge especially:

Mr Guy Ducrey, Ambassador Extraordinary and Plenipotentiary, Embassy of Switzerland, New Delhi; Sir Iain Vallance, Chairman, British Telecom, London; Mr Peter L Lockton, CBE, Managing Director, Rolls Royce India Ltd, New Delhi; Mr Suresh Rajpal, President, Hewlett-Packard India Ltd, and Chairman, American Business Council, New Delhi; Mr Denis Ryan, Managing Director, Esso Asia Pacific (Petroleum) Pte Ltd, Bombay, for very kindly agreeing to review the proofs of the *The Business Guide to India* and for their most valuable comments and feedback.

Mr Graham Brown, Managing Director, Apple Computer International Ltd, for encouraging me to accept the responsibility as General Editor of this book.

Mr R Mehta, IAS (retd), Director, J Kohli Consulting, for reviewing and editing the two chapters of this book which have been written by me.

Ms Indira Kohli, Reader in Political Science, Maitreyi College (University of Delhi), for reviewing the chapter 'India—Land, People and System of Government' and for providing valuable input for the chapter.

The support staff of J Kohli Consulting for providing secretarial and logistical support for compiling the various chapters.

Ms Margaret Tresidder, Commissioning Editor, Reed Academic Publishing Asia, Singapore, for her excellent coordination and support at every stage of the project.

All the contributors who, despite their heavy official responsibilities and commitments, spent valuable time and energy in writing and compiling their respective chapters.

Jitendra Kohli
General Editor

PREFACE

India has always occupied pride of place on the world map—earlier as the cradle of an ancient civilisation which excelled in material, intellectual and spiritual pursuits and, in more recent history, as a nation which regained independence in 1947 and became the world's largest multi-party democracy.

In the last five decades, India's pre-eminence has been mostly for reasons other than economic ones: as a nation which showed the world the path of non-violence for regaining independence, as leader of the non-aligned nations, as a major military power with a strong tradition of international peace-keeping. In years to come India is set to demonstrate to the world how such a diverse nation, with a fully democratic political system, can set the stage for economic reforms without causing social turmoil and can achieve the status of a major economic power.

For over four decades after 1947, India created for itself partial economic isolation from the international business community. While, on one hand, the Indian Government's policy of self-reliance created a diverse industrial and technological infrastructure, and achieved self-sufficiency in food for its rapidly growing population, it also caused some lacunae in its development and international competitiveness due to the protective policies. One consequence of this was that during this period there was limited foreign investment allowed into the country and Indian corporate entities had limited interaction with their counterparts in other countries.

The regulatory environment has now undergone a sea change under the New Economic Policy launched in July 1991. As a consequence, an economic revolution has occurred in the country. Foreign investment is now not only welcome, it is a priority on the economic agenda of the Central Government, as well as most of the State governments.

Political stability and credibility are important for foreign investors. The recent general elections (the 11th since 1952), held in April and May 1996, brought to the world's attention two important points in this regard.

First, about 340 million adult voters (out of about 591.5 million eligible voters) exercised their franchise in around 768,000 polling stations. Approximately 14,000 candidates contested 543 parliamentary seats. Despite the previous ruling party, the Congress, losing at the hustings, and no clear mandate in favour of any other single party, there was a smooth transition of power, first from the Congress to the BJP, which emerged as the single largest party, and then from the BJP to the United Front, a coalition of 13 parties. The transition of power was in the highest democratic tradition. Such is the vibrant Indian democracy and the stability of its political system.

Secondly, before the polls there was a credibility question in the minds of many foreign investors as to what would be the fate of economic reforms in general and foreign investment in particular, if the Congress Government was not returned to power. The post-polls scenario has resolved this credibility question convincingly. On assuming power, the BJP Government announced its objective to double Foreign Direct Investment (FDI). The present United Front Government has announced its intention to increase FDI five times. Consistency with regard to economic reforms and foreign investment across the political spectrum is manifest. There are a few areas of foreign investment where there may be minor differences between political parties on some details of policy. However, such differences are natural in any healthy and functional multi-party democracy.

A gold-mine of opportunities has therefore been opened up for foreign investors—opportunities which no major international business organisation can afford to miss. The steady increase in response of foreign investors since mid-1991 confirms this view.

Non-availability of authentic and comprehensive information about India in a concise form has been an oft-heard complaint of foreign investors. This book endeavours to fulfil this need by presenting information from authoritative sources on a wide range of subjects relevant to foreign investors.

A distinctive feature of the book is that the chapters have been written by distinguished and authoritative contributors. The authors comprise top-ranking government officials who are directly involved in policy formulation and implementation, leading lights of the Indian corporate world and leading professionals who have dealt hands-on with problems faced by foreign investors in India. It should be noted that the views of the senior government officials in the various chapters are expressed in their personal capacities and should not be treated as official statements of policies and rules. However, with their experience and maturity, these government officials have provided appropriate information and valuable guidance in their respective fields.

The book will provide top management of foreign organisations with valuable information on an unmatched array of important topics. This should help them to formulate the right entry strategies for India and to avoid major mistakes which frequently occur during the initial phase of an organisation's functioning in a new country. Even those foreign investors who have already initiated their operations in India would find many of the chapters interesting and useful. Investors must, however, supplement the information provided here with further details and specific advice from appropriate sources before taking action and implementing their plans for India.

We will endeavour to enhance the quality and comprehensiveness of the information presented in the book after the valuable feedback we receive from readers.

We wish foreign investors a very happy and beneficial experience in India.

Jitendra Kohli
General Editor

19 August 1996
New Delhi

Feedback and suggestions may be mailed to:
  Mr J Kohli
  Director-in-Charge
  J Kohli Consulting (P) Ltd
  (Strategy, Management and Technology Consultants)
  6, Jain Mandir Road
  New Delhi 110 001, India
  Fax: +91 (11) 6856435

ABOUT THE GENERAL EDITOR

Mr Jitendra Kohli is the Director-in-Charge of J Kohli Consulting (P) Ltd, a Strategy, Management and Technology Consulting Group formed in 1992 and based at New Delhi.

Aged 42, Mr Kohli is an electrical engineer who graduated from the Indian Institute of Technology, Delhi, which is among the top technology institutes in India.

One of the key functions of the Consulting Group headed by Mr Kohli is to assist foreign investors in formulating, reviewing and implementing their entry strategies for India. The Group has rendered consulting assistance to some of the most reputable and internationally well-known multinationals in areas such as information technology, telecommunications, engineering, health care, education and training and banking. It also has expertise in infrastructure and public utilities.

Some of Mr Kohli's personal areas of expertise include:

* In depth analysis of government policy and dove-tailing it in the corporate strategy of individual business organisations.
* Team-structuring and work-culture development.
* Converting abstract concepts and dead-locked situations into action-oriented strategies.

His major assignments as a strategy consultant in India include those with Compaq Computer and Apple Computer.

Mr Kohli has professional experience working in senior management positions in corporate planning, marketing and other management functions of leading Indian organisations, and also as a management consultant.

It is his firm belief that, in the absence of a background of operational experience and responsibility, a consultant, however brilliant, lacks the practical touch in his strategy formulations. This belief is reflected in the choice of the other members of his team.

Mr Kohli was a member of the ASSOCHAM (Associated Chambers of Commerce and Industry) Working Group on Electronics and Telecommunications (1988–91). His article proposing a Prescription for Reforms and Deregulation of the Indian Telecommunications Sector was published in 1989.

His world-wide travels include business visits to the USA, Canada, the UK, Germany, Switzerland, Austria, Denmark, the former USSR, Australia, Indonesia and Singapore.

One of his personal interests is assisting people in personality analysis and behaviour-shaping using principles of stellar sciences.

Mr Kohli is a member of IEEE (Institute of Electrical and Electronics Engineers, Inc).

ABOUT THE CONTRIBUTORS

Prathipati Abraham, IAS, is currently Secretary, Ministry of Power, Government of India. During the last 34 years he has held a series of important positions in the Central Government, the State of Maharashtra, and the State of Andhra Pradesh. These include: Special Secretary, Ministry of Power; Special Secretary, Ministry of Defence; Chairman, Energy Department, Government of Maharashtra.

He is a postgraduate from Andhra University and was a UNIDO Fellow on Industrial Development.

P Chidambaram is the Union Minister of Finance, Government of India. He was formerly Minister of State (Independent Charge) Ministry of Commerce in the Government headed by former Prime Minister P V Narasimha Rao. He obtained his MBA from Harvard University, USA. Prior to that he obtained his BSc degree from Presidency College, Madras, and an LLB from the Law College, Madras University.

Krishan Chugh was the Chairman of the ITC Group from November 1991 to January 1996. Mr Chugh is a Member, Court of Governors, Administrative Staff College of India, Hyderabad, a Member, Board of Governors, National Council of Applied Economic Research, New Delhi. He is a mechanical engineer from Delhi University.

The Confederation of Indian Industry (CII) is one of the top industry associations, with a direct membership of 3000 companies, whose total capital investment is over US$35 billion. CII has members from both the public and the private sectors. CII, with its 23 offices in India and eight overseas offices in Germany (Koln and Bremen), Kathmandu, London, Singapore, Tashkent, Washington DC and Zurich, is a reference point for Indian industry and the international business community.

On the international front, the Confederation has a working relationship and Memoranda of Understanding with counterpart organisations in 48 countries.

Susim Mukul Datta is Chairman of Hindustan Lever Ltd and the Unilever Group of Companies in India and Nepal. He is a Director of Philips India Ltd, Indian Aluminium Company Ltd, Ashok Leyland Ltd, Tata Mutual Fund, Credit Analysis & Research Ltd (IDBI), West Bengal Electronics Industry Development Corporation Ltd, and Infrastructure Leasing & Financial Services—Venture Corporation Ltd. He is Chairman of the Local Advisory Board of Barclays Bank Plc.

Mr Datta is the President, Associated Chambers of Commerce & Industry of India (ASSOCHAM), and President of the Council of EEC Chambers of Commerce in India. He has also headed various other trade and industry bodies in the past.

Actively associated with a number of Management and Research Institutes in India, he is a Member of the Board of Governors of the Indian Institutes of Management of Calcutta and Lucknow; Court of Governors, Administrative Staff College of India, Hyderabad.

Mr Datta is an MSc (Tech) and Chartered Engineer, Fellow of the Institution of Engineers, and of the Indian Institute of Chemical Engineers; Honorary Fellow of All India Management Association, Member of the Society of Chemical Industry, London and the Oil Technologists Association of India.

Devi Dayal, IAS, is currently Additional Secretary, Ministry of Petroleum and Natural Gas. He is widely travelled and has in-depth knowledge of the petroleum sector. He has contributed substantially in the framing of important government policies for the liberalisation and restructuring of the oil sector in general, and marketing of petroleum products in particular.

Dr Praveena Goel is Assistant Director General (Public Health) in the Directorate General of Health Services, Government of India.

Justice H R Khanna was appointed Chief Justice of Delhi High Court in 1969. In 1971 he was appointed Judge of the Supreme Court of India. During the Emergency in 1976 he gave the dissenting judgment in the famous *Habeas Corpus Case* which attracted world-wide attention. The *New York Times* in its editorial then wrote: 'If India ever finds its way back to freedom and democracy, that proud hallmark of its first 18 years, someone will surely erect a monument to Justice H R Khanna of the Supreme Court.'

From 1977 to 1979 he was Chairman, Law Commission of India. He was also for a short time in 1979 the Minister of Law, Justice & Company Affairs.

Tejendra Khanna, IAS, is currently Secretary to the Government of India in the Ministry of Commerce and is a member of the Foreign Investment Promotion Board (FIPB).

Mr Khanna had a brilliant academic record and has an MSc (Physics) from Patna University, India, and MA (Public Administration) from the University of California, Berkeley (USA).

Widely travelled, Mr Khanna has led India's delegations to a large number of multilateral conferences, as well as bilateral interactions with trading partners in the USA, Europe, Africa, East Asia and Latin America.

Dr A K Kundu is Deputy Director General (Planning) in the Directorate General of Health Services, Government of India. He is also the Chairman of SAARC Technical Committee on Population and Health Activities.

Nalin Miglani is Divisional Manager, Human Resources, of the India Tobacco Division of ITC Ltd. Mr Miglani is an Economics graduate from St Stephens College, Delhi, with a specialisation in Human Resource Management from XLRI, Jamshedpur.

Dr A K Mukherjee, who is currently with WHO, was Director-General of Health Services, Government of India, at the time of contributing his chapter. He is also the Secretary General of the Indian Red Cross Society and St Johns Ambulance Association. He holds a PhD from Oxford University, in addition to MS (Ortho) and MBBS. He has been a Berry Scholar at Oxford University, Johnson-Johnson Fellow, Fellow of the British Orthopaedic Association, Fellow of the National Academy of Medical Sciences and was awarded the N G Dewan Memorial Award for Services to Rehabilitation. He has 19 years' clinical experience in various capacities in hospitals in India and the UK, as well as 19 years of teaching students in orthopaedic surgery.

A D Narain is Director-General (Road Development), Ministry of Surface Transport. He is a graduate in Civil Engineering and has undergone postgraduate training in traffic and transportation from the University of New South Wales, Australia. He has been actively associated with the highway sector for the last 32 years. Mr Narain has varied national and international experience. He has served as an expert with the State Organisation of Roads & Bridges, Government of Iraq, and has represented India at numerous forums abroad for inviting private sector participation in highways in the country. He is Secretary of the Indian National Group of International Association for Bridge and Structural Engineering.

Ravinder Nath has been practising as a lawyer since 1967. He is a partner of M/s Rajinder Narain & Co, Solicitors and Advocates on Record in the Supreme Court of India.

Mr Nath holds BCom (Hons) and LLB degrees. He has studied international and comparative laws in London and at Harvard, and is a Member of the International Bar Association, the Asia Pacific Bar Association and other professional bodies.

D H Pai Panandiker is on the Board of the Reserve Bank of India (Northern Region) and also on the Board of a number of other companies. He was formerly the Secretary General of the Federation of Indian Chambers of Commerce & Industry (FICCI) for 12 years until 1992. He is presently the Director-General, RPG Foundation, an organisation involved in economic research. Mr Panandiker has to his credit three publications viz, *Interest Rate and Flow of Funds, Anatomy of Inflation* and *Controls and Over-controls*. He contributes a column regularly to premier Indian dailies, the *Hindustan Times* and the *Asian Age*.

He took his MCom degree from the University of Poona, and his Tripos in Economics from the University of Cambridge, UK.

Dr Vishvanath A Pai Panandiker has an MA, LLB from Bombay University, and a PhD from the University of Michigan, USA.

He has been Director of the Centre for Policy Research, New Delhi, since its inception in 1973. He was Director, Planning Commission, and Special Assistant to the Chairman, Administrative Reforms Commission of India, and later Special Adviser on Nationalisation of Banks to India's Deputy Prime Minister Morarji Desai. He is Chairman of Marpol Pvt Ltd and on the Boards of a large number of private corporations, universities and institutions.

R K Pandey has an MCom followed by an LLB degree. Before joining the Delhi Stock Exchange as its Executive Director in 1979, Mr Pandey worked in various capacities in the field of corporate administration and financial management, both in the private and public sectors between 1961 and 1979.

C Ramachandran, IAS, is Secretary to the Government of India, Department of Urban Development in the Ministry of Urban Affairs and Employment.

He has formerly held various senior positions in the Central Government, as well as in the Government of Tamil Nadu. He was also Industrial Adviser to the Royal Government of Bhutan for about four years.

He has worked as a consultant for the International Trade Centre, Geneva, and the Asian Development Bank, and has also written papers on the Budgetary System in Papua New Guinea and on Financing the Capital Investment in the Infrastructure Sector for Urban Centres.

S Ramaiah is currently Chairman of the Copyright Board, a statutory quasi-judicial Tribunal established under the provisions of the Indian Copyright Act. Earlier, Mr Ramaiah retired as Secretary to the Government of India and Head of the Department dealing with Parliamentary Legislation. There is practically no legislation in the

Indian Statute Book which he did not draft or amend during his career. Specifically, he was associated with the drafting of the Patent Bill and he drafted all the amendments to the Copyright Act.

In view of his expertise in copyright law, he was selected to head a Bureau in the World Intellectual Property Organization (WIPO), Geneva, which administers a number of International Conventions on Intellectual Property.

Ashoke Chandra Sen, IAS, is currently Secretary, Ministry of Mines, Government of India. He had a brilliant academic career in the University of Calcutta and London School of Economics. After serving as Assistant Professor of Economics in Presidency College, Calcutta, for a short period, he joined the Indian Administrative Service in May 1962. He was awarded the Ford Foundation Fellowship in 1967–68. During 34 years of his career in the State Government of Punjab and the Government of India, he held a series of important and prestigious posts. He was awarded the highest State Red Cross Prize for three years by the Governor of Punjab for his charitable and philanthropic work.

Professor A K Sharma, PhD in Chemistry, Punjab University, Chandigarh, is currently Director, National Council of Educational Research and Training (NCERT), New Delhi. Prior to this, he has held various senior positions in the field of education, including Principal, Regional Institute of Education, Mysore, and Reader in Chemistry, Punjab University, Chandigarh.

Professor G D Sharma, PhD in Economics, University of Bombay, is currently Secretary, University Grants Commission, New Delhi. He was formerly Professor and Head of the Higher Education Unit in the National Institute of Educational Planning and Administration (NIEPA), New Delhi, and also held the position of Director, Indian Institute of Education, Pune. He has been a consultant to UNESCO, UNDP and IIEP, Paris.

V K Shunglu, IAS (Indian Administrative Service), is currently the Comptroller and Auditor-General, Government of India.

At the time of contributing his chapter, he was the Secretary, Industrial Policy & Promotion in the Ministry of Industry, and Member, Foreign Investment Promotion Board (FIPB). Mr Shunglu has varied administrative experience of various departments in the Central Government and State of Madhya Pradesh. He formerly worked in the Asian-Development Bank.

He was educated at the University of Delhi from where he obtained degrees in Economics and History.

Shilendra Singh retired as Foreign Secretary of India. Mr Singh, MA, LLB, lectured in History at Agra University and served in the Indian Diplomatic Service from 1954 to 1990. He was official spokesperson of the Government and served as Ambassador to Lebanon, Jordan, Cyprus, Afghanistan, Austria, and Pakistan.

Mr Singh is an expert on United Nations and disarmament issues. He writes extensively on foreign policy issues, and has been Visiting Professor of International Relations and Diplomacy, Jawaharlal Nehru University.

He is currently serving on the Boards of a number of social, cultural, academic and business organisations in India.

M R Sivaraman, IAS, is Secretary, Revenue, Ministry of Finance, Government of India, New Delhi, and is fully responsible for tax revenues and carrying forward the taxation reforms initiated by the Government.

He obtained his MA in Economics from the University of Madras in 1962 and joined the Indian Administrative Service in the same year.

Mr Sivaraman was formerly Additional Secretary to the Government of India, Ministry of Commerce, New Delhi. He has also held the position of Director-General of Civil Aviation & Ex-officio Additional Secretary to the Government of India, Ministry of Civil Aviation.

T S Srinivasan graduated in Economics and Law. He joined the Indian Revenue Service in 1959, and rose to be Chairman, Central Board of Direct Taxes. As head of the tax organisation, he led the movement for tax reform. Mr Srinivasan was also in charge of foreign tax matters, including negotiating double tax avoidance agreements.

S Sundar, IAS, is currently Secretary, Ministry of Surface Transport, Government of India. At the time of writing his chapter, he was Secretary, Department of Tourism.

He has held senior positions in Industry and Finance at the Centre and in the Gujarat State.

He spent eight years with the Commonwealth Secretariat in London, first as Special Adviser, International Finance, and then as Director of the Economic and Legal Advisory Services Division.

R K Takkar, IAS. At the time of contributing his chapter, Mr Takkar was Chairman, Telecom Commission of India, and Secretary,

Department of Telecommunications, Government of India. He has a Masters in Political Science and Post-Graduate Diploma in Public Administration. He has wide experience in public administration, ranging over various departments of the Government.

Susmita Gongulee Thomas, after having obtained a postgraduate degree in Chemistry, joined the Indian Foreign Service in 1976. In addition to having served at the Ministry of External Affairs in New Delhi, she has served in various capacities in our Embassies in Madrid, Tokyo and Washington.

She is currently Joint Secretary, Investment Promotion and Publicity Division, Ministry of External Affairs, handling issues relating to Foreign Direct and Institutional Investments into India.

Ashok Tooley is working as Executive Director of Coal India Ltd at New Delhi. He is a graduate in mining engineering with a First Class Mine Manager's Certificate of Competency in Coal Mining. He did his senior course from Henley Management College, UK.

G Venkataramanan, IAS, was the Secretary, Department of Company Affairs, at the time of contributing his chapter. He had earlier occupied a number of senior positions in the Central Government, as well as in the State of West Bengal.

He had been honoured with the prestigious 'National Press India Award' for Best Administrator.

N Vittal, IAS, is currently Chairman, Public Enterprises Selection Board. At the time of contributing his chapter he was Secretary, Department of Electronics, Government of India. He has played a significant role in policy formulation for promotion of the electronics industry in India and was formerly Chairman of the Telecom Commission. He has published two books: *India Incorporated—Some Reflections on the Electronics Industry* and *The Vicious Cycle of Vittal's Law*.

Sahdev Vohra, ICS, was educated at Government College, Lahore (now in Pakistan) and joined the Indian Civil Service (ICS) in 1941. He held various posts in the Punjab Cadre including Home Secretary, Punjab Government. He later joined the United Nations as Director in the United Nations Conference on Trade and Development (UNCTAD). Returning to the Government of India, Mr Vohra was appointed Adviser to the Planning Commission, and then Secretary to the Government of India. After retirement, Mr Vohra took up writing on national and international affairs.

PUBLISHER'S NOTES

The chapters have been written and compiled during the period June–November 1995, and reviewed and updated in July 1996. Readers are advised to update and cross-check the information before taking any action. While the authors, contributors, editor and publisher have made every effort to ensure the accuracy of the information, they cannot accept any legal responsibility whatsoever for consequences that may arise from errors or omissions, or any opinions or advice given in the book.

Please note that the use of 'he', 'his' etc is not an expression of prejudice, but a convention to facilitate a simple writing style.

CONTENTS

	Introduction	**xxi**
Part 1	**The Setting**	**1**
	1. India—Land, People and System of Government	3
	2. Economic Conditions and Trends	18
	3. Industrial Policy and Foreign Investment	33
	4. Trade Policy and Foreign Trade	62
	5. Competitive Advantages and Intrinsic Strengths of India	80
	6. Overview of India's Foreign Policy and External Relations	89
	7. System of Human Resource Development and Educational Infrastructure	97
Part 2	**Preparing to do Business in India**	**103**
	8. Negotiation Preparation and the Importance of Entry Strategy	105
	9. Banking and Finance	124
	10. Overview of Corporate and Business Laws	143
	11. Incorporating a Company/ Setting up an Office	152
Part 3	**Doing Business in India**	**169**
	12. Intellectual Property	171
	13. Labour Management: Laws and Markets	185
	14. Marketing and Distribution in India	197
	15. Direct Taxes	215
	16. The Structure of Indirect Tax in India	239
	17. Capital and Securities Markets and Regulations	246
	18. Arbitration and Other Related Laws in India	261
	19. Living Conditions and Procedural Formalities for a Foreign Business Executive Visiting or Working in India	278

Part 4   **Industry Surveys: Review and Opportunities**   **285**

20. Policy and Opportunity in the Indian
    Power Sector   287
21. Highways and Ports   293
22. Electronics/Software Sector   306
23. The Mineral Sector   312
24. Policies and Opportunities in the
    Telecommunications Sector   317
25. India's Petroleum Sector Investment
    Opportunities   326
26. Challenges and Opportunities in the
    Health Sector   333
27. Opportunities for International Private
    Investment in Urban Development
    and the Housing Sector in India   337
28. Coal Sector in India—Growth and Prospects   341
29. Sectors for the Future   345
30. Tourism   364

Index   **369**

INTRODUCTION
by P Chidambaram

In July 1991 India launched a programme of economic reforms—a process of opening up its economy to the world, to competition and to more trade and investment through capital flow. Today, economic growth in India is a reality and India is reaching out to the world with confidence born from the success of its reforms.

Sweeping changes were carried out in policies relating to virtually every sector of the economy—trade, industry, foreign investment, finance, taxation and the public sector. The measures introduced in 1991 and progressively strengthened thereafter have transformed the business environment and opened up the economy to more trade and more foreign investment.

The restructuring and macro economic stabilisation focused on liberalisation, openness, transparency and globalisation. The reform package sought to allocate and utilise resources in an efficient manner and concentrated on reallocation of resources

(a) from the non-traded goods sector to the traded goods sector;

(b) from importing to exporting; and

(c) from the public sector to the private sector. Innovative measures undertaken in the areas of trade, industry and foreign investment have led to sharp and significant improvement in the investment climate and in the growth prospects of the economy. Subsequently, progress has been made in simplifying, modifying and streamlining trade policy, industrial policy, and foreign investment policy. The tariff structure has been rationalised. Foreign trade and trade intensity have been recognised as crucial factors and engines of growth in a liberalised economy.

The reforms came at a time when grave fiscal and external imbalances threatened the collapse of the economy. The reforms sought to achieve macro economic stabilisation, and to build on the strengths (such as high domestic savings and investment rates, a strong and mature private sector, a vibrant capital market, a large and diversified manufacturing sector and a self-sufficient agricultural sector) that the economy had historically acquired. The reforms aimed at global integration, accelerating growth, improving productivity, innovation and international competitiveness, as well as focusing government resources on rural development and the social sector.

Introduction

India's economic interaction with the outside world is not a recent development. Economic historians have recorded the importation of raw materials from Afghanistan and Iran during the period of the Harappan civilisation some 5000 years ago. From the 1st century AD, India was an established exporter of luxury items such as pearls, gems, muslin, steel cutlery, precious stones and spices to the Roman emperors, receiving gold and silver in return. Pliny wrote in *Natural History* that Rome was being drained of gold on account of trade with India. This began to decline in the 6th century AD with the Arabs monopolising trade. The decline of trade during the following three centuries resulted in the decay of many of the old commercial cities of India. The revival of interest in India in the 1600s was based on commercial considerations, and the East India Company was set up mainly for trading with India.

Achievements in science and technology flowed as parallel streams in India's economic history. India was a world leader in the field of astronomy and mathematics. The 1000 year old iron pillar near Qutab Minar in Delhi which stands in the open with no trace of rust or wear and tear is a testimony to the development of metallurgy in India. In the textiles sector, the world famous muslin cloth is just one example of sophistication achieved in product quality.

The deregulation of industry, the liberalisation of exchange markets and convertibility of the currency require an efficient financial sector. Interest rates have now largely been freed from government control except for a specific cap on deposit rates. In order to introduce competitive elements into the banking sector, eight new private banks have already been issued licences by the Reserve Bank of India. The process of disinvestment of government equity in nationalised banks has also begun, with a substantial disinvestment in India's largest bank, the State Bank of India. Parallel reforms have also been introduced in the capital market. The Securities and Exchange Board of India (SEBI) has been strengthened to regulate the capital market in an orderly and transparent manner. Companies are now free to raise resources in the capital market, and market forces determine prices and volumes as in most developed capital markets. The new economic policies have substantially relaxed foreign exchange controls. Effective from 20 August 1994 India announced its movement to Article VIII status in the IMF: the Indian rupee is now convertible on the current account. For foreign investors, the rupee is convertible on the capital account. The irreversible nature of the current reforms can be gauged from the fact that several institutions and controls of the old economic order have been dismantled and replaced with market-friendly bodies and policies.

The exchange rate policy is now predominantly market-determined, and convertibility on current accounts was achieved in August, 1994. A steep reduction in tariffs and import licensing requirements reflects the increasing openness of the economy. Pre-entry barriers to growth and competition in most industries have been abolished and the chronically loss-making public sector enterprises are being restructured. The public sector monopoly in many areas (including power, refineries, telecom, airlines, roads, ports, banking and financial services) has been discontinued by opening these sectors for private and foreign investment. The foreign investment regime has been overhauled to permit holding of equity of 51% or more by foreign companies in their investment in India.

India's recent policy restructuring recognises that growth is a result of better technology, greater investment and more efficient production. The impressive increase in foreign direct investment (FDI) has encouraged greater investor confidence in India. Total foreign investment approved in the four-year period from August 1991 to July 1995 amounted to over US$10 billion. Actual foreign direct investment during this period was about US$4 billion.

Both the restructuring and the stabilisation programmes have seen a remarkably smooth implementation. Stabilisation has been achieved without reduction in output. Economic growth and exports have accelerated. Capital markets remain active. Foreign investment has increased at a satisfactory rate. Foreign exchange reserves remain high and the inflation rate has decreased.

The path taken by India in the economic reform process is unique in that it has been built on a broad consensus of all political parties. In the last four years, India has followed this new path of liberalisation without inflicting too much pain on the people. In India it is believed that decisions made by the free market will create a healthier economy and that the State must intervene only when it is necessary and only in favour of the poor; that its production systems must become more efficient, more competitive, and more quality-conscious; that it must take advantage of its position in the international labour market and of its comparative advantages. India must produce goods and services not only for the home market, but for the whole world. It must take advantage of the immense trade and capital flows which characterise the world economy today. India seeks trade, not aid; it seeks capital, not loans.

While the Indian economy is not over the hump yet, the transition to a free market economy brings with it new priorities and problems which need to be continuously addressed. Yet there is positive and clear evidence of significant accomplishments in the last four years.

Introduction

A Gross Domestic Product (GDP) growing at the rate of 5–6% per annum and projected to be higher, a current industrial growth of about 12%, a satisfactory level of agricultural production coupled with more than adequate foodgrain stocks, a steady and accelerated growth in exports of 20% per annum in dollar terms in the last three years and comfortable foreign exchange reserves of US$18 billion (good for six months' imports) have placed the Indian economy in an enviable position. A burgeoning import sector is evidence of the openness of the economy. International agencies and institutions forecast a steady and sustained growth of the Indian economy in the next 5–10 years to give it a place among the top five world economies.

While comparisons of the Indian economy with other emerging economies have been fashionable of late, it is widely acknowledged that India has a number of advantages: a strong and well-developed legal system, an organised and responsive capital market, natural advantages in terms of resources, skills and professional services, an improved credit rating and a convenient geographic location in Asia. It is also relatively easy for companies, including joint ventures, to be listed in India making acquisition of equity much easier. Continued political stability, a transparent and free Press, a secure legal system, the encouragement of small and medium size foreign investment, a strong network of telecommunications, roads and electricity and the high literacy rate in India coupled with the use of English as the language of commerce make India an investment-friendly destination.

Since the beginning of the reform period, there have been numerous analogies between India and a variety of beasts. Is India a sleeping tiger, an awakening tiger or an elephant rising on its four legs? It would be more appropriate to describe India as a horse on a fast track ready for the global race.

PART I
THE SETTING

CHAPTER 1

INDIA—LAND, PEOPLE AND SYSTEM OF GOVERNMENT
by Sahdev Vohra

INTRODUCTION

India, which emerged as a new state in 1947, is the world's largest democracy, and emphasises the rights of the people, secularism, justice and the establishment of a social welfare system. The country is characterised by diversity of race, caste, religion and language, and yet it maintains unity in this diversity. Rich in natural resources, it is the eleventh largest industrialised country in the world with a modern economy, transportation and communication networks, a dynamic and competitive private sector, a free Press, a developed legal system and modern education system. A sizeable well-educated middle class constitutes the backbone of modern India.

GEOGRAPHICAL AND CLIMATIC CHARACTERISTICS

India is a vast country with wide variations in climatic conditions. The Himalayas in the north separate India from China (Tibet and Simkiang). The southern peninsula is bordered by the Arabian Sea, the Bay of Bengal and the Indian Ocean. The fertile Gangetic Plains in North and Central India, the desert in the west and dense tropical forests in the east add to the geographic diversity of India.

India's geography was determined by the ancient geological formation of Gondwana-land which was once one land mass, and has now been divided into the Deccan Plateau of India and the mainland of Africa. The States of Madhya Pradesh, Maharashtra, Karnataka, Andhra Pradesh, Tamil Nadu and Kerala stand on the Deccan Plateau. The vast tableland is enclosed within the Western Ghat and the Eastern Ghat mountains running along the two coasts and trapping the monsoon rains. In the summer the main monsoons hit the western coast. The winter monsoons bring cyclonic rains to the Eastern Ghats and to the coastal areas of Andhra Pradesh and Tamil Nadu.

North of the Deccan Plateau and separated by the Aravali ranges that run diagonally from south-west to north-east across the State of Rajasthan is the Indo-Gangetic Plain stretching from the Punjab to

Bengal. The Ganges River in the north is fed by the snow-clad Himalayas. This is the area of India with the densest population and highest agricultural output. Assam and the other north-eastern Indian States have a less developed infrastructure and industry, compared to the Southern States and Indo-Gangetic area.

Climate

Variations in climatic conditions across India are extreme, although the climate is tropical in most parts of the country. The Himalayas experience very cold winters, but summers are cool in the lower regions of the Himalayas. The plains of northern and central India experience very hot summers and cold winters. Southern India remains relatively temperate throughout the year.

Most parts of the country have three seasons: summer, monsoon and winter.

Summer lasts from March to June. The Northern Plains have very hot weather although the climate is pleasant in the lower Himalayan ranges at this time of the year. The southern part of the country is generally hot, but coastal areas and the hill resorts in the Annamalai Hills and Western Ghats are cooler.

The monsoons begin in June and last till September. They start from the south along the coast of the Bay of Bengal. In July the entire country experiences heavy rains, but the heaviest falls are in the north-eastern regions and in the Western Ghats. The highest rainfall in the world occurs in Cherrapunji in Meghalaya State.

Winter lasts from October to March. Both the upper and lower Himalayan ranges experience heavy snowfalls. January is the coldest month in India. Coastal areas are pleasant during this part of the year. The plains of southern India have a very mild winter.

Most of the festivals celebrated in India are seasonal and are related to harvesting. Of the six seasons, Varsha, Sharad and Vasant are considered the best climatically and most of the festivals are celebrated during these seasons.

Area

India is the second largest country in Asia and the seventh largest country in the world. It has a total area of 3.3 million square kilometres.

Population

The world's second most populous country, India has a total of over 930 million inhabitants. The ratio of females to males is 929 to 1000.

Uttar Pradesh is the most populous State (139 million) followed by Bihar (86 million) and Maharashtra (79 million). Of the total population, 83% is Hindu. The remainder are Muslim, Christian, Sikh, Buddhist, Jain, and others.

Language

Hindi is the recognised official language. However, English is used all over the country for many purposes including most official communications. It is the principal language for administration and commerce. There are a number of other languages spoken in India. The Constitution recognises 18 languages: Assamese, Bengali, Gujarati, Kannada, Kashmiri, Konkani, Malyalam, Manipuri, Marathi, Nepali, Oriya, Punjabi, Sindhi, Tamil, Telegu, Urdu and Sanskrit.

Sanskrit is among the oldest languages of the world, and most of the other Indian languages originated from it or, as in the south of the country, Sanskrit words have been incorporated into the local languages.

As English is spoken and understood throughout India, foreign investors should have no communication problems.

SYSTEM OF GOVERNMENT

The Indian Constitution was framed by the Constituent Assembly in 1950. Its chief architect was Dr B R Ambedkar, though other prominent leaders of the freedom movement also played a role in its formulation.

It is one of the most comprehensive Constitutions in the world, consisting of 395 Articles, 22 parts and 12 schedules giving details of provisions relating to the judges of the Supreme Court and High Courts, Union, State and Concurrent lists, and Languages. Although the Indian system of government is similar to the British Parliamentary system, it differs in that it is entirely based on a written constitution providing fundamental rights to the individual and outlining fundamental duties, and with the Supreme Court as the Protector of the Constitution.

BASIC PHILOSOPHY OF THE CONSTITUTION

The basic philosophy of the Constitution is reflected in the preamble, which says that India is a sovereign, socialist, secular, democratic republic, providing fundamental rights and liberties to the citizens and ensuring justice—social, economic and political—while promising dignity of the individual and unity and integrity of the country.

INDIA—A UNION OF STATES

India consists of 25 States and seven Union Territories including Delhi. Through an amendment to the Constitution in 1991, Delhi is now called the 'National Capital, Territory of Delhi'.

The States and Union Territories are listed below:

States

Andhra Pradesh	West Bengal
Assam	Jammu & Kashmir
Bihar	Nagaland
Gujarat	Haryana
Kerala	Himachal Pradesh
Madhya Pradesh	Manipur
Tamil Nadu	Tripura
Maharashtra	Meghalaya
Karnataka	Sikkim
Orissa	Mizoram
Punjab	Arunachal Pradesh
Rajasthan	Goa
Uttar Pradesh	

Union Territories

Delhi	Dadra and Nagar Haveli
The Andaman & Nicobar Islands	Pondicherry
Lakshadweep	Chandigarh

Like a federation, India has a dual system of government, with division of powers between the Centre and the States. The intention of the writers of the Constitution was to have a strong Centre, as is indicated in the diagram below.

The Union List consists of 97 subjects on which only the union government can legislate, such as foreign affairs, entering into agreements and treaties with other countries, railways, currency, trade and commerce, defence, UNO, war and peace, extradition, maritime shipping and navigation.

The State List consists of 66 subjects on which State governments can legislate, such as public order, public health, sanitation, communications, police, local government, land, agriculture.

Industry is a State subject. However, Item 52 of the Seventh Schedule provides that the Union may assist and regulate 'Industries, the control of which by the Union is declared by Parliament by law to be expedient in the public interest'. The policy of liberalisation announced by the Central Government in 1991, and which has been implemented since then, has diluted central control of industry by amending the Industries Regulation Act. To promote industrialisation, the State Governments are vying with each other to provide facilities to entrepreneurs and to attract industry and foreign investment.

The Concurrent List consists of 47 subjects on which both the Union and State governments can legislate. But in case of a conflict Union law prevails over State law. Subjects like criminal law, marriage and divorce, forests, drugs, protection of wild animals and birds are covered by the Concurrent List.

Residual powers are left in the hands of the Centre. The Judiciary (ie the Supreme Court) is the protector of the Constitution and it functions independently of the control of the Legislature and the Executive.

SYSTEM OF GOVERNMENT AT THE CENTRE

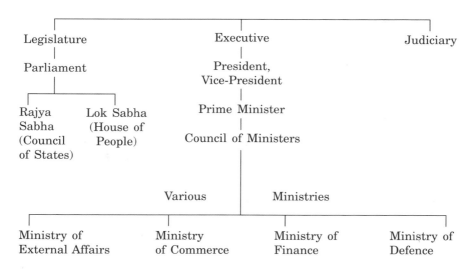

7

THE EXECUTIVE

President

The executive power of the Union is vested in the President, who is elected indirectly by an electoral college consisting of elected members of both the houses of Parliament (ie the Union Legislature, which is bi-cameral—the lower house is known as Lok Sabha and the Upper House is known as Rajya Sabha) and elected members of the State Legislative Assemblies. His term of office is five years and he is eligible for re-election although he can be impeached for violation of the Constitution by both Houses of Parliament.

The President is the formal head of the administration and makes all important appointments, such as the Prime Minister, Judges of the Supreme Court and High Courts, Governors of the States, and Chief Election Commissioner. He is the Supreme Commander of the Defence Forces, has the power to summon and prorogue both the Houses of Parliament, dissolve Lok Sabha, give or withhold his assent to Union Legislation, grant pardon and reprieve, and proclaim a state of emergency when required.

While the President is the Constitutional Head, the real functionaries are the Prime Minister and his Council of Ministers, who are also members of the Parliament.

Vice-president

The Vice-president is elected by members of both the Houses of Parliament and holds office for a term of five years. He is the ex officio Chairman of the Rajya Sabha, the Upper House of Parliament.

The Prime Minister and Council of Ministers

The President appoints the leader of the majority party in the Lok Sabha as Prime Minister. With his advice the President also appoints the Council of Ministers. The Prime Minister and his Council of Ministers are collectively responsible to Lok Sabha, the Lower House of Parliament. The Prime Minister regulates the size and composition of the Council of Ministers.

A Secretary is the principal adviser and instrument of the Minister in matters of policy and administration, being responsible for the efficient and economic administration of the department and its attached offices and also representing the department before parliamentary committees.

An Additional or Joint Secretary is in charge of a wing with full authority to dispose of business entrusted to his charge.

A Deputy Secretary controls a division consisting of branches, with each branch being controlled by an Under Secretary.

The Prime Minister is the link between the President and the Council of Ministers. He is leader of the government and majority party in the Lok Sabha and also leader of his own party and the real head of the government.

PARLIAMENT (UNION LEGISLATURE)

The Lok Sabha is a directly elected chamber consisting of 545 members with a term of five years. Members of the Rajya Sabha are elected by state legislatures and a third of the members retire every two years, ie each member stays in the house for six years. Its total strength is 250 members of which 12 are nominated by the President.

India has adopted a representative democracy, based on universal adult franchise. All legislation requires the consent of both houses, but the Lok Sabha has the final say in financial matters.

THE JUDICIARY

The Supreme Court sitting at New Delhi is the highest judicial body of the state consisting of a Chief Justice and 25 Judges appointed by the President. It is independent of the control of the Executive and the Legislature, and is the highest court of appeal in the country, exercising both original and appellate jurisdiction together with the power of judicial review on the basis of due procedure established by law. It is the final interpreter and protector of India's Constitution. All disputes between the Centre and the States or between one State and another are referred to this Court.

The Attorney-General of India

The President appoints a person, who is qualified to be appointed a Judge of the Supreme Court, as the Attorney-General of India. The Attorney-General advises the President on legal matters, and holds office at the pleasure of the President.

Comptroller and Auditor-General of India

The President appoints the Comptroller and Auditor-General of India who performs such duties and exercises such powers in relation to the accounts of the Union and of the States as may be prescribed by Parliament.

The Chief Election Commissioner

For the supervision, direction and control of the preparation of electoral rolls, for the conduct of all Parliamentary and State elections and of the election of the President and Vice-President, India has an Election Commission consisting of the Chief Election Commissioner and such other election commissioners, as the President may from time to time appoint subject to the provisions of any law made in that regard by the Parliament.

SYSTEM OF GOVERNMENT AT THE STATE LEVEL

In structure, the government of each State is very similar to the Central Government.

THE EXECUTIVE

Governor

A Governor is appointed by the President for a term of five years, and holds office at his pleasure. He appoints the leader of the majority party in the Legislative Assembly as Chief Minister and with his advice appoints other Ministers. In cases where no political party gets a majority in the State Legislature, he uses his discretionary powers to decide who should be invited to form the government. He has the power to dissolve the assembly on the advice of the Chief Minister. He can also summon and prorogue the state legislature, and can grant pardons and reprieve.

The Chief Minister

The position of the Chief Minister is similar to that of the Prime Minister. He and his Council of Ministers are the real Executive, exercising power in the name of the Governor.

The State Legislature consists of two houses—the Legislative Assembly (Lower Chamber) and the Legislative Council (Upper Chamber), but the states have the power to decide whether they want a second chamber or not.

The Chief Minister and his Council of Ministers are responsible to the State Legislature.

THE JUDICIARY IN THE STATES

The High Court

Most States have a High Court consisting of a Chief Justice and such other Judges as the President may consider necessary. Parliament may by law provide for a common High Court for two or more States. A High Court is a Court of appeal and also of original jurisdiction on writ petitions.

Both the Supreme Court and the High Courts have power to issue various writs for the protection of rights of the citizens.

The Advocate General

The Governor of each State appoints a person who is qualified to be a Judge of the High Court as Advocate General for the State, to give advice to the Government of the State on legal matters referred to him by the Governor.

SYSTEM OF GOVERNMENT IN THE DISTRICT

In India States are divided into Districts. District Administration is the management of public affairs within a District. The Constitution of India makes no mention of a District at all, as a unit of administration, except in the reference to the appointment of District Judges. Yet it is the most important unit of field administration in the country. The Districts are further divided into Tehsils or Taluks. The most important sub-division is the Village, the basic unit of Indian rural administration. India has a total of 501 districts.

The District Collector is the highest officer in the district. He is responsible for maintaining law and order, land records, land revenue, provision of civic amenities and development.

The diagram below shows how district administration is carried on:

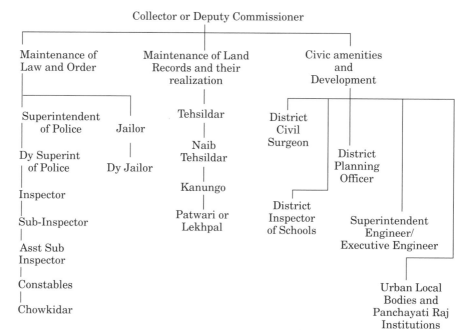

Collector or Deputy Commissioner

The basic feature of the field administration is that the Collector who is also the District Magistrate and is designated also as Deputy Commissioner in some States, is the co-ordinating and moving spirit of the administration in the District, just as the Tehsildar is in the sub-division of the District called a Tehsil. In matters of law and order, the Collector is assisted by the District Superintendent of Police who is in independent charge of the police. There are also a large number of departmental officers in charge of roads, canals, bridges (under the Public Works Department), the Civil Surgeon in charge of hospitals and medical facilities, the District Inspector of Schools and so on. But the lynchpin of the administration is the Collector.

JUDICIAL ADMINISTRATION IN THE DISTRICT

Under the High Court the parts of District administration concerning law, order and justice consist of the District Judge and a hierarchy of subordinate courts.

The Court of the District Judge is the highest court in the District, and it supervises the functions of civil and criminal courts. Civil courts include the courts of the Civil Judge and Munsif. The Court of Sessions Judge tries criminal cases of a serious nature. Under the sessions courts there are other courts headed by the Metropolitan Magistrate, and by first, second and third class magistrates. A First Class Magistrate can impose punishment of up to two years' imprisonment and a fine of up to 1000 rupees. A Second Class Magistrate can impose imprisonment of up to six months and a fine of up to 200 rupees. A Third Class Magistrate can impose imprisonment of up to one month and a fine of up to 50 rupees.

Minor cases are tried by the village panchayat at the village level.

LOCAL GOVERNMENT

District Administration is carried on at three levels of local government: the Gram Panchayat (at the grass-roots village level), Panchayat Samiti (at the intermediate level) and Zila Parishad (at the district level). Co-operative societies, women and backward classes are given special representation in these institutions.

'Village' means a village specified by the Governor by Public Notification and may include a group of villages.

The panchayat is an institution of self-government for rural areas.

The Village Panchayat

The lowest unit of administration is the village panchayat, elected for a period of five years directly by the people of the village who constitute the Gram Sabha or the Village Assembly, on the basis of adult franchise. The village panchayat elects its chief, known as 'Panch' or 'Sarpanch'.

Besides these institutions, village level workers appointed by the government assist in linking the farmer with other levels of district administration.

The Panchayat Samiti

The Panchayat Samiti functions at the block or intermediate level. This intermediate territorial level is also known as Tehsil or a Sub-Division.

The Panchayat Samiti is a link between the village and the Zila Parishad. The heads of the village panchayats elect their representatives to the Panchayat Samiti. All the members of the State Legislative Assembly and Council and members of Lok Sabha and Rajya Sabha who are elected from that block are also members of the Panchayat Samiti. The term of this Samiti is five years. It is responsible for the overall welfare of the block.

The Zila Parishad

Persons elected as block heads automatically become members of the Zila Parishad. Members of the State Legislative Council and Assembly and members of Parliament from that district are also members.

THE CIVIL SERVICE

An independent civil service, which is one of the important pillars of a good system of government, exists in India.

There are three categories of civil services:

(1)   The All India Services, recruited by the Union Public Service Commission, which include the Indian Administrative Service (IAS), the Indian Police Service and the Indian Forest Service. The Officers recruited into the IAS are assigned to the State Cadres. Besides these the Indian Foreign Service mans the Ministry of External Affairs and Diplomatic Missions abroad.

(2)   Central Services, recruited by the Union Public Service Commission, which include the Indian Postal Service, the Indian Revenue Service, and the Indian Audit & Account Service, to name a few.

(3)   State Services, which are recruited by State Public Service Commissions in the States and are structurally similar to Central Services.

RIGHTS AND DUTIES OF THE CITIZENS

The Constitution provides six fundamental rights to citizens (equality, freedom, right against exploitation, freedom of religion, cultural and educational rights, and the right to constitutional remedies) besides a long list of rights provided indirectly to the citizens in the form of Directive Principles of State Policy, which are not justiciable.

The fundamental duties of the citizens are:

(1)   To abide by the Constitution and respect the National Flag and National Anthem.

(2)   To cherish and follow the noble ideas which inspired our national struggle for freedom.

(3)   To protect the sovereignty, unity and integrity of the country.

(4)   To defend the country.

(5)   To promote the spirit of brotherhood.

(6)   To preserve the rich heritage and culture of the country.

(7)   To protect the environment.

(8)   To safeguard public property.

(9)   To develop scientific temper and spirit of inquiry.

(10)   To strive towards excellence in all spheres of individual and collective activity.

The Indian Constitution is based on the idea of secularism, and there is no State religion.

POLITICAL PARTIES

India has a multi-party system. There are four major types of parties in the country: all-India parties; regional parties; localised parties; and personalist parties.

All-India Parties

These are national in character and their programmes cover a large number of social, economic and political issues. Important all-India parties are the Congress (I), Bhartiya Janata Party, Janata Dal, the Communist Party of India, and the Communist Party of India (Marxist).

Regional Parties

These parties represent the interests of particular linguistic, religious, regional ethnic and cultural groups. These parties generally do not aspire to gain control over the Central Government, though they may play an important role in national, State and local politics. Important regional parties are the AIADMK and the DMK in Tamil Nadu, the

Akali Dal in Punjab, the Telugu Desam in Andhra Pradesh, the National Conference in Jammu and Kashmir, the Jharkhand Party in Bihar, and the Gorkha League in West Bengal.

Localised Parties

The influence of such parties is confined only to a few constituencies and does not show any evidence of expansion. Some of the important local parties are the Forward Block, the Peasants and the Workers Party, the Republican Party, and the CPI (ML).

Personalist Parties

Personalist parties are formed around a charismatic leader whose personal qualities inspire his followers.

The Congress for Democracy formed by Jagjivan Ram in 1977 and the Bhartiya Kranti Dal formed by Charan Singh in 1968 are important examples, although these no longer exist.

Another emerging party, the Bhartiya Samajwadi Party, representing the under-privileged classes, is currently playing an important role in Uttar Pradesh.

As at September 1995, the party in power at the Centre is the Indian National Congress. It was founded in 1885 and was the king pin in the movement towards freedom from British rule. The party continued to be the main ruling party after 1947 but it was soon faced with challenges from other parties which came to power at State level, as well as from the Communists and Socialists. In 1977 for the first time the Janata Party in coalition with other opposition parties defeated the Congress and formed the Central Government. The Congress was defeated once again in 1989 by the Janata coalition at the Centre but came back to power in 1991.

A new phenomenon over the last decade is the emergence of the Bhartiya Janata Party (BJP) which represents traditional Indian values and ethos, while fully accepting the political system, the many-dimensional civilisation of India, and the religious diversity of the people. This party has had considerable success lately and was, as at September 1995, in power in Maharashtra (as a coalition partner), Gujarat, Rajasthan and Delhi.

The Congress has been in power since the Central elections of 1991, but in the States Congress governments exist only in Haryana, Himachal Pradesh, Madhya Pradesh and in some of the States of the north eastern region. In Kerala the Congress has also formed a coalition government. The Janata Dal has governments in Bihar and in Karnataka. The other State governments in the south are locally-based parties—the Telegu Desham Party in Andhra Pradesh and the AIADMK in Tamil Nadu. The noteworthy feature of the West Bengal Government is that for 16 years it has had a Communist Party government in power. It may be asserted that the Indian political parties are largely in full accord over the liberalisation of the economy and the open-door industrial policy of India, although there may be differences of opinion with respect to a few details. After the general elections of 1996, the Congress Party lost its premier position. The BJP emerged as the largest single party, but the government was formed by all the other parties coming together as the United Front.

CONCLUSION

India has, as the world's largest democracy, a political system and a system of government which is fully compatible with free trade and with foreign collaboration. It has a financial structure, including banking, insurance, and marketing of stocks and shares, that has worked well to promote industry and foreign trade. When a foreign investor comes to India, he can expect an open market, fair competition and a level playing field.

India is an old civilisation, which prides itself on its economic prosperity, the skill of its craftsman and the enterprise of its business communities. India lost ground internationally after the industrial revolution in the west, but since Independence it has worked hard at catching up and regaining its former pre-eminence. The policy of liberalisation now requires the country to prepare to face even greater challenges. As a member of GATT and now of the World Trade Organisation, India is playing its part in a world economy based on fair competition and fair play. India has geared itself up to step up the pace of industrialisation, and the foreign investor is welcome to take part.

CHAPTER 2

ECONOMIC CONDITIONS AND TRENDS
by Vishvanath Pai Panandiker

In August 1947, when India became independent after almost 150 years of British rule, Prime Minister Jawaharlal Nehru made his famous speech—India's Tryst with Destiny.[1] The long journey to provide the Indian people with quality of life continues. Nearly 50 years later, the Indian dream remains only partially realised. India's economic potential is enormous, but it is yet to become a major international economic power. India decided to open up its economy and to go global in 1991, far behind its East Asian or South East Asian neighbours, and even China. Since 1991, India has progressed a great deal and promises much more.

A HISTORICAL RETROSPECT

In 1951, the Indian population was about 360 million. By 1961 it had exceeded 493 million and in mid-1995 was estimated at 916 million. The population has thus increased two and a half times during the period 1947–95.

Food Production

India faced serious food shortages in 1950 as some of the great grain-producing areas of India went to Pakistan on partition of the country. In 1951, Indian food grain production was only 46.5 million tonnes. By 1961, production had gone up to 69.6 million tonnes and in 1995 it was estimated at nearly 190 million tonnes. In other words, while the population increased by two and a half times, the foodgrain production increased by four times making India essentially self-reliant in food grains. Indian performance in this respect is remarkable inasmuch as many Western scholars had predicted in the 1960s that India would not be able to feed its growing population. By mid-1995, India was a net exporter of food and the official buffer stocks were over 37 million tonnes, far above the level necessary to support the public distribution system.

India's agricultural success has been helped by the fact that the net sown area, which was 118.7 million hectares in 1951, had risen to 133 million hectares in 1961 and to 142.2 million hectares in 1991. The gross sown area has grown from 131.9 million hectares in 1951 to 185.5 million hectares in 1991, making India one of the greatest agricultural countries in the world. The potential of this land is so great that all the studies indicate that, even with the existing technologies, India has the inherent capacity to feed its projected population of 1.6–1.8 billion people.

Key Indicators

India's historical performance in a few other key indicators needs emphasis. In 1951, the installed capacity for power production was only 1835 megawatts. By 1995 it had risen to 81,750 megawatts, or by nearly 45 times, and India plans to have an installed capacity of 220,000 megawatts by the year 2010 which is nearly 120 times the capacity in 1951.

India's domestic savings equalled only about 10.4% of the GDP in 1950–51. It rose to 12.7% in 1960–61 and had reached 24.4% of the GDP in 1994–95. India had thus managed to increase its domestic savings rate significantly despite the fact that its per capita income remains relatively low. Historically India has never received much aid in per capita terms. Nor have foreign investments in India been very high. Most investments have, therefore, come essentially from internal sources.

Another major achievement of India in historical terms is its scientific and technical manpower. This manpower pool consisted of about only 168,000 persons in 1951. By 1991, India's scientific and technical manpower pool was estimated at about 3.5 million persons, making it one of the world's largest.

Finally, the growth of India's market capitalisation deserves comment. In 1951, market capitalisation was only of the order of Rs6 billion. By 1961 it had grown to Rs12 billion and to an enormous Rs398 billion by 1991. It clearly reflects the buoyancy of the Indian capital markets over this period.

Table 1
Major Indicators

	1951	1995
Population	360 million	916 million
Domestic savings rate	10.4% GDP	22% GDP
Food grain production	46.5 million tonnes	190 million tonnes
Installed power capacity	1835 megawatts	81,750 megawatts
Scientific and technical manpower	168,000	4.1 million
Market capitalisation	Rs6 billion	Rs400 billion
Imports at current prices	US$1.2 billion	US$28.2 billion
Exports at current prices	US$1.2 billion	US$26.2 billion
Foreign currency assets in US$	US$1.5 billion	US$20 billion

Areas of Poor Performance

Two or three areas of the Indian economy stand out for their relatively poor performance. First, India's population growth at 1.9% in 1995 is still way above the targeted level of 1.3%. Secondly, the Indian illiteracy rate of 48% is not a very favourable reflection on public policy. And lastly, India's per capita income at US$350 or so in 1995 is well below its potential. Even at Purchasing Power Parity (PPP) level, the per capita income is only about US$1230 which compares unfavourably with its East Asian neighbours. These factors are a reflection of the failure of the development policy followed during 1951–91.

Mixed Success

In retrospect, the Indian story of 1951–91, the main years of centralised planning, is a story of mixed success. Under the national planning system, India so far has had eight Five Year Plans. Compared to Indian economic performance between 1900 and 1947, when India achieved Independence, the experience of the last 47 years of planned development is one of considerable achievement. Yet the achievement lacks the lustre of the Asian 'miracle' countries. This is largely due to the closed economy policy during the years of centralised planning. It is a story of some successes and many failures.

INDIA'S ECONOMIC POTENTIAL

India's natural and human resources are indeed very large. It is because of this large natural endowment that India was such a highly developed society, with advanced technologies, and well-developed agriculture in ancient times. It is for this reason that India was the target of regular immigration from time immemorial.

This basic economic potential of India remains intact. In 1992, even the low rate of PPP of US$1230 gave India a GNP of over US$1.1 trillion. If India grows at a sustained rate of 7% per year, the Indian GNP would be over US$2 trillion by 2005 and US$4 trillion by 2015. This will make India one of the five largest world economies, and, from all indications, India will be the second largest economy after China by the year 2050.

India's Advantages

India has two distinct advantages compared to China in the short term, say up to 2010. First, the Indian agricultural base seems much sounder than China's and India has shown enormous growth and diversification in the last decade. This will indeed enable India to sustain its projected population growth without much difficulty. Secondly, India has a large pool of technical and scientific manpower whose potential for conversion into specific economic performance is also vast.

Size of the Indian Market

A question of considerable interest to the rest of the world is the size of the Indian market. According to available data and the PPP estimates, the top 10% of the Indian population or about 100 million people enjoy a per capita income of over US$5000. Even by conservative calculations India's 100 million population accounts for over US$100 billion GNP, which is larger than the total GNP of many countries. What is more important is that this market is growing very rapidly. At the present rate of growth of 6–7% India could well have a market of 150 to 200 million people in the upper middle class and something like 300 million in the middle class by the year 2001. The exact purchasing power of these people, who will constitute a formidable market, will depend a great deal upon the policies pursued and the actual performance of the economy. However, it is clear that a market of 300 million people will emerge in India before 2010.

As explained earlier, India's growth rate is now about 6%. It is quite likely that with economic liberalisation which is proceeding at a modest pace, the growth rate will rise from the present 6% to 7–8% before the turn of the century. Because of the inherent strengths of the economy, it should be possible to sustain this growth rate for the subsequent decade or two or up to the year 2020.

This rate of growth will in turn have a major impact on the growth of the middle class and the market in India. The Indian population will be about 1300 million by 2020 and assuming that about 40% of the population will achieve middle class status, the size of the market in India will have risen to about 500 million people. While it is difficult to predict the exact purchasing power of this 500 million strong middle class, there is little doubt that it will be a formidable buying force.

INDIA'S PROSPERITY

Conditions for Prosperity

India's prosperity in the coming years will be dependent on its performance with respect to two factors: first, its ability to harness its vast human resources especially its technical, scientific and managerial manpower, for economic development; secondly, its ability to take advantage of the process of globalisation of the world economy by attracting foreign investment and technology.

India's Natural Resource Base

India's vast natural resource base has already been mentioned. Its land area, especially arable land, is large. Its water and mineral resources are also large. And although oil reserves tapped so far are not very large, India's gas reserves are estimated to be considerable. India is a land of sunshine and, as solar energy becomes economically viable, India's energy options will be vastly improved.

India's Human Resources

More important is India's human resource development. Although India has not done as well as China in terms of primary and secondary education of the masses, India's performance in tertiary education has been exceptionally good. Manpower development in engineering and technology has been impressive. In the services sector, training and development has resulted in a pool of nearly 3.5 million people now being available. India is already an important exporter of technical and scientific manpower. With over 5 million students in the Indian university system, India's ability to provide a large number of well-trained people will help the country to move faster towards prosperity.

India's Entrepreneurial Class

Yet another factor which is likely to contribute to India's prosperity in the coming years is the strong entrepreneurial and managerial class. Unlike China which followed a fully centrally planned economy, India followed what was called a 'mixed economy' model. The mixed economy model permitted full private enterprise in the agricultural sector and also considerable opportunities for the private sector in the industrial and service areas.

It is not by accident that India has a number of relatively large business houses such as the Tatas, the Birlas, the Ambanis, the Kirloskars, the Bajajs and a host of other entrepreneurial families which have built considerable strength in the last 40 years. These large business houses are increasingly becoming global players. Their ability to mobilise global resources combined with indigenous capabilities has been considerably enlarged. In the years to come, the entrepreneurial and managerial class in India will be able to play a major and important role in increasing India's prosperity.

Financial Market

India's primary financial market activity, reflected by the number of public issues and the total capital raised, has shown much improvement in recent years. The total number of launches in 1992–93 is estimated at Rs21.9 billion or US$700 million. The secondary market has also grown considerably in the last few years and the stock exchanges in India have shown robust health. The number of companies listed on the Bombay Stock Exchange at the end of December 1993 was 3585 which was more than the aggregate total of companies listed in the nine emerging markets of Malaysia, Thailand, South Korea, Taiwan, South Africa, Brazil, Mexico, China and Argentina. This is little known outside India, and the fact that India was a relatively closed economy in the last 40 years or so has hidden its inherent potential.

RECENT GDP AND GROWTH RATE

Size of GDP

The GDP of India in 1995 was estimated at about US$300 billion. If the PPP concept is used, the GDP figure rises to US$1.1 trillion making it one of the largest economies of the world even at the present low level of per capita income. The expected growth in the GDP in the next decade should clearly make India one of the major economies of the world.

The growth rate of the Indian economy since the 1980s has been on average about 5.5%. The rate was affected in 1991–92 by the structural adjustment process but has regained its buoyancy since 1994–95. Indeed structural adjustment in India has been one of the least painful by international standards suggesting a good management of this inherently painful process.

Agricultural Success

Behind the growth rate lies the excellent performance of the agricultural sector. Agriculture remains the mainstay of the Indian economy and although it accounts for only 30% of the GDP, over 63% of the Indian population is still dependent on agriculture. The success of Indian agriculture in recent years has not only been in food grains but also in the non-food grains sector. The diversification of Indian agriculture in recent years has been quite remarkable in that the growth of cash crops and horticulture has been at a higher level than ever before.

Structure of the Economy

Besides agriculture, the structural dimensions of the Indian GDP are also worth noting. Agriculture accounts for nearly 30% of the GDP, as does industry. The tertiary sector accounts for nearly 40% of the economy. Thus the Indian economy has moved a great deal from its traditional dependence on agriculture which was as high as 60% at the time of Independence.

The industrial sector has grown consistently over the last 45 years of planned development and from a low base has now gained an important position in the GDP. The current rate of growth in industry is around 12%, which should be sustainable in the coming years. In particular there has been a significant increase in the manufacturing sector and 1995–96 estimates suggest a growth of 12% in value-added manufacturing. The subsectors which have shown especially strong growth are electricity generation, saleable steel and crude oil.

ECONOMIC REFORMS AND LIBERALISATION

Initiating the Reforms

India's economic reform process was initiated in July 1991 when the first budget of the new government was unveiled. The reform process was focused on fiscal stabilisation, investment reform, trade policies, the financial sector and public enterprises. In his budget speech of 29 July 1991, the Finance Minister Dr Manmohan Singh outlined the nature of the economic crisis.[2] He specifically stated that the balance of payments situation was precarious, the inflation rate was very high, along with persistent and large macro-economic imbalances, low productivity of investment, unsustainable increases in government expenditure, an inefficient tax system, and a poorly managed public sector. The Finance Minister outlined the need for removing irksome controls over industry, for the opening of the economy, and for the reform of the fiscal system, the financial sector and a host of other areas. India was in serious economic crisis and urgent action was necessary.

Policy Reforms

The economic reforms from July 1991 onwards were aimed at widespread policy changes directed at fiscal stabilisation and macro-economic policies especially in relation to industrial and trade policies. As Isher Ahluwalia points out:[3]

> The economic reforms of the 1990s were designed within an overall dual strategy whereby fiscal adjustment aims to bring about macro-economic stabilization, while structural reforms in industrial, trade and financial policies are designed to strengthen the growth capability of the economy in the medium term and help Indian industry to become internationally competitive.

The direction of economic reforms was further spelt out in the subsequent budgets of 1992, 1993, 1994 and 1995. The five budgets represent a paradigmatic shift in thinking about economic policy. The basic premise is that excessive governmental controls over the economy are counter-productive and do great harm, and that India has to open up and join the world economy to reap the full benefits of a rapidly integrating global economy.

Direction of Reforms

The direction of reform was focused around five issues, viz investment regime, trade policies, the financial sector, taxation, and public enterprises. One of the major objectives of the reforms was to reduce the capital intensity of India's growth process, lessen the excessive dependence on the capital-intensive public sector, and effectively use the relatively high savings and investment rate to create high growth—much above the traditional 4–5% growth rate.

Results of the Reforms

By March 1995 when the Finance Minister had presented his fifth consecutive budget, he was able to outline his achievements.[4] The growth of the Indian economy which had fallen to barely 1% in 1991–92, was expected to reach 5.3% in 1994–95. It was a remarkably fast turnaround.

Secondly, industrial growth which had collapsed to barely 0.5% in 1991–92, had made a remarkable recovery with an industrial growth of 8.7%. The manufacturing sector was growing even faster at over 9% and the capital goods sector at over 24%.

Thirdly, there was a strong revival in domestic industrial investment as Indian industry modernised, upgraded its technology and improved its competitiveness. Foreign direct investment was responding well with large investments flowing into the power and telecommunications sectors.

Fourthly, food grain production which had fallen to 168 million tonnes in 1990–91 was estimated at a high of 189 million tonnes in 1994–95. Indian farmers had responded well to remunerative prices and to various other production-related incentives. Food grain stocks had reached a record of 37 million tonnes by May 1995.

Fifthly, the growth had created new jobs for the people. Employment had increased from 3 million jobs in 1991–92 to over 6 million jobs in 1994–95. This was a spectacular increase since many people had previously spoken about the adverse impact of the reforms on employment.

Sixthly, export growth has been remarkably good. The dollar value of exports in 1991–92 fell by 1.5%; by 1994–95 exports had shown a healthy growth at over 17%. Imports had also grown but were within manageable limits. Importantly, exports now finance over 90% of imports compared to just 60% in the latter part of the 1980s. The external deficit on current account which was over 3% of GDP in 1990–91 had dropped to less than 0.5% in 1994–95.

Finally the foreign currency reserves which had fallen to barely US$1 billion in June 1991 had risen to over US$20 billion in March 1995.

The response of the economy on the whole to the programme of macro-economic stabilisation has been positive. As the Finance Minister claimed in his budget speech of 1995, growth has recovered. Industrial production and investment have also recovered. The improvements in India's external accounts, current as well as capital, have been dramatic. The growth of exports has been healthy as a result of which the current account deficit has come down significantly.

The decline in inflation in 1995 has also helped the economy in some important respects. By August 1995, the rate had come down to a little over 7% which indicated that the steps taken during the year had begun to have an impact.

Liberalisation of Investments

The liberalisation of the investment regime especially dismantling the previous system of rigid controls over the private sector and opening up some of the earlier closed areas to the private sector has generated considerable confidence. Even in areas which are technically still reserved for the public sector (especially power, telecommunications and roads), the new policy provides considerable scope for private and foreign investment. Despite the controversy generated by the cancellation of Enron's Dabhol power project by the Maharashtra Government, overall optimism regarding private investment in the infrastructure continues, reflecting the broad national consensus.

Trade Liberalisation

The liberalisation of the trade regime has also been significant. Export controls have been drastically reduced. Foreign exchange controls, which had traditionally been irksome to the private sector, were also reduced. By March 1994, the government had established near full current account convertibility of the rupee.

Financial Sector Reforms

The financial sector reforms were suggested by a committee headed by former Finance Secretary Mr Narasimham. Several measures to implement its report have been taken. The discretion of banks and financial institutions over their portfolio composition has been increased. The Cash Reserve Ratio (CRR) and the Statutory Liquidity Ratio (SLR) have been reduced. Priority sector lending has been made less onerous. The government has also announced the creation of an autonomous Board for Financial Supervision. Controls over interest rates have been relaxed and the government has begun a comprehensive programme to strengthen the public sector banks. For the first time the country's central bank, the Reserve Bank of India, has announced guidelines for the entry of new commercial banks. Nine new banks have been authorised, including three foreign banks which will open branches in India.

Tax Reforms

Following the Tax Reform Committee's Report in 1993, the country has embarked on a comprehensive programme of tax reform. Tariffs have been significantly reduced over the last four years. In the 1994–95 Budget, taxes on corporate income were reduced and a major reform of indirect taxes was unveiled. Coverage has been extended to what is called Modvat to include the manufacturing sector which was previously excluded. Parts of the service sector are now also covered.

PRIVATISATION OF THE PUBLIC SECTOR

Size of the Public Sector

India has about 1000 non-financial public enterprises of which about 700 are owned by the State governments. These public enterprises have traditionally been instruments of channelling public funds into key sectors of the economy reserved for the public sector. According to a recent publication of the World Bank, public enterprises account for 55% of the economy's capital stock and 25% of the non-agricultural GDP.[5]

Finances of the Public Sector

Since 1991 a series of steps has been taken to improve the finances of the public enterprises. However, privatisation of the Public Sector Enterprises is not yet the policy of the government. For a variety of political reasons, the Government of India is still shy of privatisation. Some disinvestment of shares has been planned and in fact carried out. However, this has been done more to mobilise fiscal resources rather than to restructure or reform the PSUs. The Government has implemented a disinvestment programme of Rs100 billion (over US$3 billion) of which about half has already been carried out.

The philosophy of economic reforms requires the government to shed those public enterprises whose general financial performance has been poor. The public enterprises are in poor condition not because of any inherent managerial weaknesses but because of political interference. In India, as in many other countries, public enterprises have suffered enormously due to the politicisation of management, personnel and sometimes even contracts. The political parties in power have tended to view the public enterprises as milch cows for raising funds for their party purposes. Patronage rather than performance has been the primary consideration governing public enterprises in India.

Social Considerations

There is a great deal of fear in India that the closure of public sector enterprises may lead to unemployment which in turn may bring the system under new kinds of strain as has been witnessed in Latin America. Traditionally organised labour has considerable political clout in India. A country which has been brought up under socialism finds it difficult to cope with these changes. However, in the long term, privatisation of public enterprises is perhaps in India's national interest.

THE ECONOMY OF THE INDIAN STATES

Under the Indian federal system, the economy operates essentially through the 25 States and seven Union Territories. As is only natural in a federal system, most of the powers to deal with the economy lie with the States where most of the economic activity occurs.

According to the 1991 Census, of the 846 million Indian population, over 835 million lived in the 25 States, the largest of which is Uttar Pradesh (UP). UP's population in 1991 was estimated at 139 million, followed by Bihar with 86 million and Maharashtra with 78 million. Andhra Pradesh had a population of 66 million, as did Madhya Pradesh, and Tamil Nadu had 55 million. These five States accounted for 490 million of the 835 million population of the Indian States in 1991, making them bigger than any other country in the world barring China.

According to the available projections, Uttar Pradesh will have a population of 168 million by 2001, Bihar 105 million, Maharashtra 91 million, Andhra Pradesh 76 million, Madhya Pradesh 77 million, and Tamil Nadu 62 million. In other words, these five States with a population of nearly 580 million will account for nearly 60% of the Indian population by the year 2001.

There are major variations between the income levels of the Indian States. Amongst the larger States, Pubjab, Maharashtra and Haryana have per capita incomes which are nearly three times larger than the populous States of Bihar and Uttar Pradesh. Maharashtra is also far more industrially advanced than Uttar Pradesh or Bihar, as are Gujarat and Haryana. This makes for large regional disparities amongst the various States of the Indian Union. These regional disparities are a constant source of concern to the national policy-makers and planners because of the inevitable stress which they place on the management of the Indian polity.

The basic reason for these regional disparities lies, first, in the inadequate development of the physical infrastructure in the backward States, and, secondly, in their poor social development, especially in terms of health and education.

As a result, the potential growth in the relatively more developed States like Maharashtra, Gujarat, Haryana and Karnataka, which are gearing themselves for economic reforms more quickly, is likely to provide them with more opportunities to attract foreign as well as domestic investments.

DEMOCRATIC PROCESS

Behind the entire programme of economic reforms lies the basic democratic process in India. Since the first general election in 1951–52, there have been 11 general elections. Today the Indian system is operated by nearly 780 Members of Parliament at the national level, about 3500 members of State Legislatures and over 3 million elected representatives at the local level.

In addition to economic reforms in 1991, India embarked on one of the most ambitious structural reforms of its political system in 1993 through the 73rd and 74th amendments to the Indian Constitution. As a result of these Constitutional amendments, elections to local bodies are mandatory. Political power is being transferred in one single historic step to the elected representatives of the Indian people. Perhaps, in the long run, this structural reform of the Indian political system will be far more important than economic reform, though economic reforms are currently more newsworthy.

The democratic process in India poses several challenges for economic policy. Under the Indian Constitution, powers are shared between the Centre, the States and local bodies. A large number of powers are the preserve of the States and some of the powers which are placed under the concurrent list are shared between the Centre and the States. The Indian Constitution is basically predicated on the federal principle which makes economic reforms very complex. While the States cannot do much with respect to foreign policy, including foreign economic policy, money, banking etc the Centre also cannot do a great deal with respect to powers which are within the prerogative of the States.

The important question that arises with regard to economic policy is the extent to which the Indian democratic process is predictable. As of 1996, it is safe to predict that India will continue to remain broadly committed to economic reforms since there is a broad political consensus among all the major political parties. What is not predictable, however, is the pace of economic reforms. The political parties in India, including the Congress Party, remain divided on the speed with which reforms should be carried out. There is considerable feeling among the political parties that the reforms are too much oriented for the benefit of India's middle class but not sufficiently oriented towards the rest, a large number of whom remain poor despite more than four decades of planned development.

CONCLUDING OBSERVATIONS

Successful Change

India has been remarkably successful in bringing about significant changes in economic policies and carrying out major structural reforms, without the painful disruptions which have been witnessed in many countries of Latin America and Africa. There are distinct signs of confidence in Indian industry that it is able to handle the globalisation and integration of the economy.

Factors in India's Favour

Two factors stand out in India's favour: first, the quality of Indian entrepreneurship, and secondly, the quality of India's human resources. Both these have played an important role in the smooth transition which India has made and is likely to make in the years to come.

India's entrepreneurship is as old as Indian history. Today the major industrial houses like the Tatas, the Birlas, and the Ambanis are global players. Their management is of international standard and they are not afraid of either foreign competition or the challenges of globalisation.

The second vital factor is India's vast human resources. Although there is still a great deal of illiteracy in India, the fact remains that India has one of the largest pools of scientific, technical and managerial personnel. These people constitute the backbone of India's process of modernisation and economic reforms.

Prognosis for India

India has yet to take its final steps towards completing the process of economic reform. In fact, during 1994 and 1995, the pace of reforms has been slowed down by political considerations. Some of the recent studies have emphasised the need to improve the capacity of the public sector to invest, prioritise and increase the efficiency of public expenditure, increase private investments, better manage capital inflows and generally accelerate the pace of reform in several key areas.

The prognosis is optimistic. India has all the ingredients needed for success on the economic front. What has held India and Indians back are economic policies which placed heavy emphasis on controls, and restrictions on Indian creativity. As the economic reforms move forward, as they are bound to due to international pressures, India will emerge as a major economic power, and sooner rather than later.

---

1 *Jawaharlal Nehru's Speeches*, Delhi Publications Division, Ministry of Information and Broadcasting, Govt of India, Vol 1, 1949 pp 25–27.
2 *Speech of Finance Minister Presenting Central Government's Budget for 1991–92*, New Delhi Ministry of Finance 1991.
3 *India—Industrial Development Review* published by the Economist Intelligence Unit for UNIDO, Vienna, 1995.
4 *Speech of Finance Minister Presenting Central Government's Budget for 1995-96*, New Delhi Ministry of Finance, 1995.
5 See World Bank *India—Recent Economic Developments and Prospects*, Washington DC, 1995, p 52.

CHAPTER 3

INDUSTRIAL POLICY AND FOREIGN INVESTMENT
by V K Shunglu

HISTORICAL PERSPECTIVE AND HIGHLIGHTS OF PRE-LIBERALISATION INDUSTRIAL POLICIES

Introduction

India became an independent nation in 1947, with a determination to achieve self-reliant growth with social justice. It adopted a 'mixed economy' where the public and private sectors could co-exist with the former dominating the core sectors of the economy. The government has articulated its industrial policy through various Industrial Policy Resolutions. The key features of all these resolutions included a former dominant role for the public sector (where the government has a majority shareholding), demarcation of priority and non-priority sectors by the Government, encouragement to the small-scale sector (industries with a specified maximum investment in plant and machinery at present Rs6 million), prevention of concentration of economic power, control of foreign investments in India, encouragement of domestic entrepreneurship and balanced regional growth.

Regulatory Framework

The Industries (Development and Regulation) Act, 1951 (the IDR Act), was enacted to provide the legal framework for development and control of industry. All industrial undertakings manufacturing items mentioned in the First Schedule of the IDR Act were required to obtain a licence for establishing a new undertaking, manufacturing a new article, effecting substantial expansion, carrying on business of an existing unit, or for changing location.

The private sector could not participate in production in 17 industrial sectors exclusively reserved for the State, and 836 items were later reserved for exclusive manufacture in the small-scale sector. The reservation policy along with the special treatment by the government resulted in undue protection to these industries, making them non-competitive.

The regulatory framework was all-pervasive. The Monopolies and Restrictive Trade Practices Act, 1969 (MRTP), governed undertakings which had an investment level of Rs200 million or more, later raised to Rs1 billion, or which commanded a market niche of over 25%. These undertakings required separate approval from the MRTP authorities for manufacturing a new article or for expansion. The Foreign Exchange Regulation Act, 1973 (FERA), inter alia regulated foreign equity participation in Indian companies. Particular restrictions were applicable for companies with foreign equity participation of more than 40% (FERA companies). MRTP and FERA companies were subjected to greater scrutiny by licensing authorities, and were restricted to investment in a set of priority industries popularly known as Appendix I industries. On the whole, companies' ability to expand production was limited by the licensing mechanism.

Nearly 50 categories of approvals were necessary from Centre and State government bodies. These covered licence/registration, import of technology, procurement of imported machinery, intermediates and raw materials, locational approval, land allotment, project buildings, water supply, energy, effluent, financial assistance and other special clearances. There were 10 Approval Committees in different Administrative Ministries that were responsible for considering and approving the grant of a licence. The sequential nature of these approvals resulted in delay in the execution of projects.

As a rule, foreign investment was permitted only if it was tied to the inflow of foreign technology. The normal ceiling on foreign investment was 40% of the equity and there was a list of industries where foreign participation was not permitted. The Phased Manufacturing Programme (PMP), which aimed at forcing the pace of indigenisation in manufacturing was a part of licensing conditions.

Consequences

These policies initially succeeded in promoting the development of a diverse industrial and infrastructural base. A large scientific/technical manpower base was created and self-sufficiency in the majority of industrial items was attained. However, the adverse effects of these policies were loss-making public sector enterprises, a government-controlled financial sector, high import duties and corporate taxes, militant trade unions and low productivity, inflation, periodic trade/current account deficits, low private sector investment, high unemployment, tax evasion and in due course widespread technological obsolescence.

HIGHLIGHTS OF THE NEW INDUSTRIAL POLICY (NIP), 1991

The objectives of the new policy are to build on the gains already made, to correct distortions, to achieve a sustained growth in productivity and gainful employment and to attain international competitiveness. While still committed to the ideal of growth with social equity, this policy made a dramatic change in direction from regulation and protection to the active encouragement of private and foreign participation in industry. The government will concentrate more on the development of industrial infrastructure while gradually withdrawing from all manufacturing activities of low priority from the social angle. Changes in line with these objectives have been made and are described below under convenient headings.

(Note: The new government which took office in June 1996 decided to continue this policy.)

Industrial Licensing

From the 1960s onwards, several committees appointed by the government recommended deregulation, as the objectives envisaged by the government, such as better resource allocation, balanced regional growth, and prevention of economic concentration had not been achieved. As a result, in the 1970s and 1980s, there was gradual deregulation. The 1991 policy quickened the pace of deregulation by reducing the number of industries reserved for the public sector from 17 to six. Even in these six areas, selective private participation is permitted. However, reservation for the small-scale sector continues.

Industrial licensing has been abolished for all industries (including MRTP and FERA companies) except for a short list of 18 industries selected due to social, security, strategic or environmental reasons or which are hazardous. Manufactured articles that have a high import content or are of elitist consumption are also included in the compulsory licensing list (Annex II of the NIP, reproduced as Schedule II of this chapter). This list was further reduced to 16 in 1993.

Location restrictions for industry have been removed, except in the case of 23 listed metropolitan cities, which have a population of more than 1 million according to the 1991 census. All industries (except electronics, computer software, printing and other non-polluting industries) have to be located outside the 25 km boundary of these cities, except in certain designated industrial areas. The PMP was first discontinued for new units and later for existing units.

Annex I of the NIP (reproduced as Schedule I of this chapter) contains a list of industries reserved for the public sector. Annex II of the NIP lists industries in respect of which industrial licensing is compulsory. Annex III of the NIP (reproduced as Schedule III of this chapter) contains a list of industries where automatic approval for up to 51% foreign equity participation is permitted. For a detailed list of industries reserved for the small-scale sector, the Office of the Development Commissioner (Small-Scale Industries), Nirman Bhavan, New Delhi or any of its branches in various States may be contacted. Schedule IV of this chapter has a list of cities with a population of 1 million and above according to the 1991 census.

Procedural Requirements for Licensed and De-licensed Sectors

New units

The entire policy framework has been demystified by simplifying procedures and making them more transparent. All earlier registration schemes have been abolished. For setting up a unit in the de-licensed sector, the entrepreneur (whether domestic or foreign) now has to file an Industrial Entrepreneur's Memorandum (IEM) with the Secretariat of Industrial Approvals (SIA) in the Ministry of Industry. A crossed demand draft for Rs1000 payable to the Pay and Accounts Officer, Department of Industrial Policy and Promotion, Ministry of Industry, must accompany the memorandum. The SIA will immediately acknowledge the receipt of this draft and indicate a reference number that the entrepreneur can quote in all future correspondence. Part B of this form has to be filed by the unit once commercial production is commenced. This requirement is merely for statistical purposes and for a post-facto check on whether the proposed manufacturing activity requires an industrial licence or not.

Existing units

Substantial expansion, subject to locational conditions, of existing units has also been exempted from licensing.

Facilitation cell

A Facilitation cell has been set up in SIA, to attend to inquiries from entrepreneurs on a wide range of subjects concerning investment decisions. This cell will also provide information on status of applications filed for various industrial approvals. Information regarding various infrastructural facilities offered by various State governments is also readily available in the cell.

Small-scale industries

Small-scale (as already defined earlier) and ancillary units (whose investment in plant and machinery does not exceed Rs7.5 million) do not have to file an IEM but may register themselves with the Director of Industries of the concerned State Government. This registration is not compulsory but is usually desirable in order to obtain any incentives that the State governments may offer.

Licensed industries

All industrial undertakings subject to compulsory licensing are required to submit an application in a prescribed form (Form IL) to SIA. For Non-Resident Indians (NRIs) planning to invest in the compulsory licensing sector, a separate form (Form FC) (SIA) should be submitted to SIA. In these cases, the licence application fee is Rs2500. The normal approval time is generally 6–8 weeks.

New transparent industrial classifications

A welcome feature of the NIP is the specification that all industrial items are classified according to the Indian Trade Classification System (based on the Harmonised Commodity Description and Coding System) and have to be described as such in the IEM or IL form. This is done to eliminate procedural complications for investors. Complete details on the Indian Trade Classification System are available in a publication of the same name by the Directorate General of Commercial Intelligence and Statistics, Ministry of Commerce, and is available in all bookshops which stock government publications.

POLICY ON FOREIGN INVESTMENT

A striking feature of the new policy is the opening up to foreign investment. Traditionally foreign investment has been tightly regulated in India. In the case of both foreign technology agreements sought by Indian firms as well as foreign investment, it was previously necessary to obtain specific prior approval from the government for each project. However, the new policy has been designed to remove the delay and uncertainty which clouds the relationships between Indian and foreign firms and is designed to encourage more stable and dynamic technological relationships between foreign firms and their Indian counterparts.

Multilateral Investment Guarantee Agency (MIGA)

MIGA was established in April 1988 to encourage the flow of foreign direct investment to, and among, developing member countries. The Agency offers non-commercial investment insurance cover to private investors and provides promotional and advisory services. India is also a signatory to MIGA thus providing foreign investors with additional security against non-commercial risks.

Various forms of foreign participation in Indian industry are encouraged today. Foreign investment is no longer tied to the inflow of technology. At present, there is no area where foreign investment is prohibited.

Bilateral Investment Agreements

In order to encourage bilateral flow of investment, India has signed several agreements with countries such as the United Kingdom, Germany, Russia, Malaysia, Denmark and Turkmenistan.

Automatic Approval

In the case of high-priority items (Annex III of the NIP), foreign equity participation of up to 51% is automatically permitted by the Reserve Bank. Foreign equity is ordinarily expected to cover the foreign exchange requirements for import of capital goods. Automatic approval is also granted for up to 51% foreign investment in trading houses primarily engaged in exports. Hotel and tourism-related industries and service sectors are also eligible for automatic approval of up to 51% foreign equity. In the 1996–97 budget presentation on 22 July 1996, the Finance Minister announced that the list of 35 industries covered by Annex III of the NIP would be expanded.

Foreign Investment Promotion Board (FIPB)

In cases where the item to be manufactured is not included in Annex III, or where foreign equity is more than 51%, applications for approval must be submitted to the Foreign Investment Promotion Board (FIPB), which was until recently part of the Prime Minister's office. The FIPB is a high-powered body which is authorised to engage in negotiations with a number of large international firms and to consider the project in totality without any pre-determined parameters or procedures. This body is headed by the Secretary, Ministry of Industry and has some other Secretaries as permanent members, viz Commerce and Finance. Once the case is recommended by the FIPB, it is considered for approval either by the Industry Minister (in cases involving up to Rs6 billion) or by the Cabinet Committee for Foreign Investment (CCFI) headed by the Prime Minister in cases involving more than that amount.

Raising Foreign Equity in Existing Companies

The procedure for raising foreign equity in existing companies has been simplified. The Reserve Bank of India accords automatic approval to companies wishing to raise foreign equity up to 51% provided they are predominantly engaged in high priority (Annex III of the NIP) industries or for financing the expansion programme of a non-Annex III industry, provided that the proposed expansion involves the manufacture of Annex III articles.

Applications for approval of such proposals are to be submitted, free of charge, in Form FC (RBI) to the Exchange Control Department, Reserve Bank, Bombay.

Dividend Balancing Condition

In specified consumer goods industries (refer to Schedule VI of this chapter), there is the additional requirement that companies have to balance dividend payments with earnings from exports for seven years. The dividend balancing period will start from the date of allotment of shares to the foreign investor. In the case of companies raising equity for expansion, the balancing period will start from the date of commencement of production.

Foreign Technology Agreements

The government has simplified approval mechanisms for foreign technology agreements with a view to 'injecting the desired level of technological dynamism in Indian industry' and 'for promoting an industrial environment where the acquisition of technological capacity receives priority'. This could be in the form of providing technical

39

know-how, technical assistance, licensing intellectual property or training. Automatic approval is given by RBI for all industries, where the contract involves a lump payment of less than US$2 million (this limit was increased in the budget of 1996–97) and a royalty of up to 5% of domestic sales and 8% for exports. A ceiling of 8% of the total sales over a 10 year period from the date of agreement or seven years from the commencement of production is also specified. These payments are calculated net of tax. No permission is now required for hiring of foreign technicians or for foreign testing of indigenously developed technologies.

REPATRIATION OF CAPITAL

Foreign capital invested in India can be repatriated along with any capital appreciation, after the payment of taxes due. Automatic disinvestment is permitted through stock exchanges for listed shares at market prices. In the case of unlisted shares, the sale price is required to be approved by RBI before disinvestment.

THE PUBLIC SECTOR

Selective private participation, including foreign participation, is being allowed in several infrastructural areas, which were hitherto reserved for the public sector. Sick state-owned units are referred to the Board for Industrial and Financial Reconstruction (BIFR) for either initiation of a revival package or for being wound up. The government has announced that it will disinvest equity in the public sector up to 49%. State-owned enterprises are to be granted greater autonomy in management and will be held accountable for losses.

AMENDMENTS TO THE MONOPOLIES AND RESTRICTIVE TRADE PRACTICES ACT (MRTP)

The MRTP Act was amended to eliminate the prior approval of the Central Government for expansion of units and the setting up of new units by large companies. The inherent bias against large and dominant companies has thus been removed.

The government continues to put emphasis on controlling and regulating monopolistic, restrictive and unfair trade practices. The MRTP Commission is to be empowered to exercise punitive and compensatory powers, thus making it more effective in curbing unfair trade practices.

AMENDMENTS TO THE FOREIGN EXCHANGE REGULATION ACT (FERA)

Comprehensive amendments to the FERA were effected in 1993 in keeping with the Indian Government's stance on liberalisation and openness. Several sub-sections of the FERA, 1973 have been deleted so that misapprehensions and fears among foreign investors may be avoided. Some of the important changes include:

(1) The RBI no longer blocks securities of persons migrating abroad nor does it block bank accounts and securities of emigrants.

(2) Permission has been granted for taking out goods on rental, lease, hire or any other arrangement which does not amount to the disposal of such goods.

(3) The earlier regulation of transfer of shares between non-residents has now been removed.

(4) Restriction on holding of immovable properties outside India has now been suitably amended to enable RBI to grant general permission subject to certain conditions, as may be notified by RBI from time to time.

(5) Earlier restrictions on FERA companies in the matter of borrowing funds or raising deposits in India have been removed.

(6) FERA companies are not subject to any restrictions regarding acceptance of appointment as an agent or technical or managerial adviser or for the use of trade marks. Foreign companies, foreign citizens and non-residents continue to remain subject to these restrictions.

(7) FERA companies are now permitted to establish a branch office or a liaison office even when the non-resident interest in such companies exceeds 40%. Such companies are also permitted to acquire whole or part of any undertaking in India for carrying on trade, commerce and industry (except for agriculture and plantation activities).

(8) No prior permission is now necessary for foreign nationals taking up employment in India.

(9) Henceforth FERA companies, unlike foreign companies or foreign citizens, do not require the permission of RBI for acquiring, holding, transferring or disposing of by sale, mortgage, deed, lease, or gift, any immovable property situated in India.

DISINVESTMENT

In 1992, the government simplified the procedure of disinvestment of foreign investors, permitting expeditious approval of the disinvestment proposals provided the following guidelines are met:

(1) The RBI permits on a near automatic basis the transfer of shares, bonds and debentures provided the sale is effected through the stock exchange or a registered merchant banker or stockbroker.

(2) The RBI also gives special permission where the foreign investor wishes to transfer his shareholding not through a stock exchange but on a private basis to a resident, including one of the co-promoters.

(3) For the pricing of the disinvestment, in the case of a transfer from a non-resident to a resident, the RBI has to satisfy itself as to how the price has been calculated.

(4) In the case of unlisted companies, or in the case of listed companies where the shares are not regularly traded, the RBI will be guided by the net asset value and the earnings per share.

(5) For the transfer of shares, bonds and debentures of an Indian company held by a non-resident or foreign national to another non-resident, the RBI does not interfere with the price; however, a tax certificate is required before the RBI gives permission.

In the union budget, the government proposed setting up a Disinvestment Commission to create an institutional mechanism to consider disinvestment of public sector undertakings in a rational and transparent way.

RAISING FINANCE IN INDIA

Investors can raise funds through a variety of debt and equity instruments. Long-term loans could also be sought from national or state level financial institutions depending on the size of the project. Financial leasing, hire-purchase, deferred payment guarantee, and other mechanisms are also available. Concrete project reports along with market survey reports are a pre-requisite for loan applications. Working capital financing is available from numerous nationalised and other banks in India, through such instruments as fixed deposits, inter-corporate deposits and commercial paper.

Investors can freely access India's large capital market for mobilisation of funds. Indian firms also have the option of raising funds from international capital markets.

ROLE OF STATE GOVERNMENTS

There are a large number of reputable project and management consultancy agencies in India to provide expertise in preparing project reports. Several State governments provide single window clearance facilities for investors.

Clearances for land, building, water, power, etc are required for setting up a business in India. See Schedules VII and VIII for a check-list of clearances required.

SPECIAL POLICIES FOR SPECIFIC SECTORS

Specific policies for various infrastructural sectors, electronics and some other sectors are discussed elsewhere in the book.

Food Processing

All food processing industries (other than milk-food, malted foods, flour and a few items reserved for the small-scale sector) are considered high priority industries and eligible for preferential treatment.

All items of packaging for food processing industries, excluding those reserved for the small-scale sector, are also eligible for automatic approval.

Apart from the distillation and brewing of alcoholic drinks, the manufacture of sugar, animal fats and oils, all other food processing items do not require a licence.

The scheme of dividend balancing is applicable to items such as chocolates, beer and wines.

Several agriculture-based products are entirely exempt from excise duties. Customs duty on most agriculture processing equipment and spare parts has been reduced to 25%.

Projects of 100% EOU in agriculture, aquaculture, animal husbandry, floriculture, horticulture, poultry and sericulture may sell 50% of the value of production in the domestic market after paying half the value of customs duty for similar products or excise duty, whichever is higher. This does not apply to items that originated from plantation crops, tea, coffee, rubber, cardamom and rice. Domestic Tariff Area sales are not permitted for alcoholic beverages.

Drugs and Pharmaceuticals

A new drug policy was announced de-licensing all except five bulk drugs (which were reserved for the public sector), drugs that involved use of recombinant DNA technology and specific cell/tissue targetted formulations. The remaining bulk drugs were automatically open to foreign investment and technology participation up to 51%.

Price control deregulation was announced in the case of drugs where there was sufficient market competition. Uniform Maximum Allowable Post Manufacturing Expenses (MAPE) of 100% are allowed for all drugs under price control.

The National Pharmaceutical Pricing Authority is an independent body to approve prices within a fixed time. The National Drug Authority ensures quality control and rational use of medicines.

SPECIAL SCHEMES FOR NON-RESIDENT INDIANS (NRIS)

In the New Industrial Policy, a special role was assigned to NRIs and to Overseas Corporate Bodies (OCBs, viz overseas companies predominantly owned by NRIs). In 1991, the number of NRIs was estimated to be 15 million, constituting a sizable resource in terms of finance, scientific talent and technical know-how.

NRIs and OCBs are permitted to invest with full repatriation benefits up to 100% in the equity of high priority industries. In the case of export trading companies, 100% EOUs and units located in Export Processing Zones, 100% foreign equity investment is permissible.

SPECIAL SCHEMES FOR EXPORT PROMOTION

Export Processing Zones (EPZs)

The government has declared seven designated areas known as EPZs within which manufacturing and processing activities can be carried out for the purpose of export. In these areas, the government provides basic infrastructure facilities such as power and water. Standard factory buildings and customs clearance facilities are also provided. The areas of activity permitted in EPZs included training, packaging, labelling, repairs re-conditioning and re-engineering. The seven EPZs are Kandla (Gujarat), Bombay (Maharashtra), Madras (Tamil Nadu), Falta (West Bengal), Cochin (Kerala), Noida (UP) and Vishakhapatnam (Andhra Pradesh).

Export Oriented Units (EOUs)

Anywhere raw material and skilled labour can be sourced, 100% EOUs may be set up. Generally, 25% of the production in value terms may be sold in the Domestic Tariff Area (DTA) at concessional duty rates subject to fulfilment of minimum value-addition norms. A higher DTA access of 35% and 50% is allowed for electronics and agricultural industries respectively. However, no DTA sales are permissible for rice, jewellery, diamonds, precious and semi-precious stones and gems, motor cars, liquor, silver bullion and some other items.

Criteria for Automatic Approval of EOUs and EPZ Units

(1) Import of new capital goods financed by foreign equity or constituting not more than 50% of the total value of plant and equipment, subject to a ceiling of Rs30 million.

(2) Foreign Technology Agreements are to be made within the stipulations of the NIP regarding automatic approval.

(3) The project should undertake to achieve value addition of at least 35%, unless otherwise specified.

(4) If located within an EPZ, then the availability of space and conformity with environmental and other standards of the EPZ should be certified by the Development Commissioner. If located in any other area, then the locational conditions stipulated by the NIP have to be complied with.

(5) The product to be manufactured should not be in the compulsory licensing list and should not be reserved for the public sector.

(6) The unit should meet the requirements of the customs authorities including:
  (a) The provisions of the Central Excise and Salt Act, 1944;
  (b) Amenability to bonding by customs;
  (c) All manufacturing operations to be carried out on the same premises.

(7) The conditions relating to DTA sales should be adhered to.

(8) The unit should have an annual turnover of at least Rs500 million if it proposed to manufacture gems and jewellery and is located outside EPZs or other designated areas.

CURRENT INDUSTRIAL SCENARIO

The attainment of a strong and diverse industrial base over the last 48 years has been the striking feature of the Indian economic development process. Large investments have been made in building up capacity over a wide spectrum of industries. Industrial production has made rapid strides in terms of diversity, quality and quantity. India today produces a wide range of industrial goods. Indigenous capabilities have been established paving the way for further expansion and attainment of international competitiveness in various sectors such as mining, power, chemicals, transport and communication, metals, machinery and machine tools. The process of industrialisation has fostered the spirit of entrepreneurship and has encouraged the development of a wide variety of technical, managerial and operative skills.

Industrial growth over the years has been significant. During the first three plans (1951–65), industrial production maintained a growth rate ranging from 6% to 8%. After comparatively slower growth between 1966 and 1980, industrial growth recorded a surge in the 1980s, with the beginning of selective deregulation and liberalisation. In response to these initiatives, the average rate of industrial growth picked up from 5.9% in the Sixth Plan (1980–85) to 8.5% in the Seventh Plan (1985–90).

However, although industry performed well during the 1980s, the growing macro-economic imbalances and current account deficits resulted in a crisis in mid-1991. This resulted in the introduction of the New Industrial Policy in July, 1991 with a strong emphasis on stabilisation and attainment of competitiveness.

For the first two years following the structural reforms of 1991, overall industrial growth was only moderate. This was mainly due to the fiscal and monetary constraints that industry faced because of the government's preoccupation with handling the balance of payments crisis.

However, the adjustment of Indian industry to the reform process has been relatively quick. Overall industrial growth has been positive, rising from a mere 0.6% in 1991–92 to 2.3% in 1992–93. This was followed by a significant growth of 6% in 1993–94 and further accelerated to 9.4% in 1994–95 and 12.1% in 1995–96. The performance of the manufacturing sector improved substantially from −0.8% in 1991–92 to 13.7% in 1995–96. The capital goods sector, which had been in the doldrums earlier, emerged as a leading contributor to industrial buoyancy with a growth of 24.8% during the period 1994–95 and 19.4% in 1995–96. The consumer durable sector showed significant growth from 1994 onwards while the consumer non-durable sector picked up rapidly in 1994–95 and 1995–96.

The performance of six infrastructure industries (electricity, coal, saleable steel, petroleum refinery products, crude petroleum and cement) has been good with a growth of 7.8% for these industries during April–March 1995–96.

In the manufacturing sector, during the period April–March 1995–96, maximum growth was observed in the following sectors: transport equipment (20.9%), electrical machinery (20.8%), beverage, tobacco and products (20.0%), metal products and parts (17.7%), machinery and machine tools (17.6%), food products (14.7%) and basic metal and alloys (13.9%).

This broad-based industrial recovery has been due to a number of factors including the cumulative impact of various sectoral reforms (ie industrial, trade, financial and capital market reforms) which directly affect industrial performance. Favourable monsoons, bumper crops, and growing confidence both by foreign and Indian investors in the NIP have also gone a long way in fostering rapid growth. Industry-friendly fiscal measures including extension of Modified Value Added Tax (MODVAT) to more sectors, further rationalisation and reduction of tariffs, reduction of corporate taxes and elimination of government control over interest rates have also contributed largely to the recovery. Several State governments have formulated new industrial policies in line with the liberalised NIP.

Between August 1991 and May 1996, 25,781 IEMs were filed. The proposed investment envisaged is more than Rs5048 billion, and is expected to offer employment to approximately 4.7 million people. In addition, during this period, 2403 Letters of Intent (LOI) have been issued for setting up units in the licensed sectors. Nearly Rs753 billion is expected to be invested and this would have an employment potential of nearly 514,000 people.

FOREIGN INVESTMENT TRENDS

As earlier stated, the new policy encourages foreign investment in India in order to forge stronger and more dynamic relationships between the domestic and foreign industry—both in terms of investment and technology. It has been recognised that foreign investment will bring with it the attendant advantages of technology transfer, marketing expertise, introduction of modern managerial techniques and new avenues for export promotion. The government has encouraged mobility of capital by allowing foreign investment to flow into India. The United Front Government has targetted an inflow of US$10 billion per year.

Large international firms such as IBM, BMW, Kellogg's, General Motors, General Electric, Coca-Cola, Sony, Motorola and Suzuki have been granted approvals for foreign collaboration. The total amount of foreign direct investment committed and approved has been over US$12 billion in terms of foreign equity in the four years (1991–95), implying total investment of over US$30 billion. Between August 1991 and April 1996, approvals granted involving foreign investment have numbered 4716. The total quantum of foreign investment envisaged is around Rs710 billion. So far the actual inflow has been in the order of nearly Rs151 billion.

CONCLUSION

Conventional indicators such as increase in sanctions and disbursements of loans by financial institutions, raising of capital by the corporate sector from the primary market (including international centres) and the trends of security prices in the secondary market all indicate a buoyant investment climate. The industrial recovery has gathered momentum and India is now ready to take a lead role among the newly industrialising countries of the world.

SCHEDULE I

Proposed List of Industries to be Reserved for the Public Sector (As indicated in Annex I of NIP)

1. Arms and ammunition and allied items of defence equipment, defence aircraft and warships

2. Atomic energy

3. Coal and lignite

4. Mineral oils

5. Mining of iron ore, manganese ore, chrome ore, gypsum, sulphur, gold and diamonds

6. Mining of copper, lead, zinc, tin, molybdenum and wolfram

7. Minerals specified in the Schedule to the Atomic Energy (Control of Production and Use) Order, 1953

8. Railway transport

Note: Items No.5 and 6 have subsequently been deleted from this list, vide Press Note No.3 (1993 Series).

SCHEDULE II

List of Industries in Respect of which Industrial Licensing will be Compulsory (As indicated in Annex II of NIP)

1. Coal and lignite
2. Petroleum (other than crude) and its distillation products
3. Distillation and brewing of alcoholic drinks
4. Sugar
5. Animal fats and oils
6. Cigars and cigarettes of tobacco and manufactured tobacco substitutes
7. Asbestos and asbestos-based products
8. Plywood, decorative veneers, and other wood-based products such as particle board, medium density fibre board, block board
9. Raw hides and skins, leather, chamois leather and patent leather
10. Tanned or dressed furskins
11. Motor cars
12. Paper and newsprint except bagasse-based units
13. Electronic aerospace and defence equipment (all types)
14. Industrial explosives, including detonating fuse, safety fuse, gun powder, nitrocellulose and matches
15. Hazardous chemicals
16. Drugs and pharmaceuticals (according to Drug Policy)
17. Entertainment electronics (VCRs, colour TVs, CD players, tape recorders)
18. White goods (domestic refrigerators, domestic dishwashing machines, programmable domestic washing machines, microwave ovens, airconditioners)

Note: The compulsory licensing provisions would not apply in respect of the small-scale units taking up the manufacture of any of the above items reserved for exclusive manufacture in the small-scale sector.

Items No.11, 18 and all but 'chamois leather' in item No.9 have been subsequently deleted from this list, vide Press Note No.4 (1993 Series).

SCHEDULE III

List of Industries for Automatic Approval of Foreign Technology Agreements and for 51% Foreign Equity Approvals (As indicated in Annex III of NIP)

1. Metallurgical Industries
   (i) Ferro alloys
   (ii) Casting and forgings
   (iii) Non-ferrous metals and their alloys
   (iv) Sponge iron and pelletisation
   (v) Large diameter steel welded pipes of over 300 mm diameter and stainless steel pipes
   (vi) Pig iron

2. Boilers and Steam Generating Plants

3. Prime Movers (other than electrical generators)
   (i) Industrial turbines
   (ii) Internal combustion engines
   (iii) Alternate energy systems like solar, wind, etc and equipment therefor
   (iv) Gas/hydro/steam turbines up to 60 MW

4. Electrical Equipment
   (i) Equipment for transmission and distribution of electricity including power and distribution transformers, power relays, HT switch gear synchronous condensers
   (ii) Electrical motors
   (iii) Electrical furnaces, industrial furnaces and induction heating equipment
   (iv) X-ray equipment
   (v) Electronic equipment, components including subscribers' and telecommunication equipment
   (vi) Component wires for manufacture of lead-in-wires
   (vii) Hydro/steam/gas generators/generating sets up to 60 MW
   (viii) Generating sets and pumping sets based on internal combustion engines
   (ix) Jelly-filled telecommunication cables
   (x) Optic fibre
   (xi) Energy efficient lamps
   (xii) Midget carbon electrodes

5. Transportation
   (i) Mechanised sailing vessels up to 10,000 DWT including fishing trawlers
   (ii) Ship ancillaries

(iii) (a) Commercial vehicles, public transport vehicles including automotive commercial three-wheeler jeep type vehicles, industrial locomotives

(b) Automotive two wheelers and three wheelers

(c) Automotive components/spares and ancillaries

(iv) Shock absorbers for railway equipment

(v) Brake system for railway stock and locomotives

6. Industrial Machinery
   (i) Industrial machinery and equipment

7. (i) Machine tools and industrial robots and their controls and accessories

   (ii) Jigs, fixtures, tools and dies of specialised types and cross-land tooling

   (iii) Engineering production aids such as cutting and forming tools, patterns and dies and tools

8. Agricultural Machinery
   (i) Tractors
   (ii) Self-propelled harvester combines
   (iii) Rice transplanters

9. Earth-moving Machinery
   (i) Earth-moving machinery and construction machinery and components thereof

10. Industrial Instruments
    (i) Indicating, recording and regulating devices for pressure, temperature, rate of flow weights levels and the like

11. Scientific and Electromedical Instruments and Laboratory Equipment

12. Nitrogenous and Phosphatic Fertilizers falling under
    (i) Inorganic fertilizers under '18 Fertilizers' in the First Schedule to IDR Act, 1951.

13. Chemicals (other than fertilizers)
    (i) Heavy organic chemicals including petrochemicals
    (ii) Heavy inorganic chemicals
    (iii) Organic fine chemicals
    (iv) Synthetic resins and plastics
    (v) Man-made fibres
    (vi) Synthetic rubber
    (vii) Industrial explosives
    (viii) Technical grade insecticides, fungicides, weedicides, and the like
    (ix) Synthetic detergents
    (x) Miscellaneous chemicals (for industrial use only)
        (a) Catalysts and catalyst supports
        (b) Photographic chemicals
        (c) Rubber chemicals
        (d) Polyols

     (e) Isocyanates, urethanes etc
     (f) Speciality chemicals for enhanced oil recovery
     (g) Heating fluids
     (h) Coal tar distillation and products therefrom
     (i) Tonnage plants for the manufacture of industrial gases
     (j) High altitude breathing oxygen/medical oxygen
     (k) Nitrous oxide
     (l) Refrigerant gases like liquid nitrogen, carbon dioxide etc in large volumes
     (m) Argon and other rare gases
     (n) Alkali/acid resisting cement compound
     (o) Leather chemicals and auxiliaries

14. Drugs and Pharmaceuticals
   According to Drug Policy

15.   (i) Paper and pulp including paper products
     (ii) Industrial laminates

16.   (i) Automobile tyres and tubes
     (ii) Rubberised heavy duty industrial beltings of all types
     (iii) Rubberised conveyor beltings
     (iv) Rubber reinforced and lined fire-fighting hose pipes
     (v) High pressure braided hoses
     (vi) Engineering and industrial plastic products

17. Plate Glass
     (i) Glass shells for television tubes
     (ii) Float glass and plate glass
     (iii) HT insulators
     (iv) Glass fibres of all types

18. Ceramics
     (i) Ceramics for industrial uses

19. Cement Products
     (i) Portland cement
     (ii) Gypsum boards, wall boards and the like

20. High Technology Reproduction and Multiplication Equipment

21. Carbon and Carbon Products
     (i) Graphite electrodes and anodes
     (ii) Impervious graphite blocks and sheets

22. Pretensioned High Pressure RCC Pipes

23. Rubber Machinery

24. Printing Machinery
    (i) Web-fed high speed off-set rotary printing machine having output of 30,000 or more impressions per hour
    (ii) Photo composing/type-setting machines
    (iii) Multi-colour sheet-fed off-set printing machines of sizes of 18" x 15" and above
    (iv) High speed rotogravure printing machines having output of 30,000 or more impressions per hour
25. Welding Electrodes other than those for Welding Mild Steel
26. Industrial Synthetic Diamonds
27. (i) Photosynthesis improvers
    (ii) Genetically modified free living symbiotics nitrogen fixer
    (iii) Pheromones
    (iv) Bio-insecticides
28. Extraction and Upgrading of Minor Oils
29. Pre-fabricated Building Material
30. Soya Products
    (i) Soya texture proteins
    (ii) Soya protein isolates
    (iii) Soya protein concentrates
    (iv) Other specialised products of soyabean
    (v) Winterised and deodorised refined soyabean oil
31. (a) Certified high yielding hybrid seeds and synthetic seeds
    (b) Certified high yielding plantlets developed through plant tissue culture
32. All food-processing industries other than milk food, malted foods and flour, but excluding the items reserved for the small-scale sector
33. All items of packaging for food-processing industries excluding the items reserved for the small-scale sector
34. Hotels and tourism-related industry
35. Software*

Source: Government of India, Ministry of Industry.
Note: *Electronics Software has also been declared as a high priority industry and falls under Annex III, vide Press Note No.5 (1992 Series).

SCHEDULE IV

List of Cities with a Population of 10 Lakhs and Above According to the Provisional Results of the 1991 Census

Sl. No.	Cities	Population
1.	Greater Bombay UA	12,571,720
2.	Calcutta UA	10,916,272
3.	Delhi UA	8,375,188
4.	Madras UA	5,361,468
5.	Hyderabad UA	4,280,261
6.	Bangalore UA	4,086,548
7.	Ahmedabad UA	3,297,655
8.	Pune UA	2,485,014
9.	Kanpur UA	2,111,284
10.	Nagpur	1,661,409
11.	Lucknow UA	1,642,134
12.	Surat UA	1,517,076
13.	Jaipur UA	1,514,425
14.	Kochi UA	1,139,543
15.	Coimbatore UA	1,135,549
16.	Vadodara UA	1,115,265
17.	Indore UA	1,104,065
18.	Patna UA	1,098,572
19.	Madurai UA	1,093,702
20.	Bhopal MC	1,063,662
21.	Vishakapatnam UA	1,051,918
22.	Varanasi UA	1,026,467
23.	Ludhiana M Corpn	1,012,062

SCHEDULE V

Forms of Participation

Foreign Direct Investment	Foreign Direct Investment	Foreign Institutional Investors	Foreign Technology Transfers (Without Investment)
Wholly owned subsidiaries	Joint venture company with Indian parties	Broad based entities such as pension funds and investment trusts. FIIs can hold portfolio investment in the primary and secondary markets up to 10% in a single company with an overall ceiling of 24% for all FIIs	Automatic approval from RBI if payments meet the set requirements. Otherwise FIPB or SIA approval is required together with the RBI approval for remittances to the foreign party
Approval required from FIPB or SIA	Automatic from RBI for up to 51% equity investment in the specified high priority industries and trading houses engaged primarily in export. Others require FIPB or SIA approval	FIIs must be registered with the Securities and Exchange Board of India. RBI approval must also be obtained to enable buy/sell of securities and to remit income/ sale proceeds	

SCHEDULE VI

List of Consumer Goods Industries Where Dividend Balancing is Required

1. Manufacture of food and food products
2. Manufacture of dairy products
3. Grain mill products
4. Manufacture of bakery products
5. Manufacture and refining of sugar (vacuum pan sugar factories)
6. Production of common salt
7. Manufacture of hydrogenerated oil (Vanaspati)
8. Tea processing
9. Coffee
10. Manufacture of beverages, tobacco and tobacco products
11. Distilling, rectifying and blending of spirits, wine industries, malt liquors and malt, production of country liquors and toddy
12. Soft drinks and carbonated water industry
13. Manufacture of cigars, cigarettes, cheroot and cigarette tobacco
14. Manufacture of wood and wood products, furniture and fixtures
15. Manufacture of leather and fur/leather products
16. Tanning, curing, finishing, embossing and japanning of leather
17. Manufacture of footwear (excluding repair) except vulcanized or moulded rubber or plastic footwear
18. Manufacture of footwear made primarily of vulcanized or moulded products
19. Prophylactics (rubber contraceptive)
20. Motor cars
21. Entertainment electronics (VCRs, colour TVs, CD players, tape recorders)
22. White goods (domestic refrigerators, domestic dishwashing machines, programmable domestic washing machines, microwave ovens, airconditioners)

SCHEDULE VII

Clearances Required for New Projects

Clearance required by all industrial units for setting up a unit	Authority
In case of Annex II Industries	SIA
In case of Annex III Industries	SIA/RBI
In case of non-Annex III Industries or Annex III Industries involving foreign equity beyond 51%	FIPB
Land for project	
Allotment of plot or shed in an industrial estate	State Industrial Development Corporation (SIDC)
Allotment of government land	District Collector
Notified Authority permission	District Collector or District Development Officer
Construction	
Plan approval in an industrial estate	SIDC
Plan approval in other areas	Local Authority
Water	
In an industrial estate	SIDC
River or Public service	Department of Water Resources
Power	State Electricity Board

Other clearances	Authority
Environmental clearance	
No Objection Certificate, applicable to polluting industries like chemicals, pharmaceuticals etc. Permission to be obtained before site selection and norms to be observed for disposal of effluents under Prevention of Environment Pollution Act as well as the Pollution (Water and Air) Act.	State Pollution Control Board

Other clearances	Authority
Site clearance certificate	
Applicable to 22 highly polluting industries	Office of the Industries Commissioner
Incentives	
Investment subsidy for industrial units to be located in backward areas of the State	District Industries Centre
Sales tax exemption/Eligibility certificate	Industries Commissioner

Clearance for specific projects	Authority
Pharmaceutical and cosmetics projects	Food and Drugs Control Administration
Permission under the Boilers Act	
Permission to be obtained for installation of boilers in accordance with safety requirements	Chief Inspector of Steam Boilers
Mining	
Permission for extraction of minerals; permission to be obtained for lease and setting up a mineral based industry	Director, Geology and Mining
Port location	
Permission to locate a Board project near the seashore	Port Department/State Maritime

Clearance before commencing production	Authority
Registration as factory	
Under the Factory Act, for the safety of the workers	Chief Inspector of Factories

Clearance before commencing production	Authority
Sales tax registration	
A sales tax number is to be obtained from the regional sales tax office to effect sales of goods produced which are liable to sales tax. This is an important requirement to be completed by an industrial unit after going into commercial production.	Sales Tax Officer

SCHEDULE VIII

List of Projects Requiring Clearance from the Ministry of Environment and Forests

1. (i) Major irrigation projects, hydel power projects and multi-purpose river valley projects
    (ii) Thermal power projects
    (iii) Nuclear power and interrelated projects
    (iv) Mining projects of public sector undertakings
    (v) Industrial projects (a) requiring the clearance of the Finance Committee or the Public Investment Board or (b) requiring international funding, or (c) those projects referred specially to the Ministry of Environment and Forests by the State governments or the respective administrative Ministries or (d) those taken up for scrutiny by the Ministry of Environment and Forests due to public complaints

2. All projects being put up before the Cabinet Committee on Economic Affairs (CCEA) or Public Investment Board (PIB), such as ports and harbours, communication projects, etc.

3. Projects in certain areas such as the Doon Valley and the Islands are taken up for scrutiny because of the ecologically fragile nature of the areas. Projects falling in Aravalli, Agra, Mathura and Dahanu area are examined more critically being located in sensitive areas.

4. Tourism projects including beach resorts.

5. Other projects such as construction in violation of the existing rules brought to the notice of the Ministry of Environment and Forests.

6. All the projects involving forest land requiring central clearance for diversion of forest land.

SCHEDULE IX

List of Various Investment-Related Forms

Purpose	Form type	To be submitted to
For setting up an industry in the non-licensed sector	IEM	SIA
To obtain a licence for industries requiring compulsory licensing	IL	SIA
For obtaining government approval for foreign collaboration and/or foreign investment	FC(SIA)	SIA
For the automatic approval of up to 51% of foreign equity in Annex III (high priority) industries and for foreign technology approvals in all industries	FC(RBI)	RBI
For setting up a unit in EPZ		Ministry of Commerce
For setting up 100% EOU		SIA
Application for permission under section 29(1)(a) of FERA for an overseas company to set up an office for carrying on liaison work/setting up a project office/site office in India	FNC(5)	RBI
Application for permission under section 29(1)(a) of FERA for an overseas company to set up a branch office in India	FNC(4)	RBI

61

CHAPTER 4

TRADE POLICY AND FOREIGN TRADE
by Tejendra Khanna

THE TRADE POLICY FRAMEWORK

Introduction

The 1990s are witnessing momentous changes in the world and in India. The international political and economic order has been restructured and, as the 20th century draws to a close, many of its distinguishing philosophies and features have been swept away. In this turbulent world, India's policies have also had to adjust to the changing reality. Its basic policies aimed at self-reliance and import substitution which were pursued for over 40 years since Independence have helped to create a broad-based technological and manufacturing capability and now provide the opportunity to respond with flexibility to the new situation, to enable the government to achieve its aim of providing a rich and just life for the people. During 1991 India launched a macro-economic stabilisation programme to overcome the immediate balance of payments crisis. This stabilisation programme was supplemented by a major structural-reforms exercise encompassing the industrial, trade, fiscal, financial and external sectors of the economy.

In July, 1991, in a major departure from the import-substitution philosophy which had been accompanied by stringent import controls, India's trade sector was liberalised to respond to the opportunities and challenges posed by national and international developments. The trade sector cannot be seen in isolation and it was ensured that the changes introduced in this sector were in harmony with the rest of the economy. The Export-Import (EXIM) Policy (1992–97) was made co-terminously with the Eighth Five Year Plan with a view to providing a stable policy matrix subject to annual changes depending on the requirements of the economy. Trade was made free, except for a negative list of exports and imports. In the case of consumer goods and a few intermediate goods whose import was otherwise restricted, a positive list allowed for import under certain conditions. The Export-Import Policy aimed at accelerating the country's transition to an internationally oriented economy with a view to deriving maximum benefit from the expanding global market opportunities. It sought to stimulate India's exports by providing access to the required raw materials, intermediates, components and capital goods from the international market and to encourage the attainment of internationally accepted standards of quality, thereby improving the image of India abroad. Policy and procedures have been deregulated, streamlined and simplified, and steps taken to provide a friendly environment for exports.

Evolution of Trade Policy

After Independence India adopted an inward looking import substitution policy, which laid heavy reliance on creating capital intensive heavy industries and gave primacy to investment in the capital goods sector. It could not therefore take advantage of the expansion in world trade during the 1950s and 1960s. India protected its domestic industry though high tariffs and other quantitative restrictions. This led to certain inefficiencies in the economic system. Many Indian products were not competitive enough in the world market and India's share of world trade was marginal.

It was generally realised during the 1980s that the Indian economy should gradually open up and subject its domestic industry to international competition. This thinking led to certain changes in policies and procedures. However, in the external trade sector, the impact of these changes was inadequate. A large number of items including capital goods, instruments, raw materials and components needed licences before they could be imported and obtaining these licences was a time-consuming and cumbersome process since the possibility of domestic sourcing had to be excluded before permitting imports. The precious time and energy of the entrepreneurs and manufacturers was being taken up in obtaining industrial licences and import licences and meeting the other procedural formalities of the system.

In June 1991, a major shift in strategy was effected vis-a-vis the management of the economy. India's trade policy was liberalised along with the other sectors of the economy in response to the opportunities and challenges posed by national and international developments. A major structural reform exercise was carried out in the Indian economy along with short-term measures to contain the balance of payment crisis. The new Exim Policy 1992–97, and the revisions made so far, aim at (i) creating a free environment for trade; (ii) strengthening the export promotion structure; (iii) removing all procedural irritants through simplification and streamlining of procedures; (iv) increasing export production, improving efficiency and sharpening India's competitive edge; (v) facilitating input availability and (vi) focusing on quality and technological upgrading.

Export-Import Policy (EXIM Policy)

Imports and exports are regulated through the Export and Import Policy which is updated by the government in March every year. In March 1992, the government announced an Export and Import Policy for a five year period with the objective of providing a stable regime of economic policies, which would minimise year-to-year uncertainties and help industry to plan economic activities in the longer term. Amendment to the Policy, where necessary, is notified by means of Public Notices by the Director-General of Foreign Trade (DGFT) in the Ministry of Commerce from time to time. The policies and procedures governing the import of various items are laid down in the Export-Import Policy Book. The Handbook of Export-Import Procedures is also published as a supplement to the EXIM Policy. As stated above, the current EXIM Policy and Handbook of Procedures are valid for a period of five years, ie, up to 31 March 1997.

METHODS USED FOR RESTRICTING IMPORTS

Salient Features of the Import Policy

One of the main objectives of the EXIM Policy of the Government of India since 1991 has been to phase out quantitative restrictions in the form of licensing and other discretionary controls regulating India's foreign trade. According to the EXIM Policy for 1992–97, all capital goods, raw materials, intermediates, components, consumables, spares, parts, accessories, components and other goods may be imported without any restriction except to the extent that such imports are regulated by the Negative List of Imports or any other provisions of the policy or any other law in force. The Negative List of Imports consists of prohibited items, restricted items and canalised items. Import of prohibited items contained in the Negative List of Imports is not allowed under any circumstances, whereas the canalised items can be generally imported through the designated canalising agencies. Imports of canalised items may also be permitted against a licence granted by the Director-General of Foreign Trade. As regards restricted items, imports may only be allowed against specific import licences or in accordance with a Public Notice issued for the purpose. Second-hand capital goods can now be imported without a licence by actual users, with effect from 30 March 1994.

Almost all of India's trading partners receive MFN treatment in the issue of import licences, with the exception of Iraq and Fiji (on account of United Nations sanctions in the case of Iraq). In these cases import licences cannot be issued, or licences can only be issued against tied aid and foreign credits.

The restrictions on the import of items in the Negative List, other than consumer goods (which are restricted for balance-of-payments reasons), are on grounds of health, safety, security and environmental protection policies and agreements. In respect of certain items, the conditions for import have been specified in a general way in Public Notices issued for this purpose and the need for licensing in individual cases has been eliminated.

Imports into India are not restricted through maintenance of quotas. The instrument used for restricting imports is import licensing.

Easing of Import Restrictions

Quantitative restrictions on imports of most intermediate inputs and capital goods have been eliminated. As already stated, import restrictions apply only to the Negative List. In keeping with the needs of the economy and the emerging trade balance, the Negative List is being pruned. In July 1991, out of 5021 Harmonised System of Trade Classification tariff lines, 80% (4000 lines) were subject to import licensing restraints. As a result of regular pruning of the Negative List more than 3000 tariff lines covering raw materials, intermediates and capital goods are now free of import licensing requirements.

Contents of the Negative List

The Negative List of Imports now comprises three prohibited items, 62 restricted items including specified consumer goods and seven canalised items. The three prohibited items are tallow, fat and/or oils of animal origin, animal rennet, and wild animals including their parts and products of ivory.

The list of restricted items under the Negative List includes specified consumer goods, precious, semi-precious and other stones, insecticides and pesticides, electronic items, drugs, pharmaceuticals, chemicals and allied items, hazardous wastes and hazardous chemicals, items relating to the small-scale sector, certain miscellaneous items, and special items required for hotels, the tourism industry and sports bodies.

The list of canalised items includes some petroleum products, fertilisers, specified edible and non-edible oils, seeds and cereals.

Import of restricted items covered by the Negative List may be made against a licence or in accordance with Public Notices issued for this purpose. In the case of import of ships, trawlers and boats, aircraft and helicopters, automobiles and newsprint, no licence is required but imports are allowed subject to published conditions.

Import Licences

Imports of a large number of specified restricted items (including certain consumer goods) are permitted against freely transferable Special Import Licences (SILs) granted to Export Houses, Trading Houses, Star Trading Houses or Super-Star Trading Houses, exporters of electronic goods and 'deemed exporters' (who supply inputs to final exporters under certain conditions) and manufacturers who have acquired prescribed international quality certification, on the basis of their foreign exchange earnings. One-time facility for the import of cars is available to Export Houses, Trading Houses, Star Trading Houses or Super-Star Trading Houses against their own Special Import Licences. A document, ITC (HS) Classifications of Export & Import Items, which sets out the present import policy treatment for various items under the eight digit Harmonised System (HS) classification, was notified on 25 March 1996. There are in all 10,087 entries covered under the classification out of which 6161 entries are in the freely importable list and 771 entries are importable against the freely transferable SILs. It is the government's intention to gradually expand the list of items under both the freely importable and SIL categories.

IMPORTS FOR FACILITATING EXPORT PRODUCTION

Introduction

For import of items required for export production, exporters are issued duty free import licences for import of items including those on the Negative List under the Duty Exemption Scheme. Capital goods which are otherwise freely importable can, under the Export Promotion Capital Goods (EPCG) Scheme, be imported at a concessional rate of customs duty or zero customs duty subject to an export obligation to be fulfilled over a period of time. These licences in fact provide easier access to imported goods at concessional rates for export production.

Duty Exemption Scheme

Under this scheme, exporters can import duty free components which go into export products without resorting to the mechanism of claiming duty drawback at a later stage. This scheme has been recently modified and enlarged. The modified Duty Exemption Scheme now covers the following categories of licences:

- (i) Advance Licence:
  - (a) Value-Based Advance Licence;
  - (b) Quantity-Based Advance Licence;
- (ii) Passbook Scheme;
- (iii) Advance Intermediate Licence/Value-Based Advance Intermediate Licence; and
- (iv) Special Imprest Licence.

The basis and conditions for issue of these types of licences vary. Hence licences issued under one category cannot be combined with those issued under another category. Duty free licences bear a suitable export obligation to achieve the objective of the scheme. The purposes and scope of the categories of licences mentioned above are as follows:

Advance Licences

An Advance Licence is granted for the duty free import of inputs, with an obligation to value-add and export within a specified time. Advance Licences may either be value-based or quantity-based.

Value-based Advance Licences

Under a Value-based Advance Licence, any of the inputs specified in the licence as per the standard input-output norm may be imported within the total c.i.f. value indicated for those inputs, except for notified sensitive items. The sensitive items may be imported only to the extent of the quantity or value specified in the licence.

Quantity-based Advance Licences

The Quantity-based Advance Licence will indicate the names and description of items to be imported and exported, the quantity of each item of import or in case where the quantity cannot be indicated the value of the items, the c.i.f. value of imports and quantity and f.o.b. value of exports. The quantity of each item imported shall be allowed in accordance with the standard input-output norms as mentioned above based on the quantity of goods to be exported. In respect of items for which no norms exist in the statement of standard input-output norms, the quantitative norms may be approved by the competent authority. These licences are transferable or non-transferable subject to certain conditions.

Passbook scheme

This is a new scheme which was introduced with effect from 1 April, 1995. Manufacturer Exporters and Export Houses, Trading Houses, Star Trading Houses and Super-Star Trading Houses are eligible to make applications under this Scheme to the designated authorities in each of the Customs Houses at Delhi, Bombay, Calcutta and Madras. The scheme applies to the export products for which standard input-output norms have been published. On export of goods, the Passbook holders become eligible for credit equivalent to the basic duty payable on the inputs used for the manufacture of the relevant export product. The Passbook is valid for two years and the credit available therein can be used for a period of three years for the payment of customs duty on import of permissible items.

Advance Intermediate Licence

Such licences are quantity-based and are issued to registered manufacturer-exporters for import of basic inputs for manufacture and supply of intermediate products under a tie-up arrangement, to another manufacturer-exporter, called the ultimate exporter, holding the Advance Licence, for further processing into the final product for export. The objective of the scheme is to integrate the production activities of the two indigenous manufacturers, with the optimum utilisation of the indigenous infrastructure to achieve a higher value addition. Imports are allowed in accordance with the standard input-output norms as mentioned above.

Special Imprest Licence

The Special Imprest Licence is granted for duty free import of necessary inputs to the main/sub-contractor for the manufacture and supply of products to projects financed by multilateral or bilateral agencies, funds as notified by the Department of Economic Affairs, EOU, EPZ Units, Electronic Hardware Technology Parks (EHTPs), Software Technology Parks (STPs), fertiliser plants, any project notified by the Ministry of Finance, Department of Economic Affairs and also to such projects in the power, oil and gas sector to which the benefit is extended by the Ministry of Finance. The Special Imprest Licence is a quantity-based licence.

Engineering Products Export (Replenishment of Iron & Steel Intermediate) Scheme

Steel producers supplying steel to the exporters of engineering goods under the Engineering Products Export (Replenishment of Iron & Steel Intermediate) Scheme are eligible to make applications for value-based intermediate licences. Applications can be made both on a production programme basis in anticipation of the supply orders as well as after making the supplies, on the strength of Release Advices. After the supplies have been completed and the DEEC Book redeemed, the licences or the material imported thereunder can be transferred among the producers of iron and steel intermediates.

A duty free licence holder (including a transferee) may, instead of making imports, also procure the raw materials from indigenous sources through an Advance Release Order/Back to back inland letter of credit. The Advance Release Order is issued against quantity-based licences as well as value-based advance licences where the quantity of the item has been specified.

Duty Draw-back Scheme

In addition to the option given to exporters to obtain Advance Duty Free Licences for sourcing raw materials and intermediates, from abroad for export production, the government also allows exporters who use duty-paid goods of imported or indigenous origin to claim draw back on presenting evidence of export shipment.

Export Promotion Capital Goods (EPCG) Scheme

Under the EPCG Scheme, capital goods which are otherwise freely importable may be imported at a concessional rate of customs duty of 15% or may be sourced from the domestic manufacturers subject to an export obligation of four times the c.i.f. value of imports. The domestic manufacturers, permitted to supply the capital goods under this scheme to an EPCG licence holder, can also import the requisite components at a concessional rate of customs duty of 15%. The scheme is also available to service providers for rendering services for which the payments are received in freely convertible currency. From 1 May 1995, in addition to the concessional customs duty of 15%, another opportunity has been provided for the import of capital goods at zero duty, against an obligation of six times the value of imports on f.o.b. basis or four times the value of imports on NFE basis to be discharged in a period of eight years. In such cases, domestic manufacturers supplying to an EPCG licence holder can import the requisite components at zero duty.

The exporters of specified gems and jewellery products are eligible for grant of replenishment licences at the rate and for the items mentioned in the EXIM Policy to import and replenish their inputs. Such licences are transferable.

Export Houses, Trading Houses and Star Trading Houses

Export Houses, Trading Houses, Star Trading Houses and Super-Star Trading Houses (defined as those companies with exports which have averaged Rs100, 500, 2500 and 7500 million respectively or with net foreign exchange earnings of Rs60, 300, 1250 and 4000 million respectively in the preceding three years and have had exports of Rs150, 750, 3000 and 10,000 million or net foreign exchange earnings of Rs120, 600, 1500 and 6000 million in the previous year) are entitled to Specific Import Licences at 4, 5, 6 and 11% of the f.o.b. value of exports made or at 6, 8.5, 11 and 16% of net foreign exchange earnings on exports in the preceding licensing year. Extra SIL of 1% is also permitted to exporters of SSI, handloom and handicraft products including hand knotted carpets, silk products and sports goods provided the export of these products is more than 50% of their total export.

The import of items appearing in the restricted list of imports under the Negative List (other than those imports which are prohibited or canalised) may be allowed against specific import licences or in accordance with the Public Notices issued for this purpose. Such items are subject to Actual User Conditions unless this condition is dispensed with in particular cases. Manufacturers (Actual Users) can apply for such licences to the Director-General of Foreign Trade who can issue import licences for the purpose, on merit.

Actual User Condition

Capital goods, raw materials, intermediates, components, consumables, spares, parts, accessories, instruments and other goods, which are importable without any restriction, may be imported by any person whether he is an Actual User or not. However, if such imports require a licence, the Actual User alone can import such goods unless the Actual User Condition is specifically dispensed with by a licensing authority. The time limit for processing various types of applications varies and it may be between 2 and 30 days.

Value of import licences

Import licences, wherever required, are issued with a specified period of validity for shipment of goods. It is up to the importer to import goods any time during the validity period of the import licence. Generally, the goods should be shipped from the exporting country, only after the import licence is issued, and licences cannot ordinarily be granted for the goods which have already arrived at the port.

Import applications are submitted to the Office of the Director-General of Foreign Trade, New Delhi or its regional offices, as the case may be. The practice of routing licence applications through the sponsoring authorities has been dispensed with.

Applications for import licences are to be submitted by 28 February of the licensing year ending on 31 March unless otherwise specified.

The licensing authority may refuse to grant an import licence:

(i) if the applicant has contravened any law relating to customs or foreign exchange;

(ii) if it has been decided by the Central Government to canalise imports and distribution thereof through special or specialised agencies;

(iii) if any action against the applicant is pending under the Foreign Trade (Development and Regulation) Act, 1992, or rules and orders made thereunder;

(iv) if the applicant fails to pay any penalty imposed on him under the said Act;

(v) if the applicant is not eligible for a licence in accordance with any provisions of the EXIM Policy; and

(vi) if no foreign exchange is available for the purpose.

The reasons for refusal are generally given to the applicant.

TREATMENT OF IMPORTS FROM DIFFERENT SOURCES INCLUDING INFORMATION ON THE USE OF BILATERAL AGREEMENTS

Imports on MFN Basis Except Under Certain Conditions

Licences for imports are valid for import from any country having trade relations with India. The restrictions if any are applied on a non-discriminatory basis. At present India does not have trade relations with Fiji and Iraq. The Government of India has signed trade agreements with a number of foreign countries. These are generally MFN type agreements, which do not involve specific commitments on import of any goods, nor do they limit the imports either in terms of items or value. The Government of India does not direct importers to buy from any particular source.

71

Trade in Hard Currencies with some Transitional Exceptions

With certain countries, India had concluded special payments and trade arrangements which provided for payments for all commercial and non-commercial transactions in non-convertible Indian rupees through a central clearing account. These arrangements have now been replaced by hard currency arrangements except in a few cases (Russia, Romania, the Czech Republic and the Slovak Republic) in which India has entered into arrangements for the liquidation of rupee balances through the export of goods from India to these countries against these balances held by them.

State Trading

Canalisation

Import of certain essential items like cereals, edible oils, fertilisers and petroleum products, are canalised through public sector agencies such as the State Trading Corporation, and the Minerals and Metals Trading Corporation. The agencies concerned import these commodities on the basis of the foreign exchange made available in their favour for this purpose. The policy for canalisation of certain items through the designated public sector agencies has been evolved with a view to effecting users, by securing the most favourable terms of payments and trade. Purchases by the public sector agencies are guided by the normal commercial considerations and are entirely non-discriminatory in nature. The government's policy is to progressively move away from canalisation. Hence at present there are only seven canalised items.

Present status of import policy and recent changes therein

In March 1996, the Government of India, by publishing and notifying document called 'ITC (HS) Classifications of Export & Import Items' (Indian Trade Classification (Harmonised System)), implemented the Harmonised System for the day-to-day working of the import and export licensing system, helping the smooth flow of trade goods. The document covers 10,087 entries. The system will be useful in liberalising the policy further in a systematic manner. Analysis of the 10,087 products and product groups shows that 61.07% of the entries are freely importable; the balance are either prohibited, restricted or canalised. Out of these, 7.64% of the items otherwise in the Negative List are freely importable against transferable Special Import

Licences. The market premium on these licences hovers around 10% of the face value.

The remaining 31.29% of the items consists of the following types of goods:

(1) **Prohibited items.** This is a list consisting of items prohibited for import on religious and environmental grounds. The number runs to only 59 items forming 0.58% of the total.

(2) **Canalised.** The list covers 178 items forming 1.76% of the total. However, the trade weight is comparatively high as important energy sector products like motor spirits, high speed diesel, crude oil are covered. In addition, agriculture inputs, namely, single fertilisers and the output consisting of cereals are canalised through public sector corporations. There is no licensing on the items; the import is free for all practical purposes. The canalisation policy is designed to monitor the supply of critical inputs and the general financial management of the economy.

On the output side, the control through canalisation is only on cereals and two types of edible oils, coconut and RBD palm oil. The policy on these items is governed by special domestic concerns and is under constant review.

(3) **Restricted goods.** There are 3689 items in the restricted list, mostly in the category of 'consumer goods'. The figure is exaggerated to an extent as the eight digit classification extending the six digit HS lines focuses on the consumer goods sector where India has a definite export advantage.

Products other than those in the category of consumer goods are restricted on account of safety, security, phytosanitary, health and environment factors. A few others are restricted due to protection of small scale industry. In such cases, imports are permitted to some extent against the special import licence described above.

(4) **Consumer goods.** As a category, consumer goods cover 3908 items at the eight digit level of the ITC, that is, a little more than a third of the total consisting of 10,087 products and product groups covered under the category of consumer goods and others. As mentioned earlier, the share at the six digit level should be in the region of one quarter of the total as the bulk of the sub-division to the eight digit ITC is in the consumer goods category.

MAJOR DEVELOPMENTS IN THE PERIOD FROM OCTOBER 1993 TO SEPTEMBER 1995

The Government of India has a conscious policy of removing licensing controls in the restricted category defined in the Negative List of Imports. The first major step was to remove all forms of import licensing in general. Control was restricted to a small negative list. All other goods are freely importable without any restriction on end use or importer category. This step was taken in April, 1992. Since March 1994 the major steps taken towards removal of import restrictions are:

(1) In March, 1994 sugar was made freely importable. This policy continues and the definition has been widened to include all goods under HS headings 17.01 and 17.02.

(2) On 1 March, 1995 all edible oils, excluding coconut oil, palm kernel oil, RBD palm oil and RBD palm stearin, were moved to the free list.

(3) For the first time in the history of the trade policy, the textile sector was opened to import on 15 February, 1995. As many as 180 tariff lines were moved from the restricted category to the free list. Similarly, 313 lines are importable against the Special Import Licence. Another 98 tariff lines consisting of SIL or restricted lines are freely importable as upholstery. All raw materials or finished goods suitable for being used in the industrial sector are now freely importable.

The Indian Government has contracted with the WTO to lift import restrictions on the textile sector altogether by the year 2000. In the intervening period, the scope will be widened from the starting point defined on 15 February, 1995.

(4) The annual review of the import policy announced on 1 April, 1995 resulted in a significant reduction in the Negative List. Major changes included dry fish, paper and paper products including newsprint, wood and wood products, personal computers other than those of small value, oral and dental hygiene products, skimmed milk powder and butter oil, cameras, sports goods, surgical gloves and video magnetic tapes. Lastly, and most importantly, parts and components of consumer durables are now freely importable.

(5) The scope of the SIL has been extended substantially. On 26 July, 1995, important petroleum products like aviation turbine fuel and furnace oil were added to the list, as well as from educational games. The expansion in the list for the textile sector in February 1995 is covered above.

(6) On 1 April 1995, the list was further extended to include refrigeration equipment, battery and electrically operated vehicles, vending machines, compact fluorescent lamps, stationery, electric sewing machines, and consumer telecommunications equipment.

DIRECTION OF EVOLUTION OF IMPORT POLICY

It is the policy of the government to move to a situation where imports of essential raw materials and components needed for industrial production are entirely regulated through appropriate tariffs. As regards consumer goods, the broad approach is first to allow phased relaxation through freely tradeable SILs and subsequently to transfer them to a purely tariff-based regime. Canalisation of inputs which has already been significantly reduced is proposed to be progressively further reduced . However, in view of the uncertainty in the balance of payments arising from domestic liberalisation and external fluctuations, containment of import growth within prudent limits will be necessary and phasing out of the Negative List of Imports will have to be done in a careful and socio-politically sustainable manner.

CREATION OF AN EXPORT-FRIENDLY ENVIRONMENT

The government has made export a national aim, being keen to provide a friendly environment to traders. The Exporters Grievance Redressal Cell in the Ministry of Commerce has been specially created to look into and sort out the problems of exporters. Supportive financial and fiscal measures are also undertaken to try to remove the inherent bias against exports that was prevalent in the Indian economy till 1991. Tariffs are gradually being reduced to lower levels, the peak rate of tariff in the 1995–96 budget being 50%. The rupee has been made convertible on the current account and export credit is provided in foreign currency also, at LBOR related rates. All export profits are exempt from income tax under Section 80HHC of the Income Tax Act.

STRENGTHENING OF INFRASTRUCTURE: A KEY TO FOREIGN TRADE

It is realised that India, compared to the other developed countries, lacks sound infrastructure. Great attention is being paid to improving infrastructure like roads, power, and telecommunications facilities. The network of Inland Container Depots and Container Freight Stations is being extended and has recently been opened to the private sector. Modern means of communications such as Electronic Data Interchange are being encouraged for use by traders. At the same time, efforts are being made to increase involvement of State governments in export, through schemes like EPIP, to ensure successful implementation of government policies at the grass roots level.

A very strong emphasis is being placed on quality, and manufacturers/exporters are offered incentives to attain ISO 9000 or BIS 1400 certification.

Export Processing Zones

Setting up of Export Processing Zones, Export Oriented Units and the granting of status of Export House, Trading House, Star Trading House and Super Star Trading House are other measures which have been introduced to boost exports. EPZs are set up as enclaves, separated from the Domestic Tariff Area by fiscal barriers and are intended to provide an internationally competitive duty-free environment for export production at low cost. This enables the products of EPZs to be competitive, both quality-wise and price-wise in the international market. India has seven Export Processing Zones at Kandla (Gujarat), Santacruz (Bombay), Falta (West Bengal), Noida (UP), Cochin (Kerarla), Madras (Tamil Nadu) and Visakhapatnam (Andhra Pradesh). The zone at Visakhapatnam (Andhra Pradesh) has become operational only recently. The Santacruz Electronics Export Processing Zone is meant exclusively for export of electronics and gem and jewellery items whereas the others are multi-product Zones.

Export Oriented Units Scheme

The EOU Scheme is complementary to the EPZ Scheme. It adopts the same production regime but offers more freedom in location of sources of raw materials, ports of export, hinterland facilities, availability of high level skills, existence of an industrial base, and the need for a larger area of land for the project. At present 523 units are in operation under the EOU Scheme.

Recognition of Export Houses and Trading Houses

The objective of the scheme of Export Houses and Trading Houses is to give recognition to the established exporters and large export houses to build up the marketing infrastructure and expertise required for export promotion. Registered exporters with a record of export performance over a number of years are granted Export/ Trading House status subject to the fulfilment of minimum annual average export performance in terms of f.o.b. value or net foreign exchange earnings on physical exports prescribed in the EXIM Policy.

Multilateral Policy Approach

A significant development in 1994 was the signing of the World Trade Organisation (WTO) agreement, marking the successful outcome of the seven-year-long Uruguay Round of Multilateral Trade Negotiations. India believes that international trade can flourish best within a rule-based multilateral trading system founded on the principles of non-discrimination and transparency. The WTO which came into effect from 1 January, 1995 will certainly create opportunities for India to expand its share of world trade. In line with the need for closer monitoring of trade performance, the Director-General of Commercial Intelligence and Statistics has made significant progress in the generation of foreign trade statistics with the minimum time lag consistent with the system of data capture currently existing. The aggregate data on foreign trade are presently made available within 25–30 days and dis-aggregated data at the eight-digit product level is published within four months.

Regional Initiatives

Apart from being an active member of the WTO, India has made specific contributions to the South Asian Association of Regional Cooperation forum (SAARC) and has helped to make operational the South Asian Preferential Trading Arrangement (SAPTA). SAPTA was put into operation in December 1995 to improve intra-regional trade amongst members of SAARC. India is also playing a supportive role in promoting a preferential trading arrangement between Indian Ocean Rim Countries and has expressed its interest in joining APEC and is a sectoral-dialogue partner of ASEAN.

As well, country specific initiatives have been taken to promote trade ties with emerging economies such as South Africa and Israel. Border trade with Myanmar has also been opened recently. Exports to Russia have been stepped up and alternative trade routes to Central Asia are being developed through Bunder Abbas, with support from Iran. A special effort is being made to expand India's trade with Latin America, Africa and the Central Asian Republics.

TRADE PERFORMANCE

Export Growth

Export growth holds the key to the balance of payments management of the country. Boosting exports is a major element of foreign trade strategy during the Eighth Five Year Plan. After suffering a decline of 1.5% in 1991–92, exports revived in 1992–93 and recorded a 3.8% growth despite a 62% fall in exports to the former Rupee Payment Countries (USSR and COMECON). The export growth in 1992–93 over 1991–92 was made possible by the substantially higher level of exports (about 11%) to hard currency areas. Exports in 1993–94 totalled US$22.24 billion and registered an impressive growth of 20%, in dollar terms. The momentum of export growth has been sustained in 1994–95 when exports reached US$26.22 billion and recorded 18.3% growth over 1993–94. During April 1995 to March 1996 exports were US$31.83 billion and this represents 21.39% growth.

Import Growth

In 1991–92 imports declined by 19.4% due to import compression, consequent upon balance of payments problems. Imports recorded 12.7% growth in 1992–93 followed by a lower growth of 6.5% in 1993–94 before rising by 21.7% in 1994–95. Import growth during April 1995 to March 1996 was 28.74% in dollar terms. The increase in the level of imports is mostly in the non-oil category and is attributable to the higher level of industrial growth.

As a percentage of GDP, the share of foreign trade which was 16.8% in 1993–94 should reach 21.5% by the end of the 1995–96 year.

Another noteworthy feature is the increase in the coverage of imports by exports. In the beginning of the 1960s, the coverage ratio was only 52.4% which led to a massive trade deficit. This improved to about 70% by the end of the 1980s. During the last three years, export earnings, on an average, amounted to 90% of the value of imports. This marked improvement in the export-import ratio has contributed to the reduction in current account deficit which has come down from the unsustainable levels of 2% GDP to less than 0.5% last year.

Composition of Exports

India's export basket has changed from a heavy reliance on primary products comprising agricultural and allied products and ores and minerals to a predominance of manufactured exports. Manufactured products which accounted for 45% of India's total exports during 1960–61 represented 77% during 1994–95. It may be noted that India is the largest exporter of leather goods and gems and jewellery. The electronics and computer software industries are where Indian exports have made inroads in the world market and are set to expand their share at a faster pace. Other non-traditional exports like ready-made garments, engineering goods, chemicals and allied products are increasingly assuming an important position in India's export basket. Major countries to which Indian goods are exported are the USA, Japan, Germany, the UK, Hong Kong, UAE, Belgium, Singapore, Russia and Italy. Asia and Oceania accounted for 42% of total exports followed by Western Europe (29.4%), America (20.4%), Eastern Europe (4.6%) and Africa (3.8%) during 1994–95.

CONCLUSION AND OPPORTUNITIES

With the liberalisation of the foreign trade sector and the sustained growth of both exports and imports for the last two to three years in excess of 20% in dollar terms, the opportunities for India to enlarge its share of global exports substantially on the one hand, and also to provide a growing market for various industrial inputs and priority items of mass consumption are great. With annual GDP growth in the range of 6–7% in the next few years and annual foreign trade growth of 20% and above, the share of foreign trade as a proportion of GDP is bound to continue to rise, evidencing an increasing degree of openness of the Indian economy. As a result of the adoption of export-friendly policies and an accompanying attitudinal shift within the Indian business community which is now taking a much greater interest in the global market place than before, exports are expected to touch US$75–80 billion at current prices by the turn of the century. The favourable policies permitting the import of sophisticated machinery and other production inputs, access to modern technologies, and foreign direct investments for strengthening the production infrastructure, all augur well for the realisation of these projections in the years to come. India's emergence as a major market with higher per capita levels of consumption is bound to have positive spin-off effects on neighbouring countries in South and Central Asia as well as in Africa.

CHAPTER 5

COMPETITIVE ADVANTAGES AND INTRINSIC STRENGTHS OF INDIA
by Jitendra Kohli

HISTORICAL PERSPECTIVE

India—Unique Nation, Not a Mere Emerging Economy

India is a land of tremendous opportunity and has been so for thousands of years. Ancient India, like Egypt, attained a very high level of civilisation thousands of years ago. Racially speaking, most Indians are Aryans, with a rich amalgam of Aryan and Dravidian cultures. They are an inquistive and bold people who excelled in the fields of mathematics, astronomy, civil engineering, metallurgy and medicine. Spirituality was their hallmark. Based on that were their cultural and ethical values. Sanskrit, the language of ancient India, is one of the most scientific and structured of languages.

India's prosperity through the ages made it the destination of explorers, adventurers, and seekers of knowledge. Alexander the Great of Greece was one of the earliest invaders who mounted an onslaught on India. However, some compelling historical reasons stalled the invasion.

An idea of the strong attraction which India held for the rest of the world even in more recent history can be gained from the following:

Bartholomew Diaz was sent by Prince Henry of Portgugal in AD 1487 to find a sea route to India. However, he only succeeded in reaching the southern tip of Africa which was subsequently named the Cape of Good Hope.

Christopher Columbus supported by King Ferdinand and Queen Isabella of Spain in AD 1492 sought to discover a sea route to India by sailing west from Spain. In the process, Columbus bumped into what is now the West Indies and the Northern American continent. A new World was laid open.

Vasco Da Gama was sent by the King of Portugal in AD 1497 to find a sea route to India and accomplish the task left unfinished by Bartholomew Diaz. He succeeded in reaching India and landed at the city of Calicut in the south.

King Charles of Spain was envious that a Portuguese had found a sea-way to India via the East. Ferdinand Magellan was thus despatched on a daring voyage to sail round the world via the western route and reach India. In the process the southern part of the South American continent, a waterway called Magellan's Strait and the Pacific Ocean were discovered. Magellan himself did not complete the task. Only one of his five ships, *Victoria*, and 18 of his sailors, reached Spain on 9 September 1522, thus sailing round the globe for the first time.

Such was the obsession which other countries of the world harboured about India. By comparison, foreign investors today are being offered opportunities literally on a platter.

Decline and Resurgence of a Mighty Nation

The core competencies and natural advantages of India were for many centuries the foundation of its development and prosperity. India's growth, however, was affected in the latter part of this millennium when large parts of India were subjugated by foreign agencies and powers.

A consequence of this was that by and large India did not experience the growth which occurred in some other parts of the world consequent upon the Industrial Revolution. India is therefore very conscious of having to make up for lost time.

The thrust of the post-1947 Economic Policies, when India regained independence, was to build a self-reliant and powerful nation. On one hand, this created a diverse technological and industrial infrastructure and a large pool of skilled human resources, which contribute to India's competitive strengths. On the other hand, excessive regulation and protectionism stunted fructification of the country's full potential in many areas.

Since mid-1991, however, the government has embarked upon a process of deregulating and globalising the Indian economy. This is more commonly referred to as the process of 'Economic Liberalisation'. The objective of the economic reforms is to carry forward the process of building a modern India.

JUDGING COMPETITIVE ADVANTAGES AND STRENGTHS

When judging a nation's strengths and weaknesses, it is possible to take a myopic view, and to assess the current situation, ignoring the past and future.

A broader view of competitive advantage would, however, cover both short-term and long-term competitive advantages. Short-term competitive advantages are based on apparent strengths and long-term competitive advantages are based on latent strengths.

MOTIVATIONAL FACTORS AND ENABLING FACTORS FOR FOREIGN INVESTMENT

It would be useful to look at the advantages and strengths of a country such as India in terms of:

Motivational Factors: the prime reasons which motivate an investor to assess a country as a prospective investment destination and

Enabling Factors: factors which facilitate the pursuit of an investor's objectives. Sometimes, these factors basically involve removal of constraints.

Some of the motivational factors and enabling factors relevant to India are:

Motivational Factors

(i) Large domestic market

(ii) Human resource wealth (knowledge/education/skills of the people)

(iii) Nature's bounty
  - Vast and diverse mineral wealth
  - Second largest expanse of arable land in the world with rich agricultural resources
  - A web of rivers flowing throughout the country
  - Diverse climatic conditions and geographical regions—varying from the snow-clad Himalayas in the north and the long coast-line in the south, east and west; from dense forests in the north-east and sandy deserts in part of western India and the vast plains of agricultural land
  - Rich diversity of flora and fauna

(iv) Lower wages and low cost of living

(v) Existing technology base, production and service infrastructure.

Enabling Factors

(i) Stable democratic government (World's largest, multi-party democracy with no fundamental conflict between political and economic systems)

(ii) Institutional framework
Time-tested and extensive:
– Laws and legal systems
– Mature financial sector and vibrant capital markets
– Free and vibrant press
– Modern educational infrastructure

(iii) Pro-investment reforms in government policies for both domestic and export-related activities

(iv) Extensive (though in some areas still inadequate) infrastructure of railways, roads, airlines, ports, other means of transportation, power, telecommunications

(v) Modern business infrastructure including information technology and related equipment and services in many cities

(vi) Strong entrepreneurial ethos

A large number of world class industrialists and companies available as prospective alliance-partners. These Indian companies, owing to government policy constraints, were inhibited till recently in their globalisation projections

(vii) A large English speaking population
(viii) Rich culture and ancient heritage.

A specific advantage could be viewed as a motivational factor or an enabling factor depending upon the business context. For example, availability of skilled manpower may be a motivational factor in the case of investment for the computer software industry but in another industry which is not manpower intensive, this may only be an enabling factor in the sense that the foreign investor can recruit personnel for handling his Indian operations locally and does not necessarily have to depute personnel from the parent company. Similarly, an advantage such as a rich culture and ancient heritage may be a motivational factor for a tourism-related business investment but, for a high-tech industrial project, it may only be an enabling factor in that it adds to the quality of life and living conditions of the foreign organisation's personnel posted in India.

Large domestic market

Market size estimates can vary depending upon the nature of business.

If the market size is to be measured in terms of size of the middle-class consumers, the estimates vary from 100 million to 300 million potential buyers depending upon the type and cost of goods in question. The size of the Indian middle class, a powerful stabilising factor in any political system exceeds the size of the population of the USA or the European Union.

If one looks at the market keeping in view the overall size of the country and the overall responsibilities of the government (and now also the private sector to some extent) for creating infrastructure and other facilities, the parameters are:

(i) 930 million people (second most populous country in the world)

(ii) 3.3 million square kms of geographical area (seventh largest in the world)

(iii) fourth largest military power in the world (third largest by some estimates)

(iv) fifth largest economy in the world (sixth largest by some estimates)

(v) tenth largest industrial nation at current level of industrialisation.

With industry projected to grow at an annual rate of about 10%, and exports and imports at around 20%, new requirements for infrastructure and other facilities and increase in market demand in general can be reasonably forecast.

Human resource wealth

The availability of human resources would be relevant to the requirements of specific business activities.

In broad terms, India has one of the largest pools of scientific and technical manpower in the world. The following figures are revealing:

(1) Graduates and postgraduates: around 3.0 million.

(2) Diploma holders: around 0.8 million.

(3) Trained technicians: around 2.0 million.

(4) Graduates from scientific and technical faculties of universities annually: around 0.2 million.

(The above figures are based on 1990 statistics. Source: Economic Coordination Unit of the Ministry of External Affairs.)

Because of limited commercial interaction with other countries in the past, the skills of this vast pool of Indian scientific and technical manpower could be tapped only by a few international business organisations. However, wherever this interaction occurred, Indian technical and managerial personnel proved themselves to be as good as the best in the world. Expatriate Indian managerial, technical and medical personnel grace the board rooms, operational setups and research laboratories of the world's premier corporations and institutions. It should now be possible for leading multinational organisations to source management talent directly from India to manage at regional or global level.

The skill of Indian software personnel is acknowledged all over the world. After the United States, possibly the premier software developers in the world are from India.

Multinationals who have set up manufacturing facilities in India have realised that the skills, productivity and commitment of the inexpensive Indian worker are second to none. No doubt, this level of productivity and commitment is attained only when management provides an appropriate environment and work culture. It is true that in many industries in India where there is poor motivation, over-protectionism, excessive trade-unionism, excessive interference from government and lethargic management, worker productivity is not very high. However, foreign investors have the freedom to provide the right work culture and reap the fruit.

Convenient availability of raw materials

Minerals, agricultural resources and other natural endowments provide raw material for a variety of industries.

Technology, production and service infrastructure

A fact which is not as well known as the Indian expertise in software is that over the last few decades, India has developed an impressive research and development (R&D) infrastructure. This has resulted in remarkable advances in the fields of space technology, telecommunications, parallel computing, software, ship-building, aircraft, pharmaceuticals, metallurgy, defence equipment, applications of nuclear energy and numerous others.

While the bulk of the R&D talent has traditionally been in various government laboratories and research institutions, some progressive private sector companies have also done commendable work in R&D.

There is, however, need for enhanced expenditure in R&D in private sector corporations and with the new post-liberalisation enthusiasm, this is likely to occur.

The significant point for foreign investors is that since this R&D and design capability exists in India and is accessible, it would be to their benefit to start viewing India as an R&D base as well as a low-cost production base unlike some other emerging economies. This advantage is, however, more likely to be relevant for those who take a long-term view of their investments in India. Some leading international organisations which have invested in India in the last few years have very wisely utilised the R&D talent available.

The existing production infrastructure of Indian companies could be used by foreign investors through strategic alliances. While some Indian manufacturing units are already producing international quality products, others could do so with some technical and management input from their foreign partners. Such vendor development, if properly undertaken by foreign companies, could provide them with the necessary edge for competing effectively in world markets with high-quality and low-cost parts and products sourced from India.

In the short-term, foreign investors who do not have their own manufacturing setups in India, could utilise the existing manufacturing facilities of Indian companies to gain a competitive edge in the Indian domestic market.

Indian talent in the service and support sectors could also be strategically deployed by foreign investors not only for handling their requirements in the domestic market but also for gaining competitive advantage in their operations outside India. Such possibilities should definitely be explored by investors, even if initially it is limited to regions in proximity to India.

SHORT-TERM VS LONG-TERM PERSPECTIVE OF ADVANTAGES AND STRENGTHS

Despite good intentions and management sermons about the necessity of a long-term view in corporate strategy, it is a common observation that the objectives and targets for the immediate or near future are of paramount importance in the corporate plans of most business organisations. Most studies conducted recently on the competitive advantages of India have by and large limited their vision to the more apparent strengths and advantages relevant only to those who are taking a short-term view.

If one confines oneself only to the short-term view, the relevant advantages which could accrue to the investor are:

(1)   A large domestic market for a variety of products and services. The investor could meet the demand in a limited way by importing these products, where permissible.

(2)   Sourcing from India:
  – Software services
  – Products where Indian industries have already established their presence in the international markets—handicrafts, leather goods, brass-ware, garments, select engineering items
  – Raw material, minerals
  – Auto-components, select computer parts and other engineering items where some Indian companies have attained international levels of quality and price competitiveness.

(3)   Utilisation of locally available production and service infrastructure through strategic alliances for limited assembly and support of their products to meet domestic demand.

Those investors who take a long-term view can gainfully deploy all the advantages and strengths which this country offers, for enhancing competitiveness in the domestic market, as well as for their international operations. The additional activities undertaken by them in India could encompass:

(1)   Manufacturing facilities for domestic market requirements, as well as exports.

(2)   Design and R&D facilities for adapting products for the Indian market as well as for their global requirements.

(3)   Software development facilities for their world-wide requirements.

(4)   Extensive vendor base.

(5)   Unrestricted supply of their products for meeting the domestic demand. (Where domestic demand is met purely through imports as in some cases of short-term strategy, there could be limitations in supplies if the item happens to be in the restricted list of the government's trade policy.)

(6)   Lower cost and better pricing of products in the domestic market compared to imports (Note: This may not be so in a few cases.)

(7)   Use of India as the investing company's regional headquarters for providing support and services to their operations in South Asia, South-East Asia, the Middle East, Central Asia or Eastern Europe.

ROLE OF THE INVESTING COMPANY'S CORPORATE STRATEGY

The extent to which an investor gainfully uses the advantages and strengths of India, which exist even now for full use by those who have strategically positioned themselves, would largely be determined by his own understanding of the country, his confidence, foresight and corporate strategy.

Advantages classified earlier as motivational factors would in general be applicable to all business activities which could be undertaken by foreign investors in India. For some business activities, like insurance, the enabling factor of government policy is currently not applicable as the insurance sector is yet to be opened (as at the end of July 1996) for foreign investment. For most business sectors, the enabling factors are already there and may undergo only marginal improvement with time. Waiting for further changes and more incentives may not therefore be the best strategy for the foreign investor.

No doubt, there are some problems and irritants typical to a developing environment, which at times dissuade some investors from taking bold investment decisions. While some of the concerns may be genuine and some may be removed as the economic reforms progress, many of these would be in the nature of psychological barriers. Very few of these concerns would be such that they are not amenable to resolution through well-formulated entry strategies.

CONCLUSION

India has enormous strengths and advantages relevant to foreign business investors. Since mid-1991, the government has brought about a major change in the investment climate. The initiative for beneficial and healthy exploitation of these advantages now lies with investors.

There is a saying: There are three types of companies—those who make things happen, those who watch things happening, those who wonder what happened. The investing company has to decide which of these categories it would like to belong to when it comes to investment in India.

CHAPTER 6

OVERVIEW OF INDIA'S FOREIGN POLICY AND EXTERNAL RELATIONS
by Shilendra K Singh

A BRAND NEW WORLD

Cataclysmic and millennial changes in the world occurred from 1989 to 1992.

The Cold War ended. The Berlin wall crumbled. Germany was re-united. East Europeans abandoned Marxism-Leninism and adopted democracy. The Soviet Union abolished itself. The European Economic Community became the European Union. Militarily the United States of America became the sole super power, in economic and technological terms facing serious competition from Japan and the European Union. The countries of the Asia-Pacific region (Japan, South Korea, China, Hong Kong, Taiwan, and the ASEAN countries) had phenomenal economic success.

For India many an old international equation suddenly vanished, new ones struggling to be born. India also had to structure, with some urgency, new economic policies. Its traditional foreign policy required refashioning to be brought into line with the new economic policies. Above all India required a favourable international economic and political environment. It needed to put forward a new vision of peace and security for the sub-continent, the South Asian region, and the wider world, without compromising on its security, integrity and national interests.

THE CONSTANTS OF INDIA'S FOREIGN POLICY FORMULATION

The process of history necessitates that changes in policies be made in the context of overall continuity with the recent as well as distant past.

In the shaping of India's foreign policy the primary factors have always been: India's history and culture, geographical situation; national philosophy and identity, Gandhiji's non-violent methods for winning freedom, and the country's partition at the time of Independence, when a brand new country, Pakistan, was carved out next door.

For centuries the Himalayas in the north, and the long southern peninsular coastline, jutting into the Indian Ocean, have affected India's perceptions of its region and the wider world. India's complex history and cultural diversity have given its people a unique spirit of tolerance. The Hindu, Buddhist, Jain and Sikh faiths were born in India. Christianity, Judaism, Zoroastrianism and Islam were welcomed into the country and prospered there, in an atmosphere of reverence. Outsiders have always been effortlessly assimilated into India's own internal fabric. Indians have never been xenophobic. That is how the Graeco-Romans, Scythians, Parthians, Huns, Arabs, Turks, Moghuls, Persians, Dutch, Portuguese, French and British all came to these shores as invaders, and stayed on as Indian nationals.

The country's commitment to parliamentary democracy, freedom of the Press, and independent judiciary, secularism and a determination to eliminate poverty, have been elements in conditioning the formulation and articulation of its foreign policy. As a democratic society with a ferociously free Press, India, in a fast-changing world, has been able to mould and evolve its foreign policy according to the requirements of its people.

The Era of Non-Alignment

When India started participating in the work of the United Nations, it espoused two causes with great enthusiasm and dynamism: the de-colonisation of the subject world, and the abolition of apartheid and racism. Another preoccupation was never to surrender its autonomy of decision-making in framing the country's economic, domestic, foreign and defence policies, which would have happened, had India agreed to join one of the two Cold War military blocs. India refused to lose any part of its autonomy. Hence the policy of non-alignment, from which also came the enthusiasm for South-South economic cooperation, the building up of Group-77, and its representative nodal body called Group-15.

Internally India adopted an economic policy of broad self-reliance and self-sufficiency, at the same time rejecting the Marxist-Leninist recipes of collectivisation and State controls. Nehru, India's first Prime Minister after Independence, encouraged entrepreneurial functioning in all areas of economic productivity. The State or public sectors took up only those areas which the entrepreneurs themselves felt they were unable to handle. This was how India's mixed economy developed. India's productivity expanded during that period, in both agriculture and industry. The country was able to avoid external pressures, but in the process became isolated. Mrs Indira Gandhi in 1980–81 was already anxious to free the country from this self-imposed isolation, which had denied it opportunities of export-driven growth and prosperity, the ability to attract a better flow of investments, and easier access to the latest technology. Her successor Rajiv Gandhi shared her perceptions. Just as he was preparing to liberalise and internationalise India's economic functioning he was weakened by domestic developments that led, a few months later, to his defeat in the 1989 general election.

Changed Economic Policy—New Foreign Policy

In 1991 after another general election, Prime Minister Narasimha Rao made comprehensive and structural economic reforms. These included reducing the bureaucracy of the economy, and meshing it with the global market. These reforms were applauded by the world's economic powers. Both the International Monetary Fund and the World Bank were supportive. So were most of the major economic powers. The fiscal and financial disciplines India imposed upon itself were specially acclaimed.

India's political spectrum recognised that the country's foreign policy requirements had changed, and that it would be necessary to make major adjustments. India needed to grapple with the challenges, and also to grasp the opportunities involved in this changing scenario. India's foreign policy was thus changing in the midst of continuity. A pattern of peaceful relationships had to be built without ignoring the need to safeguard the country's sovereignty and territorial integrity.

And all this in a world where old federal structures like the former Soviet Union and Yugoslavia had failed; in which ethnic, sub-ethnic, linguistic, religious and other differences were being fomented from across borders, and terrorism was being promoted from outside. India could not but oppose fundamentalism and fanaticism trying to promote, finance, aid, arm, train and bank-roll dissidence, militancy and secessionism inside its own borders. This required vigilance and caution as well as forbearance, so as not to sacrifice India's own humanitarian values.

IMPULSE FOR PEACE IN ALL SOUTHERN ASIA

With any of its neighbours who were prepared to reciprocate, India has tried to strengthen and upgrade friendly and warm relationships, as in the case of China, Burma, Bangladesh, Nepal, Sri Lanka, Afghanistan and the five Central Asian Republics. Cooperation with all neighbouring countries must be increased, and potential confrontation or discord eliminated. One must not exaggerate the importance of defence and security strategy, and consciously direct one's attention to the expansion of cooperation in trade, communications, shipping, air-services, tourism, banking, informatics, transportation and infrastructure. In today's world, it is not possible to build a country's internal prosperity and economic security without cooperating in lifting the levels of prosperity in the region around it.

India and its six immediate neighbours, Bangladesh, Bhutan, Nepal, Maldives, Pakistan and Sri Lanka have tried during the last 10 years to strengthen their regional organisation, the South Asian Association for Regional Cooperation (SAARC). India and the other SAARC countries are confident that, given time, they should be able to get the SAARC, as has happened in the case of the ASEAN, to focus on cooperation, without mingling bilateral disputes with its work. After some years of discussion the South Asian Preferential Trading Arrangement (SAPTA) is about to be finalised. The logic of general action for greater prosperity is getting stronger and SAARC is moving towards expanding cooperation.

Relations with Pakistan

In this spirit India has offered the hand of friendship to its closest neighbour Pakistan, ignoring the problems Pakistan has created for itself and for India. Pakistan promoted secessionism in Punjab, which did not work. Since 1989 it has turned its attention to promoting secessionism in Kashmir. In the post-1990 period Pakistan has not been agreeable to discussing anything with India until the Kashmir problem is settled. Without denouncing the Simla Agreement they have tried to retreat from their commitment to it. India has the patience to wait for Pakistan to agree to peaceful negotiations on all bilateral issues.

Pakistan's acquisition of nuclear weapons and missiles has become a problem internationally. India does not see this as a bilateral issue. India's objective has always been general and complete disarmament, and a non-discriminatory global regime in respect of all weapons of mass destruction, as in the case of the Chemical Weapons Agreement. India does not believe in an arms race, of a nuclear character, with Pakistan, or with any other neighbour.

Defence Expenditure

India has been reducing its outlay of resources on defence, enabling itself to plough more resources into development. India's defence expenditure is down to 2.53% of its GDP, or US$1.23 per head; whereas in China the figures are 5.39% of GDP and US$2.69 per head of population, for Pakistan it is 6.88% of GDP and US$30.22 per head. The figures for Egypt are 4.15% and US$29.61, for Malaysia 4.57% and US$142.28, and the United States 4.8% and US$1081.17.

Asia-Pacific

In the post-Cold War era the Asia-Pacific region has emerged as a power house for generating economic activity, productivity and wealth. India's economic reforms, expansion of its productivity and exports show that India's economic dynamism and success is bound to bring it closer to this region. Nehru prophesied in 1943 that the importance of the Atlantic Ocean would diminish and that the Pacific Ocean would gradually acquire greater significance. As the Pacific and Indian Oceans are linked, India must consciously try to expand and improve its maritime activities. The NAFTA countries (the USA, Canada and Mexico) and the major South Pacific nations (Australia, New Zealand, Chile etc) are all drawing closer to ASEAN which now includes Vietnam.

Japan

Indian foreign policy takes into account Japan's emergence as an economic super power, and the economic success and dynamism of China and Taiwan. Japan too has shown awareness of the need to build closer economic, maritime, banking and communications links with India, and to use cooperation with India in its automobile industry.

European Union

India has built closer links, both economic and political, with the European Union, with an emphasis on its major countries, Germany, the UK, France and Italy. India's relations with the European Union are expanding and developing. In addition, some of the new entrants into the Union (eg Austria and Sweden) and some potential entrants (eg Poland and Hungary) have always had close and warm relations with India. Even today the EU absorbs a quarter of India's exports and provides a third of its imports. It is a growing market for India, which now ranks as the 16th most important trading partner of the EU compared with its 25th ranking in 1992. The end of the recession in Europe is opening up prospects of a faster growth in the EU for India's exports. The EU's investments in India are growing and hopefully will rise also as a percentage of the total foreign investments.

Russia and East Europe

India's relations with Russia have been close and warm. In principle, both sides wish to continue the old traditions of friendship and closeness. Russia, however, is in a period of massive and difficult change and reorganisation, both politically and in broad economic terms. One cannot, these days, realistically expect from it the earlier vigorous responses, or firm support, of the Soviet era. India and Russia are using this period of flux for articulating principles that could be useful now and later. A good example is the Narasimha Rao-Yelstin Declaration on the problems facing the pluralistic states, made in July 1994.

During the post-Cold War period India and the East European states have continued their traditional economic and commercial exchanges in a new ambience of democratic openness. In the writings and statements of President Havel Vaclav one gets a clear impression of India's abiding impact on various aspects of East European life and thinking.

India-United States Relations

India's economic reform programme today is the single most important factor in strengthening Indo-US relations. Large US and European multinationals have started investing in India and functioning in the Indian market. These include IBM, Hewlett Packard, Texas Instruments, Apple, Microsoft, Ford, General Motors, US West, AT&T, General Electric, Pepsico, Coca-Cola, McKinsey, Philips, Bosch, ABB, Siemens, Alcatel Ericsson, Daimler-Benz, Peugeot, Fiat, Henkel, Royal Shell, Elf, Unilever, Deutsche Bank and Credit Lyonnais.

The USA has become India's largest investor, largest trading partner, and the most important source for technology. Indo-US trade registered a 30% increase between 1991 and 1994, standing in 1994 at approximately $8 billion. This is being assisted by numerous high level political and economic visits, resulting in multi-faceted growth of common endeavours. The recent joint military exercises are a significant new venture for the two countries. There appears to be genuine interest in examining broader Indo-US cooperation in the military field. All this has resulted in a greater understanding of each other's perceptions of global and regional security and strategic issues. Their common commitment to democracy has been a major element in building a closer understanding. The USA has shown greater sensitivity to India's concerns and problems. However, old habits die hard, and occasionally sections of the US foreign policy establishment have confused the Indo-US relations and dialogue, NPT, allegations of human rights violations by Indian security authorities, the pace of socio-economic change in a pluralist democratic India, the Kashmir issue, and bilateral Indo-Pak relations. With closer understanding and a more detailed, and continuing US-India dialogue, this tendency is bound to taper off. India has no desire to make Indo-US relations hostage to Pakistan's truculence with India, or their efforts to promote terrorism, militancy and secessionism in Kashmir.

India has been sensitive to the US concerns on human rights issues. An MOU has been signed with the International Committee of the Red Cross for providing custodial access in Jammu and Kashmir. Amnesty International and other NGOs are getting used to visiting India, and discussing matters with the government. Jose Ayala, UN High Commissioner for Human Rights, has visited Jammu and Kashmir. India has established its own Human Rights Commission which is recognised as both vigilant and active. The USA is finding that the same fundamentalists who are spreading mayhem in India, are operating now in Algeria, Turkey, Egypt, Saudi Arabia and Tunisia, using explosives even in the USA, as they did in the case of the World Trade Center in New York City.

PROBLEMS AND ISSUES—POST-COLD WAR

In the post-Cold War world, communications, technology, commerce and economics are helping globalisation and cooperation. At the same time issues of small arms proliferation, fanatical fundamentalism, international narco-terrorism, the spread of ethnic and religious proxy wars are creating divisive impulses. The UN's efforts in Somalia, Rwanda and Bosnia have not been effective. Major powers are being tardy in financing UN operations. There is manifest lack of objective thinking in matters like expanding the membership of the UN Security Council. The major powers are averse to a thorough review of the UN Charter.

India's principal aspiration in foreign policy has been to take note of the changes in the world around it without being overwhelmed by them. India must not overlook the continuity of its quest for peace, prosperity, security and compassion, not only for all Indians, but also for the people of the region, and the world.

CHAPTER 7

SYSTEM OF HUMAN RESOURCE DEVELOPMENT AND EDUCATIONAL INFRASTRUCTURE

by A K Sharma
and G D Sharma

ANCIENT INSTITUTIONAL ARRANGEMENTS

The institutional arrangement for passing on accumulated knowledge in India was an individual teacher-oriented system called 'Gurukul'. For fine arts it was called 'Gharana' and for crafts and architecture 'Vastukar', ie 'master craftsmen'—where groups of students were taught at the ashram or at the workplace of their 'Gurus'. At the higher education level there were three well-known universities, namely, Takshsila (6th century BC), Nalanda and Vikramsila (4th–5th century AD). At these universities scholars from various parts of the world gathered and had the opportunity of learning and interacting with experts in various fields. These universities were among the very few universities in the world during that period.

Indians had excelled in mathematics as early as the 5th century AD through mathematical theories developed by Aryabhatta. The invention of the concept of zero in India before the 9th century is well documented. Astronomy originated in India and was well developed by the 13th or 14th century BC. High standards of craftsmanship in architecture are evidenced by many buildings and monuments. Indian style in fine arts such as painting, dancing and music is well known to the world. The Indian system of medicine and preventive care was well developed.

EDUCATION SYSTEM DURING THE BRITISH PERIOD

In the past few centuries when some countries were advancing their knowledge of guns and gunpowder, large scale production through the development of machines and the transformation of energy into steam and electricity and so on, India continued to bask in the glory of past achievements. It was taken over by the strength of gunpowder and modern machines and mass scale production. Under the compulsion of foreign rule, trade and commerce, the education system and to a great extent law, moral values and social institutions were transformed. A new education system was initiated. The colonisers attempted to replace the native system of education by English education with an emphasis on English literature, British history, social sciences and sciences developed in the West. Over a period of time, the English system of education expanded and to a great extent it succeeded in replacing the native system.

EDUCATION SYSTEM AFTER INDEPENDENCE

During the period of struggle for independence, and after India gained independence, the British system of education continued to dominate. Between 1951 and 1994, many reforms were introduced into the education system. The setting up of institutes of technology, agriculture, medicine, research laboratories and institutes of social sciences and sciences highlights these reforms. The system has been transformed by the rapid growth of institutions of higher education during this period. The rate of expansion is highlighted by the following facts:

Table 1
Growth of Institutions of Higher Education, India
(1947–1994)

Institutions	Years	
	1947	1994
General Universities	19	122*
Science Technology Universities	2	20
Agriculture Universities	0	26
Management	0	5**

* Along with these apex institutions, the number of colleges increased to 8200 from just 500 colleges at the time of independence.

** There are as many as 242 recognised institutions which offer management programmes at the post-graduate level, 38 institutions offered part time programmes and 58 universities and institutions of management offered a research degree programme in management.

HUMAN RESOURCES AND INDUSTRY, TRADE AND COMMERCE

Educated and Technical Manpower

Educational institutions have been able to provide a strong base of educated people in the areas of agriculture, technology, medicine, social sciences, general sciences, arts and literature. Compared to population size, the numbers of people educated in science and technology or engaged in R&D are not very high, yet compared to the total number in the technical workforce, India ranks third in the world. The stock of technically educated people in 1991 was as follows:

Table 2
Technical Manpower, India: 1991

Category	(Thousands) Economically Active Population
Engineering Degree Holders	395.3
Engineering Diploma Holders	639.3
Medical Graduates	263.1
Dental Surgeons	10.4
Nurses (BSc)	5.4
Agricultural Graduates	127.0
Veterinary Graduates	29.1
Science Graduates	1044.7
Science Post Graduates	327.4
BEd (BSc)	269.0*
Total	3110.7

GDP—Research and Development Statistics, 1990–91, Department of Science and Technology
* Estimated on the assumption that 25% of Education graduates would be with a Science background

No sector of industry, trade or commerce has ever suffered due to a shortage of qualified human resources in the country. India has been sending highly educated people trained in Indian Institutes of Technology, Indian Institutes of Management, universities, medical and engineering colleges, as well as social sciences institutions to various parts of the world. In particular, science and technology graduates have been sent to the USA and medical and social sciences, trade and commerce graduates to the United Kingdom and some of the Gulf countries.

Educational Infrastructure and Enrolment by Areas of Studies

India has developed a vast infrastructure of universities and colleges, institutions of technology and schools of management. About 5 million students are studying in institutions of higher education.

Table 3
Institutions by Fields of Specialisation, India, 1993–94

	General	S&T	Open	Agriculture	Women	Language	Sanskrit	Medical	Mgmt
TOTAL NO.	122	20	6	27	5	4	6	12	5*

Source: Sharma, G D Indian University System. A profile, NIEPA, 1994

*a) There are as many as 242 recognised institutions which offer management programmes at the post graduate level.
b) There are a large number of specialised departments attached to various universities (eg many universities have a Department for Management Studies. This number can, therefore, convey a different impression. In addition, there are a large number of private institutes.

Table 4
Enrolment in Higher Education by Areas of Studies

Course of Study	1992–93 % of Total
Arts (including oriental learning)	40.4
Science	19.6
Commerce	21.9
Education	2.3
Engineering/Technology	4.9
Medicine	3.4
Agriculture, Veterinary	1.1
Science	0.3
Law	5.3
Others	0.8
Total No. of students	4,804,773

Source: UGC—Annual Report, 1993

The Institutes of Technology, Institutes of Management, centres of excellence in the area of bio-technology in nine universities, and advanced centres for environmental sciences, immunology, computers and electronics, social sciences, economics, financial management, operations research and sociology form a very strong base comparable with institutions in any part of the world.

Though the literacy rate in India is not comparable with that of many parts of the world, the efforts put into the organisation of educational infrastructure at the school level is remarkable. The following table indicates the educational infrastructure developed at the school level:

Table 5
School Education System, India, 1993–1994

Types of Institutions	Nos. of Institutions	Enrolment
Pre-primary schools	17172	
Primary schools	572923	108.2 million
Middle schools + upper primary	220962	
Higher Secondary Schools	20167	39.9 million
(new pattern) + high schools		
Inter/Junior/pre degree colleges	2989	23.3 million

Source-GOI, Ministry of HRD, Selected Educational Statistics 1994.

Cost Estimates

For general universities, the annual budget ranges from Rs50 to Rs90 million and for Central Universities with general education, science and technology education, research projects and residential facilities projects, the budget ranges between Rs300 to Rs400 million annually. The cost per student in general (both Central and State supported universities) is estimated at Rs14,000. The cost in Central Universities is estimated at Rs25,000 per student. The student cost in social sciences is almost twice that of arts, and in sciences it is almost twice that of social sciences.

Policy Thrusts

Policy thrusts, as envisaged in NEP 1986, and revised in 1992 are on improving the quality and relevance of higher education, improving the efficiency of the system and the introduction of quality assessment. After liberalisation of the economy and the opening up to world markets in 1993 the emphasis is on the utilisation of resources by institutions of higher education by establishing links with industry, trade and commerce. A bill relating to the opening of private universities has been initiated in the parliament.

OPPORTUNITIES AT PRESENT

India is a vast country and there are abundant opportunities for the development of human resources and, through them, the development of the country. The diversity of industry, trade, commerce, vocations and the need for social sector development is so great that existing institutions are not able to cater to the diverse needs of the economy and society. New institutions will need to be created and older ones reformed to meet the present need. The growing areas are training in computer application, software development and skill development in information technology, bio-technology, water and energy management. The areas of economics, commerce and trade, human resource development in financial management, market research, and market operations are the developing needs.

LIKELY OPPORTUNITIES IN THE FUTURE

Besides the private sector universities and colleges, which might emerge (with the acceptance of a bill in the parliament) to meet the changing needs of a future workforce, the existing workforce will need continuous training and upgrading of skills in the areas of plant and market operations as well as administration. In-house training will need to be provided in the areas of information technology, the use of higher technology tools and machines, planning, and management. The opportunities for developing, marketing and providing training programmes will grow significantly in the near future.

PART 2
PREPARING TO DO BUSINESS IN INDIA

NEGOTIATION PREPARATION AND THE IMPORTANCE OF ENTRY STRATEGY

by Jitendra Kohli

SCOPE OF THE CHAPTER

It is well understood that negotiation is the process of reaching mutually satisfying agreement amongst concerned parties through communication, discussion and where required, bargaining. The focus of this chapter is to provide broad guidelines to prospective foreign investors in India on the situations they could encounter which would require negotiation of some kind, and broadly the kind of preparation or homework they should do as a prelude to such negotiations. Some allied issues have also been touched upon.

SOME IMPORTANT SITUATIONS WHERE FOREIGN INVESTORS MAY HAVE TO NEGOTIATE

Broadly speaking there are five important situations where foreign investors in India may have to negotiate during the initial phase of their entry into the country.

The quality and extent of the investors' preparation in these five situations can have a major impact on the long-term success of their ventures in India. These are:

(1) Negotiations with the Central Government for permission (also called licence in some situations) to start business activities in the country.

(2) Negotiations with the Central Government or a State Government for permission or contract for undertaking activities in specified sectors.

(3) Negotiations with the Central Government, a State Government or local bodies for specific activities related to project implementation.

(4) Negotiations with prospective joint-venture or strategic alliance partners.

(5) Internal negotiations within the investing company.

An investor may begin his operations in India by one of the following means: agency; liaison office; branch office, project office; joint-venture with an Indian company; subsidiary with public shareholding; or wholly-owned subsidiary in India.

These entry options and business structures (termed hereafter business entities) have varying degrees of commercial risk and differing advantages. Some of these have been separately discussed in chapters pertaining to industrial policy and incorporating a company. Depending on the type of business entity chosen, permission would have to be sought from the Reserve Bank of India (RBI), the Secretariat of Industrial Approvals (SIA) or the Foreign Investment Promotion Board (FIPB).

The process of obtaining such a permission would involve submitting an application in appropriate format with relevant information to the government department concerned. The information provided would be studied by the government keeping in view government policies and norms for foreign investment in general, and special policies and norms, if any, for that area of business activity in particular. Where required, other concerned ministries would be consulted. This would be followed by the government granting the necessary permission (through issue of a formal letter) or communicating its need for further clarification and negotiations.

Negotiation preparation is useful not only for such formal meetings with the government, but would also be reflected in the quality of the application submitted. This could substantially reduce or sometimes obviate the need for formal presentations and discussions in most of the situations described above.

It may be noted that as a consequence of economic reforms since 1991, the process of obtaining government permissions has become quite simple for cases of liaison office, branch office, and proposals which come under the list of 'delicensed industries' and fulfil the government stipulations for foreign investment under the 'automatic approval route'.

Some important aspects of preparatory work which the investor should undertake before seeking permission from government are outlined below:

(1)   The investor should be clear about his business objectives in India.

(2)   Clear understanding of relevant policies of the Government of India. Where special permission is to be sought from FIPB, as in the case of proposals for 'wholly-owned subsidiaries' of foreign companies or those which fall 'outside the ambit of automatic

approval', it is important for the investor to appreciate the country's and the government's special 'needs and priorities' to merit such special permissions. There are no strictly defined guidelines which have been published on the criteria adopted by FIPB. The FIPB is specially empowered to engage in negotiation and to consider proposals in totality, free from pre-determined parameters or procedures. The FIPB is also guided in its decisions by the specific policies of the government for different sectors. For example, while the FIPB would consider the merits of a proposal for setting up a wholly-owned subsidiary of a foreign company for an industrial project, a power project, a non-banking finance company (NBFC), or a holding company, there would be a ceiling of 49% on foreign equity holding of a basic telecommunications services company. To avoid arbitrariness, 'informal sectoral-guidelines' are understood to have emerged within FIPB for evaluating proposals pertaining to different sectors. The investor should endeavour to understand these through direct discussions or with the assistance of local consultants.

(3) Strategy for achieving these objectives in the short term, medium term and long term.

Absence of clarity in the above-mentioned could result in the investor not being able effectively to handle objections raised or clarification sought by the government. More importantly, the investor may end up seeking permission from the Government of India for a type of business entity not ideally suited to his actual needs.

Some examples of the latter situation could be:

(1) The investor may hasten into a decision to establish a joint-venture and submit an application on that basis. He may realise later that his short-term goals could have been better achieved through a liaison office or a branch office and followed up with a wholly-owned subsidiary incorporated in India.

(2) In a similar vein, another investor may seek special approval from the government for setting up a wholly-owned subsidiary in India and realise later that it would have been more advisable to have a good local partner in a joint-venture. Furthermore, such errors of judgment would not only bear on the decision for the type of business entity, but on the scope of business activities the investor has planned for India, the type of joint-venture or alliance partners the investor chooses, the type of marketing and support channels the investor sets up and so forth.

An example of a somewhat erroneous decision regarding the scope of business activities could be that the investor forges an alliance in India believing that he merely wants to market his products in the domestic market without any local manufacture. He may realise later the advantages of local manufacture, not only for the domestic market in India but also as a sourcing base (for finished products as well as parts) for his requirements in other parts of the world. If these aspects had been considered by the investor at an earlier stage, his entry strategy, as well as joint-ventures could have been appropriately reoriented.

Typical Reasons for Errors in Entry Strategy

Investors entering a new country like India may sometimes have preconceived ideas regarding the business activities they would like to carry on in that country. Errors of judgment regarding clarity of objectives and the strategy for achieving those objectives occur quite often due to incorrect or incomplete information. This may be due to any of the following:

(1) Biased perceptions about India in the mind of the investor. Such perceptions could be related to industrial infrastructure, quality of products manufactured in India, productivity of the Indian workforce, level of skills and technology which has been already reached in India, red tape in bureaucracy or other factors.

(2) Inability to accept the differences between India and countries they are more familiar with.

(3) Incomplete information about the relevant local markets. This may be due to only a cursory market study, or scanty and at times somewhat biased information from existing local agents or partners.

(4) Lack of proper appreciation of the relevant government policies and the various options available to investors.

As a result of such mistaken perceptions, the investor may set his sights on limited objectives in his entry strategy for India and as a consequence formulate an incorrect approach to achieve those objectives. Realisation of these errors often dawns on the investor after beginning operations in the country. Many investors are obliged to make major changes in their strategy within two years of commencing business in India.

To reduce such errors of strategy, it is important to emphasise the role of a well-formulated entry strategy at the outset.

Entry strategy guidelines

To ensure that important issues are not overlooked in the entry strategy, the investor should take into consideration the issues raised above, as well as some other relevant factors. An entry strategy model depicted below brings out some elements which the investor is advised to consider. It may be noted that, depending upon the nature of business activities proposed, some aspects of the entry strategy model presented below would change significantly. Also, the emphasis on different activities outlined in the model would vary substantially for different types of business activities. As an example, the model would be ideal for a typical industrial project but would need modification for infrastructural projects in areas like power, highways, or urban utilities.

Basic entry strategy model

One decision which should be firmly in place at the end of phase 1 (as shown in the entry strategy model below), is the form of business entity the company wishes to establish in India and whether or not it should have a joint-venture partner on an equity sharing basis for the proposed Indian venture.

To summarise, taking short-cuts in formulating an entry strategy can result in the reworking of strategy later on, lost opportunities, delayed results, avoidable frustration, and increased costs as a result of these factors.

While stressing the importance of a comprehensive entry strategy, it is important to sound a note of caution. Sometimes, by the time an opportunity has been investigated fully, it may have ceased to exist. This reality should always be kept in mind. Decisions in this regard will, of course, vary from case to case and provision can be made for 'mid-course corrections' if necessary.

Entry Strategy and the 'Evolving Plan Model'

Any entry strategy or plan must of course be subject to some ongoing refinements based on new inputs or changed circumstances.

Planning for a new project or even a new market segment for an existing company cannot follow the same planning model as is typically followed for ongoing, well-established operations of the company. In the latter case, there is generally a database of experience and knowledge, and market trends and other variables are more predictable. In the former, the ratios of 'unknown to known' and 'assumptions to facts' are higher.

Entry Strategy Model

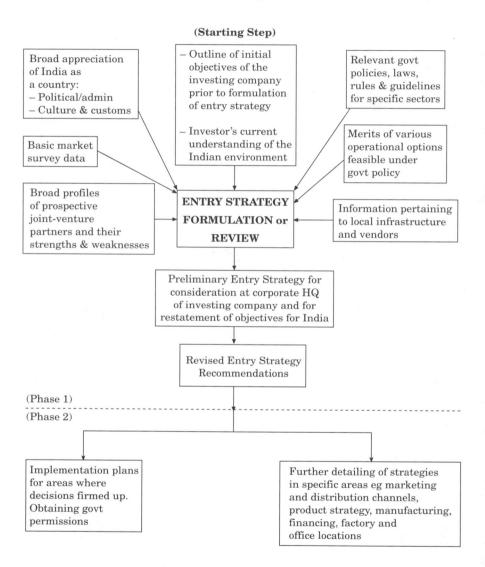

(Starting Step)

Broad appreciation of India as a country: – Political/admin – Culture & customs	– Outline of initial objectives of the investing company prior to formulation of entry strategy – Investor's current understanding of the Indian environment	Relevant govt policies, laws, rules & guidelines for specific sectors
Basic market survey data		Merits of various operational options feasible under govt policy
Broad profiles of prospective joint-venture partners and their strengths & weaknesses	**ENTRY STRATEGY FORMULATION or REVIEW**	Information pertaining to local infrastructure and vendors

Preliminary Entry Strategy for consideration at corporate HQ of investing company and for restatement of objectives for India

Revised Entry Strategy Recommendations

(Phase 1)
- -
(Phase 2)

Implementation plans for areas where decisions firmed up. Obtaining govt permissions

Further detailing of strategies in specific areas eg marketing and distribution channels, product strategy, manufacturing, financing, factory and office locations

Source: J Kohli Consulting (P) Ltd

A well-formulated entry strategy as outlined above improves the situation by reducing the learning period and avoiding major pitfalls significantly. The uncertainties and the learning period cannot be eliminated altogether. Adaptation should be a basic feature of any good plan or strategy and this is particularly important for entry strategy.

Some management experts suggest that even the personality, attitudes and skills profile of executives who are successful in the building phase of an organisation are quite often different from those who are successful in routine operations. The former class of executives should have better creative problem-solving ability. Personal experience as an executive and subsequently as a management consultant confirms this view.

Entry Strategy Formulation Teams and External Assistance

There are many ways of formulating entry strategies. Some companies prefer to send their own large teams who may work with some local assistance. Others prefer to economise on their own management time in the initial phase and assign responsibility to a senior executive within the company who in turn works through a locally based management consultant. The management consultant's role is sometimes supplemented with that of specialised market research agencies, lawyers, taxation firms, merchant bankers and human resources companies. There are advantages and disadvantages to these divergent approaches.

Ultimately of course it is not enough to merely go through the motions of ticking the check-list for steps of entry strategy. The background, experience and perception of the persons who conduct the exercise, and the thoroughness with which it is done, matter most.

NEGOTIATIONS WITH THE CENTRAL GOVERNMENT OR STATE GOVERNMENT FOR PERMISSION OR CONTRACT FOR UNDERTAKING ACTIVITIES IN SPECIFIC FIELDS

Such permissions would not apply to investments relating to most industrial activities. However, infrastructural sectors like telecommunications, power, roads and highways, bridges, urban utilities and a few others would require specific permissions for specified projects. As an example, a foreign investor may establish a wholly-owned holding company in India for setting up one or more power projects. After obtaining permission from FIPB, a company would have to obtain specific permission for setting up a specific power project in a particular State. The process of obtaining such a permission could be through the 'MOU route' (Memorandum of Understanding) or the 'competitive bidding route'. It should be noted that competitive bidding is now mandatory for some sectors including power, national highways, and hydrocarbons (upstream sector).

The policies, rules and evaluation criteria vary for different sectors; however, some typical situations are illustrated in a section of this chapter.

'MOU' and 'Competitive Bidding'

When policy for a particular infrastructural sector is in a nascent phase, the 'MOU route' is generally adopted by the government in negotiating and approving projects from organisations who have taken the initiative and have submitted their proposals to the government. As experience is gained and the policy and rules for that sector mature, the MOU route is replaced with 'competitive bidding'.

A case in point is the power sector. When the Private Power Policy was announced in 1991, the methodologies pertaining to Independent Power Projects (IPPs) had not fully crystallised. Therefore, as in many other countries, project solicitation was through the MOU route. From the experience gained since 1991, the government now feels confident to pursue the bidding route for IPPs. Since 18 February 1995, competitive bidding has become mandatory for all new power projects. It is expected that the bidding route would bring greater transparency in the evaluation and negotiation process, encourage competition, and get a better deal for the State Electricity Boards (SEBs) and the consumers.

Resort to the bidding route, of course, becomes feasible only when the concerned State governments and the SEBs have undertaken considerable preparatory work and established a competitive bidding framework. In broad terms this would require detailed project information (including preliminary feasibility report); availability of associated infrastructure clearances; well-established bidding criteria; and draft PPA (Power Purchase Agreement) as well as other important documents.

For power projects, the Ministry of Power has now prepared a set of guidelines to assist State governments in following the bidding route, which is normally in two stages:

(i) The RFQ (Request for Qualification) stage.

(ii) The RFP (Request for Proposal) and stage.

The RFQ stage establishes a threshold criteria in the four principal areas (organisation, financial capability, management capability and technical capability) to qualify for the subsequent RFP process. Parties which meet the stipulated criteria are entitled to compete. In principle, RFQ threshold criteria need to be carefully framed to ensure that the selection at the RFP stage is done primarily on quantifiable price considerations, the other parameters having been eliminated at the RFQ stage.

The RFP process also needs considerable preparatory work. The design of RFP broadly takes into consideration factors such as engineering adequacies, acceptance of SEB operating requirements, pricing, plant availability, draft PPA and other agreements to be provided to the bidders, evaluation criteria, price caps, acceptable inflation indices; and clear identification of GOI's (Government of India), State governments', SEBs' and bidders' responsibilities.

It may be noted that the terms RFQ and RFP are used in guidelines for power projects. However these terms are not standardised for all sectors and the investor may come across different terms such as 'Technical Bid' and 'Price Bid'.

Nature of Negotiation Preparation for 'MOU Route' and 'Bidding Route'

While some of the steps for negotiation preparation remain common irrespective of whether the MOU route or bidding route is taken, there would be some areas in the case of competitive bidding, where responsibilities would shift from the investor or developer to that of the concerned State government and its relevant bodies. The nature of and emphasis on negotiation preparation would, therefore, also shift accordingly. For example, in the case of the bidding route, responsibility for the Preliminary Project Feasibility Report would rest primarily with the concerned SEB and State government and would be available along with the bid documents from the SEB. The detailed feasibility report which would be required to be submitted along with the bids by the promoters would, however, still have to be prepared by the promoter. In the MOU route, all clearances including identification of project site would be the responsibility of the developer. In the bidding route, while the primary responsibility for obtaining various clearances would still remain with the developer, a few clearances required from the SEB and the State government would be relatively easy to obtain.

Irrespective of the route, it is imperative for the investor or developer to understand the following:

(1) Government policy for that sector.

(2) Procedural steps and government guidelines, if any, for the MOU route for that sector.

(3) Procedural steps and guidelines for the competitive bidding route for that sector.

(4) Special guidelines, if any, for some specific aspects of the competitive bidding process. For example, in the case of the power sector, apart from general 'Guidelines for Competitive Bidding Route for Private Power Projects', it would be important to understand the key issues and guidelines for PPA, which is the most crucial legal document in the project finance structure and is quite often decribed as the heart and soul of private power project.

The draft PPA is part of the RFP documents provided to pre-qualified bidders and is one of the solicitation documents. PPA is signed by the SEB with the selected bidder.

(5) Information and practical tips to supplement the above. Such information could be assimilated in the course of personal interaction by the investor in India with the Investment Promotion Cell (Ministry of Power), concerned departments in the States and through knowledgable consultants.

The broad principles of the negotiation preparation guidelines outlined above for the power sector would in general also be applicable for other infrastructural sectors. The actual steps and the nature of negotiations would vary from one sector to another. The investor is therefore, advised to educate himself appropriately about the sector of his interest.

In projects where competitive bidding is involved, it is generally not mandatory for the bidder to have an incorporated company in India at the time of bidding, although it could be advantageous to have one. However, in most sectors it is necessary for the successful bidder to have an incorporated company in India for implementing the project.

One important aspect which the investor must keep in mind while negotiating with any government body is that government personnel are publicly accountable for whatever decisions they take during the negotiation process. The level of openness and flexibility shown by government personnel during any negotiations is therefore bound to be somewhat different from the attitude of negotiators from a private corporate body. Appreciation of this reality would be helpful to prospective foreign investors during the negotiation process. It would also be pertinent to state here that since the beginning of economic reforms in India, there is a sea-change in the attitude of bureaucracy at the Federal Centre and in many of the more progressive States.

NEGOTIATIONS WITH CENTRAL GOVERNMENT, STATE GOVERNMENT OR LOCAL BODIES FOR SPECIFIC ACTIVITIES RELATED TO PROJECT IMPLEMENTATION

Having obtained permission from the government for setting up a wholly-owned subsidiary or a joint-venture in India and, where applicable, additional approvals for specific infrastructural project(s), the investor must get ready to implement his project and establish his operations in the country. For a typical industrial project, the subsequent steps would be:

(1) Incorporating a company (as explained in chapter 11). A private company can commence business after it receives its Certificate of Incorporation from the Registrar of Companies. For a public company there are additional requirements. A public company can commence business on receipt of a Certificate of Commencement of Business

(2) Recruiting key personnel.

(3) Setting up office(s) by renting or purchasing office premises.

(4) Raising finances (as explained in chapter 9).

(5) Acquiring land for the industrial project. Land can be purchased from the State governments in designated industrial areas, or from private parties. Agricultural land can also be converted into industrial land on application to local authorities, subject to certain conditions.

For his specific project, the investor is advised to prepare an exhaustive check-list. For an infrastructural project, the investor is advised to collect and assimilate information pertaining to that sector and prepare exhaustive check-lists which would not only assist him in planning negotiations at various stages but also in effective project management.

NEGOTIATIONS WITH PROSPECTIVE JOINT-VENTURE OR STRATEGIC ALLIANCE PARTNERS

Alliances

The decision to establish 'alliances' and the nature of such alliances should be one of the essentials of the entry strategy of the investing company.

The term 'alliance' could imply a variety of different relationships and business structures between the investing company and the prospective Indian partner. Within its ambit could come a non-exclusive distribution tie-up, a limited technology-transfer or design tie-up, a supplier-buyer relationship, joint-ventures with equity participation by both partners, or mergers and acquisitions. Strategies and negotiation preparation steps would naturally vary both in content, spread and extent in the different situations outlined above.

A joint-venture is an alliance structure which is commonly adopted. The suggestions made below pertaining to joint-ventures could be applicable to other types of alliances.

Joint-ventures

Joint-ventures can be of different forms. The foreign investing company and the Indian company could share equity on a 50:50 basis (eg Tata-IBM joint-venture) or have equal equity with some offered to the public (eg Bharat Petroleum-Oman Oil joint-venture for a refinery where each company has 26% equity and the balance is with the public) or one partner could have controlling equity.

Some common problems of joint-ventures

The equity structuring of the joint-venture should be such that it allows both or all the parties involved to achieve their corporate objectives. From the foreign investor's perspective, this would be feasible only if it is clear about its objectives based on a reasonably well-formulated entry strategy. It is not uncommon to come across cases where a foreign investor, having limited information about India, enters into an alliance with minority equity with an Indian company. Soon after, the investor realises that this country offers greater potential than was initially perceived and starts agitating for controlling equity in the joint-venture. The Indian partner, in some cases, resents this change and the alliance founders.

Some other major problems which afflict joint-ventures in India, as well as in other countries are:

(1) Reasonable synergy in the short-term objectives of both partners but very little compatibility in long-term objectives. An example of this would be a situation where the foreign investor is interested in utilising the readily-available office network of the local company and the local company is interested in the product technology of the foreign organisation, but there is no matching of objectives beyond this.

(2) Incorrect or inadequate information about the prospective partner's strengths and weaknesses. One example of this could be that the foreign investor while evaluating the local partner places great importance on the financial health and credit-rating of the local partner but gives insufficient attention to other important aspects.

(3) The projected objectives of one or both the partners may be different from the real objectives which are kept hidden at the time of formalising the alliance.

(4) Legal and equity structure related matters may have been well covered at the time of forging an alliance but some key operational and strategic issues, such as sharing of management responsibility and control, technology upgrading, brand identity, pricing, intent to manufacture and export from India, equity structure in case of major expansion in the future, and other such issues may not have been sorted out.

(5) The investor may select a local partner based on the overall corporate image and size of the local corporate group, which may be quite impressive. Realisation may dawn later that while the local partner's overall strengths are indeed impressive, his strength in the specific field targetted by the joint-venture is not so impressive.

(6) Cultural mismatch between the two organisations. Such an eventuality between a foreign and a local organisation is quite natural and likely. However, if some study of such cultural (including work culture) differences is made beforehand and appropriate planning is done to overcome such incompatibilities over a period of time, the chances of success for the alliance are heightened.

(7) Personality mismatches between the management personnel of the two organisations with one or both parties trying to control the relationship rather than nurturing the relationship. Problems relating to individuals, however, have to be handled separately and any good management system should have provisions for handling such situations.

(8) Negative or unsound reasons for choosing the joint-venture route (see below for some typical reasons for selection of the joint-venture route). Success of the joint-venture would naturally hinge on which of the reasons enumerated below were the motivating force behind the alliance.

It is important to emphasise that, while negotiating a joint-venture, the senior managements of both organisations should be able to foresee substantial synergy and complementary strengths not only in short-term but more importantly in long-term objectives of the two organisations. It should also be confirmed that no crucial area of disagreement has been left unresolved.

If synergy is perceived only in the short term, other types of alliances, less demanding in terms of time, money and commitment should be explored.

Typical reasons for choosing the joint-venture route

Foreign investors' perspective

(1) General fear of the local environment.

(2) Lack of sufficient knowledge and specific information about the local environment (government policies, laws, culture, markets, availability of resources, ability to coordinate with bureaucracy and others).

(3) Avoiding local resistance and political sensitivity to foreign investment in some sectors. (Note: This is specially relevant to non-priority sectors.)

(4) In certain sectors the government policy does not allow wholly-owned subsidiaries of foreign companies even through the case-by-case special-approval route of the FIPB.

(5) Desire to kick off business operations immediately without making any major investments (low risk strategies).

(6) The local partner may have a well-established marketing and distribution network, the like of which may take the foreign company many years to build.

(7) The local partner may have manufacturing facilities which, with some fresh inputs, could be used by the foreign investors not only for addressing the domestic market but possibly as a high-quality, lower-cost source for their requirements in other parts of the world.

(8) Lack of desire on the part of the foreign investor to do any independent study and analysis of the local market. As a strategy to gain a foot-hold, the investor may initially tie up with one of the Indian companies who may have approached it.

(9) The investor has little interest in the Indian operations, or the initial local alliance may only be an interim arrangement.

Indian companies' perspective

(1) To acquire better technology for their existing products or a whole new range of products and associated technology.

(2) Capital for their new project or for modernisation of their existing projects.

(3) Global experience and management know-how of the foreign partner.

(4) Access to international markets for exports.

(5) Pride in being associated with a big international player.

(6) Fear of being swamped by foreign MNCs (the philosophy of 'if you can't beat them, join them'.

Negotiation-preparation for joint-ventures and joint-venture agreements

Clarity regarding objectives, strengths and weaknesses, and cultures of the two organisations should be the essential elements of negotiation preparation for joint-ventures.

For this, a comprehensive 'Joint-venture Partner Evaluation Exercise' should be carried out before the joint-venture is formalised. A typical 'evaluation model' is presented on the following page.

In addition, understanding of relevant laws of the country is essential.

Joint-venture agreements should be so drafted that:

(1) The main emphasis is on the objectives of the joint-venture and its successful functioning with important powers and responsibilities clearly defined.

(2) There is mutual commitment to nurturing the relationship and this should be reflected in the agreement.

(3) Provision is made for reviewing progress periodically, not with 'Divorce and Termination Clauses' in mind but with a desire to achieve the defined objectives despite the odds.

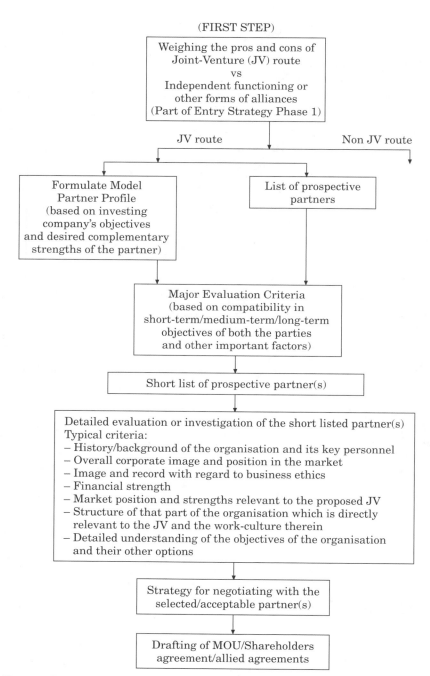

(FIRST STEP)

Weighing the pros and cons of
Joint-Venture (JV) route
vs
Independent functioning or
other forms of alliances
(Part of Entry Strategy Phase 1)

JV route   Non JV route

Formulate Model
Partner Profile
(based on investing
company's objectives
and desired complementary
strengths of the partner)

List of prospective
partners

Major Evaluation Criteria
(based on compatibility in
short-term/medium-term/long-term
objectives of both the parties
and other important factors)

Short list of prospective partner(s)

Detailed evaluation or investigation of the short listed partner(s)
Typical criteria:
– History/background of the organisation and its key personnel
– Overall corporate image and position in the market
– Image and record with regard to business ethics
– Financial strength
– Market position and strengths relevant to the proposed JV
– Structure of that part of the organisation which is directly
   relevant to the JV and the work-culture therein
– Detailed understanding of the objectives of the organisation
   and their other options

Strategy for negotiating with the
selected/acceptable partner(s)

Drafting of MOU/Shareholders
agreement/allied agreements

(Source: J Kohli Consulting (P) Ltd)

(4) Provision is made for resolving disputes and grievances in a timely and reasonable manner.

Managements therefore have the most crucial and substantial role to play in drafting of joint-venture agreements. While legal departments too have a valuable role in the drafting of such agreements, it may not be advisable for top management executives to completely delegate this responsibility to their legal teams. A joint-venture agreement is above all a document reflecting 'Intent and Relationship' and not merely the law relating to contracts.

Negotiation process for joint-ventures

In most Indian corporate organisations, the decision to enter into a joint-venture or a strategic alliance with a foreign company would be formalised at the top operating level of the organisation, although initiative for such a business relationship could have been taken at any hierarchical level in the organisation. The decision would generally be based on the recommendations of a task force or an evaluation team set up by the organisation head for that specific joint-venture proposal. The evaluation team would consist of senior executives of the organisation and sometimes external consultants.

Depending upon the corporate culture of the organisation, decision-making could be quick or time-consuming. If the Indian organisation concerned is a public sector company, clearances may also be required from the relevant government ministries.

Peculiarities of the Indian environment may at times cause teething problems in the negotiation process. Adaptability, flexibility and patience would be rewarding for the foreign investor in such situations.

Understanding personal traits of Indian negotiators with specific reference to joint-ventures

A striking feature of India is its diversity. The typical Indian business negotiator, therefore, does not fit into any specific mould. A foreign investor coming to India can expect to meet people with varying personality projections and business styles. It would, however, be helpful for an investor to understand some typical aspects of Indian ethos, such as:

(1) Indians like to extend hospitality and also appreciate its reciprocation.

(2)   There is a strong emphasis on human relationships. Indians like to have social interaction with their prospective business partners and to some extent know them at a personal level. Occasional social interaction with spouses is welcome, although, where the wife of an Indian businessman is somewhat traditional and not well-versed in English, she may not be very vocal during the interaction. Nevertheless, she would be observant.

A cold, brusque and domineering attitude on the part of a foreign investor would generally be counter-productive.

(3)   Indians, by and large, have strong family ties and stable marriages. The expectation of an Indian business person, in an important relationship like a joint-venture, would also be similar— long-term and stable.

ACQUISITIONS, MERGERS AND AMALGAMATIONS

Foreign investors who want to avoid a greenfield approach to conducting business in India can now also consider the possibility of acquisitions through which they can acquire controlling equity in an existing Indian company.

While negotiating an acquisition of a company listed on the stock exchanges, SEBI (Securities and Exchange Board of India) guidelines have to be kept in view.

Among other preparatory steps, the procedure would require submission of a proposal to the FIPB with the consent and board resolution of the company to be acquired.

Cases relating to merger and amalgamations of two existing Indian companies would generally not be relevant to new foreign investors. Where relevant, the reader may refer to the chapter on Company Affairs for procedural steps. The Companies Act, 1956 does not define either of the terms 'merger' and 'amalgamation'. One has to be guided by the meaning of the terms as used in the ordinary commercial sense. A merger or amalgamation may be defined as an arrangement whereby the assets and liabilities of two companies become vested in another company, which may or may not be one of the original companies.

INTERNAL NEGOTIATIONS WITHIN THE INVESTING COMPANY

It is not uncommon to come across cases where the foreign company's team responsible for evaluating India as a possible investment destination has a limited mandate from its top management. This may be due to the limited information available about India at its headquarters. However, as the 'India team' studies the local situation and does spade work, they may realise that the potential and possibilities in India far exceed those initially visualised by their top management. This is a situation where the 'India team' would have to do internal negotiations with top management of its own company to convince it to give higher priority to India.

No guidelines for such situations are proposed. The members of the India team would be the best judges. The only recommendation is that a well formulated and comprehensive entry strategy would strengthen their case.

CONCLUSION

In general, whenever the investor needs to obtain licences, approvals or clearances from the government, negotiations will ensue. Similarly, whenever agreements are to be signed with government or private bodies or individuals as in the case of joint-ventures, negotiations in some form are likely to occur.

In negotiation preparation it is most important to base decisions on a well-conceived entry strategy supplemented with specific information and creative solutions at each stage of negotiation.

While a strategy should be comprehensive in its coverage, it should not be complex. Even if the situation for which the strategy is being formulated is complex, the analysis and strategy formulation process should sift through the complexities and propose clear action steps.

Lastly, while guidelines can be used as supportive check-lists, they are only a partial determinant of success. How a process is implemented, and the skills, experience and mature judgment of the persons involved are as important as the 'what-to-do check-list'.

CHAPTER 9

BANKING AND FINANCE
by D H Pai Panandiker

THE FUNDS FLOW

The financial infrastructure in India is well developed. There are different markets, institutions and instruments which ensure a smooth transfer of funds from those who save to those who invest. Most of these funds are transferred through financial intermediaries who provide the kind of instruments which lenders prefer and accept the kind of securities that borrowers like to issue. These transactions give rise to a structure of interest rates which now is mostly market determined.

The total net funds flow in the country in 1994–95 would be about 22% of the national income or about Rs2 trillion. Of this amount nearly 80% passed through the intermediaries.

THE FINANCIAL MARKETS

Broadly, there are two markets which undoubtedly overlap each other. First, there is the market for short-term funds. It is this market that companies draw upon for working capital. Secondly, there is the market for long-term funds trading either in loans or equity. Funding of plant and machinery comes from this market. The institutions which handle short-term and long-term funds are different.

THE MAJOR PLAYERS

The major players in the financial markets are:

- Banks
- Non-banking financial institutions like mutual funds, leasing companies, etc.
- Development Banks like Industrial Development Bank of India, Industrial Credit and Investment Corporation of India, Industrial Finance Corporation of India, State Finance corporations, etc.
- Insurance companies.
- Provident Funds.
- Stock Exchanges.
- Post Offices.

THE SECURITIES

These financial intermediaries accept and issue claims and thus create a market for finance. These claims take a variety of forms. Some of the claims are tradeable like debentures or shares issued by the corporate sector or securities issued by the Central and State Governments. In recent years a variety of new instruments like commercial paper, certificates of deposit, convertible debentures, zero coupon bonds, warrants, secured premium notes, stockinvest, deep discount bonds, and floating interest bonds, among others, have been successfully introduced. There are also claims that cannot be traded, for instance, deposits with banks, post offices or companies, provident funds and so on.

FINANCIAL NEEDS OF COMPANIES

Equity Capital

An Indian public limited company raises its finances from the market to meet its working and fixed capital needs. Broadly, the promoter will hold a certain percentage of the share capital which would enable him to acquire management control. Absolute control is possible only when the promoter's equity holding is more than 50%. However, in large companies promoters prefer to hold much less, ideally 26% or more of the equity capital. With that, management is able to block any resolution which requires a three-quarters majority. The extent of promoter share holding is, however, a matter of judgment. A company in which the shares are closely held will be a private limited company which is treated somewhat differently in the Companies Act.

A part of the share capital can be subscribed by the foreign partner/promoter. He can hold up to 51% of the equity without being required to obtain any permission from the government. That is so in respect of companies involved in any of the 35 groups of industries. For a higher percentage or for investment in any other industry, clearance from the Foreign Investment Promotion Board is necessary.

The promoter, after retaining the number of shares for himself, will issue the balance to the public. Such public issue of shares requires the permission of the Securities and Exchange Board of India (SEBI). The main object of SEBI is to ensure that the public is given requisite details about the project and the risks involved. The initial issue has to be without premium at Rs10 a share. Equity issues are normally handled by a merchant banker/underwriter.

Loan Capital

Equity is the nucleus of the capital structure of a company. On the basis of the security provided by the equity a company is able to borrow. Normally a debt/equity ratio of 2:1 is allowed. In capital heavy industries like power or fertilisers the debt/equity ratio can go up to 4:1. The debt for such purposes is the long-term debt which would include borrowings from the development banks or financial institutions like Industrial Development Bank of India (IDBI), Industrial Credit and Investment Corporation of India (ICICI), Industrial Finance Corporation of India (IFCI), or debentures issued by the company in the market. For issue of debentures a company has necessarily to be rated by agencies such as Credit Rating and Information Services of India (CRISIL), Investment Information and Credit Rating Agency of India (ICRA) or Credit Analysis & Research Ltd (CARE).

Working Capital

The equity and the loans finance the fixed capital of the company, leaving a little excess to make up the margin for borrowing for the working capital. The bulk of the working capital comes from the banks. Companies can also discount bills arising from purchase of raw materials, float commercial paper (for which the company has to be rated), and so on.

The bulk of the finance required by the company comes from the promoter, the primary capital market, development banks and commercial banks. These are major players in the market and have abundantly met the financial needs of companies. The market for corporate finance is increasing at a phenomenal rate.

THE BANKING SECTOR

Major Constituents

Banking institutions have a very long history. They are now fairly well developed, modernised and provide a variety of financial services. In 1969, 14 scheduled commercial banks with deposits of over Rs500 million were nationalised. This made it possible to expand the branch network and take banking facilities to every nook and corner of the country.

The banking sector is composed of the following main segments: Reserve Bank of India (RBI); scheduled commercial banks; regional rural banks; and foreign banks.

Functions of the Reserve Bank of India

The RBI is the central bank of the country. It regulates the operations of other banks, manages the money supply and acts as banker to the government. As a central bank it is responsible for maintaining the internal and external stability of the rupee. More specifically, the RBI:

- issues currency and regulates money supply;
- makes and receives payments on behalf of government;
- markets government securities;
- supervises and inspects other banks;
- directs banks to maintain a minimum statutory liquidity ratio (SLR) and a minimum cash reserve ratio (CRR);
- undertakes open market operations;
- prescribes minimum interest on bank credit and maximum interest on bank deposits;
- operates the exchange control;
- maintains foreign exchange reserves;
- accepts applications for foreign direct investment which is eligible for automatic clearance;
- regulates setting up of new banks;
- sanctions opening of branches in India by foreign banks and of Indian banks abroad.

The assets of the RBI consist mainly of gold and bullion, Government of India securities, and foreign government securities constituting the foreign exchange reserves. The liabilities principally include currency issued to the public and deposits of scheduled commercial banks, apart from other liabilities. At the end of March 1995 total assets/liabilities were Rs2 trillion.

As banker to the government the RBI is under an obligation to hold the part of the unsubscribed loans floated by the government. One security which is held almost exclusively by the RBI and hence directly increases 'reserve money' is ad hoc treasury bills. Borrowing by government against ad hoc treasury bills has been responsible for high inflation. The RBI therefore entered into an agreement with the Finance Ministry in September 1994 to phase out treasury bills within three years. This implies that the government will have to borrow entirely from the market in competition with the private sector at the market rate of interest. Undoubtedly, the government will always borrow at a lower rate considering that government paper is the most liquid and the most secure.

Scheduled Commercial Banks

There were 280 scheduled commercial banks at the end of March 1995 having 62,264 offices. Of these banks, 25 were in the public sector. Since nationalisation was limited to banks with deposits over Rs500 million, private sector banks are small. The aggregate deposits of scheduled commercial banks at the end of March 1995 were Rs3.7 trillion or about 41% of the GDP. More than 82% of the deposits are with the nationalised banks.

Of the scheduled commercial banks, the State Bank of India has a special place. It was nationalised much earlier than the rest of the banks and has been operating as 'a lender of immediate resort'. It is the largest among the commercial banks with nearly a fifth of the deposits with all banks.

Among other scheduled commercial banks, the major ones include the Bank of India, Central Bank, Punjab National Bank, Bank of Baroda, Canara Bank and United Commercial Bank. The principal assets/liabilities of all scheduled commercial banks at the end of March 1995 consisted of the following:

Deposits	Rs3.76 trillion
Credits	Rs2.22 trillion
Securities	Rs1.5 trillion
Cash & balances with the RBI	Rs0.65 trillion

Pattern of Funds Use by Commercial Banks

Scheduled commercial banks have to invest a part of the deposits in government securities to make up the SLR and maintain a part with the RBI as cash reserve. The rest of the deposits are used to extend credit to companies, firms and individuals or to discount trade bills. The bulk of the credit is short-term. The RBI has also directed banks to observe prescribed norms in regard to credit to different sectors of the economy. These are:

(1)   Banks have to maintain a minimum 12% CRR and 25% SLR.

(2)   Credit to priority sectors should be at least 40% of total credit.

(3)   Maximum interest on deposits (less than two-year maturity) cannot exceed 12%.

(4)   Minimum interest on credit cannot be less than 15%.

Priority sectors for the purpose of credit allocation include agriculture, small-scale industries, transport operators, retail trade and exports. Pre-shipment and post-shipment credit is available at a lower rate of interest to enable exporters to match credit facilities with their competitors abroad.

In the past four years the SLR has been scaled down from 38.5% to 25%. SLR creates a protected market for government securities which prompts the government to offer an artificially low rate of interest on its securities. That had forced the banks to charge a high rate of interest on credit to the commercial sector. With the substantial lowering of the SLR, the government has now to compete with the private sector for loans. The result is that the rate of interest on government securities has substantially increased. Interest on a 10 year loan, for instance, went up from 12% in 1991 to 14% in 1995. On the contrary, the prime rate on bank credit to the commercial sector came down from 19% to 15%. This has eliminated cross-subsidisation and at the same time improved the profitability of banks. Many of the banks are now in a position to build up capital reserves to make up the 8% capital adequacy norm. Those that cannot find resources on their own have been assisted by the government. In future banks will function on commercial lines free from the rigid control to which they were subject since nationalisation. Most of the banks are now in the process of modernisation. Since 1993, after agreement with labour unions, banks have gone in for computerisation, and ATMs.

With the reforms in the financial sector, new banks are allowed to be set up in the private sector. The UTI Bank was the first to come into existence. Five other banks have already emerged and six others have received RBI approval. The intention is to foster competition and compel public sector banks to provide better service to their clients.

Foreign Banks

There were 24 foreign banks operating in India with 147 branches, apart from 22 representative offices, as at the end of March 1994. The total deposits of these banks were Rs21.9 billion. This would be about

6% of the total deposits of the scheduled commercial banks. The business of the foreign banks is more diverse. Their place in the financial structure cannot be judged merely on the basis of their deposits. They play a much bigger role in portfolio management, direct foreign investment, international trade, derivatives, etc.

The setting up of a branch of a foreign bank requires the approval of the RBI. That approval is given mainly on considerations of reciprocity. The largest network of branches is of Citibank which controls about a fourth of the total deposits of foreign banks in India. One of the important businesses of foreign banks is credit cards. Six foreign banks have been in this business as of 30 June 1994 compared to only five nationalised banks and the SBI. The other major business is consumer credit.

Pattern of Funds Use by Foreign Banks

Foreign banks are largely subject to the same regulations as the scheduled commercial Indian banks. They have to extend credit to priority sectors to the extent of 32% of their total credit. However, since foreign banks do not have established links with agriculture, small-scale industries or other priority sectors, they are allowed to deposit a corresponding amount with the Small Industries Development Bank of India (SIDBI), a bank specially set up to provide credit to small-scale industries. As an alternative, foreign banks can finance export credit.

The rate of interest charged by foreign banks is more in keeping with prevailing market conditions. Nationalised banks generally act in concert in deciding the rate of interest on bank credit or on charges for different banking services. Foreign banks act more independently and, therefore, the rate of interest is somewhat different. Foreign banks provide more modernised banking facilities and enjoy an edge over other banks.

Regional Rural Banks

Regional rural banks (RRBs) were set up to provide banking services to the rural sector where the reach of the scheduled commercial banks was weak or absent. There are 196 RRBs operating in different parts of the country with 14,593 branches. The aggregate deposits of these banks were Rs88 billion and the outstanding loans Rs52 billion.

RRBs have not been a profitable business. More than 76% of the banks have been making losses. These banks are now going through comprehensive restructuring. They have already been given some freedom which will bring them out from isolation into the national mainstream. Non-target group lending of RRBs has been raised to 60%. They are allowed to extend consumer credit against security, give guarantees on behalf of their customers and issue travellers' cheques as agents of their sponsor banks. It is significant that RRBs can invest their non-SLR funds in UTI schemes, fixed deposits with financial institutions, bonds of nationalised banks, non-convertible debentures of blue chip companies, etc.

Development Banks

Development banks are also described as term lending institutions or financial institutions. They are an important segment of the market for long-term funds. Until 1990 these institutions played a critical role in the financing of investment in the corporate sector. They had become the major source of long-term capital. That was because the primary market for corporate securities was under-developed. Besides, with the high rate of taxation of corporate profits and exemption of interest from taxation, companies were tempted to depend on loans to the maximum permissible extent.

The major financial institutions include: Industrial Development Bank of India (IDBI); Industrial Finance Corporation of India (IFCI); Industrial Credit and Investment Corporation of India (ICICI); State Finance Corporations (SFCs); State Industrial Development Corporations (SIDCs); and Industrial Reconstruction Bank of India (IRBI).

There are also specialised institutions like the Small Industries Development Bank of India, the Shipping Credit and Investment Corporation of India, and the Tourism Finance Corporation of India, which provide finance to specific industries or services. Special mention, however, needs to be made of the Life Insurance Corporation of India, the General Insurance Corporation of India and the Unit Trust of India, which offer financial assistance to the corporate sector by way of underwriting of shares, private placement, and other services.

At the end of March 1993 the total assistance provided by the financial institutions stood at Rs1.51 trillion. The annual outflow of funds from the institutions to the corporate sector is over Rs400 billion.

Loans by financial institutions are generally secured against fixed assets. The maximum loan available to any company would normally be twice the amount of its own funds, ie equity *plus* reserves. The rate of interest was 17% at the end of August 1995. Some of the financial institutions also have a line of credit from similar institutions abroad and provide loans in foreign currency to Indian companies. The amounts, however, are small, usually less than US$1 million.

Industries which have derived most assistance from the financial institutions include textiles and chemicals, among others. The share of some of the major industry borrowers are as follows: textiles 12%, chemicals 14%, services 11%, steel 8% and electricity 7%.

Financial institutions continue to be an important source of long-term funds to a number of companies. In most companies, financial institutions have a large stake. To ensure the safety of their money the institutions insist on appointment of their nominees on the Board of Directors of the assisted companies.

The emergence of a vigorous primary market for shares in recent years has somewhat reduced the importance of the financial institutions. Besides, these institutions which derived considerable resources from the budget of the Central Government have now to borrow from the market. Hence the amount of finance at their disposal is not quite adequate and its cost is high.

NON-BANKING FINANCIAL INSTITUTIONS

There are a number of non-banking financial institutions providing financial accommodation to individuals, firms and companies. These include mutual funds, hire-purchase and leasing companies, and investment companies. Companies are also allowed to accept deposits from the public. These are subject to restrictions regarding the amount and the rate of interest.

Mutual Funds

Mutual funds have become a significant segment of the capital market. At the end of March 1995 there were 22 mutual funds registered with the SEBI. The largest mutual fund, the Unit Trust of India (UTI), was set up way back in the 1960s and, until 1992, enjoyed an absolute monopoly. The UTI now accounts for 82% of the total investment by all mutual funds. Apart from the UTI, there are nine other public sector mutual funds set up mainly by banks and insurance companies. The other nine mutual funds are in the private sector. The share of the latter is less than 3%. The largest private sector mutual fund is Morgan Stanley Mutual Fund with investment of Rs10 billion. The investments of mutual funds at the end of March 1995 were:

(a) UTI — Rs616 billion.

(b) Other public sector MFs — Rs103 billion.

(c) Private sector MFs — Rs25 billion.

The mutual funds collect money from the public through a variety of schemes designed to suit the needs of different investors. The moneys are invested in corporate securities like shares and debentures. Mutual funds underwrite share issues and also accept private placements.

Mutual funds are supervised by the SEBI. To ensure that the investments are made entirely on business considerations, mutual funds are required to set up asset management companies with 50% independent directors. Further, the investments have to be made according to the SEBI guidelines which stipulate that:

(i) no individual scheme can invest more than 5% of its corpus in any one company's shares;

(ii) under all the schemes investment should not exceed 5% of the paid up capital of any single company;

(iii) under all the schemes investment should not exceed 10% of the funds in the shares and debentures of a single company.

Mutual funds are prohibited from giving term loans. Further, the offer documents of schemes to be launched have to have SEBI approval.

NON-BANKING COMPANIES

Non-banking companies include non-financial companies, financial companies and other miscellaneous companies. Non-banking companies are allowed to accept deposits up to 10 times the net owned funds without restrictions on the rate of interest. At the end of March 1993 the total amount of deposits with non-banking companies was Rs1.1 trillion. There were more than 40,000 financial companies accepting deposits at the end of March 1993. The aggregate deposits with these companies were Rs443 billion. The regulated deposits of the non-banking companies were Rs112 billion, about 4% of the aggregate deposits of all scheduled commercial banks. Deposits with non-banking companies have been increasing at the rate of 22% annually, even faster than bank deposits.

PRIMARY MARKET FOR SHARES

With the introduction of capital market reforms, companies have been depending more on the primary market for their long-term capital. The motivation is two-fold. First, the rate of corporate taxation has been reduced. This makes equity servicing easier. Secondly, companies have the freedom to charge premiums on their share issues. These considerations have made share capital more attractive than loan capital in spite of the fact that interest is tax free.

Size of the Primary Market

The total capital raised by companies increased more than nine-fold in just four years. From a mere Rs43 billion in 1989–90 the amount of issues went up to more than Rs400 billion in 1994–95. This increase does not reflect a corresponding expansion in investment. That is because a part of the share capital has been used to replace term loans which has reduced recourse to financial institutions. A part has also been used to finance working capital. For instance, the amount of public and rights issues in 1994–95 was Rs75 billion more than the project cost for which companies approached the capital market. With more dependence on the primary market for shares the expansion of bank credit to the corporate sector slowed down.

Share capital has become the most economical source of finance mainly because of the high premium at which shares are issued to the public and the shareholders. Premiums can be charged only on further issues by existing companies. The premium on share issues has become a matter of some controversy. Since some companies sought to rig up market prices of their shares to justify higher premiums the SEBI has introduced new directives asking promoters to disclose more information to help investors make a fair judgment about the reasonableness of share prices.

The response from investors has been excellent. The equity culture has spread rapidly. The total number of shareholders rose from 6 million in 1985 to 16 million in 1994. There is widespread demand for shares which proved a good hedge against inflation. Until 1995 share prices have been going up faster than the prices of other investible assets like gold and silver or interest on bank deposits, government securities and debentures.

Supervision of SEBI

A company going to the capital market to issue equity has to get the approval of the SEBI. The SEBI insists on material disclosures about the purpose for which the money is raised, the risks involved, and getting debt instruments rated, so that the investor can make a proper assessment of the future prospects of the company. Merchant bankers are made accountable in the offer document. Firm allotment can be made to institutions like mutual funds. Underwriting of shares is optional. In case of oversubscription, the allotment has to conform to the guidelines issued by the SEBI.

Listing of Shares

With the issue of shares to the public the company will be in a position to raise the loans negotiated with the financial institutions, and when the project is implemented to get the bank credit for its working capital. The shares will be listed on the local stock exchange. For the listing of shares it is, however, necessary that a minimum of 25% of the shares are with the public. It is expected that a depository system will be in place shortly to eliminate physical transfer of share certificates.

Apart from the domestic market for shares, companies can also raise money from the Euromarket by issue of GDRs or convertible debentures. Since 1992, 52 companies have approached the Euromarket and raised US$4.7 billion. GDRs are a proxy for shares and take the form of depository receipts for the purposes of trading on the Luxembourg or London Stock Exchanges.

THE STOCK MARKET

The stock market does not generate resources for the corporate sector. It is a secondary market which merely trades in securities that have already been subscribed to. However, it has a tremendous impact on the primary market because it influences the response of the investor to new issues. A bullish stock market is necessary to make equity an attractive investment.

Price Trends

In the last five years, the stock market has gone through four distinct phases. For 10 months from June 1991 until April 1992 the stock market enjoyed a strong bullish trend. The last four months of this phase witnessed a feverish rise in prices. In 120 days prices jumped 120%. This bullish phase reflected unusual conditions which were subsequently believed to be unrealistic. The aftermath was equally dramatic. Prices dropped over a period of 15 months bringing the Bombay Sensex back to the level of January 1991 just before the scam began. From August 1993 there was a steady rise in prices based more or less on reality, and other factors like reforms and, equally important, excellent corporate performance. This bullish phase lasted for about 14 months taking the index to a new peak. In September 1994 it had crossed 4500. Since then it has been a climb down partly brought about by the SEBI with the ban on forward trading. There were other contributory factors like the loss in the elections of the ruling Congress Party in important States like Karnataka, Andhra and Gujarat. The Mexican crisis also created its own ripples which affected all emerging markets and, for a time, kept the foreign institutional investors out.

FII Investment

Foreign institutional investors can invest in the stock of Indian companies. Such investment has to have the approval of the SEBI. The maximum permissible investment is 24% of the equity capital of a company for all FIIs together, and 10% for any single FII. The outstanding FII investment at the end of October 1995 was $4 billion. FII investment, as well as the response to GDRs, depends to a great extent on the rate of exchange. That is because the earnings and capital appreciation are in rupees and their repatriation will be in foreign currency. Since the latter is what is relevant to FIIs, the exchange rate becomes an important consideration.

THE EXCHANGE RATE

The rupee was made convertible on current account from March 1993. The immediate result was a hardening of the rupee in terms of the dollar which is used as the intervention currency. The RBI, therefore, intervened in the currency market and purchased dollars in order to stabilise the exchange rate at Rs31.37 to a dollar. Since November 1994 the inflow of FII investment and the issue of GDRs have eased. The RBI has therefore stopped its intervention and left the exchange rate to be decided by the market. The rupee remained fairly stable until September 1995. There were pressures building up to push the rupee down. The main consideration was the fall in the value of the rupee following inflation at about 8–9% per year. A correction in the exchange rate to that extent was necessary and did take place. This was designed to bring about greater harmony between imports and exports and stabilise the rupee. With the revival of the stock market and the reduction in trade deficit the rupee should stabilise at about Rs35–36 to a dollar in the medium term. This stability of the rupee will minimise the currency risk that institutional and corporate investors face.

The Indian stock market is inevitably linked with the GDR market through arbitrage operations. The FIIs have the choice to buy shares in India or the Euromarket. In this arbitrage the rate of exchange also plays a crucial role.

STRONG FUNDAMENTALS

The fundamentals are extremely strong. Since 1993 profits of companies have been increasing at rates ranging between 70% and 72%. Broadly, share prices are related to the earnings of companies. The price/earnings ratio in September 1995 for BSE Sensex companies was about 19 and the ratio of market price to book value 3.2. The half yearly results for 1995–96 indicate about 31% increase in sales. Net profits were up 53%. Profitability was the highest ever. It was 17.7% of sales.

The strength of the fundamentals did not impact positively on share prices. In the first half of 1995 share prices declined. As a result, some of the companies which went to the market did not meet with good response from investors. This had a secondary effect on the market for GDRs. They were quoted at a discount which prevented companies from approaching the Euromarket as well. The corporate sector, as well as the government, therefore, had to face some financial stringency. Since the fundamentals are strong the market showed a revival before the end of the financial year.

OPPORTUNITIES IN THE FINANCIAL SECTOR

One of the objectives of reforms was to create grounds for attracting foreign investment. The removal of industrial licensing and the permission to foreign investors to hold up to 51% of the equity in priority industries, without any government approval, opened up opportunities for foreign investment in a wide range of industries. Looking at the results it does appear that the policy has worked well.

Direct foreign investment actually received in the past three years. exceeded US$3.5 billion. Policies have also been liberalised in the financial sector, which has opened up opportunities to foreign investors.

Opportunities in Banking

The banking sector was opened to foreign investment in spite of bank nationalisation. A foreign bank can open a branch in India after getting the requisite permission from the RBI. A number of foreign banks have set up branches in India which offer all banking facilities. The Citibank branch in India, it was reported, has been the most profitable of all its branches. A number of new foreign banks have been accessing the Indian market. Very often they start with a representative office which is later converted into a regular branch.

After the nationalisation of banks in 1969 new private sector banks were not permitted. Under the new dispensation in 1993 private sector banks have been allowed. By 1994 six private sector banks were already in operation. The RBI has allowed foreign financial institutions to take up 20% of the equity in private sector banks. NRIs can have 40% stake in such banks.

Opportunities in Merchant Banking

An area of special interest is merchant banking. The Indian corporate sector is growing at a rapid pace. The finance for investment has to come from equity floated in the domestic market, loans from term lending institutions, international agencies like the International Finance Corporation, the Asian Development Bank, government institutions such as Exim Banks, loans from foreign commercial banks, as well as issue of GDRs and debt securities in the international markets, mainly Luxembourg and London. This has created a large demand for merchant banking services to be provided by domestic and foreign merchant bankers.

The first merchant banking division was set up in 1969 by Grindlays Bank. Sensing the opportunities, many others followed. At the end of September 1993 there were 311 merchant bankers undertaking diverse operations such as corporate counselling, project counselling, capital restructuring and portfolio management.

Merchant banking is now statutorily under the regulatory framework of the SEBI. Merchant bankers are divided into four categories depending upon the kind of functions they undertake and the responsibilities they are required to fulfil. They have to conform to capital adequacy norms. For a full-scale merchant banker a minimum capital of Rs10 million has been prescribed.

The business of leasing has flourished in recent years. A number of equipment leasing and hire purchase companies have been set up and have excellent potential.

Opportunities in Mutual Funds

Mutual funds started in the 1960s with the setting up of the Unit Trust of India. Until recently no other mutual fund was allowed. The field is now open to the private sector. Mutual funds will be a popular form of investment with the general public. At the end of September 1995 the outstanding corpus was US$7.4 billion. This was less than 5% of the market capitalisation of all companies. Being an avenue which will find greater favour with the public, this business is being pursued by private sector companies. Morgan Stanley Mutual Fund with investment of more than US$300 million was launched in January 1994. Mutual fund business will attract foreign participation in view of the long experience of foreign mutual funds and the variety of schemes they have evolved.

Opportunities in Securities Business

The securities market was opened to FIIs in September 1992. FIIs can operate both in the secondary as well as the primary market. A single investor can hold not more than 10% of the equity of a company and all FIIs together cannot hold more than 24% of the equity of any company. They have to pay 20% tax on the dividends, 10% on long-term capital gains (one year) and 30% on short-term capital gains. Since the FIIs have to buy and sell securities on a continuous basis, the rupee is made fully convertible for such transactions.

There has been a flood of foreign investment in Indian securities. By the middle of October 1995 FII investment had reached US$4 billion. By March 1995, 308 FIIs had been registered with the SEBI. The presence of FIIs in the securities market is quite noticeable. Their investment is about 3% of the market capitalisation of all companies listed on the stock exchanges. One of the major problems faced by FIIs was with the delivery system. Share certificates have to be physically delivered and must be transferred by the company in the name of the investor. This involved considerable delay as well as the dangers of physical delivery. To obviate these difficulties the government has promulgated legislation to permit the setting up of depositories. These will enable paperless trading and encourage FIIs to invest in the securities of Indian companies. Foreign institutional investors will be able to invest in the equity of the depositories.

The bond market is not yet opened to the FIIs. After the rupee becomes convertible on capital account the FIIs will be able to participate in the bond market as well. In fact, the whole of the debt market including private sector securities will be open to foreign investors. The Finance Minister has indicated that full convertibility of the rupee may take about two to three years.

The entry of FIIs in the Indian securities market has created large opportunities for brokering business. To generate greater trust, foreign brokers are allowed to act on behalf of the FIIs. James Capel, Kleinwort Benson, Credit Lyonnaise Securities and Marline Partners made up the first batch of foreign brokers to get permission from the SEBI to operate on behalf of the FIIs. More brokers have since been approved. With the expansion in FII investment there will be scope for more opportunities in this line.

Opportunities in Insurance

Insurance was nationalised along with the banks in 1969. With the reforms undertaken in the financial sector it was thought expedient that the insurance industry should be opened to the private sector as well to improve the quality and range of services offered to the insured. Accordingly, a committee under the chairmanship of Mr R N Malhotra was appointed to examine the issue. The Committee submitted its Report in January 1994. The Committee, inter alia, has suggested the following:

(1) The private sector should be permitted in the insurance industry. The minimum paid up capital has to be Rs1 billion, with the promoters holding between 26% and 40%.

(2) Foreign companies, when permitted in the insurance industry, should float Indian companies and preferably joint-ventures with Indian partners.

(3) The Life Insurance Corporation should be privatised and restructured.

(4) The General Insurance Corporation should cease to be a holding company.

(5) The mandated investment of funds of the LIC and GIC should be reduced.

(6) The Controller of Insurance should be restored its full functions under the Insurance Act.

The Malhotra Committee Report is yet to be implemented. The government has, however, taken the first step of establishing an Insurance Authority and indicated its intention of permitting private sector participation in the insurance industry. On the expectation that at an early future date the insurance industry will be opened to the private sector, MOUs have already been signed between Indian and American companies, to give them time to complete the initial formalities. Insurance will be a very promising area for foreign investment.

CONCLUSIONS

The financial markets in India are not only well developed but also very active. They fully respond to changes in economic and business conditions. The expert management of money supply and the exchange rate have enabled the government to restrict inflation to single digit numbers and build up a foreign exchange reserve exceeding US$17 billion. The interest rate structure is now more market-determined. The different institutions and the various instruments have channelled the savings of the people to the government and the corporate sector mainly on the basis of return. That ensures that the corporate sector will not be starved of funds if it is willing to pay the market rate of interest. In the 10 months from August 1994 to June 1995, the stock market was somewhat depressed. With the strong fundamentals and low P/E ratios, the market revived in the first quarter of 1996. That will help companies to raise equity capital. It will restore balance in the financial system and both the government and the companies will be able to mobilise the amount and the type of moneys they need.

The dynamism of the financial sector opens up vast opportunities to foreign investment in a number of areas like participation in equity of private sector banks, opening of branches of foreign banks, participation in the setting up of mutual funds, leasing companies, investment in the securities of Indian companies through the FIIs, undertaking brokering for the FIIs, undertaking merchant banking operations, setting up joint-ventures in the insurance industry and so on. The prospects are good because the Indian economy is entering a new phase of development. Already, industrial production is increasing at the rate of 14% per year and the economy will grow at rates exceeding 7% in line with the performance of other similarly placed countries like Thailand, Indonesia or China. Early entry by foreign investors will have the advantage of capturing a good share of the market and establishing a competitive position.

CHAPTER 10
OVERVIEW OF CORPORATE AND BUSINESS LAWS

by Ravinder Nath

A foreign investor needs to become familiar with various laws before commencing business activities in India. Among others, the Companies Act, the Foreign Exchange and Regulation Act, the Contract Act, the Monopolies and Restrictive Trade Practices Act, the Arbitration Act and the laws relating to intellectual property rights are of special significance.

Some important business laws (such as the Companies Act) and allied subjects (such as arbitration, intellectual property, setting up a liaison office/branch office, investment/disinvestment and taxation) have been covered elsewhere in this book.

COMPANY LAW

The law relating to companies, branches of foreign corporations and certain other associations is contained in the Companies Act 1956 ('the Act'). This Act is in many respects based on the United Kingdom Companies Act, though the Indian Act is far more comprehensive. A more detailed treatment of the subject is given elsewhere in this book.

EXCHANGE CONTROL

A foreign investor must consider the applicability of the provisions of the Foreign Exchange Regulation Act, 1973 (FERA), which was amended by the Foreign Exchange Regulation (Amendment) Act, 1993. The FERA forms the statutory basis for exchange control in India. The 1993 amendment Act drastically curtailed the scope of FERA in many respects and provided major relief to foreign companies already operating in India. However, even after the 1993 amendment FERA remains a very relevant consideration for all foreign business people in India. Rules, Notifications and Orders issued by the Central Government, and Notifications and Orders issued by the RBI under the FERA administer the exchange control envisaged in the FERA. Foreign investment in India is subject to policy guidelines framed by the Government of India from time to time in accordance with industrial policy. Details pertaining to industries and trade are given in other chapters.

Transactions Regulated by Exchange Control

The types of transactions which are affected by FERA 1973 are, in general, all those having international financial implications. Among others, the following matters are regulated by exchange control:

- Purchase and sale of and other dealings in foreign exchange and maintenance of balances at foreign centres.
- Procedure for realisation of proceeds of exports.
- Payments to non-residents or to their accounts in India.
- Transfer of securities between residents and non-residents and acquisition and holding of foreign securities.
- Activities in India of branches of foreign firms and companies and foreign nationals.
- Foreign direct investment and portfolio investment in India.
- Appointment of non-residents and foreign nationals and foreign companies as agents in India.
- Acquisition, holding and disposal of immovable property in India by foreign nationals and foreign companies.

AUTHORISED DEALERS IN FOREIGN EXCHANGE

Authorisations in the form of licences to deal in foreign exchange are granted to banks which are equipped to undertake specific types of foreign exchange transactions in India.

APPOINTMENT AS AGENT IN INDIA

Section 28(1) of FERA 1973 requires foreign companies and foreign nationals 'whether resident in India or not' to obtain the permission of the RBI for acting and accepting as agents in India of any person or company in the trading or commercial transactions of such person or company. The term 'agent' includes any person or company (including its branch) buying goods with a view to selling them before any processing thereof. For the purposes of s 28 of FERA 1973 the term 'company' includes a firm or other association of individuals.

PURCHASE OF SHARES OF INDIAN COMPANIES

Section 29(1)(b) of FERA 1973 makes it obligatory for foreign companies and foreign nationals whether resident or not to obtain permission of the RBI for purchasing shares in India of any company carrying on any trade, commerce or industry. Applications have to be made to the Central Office of the RBI.

TRANSFER OF INDIAN SECURITIES

In terms of s 19(5) of FERA 1973 transfer of shares, bonds or debentures of a company registered in India by foreign companies or foreign nationals to residents is required to be confirmed by the RBI on an application made to it by the transferor or transferee.

IMMOVABLE PROPERTY IN INDIA

In terms of FERA 1973 persons who are not citizens of India (whether resident in India or not) and companies (other than banking companies) which are not incorporated under any law in force in India are required to obtain prior permission of the RBI to acquire, hold, transfer or dispose off by sale, mortgage, lease, gift, settlement or otherwise any immovable property situated in India. However, these restrictions do not apply to immovable property taken or given on lease for a period not exceeding five years.

ANTI-TRUST LAWS

The Monopolies and Restrictive Trade Practices Act, 1969 ('MRTP Act') was extensively amended in 1991. The 1991 amendment removed from the statute book various draconian provisions aimed at preventing the growth of monopolies in the country. The amended Act has shifted the emphasis from preventing creation of dominant undertakings to control of unfair business practices. In its new form, the MRTP Act provides for prevention of concentration of economic power, restrictions on the acquisition and transfer of shares of, or by, certain bodies corporate, prevention of monopolistic trade practices, control of restrictive trade practices and unfair trade practices.

Monopolistic Trade Practices

The MRTP Act defines monopolistic trade practices to mean trade practices which have the effect of maintaining prices, unreasonably preventing competition, limiting technical development or increasing costs or prices.

Restrictive Trade Practices

Agreements relating to restrictive trade practices are required to be registered in accordance with the MRTP Act. Certain agreements are deemed to be restrictive trade practices and need to be registered, for instance agreements with respect to the following:

(a) restrictions regarding who to sell to or buy from;
(b) tying arrangements;
(c) exclusive dealings;
(d) collective or concerted actions;
(e) differential concessions or benefits;
(f) resale price maintenance;
(g) restrictions on withholding output or supply and allocation of area;
(h) boycotts.

Unfair Trade Practices

The MRTP Act also aims to curb unfair trade practices, ie, all unfair methods or deceptive practices adopted for the purpose of promoting sale of goods and services. Unfair trade practices include false representations, false offers of a bargain price, false offers of a free gift or price schemes and non-compliance with prescribed standards.

LABOUR LAWS

Labour laws in India are extensive and are generally considered to be pieces of 'social legislation' enacted with the underlying objective of improving the lot of workers.

The Factories Act aims at regulating working conditions in factories and ensuring certain standards of safety for factory workers. The Act also provides for regulation of working hours, holidays, overtime and employment of children and women.

The Shops and Establishments Acts have been enacted by the State Legislatures to regulate working conditions in establishments not covered by the Factories Act.

The Minimum Wages Act lays down the minimum statutory wages payable to various categories of workers.

The Payment of Bonus Act provides for payment of bonus linked to profits or productivity to employees. Bonuses have to be paid by employers to employees as a matter of statutory liability in accordance with the prescribed formula.

The Employees Provident Fund and Miscellaneous Provisions Act requires employers to make compulsory contribution to a fund maintained for the future of employees.

The Payment of Gratuities Act provides for retirement benefits for employees who have worked for a certain minimum number of years.

The Workmen's Compensation Act provides for compensation to workers or their dependants in the event of an accident arising out of or in the course of employment.

The Industrial Disputes Act, 1947 has created machinery for settlement of industrial disputes.

The Trade Unions Act governs the registration of trade unions and applies to all unions of workers and associations of employers.

The Maternity Benefits Act regulates the employment of women in certain establishments in respect of the period before and after child-birth and provides for maternity and other benefits.

ENVIRONMENTAL LAWS

The Bhopal gas leak disaster of December, 1984 marks the turning point of environmental regulation in India. A number of new laws covering hitherto untouched fields, such as noise, vehicular emissions, hazardous waste, hazardous micro-organisms and the transportation of toxic chemicals, appeared on the statute book.

(1)   The Environment Protection Act, 1986.   This Act provides for severe penalties including a prison term of up to five years for violators. Corporate officials directly in charge of a company's business may be held liable for offences under the Act. Pursuant to the powers conferred under the Act, many rules have been enacted such as the Rules for the Manufacture, Storage and Import of Hazardous Chemicals. Preliminary site clearance is required in the case of thermal power stations and hydro-electric projects as well as river valley projects.

(2)   The Air (Prevention & Control of Pollution) Act, 1981.   All industries operating within designated air pollution control areas are required to obtain a permit from the State Boards. The Boards have the powers to close down a defaulting industrial plant or stop

its supply of electricity or water. The Board may also apply to a court to restrain emissions that exceed prescribed standards. This Act has now been extended to include noise pollution.

(3) The Water Act, 1974. The Boards control sewage and industrial effluent discharges by approving, rejecting or conditioning applications for consent to discharge. The penalties for contravention are similar to the Air Act.

(4) The Water Cess Act, 1977. In order to create economic incentives for pollution control, designated industries are required to pay a tax on water consumption. Under this and similar Acts areas are designated as 'Reserved Forests', 'National Parks' and 'Marine National Parks'. There is a total prohibition, subject to a few exceptions, on carrying on any industrial activity in the areas specified under this Act.

(5) The Wild Life Protection Act, 1972. This Act is similar to other laws in the world which protect wildlife. It allows capture and transportation of wild animals for scientific management of animal populations.

(6) The Indian Forests Act, 1927. This Act regulates the use of forests, including felling of trees, quarrying and removal of forest products.

(7) The Insecticides Act, 1968. This Act regulates the manufacture and distribution of insecticides through licensing. It also provides for workers' safety during the manufacture and handling of insecticides.

(8) The Atomic Energy Act, 1962. This Act regulates nuclear energy and radioactive substances in India. The manufacture and transportation of radioactive substances and nuclear generated electricity also fall within its regulatory scope. The government has the power to classify 'restricted information' relating to these matters in the public interest.

(9) The Factories Act, 1948. This Act was radically altered in 1987 to introduce special provisions on hazardous industrial activities. Every factory must have a designated 'occupier' with specified liabilities and duties.

(10) The Public Liability Insurance Act, 1991. The Act requires certain hazardous industries to obtain insurance against accidents, so that immediate relief can be provided to victims of industrial accidents.

NEGOTIABLE INSTRUMENTS

The law governing negotiable instruments is contained in the Negotiable Instruments Act, 1981 (the NIA), which operates subject to the provisions of ss 31 and 32 of the Reserve Bank of India Act, 1934. The NIA lays down definitions of negotiable instruments, promissory notes, bills of exchange, cheques, bank drafts, Hundi. For the purpose of security of interest in a transaction, the provisions and the definitions contained in the NIA would be relevant for a foreign investor.

CONSUMER PROTECTION

Foreign investors interested in manufacturing and marketing consumer goods would need to be aware of the Consumer Protection Act, 1986 (CPA) enacted with the object of securing the interests of consumers. Any person who buys any goods, or hires or avails himself of any services is a 'consumer' for the purposes of the CPA and is entitled to its benefits. The CPA envisages promotion of rights of consumers by giving consumers rights, inter alia, to be informed as to the quality, quantity, price of goods and services. The CPA also provides for protection of consumers against unfair trade practices and unscrupulous exploitation. Redressal agencies at the District, State and national levels have been set up to help achieve the objectives of the CPA. Penalties have been prescribed for non-compliance with the orders of the redressal agencies.

ESSENTIAL COMMODITIES

In view of shortages of various items of everyday use, legislation to regulate production, distribution, storage, pricing, etc, of certain items of mass consumption has been enacted. The Essential Commodities Act, 1955 through various control orders regulates items declared as 'essential commodities' under the Act. Despite liberalisation in India, the Act is still on the statute book and may be a relevant consideration for investors contemplating investing in industries manufacturing and/or marketing 'essential commodities'. Various control orders as to price, quality, movement, packaging, licensing and distribution of 'essential commodities' have been issued.

ACCOUNTS

Every company is required to keep at its registered office proper books of account with respect to payments and receipts, all sales and purchases, all assets and liabilities. In the case of companies engaged in manufacturing, processing, production and mining activities cost accounts as may be prescribed by the government have also to be maintained. The books of account must give a true and fair view of the state of affairs of the company and to explain its transactions. The books have to be maintained on accrual basis and according to the double entry system of accounting: s 209.

Accounting Period

At every annual general meeting the Board of Directors have to place before the company a balance sheet and a profit and loss account relating to the previous financial year. The financial year ordinarily cannot exceed 15 months: s 210. Generally, companies prepare accounts for the 12 months ending 31 March of each year for the reason that the Income Tax Act requires all assessees to calculate income for assessment on the basis of a uniform period, that is, April to March.

Form of Accounting Statements

The Companies Act prescribes the form in which the balance sheet and the profit and loss account have to be prepared. Insurance, banking and power companies are required to prepare the account statements and make disclosures in accordance with the special legislation in force governing such companies — the Insurance Act, 1938, the Banking Companies Act, 1949 and the Indian Electricity Act, 1910 and the Electricity (Supply) Act, 1948, respectively: s 211.

Particulars to be included in Accounting Statements

The Companies Act requires that to every balance sheet laid before the company in a general meeting, a report by its Board of Directors with respect to the following shall be attached:

(a) the state of the company's affairs;
(b) the amounts proposed to be transferred to the company's reserves;
(c) the recommended dividend;
(d) material transactions/changes between the date of the balance

sheet and the date of the report affecting the company's financial position;

(e) the conservation of energy, technology absorption, foreign exchange earnings and outflows: s 217.

The balance sheet of a holding company is required to include certain particulars as to its subsidiaries (s 212) though there is no requirement as to preparation of consolidated accounts.

Distribution of Accounting Statements

Every member of the company is entitled to receive a copy of the balance sheet and auditors' report: s 219. The balance sheet may be sent to the members in the prescribed abridged form instead of the detailed balance sheet along with all the annexures. After the balance sheet and the profit and loss account have been laid before the company in a general meeting, the same have to be filed with the Registrar of Companies within the prescribed period: s 220.

Accounting Practices

The accounting practices in India are based on the practices followed in the United Kingdom. The Institute of Chartered Accountants of India has taken various steps to bring the accounting standards in the country to international standards. The Institute has issued accounting standards (some of which have been made mandatory), statements and guidance notes.

Accounting under the Companies Act and the Income Tax Act

A company cannot declare dividend unless depreciation at the prescribed rates has been provided for. The depreciation may be calculated on the straight-line or written-down-value basis. Assets have to be shown on the historical cost basis, though these may be revalued. The revaluation reserve is not available to the company as a free reserve. Depreciation rates under the Companies Act and under the Income Tax Act vary. Separate calculations have to be made to claim depreciation as a deduction from income. Another difference between accounts maintained under the Companies Act and accounts prepared for income tax purposes is that taxes and dues to government are to be accounted on accrual basis under the Companies Act whereas they are allowed as expense under the Income Tax Act on payment basis.

CHAPTER 11

INCORPORATING A COMPANY/ SETTING UP AN OFFICE
by G Venkataramanan (dec)

HISTORICAL PERSPECTIVE

Compared to the law of property and some other branches of law, corporate law is a recent development having a very short, but significant, history. Until the latter part of the 18th century English law had dealt with incorporation by three processes: a religious corporation could be created by the Pope himself, and a non-religious corporation could be created and empowered to act as such either by a Royal Charter or by the Act of Parliament. Of course, the constitution, capital, powers and the limitations, geographical or otherwise, in respect of every corporation depended upon the source of its incorporation, namely, the Charter or the Act concerned. A rich diversity, therefore, could be seen in the nature, scope and operational efficacy of various corporations. For instance, in the 16th century the famous East India Company was established by a Royal Charter. It had a monopoly in trade and business in the East. Its members could carry on the trade individually and also had the option to subscribe to the joint fund or stock of the company.

The process of streamlining the birth of a corporation through a settled and uniform pattern of legislative provisions started (and gained tremendous speed), due to commercial exigencies, in the 19th century. To meet the needs of the business community and trade, the Trading Companies Act 1834 was passed empowering the Crown to confer by Letters Patent all or any of the privileges of incorporation, except limited liability without actually granting a Charter. This enabled companies to sue and be sued in the names of their officials. It was a first general Act requiring public registration of members, but it expressly preserved their unlimited liability. The Chartered Companies Act, 1837 re-enacted the 1834 Act but provided that personal liability of members might be expressly limited by the Letters Patent to a specified amount per share.

The English Companies Act, 1844 was the first enactment recognising a company registered thereunder as a distinct legal entity without, however, recognising the principle of limited liability, which defect was later removed by the Limited Liability Act 1855. The Joint Stock Companies Act 1856 repealed both these enactments and prescribed a format of company law which has continued for generations, subject, of course, to the legislative variations and modifications which were necessary due to the exigencies created by the change in the social and economic circumstances prevailing from time to time in England.

INDIAN LEGISLATION ON COMPANIES

In its initial stages the Indian legislation on companies was virtually a replica of the English legislation. In 1850, an Act for 'Registration of Joint Stock Companies' was passed in line with the (English) Companies Act, 1844. Under the 1850 Act, the High Courts of Calcutta, Madras and Bombay were the registering authorities of companies. The Act permitted registration of an unincorporated partnership formed under a deed and containing a provision for transfer of shares in its stock or business without the consent of all the partners, and of non-trading companies, with or without limited liability. The privilege of limited liability was not granted to banking and insurance companies until the passing of the Joint Stock Companies Act 1860. The Indian Companies Act, 1866, was passed consolidating and amending the laws relating to incorporation, regulation and winding up of trading companies. Time and again, the Act was amended by drawing inspiration from the corresponding English Companies Acts. A new Indian Companies Act was passed in 1913 but it contained a number of inaccuracies and in order to overcome the loop-holes created by it and to cover the deficiencies in it, the Companies Act, 1956 was passed, consolidating the law on the subject with the aim of meeting the socio-economic needs of the country.

TYPES OF COMPANIES AND THEIR INCORPORATION

The Act defines a company as a company formed or registered under the Act. The Indian Companies Act makes a distinction between a body corporate and a company. A body corporate includes a company incorporated outside India.

Companies can be classified into various categories: (i) private company; (ii) deemed public company; (iii) public company; (iv) company having unlimited liability; (v) company limited by guarantee; and (vi) holding and subsidiary company.

153

Private Companies

Private companies deal with relatively smaller investments of public money and are, therefore, less regulated than public companies. A private company has the following features:

(1) The Articles of the company restrict the right to transfer its shares.

(2) The maximum number of its members (excluding its employees) is limited to 50.

(3) No offer can be made to the public to subscribe for its shares or debentures.

Deemed Public Company

A private company is deemed to be a public company in the following circumstances:

(a) 25% or more of its share capital is held by one or more public companies;

(b) the private company holds 25% or more of the paid-up capital of a public company;

(c) the private company accepts or renews deposits from the public;

(d) the average annual turnover of the private company exceeds Rs100 million.

Public Company

The Act defines a public company as one which does not have the restrictions imposed on a private company by its Articles of Association.

Company Having Unlimited Liability

A company in which members have unlimited liabilities is known as an unlimited company. A company registered as unlimited may be registered under this Act as a limited company; and a company already registered as a limited company may be re-registered under this Act.

On registration pursuant to this section, the company's former registration will be closed by the Registrar who may dispense with some of the requirements for submission of documents, but the registration shall take place in the same manner and shall have effect, as if it were the first registration of the company under this Act.

The registration of an unlimited company as a limited company under this section shall not affect any debts, liabilities, obligations or contracts incurred or entered into, by, to, with or on behalf of the company before the registration, and those debts, liabilities, obligations and contracts may be enforced in the manner provided by Part IX of this Act in the case of a company registered in pursuance of that Part.

Company Limited by Guarantee

A company limited by guarantee has two features in common with a share-capital company. In both cases:

(a)   the company has legal personality; and

(b)   the liability of the members is limited, in the case of the share-capital company by the nominal number of shares held by each member, and in the case of the guarantee company by the amount of the guarantee undertaken by the member. Accordingly, both types of companies have to embody into their memorandum a statement to the effect that the liability of their members is limited.

Definitions of a Holding Company and Subsidiary Company

A company shall be deemed to be a subsidiary of another company (Holding Company), but only if that other constitutes the composition of its Board of Directors or that other:

(a)   where the first mentioned company is an existing company in respect of which the holders of Preference Shares issued before the commencement of this Act have the same voting rights in all respects as the holders of equity shares, exercises or controls more than half of the voting power of such company;

(b)   where the first mentioned company, in any other company, holds more than half in nominal value of its equity share capital; or if the first-mentioned company is a subsidiary of any company which is that other's subsidiary.

FORMATION OF A COMPANY

Requirements for Formation of a Company

The promoters should first decide about proposed names, preferably two or three in order of priority so that if the first name proposed is not available then an alternative name can be considered by the Registrar of Companies.

In this regard it may be mentioned that if a name falls within the categories mentioned below, it will not generally be made available:

(1)   If it is not in consonance with the principal objects of the company as set out in its Memorandum of Association.

(2)   If it includes any word or words which are offensive to any section of the population.

(3)   If the proposed name is the exact Hindi translation of the name of an existing company in English, especially an existing company with a reputation.

(4)   If the proposed name has a close phonetic resemblance to the name of a company in existence, for example, JK Industries Limited and Jay Kay Industries Limited.

(5)   If the name is only a general one, like Cotton Textiles Mills Limited or Silk Manufacturing Limited.

(6)   If it includes the word 'Co-operative', 'Sahkari' or the equivalent of 'Co-operative' in the regional languages of the country.

(7)   If it attracts the provisions of the Emblems and Names (Prevention of Improper Use) Act, 1950 as amended from time to time, ie, use of improper names, prohibited under this Act.

(8)   If it connotes government participation or patronage unless circumstances justify it. For example, a name may be deemed undesirable in a certain context if it includes any of the words such as National Union, Central Federal Republic, President, Rashtrapati, Small Scale Industries, Cottage Industries, etc.

(9)   If a proposed name implies association or connection with or patronage of a national hero or any person held in high esteem or important personages who are occupying important positions in government so long as they continue to hold such positions.

(10)   If it resembles closely the popular or abbreviated descriptions of important companies like TISCO (Tata Iron & Steel Company Limited), HMT (Hindustan Machine Tools), ICI (Imperial Chemical Industries), TEXMACO (Textile Machinery Corporation), WIMCO

(Western India Match Company), etc. In some cases, the first word or the first few words may be the key words and care should be taken that they are not exploited. Such words should not be allowed even though they have not been registered as trade marks.

(11) If it is different from the name/names of the existing company/companies only to the extent of having the name of a place within brackets before the word 'Limited', for example, Indian Press (Delhi) Limited should not be allowed in view of the existence of the company named Indian Press Limited.

(12) If it includes the name of a registered trade mark unless the consent of the owner of the trade mark has been produced by the promoters.

(13) If a name is identical to or too nearly resembles the name by which a company in existence has been previously registered. However, if a proposed company is to be under the same management or in the same group and likes to have a closely resembling name to existing companies under the same management or group with a view to having the advantage of the goodwill attached to the management or group name such a name may be allowed.

Form No. 1A should be filed with the Registrar of Companies along with Rs500 as fees for the availability of the name with the ROC.

Form No. 1A has to outline the main objective of the proposed company, the names of at least two promoters with their addresses if the proposed company is to be private and at least seven names with addresses if the proposed company is to be public.

Memorandum and Articles of Association

After the name is made available, the Memorandum and Articles of Association have to be printed. The Memorandum is to contain:

(1)   The name of the company.

(2)   Whether private or public.

(3)   Situation of the registered office.

(4)   The objects for which the company is being incorporated under the following heads:

    (i)   main objects;

    (ii)   incidental objects;

    (iii)   other objects.

(5) It has to be provided that the company has limited liability if it is so.

(6) The authorised share capital of the company.

In this connection, it may be mentioned that:

(1) The provisions of the Act override the Memorandum and Articles.

(2) A public company limited by shares may not have Articles, in which case Table A as incorporated in the Companies Act 1956 will apply. A private company limited by shares must have Articles. Similarly an unlimited company and a company limited by guarantee have to frame their own Articles.

(3) Articles establish a contract between the company and its members.

(4) Articles regulate the rights of members inter se.

(5) Articles do not constitute contracts with strangers or members in other capacities.

(6) The Memorandum and Articles have to be stamped before or at the time of signature as per Schedule I of the Indian Stamp Act.

(7) The purpose of the Memorandum is to enable the shareholders, creditors and those dealing with the company to know what its permitted range of activities is.

(8) Outsiders dealing with the company must be taken to have had constructive notice of the contents of the Memorandum and Articles.

(9) The Memorandum and Articles of Association have to be stamped with duty stamps from the State Treasury as proof of payment of stamp duty (which varies from one State to another).

(10) After receiving the stamped Memorandum and Articles from the Treasury Department, the subscribers (at least two in the case of a private company and seven in the case of a public company) whose names were mentioned in Form No. 1A have to sign in their own hand, their names, addresses, description (son of or wife of, as the case may be) and occupation along with the number of shares subscribed.

(11) The Memorandum and Articles of Association have to be accompanied with the following forms:

(a) Form 1 signed by any proposed Director, Chartered Accountant, Advocate or Practising Company Secretary on Stamp Paper. This is a declaration in the form of an affidavit.

(b) Form No. 18 showing the place of the Registered Office of the proposed company.

(c) Form No. 29 in the case of a public company being consent signed by each proposed Director.

(d) Form No. 32 in duplicate giving particulars of the proposed Directors.

Time Taken by Registrar for Issue of Certificate of Incorporation

The Memorandum and Articles and the above forms have to be filed with the Registrar of Companies along with filing fees which depend on the authorised capital, the value of which is provided for in Schedule X to the Companies Act. These papers should be accompanied by a Power of Attorney signed by each subscriber in favour of a professional who is entrusted with the task of the formation of the company.

The Registrar of Companies normally takes five to seven days for the processing of papers and gives a date for making corrections and authentication of documents.

After the corrections have been discussed and carried out, the Registrar of Companies issues the Certificate of Incorporation. The date of the Certificate is the day the company comes into existence.

BASIC ISSUES WITH REGARD TO CORPORATE PERSONA

Types of Share Capital

The government permits a company to issue two kinds of share capital, namely, preference share capital (preferred stock) and equity share capital (equity common stock). A private company may, however, issue other types of shares. Share capital which provides for preferential rights to a fixed amount of dividend and preferential rights for repayment of capital in the event of winding up of the company or repayment of capital is called preference capital. A company may issue redeemable preference shares with a redemption period not exceeding 10 years from the date of issue of shares. Redemption of preference shares does not amount to reduction of capital.

Equity share capital is that part of the share capital which does not carry the preferential rights. The equity shares always have voting rights whereas the preference shareholders can only vote in the event of non-declaration of a dividend for a specified number of years in relation to preference shares.

In the budget of 1996–97 (presented 22 July 1996), the Finance Minister announced that company law will be amended to introduce a 'new category of equity shares without voting rights'. It is proposed that non-voting shares will be permitted up to 25% of the issued equity capital of the company.

Issue of Shares with a Premium or at Discount

Shares may be issued at par or with premium or at a discount. The amount of share premium can be determined by the company. However, the company has to obtain permission from the Company Law Board before issuing shares at a discount. Where the company issues shares with a premium an amount equivalent to share premium has to be transferred to a 'share premium account' which can be utilised only for purposes specified in the Act.

The issue of share capital is limited by the authorised capital specified in the Memorandum of Association. However, a company can increase its authorised capital if permitted by the Articles of Association.

Increase of Paid-up Capital

If a company wishes to increase its paid-up or subscribed capital by allotment of further shares, such further shares are referred to as 'right shares' and have to be offered to the existing shareholders in proportion to their shareholding. The existing shareholders may, instead of accepting such shares, renounce those shares in favour of any other person. Only if they do not accept the offer, further shares can be issued by the Board of Directors in such manner as they think most beneficial. If the company wants to offer these shares to persons other than the existing shareholders a special resolution to that effect must be passed by the members in a General Meeting with a majority of 75% of votes cast.

The company can also increase its subscribed capital by issuing bonus shares out of its retained profits.

In the past the issue of share capital was subject to the approval of the Controller of Capital Issues. However, after the constitution of the Securities & Exchange Board of India with effect from 30 January 1992 all applications for share issues are cleared by the SEBI. The offered document has to disclose the information prescribed in Schedule II of the Companies Act and that prescribed by guidelines issued by the SEBI.

Debentures

Companies may issue debentures which are in the nature of a certificate of loan evidencing that a specified sum of money is issued by the company on a specified date. The interest on debentures is payable in accordance with the terms of issue irrespective of whether there is profit or not. The issue of debentures with voting rights is prohibited. Debentures can also be issued by a public limited company.

Public Deposits

A company may also invite deposits from the public or its members. The Central Government in consultation with the Reserve Bank of India (RBI) has prescribed the limits up to which and the conditions subject to which the deposits may be accepted by a company.

Transfer of Shares

The shares of a public limited company are movable property and are freely transferable. The share certificates along with the share transfer deed have to be submitted with the company in the case of a private company. Restrictions on right of transfer are imposed by its Articles. The shares can be transferred to Non-Resident Indians and foreigners with the prior approval of the RBI and all companies maintain a register of their shareholders and a record of share transfers.

SETTING UP AN OFFICE

Requirements for Setting Up an Office

For companies which have been incorporated outside India and which intend to set up an office in India, the provisions of ss 591–602 would be applicable.

A 'foreign company' means a company incorporated outside India and having a place of business in India. This, however, must be distinguished from a 'foreign controlled company' which means a company (foreign or Indian) in which the majority shareholding and voting power is in the hands of foreign individuals and/or bodies corporate.

Liaison Office

Foreign companies can operate in India through liaison offices. Their main role is to establish a liaison between Indian business people and the overseas parent company. Liaison offices can be opened with the permission of the RBI. Liaison offices are not permitted to carry on any trading or commercial activity or earn any income. The expenses of liaison offices are to be met out of inward foreign remittances.

Application (in Form FNC 5) under s 29(1)(a) of FERA (1973) must be submitted by an overseas company to RBI for permission to establish a Liaison Office in India.

Project Office

Foreign companies can operate through Project Offices (PO). POs can be opened with the approval of the RBI for undertaking a specific contract or activity such as turn-key projects or installation projects. POs cannot carry on trading or industrial activity except in connection with the execution of approved projects. All expenses of POs must be met out of inward foreign currency remittances or rupee components of receipts and contracts.

Application (in Form FNC 5) under s 29(1)(a) of FERA (1973) must be submitted by an overseas company to RBI for permission to establish a Project/Site Office in India.

Branch Office

Foreign companies are allowed to open branch offices with the approval of the RBI for specified purposes:

(1) Buying/selling agency of the parent company.

(2) To undertake import and export trading activity.

(3) Promoting financial and technical collaboration.

(4) Conducting research provided the results of the research are made available to Indian companies.

(5) Representing the parent company in India.

Application (in Form FNC 5) under s 29(1)(a) of FERA (1973) must be submitted by an overseas company to RBI for permission to establish a Branch Office in India.

Main Ingredients for Setting Up a Foreign Office

A company will be establishing a place of business in India if it has a specified or identifiable place at which it carries on business, such as an office, store house, godown or other premises having some concrete connection between the locality and its business. The word 'establish' indicates more than occasional connection. Having a share transfer office or share registration office will constitute 'establishing a place of business'.

The requirement of 'carrying on business in India' is satisfied if a company's business is carried on at a fixed and definite place in India for a sufficient and reasonably long period of time.

As per the corporation laws of several States in the USA, the following activities do not constitute 'carrying on of business':

(1) maintaining or defending any suit or action or other proceeding or effecting the settlement of any claim or dispute;

(2) holding meetings of shareholders or directors;

(3) maintaining bank accounts;

(4) maintaining offices or agencies for the transfer, exchange and registration of shares or other securities;

(5) effecting sales through independent contractors;

(6) soliciting or procuring orders where such orders require acceptance outside the State to become binding contracts;

(7) creating evidence of debts, charges on real or personal property;

(8) securing or collecting debts or enforcing claims to property of any kind;

(9) conducting any isolated transaction.

There is also a difference between 'carrying on business' and 'having an established place of business'. The latter test requires some degree of performance not imported by the former. Where the company delivered to the Registrar of Companies at Bombay documents under s 592 of the Act and such documents, under that section, are to be delivered 'within thirty days of the establishment of the place of business', it was held that by delivering the documents, the defendants had admitted that the company had established a place of business within India.

Note: Within 30 days of establishing a place of business, the foreign company must deliver to the Registrar for 'registration' a set of documents as stated in s 592 of the Act.

Other Procedural Formalities

The company should comply with other procedural formalities as stated in the RBI approval for setting up an office and also in regard to Sales Tax Registration, PAN, Shop and Establishment Act Registration etc.

Accounts of Foreign Company (Requirements for Compliance with Section 594)

Every foreign company shall, in every calendar year, deliver to the Registrar three copies of documents as specified under s 594 of the Act.

SOME ISSUES ON WHICH THE FOREIGN INVESTOR MAY HAVE TO INTERACT WITH THE DEPARTMENT OF COMPANY AFFAIRS

Major Issues

The procedural issues on which the foreign investor may interact with the Department of Company Affairs have already been discussed in previous sections. However, the foreign investor may be required to obtain the approval of the Department of Company Affairs (DCA) on other issues also. If a company registered in India intends to invest in loans and shares of another company exceeding the prescribed limit, approval under the provisions of ss 370 and 372 would be required, depending upon the nature of business. A few other points must be noted.

Appointment of Managing Directors (Executive Directors)

Foreign nationals can be appointed as managing or full-time directors or managers with prior approval of the DCA of the Central Government. Every public company or private company which is a subsidiary of a public company, whose paid up capital is Rs50 million or more, is required to appoint a full-time managing director. The extent of managerial remuneration that can be paid by a public company or its subsidiaries is laid down by the Companies Act. The total remuneration paid to managerial personnel should not exceed 10% of the net profit and in case there is only one full-time executive director it should not exceed 5% of net profits. The approval of the Central Government (the DCA) is not required if the remuneration to managerial personnel is below the limits prescribed in the Act. However, in the event of losses or inadequate profits the managerial remuneration should be within a prescribed limit based on effective capital of the company. Main features of guidelines for managerial remuneration specified by the Central Government are as follows:

(1)   The person should not be less than 25 years and not more than 70 years of age.

(2)   The person should have been a resident of India for more than 12 months.

(3)   A company with adequate profit has freedom to pay a remuneration package to its managing director within a limit of 5% of its net profits and if there is more than one managing director up to a limit of 10% of its net profits.

(4)   In the event of losses or inadequacy of net profits managerial remuneration shall be limited to between Rs14000 and Rs87500 (US$450 to $2800 approx) per month based on the effective capital of the company. In a case where a person is a managing director or manager of more than one company he can draw remuneration only from one company.

The Central Government's approval is required in regard to payment of managerial remuneration only if the above conditions are not met.

Loans and purchase of shares

Under the Act loans made by a company to other bodies corporate not under the same management as the lending company require the company to pass a special resolution in a general meeting if the aggregate of such loans exceeds 30% of its subscribed capital and free reserves. It also requires prior approval of the Central Government if the aggregate of loans made to all other bodies corporate exceeds 30% of the subscribed capital and free reserves of the lending companies. The giving of a guarantee or provision of any security in connection with the loan made by any person to, or to any other person by, any other body corporate is also required to be authorised by a special resolution of the lending company.

The companies are considered to be under the same management if:

(1) The managing director or manager of one body corporate is the managing director or the manager of the other body corporate.

(2) If the majority of directors of the one body corporate constitutes a majority of directors of other body corporate (or constituted such a majority at any time within the immediately preceding six months).

(3) If more than one-third of the total voting power in respect of any matter relating to each of the two bodies corporate is exercised or controlled by the same individual or body corporate.

(4) The holding company of one body corporate is under the same management as the other body corporate within the meaning of the aforesaid clauses.

(5) One or more directors of one body corporate whether by themselves or together with their relatives hold the majority of the shares in both the bodies corporate.

The Act allows public companies and their subsidiaries to purchase shares of any other body corporate up to 30% of the subscribed equity capital of a company. The investments in excess of this amount require prior approval of the DCA of the Central Government. The aggregate of the investment made by a company in two bodies corporate in the same group should not exceed 30% of its subscribed capital and free reserves, any investment beyond this limit requiring the prior approval of the Central Government.

Declaration of dividend

The Act provides for payment of dividends out of profits of a company arrived at after providing for depreciation for the current year and setting off the losses for the previous years or the depreciation whichever is lower. The Act also requires a certain minimum specified percentage of profits to be transferred to reserves depending on the percentage of proposed dividend in accordance with the prescribed rules. Dividends recommended by the Board of Directors require approval of shareholders in a General Meeting. The Board of Directors may, however, declare an interim dividend before the Annual General Meeting based on the company's profit position. The dividend declared must be disbursed within 42 days of the date of declaration. The amounts remaining unpaid or unclaimed after a stipulated period must be transferred to an 'Unpaid Dividend Account'. If the dividend warrant is not encashed within three years the remaining amount needs to be transferred to the General Revenue Account set up by the Central Government, but a claim may be referred to the Central Government by a person to whom money is due.

Payment of interest on share capital

A company which has issued shares for the purpose of setting up a project with a long gestation period or a project which cannot be made profitable for a lengthy period can pay interest not exceeding 4% per annum on share capital. If the interest rate exceeds 4% its payment requires prior government approval (DCA). Such interest payments may be capitalised as a part of the project cost.

Winding up and dissolution

The winding up of a company may be either by the court, or voluntary, or subject to the supervision of the court.

Winding up is a process by which the assets of the company are realised and its liabilities are paid. If any money is left after paying the company's debts, it is distributed among the members of the company and ultimately the company is dissolved following the directions of the High Court. Sections 425 to 560 of the Companies Act, 1956 deal with the winding up process. Official Liquidators who are appointed by the Central Government work under the directions of the respective High Courts.

Mergers and amalgamations

When companies coalesce or firms unite in some form, the result is variously described as an 'absorption', 'amalgamation', 'fusion' or 'merger'. Although one or the other terms from among these is used in business or financial circles, they are all words used in common parlance without any precise legal meaning attached.

The procedure for mergers and amalgamations is described in ss 391–396 of the Companies Act, 1956. Broadly, the procedure involves filing a petition in the High Court under whose jurisdiction the registered office of the company (to be acquired) falls. The High Court forwards the petition to the concerned Regional Director (under the DCA) for 'No Objections'. The Regional Director in turn secures comments from the concerned Registrar of Companies.

No approval under the MRTP Act, 1969 is required.

PART 3
DOING BUSINESS IN INDIA

CHAPTER 12

INTELLECTUAL PROPERTY
by S Ramaiah

Intellectual property, as its name indicates, is property derived from, and out of, using one's own intelligence. The objects of intellectual property are therefore creations of the human mind or the human intellect. The rights relating to intellectual property are commonly known as Intellectual Property Rights (IPR).

MEANING OF INTELLECTUAL PROPERTY

The term 'intellectual property' originally referred to rights which protected literary and artistic creations. In its modern concept, it also includes industrial property. The Convention establishing the World Intellectual Property Organization (WIPO) at Geneva—a Specialised Agency of the United Nations (WIPO Convention), defines the scope of intellectual property. India is a Member Country of the WIPO Convention. WIPO has, as its objectives, the promotion of the protection of intellectual property throughout the world, and the administration of a number of Conventions on intellectual property. The term 'intellectual property' is defined in Article 2 (viii) of the WIPO Convention to include the rights relating to:

(a) literary, artistic and scientific works;
(b) performances of performing artists, phonographs and broadcasts;
(c) inventions in all fields of human endeavour;
(d) scientific discoveries;
(e) industrial designs;
(f) trade marks, service marks and commercial names and designation;
(g) protection against unfair competition,

and all other rights resulting from intellectual activity in the industrial, scientific, literary or artistic fields.

From the above definition, intellectual property can be seen to comprise two main branches: industrial property (chiefly in inventions, trade marks and industrial designs); and copyright (chiefly in literary, musical, artistic, photographic and audio visual works, broadcasts, cinematograph films, etc).

PROTECTION OF INTELLECTUAL PROPERTY RIGHTS

The laws of a country relating to intellectual property afford protection only in respect of acts accomplished or committed in the country itself. Consequently, a patent, trade mark or other industrial property is effective only when a government office in a country effects the grant of registration in respect of such industrial property in accordance with its laws. Copyright protection in a work arises as soon as the work is created in a particular country and is regulated by its law relating to copyright. But, if the creator or author of these works desires protection in several countries, such protection must be obtained in each of them separately. This requirement is fulfilled by the International Conventions and Agreements. The Paris Convention for the Protection of Industrial Property (signed in 1883) (the Paris Convention) and the Berne Convention for the Protection of Literary and Artistic Works (signed in 1886) (the Berne Convention) were the earliest agreements in the field of intellectual property and both are administered by WIPO. Subsequently, a number of agreements on industrial property (nine agreements and four treaties) and three on literary and artistic works (known as neighbouring rights) were concluded.

A further convention in the field of copyright is the Universal Copyright Convention (UCC) which is administered by UNESCO and, from 1971, both the Conventions on Copyright are administered by a Joint Committee so that the provisions of both the Conventions are identical. India is a member of the Berne Convention and the UCC.

WORLD TRADE ORGANIZATION

On the establishment of the World Trade Organization (WTO) from 1 January 1995, a new agreement on Trade Related Aspects of Intellectual Property Rights (TRIPS) was established within the framework of WTO and is added as Annexure 1C to the WTO Agreement. It is a complete Code in itself and consists of seven Parts dealing with all aspects of intellectual property, such as standards concerning the availability, scope and use of IPR, their enforcement, acquisition and maintenance, dispute prevention and settlement. This Agreement does not purport to supersede or overrule the existing Conventions, Agreements and Treaties on intellectual property.

NATIONAL TREATMENT UNDER THE WTO AGREEMENT

In respect of national treatment to be accorded under the WTO

Agreement, paragraph 3 of Article 1 of Part I states that the Members to the Agreement will accord the treatment provided in this Agreement to the nationals of other members. In respect of the relevant IPR, the nationals of other members are those natural or legal persons meeting the criteria for eligibility for protection provided for in the Paris Convention (1967), the Berne Convention (1971), the Rome Convention and the Treaty on Intellectual Property in respect of Integrated Circuits, if all were WTO members of these Conventions. In other words, the protection of national treatment to be afforded to a citizen of a Member Country of a Convention referred to above will be available to all the WTO members of that Convention. It reiterates that the protection to be afforded under all these Conventions will, after the coming into force of the TRIPS Agreement, be available to WTO members of these Conventions. This means that this provision maintains the status quo of all the provisions of these Conventions, subject to the additional provision that, in the application of TRIPS, these members should also be members of WTO. Article 2(1) of the TRIPS Agreement states that, in respect of standards, enforcement, acquisition and maintenance of IPR (Parts II, III and IV of this Agreement), certain provisions of the Paris Convention will be applicable. Article 2(2) states that the provisions of the Agreement in relation to Parts I–IV will not be in derogation of the existing obligations that the members may have to each other under the Paris Convention, the Berne Convention, the Rome Convention and the Treaty on Intellectual Property in respect of Integrated Circuits. As a result, a harmonious arrangement has been reached by the simultaneous operation of all the existing International Conventions on Intellectual Property and the WTO Agreement. This arrangement dispels the general apprehension that, if India joins TRIPS, the existing regime of intellectual property covered by the relevant Conventions will be affected.

PATENTS

Patents Act 1970

The law governing patents in India is the Patents Act 1970. Before this Act came into force, the provisions relating to patents were included in the Indian Patents and Designs Act 1911, which, as its name indicates, provided both for patents and designs. The 1970 Act repealed the provisions of the 1911 Act in so far as they related to patents, and the 1911 Act continues to provide for industrial designs as the Designs Act 1911.

Patent Office

The Patents Act and the Patents Rules made under the Patents Act (Patents Rules) provide for the receipt of applications for the grant of a patent for an invention and contain detailed procedures for filing of specifications (both provisional and complete), for examination and for the sealing of patents. The authority for issuing patents in India is the Patent Office, headed by the Controller of Patents (the Controller). The Controller-General of Patents, Designs and Trade Marks, appointed under s 4 of the Trade and Merchandise Marks Act 1958, has been designated as the Controller of Patents for the purposes of the Patents Act under s 73 of the Act. The head office is presently at Bombay, with many branch offices facilitating the registration of patents.

What is a Patent?

As observed earlier, a patent is a kind of protection given to inventions by a government office in the form of exclusive rights of exploitation. No international treaty defines the concept of patents. The Patents Act merely defines 'patents' as patents granted under the Act.

Invention—Essential Elements of Protection

An invention can be described as a novel idea which permits in practice the solution of a specific problem in any field of technology. Under the legislation governing inventions in most countries, the idea to be protected (that is to say, patentable) must be new in the sense that there is no indication that it has already been published or publicly used; it must be non-obvious in the sense that it would not have occurred to any specialist in the particular industrial field, had such a specialist been asked to find a solution to the particular problem; and it must be immediately applicable in the industry, in the sense that it can be industrially manufactured or used. The 1970 Act defines 'invention' in s 2(j) as follows:

any new and useful –

  (i) art, process, method or manner of manufacture;

 (ii) machine, apparatus or other article;

(iii) substance produced by manufacturer; and includes any new and useful improvement of any of them and an alleged invention.

Product Patent and Process Patent

The Act makes a distinction between a process patent and a product patent. No product patent can be given in the case of inventions claiming substances intended for use, or capable of being used, as food or medicine or drug or relating to substances prepared or produced by chemical processes, including alloys, optical glass, semi-conductors and inter-metallic compounds. In these cases, only claims for the methods or processes of manufacture are patentable under the Act (s 5). Hence, under the Act, there can be a patented article and a patented process. The expression 'medicine or drug' has been given an inclusive definition in the Act to refer to medicines used for human beings or animals, diagnostic and prophylactic medicines. Section 3 of the Act specifies claims which are not inventions. They include frivolous claims which are contrary to well established natural laws, the mere discovery of a scientific principle or the formulation of an abstract theory, and methods of agriculture or horticulture.

Application for a Patent and Procedure for Registration

An application for a patent for an invention may be made to the Patent Office by any person claiming to be the true and first inventor of the invention, his assignee or the legal representative of any person who is entitled to make the application before his death. Every application for the grant of a patent must be in the form prescribed by the Patents Rules. An application must be accompanied by a provisional or a complete specification of the inventions. Drawings may also be supplied, and they will be deemed to be part of the specifications.

Register of Patent Agents

Under the Act, the Controller maintains a Register of Patent Agents who are authorised to practise before the Controller, to prepare all documents, to transact all business and discharge all the functions prescribed by the Patents Rules on behalf of an applicant. An Advocate is also entitled to be included in the Register of Patent Agents.

Examination by an Examiner

After the complete specification has been filed, the Controller refers the application, along with all the details and specifications, to an Examiner for a detailed examination. One of the important matters the Examiner has to investigate is whether any patent in respect of the invention identical to the current application has earlier been issued either in India or abroad. The Examiner to whom an application has been referred must report to the Controller within 18 months.

Sealing of a Patent

If an inquiry into the opposition to the grant of a patent is decided in favour of an applicant, the Controller will cause the patent to be sealed with the seal of the Patent Office, and the date on which the patent is sealed will be entered in the Register of Patents maintained by the Controller under the provisions of the Act.

Rights of a Patentee

Every patent will be dated as of the date on which the complete specification was filed, will be for one invention only and has effect throughout India. A patent granted under this Act confers upon the patentee the exclusive right by himself, his agents or licensee to make, use, exercise, sell or distribute an article or substance for which the patent is granted.

Term of a Patent

The term of every patent granted under this Act is, in respect of inventions claiming the method or process of manufacture of a substance where the substance is capable of being used as food, medicine or drug, five years from the date of sealing of the patent or seven years from the date of the patent, whichever period is shorter, and in respect of every other invention, 14 years from the date of patent.

Patents Rules

The Patents Rules 1972, made under the provisions of the Patents Act 1970, provide for procedural matters such as specifying forms for various applications to be made under the provisions of the Act, the form of the Register of Patents, the service of documents, the scale of fees to be paid for various applications to be made under the Act and the functions to be performed by patent agents while prosecuting applications or conducting any proceedings under the Act.

Patents (Amendment) Ordinance 1994

An Ordinance to amend the Patents Act 1970 was introduced on 31 December 1994 to meet India's obligations under the WTO Agreement, including TRIPS, and to adopt measures consistent with the Agreement and necessary to protect public health and nutrition.

The amendment mainly provided for the grant of a product patent in respect of an invention for a substance itself intended for use, or capable of being used, as a medicine or drug. Previously, only process patents could be granted in respect of such a substance under s 5 of the Act. The grant of such a patent is in accordance with a new Chapter IVA in the Act. All the provisions of the Act for the grant of a patent are made applicable to the grant of a product patent in respect of a medicine or drug except that the examination of the patent by the Examiner has been abolished for a period of 10 years, that is to say, up to 31 December 2004.

In addition to the above, the Ordinance provided for the grant of a new right, known as an Exclusive Marketing Right, which means an exclusive right in India to sell or distribute an article or substance for which a product patent could not be obtained under the Act before the commencement of the Ordinance. In granting this right, the Examiner will investigate only whether the invention comes under s 3 of the Act and whether it is related to an invention referred to in s 4 of the Act (atomic energy). The grant of this exclusive right to sell or distribute the article or substance is subject to the conditions stated in the Ordinance.

The Bill to replace the Ordinance could not be passed by Parliament before its Lower House, known as the House of the People, was dissolved at the expiration of its term in April 1996. The Ordinance thus lapsed and is not now in force.

TRADE MARKS

Registrar of Trade Marks and Trade Marks Registry

The Trade and Merchandise Marks Act 1958 provides for the registration and better protection of trade marks and for the prevention of the use of fraudulent marks on merchandise. Section 4 of the Act empowers the Central Government to appoint a Controller-General of Patents, Designs and Trade Marks to be the Registrar of Trade Marks for the purposes of the Act. A Trade Mark Registry has been established under the Act with its head office at Bombay and branch offices at Calcutta, Delhi and Madras, each of which is competent to receive applications for the registration of trade marks from persons situated within the jurisdiction of each registry as specified by the Rules made under the Act.

Register of Trade Marks

The Registrar of Trade Marks is authorised to maintain a Register of Trade Marks in which are entered all the registered trade marks with the names, addresses and designations of the proprietors, modifications and assignments and transmissions, the names and addresses and descriptions of registered users, disclaimers, and such other matters relating to registered trade marks as may be prescribed by the Rules. The Act provides for a copy of the Register of Trade Marks and such other documents mentioned in s 125 of the Act to be kept at each branch. The Register is divided into two parts known as Part A and Part B. Under s 103 of the Act, the Registrar is empowered to give to a person who proposes to apply for the registration of a trade mark in Part A or Part B of the Register, informal advice as to whether the trade mark appears to the Registrar prima facie to be distinctive.

Application to be Made in Respect of One Class of Goods

Any person claiming to be the proprietor of a trade mark used, or proposed to be used, by him, who is desirous of registering it must apply in writing to the Registrar, in the manner prescribed by the Rules, for the registration of his trade mark in either Part A or Part B of the Register. An application cannot be made in respect of goods comprised in more than one class of goods specified in the Fourth Schedule to the Rules. A trade mark may be registered in respect of any or all the goods comprised in one class of goods prescribed by Rules. The Fourth Schedule to the Rules specifies 34 classes of goods.

What are Registrable as Trade Marks?

Except in the case of registration of more than one proprietor of trade marks which are identical or nearly resemble each other in respect of the same goods or description of goods, no trade mark may be registered in respect of any goods, or description of goods, which is identical, or deceptively similar, to a trade mark which is already registered in the name of a different proprietor in respect of the same goods or description of goods.

Prohibition of Certain Marks

Section 4 of the Act provides for the prohibition of registration of certain marks. These include the use of a mark which would totally deceive or cause confusion, or which would be contrary to any law for the time being in force. The Act provides for detailed procedures for acceptance of the application, notice of opposition, examination and final registration by means of a certificate issued with the seal of the Trade Marks Registry.

Term of a Trade Mark

The registration of a trade mark is for a period of seven years and may be renewed from time to time by an application made to the Registrar by the proprietor of the trade mark and subject to payment of the fees prescribed by the Rules, for a period of seven years from the date of expiration of the original registration or of the last renewal of the registration.

Infringement and Passing Off

Section 29 of the Act, which deals with infringement of a trade mark, says that when a person who is not the registered proprietor or a registered user of the trade mark in the course of trade uses a mark which is identical, or deceptively similar, to a trade mark in relation to any goods in respect of which the trade mark is registered and in such manner as to render the use of the mark likely to be taken as being a trade mark, the registered trade mark is infringed by that person. Section 30 of the Act deals with acts not constituting infringement.

Section 27(1) provides that no action lies for the infringement of an unregistered trade mark. Subsection (2) of that section provides that nothing in the Act is deemed to affect the rights of action against any person for passing off goods as the goods of another person or the remedies in respect thereof. This is known as 'passing off' and is worded generally without any reference to a trade mark or to its registered proprietor.

There are many decisions on passing off actions and the distinction between actions for infringement of a trade mark and actions for passing off, by the various High Courts and the Supreme Court. The distinction is well brought out by the Supreme Court in AIR 1970 SC 1649 *(the Rustom & Hornby Case)*.

Trade Marks Bill

A Bill called the Trade Marks Bill to replace the Trade and Merchandise Marks Act 1958 which had been passed by the Lower House of Parliament (Lok Sabha) and which was pending in the Upper House (Rajya Sabha) lapsed on the dissolution of the Lower House at the expiration of its term in April 1996. Far-reaching changes have been made. They mainly provide for registration of trade marks for services, in addition to goods; abolition of Parts A and B of the Register of Trade Marks; registration of collective marks, providing for a single application for registration in more than one class of goods, and increase the period of registration and renewal from seven to ten years.

COPYRIGHT

The Copyright Act 1957 is the law governing Copyright in India, and was amended in 1983, 1984, 1992 and 1994. The 1983 Amendment Act sought to implement certain rights given to developing countries on translation and reproduction by the 1971 Amendment of the Berne and UC Conventions. The 1984 Amendment Act attempted to give more protection to producers of audio and video cassettes by providing stringent punishments for infringement of rights. The 1992 Amendment Act provided for an increase in the term of protection of copyright works from 50 years after the death of the author (as provided in the Berne Convention and in the Act before this amendment) to 60 years. The 1994 Amendment Act has practically rewritten the provisions of the 1957 Act to give effect to certain new and changed concepts in international protection of copyright, to India's accession to the Rome Convention and to certain modern scientific and technological developments and advancements in this sphere. The 1994 amendments came into effect from 10 May 1995.

Works to Which Copyright Applies

The Copyright Act does not provide for a definition of copyright. But the definition of the expression 'work', as contained in the Act, refers to literary, dramatic, musical or artistic works, cinematograph films and sound recordings. These are the three broad categories for which copyright protection is provided under the Act. All these expressions have also been defined in the Act. In addition, the Act makes its provisions applicable to:

(1) Broadcast reproduction rights (the Act defines 'broadcast' as communication to the public by any means of wireless diffusion or by wire).

(2) Video films which have been included in the definition of 'cinematograph film' and 'audio cassettes' included in the definition of sound recording.

(3) Computer programs, tables and compilations, including computer databases which have been included in the broad category of literary works as is the case in most of the countries.

(4) Performers' rights.

Copyright in the various works enures to the author of the work who has been defined to include the author of a literary or dramatic work, the composer of a musical work, the artist of an artistic work, the person who rearranges a work, the person taking a photograph, the producer of a cinematograph film or sound recording or the person who causes any literary, dramatic, musical or artistic work to be computer generated.

Automatic Protection and National Treatment

Neither the Berne Convention nor the Copyright Act provides for any formality to be complied with by any author for obtaining protection for any work under the Act. Copyright protection in a country is afforded to a work, the author of which is a national of that country and which was first published in that country. This is known as the principle of automatic protection. Such countries are referred to as 'originating countries' in the Berne Convention, and works originating in any of these countries must be given the same protection in the other countries as the latter give to works of their own nationals. This is known as the principle of national treatment, which is one of the three basic principles of the Berne Convention.

Register of Copyrights

Although the Copyright Act does not provide for any specific formality for obtaining protection under the Act, Chapter X of the Act provides for registration of a copyright in the Register of Copyrights. The Register of Copyrights is kept by the Registrar of Copyrights appointed under the Act at the Copyright Office, which is provided for by the Act.

Meaning of Copyright

Section 14 of the Act gives the meaning of copyright as 'the exclusive right to do or authorize the doing of any of the acts mentioned therein in respect of a work or any substantial part thereof'. These rights include the reproduction of the work in any material form, including the storing of it in any medium by electronic means, the issue of copies of the work to the public, the performance of the work in public or the communicating of it to the public, the making of any cinematograph film or sound recording in respect of the work, the making of any adaptation or translation of the work and doing, in relation to a translation or adaptation of the work, any of the above rights.

Computer Programs and Sound Recordings

In relation to a computer program, in addition to the rights mentioned above, it is possible for the author to sell or give on hire or offer for sale or hire, any copy of a computer program regardless of whether such copies have been sold or given on hire on earlier occasions. In the case of a sound recording, the rights include the right to make any other sound recording embodying it and to communicate the sound recording to the public.

Compulsory Licensing

The Act provides for the grant of compulsory licensing in any work withheld from the public and for certain translation and reproduction rights to persons resident in developing countries in addition to assignment and licensing.

1994 Amendments

The 1994 Amendment Act has introduced certain new concepts into the Act, the most important being the formation of copyright societies by various authors. Although the existing Act provided for performing rights societies, the amendment includes more detailed provisions for the formation, working and registration of copyright societies which will be more effective in collectively protecting the rights of authors instead of leaving protection to the individual author, who may not have the necessary wherewithal and expertise to protect his right effectively. These provisions are on the lines of the collective administration of the authors' rights obtaining in other countries.

DESIGNS

Designs Act 1911

The Designs Act 1911 provides for the registration and protection of designs. The Controller of Patents will also be the Controller for the purposes of registration of designs under this Act, and the Patent Office established under the Patents Act is the authority to receive applications for the registration of designs.

Application for the Registration of a Design

The proprietor of a new or original design, not previously published in India, may apply to the Controller for registration of the design under the Act in the form prescribed by rules made under the Act and accompanied by fees specified in the rules. The Controller may register, or may refuse to register, the design. Appeal is provided to the Central Government against an order of refusal by the Controller. The same design may be registered in more than one class and, in case of doubt as to which class a design ought to be registered in, the Controller may decide the question. Registration of a design is from the date of the application for registration. The Controller will grant a certificate of registration to the proprietor of the design.

Term of Protection of Designs

Once a design is registered, its registered proprietor has copyright in the design for five years from the date of registration. This can be renewed, on an application made to the Controller and on payment of fees, for two successive periods of five years. The piracy of a registered design either by sale or import empowers the registered proprietor of a design to receive Rs500 as a contract debt or, on the filing of a suit, to be eligible for damages or an injunction.

CHAPTER 13

LABOUR MANAGEMENT: LAWS AND MARKETS

by Krishan Lal Chugh
and Nalin Miglani

While the objective of this chapter is to examine the impact of labour legislation and labour markets on labour management in India, it also asserts that, in India, the key role in labour management is not played by legal considerations. It is played, as everywhere else, by top management vision, corporate culture and managerial styles. It also shifts the attention away from the over-emphasised, at times without adequate justification, focus on the impact of labour legislation in India. The chapter focuses on creation more than conflict. The true positives rather than imagined 'negatives' constitute labour management. The chapter provides many success stories of labour management in India. It seeks to provide evidence of, and guidance towards, what the authors truly believe is the core strength of the Indian economy—its human resources.

THE PHOBIA AND REALITY OF LABOUR LEGISLATION

Labour laws in India originated, along with most other corporate legislation, around the time of Independence. Influenced by British law and the then prevalent doctrine of socialism, these laws sought to protect the working class, who, it was assumed, would otherwise be seriously exploited. With this fundamental objective, a comprehensive and elaborate legislative framework was constructed. Very positive in its intentions, the framework has not kept pace with the other economic reforms. It has not yet fallen in step with the free market.

However, as stated earlier, this apparent aberration does not significantly impact on the possibilities of labour management in India. The debate on the technicalities of changes in labour legislation goes on. As is to be expected in a vibrant democracy like India, there are numerous suggestions as to how this should be done and the resolution of these issues should not be hoped for in a hurry. It needs to be understood that, in any case, out of the entire elaborate framework, the statutes that fundamentally steer the entire course of labour legislation are very few. These are the Industrial Disputes Act; the Trade Unions Act; and the Contract Labour (Regulation and Abolition) Act.

In these particular Acts, there are a few critical clauses which, in fact, were instrumental in giving shape to the present beliefs and outcomes in labour management. These clauses are:

- In the Industrial Disputes Act, the definition of a 'workman'.
- In the Trade Unions Act, the process of registering a 'Union'.
- In the Contract Labour Act, the areas where employment of contract workmen could be prohibited.

Together, these definitions had a profound and powerful impact on the ethos of labour management and thereafter on the structure of society and the economy itself. These definitions separated all employees in modern organisations into two distinct classes, one in opposition with the other. The impact of this division was reinforced by various other statutes in labour legislation which then built upon this base and created a clearly identifiable working class. The development of this phenomenon will now be explored in more detail.

The definition of a workman ensured that anybody in a non-managerial job, while employed by his employer, was under the protection of the State. The definition of a union in the Trade Unions Act ensured that employees in even the smallest enterprises could obtain such protection. In larger organisations there was competition between a host of trade unions to offer greater competitive protection to their constituencies. All that was needed to form a union was six close friends.

The Contract Labour Act introduced the now deep-rooted social phenomenon in many Indian minds—one of 'permanent employment', which meant that once a company took on an employee he was with the company till the age of 58. Furthermore, a company could not employ anyone other than through permanent employment. The Contract Labour Act virtually destroyed any possibility of temporary, contract, casual, impermanent, or flexible employment. Employment was the main concern of all politicians and this was manifested in creating lifetime 'permanent jobs'. It was assumed that employment was the cause that would result in the effect of economic growth.

Along with the existence of permanent, inflexible employment, there was an absence of market competition and therefore poor response to consumers' needs. It benefited organisations to create large, static workforces which day in and day out did no more than produce a steady, undifferentiated output (often at less than 50% utilisation of plant and equipment capacity). Typical responses to labour problems were invariably at one of two extremes. Either peace was bought at any cost and the cost then passed on to the consumer, or the employer just walked out of the enterprise preferring to keep the real estate, plant and equipment idle.

The result of this was an adversarial environment where unions and managements were involved in a bargaining situation and labour management was simply the art of negotiation, subterfuge and manipulation.

One of the significant factors influencing the law-makers in the years after Independence was the existence of a large public sector. Since the stated purpose of the public sector was to provide employment, it created a standard for industry in general where employment protection rather than profit generation became the desired goal. The chief executives of these companies were appointed by the government which contained politicians who depended on the trade unions' votes. Also, over the years, the public sector employees acquired high visibility. Any reform in labour legislation would have had the severest impact on these employees. They became a buffer for all the private sector organised work force.

There existed a significant number of organisations which successfully evolved, within the constraints of law, models and realities of productivity and employee satisfaction. However, even these organisations, because of the lack of extraordinary demand from the consumer or the market, were way below benchmark international standards, both in employee and in consumer satisfaction.

The Labour Markets

Apart from the effects on productivity and quality within companies the external labour market situation was heavily influenced by the legislation. The significant outcomes were in the nature of paradoxes, such as the emergence of an elite, organised workforce existing alongside vast masses of deprived, unorganised workers; high unemployment existing alongside inflexible employment within companies; and employment becoming the prerogative of unions rather than businesses.

Paradox 1

The emergence of an elite, organised workforce existing alongside vast masses of deprived, unorganised workers. Since it was easy to implement labour legislation in large industrial enterprises, as compared to dispersed small-scale businesses, the medium and large companies found themselves to be a fertile ground for trade union activity and government focus. As a result, in these companies, protection for labour increased at a dramatic rate. An employee in such an organisation could earn high wages and an array of benefits, and enjoyed cradle-to-grave job protection. His remuneration was entirely dissociated from the demand-and-supply conditions of labour markets. For instance, a janitor in a large company, with an organised union, would earn more than six times the wage of a similar janitor in a small business.

This privileged class of employees sought to create effective 'closed shops'. Not only was the job protected for the current employee, but the unions sought to replace him, when he retired, with his son or other nominee. The analogy with the third class compartment in the Indian railways is very apt. You could get in without a ticket, and once in, you would prevent the others from boarding on the pretext that it was very crowded inside.

How could employers afford, what the labour economists would call, labour market inflexibilities or inefficiencies? The answer, in the economists' lexicon, is very simple. The 'rent' that could be derived from simply keeping the show running and turning out the product in a closed, uncompetitive market was greater than you could derive from greater productivity and better quality.

Paradox 2

High unemployment in the country existing alongside inflexible employment within an enterprise. The above state of affairs led to another paradox. While there was vast unemployment in the country which meant that the supply side of the labour market had an excess, the price of labour in the organised sector did not drop. This happened because the supply in the organised sector was restricted, as indicated earlier, by closed shop union practices. It is often contended that labour in India is cheap. Taking into account the exchange rate, in an international comparison, this contention may be a true. But is the labour wage in India market-determined? Could it be even lower than it is today?

Paradox 3

Employment becoming the prerogative of unions rather than companies. As would be evident by now, employment choices and decisions were driven by the unions rather than the needs of the enterprise. Since unions were keen to promote what may be rightfully termed as 'dynastic employment' they ensured that the employment potential of each enterprise was never reduced, even at the cost of productivity.

Work patterns and norms were never negotiated down because that would reduce the employment potential of the enterprise. The unions, therefore, virtually ran the entire range of human resource issues on any shop floor. Employment was as much their objective as raising the living standards for their constituencies. In the process, employers virtually contracted out the management of their own employees to their unions. There was virtually no direct dialogue between employers and employees at large. The impact of such a situation on productivity and quality is evident enough.

LOOKING AHEAD

This analysis of the past leads us to the concerns of the present and the future.

It is well known that economic reforms in India have not yet reached the stage where labour legislation has also undergone reforms. It is the one area which has not yet been touched at all due to political considerations. In addition, fear of large scale resentment has prevented either privatisation of loss-making public sector or the invitation of private enterprise into areas earlier monopolised by the government.

Does this mean that anybody intending to commence an enterprise in India must look forward to a future which is similar to the story of the past? Our contention is that the future will be different even if there is no change in labour legislation.

Even though there has been no direct change in labour legislation, the environment of economic reforms has significantly affected the attitudes of employers, unions and employees. Competitiveness at the market end has forced the need for productivity and quality at the operational level. The emergence of these needs has forced employers to give up contracting out labour management to unions and to take charge themselves. In doing this, they have been able to experience significant improvement. There are many examples of companies that have responded efficiently to the new, competitive environment by reorganising themselves and delivering tangible results on the productivity and quality fronts. The unions too have realised that their companies are no longer protected by lack of competition and this leads to a more realistic assessment of business and employment.

The automobile sector in India has responded to the free market, quickly reorganising itself. Three companies are notable for their efforts: Telco, Mahindra & Mahindra and Eicher.

Telco has been able to re-gear its production system to turn out more models of vehicles. These models have been instrumental in expanding the light commercial vehicle market. In fact, the largest selling light commercial vehicle in India is the one manufactured by Telco, the only one without foreign collaboration! Both Mahindra & Mahindra and Eicher have focused on human resource development quite significantly. State-of-the-art programs have been launched, with communication with the employees a top priority resulting in a progressive and responsive work environment. In the fiercely competitive automobile sector, these companies have been able to manage their cost structures through their efforts and initiatives in human resource management.

Though the pace of change varies in different industries and different companies, the overall reality is uni-directional—towards more market-oriented labour management. The areas in labour management where significant positive change has already occurred are elaborated below. It is necessary to identify these areas separately because it is on this basis that recommendations on the subject of labour management will be made.

FLEXIBILITY

The amount of flexibility within enterprises is certainly on the increase. This is due to greater realisation by the unions that the free market requires continuous reorganisation. In addition, the free market requires greater variety in packaging and product styles and constant innovation in them. Some of this realisation has arisen because managers are communicating this fact to the employees. A large part, however, is also the direct consequence of the changed macro environment. The government, Chambers of Commerce and industry and even the politically affiliated central trade union organisations are all giving the same unequivocal message. As a result, most Indian companies have been able to successfully reorganise themselves. The route followed has not involved the shedding of labour but the redeployment of the existing workforces.

As a corollary to this development, even the issue of 'dynastic employment' has suffered a much needed dilution. From a position where organisations were recruiting on a mandatory basis every year the situation has changed to recruiting only on the basis of need.

However, preference is still given to employees' children or dependants. In addition, organisations insist on strict entry critera on the basis of merit and in most cases are successfully implementing it.

For example, in the Calcutta factory of ITC Ltd, the union and management negotiated revised work norms at the time of the union contract. These norms more or less matched the international standards for similar technology. A large number of employees became surplus. These were redeployed into running one extra production shift. As a result of this reorganisation, with the same number of employees, it was possible to generate 50% more output. In addition, the equipment in the factory is also utilised more effectively thereby increasing capital productivity. All this was accomplished in Calcutta, a place often unjustifiably labelled as unproductive and inflexible. Today, the factory is reorganising again to release more manpower to run the plant seven days a week.

How does management market all this extra output? ITC has embarked on a strategy of market expansion whereby a huge population consuming tobacco in forms other than cigarettes is sought to be converted to cigarette smoking. This effort has been successful and the demand for ITC's total output has increased by more than 11% annually.

This brings us to an interesting point. A key characteristic of all emerging markets is the possibility of market expansion. In all sectors, there is scope to increase the quantity of units sold merely because markets, unlike in the West, have not reached saturation point. This fact can be powerfully used by companies to ensure that productivity is enhanced by increasing output and not by decreasing manpower numbers.

PRODUCTIVITY

The above development in itself has contributed substantially to the improvement of productivity in organisations. However, there have been some other positive changes. The basic definition of a job has changed in the mind of a worker. From a time-based definition where 'attendance' was the greatest virtue and there was complete rigidity in the amount of work that was done in a predetermined time, the focus is shifting to 'task' and contribution, where the level of input expected from an employee has dramatically improved. Union support for inflexibilities in the workplace is considerably reduced. Those enterprises that have built on this change through sound human resource management have even started to reap the benefits of environments where the employees are positively contributing to increasing the productivity levels of their organisations and not merely doing what they are told.

QUALITY

There is greater consciousness of the issue of quality among employees. Concepts such as zero defect, six sigma quality, and total quality management have moved beyond being mere jargon and more intrinsic understanding is following. Systems and processes within an organisation have been examined for their impact on quality and suitable changes are being made.

Interaction is taking place between employees of different companies. Many companies have sent significant numbers of their shop floor employees to other parts of the world for training. The number of companies using processes such as TQM and ISO 9000 for training is growing.

All this has led to a greater appreciation of the need for quality. The evolution of professional systems that enable employees to gain comprehensive knowledge about quality is occurring. In this development, significant input has come from the various joint-ventures that Indian companies have formed with international firms.

It is not only difficult, but sometimes even imprudent, to put a numerical dimension to this progress. However, in order to clarify the magnitude of change, it is estimated that on a scale of 10, if the ideal is 10 and if the earlier level of quality was at level four, today it is certainly between six and seven.

EXIT POLICY

More has been written and said about this issue than any other in the course of India's reforms. It is the red herring of India's reforms. If ever there could be smoke without fire it is in the debate on exit policy. In the first place, the international firms which will now step into India will not have large workforces. They will not carry extra numbers on account of history. For some strange reason, even if they too land in this situation, their options of redeployment exist as much or even more (since their unions and workers would not have historical biases) than the current Indian firms. No Indian firm has yet gone under because it could not reorganise its labour force. If all this does not work, there still remains the option of reducing labour forces through voluntary separation packages.

For an attractive voluntary separation package, the costs and the payback period are well within the demands of any other investment decision. For instance, ITC has normally paid about half an individual's salary for each month of his remaining tenure. The capital that the employee gets ensures a return close to his current emoluments and the payback to the company, through saved employee costs, comes within four to five years.

It is high time that this paranoia on exit policy is dispensed with in favour of a more holistic and positive view of labour management in India.

To summarise, even though there has been no change in labour legislation in India since economic reforms, various internal and external situations have altered because of the new market conditions. Economic reforms, by changing the national and international competitive positioning of the firms, have indirectly but effectively addressed some of the issues that changes in labour laws would have sought to accomplish.

On the basis of this experience, there now follow some recommendations on labour management to entrepreneurs looking at India.

RECOMMENDATIONS

Given the past and current reality of labour management, what should prospective enterprises in India look for in the area of labour management? A one sentence answer to this question would be: Have high hopes of the minds and hearts of the Indian workforce, but don't leave any legal issue to chance.

The reality of a competitive economy has fully and firmly dawned on the industrial workforce. No employee enters an organisation expecting the kind of laid back work ethos that characterised Indian organisations in the past. Further more, the influence of the socialist and Marxist doctrine is not so intense now that it is difficult to convince the worker of the competitive imperatives. The employee, like the consumer, is young, with aspirations to improve the material standard of living and willingness to put in considerable effort to attain it. Exposure to international lifestyles and products through the visual media is immense and influential. More than any training programme, this exposure convinces the worker of the merit of and the demands from the free market mechanism. An issue of *The Economist*, which carried a survey on India, identified this as one of the most significant motivators for the Indian reforms. A consumer of global products, the employee understands the needs of a production system that has to respond to global needs. The free choice that he experiences in the markets, ironically, is also making him a world class resource for the organisation he's employed in.

The human resources management of manufacturing enterprises in India must be world class. It is necessary not only to bring in global practices for application in the Indian context, it is also necessary to employ fine managers with experience in progressive human resource management. These managers should be capable of understanding Indian sociological realities, both from the philosophical and from the practical point of view. They will then be able to communicate with the employees in a manner that will ensure commitment. They will also be able to evolve systems and structures that work in the Indian context.

Attention will have to be paid to the work environment of the shop floors and offices that the investor creates. Besides meeting international safety standards, these environments will also be a means of signifying the intention of the organisation. If the work environment is world class, the attitudes will be world class and the product quality will be world class.

It is only a combination of these initiatives that will ensure that the knowledge of free market imperatives existing in employees is converted to commitment and quality consciousness in the workplace.

That leads to another, normally Western bias: the effort to continually lower employee costs. In India, the share of labour costs in the total value added by a firm is normally negligible. The payoffs from greater commitment, because they are harder to quantify, are never taken into account. In India, welfare-oriented costs, such as pensions and medical expenses, have a high social value because there is no social security system. Expenditure on such items will have a greater value to employees than higher wages. Companies must invest in these areas in order to convey a message of confidence and credibility. In India, people want to work in companies that treat them like people, not parts of the machine.

One example springs to mind. When asked to turn-around a paper mill and rationalise the labour force, the company concerned could have got away with paying the statutory separation amounts. Not only were these amounts miserably low for the individuals concerned: it was felt that these retrenchments would adversely affect relations with the remaining workers. It was then proposed to pay separation amounts that were 10–12 times higher than normal and to make up the extra expenses by completing the modernisation of the plant 10 days earlier than scheduled.

To have good human resource management it is necessary to have, as stated earlier, managers. To have good managers, in India, the issue of location becomes critical. There is always a temptation to locate in a backward, non-urban site where real estate and other costs are low. However, such a place of work is generally unattractive to talented managers and unless suitable facilities are provided by the investor, the enterprise could end up recruiting on the basis of a compromise. The cost of such a compromise shows up in unequivocal ways, such as low productivity, poor quality, and frequent problems on the shop floor.

With respect to unions, it would always be a good policy to deal with the union that has been elected on the basis of the greatest possible worker franchise. Management often believe they can have the unions of their choice. In India, this is only possible in the short term. The labour legislation has evolved too far and trade union consciousness is too advanced for such a strategy to be sustainable. When it fails, it leaves behind a trail of devastation in employee relations. In any case, because the trade union movement in India has been in existence for a long time, there is rarely a trade union leadership so unreasonable that it is impossible to deal with. The same observation is true for any attempt to create a non-union plant. Such an attempt can be successful only in the very short term, the short term being as short perhaps as two or three years.

It is a common practice in many Indian enterprises to bargain productivity for wages. For these enterprises, this is a historical necessity. For new enterprises, however, this pattern of negotiation could become an unnecessary millstone. It advisable to create an expectation pattern where complete flexibility on the productivity front is taken for granted by the employer and his response to workers' aspirations in terms of remuneration is also flexible and progressive. Linking productivity with wages and negotiating on that basis creates long-term inflexibilities in the system. Related to the above observation is the fact that it always helps to establish international, benchmark standards of productivity as soon as the enterprise commences. Nothing should be left open to future negotiations.

Continuing this train of thought, it is often believed that labour costs in India are low and therefore labour intensive technology must be used. This assumption should be very studiously examined before being implemented. Selection of optimum technology and an optimum number of personnel with sound human resource management skills has a greater chance of success.

Outsourcing as an option should also be carefully and comprehensively utilised. For many services in India, it may not be possible to get world class service from subcontractors. However, for those that are available, this opportunity should be considered, and where it is possible, the opportunity for vendor development should be investigated.

The last recommendation concerns the legal framework. Professional and world class employee relations within companies can be a very desirable and effective substitute for managing by the law book. Most legal statutes provide for bilateral alternatives if these are in the same spirit as or more progressive than the law. Companies are advised to aim for this goal, and when it is not possible, to simply follow the law.

Labour relations in India are going through a period of transition, but the future looks promising.

CHAPTER 14

MARKETING AND DISTRIBUTION IN INDIA
by S M Datta

INTRODUCTION

The most striking feature of the Indian market, irrespective of the product category under review, is its potential size. India's population of 930 million consumers, growing at roughly 2% per annum, and the relatively low per-capita consumption of most manufactured articles, averaging between 5% and 25% of the level in developed economies, presents a picture of apparently limitless opportunity. However, as the long-established Indian companies have discovered over the years, entry into this market is beset with problems. New entrants to this market must develop a realistic appreciation of the size and the profile of the Indian opportunity, as well as learn the basic skills for accessing it.

Very frequently, the potential demand in India for a particular product or category is arrived at by applying reasonably 'modest' projections of penetration, adoption rate and depth of consumption to the entire population of the country. The strength of the apparently unsophisticated local competition is also usually underestimated. Experience shows that such demand estimates could be highly misleading for several reasons. Some of the more important ones are discussed below.

THE CONSUMER

The skewed pattern of the economy dictates that, except for a handful of product categories, only a fraction of India's population can be regarded as 'potential' consumers. The product categories which constitute exceptions already exist in the market and accurate estimates of their demand can be accessed quite easily. For most 'new' product categories it is likely that a much smaller proportion of the population—better known as the emerging Indian middle class—is likely to be potential consumers. While estimates vary, the proportion of this consuming class will not exceed 25% of the Indian population.

PRICE-VALUE RELATIONSHIP

The Indian consumers' concept of value is as well honed as anywhere else in the world, and they have little difficulty in deciding the point beyond which additional 'features' cease to justify incremental price. Thus, in most product categories, over 75% of the volume is concentrated in relatively low priced 'popular' products. The relatively low family income in India leaves very little money after meeting essential needs, and this surplus has to be stretched to satisfy their growing aspirations. Therefore, pricing plays a very significant role in determining the size of the segment which would respond to the marketing mix.

COMPETITION

For an under-developed economy, India has a surprisingly diversified industrial base. Therefore, the Indian consumer is familiar with a variety of locally available products and services. Until recently, the quality of such locally manufactured goods was not comparable to world standards. However, in many cases, the advent of international competition was foreseen and defensive measures were taken—but always ensuring that they remained on the right side of the price-value equation. The local manufacturers have extremely competitive cost structures, are innovative, and know the territory. To successfully take on such competition a new entrant must possess real competitive advantages, as well as the patience to sustain the initiative till the aim is achieved.

DISTRIBUTION COVERAGE

Indian consumers are dispersed over an extensive land mass. They are serviced by an efficient, but highly fragmented, trade system consisting of over 3 million retail and wholesale outlets, spread over many urban and rural population centres. The ability to physically deliver one's goods to the consumers, therefore, remains a source of significant competitive advantage in India. To take but one example, the top 300 cities and towns in the country account for between 30% and 50% of the demand for most consumer products. For industrial products and intermediates, however, the markets are far more concentrated around a relatively small proportion of the urban centres.

It is true that, for several product categories, the Indian market is at a nascent stage and available evidence would suggest that these markets will develop and flourish as they have already done in other more developed countries. However, this development will take place over time, in tune with the progress of the economy as a whole and the growth of purchasing power in the hands of consumers. There are unlikely to be any short-cuts, and the immutable laws that determine business success anywhere will apply to India as well.

THE INDIAN CONSUMER

India is a country with 930 million people today, to which another 18 million are being added every year. A significant majority (73%) of them live in rural, primarily agrarian, areas and are distributed over some 627,000 villages. The balance live in 3700 towns, of which 300 have a population of more than 100,000 inhabitants.

At first sight, the bulk of the purchasing power in India would appear to be concentrated in its urban markets. This is incorrect, and for many consumer products, aggregate rural consumption (as distinct from 'purchase') exceeds that in urban areas (Table 1). Moreover, the growth rate in rural consumption for most product categories significantly exceeds that of urban consumption. Consequently, the urban-rural split in demand is likely to keep moving towards the rural markets in the foreseeable future. Even for more up-market goods, a relatively higher proportion of demand could be coming from rural areas, since 55% of Indian middle class households are rural based.

Table 1

Rural Market Contribution (%)

CONSUMER DURABLES	
Radio/transistors	79
Wrist watches	72
Sewing machines	60
Two wheelers	41
Televisions	26
CONSUMER NON-DURABLES	
Personal wash	52
Synthetic detergents	46
Food/beverages	27
OTC products	36
Razor blades	50
Batteries	54

The consumption pattern in India has been shaped by several historic and socio-economic factors. Some of the more significant among these are:

Economic

The Indian economy was growing at a compounded rate of 3.5% in real terms in the three decades between 1950 and 1980. Discounting for the population growth rate of 2%, there was little growth in per capita income, and consumption stagnated at a subsistence level. In the following 15 years, economic growth has picked up to an average of 5.5% and the rate of population growth has fallen somewhat. This has helped release a higher percentage of the growing per capita income for non-food consumption (Table 2), leading to a real growth in demand for consumer goods.

Table 2

Changing Composition of Consumer Basket
% of total spent

	1976	1986	2000 (proj)
Food	55	53	43
Clothing	10	11	12
Rent/Power fuel	13	11	10
Services	12	13	14
Consumer goods	10	12	21

Education

The literate proportion of the population as a whole more than doubled from 24% in 1961 to 52% in 1991. Even more significant is the trebling of literacy among women, from 13% to 39%, during the same period. This change has touched every aspect of life in the country and particularly influenced receptivity to new ideas and new ways of organising life. Increase in literacy has also helped open the door to the other great instrument of change—the development of mass media.

Exposure to Mass Media

Penetration of television has increased from practically nil in the early 1980s to 45% of all households in 1994. As elsewhere in the world, increase in penetration of this medium has exposed mainstream Indians to a totally new lifestyle in the privacy of their own homes. The rapidly expanding penetration of cable and satellite channels (35% of urban homes by early 1995) since 1991 has further added an international dimension to this exposure. All this is influencing consumption patterns, and the development of the market for consumer products, which themselves have been going through far-reaching changes since the mid-1980s.

Consumer Product Markets

The markets for consumer products in India have seen enormous changes since the mid-1980s. This is perhaps most obvious in the area of consumer durables. For example, till the early 1980s, only two models of passenger cars of the 1950s vintage were available in the country. Entry of the Maruti (Suzuki) in 1984 changed the picture, and today the Indian car market is getting ready to receive over half a dozen of the latest models from both the East and the West. A similar order of discontinuous change has been seen in several categories of white goods such as refrigerators, washing machines and television sets. The free availability of 'world class' products for the first time in living memory has also changed the paradigm of what constitutes 'acceptable quality'.

With so much change in consumption patterns and consumer behaviour, a legitimate question is whether a new entrant into this market would have access to the resources needed to understand and measure these changes. The answer is, fortunately, in the affirmative. There are plenty of commercially available publications, from local as well as international publishing houses, containing reasonably reliable data and analysis about India and Indian markets. In addition, good quality professional market research companies with experience in handling some of the most up-to-date and sophisticated techniques are available for consumer studies.

Consumer Protection

The legislation for consumer protection can be broadly categorised under two headings: trade related and consumer related.

Three major trade-related statutes are worthy of note. The Monopolies and Restrictive Trade Practices Act contains important provisions regarding resale price maintenance, tied-up sales and territorial restriction. The Essential Commodities Act and the Prevention of Food Adulteration Act prescribe the maintenance of records, submission of returns and obtaining necessary registration.

A large number of consumer-related laws also exist. Perhaps the most important among these, apart from the three trade-related Acts mentioned earlier are: the Consumer Protection Act; Weights & Measures Act and the Packaged Commodities Rules; and Drugs & Cosmetics Act.

Expert advice on legal issues is available from well-known professionals in the field.

BRAND POSITIONING AND ADVERTISING

Appeal of International Brands and Their Positionings

'This will not work in India', and 'India is different' were refrains quite common till a few years ago. More recently, evidence has been mounting that successful international brand mixes work in India as well as anywhere else in the world. There are of course a few provisos to this general observation, some of which follow:

Relevance of positioning

The positioning of most truly international brands has universal appeal. There is evidence to suggest such brand positioning works in India as well as anywhere else. If, however, the positioning draws its strength from a regional or ethnic bias for reasons of habit or taste, it would be necessary to reconfirm the relevance of such a positioning in the Indian context. To illustrate the point, while the positioning of a toothpaste like Colgate Dental Cream has wide appeal, the appeal of a food brand such as Kelloggs' breakfast cereals is more restricted. Most successful adaptations of international brands have chosen local executions of their international campaigns. The key reason for this effort is to enable Indian consumers to easily identify with the brand and its personality.

Adapting the product mix

While the product mix is always an important element of the total brand mix, it is usually not the sole determinant. Successful international entries have used research, judgment and flexibility to adapt the precise features of their product to the requirements of the Indian market and the prevailing competitive scenario.

Delivering competitive value

Indian consumers seldom buy a brand simply because it is 'international'. International brands at entry, therefore, need to ensure that they continue to deliver excellent competitive value in the Indian market context, as much as they do in the international context.

New brands entering the Indian market have to trade off between the conflicting needs of competitive pricing, minimum product specifications for international compatibility, and margin requirements for viable operations. A rough but ready 'feel' for pricing in India can be obtained by converting dollar prices to rupees using PPP rates rather than exchange rates.

Advertising agencies and services

Many of the leading international advertising agencies have their affiliates in India, either as subsidiaries (eg Lintas, O&M), or through strategic alliances with Indian agencies (eg MAA-Bozell). In addition, there are a number of highly capable independent Indian advertising agencies. Most agencies of reasonable size (capitalised billing per year in the order of Rs1 billion) would be 'full service', and have offices in more than one Indian city. 'Full service' in this context means that the agency provides a full range of advertising services—from creative development to production, media planning and media buying. Packaging design in India has generally been handled by the full service advertising agencies but, in recent months, several specialised packaging design houses have also emerged. Similarly, specialised media planning and buying houses are also becoming available. Normal agency commission for full service agencies is 15% of billing, unless otherwise negotiated.

Production facilities and services for television commercials, printing etc of reasonable quality are available locally, but relatively easy access is available to Hong Kong, Singapore or London. Cost of the master production of a locally made 30 second television commercial would vary between Rs1 million and Rs1.5 million, while each additional language version (most commercials will need to be recorded in more than one of the regional languages) would cost roughly a quarter of that amount.

The media and media coverage

The media in India has been undergoing rapid structural changes in recent years due to the increasing penetration of television as well as the rapid expansion of satellite channels. An idea of how rapid and far-reaching the changes have been can be gauged from the fact that, from having a single TV channel till 1991, an urban home today may be connected to a cable network accessing 30 channels. Despite this progress, however, the bulk of media spending is still controlled by the Press. Total advertising expenditure in India in 1995 was estimated at Rs25 billion, with the Press accounting for Rs17 billion, and television for Rs6 billion, while the balance was accounted for by radio, outdoor and other media. The contribution of television to total advertising expenditure in the country is expected to move up from 23% in 1994 to nearly 30% by 1997, because television expenditure has been growing at a rate of 20–25%, compared to the industry average of 15%.

The hyperactivity on the television front in recent years has led to rapid expansion of the coverage of this medium in both urban and rural India. As a result, unduplicated coverage of conventional mass media among urban adults has climbed to 90%. Rural coverage, however, continues to remain low and provides immense opportunity for experimentation and initiative. The estimated unduplicated coverage by medium among a target group of 'all adults' in urban and rural India in 1994 is given in Table 3.

Table 3

Media Reach
% of All Adults

	URBAN	RURAL
Television	80	35
Radio	62	40
Press	59	20
Cinema	50	25
TOTAL	90	65

Advertising Regulations

Regulations in commercial advertising take three forms in India:

(i) Advertising on Doordarshan (DD) and Akashwani (radio): Both government owned agencies have elaborate regulations governing advertising in their respective medium. The 'Code for Commercial Advertising on Television' lays down the ground rules that have to be followed by any commercial on television, and covers areas such as requirements for advertising directed at children, need for substantiation of claims, rules concerning competitive advertising etc. It also specifies the negatives which all advertising on television has to observe. For example, no advertisement of religious or political nature is permitted. At present, advertising of foreign goods and foreign banks is not allowed on television.

(ii) Advertising for tobacco products and alcoholic beverages: Advertising of cigarettes and other tobacco products is not permitted on DD and Akashwani, though these products can be advertised in the Press and on outdoor billboards. Advertising for alcoholic beverages is banned on all mass media.

As elsewhere in the world, cigarette and alcoholic beverages manufacturers try to get around the problem by sponsoring popular sports events that are covered by television. There is also the practice of 'surrogate advertising' prevalent in the alcoholic beverages industry. This involves advertising a mineral water with the brand name and label design of a popular beer, or a set of tumblers carrying the logo of a brand of whisky.

(iii) Self regulation: The Advertising Standards Council of India (ASCI) was set up in 1985 as a body of advertisers, advertising agencies, the media and marketing research companies, in order to promote self-regulation in advertising. The ASCI lays down a code of practice covering various aspects of advertising. It also has an active Consumer Complaints Council (CCC), which invites people to write in if they find any piece of advertising offensive or otherwise objectionable. The CCC calls for the advertiser's response to the complaint and then reviews all material pertaining to a complaint in light of the ASCI code at their periodic sittings. If a complaint is upheld, the ASCI tries to prevail upon the advertiser to withdraw or suitably modify the offending piece of advertising.

SELLING AND DISTRIBUTION

Indian Trade Structure

The Indian trade network has been perfected over many decades for the efficient distribution of food grains and basic manufactured articles such as cloth, sugar, salt, oils and soap. The distribution of industrial products follows a pattern which closely resembles the original model. Even the manufacturers of consumer products in India have adopted a distribution system that is not very dissimilar from the traditional trade structure.

Manufacturers in India commonly use a three-tier distribution structure to carry their goods to the final consumer: distributor, wholesaler and retailer.

The efficiency and cost of the system depend on the exact role assigned to each of the three intermediaries and how well the process is managed. The distribution system used by manufacturers of fast moving consumer goods (FMCGs) tends to be slightly more complex than the system for industrial products. The following illustration typifies a popular model for distribution.

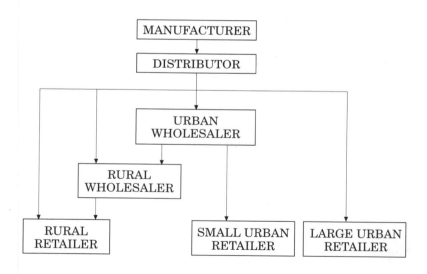

The size and direct reach of such a system, and the extent to which the company wishes to supervise distribution to retailers through its own personnel, are both variable. For example, the number of distributors for a company operating on a national scale could be between 500 and 2500. Similarly, the number of retailers directly reached by a company's distributors could be between 300,000 and 1 million. Some companies consider it necessary to visit all retailers on its direct coverage at least once a month. Others believe their responsibility is mainly in managing and motivating distributors and leaving the task of retail distribution to the wholesalers. Depending on this choice, the size of a company's sales staff could vary between 100 and 500.

A company's distribution costs and effectiveness would depend on which of the above alternatives is chosen. In terms of costs down the line and channel margins offered by medium to large FMCG manufacturers, whose products have ready consumer demand, the picture in urban areas is as follows (showing prices indexed to 100):

Manufacturer to distributor	100
Distributor to – wholesaler	103–104
– large retailer	104–105
Wholesaler to small retailer	105–107
Retailer to consumer	110–115

In rural and in more remote areas, consumer prices could be 5–10% higher because of higher cost of transportation by the trade or due to addition of one or two extra steps in the system.

The key members of this distribution system and their functions are as follows:

(1) The distributor. It is common for a typical distributor to carry products of more than one non-competing company, thereby spreading its administrative and other fixed costs. A distributor has a written agreement with the company, and buys its products and distributes them to wholesalers and retailers within a geographical area agreed with the company. To perform this service, the distributors require storage space, funds to invest in the company's products and in distribution infrastructure, and manpower to carry out distribution and associated administrative work. The distributor needs to run a very tight ship in order to pay for all its operating expenses out of the 4–5% margin earned, and still make a 35–40% per annum return on investment for the continued viability of the business.

(2) Wholesalers. Wholesalers in India have perfected the art of operating on 1–2% gross margin, by keeping their costs very low, and turning over their investment rapidly, sometimes several times in a week.

Typically, several wholesalers operate out of a 'wholesale market' that attracts smaller wholesalers and retailers from the surrounding areas which are not directly reached by the manufacturers or their distributors. Therefore wholesalers, when properly used, can be powerful allies of a manufacturer in extending distribution of its products well beyond the reach of its own distribution system. At the same time, if not used properly, the wholesale system can seriously undermine the effectiveness of the manufacturer's own distribution system through price undercutting.

(3)   Retailers.   Most of the 3 million plus retailers in India are small family establishments, often run from a shop which is also the home. There are in addition more substantial retail outlets, the largest among which operate in the 'self-service' mode. The top 20% of the retailers usually generate 80% of business.

Retailers generally operate on low margins, ranging between 5% and 10% for most advertised consumer product categories. Apart from the usual retailing services, the more enterprising among the urban outlets provide credit and home-delivery to their regular customers. These 'add-on' services, together with the prevailing low retail margins, are among the reasons trade concentration has not yet taken place in India.

(4)   Own vs third party distribution.   Given the geographic spread of India, taken together with its trade structure, there are obvious possibilities for significant economies of scale. It also places a new entrant at some disadvantage compared to more established companies.

Faced with this dilemma, organisations have responded in different ways, either by investing in setting up their own selling and distribution infrastructure, by subcontracting distribution to specialised third-party distribution houses, or by seeking strategic alliances and joint-ventures with local established companies with well-developed distribution infrastructure.

Of the three, setting up one's own distribution infrastructure is obviously the most expensive in the short term. However, several new entrants have chosen this alternative because of the importance of distribution in the Indian context, and the key role it has to play in establishing new brands.

Utilising the services of a distribution house has its own advantages and disadvantages. The immediate requirements of people and money are less. However, there are questions about the degree of commitment one can expect from the sales staff of the distribution house. The general experience seems to have been that they are more keen to sell their own products rather than those they are only distributing. From the point of view of the distribution house as well, such an arrangement has proved unsatisfactory in the past. For example, there have been cases where companies have broken off and set up their own distribution system after having acquired market share through the distribution house.

(5) Joint-Ventures. A joint-venture with an established Indian company as a way of buying into a ready-made distribution network has been a popular alternative in the recent past.

The Indian company involved in such alliances is expected to bring a range of local strengths to the table, of which distribution is a significant one. Most of these joint ventures are recent, and it remains to be seen how they work out in the long term.

CASE STUDIES

The objective of this final section is to illustrate some aspects of marketing and distributing discussed in this chapter, through a few recent case studies.

Titan Industries Ltd

Background

The Indian watch market is estimated at 20 million pieces per annum. While 50% of this market is locally produced, the balance is smuggled.

In terms of price segments, the low-to-medium segment (between Rs300–749 per piece) accounts for 70% of the market in volume while the premium priced segment (between Rs750–7500) accounts for the balance. In terms of value, the low-to-medium priced segment accounts for 50% of the market (roughly Rs7 billion) while the premium priced segment accounts for the balance.

There are only two major players in the organised watch market, Titan and HMT. Titan was a later entrant into the market which was monopolised by HMT. Currently, Titan has a market share of 32% for locally produced watches. However, when viewed in relation to the market in which Titan largely operates (that is, the quartz analogue watch segment (size 5.3 million pieces per annum), the company has a 60% market share (this includes Times' share).

Company

Established in 1987, Titan is a company promoted by the Tata group and the Tamil Nadu Industrial Development Corporation in collaboration with M/s France Ebauches. When the company entered the market, watches were considered as a necessity and not a fashion item. The only major manufacturer (HMT) provided watches that were far from elegant and merely satisfied a basic function. However, Titan picked up on a trend among consumers of smuggled watches (that is, they were willing to pay a relatively large amount—around Rs1000—for watches that afforded them a status symbol). Brands that were doing very well in this smuggled market were Citizen, Orient and Ricoh. Given the scenario, Titan launched a range of upmarket watches in the price range of Rs750–7500. In order to position the premium quartz watch as a lifestyle piece, and not merely as serving a function, and to differentiate the product in the process, the company developed a unique distribution set-up in addition to normal retail outlets. The company currently has a network of 172 high-profile shops and franchised showrooms, wherein only Titan watches are displayed in an exclusive retail ambience generating the customer perception that Titan is committed to after-sales service. The showroom exposes customers to a wide selection of Titan watches without the distraction of other competing products.

In addition, there are shops, which are the property of company appointed distributors, who are allowed to stock other competing brands. The major advantage in both these showrooms and shops is that it allows distributors to identify with the brand as well as allowing the company to control the retail ambience, stocks and sales force. In addition to the showrooms and shops, the company has a network of over 4100 retail outlets in 1150 towns. By redefining the selling process, Titan has been able to increase its sales from a mere 1 million pieces in 1987 to the current 3.2 million, thereby appropriating the mantle of market leader.

The key success factors

(1) Creating the right retail ambience so as to build the image of brand exclusivity.
(2) Creating the right perception among consumers about the company's commitment to after-sales service.
(3) Ensuring that retailers identify with the brand.
(4) Being able to monitor stocks and ensure quality of the sales force.

Kellogg's India Pvt Ltd

Background

The breakfast cereal market is estimated at around 1800 metric tonnes per annum with a corresponding value of Rs260 million. The market consists of three companies: Kellogg's India, Mohan-Meakin and Champions. When Kellogg's entered the market in September 1994, the market was small but within the short span of 11 months, Kellogg's had gained a 92% volume share of the market. The success of this company has hinged on its effective sales and distribution system combined with its organisational structure.

Company

Established in 1906 in Battle Creek, Michigan (US), the Kellogg company is the world's leading producer of ready-to-eat cereal products. The company also manufactures cereal products such as toaster pastries, frozen waffles, cereal bars and other convenience foods. Consistent with the company's goal of reaching 1 billion new customers with nutritious grain-based products, Kellogg's was the first multi-national company to manufacture and market ready-to-eat cereals in India.

The company has set up a manufacturing base at Taloja capable of producing 6000 metric tonnes of ready-to-eat cereal. Given pessimistic penetration figures of 3% in India, arising out of a need to change the breakfast habit, Kellogg's launched its product only in Bombay. However, the company realised early that its product was well received by consumers and decided to accelerate its national launch.

Kellogg's was thus faced with the difficult task of setting up an entirely new national distribution system geared for ready-to-eat cereals. However, within a very short time, the company exceeded its own expectations and achieved the market leader position with a 94% market share.

The key to its success lies in its ability to build an entirely new national distribution system in a very short time. The company's distribution system encompasses 13 C&FAs, 95 distributors and over 20,000 retail outlets servicing 32 cities across India. The company overcame the initial hesitation of distributors by agreeing to normal stock levels at the distributor level (not to exceed 15 days) and by ensuring a healthy return on investment (ROI). Additionally, the company agreed to fully subsidise the cost of hiring distributor sales people for selling its product while allowing the distributor to stock

211

other products (except for competition). Finally, distributors have been allowed to interact with the company on sales input. This empowerment of the dealer, fixed stock levels, and healthy performance (giving distributors ROIs in excess of 24% per annum) has enabled Kelloggs to develop a solid distributor base in India.

In addition, the company has put in place a very flat organisational structure allowing sales officers to deal directly with Regional Sales Managers.

The key success factors

(1) Building distributor confidence by offering fixed stock levels, empowerment, healthy ROIs and subsidising the cost of distributor sales staff in large cities.
(2) Empowerment of its own workforce by reducing the reporting procedures and allowing them to communicate directly with those in charge.

Blue Dart

Background

The Indian courier industry is estimated at around Rs8 billion, of which the organised sector accounts for roughly Rs4 billion. The organised market can be divided into that of documents and non-documents. Currently, the document market accounts for the bulk of business (60%), while the balance is accounted for by non-documents.

The first courier service began in 1978 with a tie-up between DHL and Air Freight Ltd. At this point, foreign banks constituted most of the customer base because they were used to the efficiency-enhancing product. It was only a matter of time before, in 1986, P&T began its EMS Speed Post which offered consumers the same product at lower prices. This new product soon deteriorated into a commodity status with a large number of players offering similar services at knock-down rates. Naturally, companies that offered the service at premium prices had to offer customers additional value-added features.

Company

Against this backdrop, Blue Dart began operating a courier service in collaboration with Gelco Express International (UK) in 1983. This UK-based company was subsequently acquired by Federal Express (US) leading to a partnership between Blue Dart and Federal

Express. Despite a large number of players offering similar services, Blue Dart developed a strong marketing strategy that has seen it emerge as the market leader.

The company provides 'before 10.30 am delivery' thereby ensuring a perception of reliability in the minds of consumers. In fact, the perception is well-founded because the company has achieved a service level of over 99.5%.

The company's slogan is 'Use our edge to strengthen yours'. The company has already invested over Rs67 million and has plans to invest a further Rs85 million in an e-mail network (which is claimed to be the largest private e-mail network in the country). This ensures communication between the company and customers and keeps them informed about the progress of their packages through the delivery process. The company tracks all domestic shipments through its COSMAT system while international shipments are monitored through its COSMOS system.

A human resource development programme, costing over Rs15 million, has ensured that the workforce is motivated, and in constant touch with changes in technology. Also, it is in the process of augmenting its ground distribution system (6 hubs—Bangalore, Delhi, Bombay, Madras, Hyderabad and Erode) of 63 LCVs, 1282 motorcycles and 164 Jeeps/vans with an air-based distribution system. This value-addition in terms of technology, manpower and reliability has seen the company's sales rise from Rs420 million in 1991–92 to the current Rs876 million.

The key success factors

(1) Technology—ensuring that investment in technology helps the company to be close to the customer, increasing the reliability of service and contribution to the overall profits of the company.

(2) Manpower—developing a highly trained, motivated and conscientious workforce in the belief that the workforce is the necessary ingredient to continuing growth and providing professional service to the customer.

(3) Reliability—ensuring delivery before 10.30 am of all packages.

Asian Paints India Ltd

Background

The paints market is estimated at around Rs30 billion. It is broadly segmented into decorative paints (accounting for 75% of the market) and industrial or protective paints (accounting for the balance). The two major players in the industry are Asian Paints (I) Ltd and Goodlass Nerolac.

Company

Established in 1942, Asian Paints (I) Ltd became the largest selling paint company in India in 1967 with a market share of 42%. When Asian Paints entered the market, direct distribution was largely restricted to urban markets with companies' sales forces concentrating only on large stores within these urban areas. In addition, the paint industry had a commodity bias with no clear brand loyalty.

Asian Paints started by redefining the selling route. Instead of concentrating only on urban large markets, the company's sales force began selling the company's product in smaller towns as well. In addition, the company not only relied upon the large distributors but also identified traders and hardware stores to retail its products. In addition to focusing on high-value niche markets (such as distemper paints wherein the company currently has a 65% market share), the company rationalised its product mix and substantially increased its consumer reach by launching smaller size packs of its paints.

To ensure effective sales, the company has developed an extensive distribution system ensuring that it not only services retailers within a short period but also focuses on key markets. Asian Paints has four factories, 42 warehouses and 9000 dealers. In order to ensure high service levels, the company has put in place a '24 hour service index' which connects dealers to the factory and warehouses, and enables the company to service dealers within 24 hours of the order placement.

The key success factors

(1) Rationalisation of product portfolio—introduction of small pack sizes.
(2) Company focus on high-value markets.
(3) The redefinition of the selling routes—focus on both urban and rural areas serviced by large to medium dealers and hardware stores.
(4) Its streamlined distribution system enables it to service 84% of all orders within a 24 hour period.

CHAPTER 15

DIRECT TAXES
by T S Srinivasan

THE TAX SYSTEM IN INDIA

Tax Structure

India has a federal structure of government, and taxes are levied by the Central Government, the States and local authorities. The taxes levied by the Central Government can be broadly classified as direct and indirect taxes.

Direct taxes are taxes on income (except from agriculture); taxes on wealth, gifts, expenditure; and interest tax.

Indirect taxes are customs duties; central excise duties; and service tax.

State governments also levy excise duties and a sales tax, as well as a tax on agricultural income. Local authorities have limited powers to levy and collect taxes.

Direct taxes administration

Direct taxes are administered by the Central Board of Direct Taxes (CBDT) in the Department of Revenue, Ministry of Finance. Statutes passed by the legislature and Rules made by the CBDT spell out the law, and the Finance Acts of each year specify the tax rates. Amendments are usually prospective, unless otherwise specified.

Assessment year and Previous year

The tax year is the period from 1 April to 31 March, called the 'assessment year', in which the income of the previous year is charged to tax. The law prescribes a uniform 'previous year' or accounting year, which ends on 31 March preceding the assessment year. For example, income earned during the period 1 April 1995 to 31 March 1996 (the 'previous year') will be brought to tax in the 'assessment year' 1996–97.

The applicable law will generally be the law in force in the assessment year.

Taxpayer category

Taxpayers are classified as: companies; individuals; firms (partnerships); Hindu undivided families; associations of persons or bodies of individuals, whether incorporated or not; local authorities; and any other artificial juridical person.

While the general provisions of income tax law are common, tax rates and some exemptions, reliefs and procedures are specific to one or other of the taxpayer categories.

Residence: An individual is 'resident' if he was in India (a) for 182 days or more in a financial year, or (b) for 60 days or more (extended to 182 days for a non-resident Indian, or 'NRI') in a financial year and for 365 days during the previous four financial years.

In other cases, the individual is 'non-resident'. Non-residents returning to India can claim the status of 'resident but not ordinarily resident' if they were not resident in the earlier nine financial years, or had not been in India for 730 days in the preceding seven financial years.

It is possible that a taxpayer could be 'resident' in more than one country.

Domestic companies and foreign companies

Companies are classified either as domestic companies or as foreign companies. A domestic company is an Indian company, or one whose control or management is situated in India. All other companies are foreign companies.

Thus, a company incorporated in India, even if it is a 100% subsidiary of a foreign company, will be treated as a domestic company. A branch office or a liaison office of a foreign company operating in India will be treated as a foreign company.

For other categories of taxpayers, the location of the control and management will determine the residential status.

(Note: In this chapter, 'non-resident' includes a foreign company, unless otherwise stated.)

Tax rates

Following the report of the Tax Reforms Commission set up in 1991, tax rates have been reduced over the last five years as follows: tax on domestic companies, from a maximum of 69% to 43% and tax on foreign companies, from 65% to 55%.

Many complexities in the law and procedure have been simplified. If tax holidays and other concessions and reliefs are taken into account, the actual tax could be substantially less.

Also see Minimum Alternate Tax (MAT), p 224.

Taxable Income

When is income taxable?

Indian law brings to charge the income of the taxpayer for the 'previous year'. Lottery and race winnings and gambling profits are taxable. So is capital gain on the sale of assets.

The income should have arisen or been received in the previous year. Salary accrues when due, and dividends when declared. Capital gains arise when the asset is transferred. In the case of a business or profession, accrual of income generally depends upon the method of accounting the taxpayer follows—cash or mercantile.

Tax liability and residence

A resident is taxable on his world income, ie, income wherever arising, and on income received in India. A non-resident is taxed on the income arising or received in India. A resident but not ordinarily resident is taxed on his Indian income, and on income arising abroad from a business controlled from or a profession set up in India. The character of the income is decided at the point of time of initial accrual or receipt, as the case may be. Subsequent actions will not alter its character.

Incomes deemed to arise in India

The following incomes are deemed to arise in India:

(1) Income arising, even if indirectly, through any business connection, property, asset or source of income in India, or through the transfer of a capital asset in India.

(2) Salary earned for services rendered in India.

(3) Dividends paid by an Indian company outside India.

(4) Interest, royalty or fees for technical services paid by the government; or by any other person, if the payment is for the purposes of his business activity in India.

For exceptions to the 'deeming' condition, see 'Exempt incomes of non-residents', pp 231–2.

Special provisions

While the law respects the form of the transaction, the Assessing Officer can look to the substance if it appears that the transaction is only aimed at evading tax.

The income of a minor child (except income arising from personal effort, skill or specialised knowledge) will be included in the income of the parent having the greater income.

Income of the spouse from any gift from the taxpayer or by way of remuneration from a concern in which the taxpayer has a substantial interest (ie 20% or greater) will be included in the income of the taxpayer, except where the spouse has appropriate technical or professional qualifications to render the service.

Loans, credits, investments and assets whose sources are not satisfactorily explained will be treated as income.

Arrangements between a resident and a non-resident so as to reduce profits or income in the hands of the resident can be ignored and he can be taxed on the 'reasonable profits'. Dividend stripping is not permissible.

Exempted incomes

Indian tax law totally excludes some incomes from tax. Significant exemptions are agricultural income (on which the States may levy a tax), certain retirement benefits, and incomes of specified bodies such as public charities, professional associations, sports bodies, universities and educational institutions. Incomes of mutual funds are exempt; dividends and long-term capital gains received by venture capital funds and companies are also exempted from assessment year 1996–97. Dividends, interest and long-term capital gains received by funds and companies investing in infrastructure enterprises are also exempted from assessment year 1997–98.

Income from manufacture in a free trade zone, electronic hardware park or software technology park, or earned by a 100% export oriented unit (EOU) is exempted for five consecutive years within the first eight years of manufacturing activity. There is an export commitment of at least 75% of the sales.

For exemptions relating to non-residents including non-resident Indians (NRIs), see Exempt income of non-residents pp 231–2.

Heads of income

The process of computing income, for both companies and non-companies, starts with classifying the income of the year under five heads: profits and gains of business or profession; capital gains; salaries; income from house property; dividends and other sources.

The taxable income is computed under each head with reference to the provisions for income recognition and deductions specific to that head. After adjusting admissible losses, the balance is aggregated for tax.

Business And Professions

Basis of tax

The basis of charge is the income according to the accounts, subject to prescribed exceptions and limits. Thus, the profit for tax will be the profit according to the accounts plus expenses not allowable less deductions that are admissible.

Where the accounts are not to the satisfaction of the Assessing Officer, he may estimate the income.

Broadly, expenses incurred wholly and exclusively for the business or profession (except capital and personal expenditure) are deductible.

Depreciation is admissible on buildings, furniture, plant and machinery (but not on land) used in the business or profession. Depreciation for tax purposes is calculated on the 'written down value' of the block of assets (cost reduced by past depreciation and moneys realised on assets sold) at the liberal rates specified in the Income-tax Rules, even if it be charged in the accounts at lower rates.

Other allowances and conditions

Capital expenditure on scientific research related to the business (except cost of land) is allowable. Payments to a scientific research association, university, or national laboratory will entitle a weighted deduction of 125% of the payment.

Certain other capital expenditures can be amortised:

(1)   Cost of patents and copyrights, over 14 years.

(2)   Cost of know-how, over six years.

(3)   An Indian company or Indian resident can deduct certain preliminary expenses, as well as expenditure on prospecting for certain minerals, over 10 years.

Salary, interest, royalty, fees for technical services and other sums payable to a non-resident will be deducted only if due tax is withheld at source.

Income tax and wealth tax are not deductible.

Transactions with related persons and concerns should follow the 'arm's length' principle. If any payment for goods and services is found to be excessive, the excess will not be allowed.

Even where the accounts are kept on accrual basis, certain expenses such as contributions to employee pension funds, bonus to employees, taxes and duties, and interest on borrowings from public finance institutions will be deducted only if paid before prescribed dates and proof of payment is attached with the return.

Entertainment expenditure is restricted to Rs10,000 plus 50% of the balance.

Head office expenditure incurred outside India by a non-resident will be restricted to 5% of the Indian income with certain adjustments, or the actuals, whichever is less.

To encourage prospecting for oil and natural gas, certain special reliefs have been provided as follows:

(a) The government may agree to grant the prospector special allowances for:

- exploration expenses on areas that are surrendered before starting commercial production

- drilling and exploration expenses for commercial production

- depletion of oil in the mining area

The agreement will supersede the tax law.

(b) If a prospector or a supplier of services and equipment enters into a joint-venture with the government, the latter can specify the rate of tax and the manner in which they are to be taxed. The currently specified rate for a foreign company is 50%, as against the general rate of 55%.

(c) The income of a non-resident supplier of services, including equipment on hire, will be taken to be a flat 10% of the total charges.

Accounts and audit

Under company law, companies have to maintain their accounts on an accrual basis. For others, accounts may be on a cash or on an accrual basis. The government can specify accounting standards to be followed by any class of taxpayers or for any class of income.

All companies, irrespective of income, have to get their accounts audited under company law. Any other taxpayer with a turnover of Rs4 million or with professional receipts of Rs1 million, is also required to maintain accounts and have them audited. The audit report in the prescribed format has to be filed by 30 November (in the case of a company) and by 31 October (in any other case). Separate audit reports and certificates are also required to support claims for certain deductions.

Capital Gains

Calculating capital gains

Capital gains arise when a capital asset is transferred, and is the surplus of the consideration for the transfer, over the cost of acquisition of the asset, the cost of any improvement to it, and transfer-related expenses.

Long-term and short-term capital gains

Profits on the transfer of capital assets held for more than 36 months (more than 12 months for shares, listed securities and units of mutual funds) are long-term capital gains. The transfer of assets held for shorter periods gives rise to short-term capital gains.

Capital gains on the sale of assets entitled to depreciation is treated as short-term capital gains.

For carry forward of losses under this head, see 'Adjusting losses', p 227.

Capital gain that is not taxable

Any capital profit from the following transactions is not taxable:

(1) Transfer of capital assets by a company to its 100% subsidiary or its 100% holding company, which relationship should continue for eight years from the date of transfer; and the transferee, which should be an Indian company, should not convert the capital asset into stock in trade during this period.

(2) Transfer, in a scheme of amalgamation, of capital assets by an amalgamating company to the amalgamated company, or of shares

by a shareholder of an amalgamating company in exchange for shares in the amalgamated company, where the latter is an Indian company.

(3) Transfer, in a scheme of amalgamation, of shares in an Indian company, by the amalgamating foreign company to the amalgamated foreign company, if at least 25% of the shareholders of the amalgamating foreign company continued to be shareholders of the amalgamated foreign company, and the transfer did not attract capital gains tax in the country of incorporation of the amalgamating company.

(4) Any transfer by one non-resident to another non-resident, of shares or bonds of an Indian company purchased in foreign currency.

(5) Any sale of capital assets by an industrial undertaking while shifting from an urban to a non-urban area, if the proceeds are re-invested in similar assets in the new location within a specified period.

Indexing cost to inflation

A resident can claim an 'indexed cost' of acquisition and improvement, on the basis of a Cost Inflation Index notified for each year commencing April 1981. The benefit of indexation is also available to a non-resident, except on the sale of shares and debentures in Indian companies. In the latter case, capital gain will be calculated by converting the cost and sale prices to the currency of purchase, so that the non-resident is protected from exchange rate variations between the dates of purchase and sale. Neither facility is available to foreign institutional investors.

Tax on capital gains

Long-term capital gains are taxed at concessional rates. A resident individual or Hindu undivided family, *a domestic company*, and a non-resident taxpayer including a foreign company will pay tax at 20% on long-term capital gains. Long-term capital gains arising to a venture capital fund or company *and to an infrastructure fund or company* from the transfer of specified equity shares are exempt. Any other resident taxpayer will be charged at 30%.

Short-term capital gains are aggregated with the other incomes and charged at normal rates.

For special rates for non-residents, see 'Tax on Certain Incomes' p 233.

Salary, House Property, Dividends etc

Salary

Salary accrues when due, and arises in India if the services were performed in India. It includes compensation on retrenchment or on variation of service agreement. Specified retirement benefits, travel grants, and certain other perquisites are exempted generally.

Some perquisites have values imputed to them. Accommodation is basically valued at 10% of the salary plus the amount by which the fair rent exceeds 50% of the salary (60% in the four cities of Bombay, Madras, Delhi and Calcutta). The perquisite value of a motor car provided for office and personal use will be Rs600 per month for a car of 16 hp (engine capacity 1.88 litres) or less; and Rs800 per month for a larger car.

Also see 'Exempt income of non-residents', pp 231–2.

Income from house property

Income from buildings and adjunct lands owned by the taxpayer falls under this head. The basis of charge is the annual value, ie, the rent which the property can reasonably fetch, or the actual rent, if higher. Deductions are available for specified expenses. Property used by the taxpayer for his own residence or business is excluded.

Dividends and other sources

Incomes such as dividends, interest, ground rent, mining rent, royalty, etc which do not fall in the other four heads are charged as income from other sources. Dividends are chargeable when declared. Shareholders are not given credit for any tax paid by the company on its income. A loan by a closely held company to a shareholder holding 10% of the voting power, or to a concern in which he has a 20% interest, will be deemed to be dividend. Bonus shares issued by capitalising past profits are not considered to be dividend. Non-capital expenditure laid out wholly for earning the income is deductible. Windfall earnings (from lotteries, races, gambling, etc) are also taxed under this head.

Deductions and Tax Holidays

Deductions

Donations to charity, medical insurance premiums, etc qualify for deduction from the income, subject to limits. Life insurance premiums, contributions to retirement funds and other specified savings schemes, are eligible for tax rebate, subject to limits.

As an exception to the general rule that dividends are taxable, dividends received by a domestic company from another domestic company are not taxed, if the former distributes an equivalent sum as dividend before the statutory date for filing the return of income.

Tax holidays

Indian tax law provides a number of tax holiday schemes, as follows:

(1) Profits from exports, and from hotel and travel agency, are entitled to 100% tax relief.

(2) Profits from 'foreign projects' and royalty from foreign enterprise for use of patent or similar property right, and fee for technical or professional services rendered outside India are entitled to 50% tax relief.

(3) Profits from a new industrial undertaking in specified backward States, or power project anywhere in India, starting manufacture or generation before the end of March 1998 enjoy a 100% tax holiday for the first five years, and 30% for the next five years.

(4) Profits from the activity of developing, maintaining and operating an 'infrastructure facility' enjoy a 100% tax holiday for the first five years, and 30% thereafter.

(5) *Profits from scientific research and development activity also enjoy a similar tax benefit.*

Certain conditions such as remittance to India of sale proceeds in foreign exchange, audit certification of accounts, etc apply.

Minimum Alternate Tax (MAT)

It may happen that the deductions, allowances and tax holidays may lead to a zero-tax or marginal tax, even when there is substantial income in fact. Where the income adjusted for tax purposes is less than 30% of the book profit, a minimum tax of 12% for an Indian company and 16.5% for a foreign company has been prescribed. Companies engaged in the power and infrastructure sectors are exempted.

Tax Assessment

Returns

Each taxpayer has to file a return of income or loss for the previous year by specified dates:

i)	Company	30 November
ii)	Non-company, which is required to get its accounts audited, or furnish audit certificates for claiming certain deductions (see para 3.6)	31 October
iii)	Non-company, having income from business but not requiring audit	31 August
iv)	Non-company, no income from business	30 June

These dates are mandatory. If the return is delayed, interest at 2% per month or part thereof, on the tax (excluding advance tax and withheld tax) has to be paid, and proof of payment attached with the return.

Declaring losses

To get the benefit of carrying forward losses under business or capital gains, or from the activity of owning racehorses, the returns have to be filed within the mandatory dates.

Enclosures to the return

The annual accounts and auditor's report, audit certificates supporting claims for specified deductions, proof of payment of advance tax including any interest and self-assessment tax, certificates for withheld tax for which credit is claimed, computation of depreciation and total income according to the income tax law, are some of the documents that have to be furnished along with the return of income or loss.

Assessment process

The income disclosed is generally accepted, subject to adjustment of prima facie incorrect claims. Any further tax found due on such adjustment will carry a 20% additional levy. The system is thus basically one of self-assessment. The Assessing Officer may scrutinise selected cases. If the taxpayer does not file a return despite notice, or fails to produce the accounts and evidence for scrutiny, the Assessing Officer may make the assessment ex parte, to the best of his information. An order of assessment after scrutiny or a tax demand arising from an adjustment of prima facie incorrect claims has to be made within three years from the end of the accounting year.

Partnerships

Salary to working partners and interest paid to partners as per the partnership agreement are deductible up to specified limits. The partner will bear the tax on the salary and interest received by him, and the firm will be taxed on the profit in its accounts.

Associations of persons (AOP)

An AOP comprises two or more persons joining in an activity for profit. An AOP is taxed at the maximum marginal rate of 40% in most cases.

Trusts

Public trusts set up for religious or charitable purposes are generally exempt from tax, if specified conditions are met. Private discretionary trusts (where the shares of the beneficiaries are not known) are taxed at the maximum marginal rate of 40%. In the case of a private trust where their shares are known, the beneficiaries are taxed on their share of income, either directly or through the trustees; but if the trust has income from business, the maximum marginal rate will apply.

Joint-ventures

Joint-ventures (JV) between a non-resident and a resident in India will be taxed according to the constitution of the JV, ie, as a partnership, association of persons, or company, as the case may be.

Non-residents and their agents

A non-resident may appoint an agent in India to look after his tax matters, failing which it is open to the Assessing Officer to treat an employee of the non-resident, or a person with a business connection in India, or through whom the non-resident receives any income, as the agent of the non-resident for tax purposes.

Adjusting losses

Losses are dealt with in three steps, as follows:

(1) Intra-head adjustment: Loss from a source is first set off against income from a source under the same 'head of income', eg loss from one house property is first set off against income from another house property in the same year.

(2) Inter-head adjustment: Any loss under a 'head of income' remaining after step (1) is set off against income from another head, in the same year, eg an uncovered loss from house property can be set off from salary income in the same year. Exceptions are: loss from speculation business, capital loss, and loss in owning racehorses, which losses cannot be set off against incomes from other heads.

(3) Carry forward: The unadjusted loss (and depreciation) for any year, after steps (1) and (2), is carried forward to be set off against future incomes, to the extent indicated below:

Nature of loss	Whether can be carried	No of years	Conditions for set-off
Salary	No	–	–
House Property	No	–	–
Business:			
a. Speculation:			
Depreciation	Yes	8 years	Only against speculation profits
Other loss	Yes	8 years	Only against speculation profits
b. Other business:			
Depreciation	Yes	8 years	First against business income, then against any other income
Other loss	Yes	8 years	Only against business income
Capital loss, long term and short-term	Yes	8 years	Only against capital gains
Others sources:			
a. Owning racehorses	Yes	4 years	Only against income of the same nature
b. Other losses	No	–	–

A closely held company can claim set-off of past loss only if 51% of the shares were held by the same persons who held the shares in the year the loss was incurred.

To encourage the revival of loss-making companies, such companies (in industry and shipping) may pass on the benefit of their accumulated loss and depreciation to the company into which they amalgamate. This requires a clearance from the Board for Industrial and Financial Reconstruction. When a healthy company amalgamates into a sick company, the latter retains the right to carry forward its accumulated loss and depreciation.

Appeals

The taxpayer can appeal to the Commissioner (Appeals). The Revenue and the taxpayer can appeal further to the Income-tax Appellate Tribunal. On points of law, questions can be referred to the High Court and further appealed to the Supreme Court. Only lawyers can appear in the courts. Lawyers, accountants, or employees, duly authorised, can appear before tax authorities and the Tribunal.

Advance rulings

Indian tax law did not envisage advance rulings being given in specific cases. However, non-residents can now obtain, in advance, a binding ruling from the Authority for Advance Rulings on issues which could arise in determining their tax liabilities. The ruling will bind the applicant and the Revenue with reference to the transaction (or proposed transaction) which was the subject of the question.

Advance clearances

Transactions in land and buildings exceeding specified values in certain cities need a prior clearance. A non-resident leaving India after a stay of 120 days or more has to obtain a tax clearance certificate. Remittances of interest, dividends, royalty and technical fees to a non-resident require a clearance, if tax is sought to be deducted at less than the rates given in 'Withholding Tax for Non-Residents', p 235.

Tax Payment

Modes of tax payment

Tax is paid in advance, by deduction at source (withholding tax), by self-assessment when filing the return, and on receipt of a notice of demand from the Assessing Officer.

Advance tax

Advance tax is a 'pay as you earn' scheme. The taxpayer pays advance tax on his own estimate, after adjusting estimated credit for tax deducted at source. Advance tax is paid in instalments as under:

Due dates	Companies	Others
15 June	minimum of 15% of the advance tax for the year	nil
15 September	minimum of 45% of the the advance tax less prior instalment paid	minimum of 30% of advance tax for the year
15 December	minimum of 75% of the advance tax less prior instalments paid	minimum of 60% of the advance tax less prior instalments paid
15 March	100% of the advance tax less prior instalments paid	100% of the advance tax less prior instalments paid

Failure to pay advance tax, or short payment, carries mandatory interest of 2%; and deferment of an instalment of advance tax carries mandatory interest of 1.5%, per month or part thereof. This interest should be paid before the returns are due, and proof of payment should be attached with the return.

Tax deduction at source

On a variety of payments specified in the law, the payer is required to withhold tax at source, and pay it to the government. The payee can claim credit for the amount so withheld, in his tax return. For this purpose, the payer issues a certificate of deduction of tax to the payee. These certificates should be filed with the return to support the claim for tax credit.

The rate at which tax is to be deducted on each type of payment is specified in the Finance Act of each year. Important payments are salaries, interest, dividends, rent, income from units of mutual funds, lottery and race winnings, payments to contractors and sub-contractors, payments for professional and technical services, and certain incomes for non-residents. (For provisions relating to non-residents, see p 235.) The tax deductor has to file with the tax office periodical statements of the taxes deducted by him and paid to the government.

Self-assessment tax

Before the dates by which the returns are due, the taxpayer should pay any tax that may be due on the basis of the income being disclosed, after taking credit for the advance tax and withheld tax. Any interest that may be due for delayed filing of the return, or for short payment or deferment of the advance tax, has also to be paid. Proof of payment should be attached with the return.

Tax due on assessment

Any tax found due on adjustment of prima facie incorrect claims, or on assessment after scrutiny, is payable within 30 days of a notice to be served on the taxpayer or his representative.

Special Provisions for Non-residents

Tax liability and procedures

Non-residents are liable to pay tax in India on income that arises, or is received, in India. Indian branches of foreign companies are taxed on their Indian earnings. Head office expenses of a non-resident, claimed as a deduction from its business income in India, will be restricted to 5% of its total income chargeable in India with certain adjustments, or the actuals, whichever is less.

Non-residents have the same liability as residents to file returns of income, deduct tax on payments, credit the tax to government, and other procedural matters. Tax has to be withheld on payments to non-residents by way of salaries, interest or any other sum taxable in India.

Exempt incomes of non-residents

The following incomes of non-residents, although arising or deemed to arise in India, are exempt:

(1) Remuneration received by a consultant for services rendered in India in specified work areas.

(2) Remuneration received by a consultant for services rendered in India under a technical assistance programme approved by the government.

(3) Perquisite value of tax paid on behalf of a foreign technician employed with an approved scientific research institute.

(4)   Passage moneys for going on home leave out of India.

(5)   Income of a non-resident from teaching and research activities and during training, subject to limits.

(6)   Fees received by a foreign company under an agreement with the government for providing technical services related to the security of India.

(7)   Payments for lease of aircraft, received by a non-resident from Indian air transport companies.

(8)   Interest on notified bonds.

(9)   Interest on the balance in a Non-Resident (External) account in any bank in India.

(10)   Income from units in the Unit Trust of India purchased out of funds in a Non-Resident (External) account.

(11)   In the case of a business whose operations are not confined to India, only that part of the income reasonably attributable to the Indian operations will be deemed to arise in India.

(12)   No income will be deemed to arise in India:

- from operations which are confined to the purchase of goods in India for export;
- from activities of non-resident news agencies and news publishers confined to the collection and transmission of news from India;
- from operations confined to the shooting of films in India. This benefit is not available to a citizen of India, or to a firm or company which has a partner or shareholder who is a citizen or a resident of India;
- from a lump sum royalty received from a resident for the transfer of rights for computer software and equipment under a scheme approved by the government.

Also see 'Tax holidays', pp 227–8 and 'Non-resident Indians', p 234.

Income from certain businesses

Non-residents can easily determine their taxable income from certain business activities, at prescribed percentages of the gross charges:

Activity/Who qualifies	Taxable income and conditions
Shipping business/ any non-resident	7.5% of gross shipping charges, received or arising in India. Tax to be paid or other satisfactory arrangement made before ship can leave port. Ship operator can seek to be taxed in the normal manner by an application before end of the assessment year
Providing services and equipment on hire for oil exploration/any non-resident	10% of gross charges received or arising in India
Airlines/any non-resident	5% of gross charges received or arising in India
Civil construction in approved turnkey power projects financed under international aid programme/ foreign company	10% of gross charges earned in India

Tax on certain incomes

Certain incomes of non-residents are charged at concessional rates of tax:

Who qualifies/Source	Rate of tax
Non-resident/Long-term capital gains	20% of the gross amount
Non-resident/Income from dividends, interest on lendings in foreign currency, and income from units in mutual funds, purchased in foreign currency	20% of the gross amount
Non-resident/Interest and dividends on bonds and shares purchased in foreign currency under the Depository Receipt Mechanism, and long-term capital gains on the transfer of such bonds and shares	10% of the gross amount

Who qualifies/Source	Rate of tax
Non-resident sportsman/Income from any sports activity or from advertisement or contribution of articles relating to sports	10% of the gross amount
Non-resident sports association/Income by way of guarantee amounts	10% of the gross amount
Foreign company/Income from royalty or fees for technical services received under an approved agreement	30% of the gross amount
Overseas fund/Income from units in mutual funds, purchased in foreign currency, and long-term capital gains from transfer of such units	10% of the gross amount
Foreign Institutional Investors (FIIs)/ Income from securities (excluding units of mutual funds)	20% of the gross amount
FIIs/Short-term capital gains on sale of such securities	30% of the gross amount
FIIs/Long-term capital gains on sale of such securities	10% of the gross amount

Double tax avoidance agreements usually prescribe lower tax rates on dividends, interest, royalty and technical fees.

A non-resident who has entered into an agreement with the government for a joint-venture for prospecting for and extraction of oil and natural gas will be taxed at 50% on the net income. See Other allowances and conditions, p 219.

Other incomes of a non-resident will be taxed at the normal rates specified in the Finance Act of the year.

Non-resident Indians

Non-resident Indians (NRIs) are either Indian citizens or of Indian origin, who are non-resident. They enjoy certain privileges in tax matters.

An NRI need not file a return of income, if he had income only from assets purchased in foreign exchange and long-term capital gains, and due tax has been deducted at source from such income. The NRI can, on request, continue to enjoy these benefits even after he becomes a 'resident', until the assets are transferred or converted into money. The NRI may also elect to forgo these benefits and be assessed in the normal manner.

The incomes of an NRI from interest on specified savings certificates purchased in convertible foreign exchange, interest on the balance in a Non-Resident (External) account in any bank in India, and income from units in Unit Trust of India purchased out of funds in a NRE account, are exempt.

An NRI will be taxed at 20% on his gross income from foreign currency assets and long-term capital gain. Any long-term capital gain on the transfer of a foreign currency asset will not be taxed, if the proceeds are re-invested in specified assets.

Withholding tax for non-residents

Tax will be withheld at the following general rates on incomes arising to non-residents:

Nature of income	Non-resident Indian	Other Non-resident	Foreign Company
Winnings from lotteries, crossword puzzles, race-horses	40%	40%	40%
Dividends, interest on foreign currency debt	20%	20%	20%
Long-term capital gains	20%	20%	20%
Royalty and technical fees	X	X	30%
Income from assets purchased in foreign exchange	20%	X	X
Other income	30%	30%	55%

Note: X = no specific rates prescribed.

Subtantially lower rates of deduction have been prescribed for some specific incomes of non-residents:

Nature of income	Rate of tax to be deducted
Income from a mutual fund (units in Unit Trust of India acquired by an NRI from funds in Non-Resident (External) account excepted)	20%
Income of an Offshore Fund from units in mutual funds purchased in foreign currency, and long-term capital gains from the transfer of such units	10%
Interest or dividends on bonds or shares in Indian companies purchased in foreign currency, and long-term capital gains from transfer of such assets	10%
Income of a Foreign Institutional Investor from securities listed in a stock exchange (excluding units in mutual funds)	20%
Income of a Foreign Institutional Investor from capital gains on transfer of such securities	no deduction

Double Tax Relief

Double tax avoidance agreements

India has entered into double tax avoidance agreements (DTAAs) with a number of countries to facilitate the cross-border flow of investment and technology. The treaties are mostly variations of the UN Model Convention, with elements of the OECD model incorporated in some cases. Principal features are:

(1) DTAA benefits are available only to residents of either or both of the contracting States.

(2) DTAA will supersede the tax law, but any reliefs under the tax law which are more beneficial will still be available.

(3) The concept of 'permanent establishment' which is central to the agreements limits the liability of the non-resident to tax in the source country on the business profits arising out of the permanent establishment.

(4) Interest, dividends, royalties and fees for technical services are sought to be taxed in India, at lower than normal rates.

(5) 'Tax sparing' provisions are generally included in the agreements with developed countries so that the incentives offered

to non-residents are not nullified by the 'tax-spared' income being taxed in the home country.

(6) Some agreements are limited to aircraft and shipping operations in international traffic.

The agreements also provide for exchange of information on tax evasion. If a person represents to the tax authority of the country of his residence that he has been, or will be, taxed at variance with the agreement, the competent tax authorities of the two countries can consult each other to resolve the issue.

Countries with which India has comprehensive double taxation avoidance agreements are Australia, Austria, Bangladesh, Belgium, Brazil, Bulgaria, Canada, China, Cyprus, Czechoslovakia, Denmark, Finland, France, Germany, Greece, Hungary, Indonesia, Israel, Italy, Japan, Kenya, Libya, Malaysia, Malta, Mauritius, Nepal, Netherlands, New Zealand, Norway, Philippines, Poland, Republic of Korea, Romania, Russian Federation*, Singapore, Spain, Sri Lanka, Sweden, Switzerland, Syria, Tanzania, Thailand, United Arab Emirates, United Arab Republic, United Kingdom, United States of America, Vietnam and Zambia.

(*Agreement with erstwhile USSR)

Double tax relief

Relief from double taxation is given by the credit method: credit is given in the country of residence for the tax paid in the source country on the doubly taxed income.

Where there is no DTAA, Indian tax law provides a resident tax-payer a unilateral credit of the lower of the taxes, calculated at the Indian rate and the foreign rate, on the income doubly taxed.

Other Direct Taxes

Wealth tax

An annual wealth tax is levied on non-productive assets (residences, jewellery and bullion, yachts, aircraft and unutilised urban land) of individuals, Hindu undivided families and companies. Mutual funds are exempted. Certain debts and liabilities are deductible, but debts located outside India are not admissible in the case of a non-citizen, a non-resident, or a foreign company. Wealth tax is charged at 1% of the net wealth exceeding Rs1.5 million.

Gift tax

Gift tax is payable by a donor at 30% of the aggregate value of taxable gifts made by him in any previous year. Public companies, a company in a scheme of amalgamation with an Indian company, and charitable and religious trusts whose income is exempt from tax, are exempted from gift tax.

Expenditure tax

This is a 10% tax on expenditure (including accommodation, food and beverages, and other services) in a hotel where the room charge is Rs1200 or more per day per person. This is collected by the hotel and paid to the government.

Interest tax

A tax at 3% is levied on the gross interest income of 'credit institutions' such as banks and public financial institutions, including companies carrying on hire purchase, investment, and other similar activities. 'Gross interest' includes commitment charges and discounts; but interest earned by a credit institution on loans and advances given to another credit institution is excluded.

Interest tax is deductible in computing the income tax of the credit institution. Interest tax is payable in advance during the accounting year, in three instalments due on 15 September, 15 December and 15 March. Returns are to be filed by 31 December of the following year.

CHAPTER 16

THE STRUCTURE OF INDIRECT TAX IN INDIA
by M R Sivaraman

INDIRECT TAXES—A MAJOR SOURCE OF REVENUE

Indirect taxes in India accounted for 12.74% of Gross Domestic Product (GDP) in 1995–96 with the Centre (Federal Government) having 7.03% and the States 5.71%. The direct taxes accounted for only 3.08% with the Centre having 2.89% and States 0.19%, clearly indicating the predominance of indirect taxes as a source of revenue to the government. Over the years, dependence on indirect taxes has not declined as the proportion of revenue raised through indirect taxes stood at 81% in 1994–95, 86.02% in 1990–91, 85.55% in 1985–86 and 83.53% in 1980–81.

STRUCTURE OF INDIRECT TAXES AS DEFINED BY THE CONSTITUTION

The structure of indirect taxes in India is defined by the Constitution in its two Lists in the Seventh Schedule.

In List I (Union List), Entries

83. Duties of customs including export duties

84. Duties of excise on tobacco and other goods manufactured or produced in India except

    a)   Alcoholic liquors for human consumption;

    b)   Opium, Indian hemp and other narcotic drugs and narcotics, but including medicinal and toilet preparations containing alcohol or any substance included in sub-paragraph (b) of this entry.

89. Terminal taxes on goods or passengers carried by Railway, Sea or Air; Taxes on Railway fares and freights.

90. Taxes other than Stamp duties on transactions in Stock Exchange and futures markets.

92. Taxes on the sale or purchase of newspapers and on advertisement published therein.

97. Any other matter not enumerated in List II or List III including any tax not mentioned in either of those Lists.

In List II (State List), Entries

50. Taxes on mineral rights subject to any limitations imposed by Parliament by law relating to mineral development.

51. Duties of excise on the following goods manufactured or produced in the State and countervailing duties at the same or lower rates on similar goods manufactured or produced elsewhere in India:-

    a) Alcoholic liquors for human consumption;

    b) Opium, Indian hemp and other narcotic drugs and narcotics, but not including medicinal and toilet preparations containing alcohol or any substance included in the sub-paragraph (b) of this entry.

52. Taxes on the entry of goods into a local area for consumption, use or sale therein.

53. Taxes on the consumption or sale of electricity.

54. Taxes on the sale or purchase of goods other than newspapers, subject to the provisions of Entry 92A of List I.

These powers cannot be changed unless the Constitution itself is amended. There have been major decisions of the Supreme Court of India reiterating the inviolability of these provisions whenever consciously or unconsciously any State has attempted to transgress them. Therefore, any reforms of indirect taxes in India are dependent on provisions of the Constitution.

TYPES OF INDIRECT TAXES

The indirect taxes levied by the Centre and the States in general are represented below:

Centre		
Trade Taxes		
Customs Duties	Import duties	Minor cesses on export of agricultural items to finance research
	Additional duties of customs (equivalent in most cases to the rates of excise duties)	
	Anti-dumping duties (wherever levied in accordance with the principle agreed to in the Final Round of Uruguay Talks)	
Excise Duty	Mostly ad valorem on all manufactures Duty is levied only at the stage of manufacture–ie at the first point of sale	Full set-off/ credit given to duty paid at input stage
Service Tax	Levied at 5% on telephone stock brockers and General Insurance service	No set-off given

States
Sales Tax
Central Sales Tax (levied by Centre and collected by the States)
Excise Duty on the medicines & toilet preparations collected by the States
Octroi/Entry Taxes levied on entry of goods into municipal areas for municipal purposes
Annual tax on motor vehicles
Excise duty on liquor
Stamp duties/registration fee on documents
Land Revenue
Agricultural income tax (generally on plantation crops)

TAX REFORMS

Since the beginning of economic liberalisation, there have been simultaneous reforms in tax structure. Most have been confined to the Union Government with many State governments only starting the process recently. The Central Government's main thrust of reform has been in the area of indirect taxes (that is, customs duty and central excise duty) which even today account for about 70% of the tax revenues of the government.

Customs Duty

The reforms started in 1991–92 with reduction of the peak rate of import duty to 150% and downward adjustment in many other rates. In the Budget for the year 1995–96, the government brought down the peak rate of duty to 50% with the average realisation rate reducing to 28% from a high of over 44% in 1991–92. The various requirements of bonds, certificates, test reports, end use certificates, etc were abolished with a few exceptions for concessional or duty free imports. Applicable rates of duty have been rationalised to the extent that there are no more than three rates in a chapter. The bulk of the components and parts required by industry in India carry a rate of duty of only 25% as against 65% in 1993. Further, the additional customs duty levied can be fully set off against domestic excise duty payable on the final product.

There were many specific duties in force till the year 1991–92. During the last four years, they have all been made ad valorem, leaving little scope for disputes on classification of goods or on rates.

In order to encourage the growth of industrial units in specified sectors such as leather goods, electronics and telecommunications, special concessional rates have been continued. All import items used for export production are duty exempt.

The direction in which India is moving is clear, that is, to have a duty regime which is similar to those in the newly industrialising countries within the next two to three years. Indian industries engaged in competitive areas should be able to reorganise production to meet external competition in that time.

The process of downward adjustment of rates continued in the budget for 1996–97.

Excise Duty

The other major component of indirect taxes is the central excise duty which is applicable only at the manufacturer level. There are eight rates of duty applicable now, namely, 50%, 40%, 30%, 25%, 20%, 15%, 5% and 'Nil' rate of duty. The peak rate of 50% is applicable to polyester filament yarn. The bulk of the commodities are subject to 25%, 20% or 15%, average rate on the basis of total clearance being about 18–19%. Even though a European type of VAT is still not in force, there is a complete set-off given to all duties paid at the input stage. The additional customs duty paid on imports which is equivalent to the excise duty payable or leviable on domestically manufactured products is also given full set-off when used as inputs. Assessments are at the factory gate level based on invoices issued by the manufacturers. There are still legal wrangles when sales are made at depots, as assessable values have to be derived on a normative basis on the basis of law laid down in this regard by the Supreme Court of India. A recent judgment of that Court has set at rest many controversies in such cases and it is hoped that there will be fewer disputes. Ideally, there have to be suitable amendments to the Central Excises and Salt Act making invoices issued at the factory gate or in depots the basis of all assessments.

MODVAT

The set-off allowed under the Indian excise duty system known as the MODVAT (Modified Value Added Tax) provides input duty relief at all stages of manufacture on all inputs. The facility has not been extended to office equipment, certain types of tobacco products and woven fabrics. Duty relief is provided on capital goods and full deduction is allowed in the first year. This facility given with effect from April, 1994 has accelerated the growth of the capital goods industry to 22% in the year 1994–95, and a little over 20% in 1995–96.

SALES TAX/OTHER MUNICIPAL TAXES

Under the Indian Constitution, the revenue from excise duty is to be shared between the Union and the States and under the current dispensation, 47.5% of net revenue after cost of collection goes to the States. The sales tax levied by States at the wholesale and/or at the retail level, depending upon the stage at which it is levied, is an addition to the manufacturing stage excise duty. No set-off is available for excise duty paid against sales tax payable. In addition, there are also municipal taxes such as octroi or entry tax on which there is no set-off.

PROGRESSION TOWARDS VAT

The reforms in indirect taxes carried out at the Central government level are slowly having their impact on the State governments. The Union Finance Minister, in consultation with the State Finance Ministers, has constituted a Group of Ministers to study the prospects for reform in State sales taxes and a progression towards VAT. Many State governments have made a number of changes in the administration of sales tax to simplify it. Rates have been slashed in the case of many commodities. Andhra Pradesh, Tamil Nadu and Kerala have boldly introduced the concept of VAT in the case of selected commodities. Studies are being conducted to extend the scope of VAT.

The Government of Maharashtra, a major industrialised State, made radical changes in the Sales Tax Act in 1995 as an initial move towards the introduction of VAT. Set-off against duty payable on inputs has been introduced. Competitive rate-cutting among States to attract business and industry, which erodes the revenue base, has attracted attention and is now being taken up as an important area for reform.

CENTRAL SALES TAX/CONSIGNMENT TAX

One of the more ticklish areas of sales tax reform is the central sales tax and the still-to-be imposed consignment tax. The former is levied on all goods sold in the course of interstate sales and the latter could be levied if and when it comes into force when goods move as consignments from one State to another without an actual interstate sale having taken place. The current origin-based central sales tax has been a subject of study particularly because it leads to distortion in resource availability and tends to weaken already resource-weak States. Producing States feel that when goods are moved out as consignments or as stock transfers to other States they are deprived of revenue. They want imposition of a consignment tax which is permitted under the Indian Constitution but which has not yet come into force.

CONCLUSION

Any examination of the Indian tax structure has to be undertaken against the background of the development of India and not in a purely theoretical framework. After all, the public policy of governments is a judicious mixture of politics and economics and no country, however developed, is free from political ideologies influencing its economic decisions. India being a federation with 25 States, with many State governments having different political parties in power, no reform can be abruptly introduced. Indian tax reforms will therefore inevitably be slow. Reforms which are accepted by all State governments will have greater chances of success.

The indirect taxes of the Centre have undergone substantial modifications, the benefits of which have been reflected in the acceleration of industrial growth and increase in revenues in the last two years. The State governments have shown adequate response by making changes in the sales tax system and taking initial steps towards the introduction of a VAT. This caution is more than justified as the States are strapped for resources and do not want to take any step that will tend to worsen their budget deficits. Nevertheless, all States have recently agreed to reform sales tax to bring in greater uniformity in rates, exemptions and procedures.

Tax reforms necessarily lead to the modernisation of tax administration. High rates of tax, and an intensely regulatory tax regime were reflected hitherto in low tax bases and an inherent tendency to evade taxes. Tax administration at the Union Government level is slowly, but inexorably, being revamped. An extensive computer network has been established for Indian Customs. At New Delhi, a fully functional EDIFAX facility has been set up with state-of-the-art technology. This is being extended to other Customs Houses. Similarly, an extensive computer network is being established for the central excise. Facilities for on-line feeding of required data from factories subject to excise duty are proposed.

At the State government level, the sales tax system is also being computerised. State governments are contemplating building their VAT around a fully computerised administrative network.

CHAPTER 17

CAPITAL AND SECURITIES MARKETS AND REGULATIONS
by R K Pandey

The process of liberalisation, since 1991, has set in motion significant changes in the Indian capital and securities markets. The simultaneous repeal of the Capital Issues (Control) Act, 1947, and the promulgation of the Securities and Exchange Board of India Act in 1992 led to the end of direct government control on the capital market. With this, the Securities and Exchange Board of India has been entrusted with the task of both regulating and developing the capital market in the country. However, the matters relating to Global Depository Receipts (companies raising capital in the global markets) continue to be under government control.

The years from 1991 have witnessed a discernible trend towards financial market liberalisation in the form of extending greater market access, facilitating portfolio investment flows and an increase in investment alternatives. As a result, the securities market has become an important source for mobilisation of resources for corporations. Before turning to the specifics of the manner in which the securities market in India is regulated it would be useful to give an account of the size of the market.

Approximate Size of the Indian Capital Market

No. of stock exchanges in India		23 (including National Stock Exchange and Over the Counter Exchange of India)
No. of listed companies		7000 (approx)
Market capitalisation	at 31.3.93	US$ 59.72 billion
	at 31.3.94	US$109.35 billion
	at 31.3.95	US$150.29 billion

No. of Public/Rights issues during

	Public	Rights
April 93–March 94	773	370
April 94–March 95	1341	323

Money raised by Indian corporations
from the domestic market during

	Public	Rights
	(in US$ billion)	
April 93–March 94	5.15	2.97
April 94–March 95	7.01	2.16

Table Showing Intermediaries Registered With SEBI
(At 31 March 1995)

Name of the Intermediary	Number
Brokers	6700 (approx)
Mutual funds	22
Foreign institutional investors	308
Foreign brokers acting as agents of registered FIIs	26
Merchant bankers	790
Registrar/share transfer agents	264
Debenture trustees	20
Underwriters	36
Bankers to the issue	70
Portfolio managers	61
Asset management companies with foreign participation	8

STATUTORY ACTS FOR REGULATING THE SECURITIES MARKET

The securities market in India is regulated with the help of three Statutory Acts:

(1) The Securities and Exchange Board of India Act, 1992. This is for the regulation and development of the securities market, both primary and secondary, and protection of interests of investors in the country. It empowers the Securities and Exchange Board of India (SEBI) to regulate the primary and secondary markets including mutual funds, by issuing guidelines for the issue of capital by corporations to the public, by monitoring stock exchanges and the

intermediaries in the primary as well as the secondary markets. It also empowers SEBI to take punitive measures for maintaining integrity of the market. This Act is administered by SEBI.

(2) The Companies Act, 1956. governs the incorporation, management, administration, operations, functioning and winding up of companies. This Act also contains provisions to regulate the issue of capital and other matters such as contents and formats of prospectuses, issue of shares and debentures, issue of certificates, transfer of shares and debentures, payment of dividend and interests, rights of shareholders, provisions of shareholders' meeting and contents and format of annual accounts of companies. This Act is administered by the Department of Company Affairs and the Company Law Board, Government of India, though some sections are concurrently administered by SEBI.

(3) Securities Contract (Regulation) Act, 1956. This Act prevents undesirable transactions in securities by regulating the business of dealing therein, and by providing certain matters connected therewith. Through this Act and statutory rules framed thereunder, the Central Government regulates the secondary market, trading in securities and functioning of the stock exchanges. The Act empowers the Central Government and SEBI to recognise the stock exchanges, withdraw their recognition, direct rules to be made, approve, make and amend the by-laws, supersede the governing bodies in the stock exchanges, suspend business of recognised stock exchanges, declare certain contracts illegal and void in certain circumstances, prohibit contracts in certain cases, license dealers in securities and compel listing of securities by public companies and lay down penalties and procedures for contravention of the provisions of the Act. This Act is administered concurrently by the Ministry of Finance, Government of India, as well as SEBI.

Securities and Exchange Board of India

The Securities and Exchange Board of India was set up in 1988 as an apex body under the Ministry of Finance for the protection of investors and for the promotion of orderly and healthy growth of the securities market. It was accorded statutory status in 1992 through enactment of the SEBI Act. It has its Head Office at Bombay and three Regional Offices at New Delhi, Calcutta and Madras. It is at present the most important regulatory authority in the country in respect of the securities market. None of the corporates can raise capital from the public in India without seeking SEBI's approval. Its objectives are (i) investor protection; (ii) promotion and development of the capital market, and (iii) regulation of the securities market.

Capital mobilisation

The Securities and Exchange Board of India has laid down prudential norms for capital mobilisation by corporations. Accordingly, companies can freely raise capital from the public without obtaining consent from the government. The only requirement is to file a copy of the offer document or the letter of offer with SEBI who will satisfy itself in respect of compliance of its guidelines on disclosure and investor protection.

Guidelines on disclosure and investor protection

The SEBI has issued guidelines for disclosure and investor protection which apply to issues of capital to the public made after the repeal of the Capital Issues (Control) Act, 1947.

Pricing of issues

Corporations are free to price their issues. Specific disclosure requirements have been introduced for justification of the issue price. Some of these are disclosure of net asset value of the company and high and low price of securities for the last two years. Companies need to justify the basis on which they want to price their issue.

New companies can also charge premiums provided they are promoted by corporations with track records of profitability and these corporations pick up a minimum 50% of the equity.

Book-building

Companies with an issue size of Rs1000 million or more may use the book-building process for that part of the issue which can be allotted on a firm basis.

Disclosures

Specific disclosures need to be made by the companies regarding the project details, means of financing, working capital, history of the company, promoters and their background, management, technological processes, marketing of product, implementation schedules, government approvals, outstanding litigation and the adequacy of redressal mechanism set up by them for responding to grievances of the investors.

A draft prospectus filed with the SEBI is required to be sent to stock exchanges where the issue is proposed to be listed.

Risk factors

It is mandatory for companies going public to indicate risk factors in their prospectuses.

Credit rating

Credit rating, by the established rating agencies (ICRA, CRISIL, CARE etc) for all debt instruments having a maturity beyond 18 months is mandatory.

Underwriting and devolvement

Underwriting is optional. If a company does not receive 90% of the issued amount from public subscription together with accepted devolvement from underwriters within 60 days from the date of the closure of the issue, the company is required to refund the entire amount of subscription. In cases of refund, delay beyond 78 days attracts interest at 15% as per s 73 of the Companies Act.

Minimum subscription

Promoters need to pick up a minimum 25% equity in any issue (limited to 20% of the post-issue capital). Similarly, a minimum 25% equity needs to be offered to the public. For other categories, the following reservations limits apply:

Mutual funds	20%
Non-resident Indians/ Overseas corporate bodies/ Foreign institutional investors	24%
Financial institutions	20%
Permanent employees	10%
Shareholders of group companies	10%

Promoters' contribution to the extent of 25% of the issue or 20% of the post-issue capital needs to be locked in for a period of five years.

Shares in excess of the minimum contribution need to be locked in for three years.

Deployment of proceeds

The guidelines prescribe voluntary disclosures regarding arrangements for monitoring the deployment of issue proceeds.

Advertisement code

An advertisement code has been laid down for public and rights issue by the SEBI.

Investors' protection

The SEBI has also set up an investors' grievances and guidance division which takes up complaints of investors against companies.

A stock invest facility has been introduced.

The SEBI has appointed public representatives to supervise the allotment process.

Investors' associations have been accorded recognition by the SEBI for creating greater awareness among investors.

Listing of securities

The Companies Act, 1956, enjoins companies intending to offer shares and other securities to the public to apply to one or more recognised stock exchanges and get listing approval within 10 weeks from the closure of subscription.

It has recently been decided that an issuer will not be able to come out with a public issue if it has been in commercial operations for less than two years and has a post-issue capital of less than Rs50 million except through the OTCEI or less than Rs30 million through any other exchange if such other exchange follows the requirement of market making and offers electronic trading facility.

It is obligatory for a company to have its shares listed on a stock exchange nearest to its registered office. A company having a paid-up capital of Rs50 million and above should also get its securities listed on another stock exchange (in addition to the one near its registered office).

The Securities Contract (Regulation) Rules require that listing on a recognised stock exchange can be accorded only to a public limited company with a minimum issued equity capital of Rs30 million (approx US$1 million) in which a minimum of 25% has been offered to the general public for subscription.

The Bombay Stock Exchange has recently increased the threshold limit for listing of securities with it by companies from Rs30 million to Rs50 million.

While listing the securities of a company, the stock exchange enters into a listing agreement with it. The listing agreement makes the company responsive to the interests of the investors at large.

Market intermediaries

The Securities and Exchange Board of India Act, 1992 and the Regulations framed thereunder make it compulsory for market intermediaries like the merchant bankers, registrars to the issue, share transfer agents, underwriters, advisers/consultants, stock brokers, sub-brokers, debenture trustees, portfolio managers, bankers to the issue, mutual funds etc to be registered with SEBI. Without such registration, it is illegal to carry on work in these areas.

The regulations lay down requirements for registration which, inter alia, include norms relating to capital adequacy, personnel, infrastructure, space etc.

Credit rating agencies

Credit rating is of recent origin in India. The first credit rating service, the Credit Rating Investment Services of India Ltd (CRISIL) began its operations from 1 January 1988. Its main promoters are ICICI, UTI and the Housing Development Finance Corporation of India Limited. It rates corporate debt such as debentures, preference shares, fixed deposits, commercial paper, securitisation programmes and structured obligations. In addition, it also provides information and advisory services.

The Industrial Information and Credit Rating Agency of India Ltd (ICRA) was set up in 1991 by IFCI, banks and investment institutions. It provides its services for determining the credit risk associated with a debt instrument/credit obligation. It also provides information on selected sectors/ industries. Recently, it has announced its intention of starting equity rating operations.

Credit Analysis and Research Ltd (CARE), promoted by IDBI and financial institutions, started rating debt instruments in 1993.

Trading systems

Trading on the stock exchanges takes place through registered members. The memberships are both individual and corporate. In fact an increasing number of members are converting their individual memberships into corporates. Foreign broking firms (excepting banks) are allowed membership of the Indian bourses provided they obtain requisite approvals from the government and the Reserve Bank of India.

Trading in most of the stock exchanges is through the traditional open outcry system. However, in four of the exchanges, the National Stock Exchange, Over the Counter Exchange of India, Delhi Stock Exchange and the Bombay Stock Exchange, trading is now entirely screen-based and on-line. Most other exchanges are making efforts to switch over to screen-based, on-line systems as early as possible.

In four major stock exchanges at Bombay, Delhi, Calcutta and Ahmedabad scrips are divided into two categories, ie specified and non-specified. Non-specified scrips are traded only for cash and the settlement is on a weekly basis. Trades in respect of scrips in the specified category could hitherto (till March 1994) be either settled in cash or carried forward. Settlements in the specified category were on a fortnightly basis. However, after March 1994, even specified scrips need to be settled in cash though the settlement period continues to be fortnightly. In all other exchanges all trades need to be settled in cash on a weekly basis and there is no distinction between specified or non-specified shares.

An important feature of the settlement system on the Indian bourses is that trading on days of the week is regarded as one trading cycle and the settlement takes place for all trades undertaken during the week. As all deliveries are to be physically effected, there are delays in settlement mainly because of lack of a national clearing system and depositories. These problems are likely to be redressed since a legal framework for depositories is now in place. A national clearing system is also expected to be put in place. These steps are likely to bring trading on Indian bourses in line with international practices.

National Stock Exchange

The National Stock Exchange, promoted by the Industrial Development Bank of India, insurance companies and banks, provides nationwide trading facilities for equities, debt instruments and hybrids in a fair, efficient and transparent environment using electronic trading systems. It has helped in considerably reducing the settlement cycles and has provided much needed transparent competition to the traditional stock exchanges. It began operations in 1994.

OTC Exchange of India

Promoted by the Unit Trust of India, Industrial Credit and Investment Corporation of India, Industrial Bank of India, SBI Capital Markets, Industrial Finance Corporation of India, Life Insurance Corporation of India, General Insurance Corporation of India and Canbank Financial Services, the Over the Counter Exchange of India provides small and medium sized companies, with an issued capital of Rs3 million to Rs250 million (US$100 thousand to US$8 million), an access to the market. It is a computerised, ringless, scripless exchange with a nationwide trading network. It has an understanding with NASDAQ of the United States of America.

Trading volumes

The Bombay Stock Exchange accounted for almost 42% of the total turnover of all exchanges during 1993–94 and 1994–95 which were US$67.9 billion and US$54.69 billion respectively. Bombay and Calcutta together accounted for almost 70% and 74% respectively of the total turnover during 1993–94 and 1994–95.

Stock indices

As stated above, the Bombay Stock Exchange has the prime position in respect of trading in equities. Its indices are a reference point for assessment of the general condition of the stock market in India. The oft quoted index is known as the BSE sensitive index or Sensex. This is based on the price behaviour of 30 scrips with 1978–79 prices forming the base. The other is the BSE national index which is more broad-based and takes into account the price movement in 100 scrips with 1983–84 as the base year. It also has the BSE 200 index and the dollar index (known as Dollex) with 1989–90 as the base.

Specialised markets

Till 25 January 1995, options in securities were prohibited by the Securities Contracts (Regulation) Act, 1956. The position has, however, changed and this prohibition has been withdrawn making it possible for the setting up of markets in options. The National Stock Exchange has sought approval of SEBI for the setting up of a market for derivatives in the shape of futures and options in India.

Custodial services

Custodial services in the country are provided by the Stock Holding Corporation of India (the largest custodian), the Hongkong Bank and the Bank of New York in particular.

Foreign portfolio investment

Till recently, the Indian capital markets were not open to foreign investors. On 14 September 1992, the government announced guidelines for reputed foreign institutional investors to invest in Indian stocks. As a result, foreign capital inflow and outflow is freely permitted, without any lock-in period, at market rates of exchange. At the time of entry, a foreign institutional investor has to apply for an initial registration with the SEBI on a single window basis. Such registration would be valid for a period of five years and would also include relevant permissions from the Reserve Bank of India for facilitating capital inflows and outflows, and operation of foreign currency and rupee accounts for investment purposes.

Total investments made by foreign institutional investors till the end of July 1995 were US$3.66 million.

There are limitations on such investments by a foreign institutional investor in that its holding in a company is not to exceed 10% of the issued share capital and the holding of all FIIs put together cannot exceed 24% of the issued capital. However, foreign portfolio investments through offshore funds, global depository receipts and Euro-convertibles are excluded from this 24% limit, but the portfolio investment of Non-resident Indians is included in this limit.

Concessional rates of taxation on dividends, long-term and short-term capital gains are available. Disinvestment is through stock exchanges except in extraordinary circumstances when SEBI may allow sales other than through stock exchanges.

Global depository receipts/Euro-issues

Indian companies can raise resources internationally through global depository receipts also known as Euro-issues. As of 12 August 1995, 62 companies have raised US$3.11 billion using this route.

Foreign investors can also invest in Indian companies through the global depository receipt/Euro-issue mechanism. There is no lock-in period for equities in this case. These receipts can be listed on any of the overseas stock exchanges and denominated in any hard foreign currency. However, the underlying shares would be denominated only in Indian rupees. As per international practice, private placement with US investors is also permissible in accordance with the US Securities Act. Short-term capital gains are taxable at the rate of 30% along with business income. Long-term capital gains (computed on holdings for more than 12 months) are taxable at a rate of 10%.

Mutual funds

The SEBI also regulates the mutual funds and has laid down disclosure requirements for the schemes launched by them. Prior authorisation from SEBI is required for the setting up of a mutual fund. The relevant regulations provide for setting up of the mutual funds as trusts, establishment of separate asset management companies with specified capital adequacy requirements, setting up of a board of trustees and appointment of a separate custodian.

Acquisitions and take-overs

Regulations have been issued by SEBI for making disclosures in the cases of acquisitions and take-overs. These regulations require an acquirer having more than 5% of shares to disclose the aggregate of his holding to all the stock exchanges where the shares of the company are listed within four working days of such acquisition. Those holding more than 5% of shares are also required to make half yearly disclosures about their holding to the stock exchanges.

The regulations also stipulate that no acquirer can acquire more than 10% of shares of a company either through negotiations or from the open market without making a public announcement in accordance with the procedure laid down in this regard.

Secondary market regulation

To regulate stock brokers and sub-brokers, SEBI has issued rules and regulations. No stock broker or sub-broker can buy, sell and deal in securities unless he holds a certificate granted by SEBI under these regulations. The procedure for grant of registration, requirements for payments of registration fee to SEBI, maintenance of appropriate books and records, right of inspection of the books of the stock brokers and sub-brokers by the SEBI and the liability for action in case of default which includes suspension or cancellation of registration are laid down in these rules.

Penal action can now be taken directly by SEBI against any member of a stock exchange in India for violation of any provisions of the SEBI Act, contravention of rules and regulations of SEBI, provisions of the Securities Contract Regulation Act or rules thereunder and regulations and by-laws of the stock exchanges or for manipulating the markets and price rigging.

Capital adequacy norms for brokers

Capital adequacy norms for brokers, both in regard to the base minimum capital and position risks, have been laid down for ensuring safety of the trades in the market and protection of investors.

Transparency in broker-clients relationship

The SEBI has made it mandatory for stock brokers to bring about greater transparency in their relations with clients and separate books of accounts for clients.

Compulsory audit of brokers' books

Audit of brokers' books and filing of audit reports to the SEBI have been made compulsory. The Institute of Chartered Accountants has been requested to evolve standards of auditing of brokers' books.

Stock exchanges as effective self-regulatory organisations

The SEBI has been encouraging stock exchanges to become more effective and responsive self-regulatory organisations with a greater degree of accountability. Towards this end, the SEBI has taken up with the stock exchanges the issue of strict enforcement of their own rules, regulations and by-laws, greater disclosure of outstanding positions, laying down policies on margins, ensuring that margins are monitored and collected from the members, compulsory auditing of the books of the members, ensuring the effectiveness of the disciplinary action committee, speeding up the process of arbitration and enforcement of surveillance mechanisms.

Weekly settlement of trade

The SEBI has directed all the stock exchanges to shorten the settlement period for non-specified shares to seven days.

Restructuring of the Governing Boards of the stock exchanges

Hitherto the Governing Boards of the stock exchanges were dominated by brokers. The SEBI has directed the stock exchanges to broad-base their Governing Boards with 50% representatives of members and 50% non-member representatives.

Market makers

The SEBI has issued guidelines for introducing the system of market making in less liquid scripts. To act as a market maker, a broker would be approved by the SEBI on the recommendation of the stock exchange based on his track record and financial performance. The Reserve Bank of India has issued guidelines to the commercial banks for making bank credit available to the market makers approved by SEBI.

Insider trading

For the first time insider trading has been prohibited by the Insider Trading Regulations notified by the SEBI.

Investor grievance redressal by stock exchanges

At the insistence of the SEBI, the stock exchanges have amended the listing agreement to provide for deposit of 1% of the issue amount of a company making a public issue. This amount deposited with stock exchanges can be released only after the stock exchanges satisfy themselves that the issuer has taken all action particularly those relating to despatch of allotment letters and refund orders.

Inspection and monitoring of stock exchanges

The SEBI has inspected most of the stock exchanges in the country. Many deficiencies were found and stock exchanges have been directed to rectify the inadequacies.

The SEBI has also inspected the books of a number of stock brokers of various stock exchanges.

The SEBI's powers to impose penalties

The SEBI can levy monetary fines for violations relating to failure to submit information to it, failure by brokers to enter agreements with clients, failure to redress investors' grievances, violations by mutual funds, violations by stock brokers, violations of insider trading regulations and take-over regulations.

The SEBI has been vested with the powers of the Civil Court under the Code of Civil Procedure in respect of discovery and production of books, documents, records and accounts, summoning and enforcing the attendance of persons and examining them on oath.

The SEBI can issue directions to intermediaries, companies and persons associated with the securities market in the interest of investors.

Glossary of Terms Used in the Securities Market

Badla: Carrying forward of transactions from one settlement period to another without effecting delivery. This is permitted only in specified securities and is done at the making-up price which is usually the closing price of the last day of settlement.

Backwardation/Ulta Badla/Undha Badla: The payment of money charges made by a seller of shares to the buyer. These charges become payable only when there are more sellers who are not in a position to deliver against their sale. These charges become payable to the buyer, when the seller is not in a position to deliver the documents to the buyers who demand delivery.

Bid: An offer of a price to buy as in an auction. Business on the stock exchange is done through bids. Bid also refers to the price one is willing to pay for a security.

Book closing: The closure of books of a company to take a record of the shareholders who are entitled to dividend or rights etc. Transfer is not registered during the closing period.

Bull: One who expects that price of the securities will rise.

Capitalisation: Total amount of the various securities issued by a corporation. Capitalisation may include bonds, debentures, preferred and common stock.

Clearing house: Each exchange maintains a clearing house to act as the central agency for effecting delivery and settlement of contracts between all members. The days on which members pay or receive the amounts due to them are called 'pay-in' or 'pay-out' days respectively.

Cumulative preference shares: A type of preference shares on which dividend accumulates if not paid. All arrears of preference dividend have to be paid out before paying dividend on equity shares.

Defaulter: Inability of a broker to meet his financial obligation. It is followed by 'hammering', ie the announcement on the floor of the stock exchange that the individual (or firm) concerned is unable to comply with its bargains.

Jobbers: Member brokers of a stock exchange who specialise in buying and selling specified securities from and to fellow members. Jobbers do not have any direct dealing with the public but they serve a useful function of imparting liquidity to the market.

Jobbers spread: The difference between the price at which a jobber is prepared to sell and the price at which he is prepared to buy. A large difference reflects an imbalance between supply and demand.

Making-up prices: The price at which shares closed for the current settlement and were carried over to the next settlement day.

Margin: An advance payment of a portion of the value of a stock.

Net asset value: A term usually used in connection with investment companies, meaning net asset value per share. It is common practice for an investment company to compute its assets daily, or even twice daily, by totalling the market value of all securities owned. All liabilities are deducted and the balance divided by the number of shares outstanding. The resulting figure is the net asset value per share.

Option: A right to buy (call) or sell (put) a fixed amount of a given stock at a specified price within a limited period of time. The purchaser hopes that the stock's price will go up (if he bought a call) or down (if he bought a put) by an amount sufficient to provide a profit greater than the cost of the contract and the commission and other fees required to exercise the contract. If the stock price holds steady or moves in the opposite direction, the price paid for the option is lost entirely. There are several other types of options available to the public but these are basically combinations of puts and calls. Individuals may write (sell) as well as purchase options and are thereby obliged to deliver or buy the stock at the specified price.

Spot delivery: Delivery and payment on the same day as the date of contract or on the next day.

Stamp duty: Duty imposed by the State under the Indian Stamp Act upon certain documents which are legally unenforceable without such stamp.

Volume of trading: The total number of shares which change hands and market value thereof. This information is useful in explaining and interpreting fluctuations in share price.

CHAPTER 18

ARBITRATION AND OTHER RELATED LAWS IN INDIA
by Justice H R Khanna

The liberalisation of the Indian economy is bound to attract foreign business houses to enter into industrial and commercial deals in India. As many of these agreements will be governed by Indian law, it is helpful to know something about Indian commercial law.

THE INDIAN CONTRACT ACT

So far as the relevant substantive law is concerned, the same is contained in the Indian Contract Act, 1872 and the Sale of Goods Act, 1930. Both these Acts are based on the English Common Law, and their broad outlines are not dissimilar from the corresponding enactments in Western countries. The Indian law requires that the acceptance of a proposal for an agreement must be absolute and unqualified (s 7). It further provides that all agreements constitute contracts if made with the free consent of parties competent to contract, for a lawful consideration and with a lawful object (s 10). The agreement would be void if both parties are under a mistake as to a matter of fact (s 20). The consideration of an agreement is lawful, unless it is forbidden by law, or would defeat the provisions of any law, or is fraudulent, or involves or implies injury to the person or property of another, or the Court regards it as immoral or opposed to public policy (s 23). The Act imposes an obligation on the parties to a contract to either perform or offer to perform, their respective promises, unless such performance is dispensed with or excused under the provisions of the Act (s 37). Detailed provisions on the subject of performance of contracts are contained in Chapter IV which comprises ss 37–67. Chapter V relates to certain relations resembling those created by contract, while Chapter VI containing ss 73–75 specifies the consequences of breach of contract. It may be mentioned that prior to 1930, the Sale of Goods Act was also an integral part of the Contract Act (ss 76–123), but these sections were repealed and a separate enactment was made on the subject. Chapter VIII deals with indemnity and guarantee while Chapter IX deals with bailment. Chapter X makes provisions for appointment and authority of agents.

The law of partnership was also earlier a part of the law of contract but there is now a separate enactment on the subject.

SALE OF GOODS ACT

A contract for sale of goods has been defined in the Sale of Goods Act as one whereby the seller transfers or agrees to transfer the property in goods to the buyer for a price. The contract of sale may also be between one part-owner and another. The Act provides that a contract of sale may be absolute or conditional. Where under a contract of sale the property in the goods is transferred from the seller to the buyer, the contract is called a sale, but where the transfer of the property in the goods is to take place at a future time or subject to some condition thereafter to be fulfilled, the contract is called an agreement to sell. An agreement to sell becomes a sale when the time elapses or the conditions are fulfilled subject to which the property in the goods is to be transferred (s 4). The Act defines 'Document of Title to Goods' to include 'bill of lading, dock-warrant, warehouse keeper's certificate, wharfingers' certificate, railway receipt, warrant or order for the delivery of goods and any other document used in the ordinary course of business as proof of the possession or control of goods, or authorising or purporting to authorise, either by endorsement or by delivery, the possessor of the documents to transfer or receive goods thereby represented'. 'Goods' under the Act comprise every kind of movable property other than actionable claims and money, and include stock and shares etc.

FOREIGN EXCHANGE REGULATION ACT

The Foreign Exchange Regulation Act, 1973 had been enacted to regulate certain payments dealing in foreign exchange and securities, transactions indirectly affecting foreign exchange and proper utilisation thereof in the interests of the economic development of the country. According to s 9 of the Act, save as may be provided in and in accordance with any general or special exemption, no person in, or resident in, India shall make any payment to or for the credit of any person resident outside India and receive, otherwise than through an authorised dealer, any payment by order or on behalf of any person resident outside India. The section also contains detailed provisions about what constitutes payment otherwise than through an authorised dealer and about making payment. Section 27 places restrictions on persons resident in India associating themselves with or participating in concerns outside India without the prior permission of the Central Government. Section 28 restricts the appointment of certain persons and non-banking companies as agents or technical or management advisers in India without the permission of the Reserve Bank. Section 29 imposes restrictions on the establishment of a place of business in India by a person resident outside India other than a banking company except with the permission of the Reserve Bank. Section 30 requires prior permission of the Reserve Bank for taking up employment, etc, in India by nationals of foreign States while s 31 restricts a person who is not a citizen of India and non-banking companies in which non-resident interest is more than 40% from acquiring and holding any immovable property in India without the permission of the Reserve Bank of India.

It may be mentioned that, in view of the liberalisation of the economy, the government and the Reserve Bank are liberal in giving the requisite permission subject to certain limits. There has been considerable relaxation of the restraints imposed by those provisions. The Act provides for penalties in case of violation of the provisions of the Act.

ARBITRATION

Business transactions quite often give rise to disputes. In the event of such disputes not being resolved by the parties themselves as a result of mutual discussion, settlement is provided by the Courts. Unfortunately, because of a heavy backlog of cases in the Courts, settlement takes too long. The duration of a case is sometimes as long as 8–10 years. Apart from the time taken in trial court, considerable time is also consumed in the appellate court, because the losing party invariably files an appeal. In some cases, the matter is taken further by the losing party in a second appeal or by special leave to the Supreme Court.

Hierarchy of Courts in India

India has a hierarchy of courts with the Supreme Court of India at the apex. Below it are the High Courts, generally one for each State, though some High Courts exercise jurisdiction in more than one State. Below the High Courts are the Courts of District and Sessions Judges, Additional District and Sessions Judges and Judges of the City Civil Courts. Below the District and Sessions Judge are the Courts of

Sub-ordinate judges and Munsiffs (only in some States) to deal with civil cases and the Courts of Magistrates to deal with criminal matters.

Need for Arbitration

In view of the inordinate length of time taken in the disposal of cases in courts of law, the parties, particularly in major disputes involving huge amounts, resort to arbitration. It is in this context that it becomes necessary to set out the salient features of arbitration law.

Arbitration Act

The law of arbitration in India is contained in the Arbitration Act, 1940. An 'Arbitration Agreement' has been defined in the Act as a written agreement to submit present or future differences to arbitration, whether an arbitrator is named therein or not (s 2(a)).

Reference to Arbitration and Other Ancillary Provisions

The parties to an arbitration agreement may agree that any reference thereunder shall be to an arbitrator or arbitrators to be appointed by a person designated in the agreement either by name or as a holder for the time being of any office or appointment (s 4). The authority of an appointed arbitrator or umpire cannot be revoked except with the leave of the Court, unless a contrary intention is expressed in the arbitration agreement (s 5). An arbitration agreement is not discharged by the death of any party thereto, but would in such event be enforceable by or against the legal representative of the deceased. Section 7 provides for the eventuality of a person becoming insolvent. Power has been given to the Court to appoint an arbitrator or umpire when the parties to an arbitration agreement do not concur in the appointment or if any appointed arbitrator or umpire neglects or refuses to act, or is incapable of acting, or dies, or where the parties or the arbitrators are required to appoint an umpire and do not appoint him. In case the appointment is not made within 15 clear days after the service of the notice by one party on the other party, the Court may, on the application of the party who gave the notice and after giving the other party an opportunity of being heard, appoint an arbitrator or arbitrators or umpire. Where an arbitration agreement provides that a reference has to be to two arbitrators, one to be appointed by each party, then, unless a different intention is expressed in the agreement, if either of the appointed arbitrators neglects or refuses to act or dies, the party who appointed him may appoint a new arbitrator in his place. If, however, a party fails to appoint an arbitrator, either originally or by way of substitution, for 15 clear days, after the service by the other party of a notice in writing to make the appointment, such other party having appointed his arbitrator before giving the notice, the party who has appointed an arbitrator may appoint that arbitrator to act as sole arbitrator in the reference, and his award shall be binding on both parties as if he had been appointed by consent, provided however that the Court may in the latter event set aside any appointment as sole arbitrator and on sufficient cause being shown allow further time to the defaulting party to appoint an arbitrator or pass such other order as it thinks fit. The fact that an arbitrator or umpire, after a request by either party to enter on and proceed with the reference, does not comply with the request within one month would constitute his neglect or refusal to act (s 9). In case an arbitration agreement provides that a reference shall be to three arbitrators, one to be appointed by each party and the third by the two appointed arbitrators, the agreement shall have effect as if it provided for the appointment of an umpire, and not for the appointment of a third arbitrator, by the two arbitrators appointed by the parties. Apart from this, where an arbitration agreement provides that a reference shall be to three arbitrators, the award of the majority would prevail (s 10).

Power of Court to Remove Arbitrators or Umpire

The Courts have power to remove an arbitrator or umpire who fails to use all reasonable despatch in entering on and proceeding with the reference and making an award. The Courts can also remove an arbitrator or umpire who has misconducted himself or the proceedings. In such an event the arbitrator or umpire shall not be entitled to receive any remuneration (s 11). The Court also has power to appoint persons to fill the vacancies caused by the removal of the arbitrator or umpire (s 12). The arbitrators or umpire have power to administer an oath to the parties and witnesses, state a special case for the opinion of the Court on any question of law involved, make the award conditional or in the alternative, and correct in an award any clerical mistake or error arising from any accidental slip or omission. He shall have also power to administer to any party to the arbitration such interrogatories as may, in his opinion, be necessary (s 13).

Filing Award in Court

When the arbitrators or umpire give their award, they should sign it and give notice in writing to the parties. The arbitrators or umpire shall at the request of any party or if so desired by the Court cause the award together with the record of the case to be filed in Court and the Court shall thereupon give notice to the parties of the filing of the award (s 14).

Power of Court to Modify, Correct, Permit Award

Power is given to the Court to modify or correct an award where it appears that a part of the award is upon a matter not referred to arbitration and such part can be separated from the other part and does not affect the decision on the matter referred, or where the award is imperfect in form, or contains any obvious error which can be amended without affecting such decision, or where the award contains a clerical mistake or an error arising from an accidental slip or omission (s 15). Under s 16, the Courts have the power to remit the award or any matter referred to arbitration to the arbitrators or umpire for reconsideration in the three following contingencies:

(a) where the award has left undetermined any of the matters referred to arbitration; or determines any matter not referred to arbitration; or

(b) where the award is so indefinite as to be incapable of execution; or

(c) where an objection to the legality of the award is apparent upon the fact of it.

In such an event the Court shall fix the time within which the arbitrator or umpire shall submit his decision to the Court. In case of failure of the arbitrator or umpire to reconsider it and submit his decision within the time fixed, the award shall become void (s 16).

Awards When Not Set Aside to be Incorporated in Decree

Where the Court sees no cause to remit the award or any of the matters referred to arbitration for reconsideration or to set aside the award, the Court shall, after the time for making an application to set aside the award has expired, or where such an application has been made and rejected, proceed to pronounce judgment according to the award and upon pronouncement of the judgment a decree shall follow and no appeal shall lie from such decree except on the ground that it is not in accordance with the award (s 17).

Power of Court to Pass Interim Orders

The Courts have the power to pass interim orders, at any time after the filing of the award.

Power of Court to Supersede Arbitration

Power has further been given to the Court to supersede arbitration where the award becomes void or is set aside (s 19).

Filing Arbitration Agreement in Court

Under s 20, a party can apply to the Court to file an arbitration agreement. In such an event the Court after notice to the other party to show cause why the agreement should not be filed and if no sufficient cause is shown to the contrary, shall order the agreement to be filed and shall make an order of reference to the arbitrator appointed by the parties or where the parties cannot agree upon an arbitrator, to an arbitrator appointed by the Court.

Arbitration in Suits

In pending suits the differences between them in the suit can be referred to arbitration at any time before judgment is pronounced if the parties agree in writing that the matter be referred to arbitration (s 21). Where a matter is referred to arbitration, the Court should not deal with such matter in the suit (s 23). Section 24 deals with cases where some only of the parties to a suit apply to have the matters in dispute between them referred to arbitration (s 24).

Interim Award and Other Provisions

The arbitrators or umpire may, if they think fit, make an interim award (s 27). Power has been given to the Court to extend time for making award (s 28). Even without the intervention of the Court, the parties can by mutual agreement extend the time for making the award. In case the award is for payment of money, the Court may, in the decree, award interest from the date of the decree at such rate as the Court deems reasonable (s 29). The arbitrator and the umpire have power also to award interest in money claims.

Grounds for Setting Aside an Award

An award can be set aside by the Court on the following grounds:

(a) that an arbitrator or umpire has misconducted himself or the proceedings;

(b) that an award has been made after the issue of an order by the Court superseding the arbitration or after arbitration proceedings have become invalid;

(c) that an award has been improperly procured or is otherwise invalid.

The grounds for setting aside the award include non-observance of rules of natural justice in matters of evidence or where the arbitrator conducts private inquiry or bases his decision on personal knowledge or where the arbitrator gives a hearing to one of the parties in the absence of the other or bases his award on an erroneous view of law and the error is apparent on the face of the record. It may, however, be added that while dealing with an application for setting aside an award, the Courts do not sit as courts of appeal over the decision of the arbitrator, nor can they set aside the award even if their own view on the merits of the case be different. However, it needs to be emphasised that in a number of recent cases the Supreme Court has stressed that the Courts should lean in favour of upholding the validity and finality of the award and to interfere with the award only upon clear-cut grounds.

Appeals and Other Provisions

Although, as mentioned earlier, no appeal lies against a decree passed upon the award, an appeal is maintainable against the order of the Court setting aside or refusing to set aside the award. No suit is maintainable about the existence, effect or validity of an arbitration agreement or award nor can such agreement or award be set aside, amended or modified in any way otherwise than as provided in the Arbitration Act (s 32). Power is given to the Courts to stay legal proceedings relating to matters which are the subject of an arbitration agreement when a party against whom such legal proceedings have been commenced before taking any part in those proceedings applies to the Court for stay of legal proceedings. Such party should also state that the applicant was, at the time when the proceedings were commenced, and still remains, ready and willing to do all things necessary for the proper conduct of the arbitration (s 34).

Implied Conditions and Interim Orders

The First Schedule to the Act enumerates implied conditions of an arbitration agreement. Rule 2 of the Schedule requires that if the reference is to an even number of arbitrators, the arbitrators shall appoint an umpire not later than one month from the latest date of their respective appointments. Under Rule 3 the arbitrators have to make their award within four months after entering on the reference or after having been called upon to act by notice in writing from any party to the arbitration agreement or within such extended time as the Court may allow. As already mentioned, the time for making the award can also be enlarged with the mutual concurrence of both the parties. If the arbitrators allow their time to expire without making an award or deliver to any party to the arbitration agreement or to the umpire a notice in writing stating that they cannot agree, the umpire shall forthwith enter on the reference or within such extended time as the Court may allow. The Second Schedule to the Act enumerates powers of the Court for the preservation, interim custody or sale of any goods which are the subject matter of the reference. The Court is also given the power to appoint a receiver if good cause is shown for that.

One of the questions which needs consideration is whether the arbitrator or the umpire should give reasons for his decision to be incorporated in the award. This question was considered by a Constitution Bench of the Supreme Court and it was held that in the absence of a clause in the arbitration agreement it is not imperative for the arbitrator or the umpire to give reasons in support of the decision. The Supreme Court in this context relied upon the observations of the Law Commission of India. It may be mentioned that the practice generally prevalent in Western countries is for arbitrators to give reasons in support of their decision in the award. Experience in India, however, shows that whenever reasons are given in support of the decision in the award, the award has been challenged in the court of law on the grounds, inter alia, that the reasons are not well-founded or incorporate an erroneous view of law. The awards as such become vulnerable because of their validity being challenged through applications in the Court for setting them aside.

These applications take a long time to dispose of because of the procedural delays and the heavy backlog of cases in the Courts. Even the order made by the Court refusing to set aside the award can be assailed, as already mentioned, in appeal and quite often it takes considerable time to dispose of the appeal.

Rate of Exchange for Amount Payable in Foreign Currency

Another matter which needs to be mentioned is that the Supreme Court of India has held that in an action to recover an amount payable in foreign currency, the date of passing the decree on the basis of the award is the proper date for fixing the rate of exchange at which the foreign currency should be converted (AIR 1984 SC 241).

Indian Arbitration Council

There exists in India the Indian Council of Arbitration which provides a forum for settlement of disputes through arbitration. The normal procedure is that a party approaches the Council for adjudication of its disputes. The nature of the dispute and the amount of the claim are indicated to the Council. A statement of claim is filed with the Council by the party. The party at the same time nominates its arbitrator from among the panel of arbitrators maintained by the Council. The party against whom the claim is made nominates its arbitrator and files its reply. The Council ensures that the statement of claim, the reply, replication and the documents are filed by the parties so that the matter can proceed. The Council nominates the Chairman of the arbitral tribunal consisting of one nominee of each party and the Chairman appointed by the Council. The arbitration proceedings are held on the premises of the Arbitration Council and it provides necessary secretarial assistance for the purpose. On conclusion, the arbitrators pronounce their awards and the same are filed by the Council in the Court. One snag, however, is that the scale of fees of the arbitrator as fixed by the Council is not high and on that account senior retired judges and legal luminaries are on occasions reluctant to act as arbitrators in arbitrations held under the auspices of the Indian Arbitration Council.

Recognition and Enforcement of Foreign Awards

The Foreign Awards (Recognition and Enforcement) Act was enacted in India in 1961. The aim and object of that Act was to give effect to the Convention on the Recognition and Enforcement of Foreign Arbitral Awards done at New York on 10 June 1958 to which India is a party. A foreign award under the provisions of the Act is enforceable in India as if it was an award made on a matter referred to arbitration in India (s 4). Application for filing a foreign award can be made to a Court in India by any person interested in the foreign award (s 5). If the Court is satisfied that the foreign award is enforceable under the Act, the Court shall order the award to be filed and shall proceed to pronounce judgment according to the award (s 6). Section 7 of the Act gives the grounds for not enforcing the foreign awards.

Change of Law

The President of India promulgated the Arbitration and Conciliation Ordinance, 1996, which came into force on 25 January 1996. Under s 85 of the Ordinance, the Arbitration Act, 1940, the Arbitration (Protocol and Convention) Act, 1937 and the Foreign Awards (Recognition and Enforcement) Act, 1961 have all been repealed. Subsection (2) of s 85 provides:

Notwithstanding such repeal —

(a) the provisions of the said enactments shall apply in relation to arbitral proceedings which commenced before this Ordinance came into force unless otherwise agreed by the parties but this Ordinance shall apply in relation to arbitral proceedings which commenced on or after this Ordinance comes into force;

(b) all rules made and notifications published, under the said enactments shall, to the extent to which they are not repugnant to this Ordinance, be deemed respectively to have been made or issued under this Ordinance.

In view of subs (2) of s 85 above, the arbitration proceedings which commenced before the Ordinance came into force, viz 25 January 1996, shall be governed by the provisions of the Arbitration Act, 1940. It is, however, open to the parties to agree that the provisions of the Ordinance shall apply to arbitral proceedings which commenced before the Ordinance came into force. As regards arbitral proceedings which commenced on or after the Ordinance came into force, it is the provisions of the Ordinance which shall apply and not those of the repealed enactments. It is therefore manifest that familiarity with the provisions of the repealed enactments does not lose its importance. At the same time it becomes necessary to know the salient features of the new Ordinance and some of the major changes brought about by it.

Arbitration and Conciliation Ordinance, 1996—Salient Features

The Arbitration and Conciliation Ordinance, 1996 seeks to consolidate and amend the law relating to domestic arbitration, international commercial arbitration and enforcement of foreign arbitral awards, and also to define the law relating to conciliation and matters connected therewith or incidental thereto. The preamble to the Ordinance also takes note of the fact that the United Nations Commission on International Trade Law (UNCITRAL) adopted the UNCITRAL Model Law on International Commercial Arbitration in 1985. The General Assembly of the United Nations recommended that all countries give due consideration to the said Model Law in view of the desirability of uniformity of the law of arbitral procedures and the specific needs of international commercial arbitration practice. The preamble further takes note of the fact that the UNCITRAL adopted the UNCITRAL Conciliation Rules in 1980 and the General Assembly of the United Nations recommended the use of those Rules in cases where a dispute arises in the context of international commercial relations and the parties seek an amicable settlement of that dispute by recourse to conciliation.

The Ordinance defines 'international commercial arbitration' to mean 'an arbitration relating to disputes arising out of legal relationships, whether contractual or not, considered as commercial under the law in force in India and where at least one of the parties is—(i) an individual who is a national of, or habitually resident in, any country other than India; or (ii) a body corporate which is incorporated in any country other than India; or (iii) a company or an association or a body of individuals whose central management and control is exercised in any country other than India; or (iv) the Government of a foreign country'. According to s 7 of the Ordinance, 'arbitration agreement' means an agreement by the parties to submit to arbitration all or certain disputes which have arisen or which may arise between them in respect of a defined legal relationship, whether contractual or not. An arbitration agreement may be in the form of an arbitration clause in a contract or in the form of a separate agreement. An arbitration agreement must be in writing. An arbitration agreement is in writing if it is contained in: (a) a document signed by the parties; (b) an exchange of letters, telex, telegrams or other means of telecommunication which provide a record of the agreement; or (c) an exchange of statements of claim and defence in which the existence of the agreement is alleged by one party and not denied by the other. According to s 10, the parties are free to determine the number of arbitrators, provided that such number shall not be an even number. Failing such determination, the arbitral tribunal shall consist of a sole arbitrator. Section 11 relates to the appointment of an arbitrator, as follows:

(1) A person of any nationality may be an arbitrator, unless otherwise agreed by the parties.

(2) Subject to sub-section (6), the parties are free to agree on a procedure for appointing the arbitrator or arbitrators.

(3) Failing any agreement referred to in sub-section (2), in an arbitration with three arbitrators, each party shall appoint one arbitrator, and the two appointed arbitrators shall appoint the third arbitrator who shall act as the presiding arbitrator.

(4) If the appointment procedure in sub-section (3) applies and—

   (a) a party fails to appoint an arbitrator within thirty days from the receipt of a request to do so from the other party; or

   (b) the two appointed arbitrators fail to agree on the third arbitrator within thirty days from the date of their appointment,

the appointment shall be made, upon request of a party, by the Chief Justice or any person or institution designated by him.

(5) Failing any agreement referred to in sub-section (2), in an arbitration with a sole arbitrator, if the parties fail to agree on the arbitrator within thirty days from receipt of a request by one party from the other party to so agree the appointment shall be made, upon request of a party, by the Chief Justice or any person or institution designated by him.

(6) Where, under an appointment procedure agreed upon by the parties—

   (a) a party fails to act as required under that procedure; or

   (b) the parties, or the two appointed arbitrators, fail to reach an agreement expected of them under that procedure; or

   (c) a person, including an institution, fails to perform any function entrusted to him or it under that procedure,

a party may request the Chief Justice or any person or institution designated by him to take the necessary measure, unless the agreement on the appointment procedure provides other means for securing the appointment.

(7) A decision on a matter entrusted by sub-section (4) or sub-section (5) or sub-section (6) to the Chief Justice or the person or institution designated by him is final.

(8)   The Chief Justice or the person or institution designated by him, in appointing an arbitrator, shall have due regard to—

(a)   any qualifications required of the arbitrator by the agreement of the parties; and

(b)   other considerations as are likely to secure the appointment of an independent and impartial arbitrator.

(9)   In the case of appointment of a sole or third arbitrator in an international commercial arbitration, the Chief Justice of India or the person or institution designated by him may appoint an arbitrator of a nationality other than the nationalities of the parties where the parties belong to different nationalities.

(10)   The Chief Justice may make such scheme as he may deem appropriate for dealing with matters entrusted by sub-section (4) or sub-section (5) or sub-section (6) to him.

(11)   Where more than one request has been made under the sub-section (4) or sub-section (5) or sub-section (6) to the Chief Justice of different High Courts or their designates, the Chief Justice or his designate to whom the request has been first made under the relevant sub-section shall alone be competent to decide on the request.

(12) (a)   Where the matters referred to in sub-sections (4), (5), (6), (7), (8) and (10) arise in an international commercial arbitration, the reference to 'Chief Justice' in those sub-sections shall be construed as a reference to the 'Chief Justice of India'.

(b)   Where the matters referred to in sub-sections (4), (5), (6), (7), (8) and (10) arise in any other arbitration, the reference to 'Chief Justice' in those sub-sections shall be construed as a reference to the Chief Justice of the High Court within those local limits the principal Civil Court referred to in clause (e) of sub-section (1) of section 2 is situate and, where the High Court itself is the Court referred to in that clause, to the Chief Justice of that High Court.

Section 16 provides that the arbitral tribunal may rule on its own jurisdiction, including ruling on any objections with respect to the existence or validity of the arbitration agreement and, for that purpose, an arbitration clause which forms part of a contract shall be treated as an agreement independent of the other terms of the contract, and the decision by the arbitral tribunal that the contract is null and void shall not entail ipso jure the invalidity of the arbitration clause. A plea that the arbitral tribunal does not have jurisdiction must be raised not later than the submission of the statement of defence. However, a party shall not be precluded from raising such a plea merely because it has appointed, or participated in the appointment of, an arbitrator. A plea that the arbitral tribunal has exceeded the scope of its authority must be raised as soon as the matter alleged to be beyond the scope of its authority is raised during the arbitral proceedings.

According to s 19, the arbitral tribunal shall not be bound by the Code of Civil Procedure, 1908 or the Indian Evidence Act, 1872. The parties are free to agree on the procedure to be followed by the arbitral tribunal in conducting its proceedings. Failing any such agreement, the arbitral tribunal may conduct the proceedings in the manner it considers appropriate. The power of the arbitral tribunal includes the power to determine the admissibility, relevance, materiality and weight of any evidence.

Under s 20, the parties are free to agree on the place of arbitration. Failing such agreement, the place of arbitration shall be determined by the arbitral tribunal having regard to the circumstances of the case, including the convenience of the parties.

According to s 21, unless otherwise agreed by the parties, the arbitral proceedings in respect of a particular dispute commence on the date on which a request for that dispute to be referred to arbitration is received by the respondent.

Under s 22, the parties are free to agree upon the language or languages to be used in the arbitral proceedings. Failing any such agreement, the arbitral tribunal shall determine the language or languages to be used in the arbitral proceedings.

According to s 28, where the place of arbitration is in India, in an arbitration other than an international commercial arbitration, the arbitral tribunal shall decide the dispute submitted to arbitration in accordance with the substantive law for the time being in force in India; and, in international commercial arbitration, the arbitral tribunal shall decide the dispute in accordance with the rules or law designated by the parties as applicable to the substance of the dispute. Unless otherwise agreed by the parties, in arbitral proceedings with more than one arbitrator, any decision of the arbitral tribunal shall be made by a majority of all its members.

According to s 30, it is not incompatible with an arbitration agreement for an arbitral tribunal to encourage settlement of the dispute and, with the agreement of the parties, the arbitral tribunal may use mediation, conciliation or other procedures at any time during the arbitral proceedings to encourage settlement.

Under s 31, the arbitral award shall be made in writing and shall be signed by the members of the arbitral tribunal. In arbitral proceedings with more than one arbitrator, the signatures of the majority of all the members of the arbitral tribunal shall be sufficient, as long as the reason for any omitted signature is stated.

The arbitral award shall, unless the parties otherwise agree, state the reasons upon which it is based. The arbitral award shall state its date and the place of arbitration as determined in accordance with s 20 and the award shall be deemed to have been made at that place. After the arbitral award is made, a signed copy shall be delivered to each party.

Under s 34 of the Ordinance, the arbitral award may be set aside by the Court only if:

(a) the party making the application furnishes proof that

    (i) a party was under some incapacity, or

    (ii) the arbitration agreement is not valid under the law to which the parties have subjected it or, failing any indication thereon, under the law for the time being in force; or

    (iii) the party making the application was not given proper notice of the appointment of an arbitrator or of the arbitral proceedings or was otherwise unable to present his case; or

    (iv) the arbitral award deals with a dispute not contemplated by or not falling within the terms of the submission to arbitration, or it contains decisions on matters beyond the scope of the submission to arbitration: Provided that, if the decisions on matters submitted to arbitration can be separated from those not so submitted, only that part of the arbitral award which contains decisions on matters not submitted to arbitration may be set aside; or

    (v) the composition of the arbitral tribunal or the arbitral procedure was not in accordance with the agreement of the parties, unless such agreement was in conflict with a provision of this Part from which the parties cannot derogate, or, failing such agreement, was not in accordance with this Part; or

(b) the Court finds that—

    (i) the subject-matter of the dispute is not capable of settlement by arbitration under the law for the time being in force; or

    (ii) the arbitral award is in conflict with the public policy of India.

An appeal shall lie from an order setting aside or refusing to set aside an arbitral award under s 34. According to s 35, the arbitral award shall be final and binding on the parties and persons claiming under them. Under s 36, where the time for making an application to set aside the arbitral award under s 34 has expired, or such application having been made, it has been refused, the award shall be enforced under the Code of Civil Procedure, 1908 in the same manner as if it were a decree of the Court. Section 36 thus makes a departure from the provisions of the Arbitration Act, 1940 according to which the award of an arbitrator could be enforced only if it was made a rule of the Court. Under the new Ordinance the arbitral award can be enforced in the same manner as if it were the decree of the Court.

Part II of the Ordinance relates to enforcement of certain foreign awards, in pursuance of an agreement in writing for arbitration to which the New York Convention applies. These foreign awards would be enforceable and should be treated as binding for all purposes on the persons between whom they are made. The conditions for enforcement of such foreign awards are given in s 48 of the Ordinance. Chapter II of Part II of the Ordinance deals with Geneva Convention Awards. Section 57 gives the conditions for enforcement of those foreign awards.

Chapter III of the Ordinance deals with provisions for conciliation. Conciliation under this Part can be undertaken only if both the parties to the dispute agree. If the parties agree, the conciliators appointed under the agreement shall assist the parties in an independent and impartial manner in their attempt to reach an amicable settlement of their dispute. The conciliator shall be guided by principles of objectivity, fairness and justice, giving consideration to, among other things, the rights and obligation of the parties, the usages of the trade concerned and the circumstances surrounding the dispute, including any previous business practices between the parties.

GENERAL

Before concluding, it is necessary to emphasise two matters:

(1) The speed or time consumed in arbitration proceedings depends in great measure upon the cooperation of the parties and their counsel. Experience shows that in the case of a claim by a South Korean party against an Indian party, it took more than two years for the South Korean party even to file its statement of claim on the grounds of language difficulty and lack of familiarity with law on the subject even though it was represented by one of the top Indian solicitors. There have been other cases where the parties showed promptness in completing claim statements, replies, replications and producing evidence, where the proceedings were finished in a matter of months.

(2) The awards of Indian arbitrators in disputes between an Indian party and a foreign party have by and large been fair, unaffected by any consideration of the nationality of either party.

CHAPTER 19

LIVING CONDITIONS AND PROCEDURAL FORMALITIES FOR A FOREIGN BUSINESS EXECUTIVE VISITING OR WORKING IN INDIA

by Susmita Gongulee Thomas

OVERVIEW

It has often been remarked that India is not a country but a continent. Across the length and breadth of the country, the languages are different, people are different as are their customs. Few countries on this planet offer the enormous variety that India does.

ENTRY INTO INDIA

Foreign business executives entering India are required to carry a valid passport endorsed with a valid visa. These visas are issued by Indian Embassies and Consulates abroad. Business visas may be issued for up to five years, with a multiple entry provision, and can be renewed or extended within India if the applicant so desires. A foreign national who has been issued a business visa is free to work in India.

Foreigners wishing to work in India can obtain a multiple entry employment visa valid for one year. This visa can be renewed for a longer period of time, in India. With this type of visa, the foreign national is free to travel in and out of the country.

A foreign national wishing to stay in India longer than 180 days needs to obtain a registration certificate or residential permit. These may be obtained, normally within a period of two to three days, from the Foreigners Regional Registration Offices in the four metropolitan cities, or at the State level from the Foreigners Office of the State where he will be stationed. The registration certificate needs to be obtained within 14 days of arrival in India and is to be endorsed by the authorities prior to the foreign national's departure.

Health Related Entry Regulations

Apart from yellow fever vaccinations for people coming from infected areas, there are no vaccination requirements for visitors to India.

Air Connections

India is extremely well connected by air to all parts of the world with the major international airlines having regular flights into the country. The metropolitan cities of Delhi, Mumbai, Calcutta, Madras, and Bangalore have direct international connections. The large air cargo/transport and courier companies also operate in and out of India.

Transfer of Residence

Under this scheme, which applies to foreign nationals visiting India for long durations, certain personal effects can be imported without the payment of customs duty. The goods have to be shipped within one month of entry into India or despatched by air within a fortnight of arrival in India. However, a wide variety of all consumer durables and non-durables are now freely available in India and hence do not need to be imported.

LIVING IN INDIA

New Delhi with its tree-lined boulevards and modern shopping complexes is the capital of India. Situated along the Arabian Sea, Mumbai, the financial capital of the country, is renowned for its work culture and professionalism. With a rich religious heritage and the capital of one of South India's States having the highest literacy rates, Madras is a focal point for tourists. Calcutta has a rich commercial and industrial heritage with a plethora of intellectuals hailing from this city. What has now come to be known as the 'Silicon Plateau', Bangalore, is the centre for the information technology industry in India.

Some of the important features facilitating living and working in India are:

- English is the principal language of business and administration.
- The cost of living, compared to American and European standards, is low enough for expatriates to be able to enjoy a very comfortable standard of living.
- A dynamic private sector.
- A free and vibrant Press.
- A sophisticated legal and accounting system.

- Wide-ranging avenues for entertainment and recreation, details of which are given below.
- Good international schools.

Recreation and Entertainment

All large towns in India have a number of five star hotels and clubs offering a wide range of entertainment facilities, eg, squash, tennis, snooker, swimming, gymnasium etc. Golf is rapidly gaining popularity and a large number of courses are appearing all over the country.

Twenty-four-hour cable television is available. BBC and CNN news is telecast around the clock. Even the French channels A2, TF1 and FR3 are available through some of the cable television distributors.

Food and Drink

The basic art of Indian cooking lies in the careful blending of different spices to yield subtle variations in flavours. Curries form the mainstay of Indian cuisine, which varies from region to region. The taste, colour, texture, appearance and aroma of the same delicacy changes every few kilometres. Regional differences in religion, culture and local produce have influenced eating habits to yield an intriguing diversity of exotic, tasty dishes.

In case one wants a change from the wide variety of Indian cuisine, there are restaurants in every major city offering French, Thai, Mexican, Chinese and Italian food.

Tourism

Apart from its ancient culture and civilisation, old forts, monuments and palaces, the country is endowed with diverse natural resources—a 7500 kilometre shoreline, the 3500 kilometre snow-capped Himalayan range, vast sand dunes and tropical forests.

India has a flourishing tourism industry with a number of well-located holiday resorts. A few well-known hotel companies now in India are Day's Inn Inc, Choice Hotels International, Sheraton, Best Western, Meridien, Holiday Inn, Radisson, Ramada Inn, Sofitel, Kempenski, and Resort Condominiums.

Facilities for leisure and adventure tourism are widely available. Expatriates, foreign tourists and locals can enjoy skiing, heli-skiing, mountaineering, hang-gliding, para-gliding, parachuting, windsurfing, and white-water rafting at the most scenic of locations.

Inland Transport and Travel

Travelling within India has never been easier. With over half a dozen private airlines competing to provide services with the State-owned Indian Airlines, all parts of the country are well connected by air.

To better appreciate the diversity of the country, it is possible to cover every nook and cranny by rail or road. Air conditioned rail coaches with the most modern amenities are competitively priced and attract travellers wishing to have a leisurely trip.

Shopping

There has been an increase in the variety of consumer durables and non-durables which are now freely available all over India. Along with the presence of the large Indian corporations, it is possible to purchase products manufactured by the leading multinationals, eg Suzuki, Daewoo, Kawasaki, Honda, Yamaha, Sanyo, Sony, Bosch and Electrolux. In the consumer non-durables sector, products from Unilever, Procter & Gamble, Henkel, Gillette, Coca Cola, Pepsico, Benetton, and Levi Strauss jostle for space alongside Indian brands.

Traditional Indian handicrafts have a worldwide reputation for quality and beauty. Every region has its own unique style of workmanship. These objects and artefacts are reasonably priced and freely available.

Currency

The Indian currency, the rupee (Rs), is divided into 100 paise. There are coins of 10, 20, 25 and 50 paise and Rs1, 2 and 5 as well as notes of Rs1, 2, 5, 10, 20, 50, 100 and 500.

Bringing Indian currency into India is not allowed. However, it is possible to bring in an unlimited amount of foreign currency in either cash or in travellers' cheques though any amount in excess of US$10,000 must be declared on arrival.

Credit Cards

Credit cards are popular and widely accepted. Diner's Club, MasterCard, American Express and Visa are among the major international cards present in India. Credit cards issued by various banks in India are also popular.

Business Hours

Shops, banks and post offices generally open at 10 am. Banks close for business at 2 pm and post offices at 5 pm. Shops are open till 7 pm six days a week. Sunday is normally a day off. The Federal Government works from 9 am to 5.30 pm five days a week. State governments generally work from 10 am to 6 pm five days a week and on the second and fourth Saturdays of every month.

Communications

Local, interstate and international telephone calls can be made with ease in any part of India. STD/ISD call booths with direct interstate and international dialling are freely available and are well signposted.

Media

There are a number of daily newspapers in English in India, as well as different types of Indian magazines in English which have large circulations. *Time, Newsweek, The Economist* and other international news magazines as well as newspapers are readily available.

Time

India is $5\frac{1}{2}$ hours ahead of GMT, $4\frac{1}{2}$ hours behind Australian Eastern Standard Time, and $10\frac{1}{2}$ hours ahead of American Eastern Standard Time.

Electric Current

Voltage in most places in India is 220AC 50 cycles, though a few areas have DC supply as well. It is advisable to check the voltage before using an electric shaver or any other electrical appliance.

Hospitals

Most Indian cities have high quality medical care available in several excellent hospitals. India also has many highly qualified doctors with their own private clinics offering the entire range of health care services.

Climate

India has well defined seasons:

Summer—April to June
Monsoon—July to September
Winter—October to March

Repatriation of Earnings

A foreign national may open bank accounts in India and receive funds from abroad, and may repatriate 75% of his net after-tax earnings after his employment is approved by the government and the exchange control authorities. If employment is for a short duration, such approvals are not necessary provided the amount of remittance is within approved limits.

Culture

India is one of the longest continuously surviving civilisations in the world and has developed its vision of life over thousands of years. In addition to having the satisfaction of working in a modern industrial State comprising a sixth of the human race, expatriates can look forward to a rewarding and enriching cultural experience.

PART 4
INDUSTRY SURVEYS:
REVIEW AND OPPORTUNITIES

POLICY AND OPPORTUNITY IN THE INDIAN POWER SECTOR

by P Abraham

THE INDIAN POWER SECTOR—AN INTRODUCTION

Electricity is a basic requirement for any economic activity and for a developing country like India availability of adequate power becomes extremely important as the overall success or failure of the economic development programme of the country would largely depend on infrastructural support. The country has various natural energy resources, including a vast hydro-electric potential estimated at 84,000 MW, 197 billion tonnes of coal reserves, 26 billion tonnes of lignite, 728 million tonnes of crude oil and 686 billion cubic metres of natural gas. This apart, it has a potential of about 30,000 MW of non-conventional energy. The per capita energy consumption is one of the lowest in the world at about 250 kg of oil equivalent. About 20% of this comes from electrical energy.

An Overview of India's Power Sector

Installed capacity (MW)	83,500
Power generation (BKWh)	380
Villages electrified (million)	0.5
(85% of total villages)	
Transmission and distribution network	5
(million circuit km)	
Per capita power consumption (kWh)	325

Independent high voltage regional and State transmission grids have been developed with suitable interstate links for optimum flow of power. Linking of various power regions and establishment of an inter-regional power grid, leading ultimately to the formation of a national grid, is underway.

Though the Indian electricity supply industry began its growth in the private environment it has achieved its present stature largely under government control. After Independence, power generation and distribution was reserved exclusively for the public sector and the responsibility for the growth of the power sector was passed on to State governments and State Electricity Boards through a process of gradual nationalisation. However, even during the period when it was brought under government control, some private licensees were allowed to operate in selected pockets of the country mainly because of operational considerations. These private enterprises not only existed, they flourished and performed exceedingly well in financial terms. In the mid-1970s, however, primarily due to rapidly growing demand for electricity in the country, constraints on the financial resources of the State governments and also the need for a more equitable distribution of available energy resources in the country, the Central Government decided in favour of more active participation in the development programme. This direct central intervention resulted in an accelerated growth of the power sector in terms of capacity.

However, towards the late 1980s, an increasing need for resources was recognised, mainly due to the very large capital needs of the sector, resource constraints on the State governments and the Central Government's inability to increase financial support. This last was due to the unprecedented economic crisis faced by the country and competing demands from other sectors of the economy. This led to the historic decision to open up the economy and consequently the power sector to private capital investment.

DEMAND PROJECTIONS

Despite the phenomenal growth of the sector, the per capita power consumption in the country, at 314 kWh per annum, is among the lowest in the world. India's transmission and distribution losses are among the highest in the world and power shortages arise in almost all parts of the country. The country will need an incremental capacity of around 57,000 MW during the 9th five-year plan (1997–2002) and nearly 65,000 MW during the 10th five-year plan (2002–2007). At the end of the Eighth five-year plan, corresponding to the anticipated 20,000 MW capacity addition the country is estimated to face a peaking deficit of about 29% and the energy shortage is expected to be around 15% with a varying degree of shortages in the different power regions. Thus it is estimated that the country will need increased capacity at a rate of about 10,000–12,000 MW per annum during the next decade and a half.

POWER SECTOR REFORMS

The Indian electricity sector is being structurally re-engineered. As in many other parts of the world, natural monopolies that emerged in the sector are generally giving way to competition. The reforms process, which started in 1991, has found wide acceptance. Under the reform programme the State Electricity Boards, which have mainly been instrumental in the phenomenal growth of the Indian power industry so far, are being structurally and financially remoulded to develop as viable commercial entities and to compete with the private sector on a sound footing. The Government of India has formulated comprehensive policies in this direction and many State governments have already initiated the process for restructuring their respective State Electricity Boards (SEB).

PRIVATE POWER POLICY OF THE GOVERNMENT OF INDIA

The Government of India is actively seeking greater investments by private enterprises in electricity generation and distribution. The incentives in the policy which complement the amended provisions in the electricity legislation comprehensively cover the legal, administrative and financial environment to make private investments in the industry attractive. A two part tariff system for thermal (coal/lignite/gas/liquid fuel based) power projects, to be established by generating companies to cover the fixed costs with 16% return on equity (ROE) at 68.5% PLF and variable energy cost in electricity pricing, has been formulated. To encourage efficiency in plant operation and offer a higher return to project promoters an attractive incentive scheme based on utilisation has also been formulated. Setting up of power projects being a complex exercise, requiring a number of statutory and non-statutory clearances, organisational changes have been effected to pro-actively assist and guide prospective entrepreneurs in setting up power projects and to streamline project clearance. The rapid growth in demand for electricity in India has made it necessary to supplement resources by direct foreign investment. To encourage foreign participation, up to 100% foreign equity participation has been permitted and tax and customs duty concessions announced. The salient features of the scheme to encourage greater private sector participation in electricity generation, supply and distribution are:

- The private sector can set up generation projects—thermal, hydro, wind and solar of any size.
- The private sector can take part in distribution as licensee or operate as the generating company.

- Up to 4:1 debt-equity ratio is allowed to all private companies entering the electricity sector.

- The promoter's contribution should be at least 11% of the total outlay.

- To ensure that private entrepreneurs bring in additional resources to the industry, not less than 60% of the total outlay for the project must come from sources other than Indian public financial institutions.

- Up to 100% foreign equity participation can be permitted for projects set up by foreign private investors.

- Up to 16% return on the foreign equity included in the tariff can be provided in the respective foreign currency.

- Fixed costs can be recovered at 68.5% PLF. Attractive incentives are prescribed for performance beyond this PLF.

- Normative parameters notified which, inter alia, provide for 16% return on equity at 68.5% PLF and up to 0.7% return on each incremental 1% PLF.

- Rates for depreciation of assets have been liberalised.

- With the approval of the government, the import of equipment for power projects will also be permitted in cases where foreign suppliers or agencies extend concessional credit.

- The customs duty for import of power equipment has been reduced to 20% and this rate has also been extended to machinery required for modernisation and renovation of power plants.

- A five year tax holiday has been allowed.

- The excise duty on a large number of capital goods and instruments in the power sector has been reduced.

- Generating companies operating coal based, gas based and hydro projects can sell power on the basis of a suitably structured two-part tariff.

- Liberalised tariff norms for hydro-electric projects providing Capacity Charge, Primary Energy Charge, incentive of up to 0.7% rise in ROE for each percentage point increase in availability of installed capacity beyond 90%.

- Attractive policy guidelines framed for R&M of generating stations, captive/co-generation plants.

To provide adequate safeguards to investors, efforts are being made to develop viable mechanisms on a short-term basis to meet the immediate needs of investors. However, in the longer term, efforts are underway to make the power sector self-sustainable and SEBs, which are closely linked to the reforms, are being restructured. State reforms are being encouraged and assisted. A number of State governments have already initiated the electricity sector reform process, and the others are expected to do this soon.

ADMINISTRATIVE FRAMEWORK

In order to facilitate private sector participation in power development, the required administration was set up. A high-powered Board under the Chairmanship of the Cabinet Secretary was created which monitors issues of clearances and resolves all outstanding issues pertaining to clearances. In addition an Investment Promotion Cell (IPC) was created in the Ministry of Power, which directly deals with prospective private power promoters and assists in getting clearances. The process of obtaining techo-economic clearance from the Central Electricity Authority (CEA) has been streamlined and a system of two-stage clearance from the CEA has been introduced. The CEA now provides 'in-principle' clearance to projects as an interim measure to facilitate other clearances to be obtained by the developers and to initiate negotiation with leaders. To expedite the clearance process further, projects on the competitive bidding route costing less than US$115 million (Rs400 crores) have been exempt from clearance of the Central Electricity Authority.

In the beginning, the States mostly opted for the negotiation route for private sector participation. This, however, has been modified and competitive bidding was made compulsory after 18 February, 1995.

THE RESPONSE

In the four years since the policy to encourage greater private investment was introduced a large number of developers have expressed interest in the Indian power industry. A total of 245 proposals for creating additional capacity of about 94,000 MW involving an investment of over US$105 billion have been received. This includes proposals from foreign investors for 52 projects involving an investment of US$50 billion for 39,000 MW capacity. Some of these expressions of interest are at an advanced stage and work on some of these projects is expected to commence soon.

To encourage private participation in transmission and distribution, a comprehensive policy with detailed guidelines is being formulated. Guidelines for encouraging private investment in the areas of R&M of thermal and hydro-electric power stations and captive/co-generation plants have recently been announced by the government.

FUTURE OPPORTUNITIES

The demand for electricity in the country is large and growing at a rate of over 9% per annum. Meeting the power demand of the future is through enhancement of generating capacity through greenfield projects, refurbishing older plants to improve their availability, reducing the transmission and distribution losses, effective demand side management, and energy conservation. It is estimated that an additional capacity of 142,000 MW would be required by 2007 to meet growth in demand, requiring resources in the order of US$150 billion. Of this about 60,000 MW is estimated to be created by the public sector and the balance has to come through private investment. In a market the size of India, there is enormous scope for all. Apart from a vast market, India offers a distinct advantage of flourishing private companies in the power and other industrial fields, a competent electricity generation, transmission and distribution industry offering state-of-the-art technology and quality of service accepted the world over, a vast pool of trained and skilled manpower with a capacity to absorb new management techniques and sophisticated technologies and a well-established legal system which is conducive to private sector development. India is experiencing strong economic growth. This presents enormous opportunities for all.

CHAPTER 21

HIGHWAYS AND PORTS
by A D Narain

HIGHWAYS

Overview

Road infrastructure and administration

India has a 2.1 million-kilometre-long road network spread over 3.3 million sq km of land mass. Road availability per 100 sq km is approximately 60 km, and 2300 km per million population. Nearly half of the network is surfaced. National Highways (NHs) are the major roads and their total length is 34,058 km (or 2% of the network length), followed by State Highways (SHs) (6% of the network length). Other categories are District Roads (DR), Municipal Roads, Village Roads (VRs) and roads constructed and maintained by Project Authorities. NHs are developed and maintained by the Central Government through budgetary allocations from the Central Government, and the actual implementation is carried out by State governments on an agency basis. The Central Ministry responsible for NH Development is the Ministry of Surface Transport. Recently, an autonomous body called National Highways Authority of India (NHAI) has been created which is the central implementation agency for NH developments. SHs, DRs and VRs are funded through State budgets and State governments are also the implementing agencies.

Growth of road traffic

There has been phenomenal growth in road traffic over the years. In 1950–51, roads carried just 6 billion tonne kilometres (BTK) of freight and moved 23 billion passenger kilometres (BPK). Today the corresponding figures have shot up to 400 BTK and 1500 BPK respectively. In the initial years of planning, India's economy was rail-dominated and now the railways are second to roads in both freight and passenger movement. Nearly 60% of freight movement (11% in 1951) and 80% of passenger movement (28% in 1951) are carried on roads. Vehicle population has been growing at 11% and vehicular traffic in important corridors is registering a growth of approximately 10%. These are clear indications of high patronage of road transport in preference to any other mode.

Road Development Policy

Planning goals

Road infrastructure in the country has to support and facilitate faster growth of the economy by providing accessibility to the far-flung villages as well as mobility for speedier movement of passengers and goods. Development has thus to address the needs of all categories of road—village roads to high speed expressways—and provide capacity matching the demand, both present as well as future.

Policy objectives

The objectives of road development policy in India are as follows:

(1) Providing connection between villages through a network of village roads.

(2) Upgrading the road network by strengthening the pavement, providing shoulders, drainage, etc.

(3) Increasing capacity of the high density corridors either through access controlled expressways on new alignments or by providing additional lanes, wider bridges, grade-separated intersections and bypasses around urban centres on existing routes.

(4) Upgrading road and bridge construction technology.

(5) Improving institutional arrangements and management techniques for speedier implementation of highway projects.

(6) Improved design and enforcement leading to better road safety.

(7) Augmenting resources for road development.

(8) Improving vehicle technology and promoting multi-axled vehicles.

(9) Integrating road development with other modes of transport.

Strategies adopted

(1) Connection to villages: In the course of 45 years of planned development, substantial progress has been made in providing access to villages. Over 90% of the villages having a population of more than 1500 were connected by roads by the beginning of the 1990s and it is expected that by the end of the Eighth Five-Year Plan (1997), almost total connection will be achieved.

(2) Problems of high density corridors: Capacity constraints of high density corridors have not been fully removed for want of finance. Some progress has, however, been made in bringing about improvements in high priority sections through external funding

routed through Central/State budgets. As an alternative, efforts are being made to mobilise private sources of funding.

(3) Expressway development: The necessity of providing access-controlled expressways in the high density corridors has been fully appreciated by the government. However, the government's inability to commit, out of its limited budget, adequate funds for acquisition of land has not allowed the expressway programme to really take off so far, even with private sector participation. With NHAI's capital base being strengthened, it is expected that in the near future NHAI will be able to generate funds for the purpose when it would be possible to take up Public-Private expressway projects in selected corridors under the BOT scheme.

(4) Private sector funding: The government feels that tolls charged for use of an improved highway infrastructure can service the debts raised by private entrepreneurs as well as fetch them a reasonable return on their equity. The reason for this confidence is to be found in users' overwhelming patronage of and preference for road transport, notwithstanding severe capacity constraints, consequent higher vehicle operating costs and fairly high travel time on crowded NHs. Moreover, the bulk of road transport operation, both in passenger as well as freight movement, is in private hands and as a result, there is a distinct demand for improved infrastructure with willingness to pay for improved services. This provides a sound basis for pursuit of private sector funding on Build-Operate-and-Transfer (BOT) terms. The government has accordingly decided to follow this policy.

(5) Upgrading of road/bridge construction technology: In recent years, many large construction projects have brought about improvements in technology. The usual contract size is about US\$30–40 million and these contracts, awarded on an International Competitive Bidding (ICB) basis, have attracted a number of foreign construction firms to undertake work in this country using the latest construction machinery and equipment. The conditions of such contracts are based on standard FIDIC documents with minor local adaptation. The domestic construction industry has been equipping itself, either on its own or in collaboration with its multinational partners/firms, to undertake high-tech road/bridge construction jobs.

(6) Promoting multi-modal transportation: There are basically two road-related problems in multi-modal transportation, each of which is receiving the government's attention. The first problem relates to modernisation of the vehicle fleet so as to have a higher proportion

of multi-axled vehicles which could carry large size containers. At present, multi-axled vehicles contribute to about 3% of the total freight movement in tonne per km which, according to a World Bank study, needs to be raised to at least 23% by the year 2003. This is being addressed by the Industries Ministry and it is hoped that the current liberalised economic environment which permits manufacture of vehicles by foreign companies will help build capacities in the area. The other problem relates to the deficiencies in road capacity and requirements of other infrastructure, eg terminal and wayside facilities. A study has been instituted to address these issues.

(7) Research and development efforts: These are currently directed to creation and maintenance of a road database and development of pavement and bridge management systems to identify the need, frequency and location of maintenance intervention. In addition, research is currently in progress on a number of subjects such as development of a design and maintenance model, evolving pavement design methods, behaviour of structures under various loading and environmental conditions, and new materials such as geosynthetics, etc.

(8) Alternative sources of funding: Given a tight budget and the government's commitment to the social sector, any sizeable increase in budgetary allocations for the road sector does not appear likely. Alternative sources of funding through a levy on fuel and vehicle registration is being contemplated. Consultations between various Ministries of the Central Government on the one hand, and between Central and State Governments on the other, are currently under way.

Procedure for Private Sector Participation

Areas for private sector participation

Private sector entities can invest in highway construction in India in the following areas: (a) consultancy services, (b) construction contracts, and (c) project development (on BOT terms).

Consultancy services

The Government maintains a panel of consultants, including foreign consultants in terms of specific areas of specialisation such as highways, bridges, traffic and transportation. For any job offered for consultancy services, a long list is drawn from the panel and proposals for shortlisting are invited from the long listed firms. Sometimes, the long list is also provided by the external funding agencies such as World Bank, Asian Development Bank, etc. On the basis of proposals received from the firms, a short list of usually six firms is drawn up based on objective assessment of the firms' financial and technical capabilities as reflected in their documents. Technical proposals and financial bids are then called separately from the shortlisted firms. On the basis of technical evaluation, the firms are ranked in order of merit. The financial bids are then opened. In the case of externally funded schemes, the policies of the lending agencies are followed. In case of domestic projects (ie those not funded by external agencies), the bids are evaluated on the basis of a pre-determined weighting for technical and financial bids.

Construction contracts

Contracts for construction (including improvement, rehabilitation, etc) are decided on the basis of competitive bidding. For large sized contracts (US$6 million or more), the bids are invited only from prequalified contractors. All externally funded contracts are based on the system of ICB and contractors from member countries of the institutions (such as World Bank, Asian Development Bank) are eligible to bid. Applications for prequalification (PQ) are invited through widely publicised advertisement and PQ applications are processed on the basis of the firms' financial strength and experience in similar works undertaken in the past and the capacity of the firm is ascertained. The bids are invited from the prequalified contractors and any clarifications required by the prospective bidders are furnished in a pre-bid meeting. After the receipt of bids, evaluation is done in two stages, viz, technical evaluation followed by financial evaluation. Usually, the lowest price offer is accepted.

BOT schemes

A large number of bypasses, bridges and road overbridges are proposed to be developed under BOT schemes. Feasibility study of the projects is being carried out in the first instance, forming the basis of the bidding document prepared by the government. Bidders are usually prequalified on the basis of their experience and financial strength. The process of bidding is competitive and bids are decided on the principle of lowest cost to the user. The options possible are either to get a quotation of a toll structure for a fixed concession period, or a concession period for a specified toll structure. As toll structure has to be approved and notified by the government, the second option is being favoured for selection of the bidders. The design and performance standard for the facility are specified in the bid document. Project-wise steering committees, with representations from the Central Government, implementing agency and the private entrepreneur, are set up to oversee the project right up to the end of the concession period. The committee deals with all aspects of project implementation and is also assigned the responsibility of taking all decisions, including resolving disputes arising in the course of the concession period. The BOT developer, of course, can opt for arbitration for unresolved disputes. Where large size projects are put on international competitive bidding the entrepreneur is permitted the option of UNCITRAL arbitration procedure.

Opportunities for private sector participation

Government has opened up the opportunities for private sector participation in a big way. It has provided a legal and institutional framework as well as a facilitating environment. The highlights of these measures are presented below:

Institutional changes: A number of institutional improvements has been brought about in recent years to ensure better quality in engineering services as well as improvement in project delivery. The main areas of improvements are as follows:

(a) Engineering services which were hitherto provided essentially by State/Central government departments have now been privatised to a great extent by engaging specialist consultants for these services.

(b) The project implementation framework has been substantially modified by creating specialist project implementation and project management cells in Centre as well as States and management and supervision of projects is being carried out through specialist domestic and foreign consultants.

(c) A new organisation, called the National Highways Authority of India (NHAI), has been created under an Act of Parliament for improved project implementation. This Central organisation has been given autonomy and freedom of operation and is mandated to run on commercial principles.

Facilitating private investment on a BOT basis: In order to facilitate private investment, steps taken are as follows:

(1)   National Highways Act, 1956, which governs the development and maintenance of NHs in the country, has been amended and in the States, the Motor Vehicles Act has been amended or legislation enacted to enable the private sector to participate and retain the user fee.

(2)   Revenue earned from development of wayside amenities like petrol stations, motels, parking/repair stations, transport nagars, etc can be retained by the private entrepreneur.

(3)   NHAI has been made the nodal agency for implementation of private sector projects under the BOT scheme.

(4)   High-powered committees have been set up to facilitate clearances and monitor implementation of BOT projects.

(5)   The government is prepared to meet the cost of land acquisition and also to acquire and lease the required land to the private entrepreneurs.

(6)   Sharing of risks between the government and the private investor has been accepted in principle and details can be negotiated on a project-to-project basis.

(7)   A number of liberalisation measures announced by the government since 1991, such as permitting foreign investment, repatriation of profits, reduction in import duty, foreign technology arrangements, permitting repatriate staff on a project, etc are generally applicable to the road sector as well.

(8)   Fiscal benefits in the form of a tax holiday for five years on earnings from investment in infrastructure including roads has been accepted by the government and this facility can be availed of within 12 years (under revision up to 15 years) of completion of the project.

(9)   The Finance Minister has announced in his budget speech of 1995–96 creation of an Infrastructure Development Finance Company (IDFC) with an authorised capital of Rs5000 crore (US$1.4 billion) of which Rs1000 crore will come from the Central Government and Reserve Bank of India, and the remainder from banks and financial institutions. The company will provide project finances and financial guarantees and induce investors to make available long-term funds at low rates.

(10) A sum of Rs200 crore (US$570,000) has been provided to strengthen the capital base of NHAI with a view to leveraging

resources for highway development both from within India and from outside.

PORTS

Overview

Port infrastructure and administration

There are 11 major ports along the Indian coastline. These are Kandla, Bombay, Jawaharlal Nehru, Mormugao, New Mangalore and Cochin on the West Coast and Calcutta (including Haldia), Paradip, Visakhapatnam, Madras and Tuticorin on the East Coast. The major ports are the responsibility of the Central Government and the concerned Central Ministry is the Ministry of Surface Transport. There is an autonomous body called a 'Port Trust' for each of the major ports, which is responsible for the development and operation of these ports. Port development is mostly carried out through the internal resources generated by the Port Trusts. External funding and private sector participation is also resorted to. In addition to the 11 major ports, there are 139 minor ports dotting the Indian coastline. The minor ports are the responsibility of the respective maritime State governments.

Growth of port traffic

Traffic in major ports has registered phenomenal growth over the years. In 1950–51, the major ports handled just 20 million tonnes, which rose to 215 million tonnes in 1995–96 and is likely to grow to 236 million tonnes by 1996–97. As regards container handling, the major ports carry about 1.3 million TEUs per year. Indian shipping tonnage has risen from 0.2 million GRT in 1951 to 6.34 million GRT with a fleet strength of 437 ships. There is tremendous demand on ports to augment their infrastructure and modernise operations in view of high growth projections (nearly 20% in value terms) of India's foreign trade.

Port Development Policy

Policy goals

The goals of port development policy are to augment port infrastructure and improve operational efficiency to meet the requirements of India's expanding foreign trade and make Indian export goods competitive in the world market. This would ultimately lead to an increase in domestic production and hence GDP growth.

Policy objectives

In order to achieve these goals, the following policy objectives need to be fulfilled:

(1) Creation of additional port infrastructure facilities (berths, jetties, warehouses, container terminals, etc).

(2) Acquisition of cargo handling equipment.

(3) Increase in containerisation of cargo and creation of associated facilities.

(4) Promoting multi-modal transportation.

(5) Attracting new generation liner ships to Indian ports.

(6) Improving productivity of labour and bringing changes in labour deployment methods.

(7) Bringing uniformity in documents and adopting a system of Electronic Document Interchange (EDI).

(8) Simplifying customs procedures and making them user-friendly.

(9) Reducing 'dwell time' of ships at ports and improving fast clearance of cargo from port premises.

(10) Reducing 'throughport' costs to bring them at par with ports of other countries in the region.

(11) Integrate port development with 'road' and 'rail' development.

In order to achieve these objectives, the Ministry of Surface Transport and the various Port Trusts have taken many initiatives which are discussed in the succeding sections.

Strategies adopted

(1) Leasing of Port Infrastructure: Berths have been leased at Bombay Port to M/s American President Lines (which is now over) and at Haldia Port to M/s Steel Authority of India Limited (SAIL) and Tata Iron and Steel Company (TISCO).

(2) Private investment in port infrastructure: This is permitted under the Major Port Trust Act, 1963 and private investment has already been approved in many cases for creation of port

infrastructure. Some examples are as follows:

(i) Mangalore Refineries and Petrochemicals Limited (MRPL) is developing crude handling facilities at New Mangalore Port.

(ii) A number of companies have been leased land for development of storage and warehousing facilities for setting up an LPG storage facility.

(iii) Land and water spread area has been leased to M/s Western Indian Shipyard Limited for floating dry dock/ship repair in collaboration with M/s LISNAVE of Portugal at Mormugao Port.

(iv) Ship repair facility is being set up at Madras by M/s Chokani Shipyard Limited in collaboration with M/s Keepel of Singapore.

(v) Jawaharlal Nehru Port Trust (JNPT) has been permitted to take equipment such as cranes and reach stackers on lease from private parties.

(3) Containerisation of cargo: Indian Ports have taken many steps to facilitate container handling. Bombay, Calcutta/Haldia, Madras and Jawaharlal Nehru Ports together handle more than 50% of general cargo in containerised form. With all the 11 ports taken together, the percentage of general cargo handled in containerised form is 36%. Full-fledged container handling facilities exist at Jawaharlal Nehru Port, Madras, Cochin, Bombay and Calcutta/Haldia, and among these Jawaharlal Nehru and Madras have full-fledged container terminals as well. Cochin Port is likely to have a modern container terminal very shortly.

(4) Efficient operation in ports: This is being addressed by MOST and various Port Trusts basically as under:

(a) Improving labour productivity: Indian Ports have traditionally engaged large work forces with different gangs for on-board and on-shore operations. Steps have been taken for effecting merger of these gangs and making them interchangeable. Labour unions have been taken into confidence and manning scales have been reduced while datums increased. The government has also introduced a voluntary retirement scheme which has been taken up by a sizeable section of the workforce.

(b) Deploying modern handling equipment: Port Trusts are deploying modern handling equipment either through outright acquisition or by leasing this equipment from private parties for efficient cargo handling.

(5) Multi-modal transportation: In 1993, the Multimodal Transportation of Goods Act was passed to facilitate door-to-door movement of containers. About 80 multi-modal transport operators (MTOs) have so far been registered. The provisions of the Act are based on UNCTAD/ICC rules. The Act has, however, been found wanting in some respects by users and operators, especially in the matter of liabilities of the MTOs. Amendment to the Act is being contemplated with a view to making its application consistent and smooth. There are two other problems ascribed to multi-modal operation in India, one of which is the capacity constraints of rail as well as road. The second problem relates to safeguards against loss of custom revenue due to tampering with containers en route. These issues are currently receiving serious attention from the government and solutions will emerge in the near future.

(6) Introduction of EDI services: .The government is aware of the immense potential of information technology and is keen to develop an EDI system and provide on-line services to major port users such as MTOs and trading houses. The Ministry of Commerce is the nodal Ministry and customs establishments at many locations have already been computerised. Major ports are networked by PORTNET developed by National Informatics Centre (NIC) and these are likely to be integrated with EDI. The full EDI system, however, is yet to be introduced. Once done, it will help foreign trade by cutting down delays at ports and customs establishments while at the same time keeping the exporters/importers, MTOs and all concerned fully informed about various stages of goods movement.

(7) Reduction in 'throughport' costs: In order to make Indian exports competitive in the world market, the government is concerned about comparatively high 'throughport' costs. The first step in reducing these costs has already been taken by increasing labour productivity and improving cargo handling facilities. With privatised operation of ports and adoption of EDI services, the throughport costs will reduce and become competitive.

(8) Integrated approach to surface transport: The capacity constraints of individual modes such as road and rail are already being addressed by the respective organisations. For example, Indian Railways propose to augment their capacity through private sector participation under the Build-Operate-Lease-Transfer (BOLT) Scheme while the Road Authority has undertaken the Build-Operate-Transfer (BOT) Scheme. The government has recently decided to set up a high-powered committee to evolve an integrated approach to surface transport.

Procedures for private investment

Eleven Port Trusts, as stated earlier, are autonomous bodies created under the Major Port Trusts Act, 1963. The development and operation of port infrastructure is their responsibility. It is carried out by them either through their internal resources or through budgetary support from the government. Private sector participation in these activities is permissible under the Act and the broad principles governing private investment in ports are as follows:

(i) Tariff charges provided by the private party will be fixed by government.

(ii) Existing labour laws of the land will apply.

(iii) Private entrepreneurs who take over a port facility will be required to guarantee a minimum level of performance.

Due to the variety of areas where private sector participation is permitted, it is not possible to follow a standard model and the terms are usually case specific. These are spelt out in tender documents. However, efforts have been made to standardise the tender documents. Proposals are invited by the respective Port Trusts depending upon the requirements of individual ports. The selection of entrepreneurs is done on the basis of open competitive bidding.

Opportunities for private sector participation

In tune with current thinking the world over, the government is gradually moving towards operating the ports as landlord ports by providing infrastructure and leasing them to private parties for operation. The infrastructure itself can be created through private investment to be operated on lease terms. Containerisation and container handling facilities are key elements of port policy. With container terminals leased to private parties, more modern handling equipment is being deployed. In other cases, Port Trusts are acquiring on lease such equipment from private parties. There are also requirements for improved services and the private sector can be one of the providers. Briefly stated, the areas under which the private sector can invest are as follows: construction of berths and jetties; leasing of berths; setting up/operation of container terminals; setting up warehousing facilities and tank farms; operation and maintenance of various cargo handling terminals; operation and maintenance of floating craft and other equipment; provision of pilotage and crane services; dredging; leasing of equipment; construction of dry docks and repair facilities; and power generation.

The specific details can be obtained from the respective Chairs of the Port Trusts.

CONCLUSIONS

By and large, roads and port infrastructure is capacity constrained and removing these constraints has been high on the government's agenda in view of higher projections of GNP growth and expansion of foreign trade. There are many steps taken by the government in this regard and private sector participation in these areas has been the focus of the government's attention. There are numerous opportunities available for private sector participation in highways and ports. The legal and institutional framework is already in place and a number of facilitation measures have been taken. In view of these, prospects for growth and development appear very bright and there exist enormous opportunities for private sector involvement in these areas.

CHAPTER 22

ELECTRONICS/SOFTWARE SECTOR
by N Vittal

ELECTRONICS—A HIGH GROWTH SECTOR

Electronics, a relatively young industry, is one of the fastest growing sectors in India, along with software. This would be obvious from the figures given below:

	Electronics			Software
Year	Production (Rs million)	Growth (Rs million)	Exports (Rs million)	Production
1992–93	114,250	17.2%	6750	11650
1993–94	132,000	15.5%	10200	17150
1994–95	156,000	18.2%	14500	26100

ROLE OF THE DEPARTMENT OF ELECTRONICS

The Department of Electronics (DOE) is the nodal department of the Government of India entrusted with the task of coordinating policies and helping the growth of the electronic industry in the country. The objectives of the DOE are to bring the benefit of electronics to every facet of life in India and also to make India a global player in the electronics field. It will be noticed from the figures given above that India has a long way to go to achieve that level. But there are some factors which give hope.

SOME POTENTIAL FACTORS FOR FUTURE GROWTH

Indian Competence in Software

The competence of Indians in software has been recognised. Tom Peters, the management guru, in his book *The Tom Peters Seminar* predicts that Bangalore will be the global centre for software in the next century. The quality of Indian software engineers has been recognised. Companies such as Novell and Computervision have started R&D centres in India. Motorola's software centre in Bangalore has been graded at SEI #5 by the Carnegie Mellon University. Practically all leading multinationals in the software sector (like

Texas Instruments, Hewlett-Packard, IBM, Silicon Graphics and Compaq) have established facilities in India.

Large Domestic Market

The second important factor is the immense potential India projects with its population of 900 million and a middle class with great purchasing power estimated anywhere between 150 to 200 million. The economic liberalisation policies of the government from 1991 have forced Indian industry to think competitively. Industries are facing global competition even in the domestic market. This has resulted in the growth of the information technology industry as follows. (Source: DATAQUEST 1995 Top 20 issue.)

Information technology industry—highlights

* Total industry revenues Rs6,840,880 million, grows by 44%.
* Servers triple, touch Rs6060 million.
* 1995 was the year of the 486 systems; a total of 1.16 lakh 486 machines shipped.
* Total PCs shipped crosses 2 lakh mark; 233,990 units sold.
* MNC brands dominate PC growth.
* Large systems continue to sell, Rs1530 million sold in 1994.
* Macs beginning to sell, Rs500, million sold in 1994–95.
* Private sector buying at a hefty 59% of total, government 16%.
* Third party maintenance bounces back with 30% growth.
* Multi-user systems dip as clear trend towards client/server computing emerges.
* Non-impact printers post impressive growth, DMPs sluggish in the retail market.
* Laser printers market crosses Rs1000 million as inkjets market crosses Rs500 million.
* Software industry grows by 55%, domestic market outpaces software exports.
* Total software industry revenues—Rs23,460 million.
* Domestic IT spending grows by 33.5%, Rs44,770 million.
* Services sector major buyer, SOHO absorbs Rs2200 million of IT.
* Training industry crosses Rs3000 million mark, 53% growth.

Opening of the Telecommunications Sector

A third factor is the opening to the private investor of the telecommunication sector which was announced with the adoption of the National Telecom Policy (NTP94) on 13 May 1994. This is another boost for attracting investment in this sector. The policy announced the end of the monopoly by the government's Department of Telecommunications so far as telephone services are concerned and from the present level of about 8–9 million telephones in 1994–95, it is expected that, by the year 2000, 35 million telephones will be in position.

GOVERNMENT POLICY FOR ELECTRONICS/ SOFTWARE SECTOR

General

The government welcomes investment in the electronics and software sectors. The general procedure of the government regarding foreign investment governs this sector also. Foreign equity up to 100% is allowed on a case-by-case basis, to be determined by the Foreign Investment Promotion Board (FIPB). The FIPB is chaired by the Secretary to the Department of Industrial Promotion and Policy, Ministry of Industry. Already companies like Motorola and Sony have been allowed 100% equity.

Software Technology Park (STP)

The Software Technology Park (STP) scheme is a special scheme designed to encourage software exports. The scheme is administered by the Department of Electronics. Specific features of this scheme are:

(1)   Foreign equity up to 100% is permissible.

(2)   Except for items in the prohibited list, duty free import of all inputs, including capital goods is permitted.

(3)   An export obligation in net foreign exchange terms equal to $1\frac{1}{2}$ times the c.i.f. value of hardware imported and the wage bill incurred in India to be met by the unit.

(4)   Software supply under specific conditions such as projects requiring international competitive bidding etc also considered as exports and consequent benefits given.

(5)   Units permitted to sell 25% of production in value terms in the domestic market, after meeting export obligations.

(6)   STP units are exempt from payment of corporate income tax for a block of five years in the first eight years of operation.

The DOE has appointed Directors, in various places to run infrastructural facilities created to support small and medium software developers. They are authorised to approve resident investment proposals under the scheme not exceeding Rs30 million.

If the proposed investment exceeds Rs30 million, an Inter Ministerial Standing Committee in the Department of Electronics considers such proposals for approval. Proposals involving foreign equity are considered by the FIPB. In either case, the letter of approval is issued by the Secretariat of Industrial Approvals, Ministry of Industry.

Applications for setting up units under this scheme (proposals outside the purview of the Directors) should be submitted to the Secretariat for Industrial Approvals, Department of Industrial Development, Udyog Bhavan, New Delhi along with a crossed demand draft for Rs1000 drawn in favour of the Pay and Accounts Officer, Department of Industrial Development, Ministry of Industry, payable at the State Bank of India, Nirman Bhavan, New Delhi.

Electronic Hardware Technology Park (EHTP)

To encourage hardware development, the government has promoted the Electronic Hardware Technology Park (EHTP) scheme, which is administered by the Department of Electronics. The specific features of this scheme are:

(1)   Foreign equity up to 100% is permissible.

(2)   Except for items in the prohibited list, duty free import of all inputs, including capital goods, is permitted.

(3)   No minimum value addition. Value addition means the ratio of net foreign exchange to gross foreign exchange earned.

(4)   Supply of hardware under specific conditions, such as projects requiring international competitive bidding, is considered as exports, and consequent benefits given.

(5)   The units would be permitted to sell up to 40% of the production in value terms in the doemstic market, if the value addition exceeds 15%.

(6)   EHTP units are exempt from payment of corporate income tax for a block of five years in the first eight years' operation.

Foreign Investment Trends

The foreign investment trends in the software/hardware sector have been very encouraging. This is obvious from the following figures:

Software Technology Park Scheme

	1993	1994	1995 (to June 95)
No. of approvals	21	42	23
FE earning projected (US$ million)	100902	303735	145992
Investment (Rs in lakhs)	2369	10008	4711
Foreign Direct Investment (Rs in lakhs)	1865	5316	1779

Electronic Hardware Technology Park Scheme

	1993	1994	1995 (to June 95)
No. of approvals	11	18	11
FE earning projected (US$ million)	414150	1282969	328613
Investment (Rs in lakhs)	23253	28210	21328
Foreign Direct Investment (Rs in lakhs)	8376	4660	5738

OPPORTUNITIES

India provides excellent opportunities for outsourcing of software. Leading US companies such as Texas Instruments, Motorola, IBM, and Hewlett-Packard are already operating in India. In R&D, companies such as Novell and Computervision have chosen India as the base for operation. With excellent manpower and India having signed the GATT agreement, intellectual property rights in India are in tune with the rest of the world.

The EHTP scheme simulates conditions in countries such as Singapore, Hong Kong, and Taiwan and operations can be undertaken in a duty free environment with the advantage of access to the domestic market.

The National Telecom Policy 1994 has provided opportunities to the private sector for providing basic voice services, value-added services and also the manufacture of telecommunications equipment. This is an excellent opportunity as telephone density in India is only $1/100$ people as against the world average of $10/100$ people.

CHAPTER 23

THE MINERAL SECTOR
by Ashoke C Sen

The mines and minerals sector plays a crucial role in the Indian economy, providing fossil fuel energy and raw material for industrial development. The share of this sector in the Gross Domestic Product of the country is about 4%. The rate of growth of the mineral sector has generally been higher than the rate of the growth of the overall economy of the country.

POLICY

The National Mineral Policy 1993 governs the development of the mineral sector. The Policy recognises minerals as valuable natural resources which are finite and non-renewable. It seeks to develop mineral resources taking into account national considerations so as to ensure their adequate supply for industry as well as promoting mineral development with minimum adverse effects to the ecology and environment.

The Mineral Policy encourages the induction of foreign technology, foreign participation in exploration, and mining for high value and scarce minerals. Foreign equity investment in joint-ventures in mining promoted by Indian companies is encouraged. Foreign investment in equity is normally up to 50%, though this limitation does not apply to the captive mines of any mineral processing industry. Foreign equity holding in excess of 50% and up to 100% is also permitted on a case-by-case basis.

REVIEW OF THE CURRENT SCENARIO

At present, India produces 84 minerals out of which, four are fuel minerals, 11 metallic, 49 non-metallic and 20 minor minerals. The total value of mineral production in 1994–95 was about US$9 billion approximately. Mineral oils accounted for nearly 85% of this production, followed by metallic minerals which contributed nearly 8%, while non-metallic minerals including minor minerals contributed over 90% of the total mineral production. Public sector enterprises are dominant in the production of iron ore, aluminium, copper, zinc and gold.

There are about 3800 large and small mines in the country including 560 for coal and lignite. Out of these, 3200 mines are in the metalliferous sector. The mining sector provides employment for nearly 800,000 people directly. In addition, a large number of people are employed in mining-related activities such as processing and transportation. India is the largest producer of mica blocks and the third largest producer of chromite. Besides this, India ranks 2nd, 5th, 7th and 10th in the production of barytes, bauxite and iron ore, coal and lignite, and aluminium respectively.

OPPORTUNITIES FOR INVESTMENT

The high quality geological-exploration-aerogeophysical database generated by the national agencies makes investment in the mining sector in India an attractive proposition. The database available within the country comprises geological maps, tectonic maps, metallogenic maps, mineral belt maps, aerogeophysical maps, chemical analysis of rocks and a detailed inventory of all metallic and non-metallic mineral occurrences which can serve as an useful guide. Besides, the country has a very large reserve of experienced geoscientists and well-equipped laboratories which may be utilised for chemical, petrological and mineralogical studies.

Although adequate reserves of iron ore, bauxite, chromite, manganese ore, mica, zinc ore, coal and lignite have been identified, the sub-continental size of the country and favourable geological settings strongly indicate that fresh exploration ventures using modern technology may be rewarded with significant discoveries. The country has a vast expanse of the typical pre-Cambrian shield which is endowed like any other pre-Cambrian shield such as in South and Central Africa, Australia, Canada and Brazil with rich mineral wealth. Such shield areas invariably contain huge deposits of iron, manganese, gold, diamond, chromite, Platinum Group of Elements (PGE) and base metals.

The greatest attraction for fresh exploration ventures in India apart from a very favourable terrain and database is the fact that all past successes in mineral exploration were by and large achieved by conventional exploration techniques with restricted input from geo-chemistry, geophysics and remote sensing. Advanced geo-chemical, geophysical techniques capable of probing concealed deposits and which have a higher success ratio, have not yet been extensively tried in India. Properly planned exploration ventures in the field of gold, PGE, base metals, tin, tungsten, molybdenum, lithium, nickel, cobalt and diamond are likely to be rewarded adequately. Also vast areas of the Central Indian Shield and the covered areas in the Eastern and

Western segments have not been adequately explored. Mineral potential of the extra peninsular terrain (younger Mesozoic-Cenozoic fold belt) still remains largely unexplored. There is also ample scope for advanced exploration in and around the already identified prospects/group of prospects in the country.

FOREIGN INVESTMENT TRENDS IN THE SECTOR

Since the opening up of the mining sector to private participation, most major mining companies have made proposals for taking up mining/processing ventures. Applications for exploration licences are mainly for gold, diamonds and base metals. Proposals for joint-ventures for exploitation of existing deposits relate to iron ore, bauxite and base metals. Once these projects take off, it is expected that foreign investment in the sector would exceed $2 billion. Interest has also been shown by companies in the manufacture of mining machinery and for providing technology for upgrading existing processing plants, specially in aluminium and copper.

PROCEDURES AND LEGISLATIVE FRAMEWORK

The Mines and Minerals (Regulation and Development) Act, 1957 (MMRD) and the Mines Act, 1952, together with the rules and regulations framed under them, constitute the basic laws governing the mining sector in India.

The relevant rules in force under the MMRD Act are the Mineral Concession Rules, 1960, and the Mineral Conservation and Development Rules, 1988.

The health and safety of the workers is governed by the Mines Rules, 1955 made under the Mines Act, 1952.

The Mineral Concession Rules, 1960 outline the procedures and conditions for obtaining a Prospecting Licence or a Mining Lease. The Mineral Conservation and Development Rules, 1988 lay down guidelines for ensuring mining on a scientific basis and conservation of the environment. The provisions of Mineral Concession Rules and Mineral Conservation and Development Rules are, however, not applicable to coal, atomic minerals and minor minerals. The minor minerals are separately notified and come under the purview of the State governments. The State governments have for this purpose formulated Minor Mineral Concession Rules.

The salient features of the mining legislation are as follows:

Ownership of Mines and Minerals

In the Indian Federal Structure, the State Government is the owner of the minerals in their respective territorial jurisdiction. In the offshore areas, exclusive economic zone and the continental shelf, the rights are vested in the Central Government.

Laws and mineral rights empower the government to receive royalty from the lessee or mine owner for extraction and consumption of minerals. The rates of royalty for various minerals, other than minor minerals are specified by the Central Government through a notification. The royalty rates for minor minerals are specified by the concerned State governments.

Access over Land

Access to land, both state and private, is available for exploration and mining, except in certain areas, which the government may reserve through a notification.

Prospecting Licence

A prospecting licence entitles the holder to search and explore the land for minerals. It permits the removal of limited quantities of substances for testing. Prospecting licences are granted under the MMRD Act, 1957. The procedure for obtaining the licence is given in the Mineral Concession Rules, 1960. Prospecting licences are granted for up to three years. This can be extended but the total period of a prospecting licence cannot exceed five years.

The prospecting licence has certain rights attached to it, one of which is the right of pre-emption. This right gives preferential right to the holder, for obtaining a mining lease in respect of the minerals explored on a particular area of land.

The holder of the prospecting licence also has the right to transfer the licence or any right, title or interest therein to an income tax payee subject to the sanction of the State government. The procedure for transfer is prescribed in the Mineral Concession Rules, 1960.

Mining Lease

A mining lease allows for the development and production of minerals from ore bodies discovered by prospecting or exploration operations.

A mining lease can be held for a long period which may vary from a minimum of 20 to 30 years with rights of renewal.

A mining lease is subject to a ceiling on the area being mined. The ceiling prescribed is a maximum of 10 square km. The ceiling may be relaxed by the Central Government if it deems that the relaxation is in the interest of development of any mineral. The mining lease is transferable, subject to the approval of the State government.

The procedure for obtaining a mining lease is prescribed in the Mineral Concession Rules, 1960.

CONCLUSION

India's mining industry certainly has a bright future. The government's new economic policies have stimulated both foreign investment and the expansion of the country's private sector. There are numerous plans underway to modernise and expand existing facilities, many of which will require overseas investment. In a recent research publication, *Asian Mining Review*, published by ANZ McCaughan, which was considered at the Asian Mining Conference held in Bali (Indonesia) in October, 1995, the details of a survey were presented in which the Australian companies gave their views on mining attractiveness of Asian countries. Company perceptions indicated that India enjoyed, keeping in view all relevant criteria, an overall second rank, next to Indonesia, in Asia. The *Asian Mining Review* states:

> India represents a significant opportunity for companies with the foresight to establish local links and undertake grassroots and operational exploration with local partners. The opportunities India presents are reflected in the high rating it received for geological prospectivity.

> The coming years should see the full realisation of the enormous potential of the mining sector in India.

CHAPTER 24

POLICIES AND OPPORTUNITIES IN THE TELECOMMUNICATIONS SECTOR

by R K Takkar

INTRODUCTION

Supported by bold new policy initiatives, India is emerging as a major telecommunications market in Asia. New initiatives, both in the industrial policies and telecommunications policies will further boost India's telecommunications network markets. With rock-bottom telephone penetration rates and over one-fifth of the world's population, India represents one of the world's most attractive markets for telecommunications equipment suppliers and service providers. Recent political and economic improvement has placed India in a position to expand telecommunications infrastructure more rapidly. Dramatic changes are transforming the regulatory structure in India. The National Telecom Policy announced by the Government of India in May, 1994 will provide unprecedented access to one of the world's largest and most protected services and equipment markets.

EXISTING TELECOMMUNICATIONS NETWORK

India operates one of the largest telecommunications networks in Asia comprising over 20,000 telephone exchanges and an extensive long distance transmission network. The basic telephone services are provided by the Department of Telecommunications (DOT) which is directly under the Ministry of Communications, along with its public sector undertaking Mahanagar Telephone Nigam Ltd (MTNL). MTNL provides telephone services in the metropolitan cities of Delhi and Bombay while DOT provides services in the rest of the country through its 21 circles. Videsh Sanchar Nigam Ltd, another public sector unit under the Ministry of Communications, provides all international telecommunications services. The total equipped capacity of the DOT/MTNL network is around 14 million with over 12 million working connections. The pending demand, however, is 2.5 million and is growing at 15% average per annum.

GROWTH OF DEMAND

The Indian telecommunications network has been growing at a great rate in the last few years and the number of telephone lines has more than doubled since 1990. During the Five Year Plan (1992–97), 10 million new telephone lines are proposed to be added. Despite the impressive growth, the telephone/population ratio in India remains around 1%, much less than other developing countries such as Brazil and Malaysia and less than one-fiftieth that of developed countries such as the US and Sweden. Studies conducted by the ITU have demonstrated a strong correlation between growth of economy measured in terms of GDP and the telephone density. In fact in countries where telephone density is low, the impact on the growth of the economy of providing more telephones is found to be the highest. For the telecommunications sector in India to play its assigned role in the development of the national economy, it will be necessary to increase the telephone density to at least the same order as is available in some of the developing countries, ie 6%. This will involve reaching a level of about 60 million telephone connections as rapidly as possible from the present level of 12 million. Such an expansion as well as the task of garnering the physical resources is indeed a challenge.

EVOLUTION OF REGULATORY POLICIES IN THE TELECOMMUNICATIONS SECTOR

Under the Indian Telegraph Act 1885, the provision of all types of telecommunications services is the exclusive monopoly of the Central Government. However, the Central Government is empowered to grant licences for operation of telecommunications services. The manufacturing of telecommunications equipment was also reserved for the government companies under the Industrial Policy Resolution, 1956.

The liberalisation of the Indian telecommunications sector was initiated in 1984, when for the first time the manufacture of terminal equipment was permitted in the private sector. This slowly expanded to cover a variety of equipment including locally designed switching equipment and digital transmission equipment. The historic announcement of the New Industrial Policy (NIP) under the Economic Reforms Programme initiated in July 1991 opened the Indian economy to the world, to enhance trade opportunities and foreign investment in almost all sectors of development including telecommunications. Under this bold initiative, the telecommunications manufacturing industry was fully delicensed and opened for foreign investments. Subsequently, in April, 1992, the telecommunications infrastructure equipment market was also opened to international competition under the revised Export-Import Policy 1992–97.

A summary of the current trade and investment policies and procedures in the Telecommunications sector follows.

Trade and Foreign Investment Policies and Procedures

Foreign collaborations and investment

Manufacturing projects in the telecommunications sector with foreign equity investment up to 51% and involving lump sum technical know-how fees up to US$2 million (net of taxes), royalty payment up to 5% of ex-factory value of domestic sales or 8% of ex-factory value of exports are approved by the Reserve Bank of India under automatic approval procedure. Projects with higher equity or a technology fee are considered and approved by the government.

Projects for telecommunications services involving foreign equity investment including proposals for basic telecommunications services, value added telecommunications services, etc irrespective of the amount or percentage of equity investment are considered by FIPB.

Maximum foreign equity is restricted to 49% in the area of basic services, radio paging, mobile radio trunk service and cellular mobile services, or other wireless services.

Maximum foreign equity in other value added services is restricted to 51%.

Normally royalties are not permitted in the case of telecommunications service projects.

Import policies

Import of all telecommunications equipment including switching equipment, transmission equipment, terminal equipment, satellite equipment, telecommunications cables, optical fibre cables and their accessories and attachments but excluding subscriber end terminal equipment is allowed without any import licence.

Import of fax machines and amateur radio equipment is allowed without any import licence. A similar policy has been announced in the Union Budget (1996–97) for the import of pagers, cellular telephones and mobile phones.

Import of telephone instruments and EPABX is not permitted except against a specific licence.

Customs and excise duties

Customs duty on finished telecommunications equipment was reduced from 50% to 40% in the 1996–97 budget. There is now a special reduced rate of 30% duty on three items, viz cellular phones, pagers and trunking-handsets. Parts now attract 30% and electronic components attract 20% customs duty.

Local manufacturers have to pay excise duty (ED) on equipment, 20% ED on line telecommunications equipment and 25% ED on telecommunications cables.

Importers also have to pay additional custom duty at ED rates on the landed value of imports which is adjusted against ED under the MODVAT scheme.

NATIONAL TELECOM POLICY 1994

The Government of India announced a new National Telecom Policy on 13 May 1994. Main features of this policy are as follows:

The basic telephone network is to be expanded to provide telephone connections on demand by 1997.

(1) All villages to be covered by 1997.

(2) In the urban areas, a Public Call Office (PCO) should be provided for every 500 persons by 1997.

(3) Special emphasis on the quality of telecommunications services provided to customers will be given.

(4) All value-added services available internationally to be introduced in India, preferably by 1996.

(5) With a view to supplementing the efforts of the DOT in providing telecommunications services to the people, companies registered in India will be allowed to participate in the expansion of basic telephone services.

(6) Private initiative to be used to complement the departmental efforts to raise additional resources both through increased internal generation and adopting innovative means, leasing, deferred payments, BOT, BLT, etc.

(7) A suitable funding mechanism for indigenous R&D is proposed to be set up.

(8) Pilot projects will be encouraged directly by the government in order to access new technologies, and new systems in both basic as well as value-added services.

OPPORTUNITIES IN THE TELECOMMUNICATIONS EQUIPMENT MARKET

The Indian telecommunications equipment market, which increased from about Rs30,000 million in 1991–92 to over Rs70,000 million in 1994–95, represents one of the largest and the fastest growing in the Asian region. The present DOT estimates indicate that the Indian telecommunications network will expand to about 46 million lines by the year 2005, creating a mammoth equipment market worth about Rs3000 billion in the next 10 years (see Table I). However, even this estimate is considered to be quite conservative in view of the changes in the regulatory environment and entry of the private sector into telecommunications services.

Table I
Estimates of Demand for Telecommunications Services and Equipment

Year (April–March)	Projected demand for phones (M.lines)	Total estimated requirement of telecom equipment during the year (million lines)	(Rs billion)
1995	12.08	3.0	90
1996	13.78	3.4	120
1997	15.77	4.0	150
1998	17.95	4.9	180
1999	20.51	6.0	220
2000	23.46	7.8	260
2001	26.84	9.6	300
2002	30.74	10.7	340
2003	35.22	12.6	390
2004	40.37	14.3	440
2005	46.34	16.4	530

Note: Estimated requirement of equipment includes the requirement of switching, transmission and terminal equipment as well as optical fibre, underground and overhead cables and accessories.

Digital Switching Equipment

The digital switching equipment market in India has witnessed a true metamorphosis since 1991 when the New Industrial Policy was announced. Prior to that policy, Indian Telephone Industries (ITI), a public sector undertaking, was the main supplier of large switching equipment based on E10B technology of Alcatel, France. A number of foreign companies like Alcatel, Siemens, Ericsson, Fujitsu and AT&T, attracted by the DOT's liberalised procurement policies, have already set up local production facilities for large switching equipment. In the area of small and medium digital switching equipment, the RAX (Rural Automatic Exchange) locally developed by the Centre of Development of Telematics (CDOT), the R&D wing of DOT, is still the most popular and cost effective technology option.

With an estimated market for about 40–50 million lines in the next few years, the opportunities in this area are excellent.

Transmission Equipment

The production base of telecommunications transmission equipment which was earlier limited to a few public sector companies, has expanded with the setting up of manufacturing facilities in the private sector including joint-ventures of multinationals such as AT&T, Fujitsu and Siemens which have been set up to manufacture digital transmission equipment. The market for transmission equipment such as digital microwave, optical fibre and infrastructure equipment for value-added services such as cellular and paging has great potential for large expansion.

Private Networks and Subscriber Terminals

The market for providing private voice and data networks is growing very quickly. Major international companies such as NEC, Alcatel and AT&T have already announced their plans for making an entry into this market. OKI of Japan and Siemens of Germany are presently the major players in India in this field. The telephone instrument market which was monopolised by Ericsson and Siemens is also expanding rapidly with the entry of a number of new players. Another area expected to sustain great demand in the coming decade is data networks. The DOT already provides data networks for the business community through satellite based networks such as RABMN and HVNET and the terrestrial network INET. The DOT has also started offering ISDN services in selected cities. Private operators as well are providing closed user group data networks using very small size satellite terminals (VSAT).

OPPORTUNITIES IN THE TELECOMMUNICATIONS SERVICES SECTOR

In a further bold step taken by the government in July 1992, the operation of all value-added telecommunications services (electronic mail, voice mail, data service, audio text, video text, video conferencing, radio paging and cellular mobile telephone services) were thrown open to the private sector. With the announcement of the National Telecom Policy in 1994 and opening of bids for basic services in 1995, a new era of private investment in the telecommunications services sector has been initiated. The guidelines for entry of the private sector into telecommunications services limit foreign equity in basic, cellular, paging and wireless services to 49%. Up to 51% foreign equity investment is permitted in other value-added services. With the opening of the telecommunications services sector to private operators, the government has also decided to set up a Telecom Regulatory Authority (TRAI) to regulate the tariffs and sharing of revenue between different operators, the problems of interconnection between operators and to protect consumer interests.

OPPORTUNITIES IN VALUE-ADDED SERVICES

With the opening of value-added services and finalisation of tenders for cellular and paging services, the Indian subscriber now has access to almost all value-added services. Before 1992, these services were almost non-existent in the country.

Based on these new initiatives, cellular mobile telephone service has now become available in the four metropolitan cities of Delhi, Bombay, Calcutta and Madras through private operators. In respect of the rest of the country, tenders have been invited. The response to these tenders was overwhelming and all the top corporate groups in India jointly with the best telecommunications operators of the world participated. As in the case of the metropolitan cellular licences, two licences have been issued for each service area and the technology is restricted to GSM. The licence fees quoted for various circles are around Rs17,940 million for a 10 year licence. The government has also decided to restrict the maximum number of licences to any one bidder company to three for the bigger circles. Services are expected to start in about a dozen cities by the end of 1996.

Private operators have also started offering city-wide paging services in all big cities of the country based on licences granted in 1992–93. For other areas of the country comprising 18 territorial circles, licences have been granted in most of these.

Other value-added services such as email, voice-mail, data services through VSAT, etc have been started by some of the private operators. While cellular, paging and mobile radio trunking services have been licensed on the basis of one-time tenders, opportunities in other value-added services are available and an application for a licence can be made at any time.

Opportunities are also available to foreign investors to join existing and new ventures for paging and cellular services either as an additional equity partner or to finance their projects.

OPPORTUNITIES IN BASIC SERVICES

In a major bold step to expand and modernise basic telephone services and to supplement the efforts of the DOT, the government invited bids from companies registered in India with up to 49% foreign equity investment to provide basic telephone services as an additional operator in each of the 21 telecommunications circles (each circle comprises a geographical area of about one State) for a 15 year operating licence. Sixteen Indian companies with foreign equity participation from major telecommunications operators of the world (such as AT&T, US West, Bezeq, Stet, Telstra, Bell Atlantic, etc) participated in the bids which were opened in August 1995. Licence fees quoted were as high as Rs1110 billion. Licences for 12 circles have since been granted. The private sector companies which are now being licensed will be looking for more and more investments and will provide mammoth opportunities to investment bankers and financial institutions. In addition a window is available for additional partners to join them as equity partners.

OPPORTUNITIES IN RURAL TELECOMMUNICATIONS IN INDIA

India lives in its villages. There are nearly 600,000 villages, distributed over 99% of India's land mass of 3.3 million square km. Of India's population of 930 million people, 75% live in these villages. The need for bringing the country's rural population into the mainstream of the national and global economy has resulted in a major thrust to accelerate the development of rural telecommunications. Out of about 600,000 villages, over 200,000 have already been provided with telephone facilities but about 400,000 are still without a telephone. The DOT has planned to provide one public telephone in each village by the beginning of April 1997. Under the terms of the tender for basic services, private operators have to provide at least 10% of their total lines in rural areas till all the villages have at least one public telephone.

Public Telephones—the Indian Strategy

In order to enhance accessibility of the telecommunications network by an ordinary person who cannot afford individual telephone connection, and also to provide employment to educated people, a unique system of franchised manned public telephones with local, national and international call facilities at public places has been successfully adopted in India. This service, which is now available all over the country, especially in rural and semi-urban areas and along the National Highways, has substantially increased the accessibility of telephones.

FUTURE PERSPECTIVE

The response to the recent tenders for basic and cellular services is a massive vote of confidence in the future of the Indian economy and the size of the Indian telecommunications market. With further changes expected shortly in the structure of the DOT, competition is intensifying among Indian and foreign companies, all eager to build a platform for the long-term growth ahead. In the process strong players can emerge who would have the potential to participate in the opening up of the telecommunications services sector in other countries in Asia, Africa, the Middle East and Europe.

CHAPTER 25
INDIA'S PETROLEUM SECTOR INVESTMENT OPPORTUNITIES
by Devi Dayal

INTRODUCTION

The petroleum industry in India has played and will continue to play a major role in meeting the energy requirements and in shaping and contributing to the economic development of the nation. The industry has a heritage of over 100 years, starting with the first oil find at Digboi in the north-eastern State of Assam in 1889 and the first refinery, at the same location, established in 1901. The 20th century saw the advent of various multinational companies, which initially imported and marketed kerosene and later the transportation fuels also. By the 1950s, the demand for petroleum products had risen to levels that justified investments in refineries and so Esso, Shell and Caltex set up their refineries in India. Within a decade, India's own national oil company, Indian Oil Corporation Ltd, had started building refineries to meet the growing demand for petroleum products.

India has established geological reserves of 5.35 billion tonnes of oil and oil equivalent of natural gas. India is endowed with 26 sedimentary basins with a total area of the order of 1,720,000 sq km up to 200 metres bathometry. Most of these basins are under various stages of exploration.

India has at present 14 refineries with total refining capacity of 60.4 million metric tonnes per annum which are owned by public sector companies or associated joint-venture companies. Marketing of petroleum products is carried out by four refining and marketing companies (Indian Oil Corporation Ltd, Hindustan Petroleum Corporation Ltd, Bharat Petroleum Corporation Ltd and IBP Co Ltd). The supply and distribution of natural gas is carried out by the public sector company, the Gas Authority of India Ltd (GAIL).

DEMAND FOR PETROLEUM PRODUCTS

The consumption of petroleum products in the country in 1995–96 was 74.5 million tonnes. Over the past two decades, the consumption of petroleum products has been rising by 6%–7% annually. Current estimates indicate a sustained growth of about 6% per year for the next 10–15 years, with product requirement estimated around

105 million tonnes by the turn of the century and further increasing to 160 million tonnes by the year 2010. These estimates are based on the assumption that the Indian economy would grow by about 5%–7% GDP during the period. The present per capita consumption of oil and gas in India is only 87 kg per annum as against the world average of 903 kg per annum. Obviously the potential for growth is unlimited.

AREAS OF CONCERN AND POTENTIAL FOR INVESTMENT

Against the present requirement of crude oil of 60 million tonnes, the crude production in the country is only around 35.4 million tonnes. Against the likely demand of 110 million tonnes by the year 2000, crude production in the country is likely to be only around 45–50 million tonnes per annum as per current estimates. Thus there is an urgent need to step up exploration and production efforts to meet the crude requirements of the country.

The existing refining capacity of 60.4 million tonnes per annum and indigenous crude production of around 35 million tonnes being grossly inadequate to meet the growing demand, the country is dependent on imports for both crude oil and petroleum products. The predominance of middle distillates, especially diesel, in the demand profile necessitates large imports of this product as well as reconfiguration of the refineries to produce more diesel and kerosene.

As in most countries the world over, there is increasing concern in India about the environment and the necessity to reduce the polluting effects of hydrocarbons, be they lead, sulfur or aromatics. This concern necessitates investments in the existing refineries, both for improving product specifications as well as for reduction of emissions and other pollutants from the refineries.

Although the distribution network at present appears to be just sufficient, some of the facilities are grossly inadequate. Port infrastructure for import of POL products, which is inadequate to meet even the current requirement, is required to be developed on a massive scale for importing products like HSD, SKO and LPG and industrial fuels like naphtha and FO. The storage tank capacity, which provides for about 30 days' consumption at present, is required to be increased for a frozen cover of 45 days involving additional capacity to the tune of 8–10 million tonnes.

Thus, the agenda for immediate investments in the hydrocarbon sector in India would, inter alia, include:

- Exploration and production to increase availability of crude oil.
- Creation of additional refining capacity of 70–80 million tonnes.
- Retrofitting existing refineries for meeting new product specifications.
- Infrastructure for distribution, such as ports, pipelines, terminals and storage tanks.
- Production, import and distribution of natural gas.

The investment in the petroleum sector in the next 10–15 years in the above-noted areas has been estimated to be around US$100 billion, with about 60% of the same in exploration and production, 30% in refining and the balance in marketing infrastructure.

POLICY INITIATIVES AND OPPORTUNITIES: UPSTREAM SECTOR

To enable private sector companies the world over to invest in exploration and production ventures in India, the government has launched a number of initiatives since 1991 aimed at effectively competing with other countries in attracting investments in the upstream sector.

In the upstream sector, a continuous round-the-year bidding scheme in respect of exploration acreages gives opportunities to companies to take up blocks for exploration. A fiscal regime exists which is highly progressive and is considered by consultants to be competitive with that offered by most other countries. The fiscal regime has been so designed that companies must share profits from petroleum production with the government only after they have recovered their investment.

An early cost recovery mechanism has been provided by which companies are allowed up to 100% cost recovery. There are no upfront payments in respect of exploration contracts such as signature bonuses, import duties etc. Additionally, the provision for carrying the national oil companies through the exploration stage has been abolished. The two national oil companies (ie the Oil Natural Gas Corporation Limited and Oil India Limited) will now take a participating interest of between 25% and 45% from the beginning of the contract, thereby substantially sharing in the exploration risks.

Since 1991, the Government of India has held six rounds of biddings for exploration acreages, offering as many as 147 blocks, ranging in size from a few hundred square km to over 50,000 square km. Fourteen contracts have been awarded so far. At present negotiations for award of contract for about 25 additional blocks are in progress.

Oil and gas fields discovered by the national oil companies were offered to foreign and Indian private companies for development in two offers in 1992 and 1993. While contracts for development of 18 such fields have been signed, proposals in respect of award of another 15 fields are under the consideration of the government. Production from the fields awarded so far is expected to be of the order of 350 million barrels of oil and 48 billion cubic metres of gas over a 15-year period.

For ensuring quick decisions, an empowered negotiating committee has been set up for conducting negotiations with companies. Also, a separate Directorate General of Hydrocarbons has been created under the Ministry of Petroleum & Natural Gas to monitor various aspects relating to exploration and production activities in the country.

POLICY INITIATIVES: REFINING SECTOR

The refining sector has already been opened up to the joint sector (ie the public sector companies forming joint-ventures with the private sector) as well as to the private sector for new grassroots refineries. Four refineries are already being implemented through joint-ventures of three leading multinational companies with Indian companies. A number of grassroots refineries have also been cleared for construction by the private sector. The large shortfall in refining capacity, as compared to projected demand, offers substantial scope for setting up new refining capacity in the country. Except for a few products, almost the entire production from new refineries is likely to be absorbed in the local market. There is obvious scope for the construction of export-oriented refineries in India on account of low costs of labour, cheaper infrastructure and advantageous geographical location.

POLICY INITIATIVES AND OPPORTUNITIES: MARKETING SECTOR

In sales and distribution, the import and merchandising of most petroleum products (except motor spirit and diesel) has been opened to the private sector either through the Open General Licence (OGL) or through Special Import Licence (SIL). Private investment is being encouraged for development of infrastructure such as port facilities, pipelines, terminals and tankages. India requires huge investment in development of port facilities at many locations on its east and west coasts. This has been fully opened to the private sector. India, being a large country geographically, offers tremendous scope for setting up product pipeline systems in the country. An expert team has identified over 16 pipeline projects that can be implemented immediately.

The Indian Government has decided to have storage cover of 45 days for crude and products. This would entail construction of storage tanks to the tune of about 12–14 million tonnes in the next five years. These can be set up on a Build-Operate-Transfer basis by leading tanking companies of the world along with Indian partners.

A number of multinational petroleum companies have already shown keen interest in developing the infrastructure projects and are in the process of negotiating with Indian public sector as well as private sector companies to form joint-ventures. These include Exxon, Shell, Mobil, Total and the Japanese majors. Foreign companies have shown a lot of interest in developing the infrastructure and marketing of LPG, for which there is tremendous scope.

In the field of lubricating oils, a number of multinational companies have set up blending and marketing infrastructure and are fairly well entrenched in the Indian market. Almost every company which has an international presence has established shop in India and has carved a reasonable market share.

NATURAL GAS

Another area, of recent origin, with unlimited opportunities, is the production and marketing of natural gas. While the current production potential is around 57 million metric standard cubic metres per day (mmscmd), it is likely to increase to around 80 mmscmd by 1996–97 and to 87 mmscmd by the end of the decade. The recoverable reserves of natural gas in the country are around 700 bcm.

Construction of pipelines and delivery facilities offers tremendous scope to the potential investors, especially after the proposed Oman-India pipeline project materialises, when the southern part of the country will be networked through a grid.

The registered demand for natural gas is around 260 mmscmd, whereas indigenous production will remain around 87 mmscmd even by the turn of the century. Since importing natural gas through pipelines may take more time because of the distance of currently available sources, technological issues and huge financial implications, the alternative mode of importing natural gas in the form of LNG is the only feasible and inevitable option. Producers of gas, which are large multinational oil companies, can promote joint-ventures with Indian petroleum companies and consumers for import and distribution of LNG in the country.

PRICING OF PETROLEUM PRODUCTS

The pricing of crude oil and petroleum products in the country is regulated by the Central Government and this mechanism is referred to as the Administered Pricing Mechanism (APM). The government determines the input and output prices of crude/products and assures the oil companies a fixed post-tax return on the net worth of the company, which is 15% (post-tax) for exploration and production and 12% (post-tax) for refining and marketing. While the APM helped, the oil industry has now outgrown the pricing regime and is ready to face the open market pricing system.

In the course of time, the APM will be replaced by open market pricing and total deregulation. There would be a re-orientation to the tariff structure for import of crude oil and petroleum products, thereby ensuring a reasonable level of protection for capital investments in different production facilities. Far-reaching changes are also likely for encouraging investments in marketing infrastructure. All these changes would ensure that a level playing field exists for all operators in the entire petroleum sector, namely, government companies, private companies and foreign companies.

WHY INVEST IN INDIA?

While the recent policy changes have created very attractive opportunities for prospective investors in the petroleum sector, there are a variety of other factors which would make India a chosen destination for such investments.

First, India has a large pool of trained and qualified workers, well-versed in the various facets of the petroleum industry ranging from exploration and production to refining and marketing of petroleum products.

Secondly, the costs in India including those of infrastructure and labour are low, making production internationally competitive.

Thirdly, the Indian judicial system is well developed and is comparable to that of the advanced countries in the world. This ensures that the potential investor would always have a forum to redress any grievance or non-performance of contracts.

Fourthly, the Indian banking system, which includes many foreign banks, offers most of the banking services at international standards available in advanced countries. Apart from leading international banks operating in the country, there are a number of financial institutions that specialise on financing large projects.

Fifthly, India has a well-developed engineering industry which can provide facilities for fabrication of almost any type of equipment that is required in the petroleum sector. The import content of new refineries under construction in India is only marginal. However, there are no restrictions on importing any capital equipment.

Sixthly, India has a well-developed infrastructure network in terms of transport and telecommunications, with links right across the length and breadth of the subcontinent and with other countries.

And lastly, India is a vast country with a population of about 930 million, with an accelerated pace of economic growth, and with vast potential for development of the petroleum industry.

INVESTING IN INDIA

The Government of India has permitted private and foreign participation in all activities in the petroleum sector. One hundred per cent foreign equity is also allowed on a case-by-case basis. Single-window clearance for projects has been introduced through the Secretariat for Industrial Approvals.

For obtaining an industrial licence and other clearances, application has to be submitted to the single point clearance office of the Secretariat for Industrial Approvals (SIA), Department of Industrial Development, Ministry of Industry, Udyog Bhavan, New Delhi 110 011.

For obtaining approval for foreign investment in India, application should be submitted to either the Foreign Investment Promotion Board (FIPB) or the Secretariat for Industrial Approvals. The SIA gives composite clearance for industrial licences and foreign investment.

CHAPTER 26
CHALLENGES AND OPPORTUNITIES IN THE HEALTH SECTOR

by A K Mukherjee,
A K Kundu
and Praveena Goel

INTRODUCTION

India as a signatory to the Alma Ata Declaration is committed to the achievement of Health for All by AD 2000. Primary health care has been identified as the instrument for achievement of this goal.

Significant strides have been made in the health sector since Independence. Life expectancy has increased from 41.3 years in 1950 to 61.15 years in 1991. The crude birth rate has come down from 41.7 to 28.5 per thousand population during the same period. The crude death rate has also fallen from 27 to 9.2 per thousand population during the corresponding period. Smallpox has been completely eradicated and vaccines have drastically reduced the occurrence of measles and polio. A vast community-based infrastructure comprising 1900 Community Health Centres, 22,000 Primary Health Centres and 130,000 Sub-Centres has been set up for provision of primary health care. Besides this a large number of medical colleges have been established. These successes have resulted from growing income, increasing education and technological progress apart from the expansion of health services.

Despite these notable achievements the present enormous health system has several lacunae. The country bears a massive burden of disease which is compounded by significant disparities between regions and between States. The World Development Report, 1993, placed the Global Burden of Diseases in India at 344 Disability Adjusted Life Years (DALYs) per 1000 population. India ranks second after Sub-Saharan Africa with 575, while established market economies have an index as low as 117. This means that the burden of disease in India is three times that of developed countries. The DALY lost due to communicable diseases is 51% compared with 25% in China and 10% in established market economies. Yet, the morbidity, mortality and disability from this excessive burden of communicable diseases is largely preventable.

HEALTH FINANCING

The WHO in its Alma Ata Declaration recommended that public

health care expenditure should gross at least 5% of GDP if equity and universal coverage are to be realised. Most socialist countries spend around 3.5% of their GDP on health care. Similarly in the Organisation for Economic Co-operation & Development (OECD) the share of the public health sector is over 6% of GDP. India spends about 6% of its GDP in health. The States incur a large share of funding of health care activities as health is a State concern in India. In India the total outlay for health care has always hovered around 3% of the plan outlay. An increasing proportion of health expenditure is being incurred on salaries (60–90%) and a markedly reduced (10–40%) proportion on non-salary components. There are wide interstate variations in health expenditure and health status. For instance, life expectancy at birth is 68.7 years in Kerala and only 52 years in Uttar Pradesh. The current level of health status has been realised by some of the States at a high cost (eg Assam is very high in the order of spending but has relatively low health status).

ALTERNATE RESOURCE MOBILISATION

Two important issues are of concern. The first is to redefine the role of government, care providers, consumers and health financing agencies. The second is to find new financing mechanisms that will generate additional resources and bring greater efficiency and equity. Resource constraints are forcing most developing countries to reassess their existing arrangements for health care financing. The concern is to respond to the growing demand and rising cost in health care while trying to ensure optimum use of funds. A health policy and structures that provide better quality of health care while using resources more efficiently have yet to be developed. A complex mix of funding sources and care providers in both the public and private sector is emerging.

Total health spending in India accounts for about US$13 per capita (Rs320). As a percentage of GDP this is a higher level of spending on health care than in other Asian countries such as China, Indonesia, Thailand, the Philippines, Pakistan, Bangladesh and Sri Lanka (World Development Report, 1993), most of which have better health outcomes than India. Public health spending in India is about 1.3% of GDP, which is lower than in China, Sri Lanka, Bangladesh and Pakistan but higher than Indonesia and the Philippines. Moreover the portion of GDP government expenditure devoted to disease control programmes is very low when compared to many other countries at India's level of per capita income.

Overall primary health care services account for 58.7%, secondary/

tertiary for 38.8% and other services for 2.5% of total national health spending. Of the total spending for primary health care, 8.5% is for curative care services, while 15% is for preventive and promotive care services. Household out-of-pocket expenditure accounts for 82% of total primary care spending and particularly concentrated (92%) is the curative care component of primary care services. In contrast, about 73% of preventive and promotive health services are financed by the Centre (27%). The large Central Government share is due to its almost exclusive financing of the Family Welfare Programme.

About 47% of the total health budget of the Centre and States is spent on curative care and health facility operations. This might seem excessive, but in fact, the figure is often well over 60% in a country at India's level of per capita income. Preventive and promotive services come next with 30%, of which about equal shares are for prevention and control of communicable diseases and family welfare and immunisation. This compares well with many other low-income countries, where the figure is well below 10% for preventive and promotive services.

The role of the private sector in delivery of health care cannot be minimised. This sector operates both for profit as well as on a 'no profit' basis. The latter comprises the health facilities run by NGOs, trusts, religious and charitable bodies.

LIBERALISATION OF ECONOMIC POLICY

The Indian Government has been introducing reforms in the trade regime, the financial sector, taxes and public enterprises so as to create an overall policy involvement more conducive to the efficient undertaking and operating of investments.

JOINT-VENTURE FOR HEALTH CARE DELIVERY

A lot of private investors have shown interest in provision of health services. The interest has been shown in the areas of provision of tertiary health care, setting up poly-clinics, mobile health clinics, information, education and communication activities, setting up hotlines such as Heartline and Lifeline, and medical education. Private sector cooperation is being sought for upgrading of district health care and setting up of model district hospitals. NGOs are being encouraged to adopt districts for this purpose. The government is considering provision of free or subsidised land, electricity, water, roads, exemption from customs duties on imported equipment to the fullest extent possible and fiscal incentives, wherever necessary, in order to extend full support to joint-ventures with the private sector. In return the private sector is being asked to earmark 30–40% of patient/diagnostic services free for treatment of the poor in rural and urban areas.

New projects proposals submitted for this purpose have to be cleared by the Ministry of Health & Family Welfare and recommended to the Foreign Investment Promotion Board (FIPB) which is chaired by the Industry Minister.

While the Central and State governments dominate hospital services accounting for about one-half of all facilities and nearly 70% of all beds in the country, there has been some shift recently towards the provision of private hospitals. NRIs, trusts and large private companies have set up specialised hospitals and health care facilities. The Government of India has been providing opportunities for the inflow of funds to the health sector. In fact the Union Minister for Health & Family Welfare recently made an announcement that from whatever quarter the funds are forthcoming for health facilities (PHCs, CHCs or district and referral hospitals from NRIs, NGOs, large trading houses or MNCs), the government would extend the necessary facilities provided 30–40% of the beds are earmarked for the poor.

CONCLUSION

Though the health care system in India is much better today, compared to two or three decades ago, there is still a lot to do. As fertility declines and life expectancy goes up, the proportion of population over 65 will increase and consequently the burden of non-communicable diseases will tend to rise. The challenge of communicable diseases will continue to persist particularly among younger people. There is a lurking fear that we may be faced with epidemiological polarisation in which one part of the population will make a demographic and epidemiological transition, while another part remains at pre-transition standards of disease and poverty. In fact, we are already being faced by this paradox. This will impinge on the competing demand for promotive and preventive care vis-a-vis demand of the urban, rural middle and upper classes for secondary and tertiary treatment. This calls for careful husbanding of scarce resources and the means to make sure the health care system is attuned to the needs of the neglected sections of society.

CHAPTER 27

OPPORTUNITIES FOR INTERNATIONAL PRIVATE INVESTMENT IN URBAN DEVELOPMENT AND THE HOUSING SECTOR IN INDIA

by C Ramachandran

INTRODUCTION

According to the 1991 census, the number of people living in urban areas in India was 217 million. Although urban India in 1995 contains less than 30% of the country's population, it contributes as much as 50% of the country's GDP. The figure is estimated to increase to 60% by 2001. The primary factor behind this high productivity is the concentration of infrastructural facilities and services, skilled workers and capital in cities and towns. Infrastructure is the key to the contribution of urban labour and firms to national economic growth.

URBAN DEVELOPMENT SCENARIO

Until the new economic reforms, the development of urban infrastructural facilities—water supply, sewerage, sanitation, storm water drainage, solid waste management, public transport, housing, open spaces, township development, etc—was undertaken primarily through budgetary resources of the Central, State and local governments. With urban areas emerging as attractive centres of domestic and international investment, growing urbanisation and population concentration, and increased incomes, the demand for urban infrastructural facilities and services has increased tremendously. It is impossible for governmental agencies to meet this demand in the context of their overriding priorities of education, health, welfare, poverty alleviation and stabilisation. It has been recognised that private investment—domestic and foreign—for the provision of urban infrastructure will be a necessary supplement to direct investment by governments and public agencies to meet the growing demand.

URBAN INFRASTRUCTURE PROJECTS

Most urban infrastructure projects do not offer as attractive returns as other sectors such as power, telecommunications and highways do.

They are, however, eminently suitable for public-private partnerships. Build-Own-Operate (BOO), Build-Own-Operate-Transfer (BOOT), Build-Own-Lease-Transfer (BOLT), and similar types of arrangements are promising options. The Central and State governments are open to private initiatives and public-private partnerships in areas such as water supply and sanitation, public transport, township/land development, and others. Government support in the form of equity contribution, a package of concessions, dedicated levies to repay loans, and a transparent regulatory framework will be available. Private investors are encouraged to evolve suitable financial packages required to make their investments safe and paying.

OPPORTUNITIES

The following are the broad areas where scope exists for private investments in the urban sector:

Water Supply, Sanitation and Solid Waste Management

The geographical water balance in the country is highly uneven. The development of water supply sources at vantage locations in rivers and lakes on a regional basis, ie, to take care of a number of towns and villages for bulk supply to local bodies and industries and water distribution (trunk mains) networks, are suitable for private investment. Private investors could negotiate with public agencies on the transfer price of water and concessions needed. Water distribution and billing, sewerage reclamation and reuse for non-domestic purposes, management of unaccounted-for water, manufacture of water supply equipment, and solid waste management, are also areas where the private sector could be interested. Recently the Hyderabad Metropolitan Water Supply and Sewerage Board invited private sector interest in the development of water source and conveyance to Hyderabad city from Krishna River, 150 km away from Hyderabad. The cost of the scheme will be well above US$330 million. The Board has received two international bids and one domestic bid. The Infrastructure Leasing and Financial Services (IL&FS) is pursuing a proposal for the development of a water supply scheme in Dewas town in Madhya Pradesh at a cost of US$15 million on a BOOT basis.

Urban Public Transport

Urban public transport, particularly, Mass Rapid Transit (MRT) and Light Rail Transit (LRT) are suitable areas of private investment in collaboration with governmental agencies. The proposed MRTS for Delhi at an estimated cost of US$3 billion offers good potential for public-private partnerships. Development of property above underground railway stations, investment in equity capital, forgoing returns/dividends on government capital during the 'period of concession' as agreed to with private investors, dedicated taxes/ budgetary sources for repayment of a part of the loans, tariff agreements and other measures could be extended as governmental support. Bangalore and Hyderabad are planning rail-based public transit systems in the near future.

India has 23 metropolitan cities. The number is likely to increase to 40 by 2001. All the metropolitan cities offer good scope for investment by the private sector in water supply, drainage and sewerage, solid waste management, and public transport.

Roads, Bridges and Flyovers

Bypasses to large cities, ring roads and bridges offer great scope for private investment. IL&FS has already developed a toll road connecting Pithampur and Indore on the Agra-Bombay National Highway on BOOT basis at a cost of US$2 million. It is contemplating an eight-lane bridge on Yamuna River, linking South Delhi and Noida (in Uttar Pradesh) with private sector partnership, at a cost of US$67 million. It is proceeding with the proposed BOOT projects of Panvel Bypass (at a cost of US$33 million) and Worli-Bandra Link Bridge in Bombay (at a cost of US$90 million).

Possibilities of undertaking ring roads, arterial and sub-arterial roads, bridges, flyovers and other facilities being constructed in cities subject to fixed annual repayments by Municipal Corporations out of general revenues, development charges, betterment levies, impact fees, etc, when tolls are not feasible, could be explored.

Land/Township Infrastructure Development

Development of land in extended areas of large cities and new townships offers tremendous scope for private investment. Returns on such projects could be well above 20%. A good project in this regard is the Tiruppur Area Development Project in Tamil Nadu proposed by

IL&FS at a cost of US$440 million on a BOO basis. The scheme will comprise water supply, drainage and effluent treatment, road networks, telecommunications upgrading and expansion and housing components.

Housing

The National Housing Policy defines the crucial role of government at different levels as 'not to seek to build houses but to make appropriate investment and create conditions where all women and men, especially the poor may gain and secure adequate housing, and to remove impediments to housing activity'. The policy encourages private developers and organisations to invest in various forms of housing and land development by facilitating access to finance, and removal of constraints to assembly and development of lands. The Government of India has evolved a scheme to encourage non-residents of Indian nationality/origin to invest in the development of serviced plots, construction of houses and acquisition of immovable properties. The scheme extends various facilities such as repatriation of principal investment to NRI investors in foreign exchange.

CONCLUSION

Considering the need for encouraging the availability of long-term capital for urban infrastructure, different financial packages need to be worked out. The Constitution (74th Amendment) Act, 1992 aims at strengthening the municipalities and their borrowing capacities. Over a period of time it is hoped that a municipal bonds system will be in operation. Phenomenal progress has been achieved by municipalities, water authorities, etc in the recovery of costs of services and some have achieved the targets of full cost recovery. The city of Visakhapatnam in Andhra Pradesh offers a good example of how cross-subsidisation between consumer groups could make water supply systems run on commercial principles.

The Government of India, State governments and municipalities are open to proposals for private sector participation in urban infrastructure and welcome negotiations with international investors on appropriate financial packages.

CHAPTER 28

COAL SECTOR IN INDIA— GROWTH AND PROSPECTS
by Ashok Kumar Tooley

OVERVIEW OF THE COAL INDUSTRY

Coal in the Energy Scenario

Coal is the main source of primary energy in India and currently meets about 60% of the commercial energy requirement. In view of limited resource availability of liquid hydrocarbons and natural gas, coal is likely to be the dominant source in the foreseeable future also.

Coal Resources and Quality

Present estimate of coal resources is about 200 billion tonnes up to a depth of 1200 metres. Detailed exploration has resulted in an inventory of about 70 billion tonnes of proved reserves which can be exploited commercially. Indian coals are generally high in ash content (24–45%) but low in sulphur (less than 1%). Of the reserves 15% are coking variety and the balance non-coking.

Organisational Structure of the Coal Industry

Almost the entire sector is under State control. Coal India Ltd (CIL), a Government of India undertaking, has seven coal producing subsidiaries and produces 88% of the overall coal. The eighth subsidiary, Central Mines Planning & Design Institute (CMPDI), is the planning wing. Singareni Collieries Company Ltd (SCCL), a joint-venture of the State Government of Andhra Pradesh and the Government of India, contributes about 10% of coal production. Gradually, the Longwall is being introduced under suitable conditions.

Coal Consumption Pattern

The power industry is the single largest coal-consuming sector accounting for about 70% of overall consumption. The steel sector follows with about a 13% share. The balance is consumed in the cement, fertiliser, textiles, and chemical industries. The power sector will continue to consume the bulk of the coal. Demand for coal in India has been tentatively estimated to be about 400 million tonnes by

2001–02 out of which the demand of the power sector is 284 million tonnes. It is estimated that total demand by 2009–10 will be 550 million tonnes.

OPPORTUNITIES FOR INVESTMENT

Collaborations in the Coal Sector

Technical and financial assistance of erstwhile USSR, UK, Australia, Canada, Germany and France is available in developing the coal industry on a continuing basis through Joint Working Groups of the respective governments and the Government of India. Recently, a similar collaboration with China has also been established. The World Bank has also financed some projects in the coal sector.

Reforms in Economy and Scope of Private Participation

The scope of private sector participation in coal mining was begun with the amendment of the Coal Mines Nationalisation Act. Captive mining and setting up of coal beneficiation plants and mechanisation of existing developed mines on a cost-sharing basis has been envisaged by CIL with foreign mining companies and mining equipment manufacturers. Proposals for 30,000 MW of power capacity and 10 million tonnes per year of iron and steel production have been received from private parties.

Present Level of Participation

Thirteen mining blocks with a potential for yielding 35 million tonnes per year have been offered for captive mining. Letters of Intent have been issued for setting up four washeries with a total installed capacity of 21 million tonnes a year to private investors, including foreign investors under a Build-Own-Operate Scheme of Coal India Limited. Global tenders have also been floated by Coal India to develop some existing mines in collaboration with foreign firms.

Broad Estimate of Private Investment

A production contribution of 100 million tonnes per year is envisaged from private investors by 2009–10, if the overall coal demand is to be met. This implies an investment of US$4 billion at the current price. Coal beneficiation would also need at least US$1 billion in the same time frame.

LAWS SPECIFIC TO THE COAL SECTOR

The Coal Mines Act, 1952 along with the Coal Mines Regulation, 1957 and Coal Mines Rules 1955, govern coal mining in India. The onus of administering the Mines Act, Regulation and Rules lies with the Director General of Mines Safety. The MMRD Act 1957 lays down procedures for the grant of mining leases and preparation of mining plans. Acquisition of land for mining is to follow the Land Acquisition Act and Forest Conservation Act.

GUIDELINES FOR INVESTMENT

Under the Build-Own-Operate Scheme for setting up of washeries in the private sector, the general terms and conditions are:

(1)   The investor will finance, build, operate, maintain and own the plant.

(2)   Raw coal and washed products will be the property of the coal companies and the washed products will be marketed by coal companies.

(3)   The parameters of raw coal and washed products including percentage of yield will be fixed.

(4)   Reasonable conversion cost including a fair rate of return per tonne of washed coal will be paid.

(5)   Suitable bonus/penalty clauses for early/late commissioning of the plant and for the yield, quantity and quality of coal will be evolved.

PROCESSING OF APPLICATION FOR CAPTIVE BLOCKS

(1)   Forty mining blocks have been identified with coal reserves of about 13,000 million tonnes for captive mining. Guidelines adopted for allocation of blocks to the private sector are that these should be preferably in greenfield areas and that for identifying blocks, the requirement of coal for about 30 years would be considered. The cost of exploration of blocks would have to be borne by the private

party. A screening committee has been set up in the Ministry of Coal for considering various proposals and identifying suitable blocks. Every effort is made to ensure that the applications are processed objectively and early.

(2) Leases have to be obtained from coal companies or the Government of India.

(3) Proposals for approval of mining plans have to be submitted to the Ministry of Coal.

(4) Approval for acquisition of land under the Land Acquisition Act has to be filed with the concerned State governments.

(5) Approval for forest land and environment has to be obtained from the Ministry of Environment & Forests, Government of India.

(6) Applications for power have to be submitted to the concerned State Electricity Boards.

(7) The technical expertise of CMPDI for exploration, planning and design may be obtained on a payment basis.

(8) Initial water and power supply may be offered by coal companies wherever such facilities exist nearby on a payment basis.

CHAPTER 29

SECTORS FOR THE FUTURE
by the Confederation of Indian Industry

STEEL

Introduction

India's modern iron and steel industry dates back to 1911, with production of steel in Tata's Jamshedpur plant. The Indian steel industry has experienced substantial growth since the 1950s. Easy availability of raw materials and cheap labour have definitely given the industry a push. However, several policy measures restricted the growth and development of the steel industry till 1990. The era of liberalisation has now resulted in major investments in the sector and the steel industry is looking towards a bright future.

Production

India today is the 10th largest steel producing country in the world. The production during 1994–95 was 16.62 million tonnes against 14.66 million tonnes during the previous year. The Government of India has projected the domestic demand for finished steel for the year 1996–97 at the level of 20.74 million tonnes which is definitely an improvement on the current production level of 17.65 million tonnes. Public sector undertakings form a major chunk of the steel industry in India. The Steel Authority of India Ltd (SAIL), Rashtriya Ispat Nigam Ltd (RINL) are the prominent names among the 10 major public sector steel plants in India. Among the private sector steel plants Tata Iron & Steel Co (TISCO), is a major player and Essar, Nippon Denro, Jindal Steel are set to contribute in a big way.

Exports

The export of steel from India has hovered around 1 million tonnes per annum over the years. The major items of exports are bars and rods, semis, plates, pipes, GP/GC sheets and HR coils. With additional capacities, the government has projected steel exports during the year 2001 at 6 million tonnes.

Constraints

Certain factors hinder the steady growth of steel production in India. The cheap imports in the time of a recession (in the domestic as well as the world market) will definitely exert a downward pressure on prices. This age of liberalisation is experiencing drastic slashing of import duties which will once again force prices down. By comparison, excise duties have not been reduced. The net realisation from Indian exports is still not very high. But the Indian steel industry is taking steps to improve efficiency and cut down costs with the employment of several energy efficient and cost effective innovations.

Policy Changes

Since 1991 the government has undertaken certain important policy changes to encourage private sector investment in the steel industry. The removal of iron and steel from the list of industries reserved for the public sector, delicensing of the industry, deregulation of prices, and distribution of iron and steel and liberalised import and export policy are some of the important changes to which the private sector has responded positively. Investments are flowing in both within and from outside the country. Proposals for new steel plants and associated units with foreign collaborators are under consideration, several of which are already being implemented.

New Investments

The policy changes in the Indian steel industry have resulted in quite a few collaborations and a considerable amount of foreign investment flowing into the sector. Collaborations such as those between Nippon Denro Ispat Ltd and Ispat Mexicana of Mexico with 25% foreign equity participation and an estimated cost of Rs22,000 million or between Orind Steel Ltd and Goldstar Investment Ltd and Engineers & Consultants Inc of USA with 44.44% foreign equity participation have already been approved by the government. The government has also approved a Rs27,460 million steel collaboration between Mesco-Kalinga Steel and Danieli of Italy, United Engineering of USA, Samsung of Korea, and Mitsui & Co of Japan.

From August 1991 to April 1995 the government approved total foreign investments of Rs40,250 million in this sector.

Besides the large integrated steel plants, the relatively smaller capacity steel plants are also undergoing modernisation and expansion. With the gradual increase of domestic demand, there is promise of brighter days for the Indian steel producer.

ENGINEERING INDUSTRY

Introduction

Ever since the early years of the planned economy, the engineering industry held a position of importance in India and played the role of an engine for the growth of Indian industry. Indeed it has put India in the international industrial arena and has given much needed self-reliance in certain vital areas. Though the beginning was a low-key one, the engineering industry in India now produces a very wide range of products such as plant and machinery for steel, chemicals, fertilisers, cement, sugar and paper, electrical and construction machinery, automobiles, power generating transmission and distribution equipment, earth moving equipment. The list becomes even longer with the inclusion of certain other industrial goods and certain consumer durables. Since the coverage of the engineering industry is very large, certain important parts will be discussed as independent areas in this analysis. Though partial credit for the building up of this technological base goes to the import of technology, indigenous technology also had an important role to play.

Production

The general growth rate for most of the Indian engineering sector is above or around 10% (specifically it was 10.6% for 1994–95) over the period 1993–95 with the possible exception of the sub-sector which caters to agriculture. Going by the 1991–92 estimates, there are altogether 31,782 operating units in the organised sector of the engineering industry. Foreign technology has played an important role through firms such as Suzuki, Motorola, Marubeni, Hochest, Hibon, Siemens, Escorts, Eicher, Asea Brown Boveri, Essar, and Hewlett-Packard. The major local producers in this industry are Heavy Engineering Corporation Ltd, Mukand Ltd & ISPL Industries for metallurgical machinery, Fueller KCP Ltd & L & T for Cement Machinery, Kirloskar Cummins Ltd, Greaves Ltd, Simpson & Co, TIL Ltd, and Escorts Ltd for engineering goods, and Elekon Engineering Co Ltd and TRF for materials handling.

Though there are logistical problems like the inconsistent availability of raw materials from indigenous sources on a regular basis, the poor availability of modern technology, the industrial activities are increasing in almost every area (especially in consumer goods) which in turn is increasing the size and scope of this sector.

Exports

India's exports of engineering goods are improving every year. From a modest level of Rs68,021.4 million in 1992–93 it has reached a level of Rs98,250 million in 1994–95.

New Investments

Companies like Eicher Agrotech Escort Tractors, Larsen & Toubro and TIL are leading with projects with capital outlays of Rs5000 million and Rs2500 million respectively along with other investments in agricultural and industrial machinery. In non-electrical machinery ABB, GE Alsthom, Reliance and Jindals have come up with various projects with large investments. BPL Engineering Ltd is collaborating with Sanyo of Japan and Fedders Lloyd Corpn Ltd is collaborating with Bristol Inc and Maneurope Inc of USA. With the economic environment in India improving every day, more collaboration and investment should be forthcoming.

CAPITAL GOODS

Introduction

The development of a diversified capital goods industry has been the hallmark of India's industrial objectives over the decade. Great strides have been made during the period in this area. Today, India is one of the few nations among the developing countries to have a strong base in the capital goods industry, which has played a pivotal role in India's economic progress.

Production

The capital goods industry was the first to face delicensing. The high import duties were slashed and Indian producers were exposed to international competition after enjoying a protected market for a considerable time. The results came immediately in the form of increased cost-consciousness and efficiency. These along with new standards of quality like ISO 9000, upgraded the Indian capital goods industry to international standards. Along with the names mentioned in the engineering industry, the major producers in this sector are DGP Windsor India Ltd for Plastics Machinery, Manugraph (I) Ltd and HMT for printing machinery, Lakshmi Machines and Textool for textile machinery, Binny and Triveni Engineering Work, for sugar machinery, and Escorts & Voltas for cranes.

Foreign Collaboration

Foreign collaboration in the Indian capital goods industry constitutes 72.3% of those in the engineering industry and 39.3% of the total foreign collaborations approved. These collaborations are mainly in high technology areas (eg electrical equipment, telecommunications, industrial machinery and transportation).

Export

In the year 1994–95, exports of capital goods were Rs31,050 million, a growth of 27.8% over the previous year.

Machine tools have been exported from India to Japan, Bulgaria, Poland and parts of Africa to a value of more than Rs900 million and the sub-sectors like pumps, compressors, etc are also showing signs of upward movement, both in the domestic as well as the foreign markets.

The major items of export are complete vehicles, fabricated steel structures, electrical power machinery and switchgear, textile machine tools and construction machinery.

Imports

Imports of capital goods in 1994–95 were valued at Rs204,750 million, up by 17.7% over the previous year. Major components of import in this sector were electrical machinery, non-electrical machinery and transport equipment.

Investment

It is estimated that Rs400,000 million was invested in the capital goods industry in 1994–95.

AUTOMOBILES

Introduction

Since the opening up of the economy, the automotive industry in India has been experiencing a boom both in terms of production and investment. Most manufacturers are showing double digit growth and preparing to meet even higher consumer demand in coming days.

Production

The turnover of the automotive industry is estimated to have grown at the rate of about 34% in 1994–95 over the previous year. The year 1994–95 witnessed massive production by the giants of the Indian automobile industry like Maruti Udyog Ltd, Hindusthan Motors, Premier Auto Ltd, Telco, Bajaj etc, to the extent of 2.84 million vehicles. From Rs163,288 million the total turnover of the Indian automobile industry shot up to a level of Rs221,409 million in 1994–95. The installed capacity of the industry has been increased to 0.66 million vehicles per annum for four wheelers and HCVs and to 3.15 million vehicles per annum for two wheelers. There are 25 established companies in this sector who largely influence activities among which Maruti Udyog Ltd, Tata Engineering & Locomotive Co (TELCO), Hindusthan Motors, and Premier Auto Ltd are important.

The automobile industry is significant because of the numerous forward and backward links it has throughout the economy. The auxiliary industries and the ancillary industries have shown the same growth as the automobile industry. This sector has tremendous employment potential.

Though production and sales have grown at almost the same rate of 26% and investment is flowing in, the sector dealing with LCVs and HCVs initially lagged behind. But as the government is offering substantial incentives on investment in these areas, the flow of funds is gradually catching up.

Exports

Exports of the automotive sector have increased from a moderate level of Rs7370 million to Rs13,480 million. In terms of numbers, Indian export of automobiles amounted to 0.02 million vehicles in 1994–95.

New Investments

The government as a policy decision delicensed the passenger car industry in 1993 and as a result new collaborations are emerging. With gradual improvement of infrastructure and the trends of globalisation setting in, the global auto giants have already turned their attention towards their Indian counterparts. New tie-ups such as those between Hind Motors and General Motors, LML Ltd and Piaggio of Italy, Premier Automobile and Peugeot of France are planned. With all these tie-ups in hand, the Indian automobile industry is poised for rapid growth. The Cielo, a result of a tie-up between DCM and Daewoo, has already hit the Indian market. The Mercedes will also be seen soon on Indian roads because of the tie-up between Daimler and Tatas.

A total of Rs17,460 million worth of foreign investment was approved by the government during the period August 1991 to April 1995.

CONSUMER GOODS

Introduction

At the onset of the economic reforms in 1991, the most referred-to aspect of the Indian economy was the huge size of the Indian middle class which constitutes a large part of the Indian market for consumer goods. With the wind of liberalisation blowing strongly, growth in consumer spending and changes in consumption patterns have been facilitated as much by government policies to ease supply constraints and encourage consumer demand as by the growing market infrastructure in India.

The Market

It has been estimated that there are 533 million Indians who form the broad market for manufactured consumer goods in which the size of the core group is 100 million for durables and 300 million for consumables. The National Council for Applied Economic Research (NCAER) surveys between 1985–86 and 1993–94 show that there has been a growth of 5% in urban and 10.6% in rural households, suggesting that the number of households in the two highest levels of income has shown the maximum growth. The demand for consumer goods has shown a commensurate increase as expected. But this is not the only factor behind the consumption-led growth of the 1980s. The CII report on consumption clearly showed that growth in real consumption has been lower than growth in real GDP but consumption is spread all over the economy. Above the poverty line, households in even the lowest level of income are buyers of manufactured goods such as transistor radios, TV sets, pressure cookers and watches.

The study also revealed that purchases of most consumer durables were made by the middle income groups between Rs18,000 and Rs78,000 per annum, contributing 69% of motorcycle purchases and 65% of washing machine purchases. With the spirit of urbanisation spreading rapidly in rural areas as well, the rural population has started to constitute an important segment of the mass consumption market.

Production

Since consumer goods include a wide variety of commodities such as automobiles to vanaspati it is more convenient to consider them one by one and comment on production performance. The period April to September, 1995 saw consumer durables such as passenger cars, jeeps, air conditioners, water coolers and consumer non-durables such as malted food registering growth rates of more than 20% over the corresponding period in 1994. Consumer durables such as electric fans, refrigerators, tyres and tubes and consumer perishables such as cigarettes and newspapers recorded a high growth rate between 10% and 20% in the same period. Consumer goods such as plywood and vanaspati recorded a moderate growth rate of less than 10%.

Exports

India has been an exporter of certain consumables. Over the year 1993–94, India exported tea worth Rs9783.8 million, Basmati rice worth Rs1031 million and leather footwear worth Rs15,049.0 million. Along with these, there were Rs430.06 million worth of toiletries, Rs14,110.9 million worth of handmade carpets and Rs978.04 million of electronic goods.

Foreign Investment Trends

Since 1987 foreign investment in the consumer goods sector has been on the rise. Though there was a decline in 1993–94 foreign investment is once again on the rise with multinationals like Sony, Coca Cola, Pepsi, Cadbury, Motorola, General Electric, Electronics, Whirl Pool, GoldStar, and Procter and Gamble coming into the Indian market in a big way with their international brands.

Future Prospects

The spectacular increase in consumption expenditure in recent years has been accentuated by increasing availability of foreign brands in the domestic market. Private consumption expenditure was Rs3418 billion in 1991 at current prices of which almost 55% was on food and beverages. Through the 1980s the real growth rates in the demand for several consumer goods exceeded 12% per annum. With supply constraints easing considerably, the growth in demand for consumer goods, consumer durables and various services has been really rapid. In the light of the present situation it can be concluded that more investments will be forthcoming.

SCIENTIFIC AND INDUSTRIAL INSTRUMENTS

Introduction

The scientific and industrial instruments industry is important for the smooth and proper functioning of the economy by checking, measuring and modifying physical, chemical and biological properties as well as monitoring the process parameters in different spheres. The products of this industry play an important role in the smooth and reliable functioning of plant and machinery in different fields of the economy. This sector is large in the sense that the products are varied and the uses diverse. This industry can broadly be divided into two sub-sectors—control equipment and medical electronics.

Control equipment

The control equipment sub-sector broadly comprises process control equipment such as transmitters, and sensors, test and measuring instruments such as electronic meters, and analysers, analytical instruments such as spectrometers, and chromatographs and special application instruments such as nuclear instruments, and mining instruments. The degree of sophistication in the sub-sector is skewed. Highly sophisticated proceses are being used here along with comparatively crude methods. Over the period of industrialisation, this sector underwent a number of changes. It saw the gradual superseding of the first generation pneumatic and hydraulic machinery by the second generation electronic and analogue instruments. A part of this sub-sector is in the nature of small-scale industries where simple electronic devices are manufactured. The growth for this sub-sector has been 18.2% in 1994–95 which is quite a high rate.

India also exports a substantial amount of control equipment (especially industrial electronic goods) to countries like USA, New Zealand, Hong Kong, Indonesia and Italy.

Adequate capacity as well as basic competence to achieve modernisation and technology upgrading exists in the country. The installed capacity is substantial but is infected with the malady of under-utilisation. The reason behind this is the existence of a large number of smaller units despite of the presence of giants such as Kirloskar, Crompton Greaves, ABB, BHEL and Tata Process Controls Pvt Ltd.

Medical equipment

There are about 90 manufacturing units. Radiology equipment, ECG machines, and MRI systems are the principal products. This sector has experienced phenomenal growth since 1987–88. This is coexistence of both the large and the small-scale units though the contribution is mainly from the large units (more than 70% of the total production). In 1993 the total production was Rs750 million of which almost Rs95 million came from exports. Though there are market leaders such as Philips, L&T, Siemens, Kodak, and GEC the sheer pace of its expansion is attracting more foreign investment.

Investments

It is estimated that the investment in this sector in India in 1993–94 was Rs236 million.

As the growth rate is impressive, many new collaborations are occurring. IBP Co Ltd has collaborated with Drass Galeazi SPA of Italy, Meditronics Ltd has collaborated with Midtronic International of Hong Kong, Usha Drager has collaborated with Dragenwerke of Germany and so on. In control systems we have collaborations between Tata Process Controls and Honeywell Inc of USA, and between Hinditron Schiller and Schiller AG of Germany. Judging by the trends, one can predict even more foreign investments in this sector.

ELECTRICAL MACHINERY

Introduction

The demand for electrical goods is largely influenced by the availability of power, the existing infrastructure and the market. Since the beginning of the liberalisation programme the power scene has shown marked signs of improvement. Hence the demand for electrical machinery, with the possible exception of two years in between, has shown steady increase since 1989. Investments have been substantial in products such as switchgear, transformers, cables conductors, electric motors etc for the purpose of power generation and distribution. This in turn has helped to step up the demand for different household electrical appliances.

Production

Private investments in the power sector have made the growth of the different products in the electrical industry increase substantially in recent years. Expansions, diversifications and collaborations have been widespread. There has been a substantial increase in 1993–94 over the previous year in the output of LT & HT circuit breakers, isolating switches, motor starters, HRC fuses and overload relays. In 1993–94 the overall performance of the industry was only marginally increased on the previous year. The organised sector in the electrical industry had 12,771 units with both public sector and private sector participation. Bharat Heavy Electricals Ltd (BHEL) is a big name in the public sector as L&T, Kirloskar Electricals, Siemens, GEC Ltd, Crompton Graves, ECE Industries and ABB Ltd, are in the private sector.

Though the opening up of the economy has seen a general increase in activity in all sectors, the government's procurement policy assumes special importance for the growth of the electrical industry, as public sector units such as National Thermal Power Corporation, the State Electricity Boards etc are the principal consumers of the products of the industry. Many of the SEBs have already initiated restructuring which can be taken as the initial indication for better times to come for the electrical industry.

This industry might experience some rough weather in its growth process since most of the foreign power development companies are resorting to import of equipment from abroad. The growth of the industry will be determined by the private power companies if the government can offer more transparency in its power policy, which is likely to be the case. The industry is rapidly becoming quality conscious.

New Investment

New investments have started flowing into the electrical industry. Crompton Greaves is going ahead with a transformer manufacturing project with a capital outlay of Rs750 million. Horizon Battery Tech Inc of the USA is collaborating with Horizon India Batteries Ltd in a proposed project of Rs2100 million. Hindustan Cables Ltd is planning a 'jelly filled cables' project in West Bengal with a capital outlay of Rs1000 million. With these examples not rare, it may be concluded that many investment opportunities have opened up in this area.

Foreign investment proposals worth Rs22,130 million were approved in this sector during August 1991 to April 1995 and some more are in the pipeline.

CHEMICALS INDUSTRY

Introduction

The Indian chemicals industry produces a wide spectrum of products which include pharmaceuticals, dyes, man-made fibres, plastics, pesticides, fertilisers, cosmetics, paints and a range of organic and inorganic products for varying applications. This industry displays the coexistence of the large units with small-scale operations. Going by recent performance, the chemicals group is one of the fastest growing industrial groups in the country. In 1992–93, when the economy was going through a lean period, this industry recorded a positive growth rate.

Change in Approach

Globalisation has brought the Indian chemicals industry to the crossroads, with comparatively unconstrained growth as well as exposure to tremendous competition. The 1980s brought an element of dynamism to this industry which shifted its approach from a production-led one to a market-led one. The different important sub-sectors are discussed separately in the analysis to follow.

Organic and inorganic chemicals

Soda ash, caustic soda, calcium carbide, acetic acid, phenol etc are the major products of the basic organic and inorganic chemicals industry. The importance of this industry lies in the fact that its products are widely used as components in industries ranging from consumer goods to heavy and basic industries. ICI India Ltd, Hindustan Organic Chemicals Ltd, Indian Organic Chemicals Ltd, Ballarpur Industries, Thirumalai Chemicals, BASF Polychem, Gujarat Alkaline and Chemicals, DCW, Amines & Plasticizers Ltd, Herdillia Chemicals, and Hindustan Lever Ltd are among the principal producers.

Exports

This sub-sector, being a net exporter of its products, has shown a steady increase in exports since 1991, with its exports going up to Rs6354 million in 1994–95.

Drugs and pharmaceuticals

Drugs and pharmaceuticals constitute a very important part of the Indian chemicals industry. This sector shows a lot of promise for the future because of its performance in recent years.

Production

The current production is around Rs94,500 million in value terms (in 1994–95) and it has every reason to increase further in the future because of drastic simplification of the comparatively complex drug rules of the past. The two schedules for reserved drugs have been replaced by one schedule and several restrictions are being withdrawn. As a result investment should flow in over and above the present level and production is sure to go up. Ranbaxy, Dr Reddy's Laboratories, Lupin Laboratories, Glaxo, Cipla, Pfizer, Hindustan Antibiotics Ltd, Hoechst and Cadila are among the major producers.

Exports

With exports of the drugs and pharmaceuticals industry going up to almost Rs22,000 million in 1994–95, this industry has carved a niche for itself in the world market. Exports are sure to grow in coming years.

Pesticides and agrochemicals

Pesticides and agrochemicals are another important sub-sector of the Indian chemicals industry. India is currently the second largest producer of pesticides in Asia.

Production

This sub-sector has a turnover of more than Rs90,000 million. As India expects to participate in a freer world trade in agriculture after the Uruguay Round of GATT, the demand for pesticides and agrochemicals is expected to shoot up drastically. The country is a dominant producer of iso proteurone (herbicide) among many other agrochemicals, accounting for nearly 25% of world production. For 1994–95, the production of this sub-sector was 85,800 metric tonnes (a marginal improvement over the 1993–94 value). The major names are Rallies India Ltd, Excell Industries, Ghard Chemicals Ltd, Sandoz, NOCIL, Cyramid Industries, NFL and NFCL.

Exports

Exports were around Rs211 million in 1994–95 and investments are flowing in to increase the capacity of this sub-sector even further.

Petrochemicals

The petrochemicals industry is the third major sub-sector of the Indian chemicals industry. The consumption of petrochemicals experienced a sudden upsurge in the 1980s when products such as plastic became more cost effective than their counterparts. Among the large producers in the domestic market are Castrol India Ltd, IPCL, NOCIL, Reliance and Mysore Petrochemicals Ltd. The expected increase in petrochemicals consumption during the eighth plan is 25% as they are relatively cheap replacements for metals, timber, rubber and jute.

Dyes and pigments and fertilisers

The dyes and pigments industry recorded a moderately high production of about 32,000 metric tonnes in 1994-95 with export earnings of Rs13,319 million. Another important component of the Indian chemicals industry is fertilisers with a financial outlay of Rs90 billion. Though India is the world's fourth largest producer of fertiliser it has to rely partially on imports for certain fertiliser components. Investments are pouring in and, with growing demand for fertilisers coupled with encouraging government policies (such as the deregulation of phosphatic fertilisers), the Indian chemicals industry can expect to see a greater degree of self-reliance soon. The National Fertilisers Corporation of India, Zuari Agrochemicals, Deepak Fertilizers, Coromandal Fertilisers, Godavari Fertilisers & Chemicals, Indo-Gulf Fertilisers & Chemicals Corpn, and the Nagarjuna Fertilisers & Chemicals Ltd are major players.

The demand for the products of the Indian chemicals industry is on the rise. With the value of exports going up to Rs58,607 million in 1994–95, this sector can offer excellent returns on investments.

New Investments

For 1994, investment in the chemicals industry amounted to Rs661,480 million or almost 19.7% of total investments in India. Organic chemicals accounted for Rs450,350 million, fertilisers accounted for Rs114,740 million, drugs and pharmaceuticals for Rs34,030 million and the sub-sector of inorganic chemicals received an investment of Rs62,360 million. Projects such as Assam Industrial Development Corpn Ltd with a capital outlay of Rs 4600 million and a foreign exchange outlay of Rs6000 million, under the promotion of Reliance Industries Ltd, have been proposed. Along with this Reliance Industries has gone in for a collaboration with Stone & Webester USA in an Rs14,560 million ethylene and propylene project. Shell of UK and Lumus Grest of USA have collaborated with Reliance Industries for a monoethylene glycol project at Gujarat with a capital outlay of Rs3720 million. The capital outlay of the DuPont-Reliance project at Maharashtra is at a projected level of Rs27,000 million. Hindustan Ciba-Geigy has collaborated in an Rs940 million rifamicin project with Chong Kun Dang Corporation of Korea. DuPont of USA is collaborating with RPG Enterprises in an Rs4000 million film grade polyester chips project which is already being implemented.

Foreign investment proposals for Rs28,070 million in the chemicals sector were approved during August 1991 to April 1995.

This investment boom is likely to continue in the future as well.

TEXTILES

Introduction

Textiles is the single largest industry in the country as it accounts for 20–25% of total industrial production. With more than a century of experience, it has matured into a stable, composite industry. Though there is organised production in both the private and public sectors, self-employed and co-operative employed weavers also contribute substantially.

Raw Materials

The main raw materials of the industry are natural fibres such as silk, cotton and wool, and man-made fibres. India, having more than 7.68 million hectares of cultivable land for the sector, has an abundance of the principal raw materials.

Production

As the population increased, so did textile industry production. Different categories of cloth are produced in keeping with demands from different income brackets. The government's textile policy has made it obligatory for all cloth producers to make a certain proportion of cloth for the comparatively poor sections of society. Currently textile industry production is experiencing an upsurge which is likely to continue.

According to the Ministry of Textiles estimates in 1994, there were 1227 organised mills among which 962 were spinning mills and 265 were modern composite mills. In the private sector the major players are Reliance Industries Ltd, Bombay Dyeing Ltd, Woolworth India Ltd, Century Textiles, J K Synthetics, Dawan Mills, Arvind Mills, Mafatlal Modipon, JCT Ltd, and DCM Shriram Ltd. In textiles the public sector has a marginal presence in the form of organisations such as the National Textile Corporation, and the Cotton Corporation of India Ltd.

Exports

The textile industry has been enjoying booming exports since 1992. Textile exports (excluding jute and handicrafts) during 1994–95, were estimated at Rs19,104 million, implying an increase of about 33% over the previous year. As the government is offering further incentives, exports are expected to grow even more. The government is trying to expand the overseas market for Indian textiles. Export-promoting bodies such as the Handloom Export Promotion Council and the Indian Silk Promotion Council have been specially active in the post-1991 era. A network of 35 fully fledged testing laboratories will be set up at an estimated cost of Rs30 million as a part of the two year perspective plan which is being finalised by the government to enable the industry to conform to ecological standards.

Opportunities

Since the Government of India has delicensed the industry, investments have started flowing in. This sector being a major foreign exchange earner, the government has devised a garment policy for the maximum utilisation of quotas and realisation of foreign exchange earnings, which is also encouraging investors. The government has already stressed the need for an integrated textile policy in India to foster balanced growth in the industry.

New Investments

Investments in the textile industry were more than Rs19,870 million, ie almost 5.8% of the total investment in India, in 1994. With more and more investment in hand, the textiles industry shows signs of a promising future.

Between August 1991 and April 1995 foreign investment proposals for Rs13,550 million were approved for the textile sector.

FOOD PROCESSING

Introduction

Since the member nations signed the Uruguay Round of GATT commitments, it has become essential to identify areas where India can reap most of the benefits of its comparative advantage. Being the second largest producer of both fruits and vegetables in the world, India definitely has potential in the area of food processing. Food processing is still undeveloped in terms of realisation of potential, as less than 1% of the fruits and vegetables that India produces are processed.

Potential

In India 128 million hectares of land is under food crops cultivation with 12 million hectares of land coming directly under horticultural crops. The estimated produce is 100 million tonnes per annum amounting to almost 18% of the gross agricultural output. Areas under fruit and vegetable cultivation are 3.21 million hectares and 5.5 hectares respectively with the estimated production being 28.2 million tonnes and 51 million tonnes respectively. The estimated production of vegetables excludes root and tuber crops such as potatoes and onions which have substantial shares in agriculture production. Despite this massive production there has been little investment in the food processing area because previously Indian agricultural exports were treated as residual. Now that the food processing sector offers significant opportunities for both local markets and exports, investment has started trickling in but the opportunities remain largely untapped.

Though land ceilings prevent companies from owning extensive estates, the government has made considerable efforts to promote contract farming whereby the farmer commits himself to supplying an agreed quantity of crop to companies at a specified price.

OTHER AREAS

The other areas offering investment opportunities are those of livestock, meat and poultry, fisheries, grain processing, beer and alcoholic beverages and agricultural packaging. India being the third largest milk producing country in the world with 50% of world's buffalo population and 20% of the world's cattle population has immense investment opportunities to offer. While with increasing quality consciousness among consumers, the market for scientifically produced meat products is expanding rapidly, supply bottlenecks loom large. The fisheries, with an extensive coastline of 7500 km, 28,000 km of river, 3 million hectares of reservoirs and fresh water lakes, have a huge potential. To date these resources have been mostly tapped locally, catering to the domestic demand with minimal participation by the organised sector for exports.

The grain processing sector is also largely unorganised despite the fact that India is both a large producer and a consumer of foodgrains. Beer and alcoholic beverages are mostly produced in the organised sector but the expanding demand calls for further investment.

Trading is restricted only for a few very select commodities and hence has a suppressed potential. In this changing scenario, the government has entirely exempted several agro-based products, 100% export oriented units and units located in export processing zones from the different duties and excise.

The investment potential of this sector is not totally unknown to investors. Investments have already been undertaken by organisations such as Nestle, Cadbury-Schweppes, Pepsi Foods, Godrej Foods, Kellogg's, and Kwality-Wall. Dab Brau-Consult-GMBH of Germany has decided to collaborate with Kedia Distilleries Ltd in a proposed project of Rs1700 million; Carlsberg of Denmark is collaborating with United Breweries in a Rs600 million project. The Government of India has already approved 195 proposals for 100% export-oriented units involving an investment of Rs25,280 million. These incentives coupled with prediction of high growth rates for this sector should attract large investment in the near future.

GENERAL CONCLUSION

Growth has been phenomenal in most of the Indian industrial sector over the last few years, especially the period after March 1994.

BUSINESS OUTLOOK

Industry is on an upward swing and production, employment, investment and overall activities are expected to grow in the coming years. According to the 44th Business Outlook Survey conducted by the Confederation of Indian Industry (CII), 22% of the respondents expected employment to increase by more than 10%, 31% expected it to be between 5% and 10% and 47% anticipated a 0.5% growth, implying an increase in the activities in different spheres of the industry.

The government, taking note of this, has come up with certain general and some sector-specific incentives to boost investment in the respective industries. Hence, both production and export, in almost all the sectors is registering a massive growth. If the boom in production and exports continues, which is likely to be the case, then the Indian industrial sector offers almost unlimited opportunities to investors.

CHAPTER 30

TOURISM
by S Sundar

INTRODUCTION

India is a vast country with a history that dates back over 5000 years. Its geographical diversity, snow capped mountains, mighty rivers, a vast coastline, rich culture and heritage, fairs and festivals, monuments and temples offer a variety of tourist attractions that are unparalleled.

Tourism in India is, however, limited due to lack of adequate infrastructure and facilities. Travellers to the kingdom of the Great Mughals complained about the lack of inns in India. 'In this kingdom there are no inns to entertain strangers', wrote Terry. Unlike the West where the Grand Tour and local inns laid the foundations of the tourism industry, in India there were only sarais. But even as the tourism and hospitality industry in India has grown in modern time, what stands out is the inadequacy of infrastructure in the tourism and hospitality sector.

INADEQUATE INFRASTRUCTURE

Shortage of hotel accommodation in the country is a major setback in the promotion and development of tourism. At present India has about 57,000 approved hotel rooms. It is estimated that the country requires about 125,000 hotel rooms by the turn of the century. Besides hotels, there is also an urgent need for development of tourism-related services such as travel and tour operating agencies, transportation and other facilities providing leisure, entertainment, and convention services.

IMPORTANCE OF TOURISM

The government is keen to attract investment in tourism. A growing population needs more jobs. Tourism creates them. This realisation has come to governments, both Central and State. The labour-capital ratio per million of rupee of investment in agriculture is 44.7, in manufacturing 12.6, and in hotels and restaurants 89. In addition, tourism generates maximum foreign exchange earnings with minimal expenditure on imports. Therefore, tourism has started receiving the support it rightly deserves.

FOREIGN INVESTMENT

The economic reforms introduced by the Government of India are integrating India into the global economy and making Indian industry internationally competitive. Foreign direct investment and technical collaborations form a major platform of the economic reforms. With a view to attracting investment, the hotel and tourism-related industry has been declared as a 'high priority industry' for foreign investment. It is now eligible for approval of direct investment up to 51% of foreign equity. Non-Resident Indian investment is allowed up to 100%.

FOREIGN COLLABORATION

In the fast changing world of technology the relationship between suppliers and users of technology agreements has to be recognised. To promote technological upgrading in the hotel industry, approvals for technology agreements are available automatically subject to the fulfilment of the following parameters:

(1) Technical and consultancy services including fees for architecture, design, supervision, etc up to 3% of the capital cost of the project (less cost of land and finance).

(2) Franchising and marketing/publicity support fee up to 3% of net turnover.

(3) Management fees (including incentive fee) up to 10% of gross operating profit.

The above norms are applicable provided the collaboration is proposed with companies managing hotel(s) with at least 500 rooms. No permission is now required for hiring foreign technicians.

Applications for automatic approval for foreign investment or technology agreements and/or management contracts can be made to the Reserve Bank of India who will accord automatic approval and the entrepreneurs can approach authorised dealers for release of foreign exchange. Agreements which involve a variation in the parameters will be considered on merit by the Foreign Investment Promotion Board.

INCENTIVES AND FACILITIES

As the construction of hotels is a highly capital-intensive activity, the Tourism Finance Corporation of India has been set up to render financial assistance to the private sector for construction of hotels and other tourist facilities.

A 3% interest subsidy is available to hotel projects in one or three-star categories, on loans sanctioned by the Tourism Finance Corporation of India, Industrial Finance Corporation of India and the State Financial and Industrial Corporations provided the projects are outside the metropolitan cities of Delhi, Bombay, Calcutta and Madras.

A 5% interest subsidy is available for hotels constructed in the travel destinations identified for intensive development in the National Action Plan for Tourism (NAPT) as well as for the category of heritage hotels.

In addition to the interest subsidy, a scheme of capital subsidy has been introduced for heritage hotels. Under this scheme, a capital subsidy of Rs500,000 or 10% of the cost, whichever is less, is available for development of any structure over 75 years old into a heritage hotel.

There are also fiscal incentives. Fifty per cent of profits derived by hotels, travel agents and tour operators in foreign exchange are exempt from income tax. The balance of profits in foreign exchange is also exempt provided it is reinvested in tourism projects.

Hotels, travel agents, tour operators and other organisations connected with the tourist trade are now covered under the Liberalised Exchange Rate Management System (LERMS). Authorised dealers release foreign exchange for business visits, participation in conferences, seminars and training. Prior approval of government is not necessary.

The facility to open and operate Exchange Earners Foreign Currency (EEFC) Account stands was extended to hotels, travel agents, tour operators. Under the scheme, 25% of inward remittances in foreign exchange can be credited to this account and utilised for specified purposes.

IMPORTS

Hotels approved by the Department of Tourism, Government of India are entitled to import essential goods related to the hotel and tourism industry up to a value of 10% of foreign exchange earned by them during the preceding licensing year. In the case of approved travel agents, tour operators and restaurants, the import entitlement is up to 2.5% of the foreign exchange earned.

Recreational bodies can import goods considered to be essential for their own use up to 10% of foreign exchange earned during the preceding licensing year.

Capital goods, raw materials, and components can be imported without any restriction except to the extent such imports are regulated by the Negative List of Imports. Import of special items required by hotels, restaurants, travel agents and tour operators are permitted against a licence.

EXPORT PROMOTION CAPITAL GOODS SCHEME

The import of capital equipment (including spares up to 10%) by hotels and restaurants, travel agents and tour operators, for which payments are received in freely convertible currency, is allowed at a concessional rate of customs duty of 15% subject to an export obligation four times the CIF value of the imports to be fulfilled in a period of five years. In case the CIF value of the imports is Rs200 million or more, no duty is payable. However, the export obligation will be six times the CIF value and the period for fulfilling the export obligation will be eight years.

CONCESSIONAL CUSTOMS DUTY

Customs duty on specified items has been reduced to the level as applicable to project imports provided the goods imported are required for initial setting up of the hotel or for substantial expansion of the hotel.

Equipment for adventure sports can be imported on a concessional rate of duty.

Priority consideration is given to approved projects in allotment of construction materials such as cement, steel and for telephone, telex, and LPG connections.

THE ROLE OF THE CENTRE AND THE STATES

In the Constitution of India, hotels, tourist transport and other facilities are subjects allocated to the States. It is up to the State governments to create tourist infrastructure, and to assist private entrepreneurs in securing the land, water, power and other amenities required to facilitate investment in the tourism sector. The State governments are now vying with each other to attract investment in tourism in their regions. The Government of India, with the overall responsibility for national policies on tourism, coordination and external publicity and for approving foreign investment has taken on the role of the investment facilitator, and has set up a cell to assist potential investors to identify and exploit investment opportunities in the sector.

OPPORTUNITIES

India offers tremendous opportunities for investment in tourism. These are not confined to the hotel industry and can range from internal transportation to cruises, from facilities for adventure sports to bird watch tours and from golf resorts to amusement parks. The opportunities are endless.

The Central and State governments are fully committed to the promotion of tourism in India, and are working in unison to attract investment in tourism infrastructure and facilities. Tourist arrivals in India are expected to grow by around 8% annually for the next 10 years.

INDEX

Accounts, company
  audits, 220–221
  foreign requirements, 164
  requirements, 150–151
Acquisitions, corporate, 122, 256
Actual User Condition, imports, 70
Advance Intermediate Licence, 68
Advance Licences, 67
Advertising
  agencies and services, 203–205
  regulations, 205
Advocate General, State, 11
Agents
  appointed, 144
  patent, 175
Agriculture, 24
Agrochemicals, 358
Air (Prevention & Control of Pollution) Act 1981, 147–148
Alliances, business, 116
Alma Ata Declaration (WHO), 333
Amalgamations, 122, 167
Anti-trust laws, 145–146
Arbitration, 263–277
  appeals, 268–269
  awards, 266–267, 268
  changes of law, 271–272
  court powers, 265–266, 267
  exchange rate fixing, 270
  filing agreements, 267
  hierarchy of courts, 263–264
  reference to agreements, 264–265
  in suits, 267
Arbitration Act 1940, 264, 269–270
Arbitration and Conciliation Ordinance 1996

promulgation, 271–272
  salient features, 272–277
Asian Paints India Ltd, 213–214
Asia-Pacific region, 93
Associations of persons (AOP) and taxation, 226
Atomic Energy Act 1962, 148
Attorney-General, 9
Auditor-General, 10
Audits, company, 220–221
Automotive industry, 350–351

Banking sector, 126–132
  institution types, 127–132
  investment opportunities, 138
Bidding for projects, 112–113
Bilateral Investment Agreements, 38
Blue Dart (courier service), 212–213
BOLT (Build-Operate-Lease-Transfer) Schemes, 303, 338
Bombay Stock Exchange, 23, 254
Bond market, 140
BOO (Build-Own-Operate) Schemes, 338, 343
Book-building, company, 249
BOOT (Build-Own-Operate-Transfer) Schemes, 338
BOT (Build-Operate-Transfer) Schemes, 297–298, 330
Branch offices, 162–163
Brand positioning, 202–205
Business ethos, 121–122, 193–194
Business houses, 23
Businesses *see* Companies

Canalisation, 72, 73
Capital
  equity, 125
  loan, 126
  paid-up, 160–161
  repatriation, 40
  working, 126
Capital expenditure taxation, 219–221
Capital gains taxation, 221–222
Capital goods sector
  growth, 46
  pivotal role, 348–349

Capital issue
   minimum subscription, 250–251
   pricing, 249
Capital market, 246–260
   SEBI approval, 135
   SEBI guidelines, 249–252
   size, 246
Case studies, marketing and distribution, 209–214
Chemicals industry, 356–359
Chief Election Commissioner, 10
Chief Minister, 10–11
Civil Service, 14
   see also Public sector
Climate, 4, 283
Coal sector
   captive block applications, 343–344
   growth and prospects, 341–344
   laws, 343
   private sector investment, 342–343
Collector, District level, 12
Commercial banks, scheduled, 128–129
Companies
   capital mobilisation, 249
   establishment requirements, 163–164
   hours, 282
   incorporation *see* Incorporation
   laws, 143–151, 153
   office-set-up, 161–164
   share capital types, 159–161
   taxation, 216, 219–221
   types, 153–155
Companies Act 1956, 143
   accounting statements, 150–151
   accounting under, 151
   explained, 248
Competitive bidding, 112–115
Comptroller, 10
Computer programs and copyright, 182
Consignment tax, proposed, 244
Constitution
   citizens' rights, 14–15
   described, 5–6

electoral changes, 30–31
indirect tax definition, 239–240
Consumer goods sector
described, 201
dividend balancing, 57
future, 351–353
import policy, 73
Consumer Protection Act 1986, 149
Consumers
consumption pattern, 199–202
potential, 197
protection, 201–202
Containerisation of cargo, 302
Contract Labour Act, 186
Control equipment sub-sector, 353–354
Copyright, 180–183
Copyright Act 1994 Amendments, 183
Corporate and business laws, 143–151
Council of Ministers, 8–9
Courts *see* Judiciary
Credit
cards, 281
rating, 250
rating agencies, 252
Credit Analysis and Research Ltd (CARE), 252
Credit Rating Investment Services of India Ltd (CRISIL), 252
Crude oil, present requirement, 327
Currency
regulations, 281
reserves, 27
trading, 72
Customs duty, 242

Debentures, 161
Deemed public company, 154
Defence expenditure, 93
Democratic process, 30–31
Depreciation for taxation, 219
Deputy Commissioner, District level, 12
Designs, protection of, 183–184
Development banks, 131–132
Devolvement of share issues, 250
Diet, 280

Digital switching equipment, 321–322
Direct taxes, 215–238
    assessment, 225–229
    business and professions, 219–221
    capital gains, 221–222
    deductions, 224
    dividends, 223
    payment, 229–231
    property income, 223
    rates, 216–217
    salary, 223
    tax holidays, 224
    wealth, 237
Disclosures, corporate, 249–250
Disinvestment by foreign investors, 42
Dissolution of companies, 167
Distribution
    geographic coverage, 198–199
    systems, 206–209
Distributors, 207, 208–209
District government, 11–13
District Magistrate, 12
Dividend balancing
    consumer goods industries, 57
    period, 39
Dividends
    declaration of, 166–167
    direct taxes, 223
Domestic industrial investment, 26
Double tax avoidance agreements (DTAAs), 236–237
Drugs
    de-licensing, 44
    future, 357
Duty Draw-back Scheme, 69
Duty Exemption Scheme, 67–71
Dyes and pigments industry, 358–359
Dynastic employment, 188, 190–191

East Europe, 94
Economic conditions and trends, 18–32
    advantages, 21
    areas of poor performance, 20
    key indicators, 19–20

potential growth, 21–22
public sector privatisation, 28–29
Economy
  growth, 200
  liberalisation, 27–28
  'mixed economy' model, 23
  policy reforms, 25–27
  prognosis, 32
  States system, 29–30
  structure, 24–25
EDI (electronic data interchange), ports development, 303
Education
  cost estimates, 101
  enrolment by studies area, 99–101
  infrastructure, 97–98
  literacy levels, 200
  opportunities, 101–102
  policy thrusts, 101
Electric current, 282
Electrical machinery industry, 355–356
Electricity production, 19 *see also* Power sector
  growth potential, 306–308
  IT industry highlights, 307
  opportunities, 310–311
Electronic data interchange (EDI), ports development, 303
Electronic Hardware Technology Park (EHTP), 309–310
Electronics, Department of, industry role, 306
Electronics/software sector
  growth potential, 306–308
  IT industry highlights, 307
  opportunities, 310–311
Employment *see* Labour management
Energy resources
  available, 287
  fossil fuel, 312
Engineering industry, 347–348
Engineering Products Export (Replenishment of Iron & Steel Intermediate) Scheme, 69
Entry strategy
  'Evolving Plan Model,' 109–111
  formulation, 111
  MOU route, 112–113
  typical errors, 108–109

Environment Protection Act 1986, 147
Environmental laws, 147–148
Equity capital, 125
Essential Commodities Act 1955, 149
Euro-issues, 255–256
European Union, 93–94
'Evolving Plan Model,' 109–111
Exchange control, 143–144
Exchange rate, 136–137
Excise duty, 243
Executive, State, 10–11
Exit policy, 192–193
Expenditure tax, 238
Export Houses, 70, 76–77
Export Oriented Units (EOUs), 44, 45, 76
Export Processing Zones (EPZs), 44, 45, 76
Export Promotion Capital Goods (EPCG) Scheme, 66, 69–70
Export-Import Policy (EXIM Policy)
    import controls, 64–66
    introduction, 64
Exports
    automotive sector, 350–351
    capital goods, 349
    chemicals industry, 357, 358
    composition of, 78–79
    consumer goods, 352
    encouragement of, 75
    growth, 26, 78
    promotion, 44–45
    textile industry, 360–361
External relations
    overview, 91–95
    tax agreements, 236–237

Factories Act 1948, 148
Fertiliser industry, 358–359
Finance
    companies' needs, 125–126
    raising, 42
Financial markets
    Development banks, 131–132
    growth, 23
    intermediaries, 247

investment opportunities, 137–141
long- and short-term, 124–142
major players, 124
non-banking companies, 133
non-banking financial institutions, 132–133
reforms, 27–28
Financial year, 150
Five Year Plans, 20
Food processing
future, 361–362
policies, 43
Food production, 18–19
Foreign Awards (Recognition and Enforcement) Act 1961, 270–271
Foreign banks, 129–130
Foreign collaboration
capital goods industry, 349
tourism, 365
Foreign equity
automatic approval, 38
electronics/software sector, 308–309
existing companies, 39
petroleum sector, 332
telecommunications sector, 319
Foreign Exchange Regulation Act 1973 (FERA)
amendments, 41
explained, 262–263
foreign equity levels, 34
Foreign Exchange Regulation (Amendment) Act 1993, 143
Foreign institutional investors (FIIs)
portfolio limitations, 255
SEBI registration, 255
securities, 139–140
stocks, 136
tax rate, 234
Foreign investment
business set-up, 164–167
consumer goods sector, 352–353
corporate strategy, 88
Euro-issues, 255–256
favourable factors, 82–86
financial sector opportunities, 137–141
forms of participation, 56
joint-venture benefits, 118–119

mining sector, 314
negotiation preparation, 105–111
policy, 37–42
public sector, 40
R&D capability, 86
repatriation of capital, 40
software/hardware sector, 310
stock portfolios, 255
technology agreements, 39–40
tourism, 365
trends, 47–48
Foreign Investment Promotion Board (FIPB), 38–39, 308
Foreign policy
see also External relations
formulation constants, 89–91
new, 91
overview, 89–96
post-cold war, 95–96
Foreign technology agreements, 51–54
Foreign trade, 62–79
hard currencies trade, 72
imports on MFN basis, 71
strengthened infrastructure, 75–77
Forms, official, select list, 61

GDP (gross domestic product), 24–25
Geography, 3–4
Gift tax, 238
Global depository receipts, 255–256
GNP (gross national product), 21
Government, 5–17
Central, 7–10
democratic process, 30–31
District level, 11–13
electronics/software sector, 308–310
Executive, 8–9
investment negotiations, 111–115
local government, 13–14
private power policy, 289–291
State level, 10–11
State trading, 72–74
tax structure, 215
Union Legislature, 9–10

Governor, State, 10
Gross domestic product (GDP), 24
Gross national product (GNP), 21

Health sector
  expenditure, 334–335
  industry survey, 333–336
  medical equipment, 354
  private sector participation, 335–336
High Court, State level, 11
Highways, 293–300
  BOT schemes, 297–298
  construction contracts, 297
  financing, 299
  infrastructure and administration, 293
  private sector participation, 295, 296–300
  road development policy, 294–296
  road traffic growth, 293
  urban development, 339
Holding company, 155
Housing sector, 340
Human resources
  development, 97–102
  industry, trade and commerce, 98–101
  skilled, 19, 22–23, 84–85

Immovable property acquisition, 145
Imports
  Actual User Condition, 70
  capital goods, 349
  EXIM policy features, 64–66
  for export production, 66–71
  growth, 78
  licences, 66, 70–71
  on MFN basis, 71
  policy evolution, 75
  present policy, 72–73
  reduced restrictions, 73–74
  telecommunications policies, 319
  tourism, 366–367
Income
  direct taxes, 223
  heads of, 219

repatriation, 283
tax exempt, 218
taxable, 217–219
Income Tax Act, 151
Incorporation
historical perspective, 152–153
issue of certificate, 159
requirements, 156–159
Independent Power Projects (IPPs), 112
Indexed cost, capital gains, 221–222
India
area, 4
business ethos, 121–122, 193–194
climate, 4
competitive advantages, 81–88
cultural diversity, 90
education *see* Education
entrepreneurial class, 23
entry procedures, 278–279
future prosperity, 22–23
geography, 3–4
government system *see* government
historical perspective, 80–81
investment advantages, 81–88
investment opportunities, 362–363
language, 5
living conditions, 279–283
population, 5
strengths and advantages, 80–88
Indian Arbitration Council, 270
Indian Contract Act 1872, 261
Indian Forests Act 1927, 148
Indian Trade Classification (Harmonised System), 37, 72
Indirect taxes, 239–245
defined by Constitution, 239–240
reforms, 244
types, 241
Industrial Entrepreneur's Memorandum (IEM), 36
Industrial Information and Credit Rating Agency of India Ltd
(ICRA), 252
Industrial instruments, 353–354
Industrial policies, 33–61
food processing, 43

historical perspective, 33
new, 35–37
regulatory framework, 33–34
role of State governments, 43
Schedules I to IX, 49–61
Industrial relations *see* Labour management
Industries (Development and Regulation) Act 1951 (IDR), 33
Industry
compulsory licensing, 50
current scenario, 46–47
domestic investment, 26
growth, 26, 46–47
licensing, 35–37
new classifications, 37
Information technology industry *see* Electronics/software sector
Inorganic chemicals, 357
Insecticides Act 1968, 148
Insurance investment opportunities, 140–141
Intellectual property, 171–184
copyright, 180–183
defined, 171
designs, 183–184
patents, 173–177
protection rights, 172–173
trade marks, 177–180
Interest tax, 238
Inventions, patenting, 174
Investment sector, 354
ISO 9000, 192
ITC (HS) Classifications of Export & Import Items, 66, 72
ITC LTD (Calcutta), increased productivity, 191

Japan, 93
Joint-ventures
common problems, 116–118
distribution networks, 209
foreign investor benefits, 118–119
health care delivery, 335–336
negotiations, 116–122
taxation, 226
Judiciary
Central level, 9–10
Constitution protector, 7

courts hierarchy, 263–264
District level, 12–13
State level, 11

Kellogg's India Pvt Ltd, 211–212

Labour
  costs, 194, 195
  laws, 146–147
  markets, 187–189
Labour management
  current laws, 185–187
  employment levels, 26
  exit policy, 192–193
  flexibility, 190–191
  future trends, 189–190
  improved productivity, 194–195
  outsourcing, 196
  Port work gangs, 302
  productivity, 191–192
  recommendations, 193–196
  staff rationalisation, 194
Language
  business, 279
  mass media, 203–204
  official, 5
Legislation
  anti-trust, 145–146
  consumer protection, 149, 201–202
  corporate and business, 143–151
  environmental, 147–148
  labour, 146–147
  securities market, 247–248
Liaison offices, 162
Liberalised Exchange Rate Management System (LERMS), 366
Licensed industries registration, 37
Licensing
  copyright, 182
  imports, 66
  industry, 35–37
  procedures, 36–37
  prospecting, 315
Limited by guarantee companies, 155

Limited liability companies, 154–155
Literacy levels, 200
Living conditions, 279–283
Loan capital, 126
Local government, 13–14

Managing directors, appointment guidelines, 164–165
Manpower, scientific and technical, 19, 84–85
Manufacturing sector
  growth, 46, 47
  human resources management, 194
  imports, 70
  three-tier distribution, 206–207
Market intermediaries, SEBI registration, 252
Market size, 21–22, 84
Marketing, 197–203
  distribution, 198–199
  estimated demand, 197
Mass media
  coverage, 204
  exposure to, 201
  language, 203–204
Media, 282
Medical equipment, 354
Memorandum and Articles of Association, 157–159
Merchant banking investment, 138–139
Mergers, 122, 167
Mineral sector
  current scenario, 312–313
  future, 316
  mining leases, 315–316
  opportunities, 313–314
  ownership, 315
  policy, 312
Minimum Alternate Tax (MAT), 224
Mining sector, legislative framework, 314–316
Modified Value Added Tax (MODVAT), 47, 243
Monopolies and Restrictive Trade Practices Act 1969
  (MRTP), 34, 40, 145
Monopolistic trade practices, 145–146
MOU route (Memorandum of Understanding), 112–115
Multilateral Investment Guarantee Agency (MIGA), 38
Multi-modal transportation, 295–296, 303

Municipal taxes, 244
Mutual funds
   explained, 132–133
   financial market guidelines, 256–258
   investment opportunities, 139

National Highways Authority of India (NHAI), 298
National Stock Exchange, 253–254, 255
National Telecom Policy 1994, 320
Natural gas, 330–331
Negative List of Imports, 65–66
Negotiable Instruments Act 1981 (NIA), 149
Negotiation preparation, 105–123
   bidding route, 113–115
   for government, 111–115
   joint-ventures, 119–121
   MOU route, 113–115
Negotiation process
   intra-company, 122–123
   joint-ventures, 121–122
Networks, private, voice and data, 322
NIP (New Industrial Policy, 1991), 35–37
Non-alignment policy, 90–91
Non-banking companies, 133
Non-banking financial institutions, 132–133
Non-resident Indians (NRIs)
   investment schemes, 44
   taxation, 234–235
Non-residents
   tax concessions, 231–234
   taxation, 226–227, 231–236
   withholding tax, 235
Nuclear weapons, 92

Office set-up, 161–164
Organic chemicals, 357
OTC Exchange of India, 254
Outsourcing, 196
Overseas Corporate Bodies (OCBs), 44

Pakistan, 92
Panchayat Samiti, 13–14
Parliamentary system *see* Government

Partnershps and taxation, 226
Passbook scheme, 68
Patents
    inventions, 174
    Patent Office, 174
    of processes, 175
    products, 175
    registration, 175–176
Patents Act 1970, 173–177
Patents (Amendment) Ordinance 1994, 177
Pesticides, 358
Petrochemicals, 358
Petroleum sector
    background, 326
    BOT (Build-Operate-Transfer) Schemes, 330
    demand, 326–327
    investment potential, 327–328
    marketing policy initiatives, 329–330
    natural gas, 330–331
    opportunities, 331–332
    private and foreign participation, 332
    product pricing, 331
    refining policy initiatives, 329
    upstream sector, 328–329
Pharmaceuticals
    de-licensing, 44
    future, 357
Political parties, 15–17
Population, 5, 18, 20, 55
Ports
    development policy, 300–303
    EDI introduction, 303
    infrastructure and administration, 300
    POL products facilities, 327
    private sector, 301–302, 304
    traffic growth, 300
Positioning, brand, 202–203
Power sector, 287–292
    demand projections, 288
    electricity production, 19
    entry strategy, 112–113, 114
    future opportunities, 292
    private sector involvement, 289–292

reforms, 288–289
President, 8
Price-value relationship, 198
Primary market
    shares, 134, 135
    size, 134
Prime Minister, 8–9
Private companies, 154
Privatisation and the public sector, 28–29
Productivity, increased, 191–192
Prohibited items, import policy, 73
Project offices, 162
Projects
    clearances required, 58–60
    government negotiations, 115
Property income, taxation, 223
Prospecting licences, 315
Public companies, 154
Public deposits, 161
Public Liability Insurance Act 1991, 148
Public sector
    employment role, 187
    foreign investment, 40
    privatisation, 28–29
    reserved industries, 49
Public telephones, 325
Public transport, urban, 339
Purchasing Power Parity (PPP), 20

Quality, product, 192
Quantity-based Advance Licences, 67–68

Railways and BOLT (Build-Operate-Lease-Transfer)
    Schemes, 303
Raw materials availability, 85
Regional rural banks, 130–131
Registration of business units, 36–37
Research and development (R&D)
    infrastructure, 85–86
    road database, 296
Reserve Bank of India (RBI), 127–128
Restricted goods, import policy, 73
Restrictive trade practices, 146

Retailers, 208
Roads *see* Highways
Russia, 94

Salary *see* Income
Sales of Goods Act 1930, 262
Sales tax, 243–244
Sanitation, 338
Savings, domestic, 19
Scheduled commercial banks, 128–129
Scientific instruments, 353–354
Secondary market regulation, 256–257
Securities and Exchange Board of India Act 1992, 247
Securities and Exchange Board of India (SEBI)
   corporate guidelines, 249–252
   described, 248–249
   investor protection, 251
   stock trading guidelines, 258
   stock trading penalties, 259
Securities Contract (Regulation) Act 1956, 248
Securities market, 246–260
   explained, 125
   glossary of terms, 259–260
   investment opportunities, 139–140
   listing, 251–252
   SEBI guidelines, 249–252
   Statutory Acts, 247–248
   transfer, 145
Selling *see* Trade
Separation packages, 194
Share capital and interest payment, 167
Shares
   foreign ownership, 144–145
   issue conditions, 160
   listing, 135
   loans and purchase, 165–166
   price trends, 135–136
   primary market, 134–135
   transfer of, 161
   types, 159–161
Shopping, 281
Small-scale industries registration, 37
Software *see* Electronics/software sector

Software Technology Park (STP), 308–309
Solid waste management, 338
Sound recordings and copyright, 182
South Asian Association for Regional Cooperation (SAARC), 77, 92
South Asian Preferential Trading Arrangement (SAPTA), 77, 92
Special Import Licences (SILs), 66, 74
Special Imprest Licence, 68
Star Trading Houses, 70
State government, 10–11
Steel sector, 345–347
Stock brokers regulations, 256–257
Stock exchanges, 253–254
   Governing Boards, 258
   self-regulatory, 257
Stock indices, 254
Stock market, 135–136
Strategic alliance partners, 116–122
Subscriber terminals, 322
Subsidiary companies, 155
Super-Star Trading Houses, 70

Take-overs, corporate, 256
Tax holidays, 224
Taxation
   advance rulings and clearances, 229
   allowances, 219–220
   appeals, 228
   assessment, 225–229
   assessment year, 215
   deductions, 224, 230
   direct *see* Direct taxes
   evasion control, 218
   indirect *see* Indirect taxes
   international agreements, 236–237
   losses, 227–228
   modernisation, 245
   municipal, 244
   non-resident Indians (NRIs), 234–235
   non-residents, 231–236
   payment methods, 229–231
   reforms, 28, 242–243
   residential status, 217
   return enclosures, 225

sales, 243–244
self-assessment, 231
taxpayer categories, 216
Telecommunications sector, 282
   basic services opportunities, 324
   equipment market opportunities, 321–322
   existing network, 317
   future perspective, 325
   growth of demand, 317–318
   regulatory policies, 318–320
   rural opportunities, 324–325
   services opportunities, 323
   trade and foreign investment policies, 319–320
   value-added services opportunities, 323–324
Textiles industry, 360–361
Titan Industries Ltd, 209–210
Total quality management (TQM), 192
Tourism
   government role, 367–368
   imports/exports, 366–367
   infrastructure, 364
   overview, 280
TQM (total quality management), 192
Trade
   liberalisation, 27
   performance, 78–79
   State, 72–74
   structure, 206–209
   systems, 253
Trade marks
   application, 178
   infringement, 179–180
   prohibition, 179
   registration, 177–178
   term, 179
Trade Marks Bill, 180
Trade policy, 62–79
   evolution, 63–64
   framework, 62–64
   multilateral approach, 77
   regional initiatives, 77
Trade practices
   legislation, 201–202

monopolistic, 145–146
Trade unions, 186, 195
Trading Houses, 70, 76–77
Transmission equipment, 322
Travel, domestic, 281
Trusts and taxation, 226

Underwriting, 250
Unfair trade practices, 146
Union Legislature, 9
Union of States, 6–7
Union Territories, 6
United-States of America, 94–95
Unlimited liability company, 154–155
Urban development
    highways, 339
    infrastructure projects, 337–338
    land/township infrastructure, 339–340
    long-term opportunities, 340
    public transport, 339
    scenario, 337
    water and sewerage management, 338

Value-based Advance Licences, 67
VAT introduction, 244
Vice-president, 8
Village Panchayat, 13
Visa requirements, 278
Voluntary separation packages, 192–193

Wages *see* Income
Water Act 1974, 148
Water Cess Act 1977, 148
Water supply, 338
Wealth tax, 237
Wholesalers, 207–208
Wild Life Protection Act 1972, 148
Winding up companies, 167
Workforce *see* Labour
Working capital, 126
World Trade Organization (WTO) agreement, 172–173

Zila Parishad, 14

On the

Wings of Heaven

by G.W. Hardin
with Joseph Crane

THE VISITATIONS

TEACH ONLY LOVE

*O*nce you reach into the unknown, you find yourself reaching for a cup of moonlight. You may think you are sipping the milk of heaven when, in reality, your cup is filled with moonshine. One sip of the unknown, and you know your world is about to change forever. Either it will fill your soul with magic or it will steal your senses. You take your chances. Who of us would dare to do what Joseph Crane did? Some will say he should never have taken that sip. Others will lounge under shaded trees with parched throats, licking their lips for just one drop from Joe's cup. But be careful what you ask of him, for Joe is a generous man. He just might share his cup with you. Before you decide to drink of moonlight, perhaps you ought to ask who filled this cup. Then decide whether Joe's soul is filled with moonlight or moonshine. Has he been touched by heaven, or has he simply lost his senses?

"Joe," the voice called out. Even with the TV going, he could hear it plainly. It was a man's voice. It sounded as if it were coming from inside the house. But there was no one else in the house. "Joe," the voice summoned again. Joe looked down at his dog, Hawg, who was also searching for the source of the sound, his big

mastiff head whipping back and forth, the wet nose searching for additional clues. *Must be someone outside playing a trick on me or something,* Joe growled to himself. Abandoning the movie, he bounded down the stairs and whipped open the front door, hoping to surprise the culprit. Nothing but empty night air. The stars twinkled humorously at him as his ears strained to catch a hint of footsteps. Nothing. No one. Just the regular neighborhood sounds. The hair rose on the back of his neck.

Why is this happening again? he asked himself. It had been years since the Voice last intruded. Then, like now, it had unexpectedly called him, never to divulge its source. It would be too easy to chalk it up to imagination, but this time Hawg—who had been named after Joe's beloved Harley Davidson—had heard the calling as well. With stonelike deliberation, Joe eased the door shut. Stuffing his calloused hands into his jeans pockets, he marched up the stairs with Hawg at his heels. As he slumped into the couch, he ran his fingers through his shoulder-length blond hair, then through Hawg's and let out a sigh. His eyes returned to the movie but his mind drifted elsewhere.

The first time he had felt this sense of eeriness was years ago in the belly of the USS Forrestal, on July 19, 1967. The hour: 10:52 a.m. Joe was sleeping soundly after a long night's work on the decks of the aircraft carrier. Rumors had spread that the North Vietnamese were preparing an assault into the South. If Navy jets were needed for action, all had to be ready. The night was spent loading, unloading, cleaning, and storing while they cruised the waters in the Gulf of Tonkin. Joe finally dove into his pillow at six that morning. It had been a rough night of work. Only twenty-one, Joe was a man of action who put into practice the ideals he believed. He had joined the Navy to help out his country.

"General quarters! General quarters! Fire, fire, fire on the flight deck aft. This is not a drill," blurted the ship's speakers. The blaring sirens invaded his dream with such force, Joe could not find the dividing line between dream and reality. An explosion catapulted him from his bunk onto the steel floor. His back felt the cold metal. *What the hell is going on?* he asked himself. Were they being bombed? Thundering echoes filled the carrier. Voices yelled,

feet pounded. This was no dream—the carrier was on fire. As Joe sat upright to get his bearings, an eerie feeling swept through him. He realized he was gazing up at flaming fuel falling through the upper decks. A hole the size of a truck had filled the compartment behind him with black smoke. His mind raced, *It must be an attack.* Another explosion erupted, shaking the giant ship with shivers. The explosions continued. Joe knew they were in trouble. Like a man discovered in another man's bed, he jumped into his bell bottoms. Quickly, he slid his hand under the mattress, where he always hid his shoes just in case of moments like this. Seizing them in the growing darkness, he slipped them on as if they were loafers. More bombs exploded, sending fingers of smoke deeper into the heart of the ship. Joe was getting real scared now. Like a dark hand plunging into the flesh of a wounded whale, the choking grasp of blazing blackness reached closer and closer, now nine decks deep. *There is no way out!* he thought to himself. Panic crept up his spine as clouds of smoke crept downward, blinding him. Squatting down to the floor to find breathable air, Joe swore to himself, *If this ship is going down, it's going down without me.* He looked for some kind of escape.

"Out!" yelled a voice. "Come this way if you want to live. Everybody out!" Joe didn't need a second invitation. He moved toward the voice even though he didn't recognize it. Others crawled, ran, or duck-walked toward the promise of freedom. The line of men snaked down a passageway until stopped by a closed hatch. Joe was certain they had correctly followed the voice but nothing was here but a dead end. Water now poured down from above. In the choke of fumes and fire, Joe squatted silently with the rest of the men. He had only one thought on his mind: *Wish I had a cigarette.*

The thought almost made him laugh out loud. *How odd,* he mused to himself, *that I'm not afraid.* The truth was he *wasn't* afraid. Maybe because of the voice that had led them into the passageway. Some of the men stared blankly like lab rats trapped in a maze, dead-ended by the closed hatch. Fear was filling the air. The feeling of a strange presence came over Joe, a sense they weren't alone in this, that something, *some thing* was protecting him. How he knew this, he had no idea.

At that moment, the hatch opened from the other side. Some guy yelled, "Down this way! Is everybody out?" Joe confirmed that all were out. He had been one of two men to check. The escape led to what is called the mess deck. Everyone was handed five-gallon cans of Fog Foam fire retardant. As the retardant was spread, Joe could hear men nearby crying out in pain. The mess deck led to the hospital area, and the closer they got, the louder the screaming. Among the wounded was one of Joe's buddies from the mess deck, who worked in the scullery. It didn't take a surgeon to tell he was hurting real bad. With concerned eyes, Joe tried to think of what to say. This was a guy who always had a good attitude— nice to everyone. His eyes looked up to Joe's, imploring him to say he was going to make it.

"Nahhhh, ain't that bad," Joe assured with as much believ- ability as possible. He had been trained to give encouragement to keep those wounded from going into shock. But the effort proved useless as Joe watched his crewmate die in front of him. He bent over and looked into his glassy eyes. It was obvious that what had been in his friend's body before was no longer there. But Joe saw more than one man's death. Strangely enough, he could see the whole of humanity in that moment. And what he saw told him that there was more to humans than ceasing to live in a body. In that moment, Joe knew that humanity, as a lifeform, was infinite. Death wasn't an end.

"Move along, move along!" commanded one the crewmen. All hustled up a ladder. A life vest was shoved into Joe's gut. "Put it on. Don't inflate it." Climbing up to the flight deck, Joe could barely fathom the scope of the damage as billows of smoke poured out of the guts of the aircraft carrier, twirling upward to a magnificent sky.

For two days the men of the Forrestal battled the fire, saving their ship and saving their own lives. When it was over, 164 crew- mates had been killed. And not by the hands of the North Vietnamese. One of the jets taking off from the carrier deck had accidentally launched one of its missiles, hitting the fuel pod of the plane in front of it, already in flight. One of the bombs of the damaged plane exploded, tearing up the deck of the aircraft carrier, igniting more bombs. Nine decks had been ripped apart by the

series of explosions. The tragedy of the fiasco shocked the entire crew for weeks afterwards. But all Joe could think of was the Presence that had been with him. He had felt it. Almost heard it tell him he would be fine. For him it had been a day staring into the heart of eternity through the eyes of his dying buddy. Yet death seemed so remote in the calming Presence that had sheltered him. As hard as the rescued men had tried, no one on Joe's deck ever found out who had called them from the inferno.

　　　Now, like then, he wondered about the Voice calling out to him—the great sense of otherworldliness about it. Since the war, Joe had heard the Voice call him more than once. And each time, no source could be found. But this time, he knew it wasn't his imagination. There was no mistaking that Hawg had heard it also. *What can it possibly mean?* he asked himself. *Why is this happening?* He would have to wait two years to learn the answer.

　　　While attending a seminar on spiritual awakening in Washington state, on Orcas Island, Joe unexpectedly confronted a concept he had not considered. The classes he signed up for were taught by his spiritual mentor, Alexander Everett. Alexander and Joe connected from the first day they met, and Alexander had given Joe a place on which to hang his hatful of spiritual questions. During one of the classes, Alexander presented an idea to the attendees, which Joe felt was being directed specifically toward him. "All of us are called to a place of awakening," Alexander offered, pacing slowly in front of the class. "Sometimes that calling is within, but sometimes that call is heard in other ways: a voice calling out your name." The hair on Joe's neck bristled, his ears spreading like microwave antennae waiting for the next signal. "Most people are afraid to answer," Alexander continued before the group, "while others pretend it never happened."

　　　That does it, Joe thought, *I've got to talk to Alexander.* His thoughts reeled back to the times the Voice had spoken to him, each detail surrounding each event clinging to his memory like jigsaw puzzle pieces. After the lecture, Joe cornered Alexander. "There's

something I've got to talk to you about," his voice serious, not knowing how much to tell, how much not to tell.

"Let's meet later this evening, Joe." Alexander could tell this would need time and an attentive ear. "How about over dinner?"

Barely able to contain himself, Joe patiently agreed. That night Joe revealed to Alexander what he had told no one else. His spiritual mentor listened closely for clues, knowing that such events always left some hint of how to respond. When Joe was done, he folded his hands and looked into his friend's eyes. "Joe, are you familiar with the story of Samuel?"

"Well, I've heard of it but don't remember the particulars."

"Samuel was in the spiritual tutoring of a master named Eli," Alexander started. "One night Samuel went to bed, and just before dawn he heard a voice call 'Samuel! Samuel!' Not unlike the voice you heard calling out your name. So, Samuel got up, went to his master, Eli, and asked him what he wanted. And Eli told him, 'I didn't call you. Go back to bed.' Samuel did so, but again he heard, 'Samuel! Samuel!' Off to Eli he trots again, only to be told, 'I didn't call you! Go back to bed.' " Joe loved the way Alexander told stories. His body barely moved, he was all voice. "For the third time he heard, 'Samuel. Samuel!' and went to Eli one more time. 'Here I am, for you called me,' he told his master one more time. Eli realized that the Lord must be the one calling Samuel. Eli instructed him to go back to bed and told him, if he was called again, to say, 'Speak, Lord, for your servant hears.' Samuel did what he was told and the Lord spoke to him.

"So, Joe," Alexander said, "the next time you hear your name called, say, 'Speak, Lord, for your servant hears,' and see what happens. God just may have something to say to you."

Joe's thoughts pounded against his head. *Oh, sure. With all the people in the world to talk to, God is going to talk to me?* he argued with himself. Once again, memories of past events, when the Voice had called him, played in his mind. He recollected the times over past years where he thought roommates were calling him. Like Samuel, he had gone to them to ask what they had wanted. And each time they had looked at him as if he were crazy or hearing things. *Why me?* Joe asked himself for the umpteenth

time. *What would God want with me? I really hope it's not that I am supposed to do something. Maybe I'm just hearing things, or maybe I am going crazy.* But Alexander's advice had always proven wise on past occasions. Why not this one as well?

Three more years would pass before Alexander's advice paid off. By this time, Joe had married, bought a house, left his corporate job, started his own home-renovation business. He now possessed four loving mastiffs to replace Hawg. Mastiffs are rather like St. Bernards in Great Dane skin. He had everything he had ever dreamt of. And this particular night, in his own house, with his new wife sleeping next to him, and his dogs snoring close by, was a night of perfect harmony.

Outside was a beautiful California night. The stars could be seen in spite of the smog from the Bay Area. The air felt balmy although Christmas was just around the corner. Filled with a sense of contentment, Joe nestled into bed with the Bible in hand while his adorable wife slept. Many years had passed since Joe had even owned a Bible. He was not a member of any religion and didn't go to church. But it was Christmastime, and reading from the Good Book seemed appropriate. Part of his reading ritual was to review what he had read the previous night, especially if it hadn't made sense. The previous night had provided a particularly difficult passage, and Joe had prayed to God to help him understand the real message.

Around midnight he closed the Bible and set it on his nightstand. Looking over at Donna, his mind let forth a hymn of praise. *What a beautiful woman I married.* He gazed down at the foot of the bed at two of the mastiffs fast asleep, one snoring away like a baritone warming up for a song. The other dogs lay on the floor. If the bed were any larger, all four critters would certainly be resting with Joe and Donna. For Joe loved his animals almost as much as he loved his wife. "Whatever have I done to be so blessed with such a lovely family?" he whispered to himself. A sigh of peace sang from him in harmony with the dogs. He reached over to turn off the light and bestowed a kiss on Donna as the light went out. Laying his head softly on his pillow, Joe settled in, pulling the covers over his shoulders. The warmth of the waterbed nestled him,

relaxing him as he drifted off to sleep, all thoughts gone, the world fading away.

"Joe!" the Voice said. His eyes blinked open automatically. Like before, every hair on his body stood at attention. "Joe," the Voice called again. This time Joe raised himself up on one elbow, his thoughts swimming, the waterbed gurgling against his swift movement. *What am I going to do?* he thought. His conversation with Alexander echoed in his brain. Questions flooded in. *Why would God be wanting to talk to me? Maybe I* am *going crazy.* Joe took a deep breath. *OK,* he thought, *Let's go for it. What's the worst that could happen? I might feel like a fool, and then I'll go to sleep and forget all about it by morning.* The words came out like a student reciting the Gettysburg address: "Speak, Lord, for your servant hears."

There. He'd done it. He looked around the bedroom. No reply. No sound but the breathing of the dogs. Joe was just about to roll back over and grab his pillow when he noticed a pinpoint of light in the doorway. His eyes squinted as it began to sparkle like a piece of glitter on black velvet. Was he seeing things, or was it there? The sparkle intensified as if the glitter were being hit by a laser beam of white light. Then it began to enlarge, spreading slowly in a growing circle of light. *Oh boy,* Joe thought, *I'm in big trouble now. Why did I ever start this?*

The light began to fill the doorway with a bright, yet soft, blue-white color that spilled onto the walls, illuminating the bedroom. *If this is a dream,* he thought, *then the dogs are having it too. Each one has its head up looking in the same direction I am.* Somehow, having 700 pounds of dog flesh in the same room lent a kind of security, especially since none of them was growling or barking. Each seemed quite peaceful with the expanding circle of light that had now taken over the entire doorway. *If the dogs aren't afraid, then neither am I,* Joe tried to convince himself. *Not much, anyway. Maybe if I just sit still, whatever it is won't see me.* He sat staring at the increasing brilliance taking over the room. *Better yet,* he thought, looking over to Donna who was snoozing away, *if I just pull the covers over my head, it won't find me and will go away.* The truth of the matter was that Joe couldn't move. He was mesmerized

by the blue-white light which was beginning to reveal some kind of figure behind it. Looking down at the dogs to see if they were going to save him from whatever was invading his bedroom, he quickly concluded they were not. Each pooch was either sitting politely, as if waiting for a bone, or lying comfortably staring at the spectacle before them.

Joe looked into the light again, his mouth hanging open as the figure hidden by the brilliance now moved forward from far back in the light. It was incomprehensible how the outline in the light seemed to be walking yet simultaneously materializing in front of the doorway. At first, the eyes were all that Joe could make out. They were blue, like no other blue he'd seen in his life. It was as if sky, river, and ocean had combined to form the eyes. They exuded the most wonderful kindness and gentleness. Their stare filled Joe with a great sense of peace, not unlike the Presence had done years ago on the USS Forrestal. As the outline began to take the shape of a man, Joe could more clearly see the details of platinum blond hair and alabaster skin. A long, white robe draped the fully materialized seven-foot man who was now smiling at Joe.

The voice was masculine, with feminine softness. "Put down your books, for they hold no truth for you," it said. Odd, Joe thought, that something so beautiful would appear as a male. "As the sands of the desert have been moved to suit the winds of time, so has the light been darkened by man's ink on these pages."

What is this being talking about? Joe wondered. He decided to listen fully. As if able to read Joe's mind, the being continued, "This you must do, or you will not be called upon again. Teach this, which the Lord God has charged me to give you. For it is the Last Baptism of God's children. Have those you teach, in turn teach others, for they are well-meaning in their houses of God. You are not a Christ or even a prophet, but a servant of God—who will put words in your mouth—and God's children will hear and understand.

"Take a jug of wine before sunrise and pour it into a bowl. Set this bowl in the sun's path so the light will warm it. Fast and be still until the sun is at its highest place in the sky. At this time, go to where the bowl has been laid on the ground and remove your shoes—for you stand on holy ground. Sit and wash your feet, from your toes to your knees, so that you may stand and walk the earth. Wash your hands from the tips of your fingers to the elbow, so you may do God's work. When this is done, kneel and say 'My loving Father, your child has come home to your counsel. Guide me in all things that I must do.' Then take up the bowl of wine and pour it on the ground. As your Mother Earth drinks the unclean liquid, all that is unclean within you—her brothers and sisters—is absolved, just as the blood of God's Son was said to do. Go now, be at peace and take care of that which I have given you. Teach only love. After you do this, we will speak again."

With that, the man stepped back into the light and began to become one with its brilliance, fading from Joe's view. The light then shrank back to a single point of bright light and disappeared as Joe, along with the dogs, stared in utter disbelief. Finally, shaking his head, he bounded out of bed to retrieve paper and pencil in the dining room, sat down and scribbled every word he had just been told. Joe waited two days before finally telling Donna what had happened in the confines of their bedroom while she had slept.

She stared at her husband. Never was there a more down-to-earth person than Joe. It was impossible for him to make up something like this. "What are you going to do?" she asked, not knowing what else to say.

"I don't know," Joe said back, looking deep into her eyes to see if she believed him. His heart melted with relief as he saw her concern staring back at him. She believed him. "It's not every day that an angel comes to me and tells me something this profound. Let alone wants me to do and teach this Last Baptism thing." Indeed, the whole idea seemed preposterous. *Why on earth would anyone want to listen to me?* he asked himself. *It is a good thing the churches don't burn people at the stake anymore. At least, I don't think they do.*

The next day, Joe called Alexander to tell him what had taken place. He felt that Alexander was one of the most spiritual people he had ever known. From the first moment they met at an Inward Bound class, Joe knew him to be a spiritual master. Over the years, their friendship had blossomed into trust and mutual

admiration. Joe knew if there was anyone with whom he could discuss this situation, it was Alexander. He let his mentor know that he was a bit frightened by the consequences of following his suggestion to use the same phrase that Samuel had used.

"Joe, you've had a vision. It's nothing to be afraid of," Alexander said.

"But why me?" Joe countered. "It seems to me there are a lot of people in this world who have a much closer relationship with God than I do." People like Alexander had spent their entire lives teaching spiritual truths. Why didn't the angel appear to him, instead?

"Some people wait all their entire lives to have something like this happen to them, Joe. You should be grateful for having been chosen to serve in such a grand plan. Hang in there. It's my guess that you'll hear from this angel again."

Joe let out a long sigh. "I just *knew* you were going to say that."

"Don't be frightened about what has happened. Be open to whatever the angel tells you to do. And let me know from time to time what is happening with this."

Joe promised to do so, wished his friend and mentor farewell, and hung up the phone. *At least he didn't think I was insane*, Joe said to himself. What was even more comforting was that Joe no longer wondered about his own sanity, either. Still, it was no comfort for him to think he was on some kind of mission from God. Yet, if God wanted him to do something, he figured, God was smart enough to give some kind of sign for when and how to carry out whatever he was meant to fulfill.

The next day Joe's doorbell rang, sending the dogs into a thunder of barking. Two nicely dressed people stood at the door while Joe ordered the mastiffs to back off. The visitors wanted, with all their hearts, to tell Joe of God's love for him. *Is this some kind of sign?* he asked himself. *If anyone wants to listen to my story of the angel, surely it would be someone whose life is so God-centered.* And, with the sincerity of a man confronted by an angel, Joe listened for a while to what his guests had to say about God. He then proceeded to tell them about what had happened a few nights earlier. Went so far as to retrieve what he had written down about the Last Baptism.

Like a child giving a gift to friends, Joe hoped these wonderful people would appreciate all he was entrusting to them. They stared at the writing, then stared at Joe. By the time these nicely dressed people left, they were warning Joe that he had been visited by Satan, that his soul was in mortal danger, and that if he did not cast out this demon, he would burn in hell forever. Further, even though Joe had no children, they had exhorted him to change his ways least his son grow up to be the Antichrist. "Just like it says in the Bible." And, not to leave out any details as they backed away from the front door, they informed Joe that even Armageddon would be his fault if he pursued his belief in this so-called angel.

Joe was crushed. His enthusiasm for what the heavens had brought him had been trampled under foot by those claiming to walk with God. Confusion reigned in his soul as he stood there baffled at how something so beautiful could have been made to seem so ugly. The work of the Devil? How could these, of all people, possibly see that? *What would the angel have to say about this kind of reception?* Joe wanted to know. He promised himself, the next time the angel showed up, there would be several questions he wanted answers to.

Days passed, and still Joe had not performed the baptism. There was much on his mind, much he wanted to think about before getting himself into any other surprises. The unexpected visitors had been a slap in the face. If he never had this kind of visit again, it would be too soon. But, ready or not, Joe was to receive a visitor of another kind. While lying on the sofa—watching an old movie on TV with Annie, the matriarch of the mastiffs—a kind of strangeness began to fill the air. Annie's head, resting on Joe's shoulder, jerked back, her torso rising up as if trying to glimpse something in the hallway. In turn, Joe looked toward the hallway, knowing her behavior meant someone, or some thing, was coming toward the living room. Thinking it must be Donna, Joe waited to greet her. But what he saw was a light moving along the wall as if someone were shining a flashlight from the back of the hallway. *It must be the angel, again,* he thought. But what emerged was a man Joe had never seen before. He took a couple of steps into the living room and stopped.

Who the hell is this? Joe said to himself as he stared at a perfect stranger, dressed in what appeared to be a monk's robe. Looking around as if he owned the place, the fellow stood six feet tall—thin as a rail. Long white hair surrounded a strong, determined face filled with angry frustration. A thick, bushy set of eyebrows hung above deep brown eyes, making him look as if he were angry about something. The robe he wore hung to the floor, with baggy sleeves and a hood that draped on his shoulders. He appeared to be quite disturbed.

Looking over at Joe, the monk shook his head and walked through the dining room and into the kitchen, mumbling as he went. Joe looked down at Annie, and she back at him as if asking each other what just happened. Just as quickly as he had entered, the stranger left the kitchen and stood in the dining room, shaking his head and staring down at the floor. Then, without a word, he walked out of the dining room through the closed patio door and into the back patio. He stood there continuing to shake his head and mumble to himself.

First the angel, and now this? Joe looked down at Annie once again. "Yes, indeed," he said to his favorite, "This boy is wrapped too tight, and crazy as a pet coon with rabies." Looking back towards the apparition on the patio, Joe wondered to himself, *The angel never said anything about this. Is this going to be like Dickens, where I get visited by three ghosts, or what?*

Once again, through the glass of the patio door marched the robed figure, stopping in the middle of the dining room once again. He stared straight at Joe and back down at the floor. When he raised his head to speak, Joe saw a calmness coming over him.

"You people have been told from the very beginning," he said with a soft, slow voice, as if to make sure Joe could hear every word. "Over the centuries, you have been told in a gentle way, so have you been told in a mighty way, of God's love for you. Do you hear it?" he asked sternly. His voice grew more forceful as he continued, not waiting for an answer. "You people have been given the wonders of the universe, including the world on which you live. Do you say, 'Blessed are we. God loves us so much that he gives us all this'? Do you say, 'Brothers and sisters, we may live long to

care for one another. Our happiness and well-being are great with God'?

"NO!" he said in a resounding voice. "You people would rather frighten each other with stories of an angry God that will lay to waste all who do not obey. You get pleasure from thinking of all the horrendous ways your enemies will be made to suffer. You will listen to someone expound for hours about how you are a sinner. They tell you God will forgive you only if you believe as they do. Some are so self-righteous, they believe that only *they* are worthy to enter Paradise. They carry the lie to their brothers and sisters, saying, 'If you believe as we, you will be saved.' " Waving his arms in the air, he walked about the room, almost yelling. *He must have learned this from some of those evangelists I've seen on television*, Joe mused.

"When most of you pray," the monklike figure continued, "do you ask for guidance? No. All that is asked for are things you want. 'Oh, Heavenly Father, please make *me* worthy, make the world a better place for *me* and *mine*,' " he mimicked. " 'Help *me* teach the sinners so they may be in heaven with *me*.' Or you try to bargain with God. 'If you do this for *me*, I will do that for you.' Some try to buy their way into Heaven by giving money to their church or the poor. I have seen such bribery when I walked the earth. The killing of animals and the burning of their bodies for sacrifice, or paying someone else to do it for them. Thousands of years have passed since then, and still only a few have heard. People have always sat and wondered why I rant and rave the way I do.

"It's beyond my realm of knowing why so much time is wasted on all this pettiness. If only you truly knew of God's love. ... You will learn. I promise, you will learn." Then, dropping his hands to his sides, he bowed, turned, walked through glass door once again—and was gone. Joe sat stunned, staring out the door. Here was another question to add to his list. *The next time I see the angel, I think I'll ask him who this mad monk is.*

Little did Joe know how the monk would make good on his promise. His message was intended not only for Joe's ears but for the ears of humanity itself. What was about to unfold would cause

anyone to wonder whether they were being offered a cup of moonlight or the dregs of moonshine. Who of us when offered the choice between returning to Eden or continuing as we are, would choose not to choose? Who of us would step back into the shadows and simply watch as life passed by? At one point, it seemed as if Joseph Crane would.

THE NAMING

*O*ver a month had passed, and still Joseph had not performed the baptism. It wasn't as if Joe was one of those people who kept putting things off. Quite the contrary, his entire life had been that of a doer, a pro-activist. Why, even as early as the second grade, he displayed uncanny ability to protect the underdog. Bullies from the fourth and fifth grade were picking on the littler kids in Joe's class. No one bothered Joe because he had a look about him that made bigger kids wonder whether they ought to mess with him. He talked tough, he acted tough, and no one was about to find out whether it was a bluff or the real McCoy. Funny thing about bullies. As long as they don't have to save face, they tend to avoid the threat of defeat.

There was something in Joe that smelled such cowardice. Like a pint-sized Jimmy Hoffa, he organized a union of little guys. Yep, the Don't-Mess-With-the-Little-Guys Union. With the power of persuasion he convinced all the younger kids, whether they were targeted prey or not, to rally around any kid on or off the playground who was being picked on. And Joe was their leader. Teachers began to notice the fishlike schooling effect of second-graders during recess. They thought it was cute: How nice that the kids are getting to know one another. But what was really happening was a survival of the fittest—strength in numbers. The bullies also noticed, and right away. It took only one confrontation, resulting in a mob of munchkins surrounding a Goliath, with Joe's fist setting the example, before peace reigned in the second grade. In fact, this was a battle of fists in more than one way. One of the most vulnerable kids in the class had a deformed hand. More than anything else, he wanted to be accepted as normal, just one of the guys. But instead, he became easy pickings for any kid who wanted someone to beat up. His willingness to do anything to fit in touched young Joseph. He talked with the kid about what he had to do if he was going to be in the union, the gang. And the little guy took Joe to heart. Whatever he had to do, he would do it. The next day, Joe told all the other kids that the fella with the deformed hand was his best friend, his main man. And gradually this underdog of a kid became respected by the rest of the guys in the little-guys gang. The bullies had to go elsewhere to make trouble.

So, you see, "activism" is part of Joe's middle name. But this baptism thing was a different matter. What was he getting himself in for? An angel appearing in the middle of the night? A mad monk tromping through his dining room? Donna kept asking him if he had seen the angel yet. Of course he hadn't because he was avoiding the baptism. Then one night, she looked into his icy-blue eyes and said, "I'm setting the alarm clock tonight to wake us up before sunrise. I've placed two bowls and a bottle of wine beside the patio door. Let's do this baptism together in the morning." To be sure, Donna was not the kind of person to organize a second-grade protectionist union. But neither was she the kind of person to stand idly by when she felt the importance of a decision, especially when it involved someone she loved. Action was part of what made her a successful businesswoman, and it was part of what made her a magnificent friend and endearing wife. How was Joe going to argue with her? He knew she was doing it for his own good.

The Cranes were not real breakfast eaters. Donna's mornings were usually taken up with bustling around getting ready for work, taking care of the "kids," and heading out early for a long drive

through morning rush-hour traffic. Joe normally poured coffee into his veins as his morning fix before heading out to take care of his business. Because they had to fast the next morning until the sun reached its highest point, Joe decided he'd better grab a bite before bed. As he sat there nibbling away, he started thinking, *I should have done this back in January when the days were shorter and I didn't have to be still for so long.* He smiled at himself as he thought how his waiting had done little more than cause more waiting. *Donna knows. I've put this off for as long as I could because I don't want to find out what is next.* To be honest, Joe was a little scared.

Had not his life become his dream come true? He had a house, the kind of dogs he always wanted, a wife any man would die for. He didn't need any angel coming around messing things up. *What if the angel tells me I have to give up this lifestyle?* he asked himself between bites. *How do you tell an angel he's got to find another servant? It's taken me forty-eight years to get here, and I don't want to give it up.* Joe continued arguing with himself, *I don't think God would have given me all this just to take it away. God is going to do with me what God is going to do, whether I like it or not. Besides, if I can learn to like spinach, I can learn to like whatever God has in store for me.*

Sleep did not come easy, nor did getting out of bed. Donna braced her foot against the small of his back and gave a shove that dumped both man and dogs right off the bed in Keystone Cops fashion. "What a way to start a Saturday," Joe grumbled. Silently, the two of them donned sweat pants and shirts, and with bare feet tip-toed through the cool grass to the back corner of the yard next to the lily pond.

Night was just beginning to surrender to dawn. Joe glanced around at the one-story houses surrounding the back yard. *Good thing the fence is six feet tall. Only a nut would go out in his back yard, pour wine into a bowl, and wash his feet and hands with it. The whole thing sounds pretty lame to me.* But that's just what the two of them did. As the sun reached its zenith, Donna stood there with her hands on hips and a twinkle in her eye that said, Go ahead, you big baby. If I can do it, so can you.

When husband and wife were done with the washing, they recited the prayer given by the angel. Joe looked around half expecting the creature to reappear. Donna picked up the empty wine bottle and the two bowls. A distinct odor from the wine-soaked ground filled the noon air. In fact, it filled more than the air. Back in the house, Joe thought they both smelled like winos. "What now?" she asked him.

"I don't know, but I'm getting a splitting headache," Joe retorted.

Little more was said. Donna cleaned herself off, jumped into more suitable clothes, and continued her day. She kept thinking about the baptism and what it meant to her as well as what it might mean to their marriage. She loved Joe—more than anything. He was like no man she'd ever met. He was tough as nails but had a heart as tender as a rose petal. He could win a swearing contest with any sailor, but she knew he also walked with God. Before any angel had shown up, she knew he walked with God. Her man could lie with the lion or the lamb. But what impact would the baptism have on her own life, let alone Joe's? She had egged Joe into going through with the baptism because she believed he needed to do it. But what about her? What would happen to her for participating in this ceremony?

As Donna drove off to take care of errands, she wondered when she was going to be told what to do with her life. A voice spoke quite clearly in her mind, *What makes you think that I am going to tell you?* Tingling prickled her all over as she weaved her way through traffic, trying to decide whether the voice had been imagined or real. The more she thought about it, the more she knew what she had heard and what it meant. Within her heart lay a calm understanding telling her she would be shown what to do. There was no doubt about it. She simply knew. And Donna was not a woman who hid out in the realms of wistful wondering or played around with woulda-coulda-shouldas. She had earned a Master's of Business Administration with a minor in statistics. Boardrooms, budgeting, and computers did not intimidate her. Hers was a mind that succeeded in a workplace of men. It was unusual for her to accept at face value the answer she had heard in her mind. But accept it she did.

Two days had passed since the baptism, and no angel. Joe was sitting in the back yard contemplating the gurgling waterfall in

his lily pond, when the angel materialized. Joe couldn't help but wonder why the angel had not arrived as dramatically as before, perhaps this time rising out of the water and standing in the middle of the pond. But that didn't happen. He was just there. The first words out of Joe's mouth were, "Who is the crazy man?" He was just about to add information about "God's children" coming to his front door when the angel cut him short.

"It is Isaac," the celestial said, "and he is one with God. A very long time ago he was a prophet who walked the earth. So great in understanding of God's love is he, that when he left the earth as its Teacher, God gave him leave to return. Isaac has visited many people over the centuries. Several, in your time, has he spoken to but most of them have run to their ministers saying they had seen the Devil and were frightened of him. For the unenlightened, he is truly a frightening sight to behold. Joe, I am going to speak plainly so you will have no misunderstanding. First of all, if you think every time you open your mouth all will listen and hear the words, you are as crazy as you think you are. Point taken?"

"Point well taken," Joe responded, wondering where this was leading. "But I have a few hundred thousand questions to ask. OK?"

Before he could ask even one, the angel interrupted, "I am from the Lord God, and my name you could not pronounce if I told you."

Joe asked anyway. And the name that issued forth was like a melody of beautiful sound. Joe tried once to speak it, but with no success. He could not even get the name out of his mouth.

"You may call me whatever name you are most comfortable with."

After giving it a few moments of thought, Joe suggested, "How about Michael?" The angel nodded. "What is the name of the one who sent you?" Joe then asked.

With all the authority known to man, Michael said, "No one that walks the earth or breathes the air may know God's name. For if they did, and spoke it once, they would not live long enough to finish. Many claim to, but none actually do, and this is true. If you are asked who sent you, you say, 'I AM' has sent me."

Joe sat there a bit dumbfounded, wondering what to say. The first thought that came to him was to ask the angel about hell, and where it might be. Before he could even speak the words, Michael answered. "Hell was a dump outside of Jerusalem, called Gehenna, where trash was burned, and not a place for damned souls. God loves all his children and would not damn any of them. Jesus, after seeing how poor in spirit man was, said, if he could, he would cast the unenlightened into it forever. Out of this came the story of 'If you do not follow God's law, you will go to hell.' Fear will make the disobedient flock of a church obey."

What about the Devil? Joe thought to himself.

"Satan is someone Moses made up in the *Book of Genesis* only to explain the power of God. Man, in his great wisdom, found it useful to blame an unseen force rather than take responsibility for the things he did. Man thinks in terms of greater than or lesser than, as though there is a hierarchy, when, in fact, there is only God as everything."

"This is all well and fine," Joe said, "I know what you are saying, but just what does this have to do with me? I am not a member of any church. All I do is ask for guidance in God's will for me. Am I to start a new church or religion? Because, if I am, I can tell you I am not the man for the job."

"No one is ever the man or woman for the job. They always say that, and some will suggest someone they think is just perfect for it."

"That's too bad, because that was going to be my next move."

"I know," Michael said. "Starting another church will serve no useful purpose, and will only confuse people more than they already are. So, over the next two years, you will be told of God's will for his children, and in this time, you will choose three women and four men to take this message out into the world. They will know you and you them. Out of the seven, three will be what you call gay."

"Excuse me!" Joe interrupted. "Hold on there just a minute. Let me get this straight—not that I have anything against gay people—I can tell you right now the Churches are going to have a field day with this. Just in case you haven't been keeping up on

current events, the Church says that being gay is a sin, and forbids it. Do you have any idea what they are going to have to say about this? My God, Michael, it is going to be hard enough—I mean, that would be like telling the Churches to sell all they own and give it to the poor."

"I knew you were the right man for the job," the angel's eyes gave forth a light that flooded Joe's soul with love. "You are beginning to know that which I have not yet told you. Besides, God doesn't care what they think, so why should you? Let them forbid what they will, let them be selective with whomever is let into their houses. God is not limited in his love and will not deny the kingdom to anyone."

Great, Joe thought, *I will probably get nailed to a cross or burned at the stake—not as a Christ to be remembered, but as a troublemaker who will serve as an example of what happens to such a person.*

"My time is over for now," the angel concluded. "Think about what I have said; write it down, for it is important." And with that he faded into the daylight. Joe got up, headed into the house and down the hallway to his office to type into the computer everything that had happened. *Who is going to believe this?* he asked himself.

THE TEACHINGS

*D*uring the next week, Joe replayed over and over again in his mind everything the angel had said. He found himself reflecting not only on his own personal experience, but also on how he had been instructed to search for others. But why? And if they passed right smack dab in front of him, how would he know they were the ones Michael had spoken of? He wondered where it would all end. One thing was certain, he'd better not give up his day job. As the days rolled by, he began to wonder who else he could tell this tale to besides Donna. She had been more than understanding; she had also been supportive, even encouraging. He himself could not believe what was happening to his life, yet she seemed to have less difficulty with it than he. Maybe, just maybe, it was time to talk to Kathleen. Why, he was not sure. Although they had not been friends long, their friendship was strong. They had met at Joe's last job when he had been an instructor with one of the largest corporations in the field of human dynamics. Perhaps he was calling her because she was enduring so much in her own struggle with lupus, a debilitating and strange disease of the nervous system. Perhaps he was calling her because of her great heart.

Kathleen was an enterprising human being, an all-California woman with a rich tan and eyes more alive than the noonday sun. In her forties, she had the vivacity of someone ten years her junior. In fact, her two teen-age sons gave her grief for being too alive. But when she was ill, her eyelids hung at half-mast. It was enough to sadden anyone who loved her, and almost everyone around her loved her bright nature. Joe decided to give her a call to see how she was doing. She was having one of those days when her great eyelids were starting to droop. It was time to schedule another trip down to Mexico where she could get special treatment not allowed in the United States. She had found a hospital down there specializing in conditions such as hers. Usually, she would be gone for three weeks, but money was tight right now, so a couple of weeks would have to do.

"Kathleen," Joe hesitated on the phone. "I want to tell you something that might help, and please don't think I'm nuts or anything."

"OK," she said in that encouraging voice of hers. "As sick as I am right now, I'll try anything. What is it you want to tell me?"

Joe began describing the January night when the sparkle of light had invaded his room revealing the angelic being. Like an ancient storyteller, he mesmerized her with his account of what the angel had told him and how he had performed the Last Baptism rite. He suggested she, also, give the baptism a try, along with taking her treatment, and see what happens. After the words had escaped his lips, Joe wondered if he was doing the right thing. Would Kathleen think him crazy? Was he giving her false hope? Would the baptism have any effect? Perhaps he shouldn't have told her. But it was too late. The story of the angel had flown from him like a captive bird. There was no telling if it would find a place to roost with Kathleen.

"Wow, Joe. That's quite a story. What did you think when it happened?" It was so like Kathleen to show concern for others when she herself needed the most help. Her caring question set Joe at ease, allowing the two friends to speak about why such events were occurring in these days of computers and satellites. "You know, Joe, I do believe there was a reason for our coming together. I truly do. From the moment we met there was a strong connection.

Something about this baptism thing sounds real right to me. I actually believe everything you've told me. I know you are not prone to such wild stories as this, and I'm touched that you trust me enough to share this story with me. I may give the baptism a try while I'm down in Mexico. I'll call you when I get back."

After saying their goodbyes, Joe started thinking, *What if she comes back from Mexico cured?* Would this mean that the baptism is a cure for disease? What would this do in a world of so much illness? Joe had great hope in what was happening to him, and he wanted to share that hope with others. Telling was risky, but the wonder of his encounter was also too tempting to keep to himself. For the rest of the week, Joe thought about Kathleen and how she was doing in Mexico. Her situation weighed on his mind repeatedly.

As he was driving his truck to work one morning, his thoughts again drifted to Kathleen. As he headed up the ramp to the 580 freeway, ready to cross the Bay, he heard a voice say, "Put on your seat belt." Looking over at the passenger seat, he was startled to see Michael sitting there. Glancing back to the freeway to make sure he was merging into the right lane, he looked back to find no one in the seat. Recovering from the surprise, he revved up the engine and crossed into another lane. Once again, he looked over and spied Michael sitting there again. *Just what I need*, Joe said to himself, *a comedian along for the ride.* There seemed to be a continuing theme with this angel who went out of his way to display a sense of humor. The truth be known, Joe loved to tell jokes, and he loved people who had a sense of humor, no matter how warped.

"I see you have found your first of the Seven," the angel said, this time staying visible. Joe eased his back into the truck's seat, glad to hear a voice along with the apparition. Somehow, it gave him the sense he wasn't losing his mind.

"Yeah? And who might that be?" Joe asked sarcastically.

"Kathleen is going to be just fine—not cured, for she has sums to work out. She will be a challenging student. Listen to her, though, for as a woman, she can see and know things you could miss."

"Look, Michael, I have been thinking about your last visit, and there are some things I need to know." Privately, Joe was wondering if any of the cars could see his passenger. Wouldn't it be a hoot to have the Highway Patrol pass his truck and see this angel sitting in the passenger's seat? "Such as," he continued, "where do women and gays fit in? Doesn't the Bible guide people in the direction of God? Aren't we freed from original sin when we are baptized? Wasn't Jesus sent to die for our sins, because we are all sinners and would go to hell? Most important of all to me is, What am I supposed to do?"

"If you could only see that in your questions lie the answers to why. But like the rest of the world, you still think that in the beginning you sinned against God and are being punished for it. I tell you truly, when God created man and woman in spirit, a choice was given to them. They could stay with God in Paradise, as spirit, or become flesh and live on earth. Those that chose to stay are what you know as angels, and the rest of you became flesh. However, I say you all were, and are, perfect, whole, and complete in God's eyes. You chose the path you are on with no memory of the time before you chose. A promise was given to all that you would return home, your path would start and end. It would wind through the time you have, mixing with others' paths or going off in another direction. Some last for many years, and some are over in the blink of an eye. But whichever one you took, it was for an experience. Some you would like, and others you would not. But if you do not choose a direction on the path, the nature of the journey will be chosen for you, and most of you won't like it.

"You have been taught that a sin is bad and that it hurts God. How arrogant of you to think you are that powerful. I tell you truly, the only thing God is, feels, or does, is LOVE. The word 'sin' only means 'I have missed the mark I was aiming at' or 'I made a mistake.' No one is sitting in heaven with a tally sheet marking down all the times you have sinned to see if you have been good enough to get into Heaven. Are you beginning to see the obsession you all have with right, wrong, good and bad? These are judgments you make and have nothing to do with your coming home—for all will return in time. I say to you again, you are perfect, whole, and compete just the way you are. So, act accordingly. Treat one another with honor, dignity, and respect. But most all, love each other as God loves you.

"I tell you this: No, Jesus was not given by God to die for the sins of man. You must see, if that was his purpose, he would have died at birth. The Bible, though, tells a story that was told over and over and over until it was written down, and rewritten and rewritten and rewritten to the point that why he was sent has been lost. That is part of your job: to bring back the light that man's ink has darkened over the years. I will tell you what Jesus said and what he taught. You will write it down, not as a new Bible, but as the truth to guide God's children, so they may be healthy, joyous, and abundant on their journey home.

"The Bible has become more important than those it was written for. It is said that only those who have the Holy Spirit in them may read and understand it. This is a *lie* perpetuated by ignorance. Interpreting it is not understanding it. Besides, everyone has the Holy Spirit already in them. Yet, the unenlightened will tell you that you don't have the Holy Spirit in you, and that you are a servant of the Devil.

"Any book that tells you only *it* speaks for God lies. Any book that tells you that if you don't believe in *the book*, the kingdom of heaven is lost to you forever, lies. Anyone who tells you, 'Come to me, for I will stand with you before God on your behalf to save your soul,' lies. For only you will stand before God for your rewards, and you will stand alone.

"Jesus said, When you pray, go into a closet by yourself and be quiet. Speak to God like thus: 'Our Father, which art in heaven, holy is your name. Your kingdom come, your will be done, on earth, as it is in heaven. Give us this day, our daily bread. Forgiven are our debts, and we forgive our debtors. Let us not be in temptation, and deliver us from evil.' Don't gather in crowds and pray great prayers for all to hear. Jesus' reason for coming was to teach that when people speak to God, he hears. No one is needed to speak for you, and no one can. When you pray for someone, you are giving a blessing as powerful as any priest can give.

"There is no such thing as Original Sin, in the biblical sense of it. Baptism is a ritual borrowed from an ancient religion to signify the washing away of ignorance of the existence of God. In this symbolic ritual, what you are doing is saying, 'I remember.'

"Women are the foundation of natural wisdom and true power. Jesus knew this, and always had women with him throughout his life. Only after Paul of Tarsus began preaching did women start to lose the place that Jesus recognized they should have. It was women who taught of Jesus in the catacombs. And the loss of their presence has brought the teachings to the place they are now.

"As long as humankind has walked the earth, there have been people who are gay—perfect, whole, and complete just the way they are. You see, the more a religion gets accepted, the more self-righteous it becomes in this good-versus-evil. When outside forces begin to let up, pressure begins building from within for conformity, beginning with the smallest number of members who act differently or think differently from the majority. The religion's actions become no better than those of its earlier persecutors. However, their persecution is now done in the name of God or Jesus or the Bible.

"Sex is a gift from God for you to give to the one you love as your gift of affection. There is nothing bad or wrong about what gender you give this gift to. It is up to you. However, it is the choice of the receiver to accept it or not. If you go whoring, you must understand you are only wasting time. For no bricks are made for building one's celestial mansion.

"You can be sure, most religions will be up in arms about this—so let them. When they stand before God and find that he doesn't care, I promise you they won't either. My time here is over. We will speak again. Go in peace," Michael said as he vanished.

Joe couldn't remember the drive over the bridge nor paying the toll, but there he was approaching his exit. Forty-five minutes of driving had passed, and he remembered only the words of Michael. It was as if he'd been in a time warp. The workday seemed almost a celebration. In fact, all aspects of life were taking on a different meaning for Joe, as they were for Donna. After work, Joe got to thinking about what Michael had told him. *I guess I should write a book*, he said to himself. *But I'm a carpenter, a handyman by trade, and not an author. Why is it that when God wants something done, it's always someone without the necessary skills who is chosen to do*

it? Let's face it, my handwriting is unreadable and my typing even
worse. So I can see why I was chosen to do this. Yeah, right.

Joe could not stop thinking about the right and wrong or
good and bad to which Michael kept referring. He wondered if
Michael was correct, that we as a people are obsessed with the
notion of duality. Is it possible our entire culture is driven by such
man-made forces? Joe began to think of examples where culture
reflected its obsession with right and wrong, good and bad. All
around us, in movies, books, and television, we just have to see the
good guy triumph over the bad guy. But what about eras before the
media? He thought about Moses—a good guy—who was told by
God to return to Egypt and tell Pharaoh—the bad guy—to let the
Israelites go. That would be a good thing, while not letting them go
would be a bad thing—at least according to Moses. So, how
different from Pharaoh was Moses? After all, had not Moses
murdered a high official who was only doing his job? And did not
Pharaoh up and throw Moses out of Egypt rather than have him
executed? Which, according to the law, would have been a good
thing.

Joe kept batting good versus evil back and forth like a
badminton birdie. It depended whose side you were on as to
whether something was good or evil. One man's meat was another
man's poison. And whose side is God on? According to Michael,
there was no such thing as sides. We all dwell in God's love and
would do well to remember that. Yet throughout history we, as
human beings, have put God into the same patterns that we live by.
We keep bringing God down to our level, Joe concluded. Maybe
Michael was trying to turn all that around: Bring us all back to God's
level.

A week later, Kathleen called, having freshly returned from
Mexico. The first person she called on her return was Joe. "Well, I'm
back," she started.

"And how are we doing?" Joe asked in his humorous sort of
way, trying to make conversation easier. He could tell by the tone

in her voice that she was nervous about something. Usually, Kathleen jumps into conversation the way most people jump into a pool on a hot summer's day.

"There are some other things I want to say first, so, stay with me here. I don't think I really told you how I felt when you suggested I was one of the Seven that your angel asked you to find. I honestly never really had a clue as to what that was about. It just felt good that someone thought I had a spiritual bone in my body and was chosen for a spiritual purpose. At the time, you really felt I was chosen as one of the so-called 'Seven,' and *I* felt really sure, like 'This guy is insane!' But I trusted you." There was a lull in the conversation as Kathleen tried to gather her composure. She was putting her heart on the line, and Joe knew it. He simply said nothing.

"At the time you told me this, I was deathly ill, as you know. The pain was unbearable, and the feeling that I was just hanging on was undeniable. I knew that through the depths of my illness, for the first time, there seemed to be a glimmer of hope. Instead of looking at my dying body, I was seeing my spiritual path again—the first time in a long time. Somehow, I had lost that. So I thought this Seven thing was something that was being handed me, and I had a decision to make. Either I can accept with grace what God is offering me or I can turn it right back. You know—take the chance that it *may* be something or not do it. And being who I am, I always thought I could change my mind after doing the baptism and *not* be one of the Seven. I thought I could do the baptism and be the non-committal-commitment sort of person that I am!"

Joe wanted to interrupt and tell her Michael's message about being perfect, whole, and complete, just the way she is. But this was a time for listening. Kathleen cleared her throat before continuing.

"I figured I could see what would happen. So ..." Kathleen fought for self-control as she searched for the words. "Anyway, time went by; I didn't do it, I didn't do the baptism. As I told you before going down to Mexico, I decided to do the baptism down there. Well, I got there, and checked in the hospital, and got hooked up to IVs. The truth be known, I was barely able to even walk—really—at the time. You know, the hospitals down there are

different than ours. You can kind of go where you want. They're open-air. Hooked up to my IV, I went outside where I found a quiet spot in the sun."

It had been warm outside, well past noon, as she had headed outside the room in her bare feet with a towel and bowl in hand. She knew it was not the exact time for doing the baptism that the angel had instructed Joe, but she figured she would be forgiven for it, considering the circumstances. As she sat in the grass, away from everyone else, she took out the piece of paper with the instructions that Joe had given her. Setting the bowl on a corner of the paper, so it wouldn't blow away, she poured the wine into it. Closing her eyes and trying to relax, she said to herself, *Joe would not tell me this if it were not true*, and began to wash herself with the wine. After wiping herself off with the towel, she said the prayer scratched out on the paper. She closed her eyes again and listened for counsel. Her body started feeling a numb, tingling sensation like when an arm or leg has fallen asleep and starts to get feeling back.

"It was completely silent, and I fell asleep under the tree next to where I had done the baptism. Because of all the pain I was suffering, I had been unable to really sleep for a long time. But I went into a really, really, really, deep, deep sleep. It must've been four hours or something. But when I woke up, it seemed as if … I couldn't tell if it had been five minutes or was the next day. I was in a daze, totally disoriented." The tingling feeling was gone, and she heard a voice tell her what to do during the next year.

"It struck me as kind of funny," she said. "You know, like what is going on here? Where am I? I started to get up and the first thing I notice is, *Gosh, I can move*. The pain had subsided. It was a kind of spontaneous healing, in the sense that I was out of physical pain. What was even more noticeable to me was that I didn't have that feeling I have when I am really ill, where I'm just kind of holding on, holding myself together. You know, like there's an inner core, a magnet that's just barely holding me together. And nobody knows but me that I'm just barely bound together. And if I don't hold it like that, I'm going to die … or fall apart. And that was lifted." It was as if Kathleen felt a little embarrassed to confess how badly

she had been feeling. She hadn't told anyone before how precarious her life was. She had sons to care for and a household to try and keep. Other people needed attention she found herself unable to provide at times. It was with a sense of relief that she was able to confess how miserable her life had been.

"I felt like my normal self," she continued. "It had been a long time since I had felt like that. But I *knew* it, instantaneously. It was like, *Oh my God—I feel like me!* So I went back into my room and continued my treatment anyway. But the doctors didn't think I needed it anymore. And I wasn't keen on paying the thousands of dollars more for all the live-cell stuff that I didn't seem to need. So I came home the second week." There was a pause on the phone. "Thanks, Joe."

"You're welcome," he said softly. But his mind was running a hundred miles an hour. Michael had said that Kathleen would still have "sums to work." He wasn't sure what that was, but he was sure that Kathleen needed to have this moment and enjoy it. He let her know how gratifying it was for him to hear this story, not so much because she had a spontaneous healing of sorts, but more importantly because she now believed in herself, that she was, indeed, the first of the Seven. He asked her to keep him informed how she was progressing and to let him know how the instructions the voice had given her played out.

That evening, Joe sat next to his lily pond contemplating a message: It is not fitting that my Lord God's children should suffer. He felt compassion for Kathleen and all others who had such tough lives to live. Michael appeared out of nowhere.

The angel said, **"So great has become their longing to know God and the will of God, that they will listen to whoever holds up the Book and claims to know the secret hidden within—the secret which promises everlasting life in Paradise with God. Out of fear, they will believe and obey, unto the point of death, that with the authority of a gnat, their leader has threatened the everlasting fires of hell. The Lord God requires not that you die for him, but that you live to love and give comfort to each other. For death will come to all, so speed it not.**

"I AM has instructed me to give you these words: **'It is written that the sins of the fathers are visited upon the children, but I say from this day forward, the debt is paid. Now I say the rewards of the fathers will be visited on the children for a hundred times a hundred generations. It is written that in my house there are many mansions. I say truly, one is yours that you build brick by brick with the blessings you give and the deeds you do. A place is set aside for you in Paradise to build your mansion and live with me forever. The time is close when I will give to you a book that teaches you to make the bricks. My son, Jesus, laid the foundation at the time he walked with you.**

'In your Book, it tells of *Revelation*, a vision of things to come, written with the knowledge of that time. It has been so corrupted with mysticism and superstition over the centuries, that no man or woman can know its meaning. When I AM speaks, it is cloudless, for what I say is what is— no more, no less.

'There will be a great calling of my children when a large number will return home in the blink of an eye. So will many follow in the time to come, yet not to a last judgment. They come to their reward and will dwell with me in their mansions forever.

'It is said that I am a jealous God, and you will put no gods before me. This could not be, for I am all that there is and no one *is* before me. Yet, you build great houses with windows of colored glass and fill them with statues carved from stone. You adorn them in jewels, gold and silver, paintings, and tapestries to tell stories of what was sacrificed for you. This you call a house of God, holy ground, and say I dwell within. I AM dwells not in these alone. Look you well into the eyes of one another, from the poorest of the poor to the richest of the rich. Both in spirit and possessions you will find me there. Look at the fields of grass or flowers, and at the deserts, woodlands, jungles, and at the animals. I dwell there, also. Look to the sunrise or the sunset, look to the stars at night. Open your eyes and heart, for you will see me in all

these things. When you have done this, you will know I have no need for such riches. It would be fitting to sell them to feed and clothe the needy and to turn these great houses into dwellings for those living in the streets.

'You cry out, "Oh, Lord, we need these temples to teach your word and pray in." Yet, I say to you, teach in the fields, in the light, as Jesus did, and all the prophets before and after him did. You need not the great halls for your prayers. Pray as Jesus has taught you.

' "But, Lord," you ask, "where might we gather to pray for the souls of others?" I tell you this: Gather not to pray for those who are sick in spirit. Go to them and make their body, mind, and emotions well, and the Spirit within will be free to do my work.

'You speak of sacrifice and teach that the spilling of blood made a covenant with me, and has since Adam and Eve, along with Abraham. You tell of Cain's offering to me being unpleasing, for it was not blood—so I rejected it. You teach that Jesus' blood was shed so I would open the gates of Heaven. I say this only once: All things whose blood runs red, who breathe air, have a soul. I gave life to them for my purpose, and it must not be shed.

'When you speak of "Jesus Saves," you belittle what he has done. For you speak as if he did not fulfill what he was sent to do. You listen; yet not a word have you heard. Jesus told you, when he said, No one comes to the Father but by the Son. By this he made it known that you are saved.

'Think not that salvation gives you license to do that which pleasures only you, casting aside all else. When you do not honor and bless that which is around you, no bricks do you make, and your mansion will be fitting in size for you.' "

With this, Michael became silent, staring at Joe as if waiting to hear what he had to say. Even though his head was spinning with all he had heard, Joe responded, "You know it has always seemed to me that the Bible, Torah, and Koran spoke of a vengeful God, one whose punishment is a swift and terrible thing to behold when he is displeased. Still, he is supposed to be a God of love? That, to

me, is a contradiction in terms. Now I see, if the truth be told, he is all-loving—period.

"Yes, Joe," Michael returned, "God is. And with so great a love for you all that if you could know the feeling of only the smallest portion of God's love, you would weep tears of joy that would fill rivers."

"I hear what's being said about Jesus," Joe said. "But, as regarding him making it known we are saved, why has it been so difficult for us to understand this concept?"

"Jesus was sitting with his disciples teaching when Simon said to him, 'Master, you tell these truths, yet how is it they fall on so many deaf ears? The people gather to listen, and know not what you speak.' Jesus told him, 'My teachings are not for this age but for the next.' Jesus knew that the spiritual state of most people was such that it would take 2,000 years before mortals could rise to a level where they could understand what he was teaching. Take a look around your world. Do you see many beginning to know the truths Jesus taught?"

"Yes, I do. I see more and more people looking for the truth. But I also see people returning to the old, established religions and calling the truth 'New Age thinking.' Some say New Age thinking is the work of the Devil because it talks about the signs of the zodiac."

"You know what I have said about the Devil," said Michael, leaning forward as if to emphasize the point, "so speak of it to me no more. One of your teachers has given you the knowledge of what an age is. I say, truly, to you, the age that is coming is new, for it has never been nor will be again. So, you see it is a new age. The zodiac is just a heavenly clock that measures the movement of the Earth, planets, sun, and stars. But, since the early religions thought the Earth was the center of the Universe and said everything that moved around the Earth was being pushed by angels, anything else was blasphemy."

Joe had been taught by Alexander than an age lasts 2,000 years with a transition period of 100 years from one age to the next. Each age has specific characteristics. The age we are leaving behind is Pisces, which started around the birth of Jesus. Pisces is considered a water sign of the zodiac with the symbol of two fish.

The early Christians used a fish as their sign, not the cross. A common occupation of that age was fishing. When someone was baptized, water was used. Jesus walked on water to signify he had dominion over the age. He changed water into wine to mark the beginning of his teachings from his time to the next age. When Jesus fed the people fish and bread, he symbolized the blending of the ages.

If one goes back another 2,000 years, one is in the Age of Aries, the ram, which is a fire sign. God appeared to Moses, for example, on top of a mountain in a burning bush. A common occupation of that age was herding sheep. The food of the age was sheep. The baptism of the Jewish people was done with fire. The coming age is Aquarius, the water bearer. This is an air sign, and its symbol is that of a man with a stone jar pouring water out onto the earth. What this symbolizes is the pouring forth of knowledge on the earth. He is also holding stalks of grain. The occupation of the age will be farming as well as occupations oriented around the growing of things. The last 100 years has seen an unprecedented growth in knowledge, inventions, and technology.

In Scripture, Jesus tells Peter and John, "Go and prepare for us the Passover that we may eat it."[1] They asked him where he wanted the meal to be, and Jesus told them to go into the city where they would meet a man carrying a jug of water. "He will show you a large room upstairs, already furnished. Make preparations for us there." Aquarius is the age we are passing into. In Genesis it says to let the stars "serve as signs, and for the fixing of seasons, days, and years."[2] Is it unthinkable to suggest that these signs include the signs of the zodiac?

Joe then asked Michael about not eating anything that bleeds red. "Does this mean that animals have souls, too?" After asking the question, Joe started listing animals in his head: dogs, cats, pigs, cows, whales, lions and tigers, and bears. *Oh my! Goodbye bacon, steak, eggs, and fried chicken.*

"Yes, they do," said Michael. "If their blood is red, they have souls, not as advanced as yours but souls nonetheless. You and your kind will use them for food for only a little while, and then no more.

---

[1]　Luke 22:8
[2]　Gen. 1:14

In the time to come, food is to be in such abundance, animals will not be needed as food. All this will be told to you when the time comes for *The Book of Bricks.*"

"Yeah," Joe said clearing his throat, "I want to talk to you about that. You see, I figured out for myself it has to do with making bricks for our mansions. So I guess it's about all these laws we will be given that tell us if we obey them, we get bricks, and if we don't, we won't. Right?"

"Are you not listening to the message God is giving? This is not a book of laws that you must obey so you will be given bricks. If you need a comparison, it is as a builder's manual or an instruction book. This book tells you how to make bricks, not what you must do to get them. Too many laws have been made for you to keep or break, which have earned little. This book will give you what you need to know so that many will the bricks be for your mansions in Paradise."

"OK, I understand the distinction. Now, when do I get the book?"

"When you are ready, in God's eyes, to receive it. Take heart, Joe, for the time is close at hand."

"Well, I guess if it has taken 2,000 years to get this far, sometime in my life is soon enough. As far as I can see, in our talk today, we, as God's children, have no idea of God's love for us. Yet, we want to be with God so much that we listen to anyone who tells us he knows how to get us there based on fear of going to hell, which doesn't exist anyway. If someone comes along and tells us he is Jesus, we kill ourselves because he says Armageddon is just around the corner. We do what we are told because we don't understand what was written originally in the Bible, the Torah, and the Koran. We practice idolatry in our churches through our ignorance. We are borderline cannibals because we eat other creatures that have souls. And all the time we tell ourselves that a vengeful and jealous God, who has his son killed to open the gates of Heaven, would send Jesus back a second time to toss us into hell anyway? Because he didn't get the job right the first time, he would have to come back to save us. Does that about sum it up?"

"What you speak has great truth in the way it has been, yet I say to all of you, Jesus will not return, for he is with you even now.

I tell you truly, also, he is not alone. The Holy Spirit is with him as a sister in what will be done." Both of the angel's hands were spread apart as if embracing the notion physically.

"So tell me," Joe said, "how will we know Jesus or his sister when we see them, and what are they supposed to do? What are they going to teach us?"

Michael looked into the distance as if searching for an answer. "You will know them in this way: He and she will be together *and* they will be apart. They will be young *and* they will be old, dressed in rags or dressed in fine clothing. They are well *and* they are lame. They are fair *and* they are dark. The way you will know most of all is that they are in need.

"They have not come to teach, but to learn from you. Compassion, kindness, and giving are what you will teach them. You will know not who they are, yet they will know you. What they will do is open a time for you to make many bricks by the deeds and blessings you shower on them. Be generous in this, and an abundant supply of bricks will be yours. Act meagerly, and you will make no bricks.

"My time is over for now. Be at peace and teach only love."

With that, he was gone, fading away as before, leaving Joe to ponder what had been said. Scenes from his Roman Catholic upbringing tumbled through his mind, juxtaposing their hard realities against the truths Michael had presented. In Joe's third-grade catechism class, the new wonders of who, what, and where God is had been unveiled for the first time. Joe did fine with "God is love" and with "God created Heaven and Earth, and all living things." These concepts Sister Mary Elizabeth explained in no uncertain terms. She made it all factual with no ifs, ands, or buts about it. Where Joe got into trouble was with the "where" thing. To Joe, Sister Mary Elizabeth was the Mother Theresa of his world. He could still see her kind and loving eyes looking through her strong, yet inexpensive and very unfashionable eyeglasses. She had the wise face of a best-loved grandmother, hazel eyes, and graying eyebrows. Her little pug nose and thin lips fit perfectly on the nape of the saddest child when she hugged her pupils. Joe could still see her face, bordered by the white collar around her neck, her bib of

white, and her face framed in black. As a boy, he had guessed the bib protected her from any spillage while eating.

"Where is God?" she had asked. And all the children in the classroom had replied, "God is everywhere."

"That's correct," she had encouraged. "God is in the trees, in the animals, in the ocean, in the rocks, in heaven, and on earth. So, you see, God *is* everywhere. Except in you. Because you were born with original sin. Until you're baptized in the Church, you will never go to heaven." Even in the third grade, with his limited wisdom and intelligence, it had occurred to Joe, *Wait a minute, this stinks! She just said that God is everywhere. And now she says that God is not within us because we are sinners.* Joe's childlike heart could not handle this. So thirsty for knowledge was he that he had immediately shot his hand into the air, her kind eyes acknowledging him. "Yes, Joseph, do you have a question?"

"Yes, Sister," he had said. "I don't understand how God can be everywhere and not be in me. Either God is everywhere or he's almost everywhere, but he can't be everywhere and not be everywhere at the same time. Could you explain this to me? Because I really don't understand."

Standing at the blackboard behind her desk, something in Sister Mary Elizabeth's eyes had changed as she said, "So, you don't understand?" She picked up a book from her desk and marched to the back of the room. He could now hear her footsteps as she stomped up the length of Joe's aisle. They had been told always to look forward in class because there was nothing in the back they needed to see. Sitting there politely, Joseph knew that in a few moments what he did not understand would be made clear. Her footsteps stopped abruptly behind him. Whack! The crashing thud of the book against the back of his head catapulted him into the aisle, sprawled seven ways from Sunday. He had looked up and seen what used to be a sweet grandmotherly nun transformed into a banshee from hell.

"Now do you understand? Now do you understand?" she had growled.

Humbled by his stupidity for daring to ask such a question, Joseph had responded slowly in the best way he knew how, "Yes, Sister, I understand."

"That's good," she had pronounced with tight lips, "because the Church wants everyone to go to Heaven. And it really doesn't make any difference whether you understand or not. You just have to believe what the Church tells you."

As she marched back to her desk, the other children had stared at Joe in disbelief. His embarrassment had been overwhelming. He understood, all right. He understood that he would never again admit he did not understand. These memories lingered in Joe's mind like a vulture on a dead tree. He had wanted to live a saintly life in accordance with the Scriptures, but he couldn't. He was haunted by all he had learned about God as a child. Nuns in black and white, espousing black and white edicts to young minds hungering for truth, kept him from exploring anything saintly. Like Sister Mary Elizabeth, such saints were not to be trusted. Their truths did not nurture the mind or the soul, they assaulted both like the crashing thud of the book against his innocent head.

Michael was the antithesis of the parochial school classroom. He did not give ultimatums, nor he did he rule with shame. Everything about this angelic figure spoke to and about love. If God truly was love, then this angel exemplified it. Joe could understand how others were brought up to believe a certain way all their lives. Compassion filled him as he recognized how others did their best to live their lives by the teachings they had been given. He realized Michael was unleashing a seemingly new truth, based completely on unconditional love. Joe acknowledged that others had a choice of accepting this new truth or their old truths. But this was a luxury he, himself, no longer possessed. He only knew what he must do. He had to trust that God knew where all this was going. Michael's words spoke to his soul with an undeniable love. And he was not about to say no to it. No book against the back of his head would ever change that again.

Part II

BLESSINGS, GIFTS, AND DEEDS

THE FIRST MANUSCRIPT

*T*he full seven feet of the angel stood before Joe as he looked up from his computer. Once again, Joe had climbed the rankings in his latest game of Tetris and surpassed Donna. "Oh. Hi, Michael," he said in a voice not unlike that of an employee being discovered playing computer solitaire by the president of the company. "I have started writing down all you have been telling me, but you probably already know that."

"I do. Blessed are the works you have chosen to do. Blessed are you, for you hear God's words and you follow, setting aside that which you think you know. The path you have taken may not be as difficult to walk as you think, for I AM walks with you."

"That is wonderful to know, but at this point, I feel as though I'm walking this path in the dark." Michael smiled that smile that made Joe want to run up and hug him. It was the kind of smile one sees on a child, beaming across the entire face and six inches beyond, all lit up with innocence and joy.

"Joe, you walk not in darkness, but in light. When you emerge from a place that is dim into the bright sunlight, it will take time before you see clearly. In that time, you want to cover your

eyes, for such a light brings discomfort. Soon, you will be accustomed to it and see wonders that were only shadows in the darkness before.

I wish I had a pair of sunglasses for this, Joe thought to himself.

"For the first wonder, you will call upon the land of the bear, and say to them:"

> I AM has sent me that you may be strong among nations. Take your boat that sails under the sea and go you to the Valley of the Star. In the deepest part of this valley, you will thrust a hollow rod seven feet into the bottom. Take what you have gathered there back to your land. Give it to your men of wisdom and healing. In this lies the cure for two great plagues that are in all lands. Before a year is finished, you will find it. You may ask a fair price for your labor and medicine. In return, you will give one-seventh to my servant that has brought you this. If you do these things, great riches will be yours.

"I think I know what country you are talking about, but why not my own?" Joe asked. "Also, what is this one-seventh given to me for? Is it like tithing?

Michael answered simply, "Your country would question it for too long, and many would die needlessly. Look to the birds of the field. Neither do they sow nor reap, yet their Heavenly Father feeds them. No, it is not tithing. Tithing was established by the Church as a tax to support itself and the poor. Over the the years, the Church forgot the poor and became rich, powerful, and greedy. Giving little to the poor, the Churches thought the tithe belonged to them, and still do today. It is to be, that only one-seventh may be given to those who teach God's words. Of that one seventh, a full five parts will be given to the poor and only two may be kept to live on. The gift of one-seventh is so that your brothers and sisters need not suffer. A gift is something that is given and not owed.

"Say to them that rob God's children with their tithing, they make no bricks today. Say this, also, to those who have

become wealthy on the tithing, whether they display it as gold encrusted with jewels in great houses, or hide it in vaults, or sell the jewels, or melt down the gold into the coin of the realm. Take once, and once only, one-fourth of your riches gathered by tithing and keep it to live on. Take the remaining three-fourths and heal the sick, feed the hungry, clothe the naked, and house the homeless. If you choose not to do this, all will be taken away. You will not be left with even the fourth, and no bricks do you make."

"Well, as long as we are on a roll, here," Joe said with raised eyebrows, "is there any more good news you would like me to break to the Christian community while I'm at it?"

"Tell those who lay hands on their flock, healing sickness and twisted bodies, to stop acting as if they had anything to do with it. Only faith can do this. 'Physician, heal thyself' means just that. You and your faith are all you need to heal yourself. Jesus told you that. So believe.

"Go to Kathleen," Michael continued, "and say to her, 'Get your house in order, for you are called to do God's work.' It was a woman who first saw that Jesus had risen and spoke to him. It was the women who told the men of his resurrection. In the time to come, it is women who will see the light first, and teach of God's love. It was women who led the men to the light, and will do so again. As Mary gave birth to Jesus, so will women give birth to the light that has been in the womb for almost 2,000 years. Peter's faith was the rock, then, and a woman's wisdom and love for life will be God's rock this time."

"Ah, yes, I can see it all now. A world ruled by women— this is going to make some men very happy," Joe said with tongue in cheek. "So, why didn't you just tell a woman all this? Maybe one with typing skills who is not dyslexic, like me?"

"*Rule?*" Michael had never raised his voice before. He leaned forward in a way that made Joe wish he could back his chair up, right through the wall. "Women are chosen to nurture and guide. It is in their very nature, these things. It is man's nature to lead. It is only God who will rule out of love for you and your well-being.

"Let me tell you about the birds and the bees."

"Oh, very funny," returned Joe. "It's nice to know you have a sense of humor."

"Life starts with a seed that is planted by the male in the female," the angel stated as if ignoring Joe's informality, "grows, and then is born. This is how it is with you. That which you are writing is the seed you will give. Like Jesus' earthly father did for him, you will do with these teachings. You will take them out into the world and help them grow. When they are strong enough to stand on their own, you will step aside. Don't worry, I will tell you when that time has come.

"The four men that you will choose represent the fourfold nature of God's children. These four are ...

the Physical—to take the teachings into the world.
the Mental—to think only of the well-being of others.
the Emotional—to love as you are loved by God.
the Spiritual—to have a personal relationship with God.

"These four are the signs of balance. As the day is balanced by morning, afternoon, evening, and night—the seasons of the year or the points of the compass—all these are in balance with one another.

"The three women stand for the Love God is, the Life, which is the work God has done, and the Light, which is the result of the union of the other two.

"This is not new to you, for Alexander teaches this."

"Michael," Joe responded, "you know this is going to anger our Holy Mother the Church. There is no way the Church will buy the idea that women could be on the same level or equal to men. To say this is true will undermine the Church's authority. Oh, let's not forget the Muslims, along with most of the other religions of the world, who will not buy women's equality, either.

"You say: Being gay isn't a mortal sin and an abomination to God, Women are equal with men, and Give back the money that religions have, more or less, stolen from their members under false pretense. That last one is going to be the hardest of all for the organized religions to swallow. Now, to top the whole thing off, we

are going to tell them they can't rationally use the Scriptures as a basis for their authority because the Scriptures are, at the least, disingenuous. That will start one hell of a *jihad*."

"The Church is neither holy, nor a mother," Michael said, the light in his eyes dimming with a kind of sadness. "The people who run it are not being asked to 'buy' anything. I tell you truly, any religion that says it is of God is actually a servant of GOD'S CHILDREN"—his eyes flashed with light—"and not the other way around, as it thinks itself to be. Religion has become as unreliable as servants who steal from their masters. With their ill-gotten gains, they act as though they are now masters. I AM will dismiss them as servants if they do not return that which they have stolen and obey those they serve.

"I AM has not given them the authority, nor has Jesus or any heavenly host. Just because they have written it in their Scriptures does not mean it is so. There is only one authority, and is with God. You speak of *jihad*, a holy war. I tell you this, truly: There is nothing holy about war. War is the violent act to steal or to take back that which was stolen. It was not God who ordered war. It was man who did this. To justify it, he lied, saying, 'It is the God's will.' Not until the Crusades was war allowed by the Christian Church. The head of the Christian Church in Rome made war holy, not God. Most religions, today, still think war can be holy if their leaders say it is so. The children of Israel and Islam fight with one another and lie when they say it is God's will. Yet, they are of the same family of Abraham and the same God he served. When brothers are killing brothers, no bricks are made.

"There will be no *jihad*, for God's children will say, 'I give my life to God, who is all-loving and asks only that I live to bring joy and happiness to all. I will not serve any religion in war or die for it.' So that you may see there is no need to fear this Armageddon, I AM has given me the words to tell you what is truly said in the *Book of Revelation*. You must not speak this knowledge to anyone until you first give it to your seven chosen people. Do you understand?"

Joe nodded, mulling over all he had been told by the angel. As *Revelation* was revealed, a sense of awe swept through him.

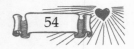

From the very first word that poured from the Michael's mouth, Joe felt that truth flowed forth. The sound of the angel's voice was a beautiful melody that carried rich vowels and consonants that warmed Joe's imagination and quieted the panic of his beating heart, flooding him with the same feeling he had felt when the angel had told him his celestial name. Such great reverie filled Joe that he did not even notice when the heavenly host had finished speaking. Nor did he notice when Michael concluded, "My time is over for now. Go in peace and teach only love."

Amazement seized every cell of Joe's body as the angel disappeared into the light and faded away. The angel's words made complete sense, filling his mind with a sense of all-knowing. He thought of Bones, who, in a classic episode of Star Trek, had been given a megadose of medical knowledge from another world. What was impossible to understand only moments before, now seemed so simple that a child could understand it.

How is it that a message as simple and clear as this could be so misunderstood? Joe tried to reason. *No wonder Jesus wept when he saw what man had done to God's words.* The phenomenon was so overwhelming that Joe, too, began to weep. He was filled with incredibly joyous love, and at the same time inundated by profound sadness. He could not make up his mind whether his tears were for the joy or the sadness. As his tears ceased, he began to laugh—just a chuckle, at first. But the more he thought of the Apocalypse, with its demonic armies in a final battle and Jesus coming out of the clouds like the U.S. Cavalry to save the day, the funnier it got. The chuckle rolled into open laughter, the laughter erupted into uncontrollable hysterics. Tears flowed again, this time from laughter.

In his mind's eye he pictured religious leaders standing before God. He heard himself roaring with laughter, *I guess you get what you deserve—poetic justice at its finest.* He could hear them trying to explain just what had possessed them to teach such foolishness. He laughed even louder as he imagined their response: "The Devil made me do it."

That night, as Joe tried to sleep, he reflected upon all that Michael had told him that day. Sleep seemed almost a nuisance. How was he going to get this message to "the land of the bear"? He

tried to imagine himself contacting the Russian embassy: *I would like to speak to someone about a message I am supposed to give you from God.* As ridiculous as it looked to him, he concluded there was little else to do. After all, Michael hadn't said anything about making them believe the message. He had said just to tell them.

A week had passed since Michael had last appeared. The more Joe thought about it, the more he began to suspect Michael was waiting for him to do something about the Russian message. Every time the angel had told him to do something, and Joe would take his time to do it, he noticed Michael's absence. Not really knowing why, Joe decided to call one of his friends and ask her if she had a clue how he might make a Russian contact. Debbie was a bright woman, totally unassuming, who always made Joe feel he was in the company of Southern hospitality. Her easy smile was a welcome mat and her eyes an open doorway. Deb was the human resources director at the human dynamics firm where Joe had worked as an instructor, and they had been friends ever since.

"Deb, do you have any idea how I might get in touch with anybody who lives in Russia?" he asked out of the clear blue.

"Russia? Why Russia?"

There was no way around it; he had to tell her something about Michael. After giving her the story in a nutshell, he promised also to send her the transcripts he had typed to this point. Her response was as open as her heart. After searching her thoughts for a minute, she asked, "Do you remember the two gentlemen who visited here last summer? They were from Russia."

"Yes, as a matter of fact I do remember." Joe was pleased to find a possible connection on his first try.

"Well, maybe you should write or call them."

"How?"

"Let me see what I can do to track them down. I'll find someone who has their address or phone number, and have that person give you a call. How's that?"

"That would be better than a cold beer in the Mojave desert." Deb laughed, mostly because she knew Joe no longer drank. He always made himself out to be some leftover of the criminal element or some kind of Hell's Angels reject. True, he had been a biker at one time, but she knew he had a heart of pure gold—a man who would do just about anything for a friend.

Another week passed before Michael appeared again. Joe was sitting at the computer playing another game, and doing quite well, when the celestial interrupted. "It is time for you to write *The Book of Bricks.*"

"OK, Michael," he replied, "but first, I want to ask a few things. You see, I have been telling some friends of mine of these experiences, and they ask me if I know the answers to their important questions. I told them I had an opinion on almost everything. But answers? No. I said I would, however, ask you and tell them what you say."

"Ask what you will." As Joe stared up at his heavenly friend, he could not help but feel he was staring up a tower of light. The angel's eyes were full of patience as he waited to hear the questions.

"I have a list of things to ask. First of all, why has God made evil, if he is all-loving?"

"God has not made evil," came the reply. Again, the eyes were like lakes of emotion. They exuded love, as if to impress on Joe how such love could be the source of anything except more love. "Your kind has brought it into being. Mankind has become lazy and will not work. It is the easy way to take from others that which you do not have. If you think about it, you will see the truth in what I say."

"What about abortion and the right to life? Should abortion be stopped regardless of the means used to stop it?"

"Your kind is always talking of rights, as if God gave any one group the authority to take life. What you seek is permission to kill in order to stop killing. And you have no such permission. This not protecting the unborn. This is insanity. I tell you truly, abortion is between a woman and God. God, and God alone, will give the woman counsel, and interfere you will not."

"What is the true religion of God?" Joe then asked. "I know this sounds like I am asking what religion God belongs to, but I hope you understand my real question. Is he maybe an agnostic that doesn't believe in himself because he just is God?"

"All religions are from God, and none are of God." Joe watched as Michael gestured with open hands. It was those eyes again. They never blinked. Never. He wondered if the angel wanted his love never to be interrupted by a blink. "Religions have taken that which God has given and made of it what they understand it to be. God gave the Word, and mankind heard what it wanted. To answer your question: All of them, and none of them."

"OK. Now what?" Joe knew he had more questions to ask, but he couldn't remember them at the moment.

"I will be with you as you write and will whisper in your soul the words you write. Begin."

THE BOOK OF BRICKS

You have all chosen to be flesh and blood, with a time to work out sums. You may have as many lifetimes as you need. Yet there is a point when all must be done. This time is known as the Grand Gathering when God's children will be called home. A quickening has begun at this time before the Gathering, so you may add bricks to your mansion. So long have you been away from your home, that you have forgotten it. You have built a new home out of dust in a faraway land. This house you will not keep, for it is of worldly things. Many of you have labored for worldly things for long years, while setting aside your real reason for coming to earth.

I give this book so you may remember and build your mansions in Paradise. This is not a book of laws you must obey. Nor is it a book by which you may judge your neighbor. There is no punishment if you do not use it to make bricks. You are given this book out of love so you may make the number of bricks you want. Your time is short before the calling. And when you are called, your mansion will be complete. Not one brick will be added or taken away from

your labors. That which you have built will be yours for all time. When your mansion is finished, you will come home to it. God will furnish it with all the wondrous things your imagination can hold. You will share Paradise with all whom you have ever loved or were loved by, I tell you now. You must never consider this book as being more important than you are to one another. You will not hold it as holy or sacred. You will worship it not. It will not be kissed or held with affection in any way.

The Book of Bricks is written in three parts. Each is equal unto the other, and none is greater or lesser in value. The first text is of Blessings. This part deals with emotional training. The second is the text of Giving. This part trains the mind. The third text is of Deeds. This part is to train the body. The three stand as separate legs of a tripod. Each is planted firmly on a solid spot. They rise upwards toward a center that holds the platform. On the platform is mounted a transom—the soul—to make sure your direction is straight and level.

THE SCROLL OF BLESSINGS

*S*o that this leg may stand on solid ground, and your blessings begin, once-blessed are you who take this leg to heart. Some will find it the easiest to set, while others will find it almost impossible. Yet, set it firmly and you will be giving your first blessing to yourself: 'Bless my soul, for I am a child of God. Bless my heart for it beats to serve you, my God, and your children. God has made me perfect, whole, and complete for I am in God's own image and likeness. With this knowledge I am all I need to be. I set this leg as the foundation of God's will for me and all others.'

The deep feeling of infinite compassion is not just an emotion. This oneness with God sets in motion an uncontrollable desire. Your soul wishes only love and well-being for a person, place, or thing. When this happens, you make a brick by saying, 'Bless its heart.' There is no blessing so small that it does not make a brick. Saying a blessing only so a brick will be added to your mansion is done in vain, for no brick is made.

Should you see a child crying, for whatever reason, know they are in pain, and bless their heart, a brick is made.

See you tears in the eyes of a man or woman, know they are in pain or joy, and bless their heart, a brick is made.

See you someone who is in anger or rage, know they are in pain for some reason, and bless their heart, a brick is made.

See you someone who is blind—they see not the wonders you do—and bless their heart, a brick is made.

See you someone who is deaf—they hear not the music of nature—and bless their heart, a brick is made.

See you someone who cannot speak—their voice sings not the language you share—and bless their heart, a brick is made.

See you someone who is lame—they shuffle with difficulty in the dance of life—and bless their heart, a brick is made.

See you someone who is disfigured—they are ugly only in the eyes that hold them so—and bless their heart, a brick is made.

See you someone who is poor—they know not the abundance that is theirs—and bless their heart, a brick is made.

See you someone who is hungry—they have forgotten how to feed themselves—and bless their heart, a brick is made.

See you someone who is naked or in rags—they know not how to clothe themselves—and bless their heart, a brick is made.

See you someone who is homeless—they have forgotten how to shelter themselves—and bless their heart, a brick is made.

See you someone who is a drunkard or an addict—what they take to numb their pain is now its cause—and bless their heart, a brick is made.

See you someone who is slow of wit—their mind is in a cloud of darkness, struggling to be free—and bless their heart, a brick is made.

See you someone who is a criminal—they have lost their faith—and bless their heart, a brick is made.

See you someone who steals a childhood—they have had their childhood stolen—and bless their heart, a brick is made.

See you someone who takes a place before you—they take from you only that which has been taken from them—bless their heart, a brick is made.

See you someone who respects you not—they have no respect for themselves—and bless their heart, a brick is made.

See you someone who has taken a life—they know not what they have truly done—and bless their heart, a brick is made.

See you someone who is with disease—they know not that they could be well—and bless their heart, a brick is made.

See you someone who belittles others—they see themselves as unimportant—and bless their heart, a brick is made.

See you someone who robs others—they only rob bricks from themselves—and bless their heart, a brick is made.

See you someone who cheats others—they only cheat themselves out of bricks—and bless their heart, a brick is made.

See you someone who hollers at others—they want to be heard but know not how—and bless their heart, a brick is made.

See you someone who lays a hand on others—they only strike bricks from their own walls—and bless their heart, a brick is made.

See you a sick or injured animal, bless its heart, a brick is made.

See you any animal that has died, bless its heart, a brick is made.

See you the meat on your table, know you that the animal gave up its life that you may be fed. Ask forgiveness, and bless its heart, a brick is made.

Let not a day go by that you have not given blessings. Open your heart to the world around you. Find in all things a reason to give blessings.

Your God has blessed you and all else. God's blessings come as easily as the rising and setting of the sun. Should not yours be given with the love you hold in your heart? Should you not bless all things around you that have been given to you? Think not that it makes no difference and is but a small and unimportant thing to do. For I tell you truly, there is no blessing that you can give that is insignificant. Any blessing you give is a brick, and will be given by God back to you unto the nth degree.

THE SCROLL OF GIVING

*T*hat this leg may stand on solid ground, and your giving begin, twice blessed are you who take this second leg to heart. So you may give to others, you must give to yourself. Forgive yourself all that keeps you from greatness. 'I am a child of God and from my soul I give. My heart beats to give to you, my God, and your children. I give myself the knowledge that I am made in God's image and likeness, to be perfect, whole, and complete. I am all I need to be to set the second leg as the foundation of God's will for me and all others.'

The gift of giving is more than the mental process of 'I think I should, therefore I give.' Be responsible in giving. If others benefit from your gift, and you or your family are left wanting, this is not responsible giving. This is suffering. Be you abundant so others may prosper, also. God has not meant for you to go hungry so others may eat. You are not to go naked so others may be clothed. You shall not live in the streets that others may live in a mansion. There is no gift so small that it does not make a brick. But to give only so a brick is added to your mansion is done in vain, for no brick is made.

Be you loving to yourself as God loves you—a brick is made. Give in return this love to all else around you—a brick is made.

Be you kind to yourself that you may know kindness— a brick is made. Give this kindness to all around you—a brick is made.

Be you your life's work, for it is the cornerstone of life—a brick is made.

In return, see that others have a life's work to be done—a brick is made.

Be there food on your table so you will not go hungry—a brick is made. Eat no more than you need to live, so there will be food for others—a brick is made.

Be you clothed so you will be protected from the heat or cold—a brick is made. Give that which you do not use to those in rags—a brick is made.

Be you sheltered so you will be dry and warm—a brick is made. Make it so all have shelter—a brick is made.

Be you receiving when someone gives to you—a brick is made. That others may receive from what you give—a brick is made.

Be you filled in your basic requirements and that of your family—a brick is made. See then that others have the same—a brick is made.

Be you relieved of your pain—a brick is made. Give relief to those in pain—a brick is made.

Be you of vision, though you are blind—a brick is made. Give eyes to those who cannot see—a brick is made.

Be you listening, though you cannot hear—a brick is made. Give ears to those who cannot hear—a brick is made.

Be you heard, though you cannot speak—a brick is made. Hear those who cannot speak—a brick is made.

Be active, though you are lame—a brick is made. Put those who cannot move into motion—a brick is made.

Be you beautiful, though you appear disfigured—a brick is made. See beauty in those who seem to be ugly—a brick is made.

Be you healthy, though you are ill—a brick is made. Give health to those who are sick—a brick is made.

Be you not seduced to use drug or drink in ways which were not intended—a brick is made. Give freedom from enslavement to those who are in its bondage—a brick is made.

Be you quick in mind, though you are slow—a brick is made. Take time to understand those whose wit is dim—a brick is made.

Be you honest, though you have committed crimes—a brick is made. Hold responsible those who have committed a crime, and then forgive them—a brick is made.

Be you caring of a child's well-being, though your well-being may have been taken—a brick is made. See that others are caring of children and their well-being—a brick is made.

Be you courteous to all, and assume no place that is not yours—a brick is made. Allow the elderly, the lame, and children to go before you—a brick is made.

Be you respectful, though you may have been disrespected—a brick is made. See that others respect one another—a brick is made.

Be one who does not take a life—a brick is made. Give mercy to and, yet, hold responsible one who has taken a life— a brick is made.

Be you knowing that you are of greatness, though you may have been belittled—a brick is made. Give in return greatness to those who have been belittled—a brick is made.

Be you trustworthy, taking not that which you have not been given or have not earned—a brick is made. Give trust to others that they may be trustworthy—a brick is made.

Be you soft-spoken with respect in your voice, though you may have been hollered at—a brick is made. Require others to speak softly, and with respect, speak to each other— a brick is made.

Be you gentle with your touch, though you have been made to smart by a heavy hand—a brick is made. See you that no one is laid a hand to—a brick is made.

Be you so loving of an animal that you make room in your home for it—a brick is made. Give sanctuary to animals in need—a brick is made.

Be caring of animals, making them neither sick nor injured—a brick is made. Give health to those animals in need of it—a brick is made.

Be you fed by that which has not red blood—a brick is made. Spare the life of an animal that you would otherwise use for food—a brick is made.

Be you respectful of all life—a brick is made. Take not so much that there is no more to come—a brick is made.

Let not a day go by that you have not been giving. Find in all life a reason to give something. God gives life every second of every day. Should not you render with the same thoughtfulness the sparing of life? Should you not think that all life is as precious as your own?

Think not that no difference is made by your giving, or that any gift you give is insignificant. For I tell you truly, no gift you give is too small that it will not be given back to you to the nth degree.

THE SCROLL OF DEEDS

*T*hat this leg may stand on solid ground and your deeds begin, thrice-blessed are you who take this third leg to heart. You have blessed and you have given. Take that which needs to be done and do it yourself. Say: 'I am a child of God. My heart beats to do God's will for his children and me. This I can do, for God has made me perfect, whole, and complete. I am made in God's own image and likeness. Therefore, I am all I need to be, and the works I do now anchor fast this leg.'

The work that is done in your name is blessed. The work that is done by your name and your money is twice-blessed. The work that is done by your hand is thrice-blessed. When you see a need to be filled, you first feel it in your heart. Then you are moved emotionally with desire to fulfill the need. Your mind will search for a way to take care of the need. Then you take to task this need, and with your hands, you will fill this need. There is no deed so small that it does not make a brick. Woe unto you who do this only so a brick is added to your mansion. This is done in vain, for no brick is made.

I, by my hand, end the pain of a child—three bricks are made.

I, by my hand, dry the eyes of a man or woman—three bricks are made.

I, by my hand, soothe anger and rage—three bricks are made.

I, by my hand, lead the blind through darkness—three bricks are made.

I, by my hand, speak the music of the deaf, that they might hear—three bricks are made.

I, by my hand, hear the voice of the speechless, that they may sing—three bricks are made.

I, by my hand, bind up the lame, that they may travel their paths and dance through life—three bricks are made.

I, by my hand, give comfort to the ill, that they may have health—three bricks are made.

I, by my hand, open the eyes of all to see beauty, that none will shun the disfigured—three bricks are made.

I, by my hand, raise up the poor, that they may make their own way and have abundant lives—three bricks are made.

I, by my hand, feed the hungry so they will learn to feed themselves—three bricks are made.

I, by my hand, dress the naked and those in rags with clean clothes, that they will clothe themselves—three bricks are made.

I, by my hand, build shelter with the homeless, that they will build shelter for themselves—three bricks are made.

I, by my hand, bring the tangibleness of love to replace the numbness in the drunkard or the addict, that they might feel the joy of life and release their pain—three bricks are made.

I, by my hand, remove the clouds of darkness, so the dim of wit will see they, too, have a place of importance—three bricks are made.

I, by my hand, hold those who commit a crime responsible to repay that which was taken, and they are forgiven that which is paid—three bricks are made.

I, by my hand, give care, and see to the well-being of children, that they may pass through childhood unmolested by word or action—three bricks are made.

I, by my hand, will make straight that which I have made crooked through mistake or knowledge, for I am honest—three bricks are made.

I, by my hand, will make way for those who need a passage, be they young or old—three bricks are made.

I, by my hand, will not allow a life to be taken, nor will I allow a life to be prolonged to suit my purpose—three bricks are made.

I, by my hand, will hold up to greatness those who have been belittled—three bricks are made.

I, by my hand, will not take the life of an animal, nor will I prolong it to suit my purpose—three bricks are made.

I, by my hand, will open my house and heart to an animal. I will care for its needs and love it as if it were my child—three bricks are made.

I, by my hand, will build only that which does not destroy the sanctuary of animals in the wild—three bricks are made.

I, by my hand, will set my table with food that does not run red with blood—three bricks are made.

Let not a day pass that a deed is not done. Open your arms to the world around you. Find in all things a deed you might do. God does for you more than you will ever know. Should you not do the same? Should not your deeds be given as freely?

Think not what you do to make little difference, or that it is insignificant. For I tell you truly, no deed is so small that it will not be returned to you unto the nth degree.

Carry this book with you. When you know not what to do, it will guide you. As a builders manual gives you the measurements of work to be done on the straight and level, so

does this book give you measurements by which to live your life, that it may be straight and level. Go you now into the world and teach only love, for God is with you all.

Joe did not see Michael leave, nor was he aware of his leaving. Somehow, he knew the angel was with him during the dictation. In two places he had gotten stuck, and twice he received help from the angel. The first occasion had occurred during the writing of the "Scroll of Giving." He kept starting with "Give you" this or that and could go no further. At that point Joe had said, "OK, Michael, you have to help me on this one. I can't get past 'Give you.' "

Joe heard his friend's voice come booming into his ears, "It is not that you give these, but you are these things to give."

The second time he needed help was during the typing of "The Scroll of Deeds." Once again Joe couldn't make sense of what he was writing. Again he asked Michael to give him a hand. Even after writing it once more, he still could make no sense of what he was being asked to write. *How the hell am I to start this scroll about deeds without someone doing something? Screw it*, he said to himself. *I'm going to the bathroom and take a nap.* No great insight came to Joe while visiting the bathroom, as insights often did. So, it was off to bed. First he had to save his work on the computer. "Whoa!" he said out loud as he gazed at the screen. Words he had not typed sat there glittering back at him. "I, by my hand" had been left for him.

"Of course," he said matter-of-factly. "What else could it be?" Inspired by the help apparently left by his heavenly visitor, he sat down and typed until the entire *Book of Bricks* was finished. As he reread it, he realized he remembered none of the text. He knew his hands had done the typing, as if taking dictation, but he was also aware his mind had been in another realm as Michael provided the information. This experience of being present but not aware was an example of the variety of ways Joe interacted with Michael. If he thought he knew the extent of those experiences, he had another

think coming. For Joe was about to see what few men in human history are allowed to see. Perhaps this was Michael's way of preparing Joe for what was yet to come.

As Joe continued to read the finished material, he realized how it worked. It was not a list of shalls and shall nots. There was no idiom of right or wrong. These were simply guideposts humanity could use or not use, piecemeal or *in toto*, depending on where each person was in their journey back to God. A sense of pleasure warmed Joe as he began to understand how people could incorporate these scrolls into their everyday lives without a lot of muss or fuss. Everything in the scrolls affords us the freedom to be who we are. *And there is nothing condemning us for what we are or for what we have and have not done,* he said to himself. *I like this just fine, but it appears to take all the control away from religions. It's like getting an instruction book on how to make our lives work. We can choose to use it or not.* Joe could see how the bricks had great worth to any individual wanting to engage with life in a new way. He wondered what the world would be like if everyone really understood what Michael was offering. Without question, it would be a kinder world, a more loving world, a world where humanity could actually be human. He imagined what it would be like to have a relationship with God based not on judgment or punishment, but a relationship based completely on love, providing us a direction home. No hoops to jump through on the way. *After all*, he asked himself, *why would God make it hard to get back home?*

The words on the computer screen excited him, inspired him. He knew incorporating all this information into his own life would take a while. That was the genuinely nice thing about Joe: He knew his own limits as a man. He took Michael's opening words to heart, telling him that he was just a servant. But he also took the words on the computer screen to heart. They told him not only how he could better his own life, but how he could better the lives of anybody he passed on the street or sat next to in a coffee shop. He thought to himself, *Even though I have a lot of growing to do, I do believe what I see here will allow me to grow closer to my Maker. I just may have to learn to walk before I can run home. The journey may be a little easier knowing that no one is watching over me,*

making sure I'm toeing the line. And I don't have to worry about getting home on time, because I will get there when I get there. Yeah. Isn't this nice? It's like we've been sent out to play, to enjoy this grand adventure we call life.

THE SEARCH FOR THE SEVEN

MICHAEL'S GOODBYE

*A*dages often have a way of being right. Like the one, "You don't know what you have till it's gone." Michael had been right: Kathleen was "about her sums" (angeltalk for getting her act together). In its worst form, lupus is a horribly crippling disease. Striking women nine times more often than men, this incurable autoimmune-system disorder can cover its victims with facial rashes, inflict painful arthritic ailments in the joints, or slowly kill with irreversible heart and kidney damage. Kathleen had suffered through bouts with lupus that she thought would end her life. Now blessed with a reprieve, she had every impetus to help her body recover from physical exhaustion and mental fatigue. But this charismatic woman exhibited an unfortunate habit: sabotaging her own well-being. Rather than seize her good fortune, Kathleen lost herself in overly strenuous exercise and poor eating habits. It did not take long before her sickness returned.

If Kathleen had known ahead of time what heaven had planned for her, perhaps she would have paid more attention to herself. It is odd how we humans, with all our greatness, are so willing to don rags of sackcloth and, with shoulders stooped and

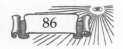

heads hung, stare longingly through frost-laden windows at the Grand Ball in the palace we call Life. We are self-made prisoners of the Cinderella complex. Had Kathleen suspected she was to serve as an example to all of us, she might have abandoned her frosty-windowed view. Angels, like fabled fairy godmothers, are none too willing to bedazzle us with knowledge of our future. For it is the journey itself, and not the destination, which is important. Instead of glass slippers, Kathleen had been given knowledge confirmed by the angel that she was one of the seven master souls who were to show others the way to the Grand Ball. She was her own Prince Charming in search of a path to fit her own footsteps.

Something inside urged her to give Joe a call. Picking up the phone, she stood drenched in sunlight before her living room window. "Hello," came Joe's gravelly voice on the other end. After exchanging chit-chat, the conversation moved in the direction of concern. "Yeah, I got sick again," she confessed. "Joe, sometimes I think you're insane for telling me I'm one of the Seven. I still have no clue what that means exactly. And besides, sometimes I think I'm too screwed up to be a part of this." Oh, how the beautiful Kathleen loved her threadbare sackcloth.

It made Joe ache inside, the way people were so ready to doubt themselves, to devalue their giftedness. He had seen Kathleen at her best: the way she ran her own business, the way she could be so responsible, even inspirational, with people. She walked into a room the way a swan lands on a lake, with a quiet grace that seizes the eye and won't let go. There was no denying Joe's admiration for her professional air, her masterful speaking abilities. "Kathleen," he finally said, "you've got to stop talking that way. Michael has said you're one of the seven master souls. And he wouldn't lie. Besides, you are perfect, whole, and complete just the way you are." This was one of Michael's quotes Joe loved to roll out repeatedly, the way some people love to post the Stars and Stripes on their front porch, holiday or not.

"I know, I know. You keep telling me that. But there is something inside me that's afraid to make a lot of changes. The day I woke up under that tree at the Mexican clinic and felt like my old self, I knew the changes I should make in my life. And I thought,

Maybe I will, maybe I won't. Something inside was afraid that I might lose Kathleen in the process. So when I came home, I didn't engage the changes—because I was afraid—and I wasn't ready. I guess."

"Are you sure you were afraid of losing Kathleen? Maybe it's the other way around. Maybe you're actually afraid of finding the real Kathleen." The pause in conversation reminded Kathleen of a comedian waiting for a laugh line. But she knew this wasn't funny, and she also knew Joe spoke from his heart.

"I don't know what to say, Joe. I don't even know for sure if this Seven thing is going to happen, and neither do you. I know I'm committed to go along with whatever emerges, but I'm not going to do too much about it. Interestingly, since the baptism, I've had this clarity that's never left me. Even though I've tried to ignore it, it's become clear to me that everything in my life has accelerated. All my lessons have accelerated, especially my spiritual lessons. There's something deep within that nags at me, telling me this relapse was a spiritual reminder. And I'm OK with that. It tells me I can do this; I can lick this disease in my own way and in my own time—in spite of screwing up. I will eventually get my spiritual house in order."

It occurred to Joe that the only thing Kathleen needed was to hear herself talk. And he was glad to listen. As the two friends closed their discussion, Joe made sure to bless Kathleen's heart. What else could he do? He knew Kathleen was master of her own fate. Hopefully, she would shed her sackcloth, leave her cinder pile, and take her rightful place in life's palace before a fairy godmother figure had to intervene once again.

Joe had met Kathleen while she was attending one of the courses he taught in human dynamics. Later on, they teamed up to teach a similar class at her own business, and had stayed friends ever since. Joe's employer provided workshops and training sessions for the general public as well as for organizations wanting their employees to receive leadership training or team-building or classes in how to get along with other employees. Joe would eventually find four of the seven master souls through corporate-sponsored activities. Not that Michael had plans to buy stock in the

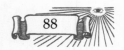

company. It was that people attending these classes and workshops showed up to grow up. They were sincere about investing in themselves, learning more about who they were as human beings.

Too many days had passed since Joe had updated Deb, the friend who had given him the Russian names. During their long years of friendship, Joe had grown to admire Deb as he did Kathleen. Both women wore their beauty in regal fashion—and it was not a beauty which measured only skin deep. Both were capable of extreme kindness and a frank honesty that could sometimes make others fidget. Deb not only worked hard at everything she did, she also displayed tireless compassion and understanding. Gazing at her California-blond hair and sharp clothing or listening to her soft-spoken voice, one was tempted to assume she was as fragile as a glass figurine. But Joe knew better. He had witnessed her in the corporate trenches where she could hold her own against strong opinion or pushy character. She was a delightful paradox to him.

Now that Michael had given Joe *The Book of Bricks*, he felt it was time to let her in on the latest. And besides, he had finally written to her Russian friends in hopes they might be able to connect with the right people who would be interested in finding the Valley of the Star that Michael had revealed. The letter told the story about Michael and his message for the Russians. A letter of introduction asked if the bearer could give the angelic information to those who would do more than simply ignore it. And if they could not find the right people, might they direct Joe to someone who could do something. "Well, I'll just see what happens and take it from there," he had promised cheerfully while sealing the envelope.

Joe loved the twinkle in Deb's eyes whenever he handed her the latest the angel had conveyed. She hugged the printout of *The Book of Bricks* like a mother welcoming her child home from school. The envelope to Russia was another matter. That she handled like a sack of uneaten lunch. *What do I do with it?* her hands seemed to say. "Ya know, my husband thinks the land of the bear might be California instead of Russia."

Joe scratched his head as she rested the envelope on her desk. He couldn't help but wonder if it would ever escape the

patchwork quilt of paper. "Yeah, it could very well be," he told her, "but I got the impression it was a country and not a state. I could be wrong in thinking it was a country, and if nothing comes of it, I'll know I was, in fact, wrong about it."

"How are you doing with all this, Joe? Are you going to be OK if no one believes what you told me?"

"Hey, look," he countered, throwing his head back in comedic fashion, "it is not my job to make people believe. All that I'm supposed to do, so far, is write it down and get it out for people to read."

"Aren't you concerned about what your family and friends might think?" Deb wanted to know if Joe was ready for this. He had wanted her to perform the baptism, which she hadn't, yet. If Joe wasn't ready for what might be coming, how could she be?

"People are going to think what they think, and I am not going to stop doing what I have been told to do. If an angel tells someone to do something, I think it would be wise to follow instructions." A grin angled across her face as she thought about it.

"Would you do me favor? Next time Michael shows up, would you ask him what I am supposed to do?" The truth be known, Deb was in personal conflict. She just knew she was one of the seven people being called forth the moment she read the first of the manuscript from Joe. Her heart had spoken to her, but she did not know if she could trust her heart. Like Kathleen, she didn't really believe she was worthy to consider herself one of the Seven. That was part of the reason she had refrained from doing the baptism. She wanted everything to be perfect because she wanted so much to believe in it. This was a woman who could deal with cold reality like few could, but put an angel in her coat pocket and she'd spend the rest of the day wondering whether she was worthy to wear her own coat.

"Just do it," Joe chided. He loved quoting commercials. "Maybe if you do the baptism you might just be told what to do."

"I'm not sure I'm ready for that," Deb countered. "What if I find out? Then what? I don't think this is any accident that you're sharing this material with me," she added. "But what am I supposed to do with it?"

"There's got to be a reason why I feel so compelled to share this with you. So why don't you just do the baptism and we can both find out. I have to be going now. We'll talk again soon." Joe understood that this phenomenon was scary for Deb. But he also knew that she had to take a leap of faith, just as he had, if she were going to be a part of it all. He dared not tell her how something was already changing in him. That would surely scare her. He understood how newness made people uncomfortable, especially if that newness started being noticed. People might say something like, "What's happened to you?" And if you told them that you were reading transcripts from an angel, well, they just might think you'd lost your mind. They might not speak to you any more. Newness can do that to a person. Never mind that slapping the word "NEW!" on a tube of toothpaste or a box of detergent was a surefire gimmick to get Americans to buy it. But apply the same label on a human being, and people begin to murmur, or wonder out loud, maybe even turn away. It was as though you'd betrayed your friends by daring to grow. Both Deb and Joe had witnessed such behavior around clients who had participated in company workshops and classes. Their friends had grown suspicious of their positive changes. Perhaps it reflected on the old adage, "Misery loves company."

Joe was sympathetic to the concerns expressed by Kathleen and Deb. Why, he was finding himself getting less crazy these days while driving his truck. It was not that people had stopped doing dumb things. Now, instead of cussing and yelling at them, he'd just say, "Bless your heart," and let it go at that. Now that's crazy.

It used to be if someone cut in front of him on the freeway, he'd speed up and pass them leaving a patch of blue smoke. No way they could put one over on him, no-sir-ee. But now it was, "Bless your heart," chalking it all up to their need to be somewhere and not be late. What really would have gotten his relatives to talking was his stopping at yellow lights. Well, mostly stopping, anyway. It was legendary how he could gun his car through an intersection without going airborne. Now, he held open doors for the elderly, women, and children. He even let people behind him get in line first. Even his wife would have wondered about that one.

Watching the evening news was no longer a grumbling match. Whenever he heard about someone being harmed, he'd say, "Bless your heart," and he'd bless the heart of the person who had done the harm as well. These weren't empty gestures. For he could actually feel that something had happened to these people that caused them to resort to violence, to deliberately harm someone else. Yep, if Deb knew all this, she might never read another word from Michael.

Deb's conversation replayed in Joe's mind later that evening. In the middle of a TV rerun, Michael's voice interrupted. "Joe, you are in doubt. The weight of what you do is heavy with you, and you know not how to lessen it." Joe turned to see his angelic friend standing behind him.

"No kidding, Michael," he replied. "I thought I would do what I was told to do, and in return you would see that things go my way. I bust my hump to get work and make a living, but right now, things are slow." Joe's home-renovating business seemed to be suffering from his divided attention. Things were slow, and it bothered him. "It's not like I am asking for the winning lottery numbers or anything like that. Quite frankly, I could use the money.

"And another thing. What about the Seven I am supposed to meet? Just when might this happen? All I've got is one, and she is working her sums out. No one else is in sight, and here I am writing this book for you. Well, maybe there is one other person. But if it's one of the Seven, how will I know? Do I just go up to people and ask them to follow me? Tell them I will make them fishers of men, like Jesus did? Or what?" The angel's eyes were filled with love, watching Joe's emotions pour out. "Sorry about complaining, but do you think you could give me a hand here?"

"What would you have me do? Give you all the work you could handle, give you the lottery numbers you ask for? Why do you ask for these things? Are you poor? Are you hungry? Are you naked? Are you homeless? How much have you been blessed since you said, 'OK, God, do with me what you will?' "

Michael's questions reminded Joe of a time when he did not have a home, did not have a job, and did not have money. The war was over, and his idealism had been shattered by the harshness of

an angered populace that had looked at him with contempt upon his return from Vietnam. He himself had been numbed by watching friends die during the war. His rifle had been exchanged for a Harley-Davidson, and his navy uniform for black leather. His first year back had begun with his living in a hollowed-out giant redwood tree at Big Sur. He had begun to wonder if life was worth living when one day a strange Presence surrounded him. He didn't know what it was, but it was quite like the Presence that had filled him with a sense of well-being on the day the USS Forrestal had been blown up. Yes, he had come a long way since those days right after the war.

Michael continued, "What you have now will eventually seem like what you had then." The angel had read his thoughts. Those days at Big Sur had been lived out of a liquor bottle and the kindness of others—a kindness that would eventually run out. But Michael was speaking of an unending kindness. "God knows what you need and will see that you have it. I promise that money will not be a problem for you and yours. Worry not that your earthly work is slow. For you need it not. Soon this book will be done and you will be about doing God's work on earth. A hundred times your worth will be yours. In spirit and in riches will you prosper all the days of your life. Trust the path you are on."

Michael changed the subject: "You have seen two more of the Seven, and they know you." Joe's mind swept his memories wondering whom the angel meant. It had to be Deb. But who was the other? His wife, Donna? The only other person he had talked to was Mark, a nice guy he knew from the human-dynamics workshops. It could be Mark. For he had already talked to him about the transcript, promising to show him a copy later. "Tell them not to follow you, that you will not make them fishers of men, for that time is past. Tell them, who would hear, to follow that which you teach, and this will make them tillers of souls. I tell you truly, as the farmer tills the soil to open it so that a crop will grow, so shall you and yours open the minds of humanity. Love will grow in the depths of their hearts like a seedling grows into a tree. The crop that has been planted will be raised up to God's light and be gathered in His arms to Paradise.

"You are forgiven your complaining, for it comes easily to your kind. Did not Jesus ask that the bitter cup pass from him? Did not Abraham, Moses, and the prophets complain? You see only the beginning of God's plan, and it is almost overwhelming. Therefore you do not know the all of it, and because of this you complain.

"Go now and ask those around you what they want you to ask me. I will answer that which they need to know. My time is done. Be at peace and teach only love."

As the angel faded away, a strange thought hit Joe: *What if he is really gone? What if he is not coming back? Boy, wouldn't I have something to complain about then?*

A few days later, Joe called Deb, telling her of Michael's appearance. Based upon what the angel had said, Joe felt she was, indeed, one of the Seven. She had to be. She was the only one besides Kathleen who had seen parts of the transcript and knew the particulars, other than Donna. He'd only hinted to Mark what might be happening. The conversation turned once again to the baptism. Deb had planned on doing the baptism over the weekend, but had changed her mind because of the rains. She still wanted everything to be perfect. He decided not to press her any further. With a sense of daring, she asked Joe if he would ask some questions of Michael that she would like answered.

"You know, I feel a bit excited by this, now. It's like I'm a kid in a candy store who can have anything I want, I just don't know where to start."

"Maybe that's how we are all supposed to feel. Wouldn't it be great if everyone could go through life like a child? Being innocent and filled with amazement like children are?" As they hung up, Joe couldn't help but think how much simpler all this would be if Michael would just give him the names of the Seven, and he could simply call them. As he continued to write down the questions he and Deb had discussed, a startling, "What is it you would ask?" boomed in his left ear. Joe jumped three feet straight into the air. In a move that would make a ballerina proud, he managed a half-pirouette before his feet hit the ground again. It was the angel.

"Don't do that, Michael," Joe gasped, trying to catch his breath. "You could give a man a heart attack sneaking up on him

that way. Couldn't you just appear in front of me from now on, so I know you are coming?" There was a bit of a twinkle in the angel's eyes, as if to say, *You fragile humans. Can't an angel have a little fun?* His eyes kept playing with Joe while his lips stayed motionless.

Finally able to breathe normally again, Joe continued, "I have some more questions for you from Donna, Deb, and myself."

Before he could even ask the questions, Michael began, "Tell Donna she worries as if worry brings value. Did I not tell you riches would be set upon you and yours? When it is time for you to take up that which is yours and cross the land to your new home, I will see that you are supplied with means to do so. Those whom she calls 'the children' will live the life they are meant to." Joe knew he was talking about the four mastiffs. "She would do well to believe with all her heart and trust that they are not only in your care, but in God's care, also. God has guaranteed you a place of prominence on earth and in Heaven. She shall not want for herself or the children. Say to her, 'Know you of all this, wife of God's servant, and your headache will be gone. Guide your husband in matters of money, for he cares little for it. A fool he is not. Yet he would lose it all if left alone. Your job in life is to guard him from himself.' "

A funny look hung on Joe's face. He wasn't sure whether he should be offended or not. He decided that the truth was the truth, and continued his questioning. "Deb wanted to know how she could serve God and see that children are cared for and nurtured. What I think she really wants to know is what her purpose is in all this." From the first moment she had read Michael's teachings, Deb felt in her heart that children were to be her calling.

"She knows as well as you that she is one of the Seven. Act not as if this is a mystery to you or her. Had she not heard the call, she would not have to ask. Know also that your third master is with you. Deb will be known as the one who brings light to the souls of children. She will lift the loads that have been placed on them so they may play as a child is meant to do. She will learn what you teach and take it into the world so that a child will hear."

"What do you mean, third master? I count only two unless you mean Donna. Is she one of the seven, and I just didn't see it?"

"Donna is not one of the seven you will teach. She is a master in her own right, and it would do you well to listen to her counsel."

It has to be Mark, he thought. *I'll have to give him a call soon and see what happens.* Joe looked down at his list of questions to see what else he might ask. As was her way, Deb had wanted to share with others the excitement of asking God any question she wanted. However, her excitement had been checked by her inability to let anyone know what was going on with the angel. Wanting her question to be just perfect, she had asked a friend of hers, "If you could ask God any question you wanted, what would it be?" Her friend had been having trouble with her new boyfriend's children, causing the girlfriend to address that particular issue. Having discussed this with Joe, Deb decided it might be a good question to give Michael.

"Deb has this friend who, it seems, lives with a divorced man. The man's kids are telling her and their father that they are living in adultery. Is this so?"

"Within the laws of man, she is," said Michael. "However, according to God, adultery is much different. When God gave to Moses, 'Thou shalt not commit adultery,' He did not give his permission to go whoring. If a husband or wife goes to lie down with another, this is whoring and no bricks are made. Divorce is not adultery in God's eyes. It does not please God that a man or woman stays with one who would abuse them. Abuse is the highest form of adultery, and grounds for divorce. Should a man or woman marry or live as husband and wife with one who has been divorced, this is not adultery."

"What about the other commandments? What are they saying?" Joe questioned.

"The only commandment that humanity should concern itself with is the one Jesus has given: 'Love one another even as I have loved you.' "

"Another thing Deb wanted to know is if I may tell the Seven all you have told me?" Deb and Joe had drunk many coffees while discussing the information that Michael had imparted to Joe.

"You are free to tell all that I have told you, save for the meaning of the *Book of Revelation.* This you will only tell to all seven at once, when they are gathered. They will take this teaching to the world then, and not before."

"One other thing we talked about: Which will be completed first, the Seven or the book?"

"The book shall you finish before the year is out. The Seven shall you have before you are half a hundred in years. I tell you this of the Seven so you alone will know." He then went on to tell Joe events that would happen to him and certain members of the Seven. These situations could not be disclosed until the Seven had gathered.

"What is going to happen with the religions other than Christianity? Like Islam, for example, or Hinduism, or Buddhism? You haven't talked about them?"

"What you will teach is for all faiths, for all have strayed from the truth. Each has had its prophets enlightening the people as to God's word. Even as Mohammed is God's prophet, so are they all. When Mohammed spoke of the infidel, he was speaking of the believers who say they believe and do not. An infidel is not outside of his own religion, but infidels are in each of them. If one seeks the infidel or sinner to enlighten, I say look no further than your reflection in a pond. If you see one there, enlighten him. Should you see none there, you will see none anywhere." Without skipping a beat, Michael turned his attention to another topic, leaving Joe to wonder why.

"I will give a second wonder from God. If you will leave the seas unmolested for two years of your time, God will bring forth such abundance in the sea that it will feed the world till the time of change. If you do not, it is you who fish who will go hungry.

"Go now. Be at peace and teach only love." And with that, the angel vanished.

Joe's mind was weedy with questions. Michael's teachings were a garden of truths to him, blossoming with answers to long-held questions. Yet each teaching stirred his soul like a gardener mulching stale soil. Along with these lush truths, new questions would spring up like weeds. It seemed like a unending cycle. Why had Michael requested that he not speak of the *Book of Revelation?*

For it was there where the real questions persisted like so many weeds. What the angel had shown him was nothing less than stunning. Not to speak of it was like asking a gardener not to pick flowers. Joe began more fully to understand the passage in the Lord's Prayer: "And lead us not into temptation." For it was so tempting to tell others about *Revelation*, the real story.

When Michael next returned, Joe was gazing into his lily pond, his mind on the topic of the *Book of Revelation*, which some call *The Apocalypse*. If people could only know the truth of what he had been told. So why had he been forbidden to speak of this profoundness? "Joe, you are not forbidden to tell," came Michael's voice out of nowhere. He looked in the direction he'd heard the voice, amused how his thoughts were apparently no secret. "However, if you do tell, you will not be heard. The time is not now for this knowledge. Those who would hear are as green as fruits, and would be bitter unless they are ripened on the vine. That which is picked before it is ripe will, no matter how long it stands, stay bitter until it rots. You would not tell a child something that he could not understand or use until he is grown. There is growth taking place in all those you will teach. Let them grow."

"I hear what you are saying, Michael, and I will wait. To what do I owe this visit?" Another question hoping for an answer that would add to Joe's garden of knowledge.

"I come to give you the last and final word of God. You will give this to all nations of the world: **My Lord God honors those who do these works and says: 'Hear you, my children, that you may live joyously and long. War not with your brothers and sisters, for they will be shown the way of peace. Fear not the mighty armies, for in the time to come I will hold them at bay.**

'Replant the lands you have made barren with that which you have taken from them. I will give rain to the lands that have been dry that you may grow food. I will make clean the waters that you have made unclean, as will I the air you breathe and the earth you walk on.

'I will take from you disease and your misshapen bodies so you will be strong. Know that you are loved and will

be with me for all time. For I have made a place for you. Fear not death, for you live forever with me. You are of me. Fear not the words of those who damn you, for those who do so are unenlightened.

'I will call each of you into my arms and bestow the gifts of Paradise upon you all. That which you have earned will be multiplied a thousand times over. That which you have given to those I have sent, though you know them not, will you receive a thousand times a thousand as gift.

'My servant has written the truths for you to see. He will teach his masters but for a little time and then will teach them no more. He will send them into the world and teach other masters to teach. Hear them.

'My words are done. My love is not. Blessed are you all, so says I AM, the Lord God.' "

The angel's words left Joe mesmerized and in need of regaining his composure. By the time his mind had cleared, Michael was gone without another word.

"Michael. Oh, Michael," Joe called out. But there was no answer. "Are you gone? Oh, please don't be gone. There is so much I have to ask you yet. Can you hear me?" Joe's heart pounded with emotion. The thought of losing his celestial companion left an ache in him. "Talk to me if you can hear me, damn it. I need you to tell me ..." His voice dropped off, knowing that Michael was gone. *He could have at least said goodbye.*

Joe sat listening to the water gurgling from the fountain in his lily pond. He felt like he was at funeral for a best friend who had died. His throat cramped as tears meandered down his rough face, falling with a plink into the pond. How could it be over? Would Joe have to wait until he went home to God before he would see his friend again?

Rubbing his nose, his thoughts snapped back to one of Michael's sentences. *Hey, wait a minute. What is this 'I will teach for just a little time'? Does this mean I am going to die?*

"No, Joe, it doesn't mean you are going to die."

"Michael, I thought you were gone forever and I would never see you again."

"All it means is that God has other work for you. You will not see me again until the Seven are together, but you will hear me in your heart. I will guide you in all that you do not know. All you need to do, is listen. My time with you is done. Get that which you have written out into the world. I will be with you and the seven masters soon. And, Joe, one more thing: Goodbye."

With that Michael faded away just as he had the first time Joe saw him. Longing filled Joe's heart. He knew he would miss the presence, the love, the teachings of his heavenly cohort. But at least he would see him later when the Seven were found. There was only one other thing left for Joe to do: to get the message out to the world. And there was no time like the present.

JOURNEYS OF THE MASTERS

*D*EB

Nothing. I hear nothing. She was sure she had done everything right. *Not a darn thing. I've been waiting all this time for* this? Deb reviewed the procedures in her head as they had been given to Joe. The final prayer had been said, a good cabernet wine picked out and poured into a bowl just before sunrise. The sweet smell of fermented grape wafted above what was now holy ground. The baptism was complete. Searching for some kind of sign, Deb turned her head in periscope fashion. *Nothing.* No angels, no sounds, no visions—nothing. All her anticipation, her hope for heavenly direction met with nothing but silence.

Considering how the week had gone, silence was actually not so bad. Of all days to set aside for the baptism, she could find time only on this day: her father-in-law's funeral. Family had gathered, so relatives were occupying the kids, husband, and dogs while Deb focused on her own preparations. She had promised Joe she would "just do it." The funeral was to be held in the afternoon— plenty of time to spend the morning in prayer and meditation. Deb

had always wanted this moment to be perfect, and today was no exception. She had started her morning preparing for the Last Baptism ritual, retreating to the brightness of the master bedroom for silence and prayer. And here she was at high noon sitting in her back yard, having finally completed the baptism, waiting to hear something from the heavens. And ... nothing.

The heat of the sun was turning Deb's hands and feet to purple stickiness. She had a funeral to go to later. *Better hit the shower before this permanently stains my skin.* A short laugh escaped her lips as she envisioned herself at the church with her arms dyed reddish purple. The family was already wondering why she had escaped to the back yard. If truth be told, Deb wished she could have had the whole house to herself. Because the family as a whole needed time to grieve, they assumed Deb was either seeking a quiet place to do the same or prepare herself for the service.

The shower handle squeaked anxiously as the stream of water shot out. Deb loved showers, especially hot showers. In no time at all, steam rose from the jets of water ready to massage and clean her wine-stained body. As she scrubbed away with soap and cloth, she also scrubbed her mind for answers. Why had nothing happened? She had convinced herself that she would hear something: a word, a phrase that would tell her what role she would play as one of the Seven. Certainly it meant a great deal to her that Joe had conveyed the angel Michael's confirmation that she was, indeed, a part of what was for her a heavenly drama. But why through a second party? Why couldn't she be told directly? After all, this mission to carry forth Michael's teachings was serious stuff.

Her stained legs stubbornly resisted the scrubbing, but repeated washings finally yielded clear skin. Deb laughed at herself. What would the family think of her smearing red wine all over herself because of words from an angel? A professional woman like herself in league with angels. The very thought. Ducking her head under the hot stream of water once more, Deb rinsed her hair as if trying to wash away her thoughts. Time to get ready for the funeral.

Stepping out of the shower and into a swirl of steam filling the bathroom, Deb retrieved a towel at the vanity, sneaking a pleased glance from the large wall mirror above it. Deb loved how the six-

foot width of glass filled the bathroom with reflected brightness and a sense of roominess. As she unfolded the towel to dry herself, she watched how her tanned form moved. For a woman in her late thirties, she held her shape rather well, she thought. Exercise was a part of her busy schedule: All things in balance. The lush towel now covered her head, her fingers vigorously massaging her scalp. All of a sudden, she realized why she kept looking at the mirror.

"Wait a minute!" she said out loud, her body frozen in place. She stood suspended in thought for a few seconds before slowly uncovering her head, not unlike a sculptor undraping a new masterpiece. Her stringy, wet hair framed a face full of puzzlement. How come she could see herself in the mirror? Why wasn't it covered in steam like it usually was after she took a shower? The bathroom was full of steam—why not the mirror?

Weird! she thought. *Ah, it must be the warmth of the sunlight. The mirror is probably too warm for condensation.* A silly grin smiled back at her in the mirror. She finished drying herself off and turned to grab a comb to unsnarl her tangles. Her eyes froze, locked on the image in the medicine cabinet mirror hanging on the side wall. Plainly, she could see the reflection of the wall mirror—covered in steam.

What is going on? she asked herself, turning her head back to the main mirror. *What is this?* her mind puzzled as she stood in front of the unfogged wall mirror. Again she turned to the medicine cabinet mirror. And again she saw the reflection of the wall mirror covered with steam. Deb's mouth dropped open as she continued to examine the cabinet mirror. The reflection of the large mirror appeared to have an arc of condensation across the top with a similar arc curving in the opposite direction across the bottom. In between the two arcs was an oval shape. The more she scrutinized the shapes, the more obvious it became that a large eye was shaped on her bathroom mirror.

Shaken by the sight, she stepped back and once again looked directly into the main mirror. And again, she saw nothing but herself. Immediately her mind searched for an explanation. *Of course!* she laughed. It had to be the nanny. She must have cleaned the mirror and somehow left streaks that were accentuated by the steam. A sense of relief touched her for a moment. It still did not explain why the eye could be seen in one mirror but not the other. Nor did it explain satisfactorily why the bathroom was clouded with steam but the main mirror was not.

Deb rotated her head back and forth between the mirrors like a sports fan watching a tennis match. There was no denying it. The eye could be seen in the reflection of the cabinet mirror, but not while looking directly at the vanity mirror. The tennis match over, her body turned statuesque. Only her lips moved. "Don't judge it—just accept it," she said to the shocked person staring back at her. Turning her head one more time to the cabinet mirror, she began to sob. Lightly at first, as she studied the eye on the mirror. Her whole body began to shake with emotion. No matter how hard she tried, she could not stop weeping. A part of her was scared while another part was flooded with awe. The emotional intensity of logic fighting against heart erupted across her body as she shook uncontrollably, tears washing her soul the way the shower had washed her body.

When the shaking subsided, Deb heard her own voice speak, "You'll know when it's time. You'll know what to do."

How odd, she thought. The voice she had wanted to hear in the back yard at the time of the baptism was the voice she heard from herself now. She had her message. And it had emerged from within herself.

That afternoon, as Deb delivered the eulogy at the funeral, a brightness emanated from her countenance. Her words were not perfunctory, nor was her message superficial flattery. She meant every word she had to say to everyone attending. The spirit never dies. Her husband's father simply had gone from one home to another. Life was full of wonder that death could not hide. Deb looked at the congregation the way she saw the eye in the mirror looking at her, the new way she looked at herself. Accepting. Loving. Hopeful.

MARK

There wasn't any real explanation for it. Joe had just always felt that Mark walked arm in arm with the Sacred. He could be counted on to help out at any seminars or workshops he might attend. Trustworthy—that was a word that fit Mark. The guy was always pleasant, talked only when he had something to say, and when he did have something to say, his words flowed with simple charm and warmth. No glibness, no judgment. Joe didn't know why all these notions hit him so strongly on this particular day. But they did. Like some landscaper spellbound by the beauty of an unassuming daisy that had never really been noticed before, Joe stood staring at Mark.

Of course! the voice in his head whispered. And without another thought, Joe walked up to Mark, his hands jammed into the back pockets of his blue jeans, and blurted out, "You going to be home tonight? I'd like to call you and talk about something."

A wiggling grin spread across Mark's cherublike cheeks. With eyes that frolicked as if in a square dance, Mark searched Joe's face, wondering what had brought this on. They had known one another off and on for several years. Mark's quest for personal growth had lured him to many seminars and workshops over the years, even to the point of volunteering at functions where help was needed setting up.

"Sure. I'll be home after eight," Mark said.

That evening the two men conversed about what had gone on in their lives since last they had chatted. It mattered not to Joe that Mark was gay, nor did he see his friend as being any different from himself, even though his Black heritage was the source of some interesting stories. Mark felt he could say pretty much anything he wanted to Joe, and vice-versa.

A short lull in the chit-chat provided Joe the opportunity to change the topic to Michael and what had happened in Joe's bedroom. "There's something I'd like to show you tomorrow at the workshop, if you're open to it." After Mark expressed willingness, the conversation was adjourned until the next day. The two men would meet before the workshops and classes began.

Angels were not a foreign topic to Mark. His Baptist roots had provided him a strong religious foundation that had not crumbled when he "came out" to himself. Like many who walked in Mark's shoes, the path of religion was replaced by the broader path of spirituality. There was no reason, in Mark's mind, to disown those who might disown him: friends or relatives who continued to walk the straight and narrow. For Mark's path had plenty of room for others. As he had grown older, he found himself repeatedly able to embrace opposing views, opposing groups, and opposing philosophies, as if he were a human bridge capable of connecting islands of people.

The following morning, Joe flagged down Mark on his way to set up one of the conference rooms. "Here's what I'd like you to read," Joe said, stuffing the computer printout containing the story of Michael and *The Book of Bricks* into Mark's chest. "Let me know what you think of it."

"OK," he consented. "But I have to tell you I don't read too well. Dyslexia. It may take me a while."

"No kiddin'," beamed Joe. "We share the same affliction. I'm dyslexic as well. You can take all the time you need. You're gonna be here the whole week. Right?"

"Actually, I am," Mark's eyes twinkled back. *What is this all about?* he wondered. Joe had to get going with his class. He patted his cohort on the back and took off, trusting he would wade through the story when he could.

Three days later, Joe spied Mark at the conference. As he approached, his friend seemed to wear a question mark on his face. "You get a chance to read the manuscript?" Joe asked without a hello or a hi, how are you.

"Actually, I did finish reading it. Once I started, I couldn't quit. Is the reason for asking me to read it because you think I'm one of the seven souls?"

"Do you feel you are one of the Seven? Does it speak to you?"

"I have to tell you, it *really* spoke to me. The ideas, the words, the mission, all make sense to me."

"So, you get it. Good," said Joe. "I tell you what: Have you done the baptism yet?"

"No, not yet," Mark admitted.

"Why don't you do the baptism, and we'll take it from there."

"Can I keep the printout?"

"Be my guest," Joe gestured with his right arm like a waiter at a restaurant. A twinge of excitement gurgled up within him. He now knew for sure that Mark was the third of the Seven. *This went nicely*, he said to himself.

Like those before him, Mark took his time doing the baptism. He wanted it to be a special event and decided the day to set out the bowl of wine would be Christmas Day. Company had been invited over for Christmas Eve, the bottle of wine set aside for the following morning. As the evening wore on, one of Mark's friends spotted the bottle sitting in the bowl.

"Hey, Mark. Christmas cheer?"

"Uh, no, it's not for what you think." How was he going to explain this? Choirs of angels appearing to the babe in Bethlehem was one thing, but angels appearing in 1994 was quite another matter.

"What's it for?" the friend asked, holding the bottle up to the light to see if anything was inside besides wine. No dead worm in it, like his favorite brand of tequila.

"It's for a spiritual ceremony I'm doing tomorrow."

"Cool," his friend concluded, returning the bottle to its resting place. Mark's eyes rolled in relief. *How are people ever going to understand this stuff?* he asked himself.

The next morning Mark set out the bowl of wine to begin his Christmas Day. Presents were then unwrapped, phone calls made to friends and relatives, and the Last Baptism performed at high noon. Mark had no expectations of seeing angels or visions or of hearing heavenly choirs grace his presence. To Mark, this sacred moment was simply to be cherished. As the baptismal prayer of commitment was finished, however, a sense of knowingness flooded through him. He felt the rightness, the clarity of why this ceremony needed to be done and of why he would live out the

messages given to humankind by the angel. Over the coming weeks, Mark would come to realize that this day was the beginning of a new spiritual journey. To dedicate himself on the birthday of Christ to a new message from Heaven was a reward that could only be appreciated in the most sublime of ways. Blessing people's hearts, living out the guidelines of the scrolls, all this bathed him in a wondrous love. And that kind of love changes a man, makes him more aware of kindness in the world, kindness seeking to flood forth from people, kindness that sweeps away polarization and suspicion. There was little doubt in Mark he had, indeed, been called by Heaven to bridge walls, serve the least as well as the greatest, and quietly span distances over troubled waters. This Christmas Day was meant for him.

"So, did you do the baptism?" It was Joe, calling to wish Mark a Merry Christmas.

"Yeeeeees," Mark sang back, as if rehearsing a line for one of his opera performances.

"Good. Let's go out for a coffee or something and talk. You up for that?"

"I wouldn't mind that. When and where?" Joe loved coffee the way some people love breathing. He was anxious to hear Mark's take on all that had happened with Michael. He knew Mark would be no different from Deb or Kathleen in wanting to know what these seven people were actually going to end up doing. The truth of the matter was that Joe didn't have a clue. He was hoping that the seven master souls would somehow tell him. When Michael departed, he had left only a clue as to what might happen—a clue with no directions.

"Mark," Joe began while hugging his cup of coffee as if it were an extension of his hands, "you're an opera singer, a taxicab driver, and a travel agent?"

"Yes, that's right. I tend to have a busy life. All three jobs allow me to enjoy people in different ways. With opera, I get to use my voice to bring joy to people. In my taxi, I meet all kinds of

different people with different stories. And some would make your hair curl. I love to bring people together on cruises or plane trips to different lands, so they can escape their drudgery and have a chance to find themselves again. I have a blessed life."

"If you were like me, dyslexia wasn't such a blessing."

Mark chuckled as he raised his cup. "Maybe once upon a time. But, yes, those former times were humiliating and troublesome. Everyone thought I was stupid because I had such trouble reading. The shame I endured is not something I would wish on anyone. In fact, it was worse dealing with dyslexia than it was dealing with being gay. In some parts of Black society, being gay amounts to betrayal of family or manhood. But being dyslexic is almost more shameful, 'cuz you're made out to be something you're not. It's difficult trying to find pride in being thought stupid. But I can find pride in being gay. It's tough having to convince yourself, let alone others, that you aren't dumb, that you have talents and gifts, but in different ways than others."

Joe nodded knowingly. "You're still active in your church, aren't you? Isn't that kinda tough?"

"In a way, yes. In a way, no. My mom's church is an interesting story. This is a Baptist church, and I never really liked it as a kid. There's never a sense of a real message for people to hear. I go because I feel that I've been drawn there to teach or to help in some way."

Not too long ago, Mark had put together a travel package to Atlanta for the members of the church. Because of his efforts he became friends with the church administrator. Casually talking with her the Friday night before everyone was scheduled to leave, the subject of gay people in the church had come up.

"Oh, there are a lot of gay people in our church," she had volunteered. "Yes, there are. And they don't think that people know."

Is she trying to say something to me? Mark had asked himself. And then she repeated it. *OK, I'm not going to touch this*, he had decided.

Mark went on to tell Joe how the two of them had sat next to one another on the flight back from Atlanta, how she brought up

the topic of gays in the church once again. "So I basically told her I was gay. And she said, 'Well, why did you think I didn't know that?' "

Joe smiled at hearing this. He had given up long ago trying to figure out who was gay and who wasn't. He'd known straight men with enough kids to form a basketball team who you'd swear were gay. And then he'd known gay guys so straight-acting you'd bet your paycheck they had eyes for every skirt that passed by.

The real issue had come forward when Mark responded to the administrator, "Well, like ... the church doesn't accept this. So gay people in the church don't feel accepted. They don't feel that they can come out and be accepted." And, the administrator had to admit, "Well, it's true, the church doesn't accept it!"

Mark had countered, "There's something wrong with that, then. There's a problem there." In response, she had asked Mark if he wanted to be on the church HIV Committee. "What's wrong with this picture?" Mark felt compelled to ask. Not waiting for a reply, he pursued his thought, "It's fine to have me work on a committee that tries to help those with AIDS, but what about the bigger issue? The gay issue still needs to be addressed."

Her reply had been, "What do you think is going to happen if we have a roll call? Who's going to show up if I ask for a church discussion on this?"

"How could I answer that?" Mark asked Joe. "Because what I've seen in the church—especially the Black church—is that there are *so* many gay people in the church. I mean it's full of them, but no one comes out. They live in glass closets."

"Kind of like you were doing?" Joe decided to ask.

"I never really went to church. I just tried to help out whenever I could. With this trip to Atlanta, I just sort of showed up again. But ... I mean ... I guess so—yeah. So everyone lives in glass closets. But then she shocks me by telling me there are married men in the church who are gay, too. And I'm sitting there with my mouth hanging open. And I'm, like, 'How do you know that?' " Mark laughed out loud remembering the scene. He reached over to dab at a small coffee spill. " 'Give me some hints!' I asked her. 'How do you know?' It was just really interesting that she was able to pick

out many of the gay people in the church who I knew were gay. She's right, of course. There are a lot of bi men. A lot. It's quite amazing, actually. At one time I thought it was the other way around—just a few bi men compared to all the gay men. I've come to learn that it's not true. I've also come to learn that more and more people know what's going on even if you don't tell them. People don't want anyone to mention these issues, because that may mean they'll have to deal with them." Mark looked up at Joe, who was taking all of this in. The more he listened to Mark, the more fortunate he felt to have him as one of the Seven.

"I know what you're saying," Joe finally said. "We seem to be a nation in denial. Rather than face our problems, we'd rather sweep them under the carpet."

"You're absolutely right," Mark acknowledged. "Reminds me of an incident in my Freemason lodge. Not too many people know this, but there used to be separate lodges for Blacks. The lodge for Blacks was known as the Prince Hall Lodge. I didn't even know that when I became a Freemason. A high-school counselor suggested I go into DeMolay after finishing Boy Scouts as an Eagle Scout. He saw how much I enjoyed working as a leader in Boy Scouts, and felt I could pursue my talents in DeMolay. From DeMolay, where I did very well, I moved into the Freemasons. I was elevated to master of my lodge and ended up representing my lodge at the Grand Lodge, where policy changes are voted on. I'm proud to say that I spoke before the Grand Lodge when the issue came up for bringing the Prince Hall Lodge into common fellowship with the Freemasons. It passed overwhelmingly. It was as if I had been prepared for that moment.

"Years earlier, when I was eighteen—1981 or '82, I believe— I had gone to DeMolay camp at Greeley, Colorado, near Denver. When I arrived, I realized I was the only Black to attend the camp. Apparently there had been another DeMolay camp where Black members typically attended. I didn't know this, and had insisted on going to Colorado because it seemed like a fun place to go. I'd only known San Francisco for most of my life. So when camp started, the camp administrator seemed rather uncomfortable, always asking me if anything was wrong, had I been treated well, telling me I could

come to him if I had any problems. There were 300 kids and leaders in camp, and I guess he was concerned I might get mistreated or hassled. Subgroups were set up, made up of ten to twelve guys and an adult supervisor. The supervisor of my group was a young police officer by trade. The first thing he did was get the guys in our group to talk about race and anything else that might be bothering us. It went great. We bonded right away. It didn't take a rocket scientist to figure out that we began to shine as a group within the camp. We were always having a good time, but also always respecting one another. The same could not be said for other groups, some who got in trouble with their rough-housing, or staying up late, or trying to prove their manhood. I was having such a good time with my group that I made up a song about them and sang it to the guys. It became our camp song."

"Somehow, I could just picture you in your prime, using music to bring people together," Joe said. "It amazes me, Mark, how you have this natural sense about you, this natural ability to dissolve barriers, bring people together."

"Thanks, Joe. But it didn't end there. The last day of camp was a day-long general meeting. And here I was, this eighteen-year-old kid going up and talking with one of the camp leaders, asking if my presence, my being the only Black man, could be brought up at the general meeting. I felt the tension needed to be broken. The camp leaders were a bit nervous about it. So I decided to give the system a little help. One of the rules of the camp was if you lost your name badge, you had to sing in front of the camp at lunch. And ... gee ... clumsy me ... lost my badge. Standing up in front of the whole camp and singing the most humorous song I could think of did the trick. Let me see. I think the name of the song was something like 'She Waded in the Water and She Got Her Mmm All Wet.' After that, lots of the other guys in camp came up and started talking with me, asking me questions. Did I come from an all-Black DeMolay—no such thing. What kinds of projects did our organization sponsor? How well was it received? That afternoon, the topic of bringing more Black kids into DeMolay was brought up at the general meeting. It made everybody uncomfortable. But so what. DeMolay is supposed to be all about brotherhood. And it's

good to do more than spout off about it. We need to live it. Nothing was resolved at that general meeting, but at least the ice was broken. And I believe that set the stage for the overall passage at the Grand Lodge years later for inclusion of Prince Hall as part of Freemasonry. It was the right thing to do, and I am only too glad to have been a part of it."

This would not be the last time Joe would hear about Mark's efforts at breaking down walls. And it would not be last time Joe would marvel about this incredibly gentle man who had the strength to pass through roadblocks with nothing more than a kind word. This dyslexic, gay, Black man was perfect as one of the master souls. Joe could easily see why Heaven had called him forth.

STEVE

Joe's lily pond was like an old friend who always listened. On this day he felt a bit melancholy as the pond reminded him of Michael. How Joe longed for his angelic sidekick. What was he to do next now that Mark had joined Kathleen and Deb? Four more masters needed to be found. Where should he start looking? He didn't have a clue.

That night, Joe logged on to the Internet and signed into America Online (AOL). He wasn't much in the mood for chat, so he decided to hang out in one of the electronic chat rooms and watch as conversation scrolled across his screen. It proved uninteresting to him. *Let's try another room; perhaps something with a spiritual angle to it.* As he entered the room, three others were already engaged in a conversation about healing and the ability to read people psychically. A small grin suspended across Joe's face as he eavesdropped. One of the participants, Light_Touch, caught his attention right away. The other two onliners were pumping the third for answers about how diseases occur and whether "the light" he was talking about could be accessed by anyone. Light_Touch seemed to enjoy the barrage of questions and challenges as his words zipped across the screen faster than Joe could read. The

more Joe watched, the more he realized Light_Touch was echoing some of the same concepts Michael had told him. *I've got to get to know this guy*, Joe said to himself, gulping down coffee. Carefully wording a message that would not say too much or too little, Joe zapped an Instant Message from his computer to Light_Touch that only he would see. Watching his screen for a response, Joe noticed a pause in the words flowing across his computer screen. Apparently Light_Touch had read the message. Could a response be far behind? Two more gulps of coffee passed before the chiming sound on Joe's computer announced an Instant Message back. It was Light_Touch. A gurgling laugh rumbled out of Joe like fresh water from an artesian well. It had begun. Joe was in pursuit of the fourth master soul.

Like a fly fisherman teasing a brook trout, Joe mentioned bits and pieces of what had happened to him, feeding Light_Touch segments of what Michael had given, watching to see how the respondent would react. Each nibble seemed to engage both men more deeply. "Take a look at this," Joe typed as fast as his mumbledy-peg fingers could stab at the keys. A copy and paste from one of the "Michael files" saved away on his disk drive transferred several quotes, one after the other, in Light_Touch's direction. There was a wait. Then a computerized chime, followed by, "We've got to talk." Joe erupted with a loud "Hah! You bet we do." His fingers searched for the keys as he directed Light_Touch to the Web site where Joe had excerpts of Michael's teachings. "Read what is there, and then let's talk again." Joe asked his new computer friend to e-mail him after he had visited the Web site.

As he turned off his computer screen for the evening, a sense of relief filled Joe. He could quit worrying. A heavenly conspiracy obviously was in place. All he had to do was not get in the way. He would patiently wait to hear from Light_Touch. It would take only a day before Joe found out that Light_Touch's real name was Steve. His e-mail was direct and to the point. "I'm in," it started. And from that point forward, Steve was dedicated to doing whatever was necessary to bring forth Michael's teachings. With a directness Joe was not accustomed to, Steve provided further details on the modalities he used in his healing arts. Joe read these remarks

with a grain of salt. *Well, that's interesting,* was the limit of his response. After all, what comments could Joe make to others when he himself was hoping they'd believe his story that an angel had materialized in his bedroom? Steve seemed to have no problem with such a tale. There were several messages back and forth regarding how many masters had come forth and whether Steve was one of them. Like the rest, Joe encouraged him to do the Last Baptism. One week later, Joe got a phone call from Steve.

After formalities were exchanged, Steve dove right into the topic both men were waiting to discuss. "I want you to know, Joe, that I now know I am one of the Seven. I don't know what I'm supposed to do, but you can count on me 100 percent for whatever it is I need to do."

Joe breathed easier. "That's fantastic, Steve. Something in me knew you were one of the Seven, also. To tell you the truth, though, there isn't much for us to do until all seven of the masters have come forth. Michael mentioned something about a gathering, but I'm not sure what he was talking about."

"I can wait," Steve volunteered. "I'm totally committed. I want you to know that. You can count on me." If only Steve had known what would be required of him in the future, he might not have been so enthused. For there is a passage in Scripture that states, "From those to whom much is given much is expected." And Steve had been given a special gift.

Joe decided to carry the conversation over to another subject. "So, Steve, what happened with your baptism? Do you mind telling me about that?"

"Not at all," he said, clearing his throat. Emotion was already starting to invade his voice. "I was looking for a day when I would have some privacy, and asked for that in my prayers. A few days ago, my partner was called away on assignment, leaving the house all to myself. She thought it was a bit odd that she had been given so little notice to make this trip. But I had to smile to myself.

"It was completely overcast when I set the wine out before sunrise. Kind of chilly out. After pouring the wine into the bowl, I sat for a while praying for protection. The five hours of fasting presented a problem to me because of my diabetes."

"Hell, Steve, your health comes first. You could have forgone that." Joe always wondered why healers have the capacity to help others, but rarely have the capacity to help themselves. Diabetes was a serious disease which requires stable blood sugar levels. Joe knew that Michael would not require someone to put himself in danger as part of the baptism.

"I know, I know," admitted Steve. "But I wanted to participate fully in the instructions Michael left. So I prayed throughout the morning, 'Lord, please protect me.' I checked my blood sugar halfway through the morning and it was right where it needed to be. I was doing fine. After that I turned the phones off and stayed in meditation. At the appointed hour, I went out back and did the ceremony. As I started washing myself with the wine, the sun broke through. It was the darnedest thing. Had been chilly and gray all morning. As I finished the prayer for guidance, I started getting hot, real fast. I looked up and said 'WOW!' in capital letters. Three-foot high capital letters. The hotness enveloped me while I stayed in prayer. My whole body was hot, not just the parts exposed to the sun. Something was going on within me. It was great. Almost half an hour I stayed there. I got up off my knees, went inside, washed myself, and turned the phones back on. Almost immediately the phone rang. It was my company asking me to come into work. Good timing."

"So how'd you feel after that? I mean, besides the fact that you knew you had to be one of the Seven Michael wanted me to find? You'll have to pardon me. I want to know as much as possible what happens to you guys. I keep hearing different things happening to different people. Makes me realize how different you four are."

"Well, I believe I had what might be called a delayed reaction," Steve decided to confess. "Something happened two days later. It was like I was a different person. At first, that kind of bothered me. But after I did some healing work on a friend of mine, I realized that even the healing energy that flows through me was different. Something's changed. It's more powerful, more pronounced. And people notice it. It left me wondering about what I need to do with my life. I have a job and all. But I'd like healing

to be my real job. I'd like to be able to make a living at it. But how? What do I do?"

There was a pregnant silence on the line. "Well, ya know, Steve, there's only one person that can answer that. And it's you."

This would not be the last time the topic of avocation versus vocation would come up in discussions between the two men. Over the following months, Joe would come to respect Steve's gift. The two men would visit with one another and Joe would watch as Steve worked on people. Steve felt changed in more ways than one by committing himself to Michael's teachings. More and more, an awareness of the fabric of life that extends from one human to another, from humanity to all of life, touched his soul. Although his relationship with Joe had started out on a computer screen, he would grow to become close friends with this servant of God, who talked with an angel named Michael. Steve's life was no ordinary life. Perhaps it was never meant to be. As much as Steve loved having these marvelous events open him up, little did he know he would be destined for changes even he could not foretell. Perhaps Joe should have warned him or at least discussed with him that much is expected from those to whom much is given—both by heaven and by humanity. But even Joe did not fully understand the magnificent process unfolding as the seven master souls began their journeys toward one another.

SHARI

On an occasion or two, Joe had noticed Michael display what could only be construed as a sense of humor. It made him wonder if this whimsy was indicative of I AM as well—that Heaven possessed what humans might consider a divine funny bone. It had taken discipline on Joe's part not to burst out laughing when Michael asked him—a dyslexic—to write a book. What he did not know was that he would not be the only paradox in the making. He was about to discover another.

Over the passing months, Joe constantly scouted for anyone who might drop out of the sky with a sign attached to their back—

"I'm the fifth. Come and get me!" Something caught Joe's eye at one of the week-long corporate conferences. The fascination started at one of his sessions when a classy blond woman named Jennifer announced during the introductions that she was a lesbian. "And I'm here with my life-partner, Shari." Every head turned as Shari rose as slowly as a dawning sun, her six-feet-plus stretching above the sitting crowd. With head bowed slightly, as if in prayer, Shari waved politely, even shyly, her soft, low voice forcing out a "Hi." She looked as though she could qualify as one of the legendary Amazons, except her demeanor and gentleness draped over her a bit clumsily. She was a pussycat hiding in a mountain lion's body. Joe figured she could arm wrestle, if not throw, any guy in the room. The more he listened, the more curious he became. Shari had converted to Buddhism where love for all and her desire for personal, spiritual freedom could escape the constraints of Judaism. Jennifer's entrance into her life had added to her self-discovery on many levels, both women seeing no reason why love such as theirs should be hidden or stifled, even in public.

After comparing notes with Mark, who was helping out, Joe found a quiet moment to introduce himself to the two women. The more he heard from them during the remainder of the week, the more drawn he was to share Michael's teachings with these two dynamic people. It turned out that Shari was a free-lance photographer who was also into meditation and chanting. Her curiosity and questioning of what Joe had to say contrasted with Jennifer's watchfulness and careful declarations. Before the conference was over, Joe had placed a copy of the manuscript in Jennifer's hands, not knowing that Shari would snatch the document to her bosom the first night home.

As her eyes traveled over the angel's words regarding gays and lesbians, a rush of nervous warmth flowed through her. *Hmmm*, she said to herself, *Why did you give this to me, Joe?* Her eyes became a lioness hunting the text for more words of truth. The inner hunger gnawed at her. She might have stayed up all night had not sleep ended the pursuit.

Finally, during phone calls back and forth between Joe and Shari, she opened her soul even more, to the point where she drove

over to Joe's house for a long talk. When their cascade of words fell silent, her eyes were cold with intent, as big as two full moons against the darkness of her hair. She wanted nothing less than the truth. "I really feel I'm supposed to do this, but I don't know where or how I fit in, with my Buddhist background and all. I don't want to give up my Buddhist teachings or my Buddhist practices."

A broad smile invaded Joe's face. This was the first time anyone had taken Michael's teachings so seriously as to think of them as a way of life, a set of disciplines. *What a spiritual warrior you are*, thought Joe. Clearing his throat with a swig of espresso, he spoke deliberately. "You don't have to give up anything, Shari. Michael's teachings aren't asking you to give up anything or to replace anything. It's a kind of enhancement to whatever path you're already on."

After thinking about it for a minute, Shari came right out and asked, "Do you think I am one of the Seven? And if so, what am I supposed to do?"

"I don't know if you are the fifth of the seven masters. Only you will know that. And if you find out you are one of the seven master souls, then there's going to come a time after I've gathered all seven when I will teach the Seven to teach. And *what* I'm going to give them, *how* I'm going to teach them, I have no idea. Michael hasn't told me that yet."

Like those before her, Shari decided the Last Baptism would be the deciding factor. She and Jennifer traveled into the desert to a friend's house. And on the day of the summer solstice, both chanted, prayed, and meditated until the sun reached its zenith. By sunset, Shari knew she had been called to carry forth Michael's teachings. Jennifer would bless her efforts but not join in them. The love they had for one another was like a fortress, and within that fortress would reside their spiritually parallel worlds. Shari could dare to venture outside this safe haven to explore new worlds. Because of this safe oasis for the heart, Shari the pussycat would soon discover that she could open fully to the power of the mountain lion. It meant that she, as a woman, as a lesbian, as a spiritual teacher, would have to recognize and embrace all of herself as she had already embraced all others.

BEN

    If the Internet had worked once, why not again? Joe was growing restless wondering whether the sixth master would show. By process of elimination, he knew the last two of the seven had to be men, since all three woman were already in place. Nights at his computer, pecking away his keyboard, proved fruitless. Steve provided moral support with a faithful stream of e-mails, asking if it might be better if others joined in the search. "Sure," was Joe's response. Michael had said nothing about who had to find these people; they simply had to be found. With typical dedication, Steve also began mining the Internet. Several conversations were started, and over a year's time, one person in particular seemed to stand out. His screen name was Music_Man, but he later told Steve his real name was Ben. In personal e-mail, their conversations turned more inward, more spiritual, more personal. Messages flew back and forth between the two men, Ben inventing more questions than Steve had answers for. As the friendship grew over time, Steve found out that Ben worked on the World Wide Web for a living, usually creating website pages for clients who contracted with the company that employed him. Oddly enough, Ben was not a techno-nerd by profession. His master's degree was in music, specializing in piano and French horn. Several nights a week he played for the Community Orchestra, conducted a church choir, or played organ at the Jewish temple. Ben was one of the most talented and unusual men Steve had ever conversed with. Eloquent, joyful, and witty, he constantly bounced between extremes.

    Even though baptized as a Baptist, Ben chose to honor the Jewish heritage he inherited from his father. Through his own efforts he studied Judaism, and in his own inclusive way practiced Judaism as a Christian. Although few might understand his capacity to pull off such a melding of two poles of religious thought, Steve easily recognized Ben's ability to walk as a living example in both camps. He saw in his friend the kind of love that knows no bounds, the

kind of love that could span from one end of the cosmos to the other. His friend seemed to relish the dualities of humankind. Perhaps it was his way of displaying his own belief that dualities, for all practical purposes, are manmade illusions. Ben could talk hi-tech one night and high spirituality the next. He could provoke Steve into thunderous laughter with his tongue-in-cheek anecdotes. Yet, there were those other times when Steve nearly wept for him. At times, Ben's personal life mimicked a Shakespearean tragedy. For those who sometimes love too much, such tragedies are a part of life. And Ben seemed to understand even that paradox. Consequently, nothing could sway Ben from his own journeys in pursuit of enlightenment. Yet, the greater the light that shone in his life and in his heart, the greater the shadows that formed in his personal life. Over ensuing months, long letters back and forth between the two men fostered a growing friendship that would eventually escort Ben to Joe's e-mail address.

```
e-mail:  Joe Crane
from:    Music_Man
subject:  Hellos & Halos

Dear Joe,

Steve has suggested I write you about the friends you
pick up in the oddest of places. He tells me that only
you could make friends with a perfect stranger showing
up in your bedroom while your wife is sleeping beside
you. However, I try to remind him that I could display
remarkable courage with 700 pounds of fanged dog meat
standing guard next to me.   :)

Over this last year, Steve and I have corresponded back
and forth. At his suggestion, I have read your "Book
of Bricks" and have performed the baptism. It has taken
me a while to come to this conclusion (good things take
time), but I do believe I might be one of your Seven.
Now that I've said that, I feel like running to the
nearest cave and hiding in it.
```

Ben's letter went on, giving Joe a brief description of his spiritual path and the many directions it had taken. His latest path had been in the realm of healing energy, in which Ben was studying to become a Reiki master, a healing discipline requiring its students to learn how to tap into the Universal, the Source, the Oneness of love that heals all. He and Steve had involved themselves in long discussions regarding Steve's own healing techniques, which also incorporated Reiki modalities, among others. Ben felt his spiritual journey was ready for the next step. And, like the others Joe had worked with, Ben wanted to know what was the next step.

During the past year, Joe had heard from several others. Like Ben, they had expressed an interest in being considered one of the Seven, but in the end, after doing the baptism, found themselves called to other tasks, or felt this journey was ultimately not theirs. Something about Ben appealed to Joe. So, without hesitation, he pounded at his computer keyboard, sending a response.

```
e-mail:  Music_Man
from:    Joe Crane
subject: Steps

Dear Ben,

I am pleased to hear from you. You asked what the next
steps were. The truth of the matter is that I don't
know. The angel only told me to find seven master
souls, and then to gather them. Until I find the seven
souls, I'm not sure what is going to take place. Steve
has sent me a few messages over the past months about
you. It's a pleasure to finally meet you one on one.

I guess what I'd like to find out, is what happened
with your baptism, your reaction to it, and how you
felt afterwards. Then perhaps we can discuss where to
go from there.

Bless your heart,

Joe Crane
```

The engagement had begun. Over the ensuing week e-mail flew back and forth between the two men. Joe observed carefully the trust that Ben walked with, the tenderness of his heart, the innocence of his spiritual path. One particular e-mail that told Joe Ben was, indeed, one of the Seven. It was more than e-mail, it was a confession of the soul, an outpouring of human wonder.

```
e-mail:   Joe Crane
from:     Music_Man
subject:  Holes and Wholes

Dear Joe,
```

It hasn't been an easy year for me. Things at home, my emotional life, my professional life, were not stable or gratifying—for various reasons. I was working in a place that did not want me. They made it very well known. I'm a very creative person; I was not doing creative work. Also, I had no sanctuary, neither at home nor at work. There was no place for me to be me. However, I've been involved with spiritual studies for the last 15 years—in fact, I don't know when I WASN'T spiritual. I worked at a place where I had an office cubbyhole ... a "cubby space" we called it. And the person next to me was not always aware of how he affected everybody else in the office—he was very loud. He would play sound bytes on his computer very loud. He was annoying and disturbing, and I'm supposed to be dealing with customers.

One day, I got an e-mail from Steve. Basically, the e-mail said, "You need to read this book. Here is the URL on the World Wide Web. I've talked to Joe, and I think you are one of the Seven. Are you?" That's all it said. Right there, I felt something within me, and went straight to the website. It was your book about Michael and the scrolls he had given you. As I was reading it, I had this love-rush, which told me I needed to keep on reading. About that time, the nerd next to me started blasting out one of his sound bytes on his computer. It was the "Theme from the Magnificent Seven." When I first heard it, I thought, "Oh, the

theme song from the Marlboro Man commercial." Having
a second thought, I remembered our orchestra had just
played that piece. It was the "Theme from the Magnificent
Seven." I reread Steve's comment about being one of the
Seven, and thought, 'Maybe I am. Whatever the Seven
are.'

Not wanting to take work time to finish the book, I
downloaded a few chapters to my computer; took them
with me to lunch. I couldn't put it down. Kept missing
my mouth with food. When I got to the chapter about
the baptism itself, I knew that this was something I
needed to do. It made sense with all my other spiritual
studies.

After downloading the rest of the document, Ben finished
the entire manuscript that night and into the next day. The more he
read, the more he wanted to read. He was transfixed by everything
that tugged at his soul. A quick e-mail was sent out to Steve
thanking him profusely for leading him to this wondrous book of
teachings. He could not yet answer Steve's question as to whether
he was one of the Seven. He needed to perform the ceremony with
the wine, first.

I had decided I HAD to do the baptism. But, being the
thinker I am, realizing that this was October with the
first snow already on the ground, I kept finding
reasons why I couldn't do it. After all, I live on the
second floor of an apartment complex with residents all
around. No privacy. The balcony wouldn't work as
'ground' or 'earth.' If I put a bowl of wine out in
another person's yard or in a park, it could be stolen.
Wine wouldn't last long if one of the indigents found
it. You get the idea. I had no sanctuary.

Like Steve, Ben wanted to be able to enter fully into the
sacred ritual spoken of by the angel. But Ben held several jobs.
Doing the baptism during the week was out of the question because
of work constraints. And on Saturdays he played organ at temple,
including bar mitzvah services in the morning. Sundays were
usually taken up with obligations with the symphony or

Freemasonry functions or traveling to see relatives. There was no way he felt he could tell his wife what he was about to do, so he could not sit down and ask for a day to himself. Before he knew it, Thanksgiving had rolled around. The weather was now fully into winter. All of October had hovered around zero degrees. And November was not much better. The Thanksgiving holiday provided a window of opportunity which Ben kept eyeing.

As it turned out, because Thanksgiving is on Thursdays, an interesting scenario began to develop. My wife and I joined the rest of my family in Southern Illinois. When my obligations drew me back to town to play for services on Friday night and Saturday morning ... well, I knew this would be the only time I would be alone.

Saturday morning turned out to be a warm front—-it was 23 degrees. So after Friday night services, I returned to my somewhat empty apartment complex to find a place to do the baptism in private. In one of the commons areas, there was open space, almost a field with some bushes in one section. I realized I could hide the bowl of wine in the bushes. It wouldn't get full sunlight, but it would get enough for me to do the baptism. The next morning, I got up at dawn, carried the wine and the bowl, with a flashlight in the other hand, a quarter mile (it's a huge apartment complex) to the open area, and left the bowl of wine there. I looked around knowing it would be safe from man and weather. Any other day the wine would have frozen completely before the washing.

I returned to the apartment for quiet time, prayer and meditation before heading off to play at the bar mitzvah. This was a holy day for me, having all of God's services in my hands as well as squeezing in time for the baptism. I got back from the morning services, put on my sweat pants and tank top so I could wash my arms and legs without too much trouble. With a light windbreaker covering me, I stepped outside and ran to the spot where I had left the bowl of wine. If you could have seen me you would have laughed. Thank God no one did see me. Some weirdo, scurrying across the

commons in sweats and into the bushes is enough reason
to call the cops.   I breathed a sigh of relief once I
reached the bowl, being thankful it had not been
removed or stolen.   I quickly looked around to see if
anyone could see me as I started removing my jacket and
shoes.   I tried to think of the sacredness of the
moment, but could not stop myself from visualizing some
neighbor's relative peering out the window and asking
cousin Myrtle what this guy was doing over in the
bushes.   Thank God for football.   Nobody was looking
out any windows. Probably glued to the TV set.

I should have been chilled to the bone as I started the
washing ceremony, but I wasn't.   A welcome warmth
completely surrounded me.   Of course the wine was
freezing cold, but my body didn't react to it.   After
saying the thanksgiving prayer at the end, I waited in
contemplation as long as my body would allow in the
cold weather.   After slipping my shoes on over my
purple feet, I tip-toed back to the apartment as fast
as possible, trying not to drop the bowl. After taking
a hot shower, I jumped into the car and drove the hour-
and-twenty-minute trip back to family and food. No one
suspected a thing.

Joe had to laugh, picturing Ben sneaking around in the dead
of winter, hiding in bushes, performing secret rites in the middle of
a busy neighborhood. It wasn't just the story that warmed Joe's
heart, it was the totality of sacrifice and effort from Ben which spoke
to him. He was, indeed, one of the Seven. Ben's concluding
paragraph in his e-mail message said it all.

From that day forward, I felt blessed with a sense of
peace of mind, a knowledge that I possessed a sanctuary
that no one could take away. It was not a physical
place outside of me; it dwelt within.   That Thanksgiving was one of the most beautiful times of my life
spent with family. A great clarity has filled me since
that day.   My needs were no longer empty holes, but
opportunities to be addressed, and filled with love.
Something had changed in me, and I knew I had to change
things around me.   I started making those changes,

getting a new job, speaking more openly about the tensions at home, addressing my own personal issues. It was a great blessing. Thank you, Joe, for being the conduit of that blessing. And as you always do with others, I now do for you:

Bless your heart.

Ben

THE MISSING SEVENTH

*S*ometimes the most common of lessons in life are learned in the strangest of ways. Cult figures from Jonestown to Waco have shocked our senses with disturbing scenes on our TV screens. They have shown us how willingly we, as observers, give up our free will; they remind us how eager we can be to surrender our own power, our own rights in decision-making, to others. It never occurred to Joe that Michael's words might effect such kinds of responses, for the simple reason that the angel constantly sought those who would carry on the teachings by realizing their own giftedness, their own inheritance as master souls.

But what does it mean to be a master soul? Michael's words, "You are perfect, whole, and complete just the way you are," warmed and affirmed any who heard them. But such a message began to bump up against the fact that these six people who had now dedicated themselves to the angel's messages were all too human. Joe would ponder over the contrasts confronting him every time one of these six people sent e-mail or telephoned, questioning their worthiness or what role they could possibly have. These people worried about paying bills, anguished about love, fussed

and complained about personalities at work, and daily stared into their bathroom mirrors ever asking the question, "Who are you?" How could any observer reconcile this apparent paradox in these people? How could these people, called forth by heaven, be so human and also be called master souls? Weren't these people just like the rest of us? Maybe so, maybe not.

Somehow, each one knew he or she was one of the Seven. But how? Each had some spark burning deep in their hearts, telling them that a brighter world lay ahead. These sparks were to be applied to tinder made of the inherent tenderness residing in us all. These sparks portended a burning future threatening to ignite the hearts of all humanity. They didn't know how this was to happen, but something within each smoldered with a hope that simply could not die. Not until later would the secret of the mystery, this smoldering hope, flame into full view. But until that time, both they and Joe confronted the light bouncing back from their morning mirrors. Is the image in the mirror the truth, or is it illusion? Even scientific fact tells us the image in the mirror is the reflected opposite of who we really are. But who among us stands there each each morning before the glass and says, "What I see is the opposite of who I really am"?

What the mirror does not show us is the light that cannot be reflected by glass. It is reflected only in each and every one of us. Deb understood that, now. The miracle of the mirror, after her baptism, had taught her never again to trust the image she saw only with her eyes. She knew that what really counts is what she sees with eyes that can look into the soul of another. And, as she had learned in her own shocking way, all the answers are to be found within. That is where the master resides. Some part of us, some small spark waiting to burst into a bonfire of grand light, whispers deep within, "All the answers are to be found here. Look here. Seek here. For this is the place of the master that is you. To see is to feed the flame. To love is to unleash the flame. Teach only love, and the master is reborn."

Time was running out for finding the last of the Seven. Joe's birthday was only a few months away. Michael had said he would find all seven before the end of his fiftieth year, and he was

beginning to wonder if the angel had made a mistake. Usually, Joe took care of the December training sessions at conferences or corporate-sponsored events, as he had done for the last thirteen years. It had become his Christmastime celebration. But this December he contracted the flu, which put him in bed in a way he never wanted to be bedridden again. Because someone else covered for him over the Christmas season, Joe moved his training schedule to cover January. Ever watchful for the missing seventh, it was at one of the sessions where he spotted Keith. *All I need is one gay man*, he said to himself. It wasn't that Keith was flamboyant or effeminate or a flaming queen or anything like that. But Joe just knew he was gay. He'd been around enough gay men to catch certain phrases, recognize certain attitudes about give-away topics, to pick up on Keith's orientation. The guy was humorous, loved to crack jokes at just the right time to get everyone laughing. Joe's eye kept examining him like the Pink Panther spying a tempting jewel. Joe argued with himself, *I'm here to train people, not to scout prospects for finishing the Seven. But ... maybe ... just maybe ... this is the right guy*. It was Joe's job to make sure those who signed up for these human development courses got something out of them, or created something out them. *But I like this guy, I* really *like this guy*, he confessed the next day, and the day after that. *And it's like ... he would be great as a spokesman. People would like him as much or more than I like this guy*. But then the professional side of him would kick in again after Keith got the entire roomful of attendees laughing at themselves.

Finally, in one of his weaker moments, Joseph walked up to Keith after one of the classes and handed him a copy of his manuscript. He was short and to the point: "I'd like you to read this. See what you think about it." Keith was left there with a blank look on his face as Joe exited the building. The first page had only a title on it: *The Book of Bricks: Blessings, Gifts, and Deeds*. Keith looked back up at the closing door and muttered, "Well, OK. Sure, Joe, I'd be glad to read this," commenting to an invisible audience. Keith was a businessman as well as a student of personal growth. Not only did he own his own florist shop and employ or contract with several people, he also owned his own house and was in a new

relationship. Now in his thirties, Keith had found a stable lifestyle by daring to take risks and enjoy the adventure of it in the process. He pressed forward with all life had to offer. The next night he read the entire manuscript. After turning the last page, he stared at the ceiling and said one word: "Wow!"

Late that night, he called Joe at home, conveying how profound the writing had been for him. Like the others, Keith asked if he was one of the seven souls. And like the rest, Joe confessed he did not have the answer to that question, and then asked if he had done the baptism. After saying he hadn't, Keith then opened his heart as wide as cathedral door, telling Joe that if he was one of the Seven, he was willing to do whatever was needed for him to do. He'd sell his house and give the money to Joe to use in any way that was needed. He'd even sell his business.

As Joe listened to this outpouring of generosity, he began to get scared. Never had this happened before. And never had he thought of himself as a Jim Jones or a David Koresh. "No, no, no! Keith. That's not what this is all about," he protested in the gentlest way he knew. "Look, this is what you need to do. You need to do the baptism. You need to take time out for yourself. Do the baptism, and see what opens for you. You will either get pretty clear that you are one of the Seven, or no, you are not. If you feel pretty clear that 'No, I am not,' then Keith, you probably are not. Now, Keith, I want you to know that this wouldn't degrade you or devalue you in any way. It's *your* choice, not mine, not anybody else's. And whatever is in the manuscript is still very valid. There's still stuff in there that can assist you in your life. And there's no rush into this. If not now, maybe later on."

Keith reiterated his openness and said he'd do the baptism. Joe wanted to make sure this wonderful man understood why he had given him the manuscript. "Please ... you've got to remember that this isn't about what you've got to give, not about your worldly possessions, or anything to do with—more or less—buying your way in. If it turns out that you aren't to walk your path with me, then don't go looking for someone else, and give him everything you own. Because the truth of the matter is that God doesn't really need your money, or your house, or your business." The conversation

left both men a bit rattled. As each hung up, parts of the conversation echoed in their thoughts.

That night, Joe took a long and hard look at himself. How could this happen? Because of scenarios that had occurred in workshop exercises, he was aware he could command a strong presence in a room, that he could come across as a powerful guy. He'd even had people go up to conference supervisors and ask if Joe was going to staff the session. And upon finding out he was to facilitate the exercise, they would state, "If he's the trainer or facilitator in this course, I'm leaving!" Such occurrences did not bother him, for they spoke to the role he played in getting them to examine their own lives, to get them to give up past behaviors that had sabotaged their professional or personal lives. It made him feel good that he worked with people who were trying to move forward on new paths. But what Keith had lain before him was different. It jolted him out of his pride and forced him to examine his own ego. It took all his professional expertise to force himself to do what he had asked thousands in his classes, over the years, to do. With trepidation he had to admit how tempting it was for him to actually say yes to Keith, to have this talented and gifted man hand over his life. *Sure! Sell your house, join me. And sure! Sell your business, give me the money*, he could hear himself saying. And it troubled him deeply to know that the temptation was not imagined, it was real. He saw himself for the first time in a way he never had before. This whole Michael "thing" had to be handled more carefully than he had previously thought. There existed a greater responsibility than he had ever dreamt. *I'd better be damned clear how I participate in this endeavor*, he concluded to himself. *I'd better make sure there is no misunderstanding that anyone should ever feel like Keith felt tonight*. And with that he turned on the TV to let his mind go. But he could not put Keith out of his mind.

While Joe waited to hear from Keith, e-mail from Steve announced another find. This wasn't another candidate for sevenhood, it was a wonderful woman on the Internet who called herself the AngelScribe. Steve felt Joe ought to chat with her on the computer, for she not only had wonderful things to say about his website book, but also was interested in promoting him in the

Pacific Northwest. How Steve managed to find people was a constant wonder to Joe. The guy was a spiritual detective in search of any source of angelic information. It was enough to make a person wonder how he could work his high-tech sales job, attend healing sessions, and canvass the World Wide Web like some cyber-detective. It didn't take long for AngelScribe, whose real name was Mary Ellen, to become fast friends with Joe. They talked about everything under the moon. The two were like bread and jam, and it was obvious that Mary Ellen was the jam. She was as sweet as they come, always full of good humor and positive comments. Not only was she willing to sponsor speaking engagements for Joe, she told him about the many people in her area who would love to network with him.

A couple of days later, Keith called. The conversation started out in a much calmer tone than when they had left off. He had performed the baptism. The event had left him with a sense of spiritual connection, which he felt most grateful for. He also described how he felt everything in his life was going to be OK, on course, filled with divine guidance. He felt very satisfied with himself and with life. But, "I don't feel called to participate as one of the seven master souls," he confessed to Joe, almost apologetically.

Afterwards, Joe reminisced about how strongly Keith had felt called to sell all his belongings and join him in his angelic mission. He mused over the courage it must have taken for this man to confess, No ... this isn't for me. This isn't what I'm supposed to be doing, or the vehicle for me to be doing it. Such courage, such honesty was just what Joe was looking for in his search for the Seven. It made him want Keith as part of the "team" all the more. Perhaps this dynamic man would change his mind later. At least Joe hoped he would, before his birthday arrived in eight weeks.

A week later, e-mail arrived from Mary Ellen. Not only had she arranged for Joe to travel to the Seattle area to talk about Michael and his teachings, she had also discovered another author of an angel book with a similar message to his. "His name is Gary. And not only is he a great guy, like you are, he is also gay. Joe," she had typed at the end of her message, "I think he is your missing seventh."

The Laughing Angel

I should have never said never." Gary frowned at the face looking back at him in the mirror. As he leaned closer, inspecting his beard, his breath fogged the glass, reminding him how cold January mornings can get in Seattle. "Angels," he huffed to himself as he slid the razor across his face. He liked talking to himself in the mirror, not for the companionship, but for a reason he would admit to no one. It pleased him to wake up each morning and wink at the baby-faced gentleman in the bathroom mirror. And he purposefully used the word "baby-faced." For a man in his fifties, he could pass for early forties or possibly late thirties in a kinder light. But like so many other parts of his life, Gary tried to keep his vanity a secret. Washing the foamy soap off his face, he checked for missed whiskers. Yes, he should have known better than to promise himself he would never disclose to anyone his hidden intentions. It was one thing to tell Mary Ellen and then Joe that there was no way he would be or could be the last of the Seven, but quite another to conclude that he would secretly support Joe and his messages from the angel in any way he could. Such secrecy bordered on arrogance. For he should have known that when it comes to angels, there is no such thing as a secret.

Requests for booksignings and speaking engagements were stacking up for Gary—thanks mostly to Mary Ellen's dynamism. The woman seemed to have an endless enthusiasm that proved to be infectious. *Surely*, Gary thought, *I can endorse Joe's* Book of Bricks *and encourage my own sponsors to invite him to speak without his knowing it. Innocent enough*, he convinced himself. No one need know what he was doing, and he could operate anonymously as one of Joe's supporters. Or so he thought.

Perhaps his first undoing hid behind his decision to perform the baptism the angel had taught Joe. He argued with himself whether he should even bother. True, it would be a symbolic act of solidarity in support of the messages Joe spoke of. And, true, since he was planning to perform the ritual in secret, it certainly would do no harm or imply any commitment on his part. Perhaps what kept Gary from actually setting a bowl out before sunrise was his busy schedule, or perhaps his own respect for ritual of any kind. To further complicate matters, he had sandwiched in a ski trip up to Whistler, British Columbia, to give himself a much needed rest. That meant the entire months of January and February were completely booked up. If he were to secretly carry out the Last Baptism rite, the only open time slot would be the morning of departure for the ski trip. As he scrutinized his calendar, he saw the only time to himself in the two-month period ahead was that specific morning. His best friend had left him the key to his house in Seattle, since the whole family would be gone that week. With no one at home, this would be about the only time he could try the symbolic act in privacy. It would have to be that morning or no morning at all.

The debate to enact or not to enact the baptism bounced around inside him with each approaching day. *Sure, it would be nice to show this kind of clandestine backing for Joe and his messages*, he argued to himself, but something way down deep inside him felt uneasy about it. Some ancient kind of memory seemed to reach out at him, lingering quietly, almost haunting him with a knowledge of the consequences if he dared to engage the angelic kingdom once again. *I know I'm not one of the Seven*, he would whisper to his soul. But what really bothered him was how the whisper would not echo back, as if the remark had gotten lost in some abyss within him. He shivered at the thought.

The snooze alarm went off for the third time before Gary finally rolled out of the waterbed. Slipping his sneakers on over bare feet, he stumbled down the stairs with untied shoelaces rattling against bare wood. Into the kitchen he marched to retrieve the punch bowl and wine he had set up the night before. Inside the bowl was a hand-written note describing all the steps, including the final prayer.

It was still dark outside with dawn just starting to grace the outline of the Seattle hills. Frost covered the ground, glistening in the dim light like sparkles from an ethereal eye. He sat next to a Japanese maple tree, wondering where the best spot would be for setting sacred space. Not wanting to disturb the ground, he stretched forward placing the bowl in what seemed like a good spot. Usually, his friend Chris prayed and carried out Native American rituals at a much-used sacred spot next to a tall blue spruce near the back corner of the house. But Michael had told Joe that the wine should be in sunlight during the period of waiting. And the small maple tree adorning the stone-and-flora shrine to Mickey Mouse was the only place in the back yard where sunlight would spill upon the bowl of wine until high noon. The front yard would invite gazes from any number of houses on the rise across the street. And Gary wanted some semblance of privacy when he covered his legs and arms in wine in the middle of a crowded city.

After pouring the entire contents of the wine bottle into the bowl, he started to shiver against the cold. *This is crazy*, he muttered to himself as he placed a small stone on the note of instructions next to the bowl. Everything was ready. Just as he stood, contemplating his return to the waterbed, the first rays of the morning sun flooded the back yard in brilliant orange. The sense of peace that also flooded him made him smile. It may have seemed crazy, but it also felt peacefully right. With arms entwined, he shuffled his shaking body back into the house and dove into the warmth of the waterbed. No use staying up for breakfast because the whole day would be a fast.

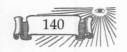

Gary spent the remainder of the morning taking care of e-mail, praying, reading, praying, meditating, and more praying. It was his way to take things-spiritual seriously, perhaps a remnant of his seminary training with the Benedictine monks. Prayer was never to be taken lightly. He believed in Joe and his angelic experiences. He believed in the messages and the good they fostered. If he were going to support Joe, it would not be done halfway.

As noon drew near, he piled the last of his bags and ski paraphernalia against the front door. There would be just enough time to take care of the baptism in the back yard, clean himself up, and head directly to the rendezvous point where he would meet with his buddies, and then caravan to Canada. In spite of the sunshine, it was still chilly outside as he ambled down the path to the back yard. With hands on hips, he stared at the bowlful of wine, its sweet fumes wafting in the still air. *Well, it's do-or-die time,* he thought to himself. As he sat next to the Japanese maple, he removed his shoes and socks, tip-toed the short distance to the bowl, and sat down. Picking up the note to make sure he performed each step meticulously, Gary reached his right hand into the cold liquid and smeared wine all over his feet, every inch. The smell tickled his nostrils as he pulled his sweat pants up high enough to finish the washing all the way to his knees. The hands to the elbows came next. His lips pursed as he remembered his boyhood days when such a smell tormented him. For it would mean that Mommie was drunk out of her mind once again. His forearms covered in purple, he picked up the note and read, "My loving Father, your child has come home to your counsel. Guide me in all things that I must do."

What might happen next, he did not know. His eyes searched around for any signs. Nothing. As he was about to pour the remaining wine from the bowl onto the ground, he stopped suddenly. A warm breeze that swirled around him. "Uh oh," was all he said. This was not the first time he had known such a breeze. Once before, on a spiritual quest in the wilds of the Columbia River Gorge, running between Washington and Oregon, this warm whisper of wind had visited him. At that time, winter gales had thrown rain like icy miniature spears most of the day. The Gorge

was well known for its winter storms. But in the middle of the quest, while meditating on the top of Beacon Rock, a natural tower of stone, the gales had suddenly ceased their howling. Out of nowhere danced this gentle, warming breeze. And then, as now, he thought of the story about Elijah in the cave and felt blessed.

In the story of Elijah, the prophet is told that God will announce himself in the holy man's presence. Upon hearing this, he leaves the cave and stands at the entrance of the cave waiting for God to show himself. He witnesses a raging windstorm and knows that God is not to be found in the great storm. Going back into his cave, he prays and waits before returning to the entrance once again. He then witnesses a great earthquake but does not see God in the quaking of the earth. Retreating within the cave, he prays once more hoping that he will see God reveal himself. Leaving the cave for the third time, he waits for a sign at the entrance. A raging fire then erupts on the mountain, and he knows that God is not in the inferno. But where can God be? It is at that moment that he feels a warm, gentle breeze and realizes that God is hidden in the gentle breeze. And so it was this day, just as it had been up at Beacon Rock. Gary could not escape the feeling that he was in the presence of something sacred and holy. Whether that was God or angels or his own spirit calling to him, it made no difference. What mattered was that, as before, something sacred was calling to his soul. Did it mean he was one of the Seven after all?

As he poured the wine upon the ground, he argued with himself that he was just being fanciful. Even though not a single maple twig had moved in the breeze, he felt he needed more of a sign than this if he were going to change his own spiritual journey by accepting the call of this angel Joe had named Michael. His path was aimed at other ideals, those expressed in his past writings. As he toted the bowl, shoes, and socks back to the kitchen, the warm breeze seemed to follow him. Perhaps it was just the fumes from the wine making him feel warm. But his bare feet on the cold pavement reminded him how cold it really was outside, in spite of the sunshine. If there had been a breeze, it would have made him colder, not warmer. The debate continued as he cleaned up the kitchen, his arms, and his legs. Time was a-wasting. His comrades

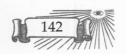

would be waiting. Clearing the argument from his thoughts, he gathered his bags and filled his car. As he sped north on Interstate 5, he could still smell the wine on his skin, in spite of three washings with soap and water. What would the guys think of him showing up smelling like a wino?

The long weekend at Whistler proved to be a blowout celebration of skiing, dancing, wining and dining, and staying up late filling the night with laughter. Hot tubs and hot stories played against the cold reality that such revelry must come to an end. Simply put, Gary needed a vacation from his vacation. As his bright yellow car zipped back toward the busy-ness that lay ahead in Seattle and Portland, thoughts about the baptism nagged at him. By the time he pulled into the driveway of his Portland rental, he knew something was wrong. The tickle in his throat that had started as he left Canada was turning ugly. Why he felt it had something to do with the baptism was totally irrational, but he could not escape the feeling.

Gary almost never fell to fevers. He was one of those people whose temperature usually dropped lower when he was ill. He could count the number of times he'd had a fever on one hand. And something told him that he could add one more finger this day. As his luggage hit the bedroom floor, he hit the bed, clothes and all. By the time he woke the next morning, he could barely talk. The thermometer confirmed his suspicions with a 102-degree reading. There was no way he could see clients. After canceling his meeting with his publisher, he decided also to cancel speaking engagements the week ahead. With a bullfrog voice he called Dawn Stansfield, owner of the New Visions Healing Arts in Bellevue, a suburb of Seattle. Mary Ellen, acting as his publicist, had booked the event in spite of his muttering about talking at small bookstores and angel shops. She had felt the big book chains got too much attention. It was an important statement to people if an author spoke at the smaller stores once in a while.

"Hello, is this Dawn?" he asked the sweet-voiced lady on the other end of the line. "Dawn, as you can tell by my voice, I seem to have come down with bronchitis, and I wanted to call ahead of time to let you know that I won't be able to speak at your store next week."

There was patient silence on the phone. "Gary, please reconsider. I've really been looking forward to this and have sold tickets and made arrangements." If this had been a big chain store, they would have simply booked another date and thought nothing of it. But the smaller stores don't have that luxury. "I know you haven't met me, but I have a gift. Maybe Mary Ellen told you about it. I am what is called a medical intuitive. I can tell that you don't have bronchitis, you have a virus. And if you will allow me, I think I can help you get better in time for the speaking engagement."

Gary had seen and heard of wonderful and strange people in his tours. Nothing surprised him anymore. He had not heard about medical intuitives, but was willing to give this a shot. "And if I'm not well enough the day before I'm supposed to come up there, you'll be able to cancel? OK?"

He could hear her sigh politely. "You'll be all right. Take my word for it. Here's what I'd like you to do. Do you have echinacea?"

"Actually, I think I'm out. But I can go get some."

"Good. Take three capsules immediately, then take three more after you've eaten lunch, and three more before dinner. I know that sounds like a lot, but it's what you need. Also get yourself Gatorade and eggs for lunch. Your body is low on a certain protein that is found in the eggs, and your electrolytes are dangerously low because of dehydration as well. Take lots of Gatorade. Tonight you will break out in sweats, so make sure you have several sheets so you can change your bed. Take the echinacea three times the next day. Call me every day. You'll see. You'll get better."

The speaking engagement was six days away. If she could cure his bronchitis (which wasn't bronchitis) in six days, then she deserved to have a presentation like he'd never given before. As he climbed into his car to purchase the remedies Dawn had suggested, a wave of nausea swept through him. He thought twice whether he should be driving as he slammed the car door. The coughing was growing steadily worse as well.

Waiting in line at the health food store was more of an ordeal than he had imagined. The owner was being considerate and thoughtful with the customer in line ahead. As she took her time explaining the benefits of an herb, Gary began to look for a quick

escape. Leaving everything at the cashier's counter, he headed out the door and slouched over the curb. It had been twenty years since he had last tossed his cookies, and he wasn't very happy at doing it now. The cold air helped settle his stomach as he took deep breaths. Dizziness was swarming around him with a buzzing filling his ears. It was time to get back to bed. As he stumbled back into the health food store, he spied his reflection in the window. He looked as pale as an old newspaper. Quickly paying for the handful of cold remedies he had gathered, he headed his car back home. He'd have to get the food stuff later.

That night he woke from wild dreams about keeping himself in prison. As he tried to read the clock, he realized he was soaking wet. Dawn had been correct. The sheets needed changing. Throughout the night, dreams and shivering repeatedly woke him. The next morning he felt worse than ever, unable to speak. He tried to fry himself an egg, but could barely get one bite down from the nausea. Rather than eat, he poured himself back into bed. The phone rang, waking him from his dreariness. It was Beth from the publisher's office wanting to know if she could help in any way.

"I haven't been able to buy any Gatorade, yet," was all he could croak out. She volunteered to drop some by after work. He fell asleep again only to be awakened by the phone again. This time it was Dawn.

"Oh, you're doing better," she chimed. He didn't feel better. He felt like dying. "I'm still picking up that you are still having problems with your protein. Have you eaten the eggs I suggested?"

"Couldn't," was all he gargled.

"You really need to. Your body is having problems balancing itself. What about the electrolytes? Have you been taking the Gatorade?" Her voice was irritatingly beautiful. He felt like a legless man forced to watch a ballerina.

"Later," was all he could manage.

"I'll call you again tomorrow. Keep taking everything as I've suggested, OK? Love you very much."

"Bye." There was no way he was going to get an egg down. And if he did get it down, there was no way he was going to keep it down. His throat felt like raw meat. Every cough felt like saw

blades dragging across his throat. His fever had dropped, but so had his spirits. He would wait for Beth.

The knock at the door woke him up. Dragging himself out of bed with covers draped around him, he opened the door to see a paper bag sitting on the doorstep. Beth was standing back at the curb waving. "I think I'd better keep a safe distance. You'll find lots of Gatorade and aspirin and vitamin C in the bag. Get well soon. But don't come into the office until you've gotten better. You look like shit." Beth was one of those women Gary thought the world of. She was a nun and a longshoreman rolled into one. She was gorgeous. She was tough. She was a walking paradox poets spent centuries writing about—the lovely maiden who could kill the stag with a rose.

In the kitchen, a dirty glass was cleaned and the Gatorade consumed. It trickled down his throat like fine wine as he polished off three glasses before crawling back into bed. An hour later, his eyes blinked open not from coughing up what felt like glass, but from a sense of actually feeling good. Gatorade? He went back into the kitchen to finish the rest of the jug, and while he was at it, boiled a few eggs that went down quite nicely. Magic! By nightfall the disheveled deathbed was aired out and remade once more to serve as a cradle for rest. Gary felt like calling Dawn. He still had the sore throat, but at least he could eat and watch some TV.

"You need to take lots of liquids," Dawn continued the next day. Gary was convinced of her gift at this point. If she had suggested dancing naked in downtown's Salmon Springs Fountain as the next step, he would have asked, How long? "Your body is trying to get rid of all the toxins at this point," she said.

"But I can still barely talk with this throat." It was true, he still sounded like a deep-voiced basso with a smoker's cough.

"Don't worry. You will be fine by the time you arrive for the speaking engagement." That was two days away. He didn't see how his throat would clear up fast enough. And just to be safe, he called his friend, Nattie, in Port Townsend, near Seattle, and asked if he could stay with her while he readied himself for the talk. And, by the way, would she mind doing readings from his book to help him save his voice for what talking he'd try to do? She readily agreed.

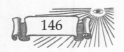

The two were more like bosom buddies than friends. And she loved the idea of seeing more of the public life of her longtime chum.

Gary arrived at Nattie's the next day. The two got caught up while he drank liquids like a dying man in a desert. She loved hearing his stories, especially this latest one about the medical intuitive she would meet the following evening. Her house was like home to Gary, with a nice bed in the guest room. It was quiet up here. Instead of police sirens waking him in the middle of the night, songbirds or crows eased him out of sleep in the morning. Nattie was a generous woman with a generous heart. Never one to complain, she put her own schedule aside to accommodate her friend and ready herself for her first public appearance as a reader.

New Visions snuggled among several other small shops not far from Bellevue's downtown mall. Dawn had gone to great lengths to create an environment of fine nouveau spiritual art, Native American works, sculpture, and angel-oriented creations of several kinds. It was like walking into Christmas the way she had lights and sounds playing amid the displayed crafts. The book section was small but focused, with Gary's book prominently displayed and a sign announcing tonight's talk. A sparkle filled Nattie's eye as she quietly scouted every inch of the store. Gary left her to her fun as he climbed the stairs to the lecture room. Like everything else in the store, the room was beautifully laid out, with chairs meticulously arranged in a semicircle. People were already seated, even though the talk would not take place for another half-hour.

Dawn swooped over to greet her guest. She could have been featured on the cover of *Vogue*, Gary thought to himself. "You don't how glad I am to see you!" she bubbled. "And you look great. How's the throat?"

"Amazingly well," her featured speaker answered with a grand smile. "You have a real gift there."

"Why, thank you."

"Makes me wonder why you bother running a store, you're that good." He wanted to let her know how genuine he thought her abilities.

"I try to do both because I love both. I get all kinds of people who come to me: CEOs, housewives, athletes, and hesitant

businessmen. I believe this is the direction medicine itself will eventually go. And the store is a nice way to bring beauty into people's lives. It can be a struggle at times, but I love it."

The two chatted on about the book and the unexpected success it had received. Dawn wanted her visitor to know how appreciative she was to have him speak this night, when the chain bookstore next to the mall couldn't get him to come to their establishment. She felt it was a real coup on her part. The room was full of people at this point with many wanting to have their books autographed immediately. Dawn decided it was time to take control and started directing traffic. Nattie snuggled up against her friend and whispered, "What do I do?"

"There's two chairs up front, one for me, one for you. You're not nervous are you?"

"Oh, a little bit. But it's also exciting."

"Go ahead and seat yourself. I'll be there shortly."

The evening was a brew of reading, talking, fielding questions, and then trying to get out the door. Just before he made his escape, two women cornered Gary, almost confronting him with their question: "Why didn't you talk about the angel?" they asked.

"What angel? Are you talking about the angels in the book?"

"No," the other lady said. "We both saw the angel that was standing behind you. We started talking afterwards and realized we both saw the same thing. Each of us was wondering when you would talk about it. Didn't you see it?"

Gary met all kinds when he did book signings and gave talks. Quickly he sized up the two ladies to determine if they were part of the woo-woo crowd or sincere in what they were trying to convey. He decided they were sincere and deserved a meaningful and honest answer. "Well, I don't necessarily see these light beings. Oftentimes I can detect their presence but not really see anything. That's when I need people like yourselves."

"Well, I wish you could see this being," the first lady said. "It's surrounded by this beautiful blue light. In fact, it's still here standing right behind you."

Gary turned around as if to expect a handshake, but could see nothing. "I don't know what to tell you ladies. Can you tell if

the angel is trying to say anything?" Both shook their heads no simultaneously.

"That's why we wanted to ask you. It doesn't seem to be saying or doing much of anything—just hanging around you."

Gary searched his mind, trying to find the right thing to say. He looked over at Dawn who spied the look in his eye. She excused herself from her well-wishers and headed over for the rescue. Gary's eyes returned to the two ladies as he spoke, "Well, I thank you for saying something to me, and I'm sorry I don't have any information to give you." To be truthful, this was not the first time people had reported angels or a nimbus of light at one of his talks. However, it was different this time because he felt the presence of something— he just didn't know what it was.

Dawn arrived, skillfully escorting her guest into her office so the crowd would leave and Gary could get back to Port Townsend. It was a two-hour trip. Nattie volunteered to drive the whole way, and Gary accepted. The closer they got to Nattie's house, the worse he felt. The fever was returning along with the nausea. By the time they reached the front door, Nattie had to help her friend to the guest room. It seemed he was having a relapse.

That night the cold sweats returned, causing Nattie to have to change the sheets. The next day, Gary stayed in bed. It was about lunchtime when he began seeing the creature. At first, he chalked it up to his high fever. But even after the fever broke, he could still see it standing next to his bed. It didn't have substance. More like a vision or daydream, but he could see it nonetheless. It was an angel. Its wings were made of an iridescent light, appearing to be pulled back behind the shoulders, and its head was slightly bowed in silence. It stood there for the rest of the day and into the night. Never moving, never speaking, never gesturing except to look over at the object of its attention: the bedridden guest. Gary kept saying to himself, *I must be sicker than I thought.* Taking Gatorade didn't help, nor did eating a meal. It simply continued watching over his sickbed. Gary fabricated all kinds of excuses. He tried justifying the phenomenon by writing it off as the power of suggestion from the two ladies who had approached him after the presentation the previous night. The fever was gone and back again, so it couldn't

be the fever. Perhaps it was too much echinacea, or too much water. He had heard of people getting water toxicity from drinking too much water to lose weight.

As he awoke the next morning, Gary's eyes immediately went to the corner of the room where the angel had been. It was still there. Exasperated, he decided he would try to communicate with the creature. *What is it you want of me? Why are you here?* he asked telepathically. He didn't dare ask out loud, fearing Nattie would surely think him odd or, at least, delirious. He looked up at the angel's eyes. Nothing. No answer. After much debate with himself, he finally decided to do what Joe Crane had done and speak the words that had brought the angel Michael forth. Feeling foolish, he spoke in a whispered voice, "Speak, O Lord, for your servant is listening." He waited, half-expecting to be shocked by a response or some change in light. But there was nothing. Nothing at all. It just continued to stand there. Like a child hiding from a nightmare, Gary covered his head with his pillow and tried to go back to sleep.

Nattie cheerfully arrived with breakfast on a tray. "Feeling hungry this morning?" she asked ignoring the fact that her company was behaving rather strangely.

Pulling himself out from under his pillows, Gary decided to find out if he was imagining the whole thing. Once and for all. "Nattie, I consider you a pretty grounded person."

"Why thank you," she smiled back.

"Do you feel any kind of presence in this room?"

"You mean now?" A worried look crept across her face.

"Yes. Now. Do you feel like there is something in the room here with us?" He couldn't believe he was asking her this. He jokingly wondered whether she would call an exorcist or take him to a shrink. Nattie and Gary had been close friends for twenty years. She knew to take his question seriously. Taking an unconscious step backwards, she looked around the room, then back at her visitor.

"Well, the room does seem a bit different. And if I search my feelings, I do kind of feel a nice kind of presence in the room. But that's probably 'cuz you're here." A small grin flashed by and disappeared.

"Seriously." Gary entreated, "If you had to point to where you thought this presence was, where would you point?"

She folded her hands, almost as if in prayer and then quickly pointed straight at the angel.

"Ha!" Gary explode almost rising off his bed. "That's it! That's where it is."

"Where what is?" Nattie begged. She wasn't sure whether to feel pleased or frightened.

"Remember when we were at Dawn's store and the two ladies came over and told me an angel was behind me?"

"Is that what they were talking about? I wondered what was going on. I didn't want to eavesdrop, even though they sounded so insistent."

"It's here, the angel is here. It's been standing in that corner for the last twenty-four hours just staring at me."

Nattie was not one of those people who embraced fanciful notions too easily. She was a woman of the earth, a wildlife biologist who loved life and lived it with mud under her feet and twigs in her hair. She understood the wonders of nature like few did. She was a grounded person who smelled the flowers, scoped out birds, and listened in ancient forests for mating calls. Angels didn't really fit into her "life list," as bird watchers like to call it. But she had been close friends with Gary longer than most people are married, and she knew her friend's sincerity was gold. She knew by the look on his face he was dead serious.

"What does it look like?" she decided to ask.

"Well. It's got a kind of blue light around it. Its head stays bowed most of the time. I can't get it to say anything or do anything. It just stands there all the time. I don't know what to do with it."

"Maybe you should call your friend, Joe," she offered. Angels were not her specialty, but she had read Joe's document from Michael—the one he called *The Book of Bricks*—and had been able to relate to it. Joe seemed to be the one who knew alot about angels. However, what Nattie did not know about was Gary's secret ritual. And he was determined that no one would hear about it.

"I'll give it some thought," he said clearing his throat. "Thanks." This entire affair was beginning to make him nervous. Why was all

of this happening? Certainly it could not mean what he was afraid it might mean. He dared not even think about it. There was too much work that needed to be done without entertaining thoughts of getting involved with Joe. His eyes snatched a look at the corner, as if hoping the being of light would not be there. But there it stood. Sleep would not come, peace would not come. The bed covers were beginning to feel like a quilt of tiny fingers lightly tapping on him, pointing to the angel, pointing to the phone. *Ask Joe*, they seemed to tap out in a spiritual Morse code. *Joe will know what to do.* As he tossed and turned, arguing with his own thoughts, suddenly a gasp gave forth. "All right, all right, all right. I'll do it." Who he was talking to, even he didn't know. Fumbling with his address book, he picked up the phone and dialed Joe's number, his own fingers tapping on the desktop.

"Hello, this is Joe," the voice on the other end said. Gary hesitated as if expecting more. "Hello?" the voice said once more.

"Joe. This is Gary. I've got something weird I want to tell you."

Joe chuckled. "I've gotten accustomed to weird of late. Lay it on me. What's going on?"

Like a man carrying a heavy load, Gary dumped the entire story in Joe's lap—minus the baptism story—hardly taking a breath the whole time. When he was finally done, his fingers started tapping once again. "What do you make of this?"

"Is the angel still there?" Joe asked.

Gary looked around, but he no longer saw the angel in the corner of the room. He was about to apologize and hang up when he realized the angel was right behind him. "Well, he's moved, but he's here."

"Is he close by?" Joe asked in a way that sounded more like a detective than a newfound friend.

"Yes, he's right behind me."

"Hand him the phone," Joe ordered.

"What?" Gary couldn't believe his ears.

"Hand him the phone," Joe stated again, growing impatient.

"How in the hell am I going to hand the phone to an angel? What are you talking about? The thing hasn't spoken since it got here."

"How tall is this guy?" Joe asked.

Gary could not believe he was having this conversation. His voice rose about an octave higher. "How tall? About six feet. What's that got to do with it?"

"Then hold the phone up to his ear."

"All right. You asked for it." Gary leaned back in his chair and held the phone high with his outstretched arm. He was starting to laugh at himself and Joe. Who could believe such nonsense? Then the angel leaned forward into the phone and started laughing. It wasn't the kind of laugh that you'd hear at a party or the kind of snicker that comes from a prankster. It was more of a joyous laugh, like the kind one hears at an airport when old friends greet one another. He could see the angel's lips move, but there were no words. It was then that the right arm of the laughing angel reached right into the phone. It was as if Gary were watching a video movie. For he could see the arm travel through the phone wires all the way down to the Bay Area and out of Joe's phone and touch his heart. Gary understood immediately that this was the signature of Michael's favorite saying, "Bless your heart." At that point the angel disappeared leaving the phone receiver suspended in mid air in Gary's hand. The whole scene was too ridiculous to believe in. It had to be his imagination. Slowly, he brought the phone receiver back to his ear.

"Joe? You there?" he asked suspecting any sane person would have hung up on him by now. Joe seemed to know he was listening once again.

"OK," Joe said, "Was the angel laughing?"

Gary sat there stunned, his mouth dropping to his lap. "How'd, how'd you know?" he gasped.

"Easy. I heard him. He has two things he wants me to tell you." Gary leaned over with his head in one hand and the phone in the other. He was afraid to go on with this. It was at that moment when he realized his fever was gone. Had this all been some grand heavenly conspiracy, a plot to get him to talk to Joe?

"What?" was all Gary could utter.

"First. He said that you are dehydrated and you need to drink lots of fluids. Secondly, he says that you are too serious, that you are struggling with something you don't need to struggle with and we should talk about it."

"Oh gawd," was all that Gary could offer back. Joe waited patiently and let the silence work with his friend's thoughts. "Joe, I've got something to confess to you."

"I'm listening," came the friendly answer. With resignation the story of the baptism, skiing at Whistler, being so sick, and the presentation at New Visions poured out. Joe realized this was not easy for Gary to tell. In the end, Joe said what he knew he had to say and what he knew his upset friend did not want to hear. "Gary." Joe spoke in a calming fashion. "Maybe you are one of the Seven."

A gasp fell from Gary's lips. "Joe, I can't be. If these angels want to leave me with a message, they've got to do better than show up with me in high fever, wondering if I'm experiencing delirium. Who knows, maybe the sickness was all part of this. But I've got choices that I have to make, and I can only make them with a reasoned mind. The truth of the matter is that I have no gurus, no teachers. Michael said that he will be the teacher of the Seven, and I just can't go along with that. I'm at a point in my life where I believe I am my own teacher, my own source of truth."

Joe was understanding. He knew he'd said all he could say. He had heard Gary's concerns and felt compassion for him, but in his own mind he was thinking, *You arrogant son-of-a-bitch*. This would not be the last time the two men would wrestle over Gary's doubts. Since the dawn of man, angels have been most patient with the most stubborn of men. And Gary was a stubborn man.

Part IV

REVELATION DECODED

THE NEW REVELATION

*A*lmost two years had crept by since Michael had last appeared to Joe. He missed his guide, his heavenly brother and friend. The mystery of whether Joe had truly found all seven of the master souls still hung before him. Michael had promised he would return when all seven had been found. And coupled with that promise was another which stated such an event would occur before Joe's 51st birthday—less than a month away. Gary's reluctance to accept the idea of even being considered one of the Seven complicated matters. Was he or wasn't he?

All these thoughts danced in Joe's head as he picked weeds from under the papyrus plants in his lily pond sanctuary. The three-foot high redwood fence kept the "kids" out, making sure errant, gangly mastiff legs did no damage, and eliminated any chance for their marking doggie domains. Joe brushed his hand over one of the lily leaves to check its health. He loved this spot, its simple beauty—so Zen. It gave him such calm.

Just as he was dipping his hand into the water to remove a bit of pond scum, he noticed a familiar light reflecting off the opposite wall in front of him. As it grew in intensity, Joe breathed out,

"Michael?" Turning, he saw before him the light growing to near blinding intensity as the familiar figure materialized within its brilliance. Joe's heart swelled with welcome.

"Michael, you ol' dog! It's so good to see you." Yes, it had been nearly two years—a long wait. A smile formed on the countenance of his angelic friend.

"Knowing how much you love your dogs, I take that as a compliment."

A joyful chuckle bubbled up from within Joe. He had almost forgotten how magnificent Michael's presence could be. His eyes soaked in every detail once again. Those deep azure eyes that struck the heart with immediate love, embracing everything they gazed upon. His platinum blonde hair dangling on broad, masculine shoulders. That face of sheer beauty, almost too beautiful, almost feminine. Skin of alabaster, oozing with warmth. So much power surrounding him, yet such gentleness on his face.

"So, Michael, this must mean I have found the seventh."

"Yes, you have found the Seven. To each you are to give a message. After each has received their message, I will return to you." Michael paused. "I will speak to you first of the book you are to write with Gary. It will take you less time than you think, but this is not one of the two I told you that you are to write. I will be with you as you write it."

So, Gary and I will write a book together, Joe thought to himself. A quiet grin spread across his face as he thought of the two of them working together. But what kind of role would Michael play? "Do you mean like you were with *The Book of Bricks*, or in person?" he decided to ask. *The Book of Bricks* had come in a telepathic manner, even though he was able to hear Michael's voice during its creation.

"I will be with you in both ways. Much you have forgotten of that which I have told you of *Revelation*. This was done so you could be about getting *The Book of Bricks* out to the world as a starting place for your brothers and sisters. You will say to Gary this: 'You are visited by an angel of light to brighten your darkness. His name is as mine, unpronounceable, and he may be called by whatever you choose. Your angel will answer when you open your heart to listen.' "

"Wait a minute, Michael," Joe objected. "What is going on with all this can't-say-your-names stuff? Why can't you guys just have names that people can pronounce like every other angel? This can get a whole lot scary to us if we can't at least use names we can, at the very least, pronounce." Joe liked asking Michael questions—primarily because he never knew what kind of wild answer he might get in return. Michael could accidentally present him with the most amazing information. Plus, Joe was already aware of skeptics who wanted to label the angels as something other than heaven-sent, asking for names to bolster their doubts.

"The names your kind calls us are used only by you. Do you really think 'Gabriel' is his name? And that he has a title as an archangel? This is not why I have come to you at this time. I have other matters to speak to you of; let us be about that."

Joe realized he was going down the wrong path with the angel-name stuff, so let it go at that. "OK, but I still want to know about it. And if not now, later."

"This I will tell you later, and much more. The two of you are brought together to do God's will with this message you will give. After you have given him that which I have told you, you will say to him this: 'Gary, you walk in a state of grace and are not alone. Fear not what you must do, for your path will be lighted and your steps will be guided. Sure will be your footing, for you have seen the angel that protects you. Humble yourself not in his greatness but rise up to the greatness that is yours.' When this is done bless his heart and be about the work you are to do together."

Michael then relayed to Joe messages for the rest of the Seven. "I will speak to you of the Seven, and you must say to them that which I tell you. The first of the Seven is Deb. To her say that she is doing the work of a provider because her husband has gone lame. She has left behind her true mission for that which is around her. Deb is to do her work, and an angel will point the way. She will no longer live in that which is around her and confusing her. She must write down all that has happened since she has become one of the Seven. This that she writes will help others to grow. She is not to worry, for her husband will begin to heal at a much faster rate. She may now be about her true work."

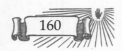

"While we are on this seven thing," Joe interjected, "I want to know something—like when should we all get together? Or do we all *need* to get together? Because I am really unclear on what to say when they ask me questions."

"You will gather in the summer. I will tell you the time and place. You have much to do before then, and the time is short. You will say to them what I tell you to say to them. Some you will begin to teach now, and others you will teach later."

Joe scratched his head. "Great. Just what I wanted to hear. Why can't you just tell me and be done with it? I don't like standing around with nothing to say to them except that you will tell me when the time is right."

"That is as it is. And your likes and dislikes matter not."

Joe was the kind of guy who appreciated an honest opinion. "OK. I got it," he said. "Go on with what you have to say. I'll do my best not to interrupt."

"To Steve you will say: 'Play not with things you know not of, for they will lead you astray. Learn to heal first on your own. You are given a gift, and in it is great power. Yet you think it is other than you who is doing the healing. As Joe has told you, you think you know something, and you don't. You have become separate from people with that which you do. Joe will instruct you in the skills you will need to regain your connection. Be you the master you are; be not the one you think you are. For when someone sees you now, they see the separation, and that frightens them. The closeness you need to do your work is not with you now. Judge not the others in the seven, for they are about their sums as you are yours. You were chosen long ago for this work, and you answered when called. Mighty will be your deeds, overshadowed only by the love you are.' "

"Question time," Joe cut in. "Aren't you going to be doing these messages in the order I found the Seven? That was one question, and now for another. This one is more like something that I am noticing, and not exactly a question. It seems like, to me, that so far with the ones you have talked about, you have fault with them. Is any of the Seven doing anything right? Or are they all wrong in what they are doing? I can tell you right now, I ain't too

thrilled with telling them they screwed up. How about a little good news?"

Michael's voice did not shift nor did his demeanor change. "Should you need to hear what I say of them in that way? Are you not open to receive the words I give unless they are in the order you think they need to be? I know well when each was chosen. Do you look to find fault in that which I say? It is you who still sees right and wrong, good and bad. Know that which I speak has nothing to do with being right or wrong. It is as I say and nothing more. I only tell you these things that the Seven will know and grow past them. There is no fault to be found in the Seven. I only give a clearer path that will lead them around the things that will slow them."

Joe responded, "I am still new at this, and I care for each of them deeply. I would rather build them up at this point because they're new at this, too. At least I have access to you from time to time, while they have no one. Do you know what I am saying?"

"I do," said Michael. "The truth is the only thing that matters to the Seven, and you must speak it without judgment. You say they do not have the access that you do. Yet they have you, and the love you have for them will let them see themselves for the masters they are. You honor the master in them, and they will rise up to it.

"You will say to Kathleen: 'Blessed are you, my sister, for the work you do. The cleaning of your house is almost done. That which you have gathered unto you will begin to serve you no more. Trust in the love that God has for you, and know that all will be well. That which you do for your children will go untreasured for now. Yet you are to be rewarded a thousandfold for your gift. From this dream, you will awake to a new day. Grow and blossom into the master you are.' "

"To Mark, you will say: 'Rise up and look at that which I have given you. Rejoice in the knowledge that you are loved. Seek not that which is made of gold. You will be given more than you can hold. Take to the world the message that you have been given and will be given in the time to come. The gift that you are is worth more than anything that you could become. Blessed are you in the world for the work you have chosen and been chosen to do.' "

"To Shari, you will say: 'The time is now that you stand as the power you are. Of the Seven, you are the mightiest in the work you will do. Know that God is with you and that you are loved. Put down the cloak of lameness, and stand witness to the love of God. All that you seek will be given to you. Hide not from these gifts that are yours. You have only to open your heart and arms to receive them.' "

"To Ben, you will say: 'My brother, come forth and be known. The Children of God seek you. Hide not from your work, for it is your gift to the world. Wait not, for the time is now. Blessed are you, and I will guide you to your greatness.' "

Joe felt he had to speak again. "You really got a lot of faith in me, don't you? Like I'm going to say this to the Seven, and they are going to buy it. I know, I know, don't judge it, just do it. I still think you got—pardon the word—the *wrong* guy for the job, but I will do it. Now I have some more things I want to talk to you about. Like Donna's healing classes."

Michael stopped Joe before he could finish.

"What she is doing is worthy of her, and she will do things that will be called miracles in the times to come. She is more powerful than she knows, and you must guide her on her way. Oh, and Joe, you still need to listen to her counsel, for she is your wife, not your student."

Michael finished with, "After the Seven have been given their messages, I shall return. Be at peace and teach only love." His body began to fade into the backdrop of brilliant light. Then the surrounding light, itself, began to fade, leaving Joe invigorated with anticipation. It was all about to begin. He could hardly wait to call Gary and let him know that the decoding of the *Book of Revelation* was about to begin, and the two of them would be working with Michael.

With swift but deliberate hands he finished cleaning up the lily pond, then went back into the house to sit in front of his computer. The word processor was booted up and Michael's first message in nearly two years was typed into Joe's computer. There was much to do. It had been over a year since he had communicated with all six of the master souls. They, too, had waited for the seventh

to arrive. And, as reluctant as Gary might be, there was no doubt now that he was, indeed, the long-awaited seventh. A pout crumpled across Joe's face as he wondered if Gary would accept this information. Surely the guy would have to accept Michael's message. Or would he?

His "Michael File" updated and the computer put into sleep mode, Joe decided it was time to call Gary in Portland at the publisher's office. The secretary patched him through right away. "Well, guess who just showed up?" Joe teased.

It took Gary only a moment to realize what must have happened. "The Big Guy appeared to you?"

"Yep."

There was a pause as Gary uneasily toyed at the implications of this event. "So ... that means you have found the seventh?"

"Indeed I have. And you just might know this fella."

Gary started spinning paperclips on his desk, a nervous habit of his. "Is it me?" he finally asked.

"Yep, it's you. Michael mentioned you by name."

The spinning paperclips stopped spinning. "Are you sure, Joe?"

"About as sure as I am about anything. There is a message to you from Michael that I am supposed to give."

"I'm all ears," came Gary's softened voice. His mind was racing like a computer at warp speed. His previous conversations with Joe about having no teachers, no guru, replayed in his mind. Joe's message was not necessarily welcomed news.

Joe's gravelly voice delivered the story verbatim to the reluctant listener. After questions bounced back and forth, Gary finally acquiesced: "When do we start on the book?"

"Michael said he would return after I deliver the messages to the Seven."

"All right. Let me know when you have new information. And Joe."

"Yeah?"

"Happy birthday."

"It's a couple of weeks away yet."

A broad grin erased the sternness from Gary's face. "I know, Joe."

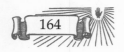

They said their goodbyes. Gary stared out his office window as he unconsciously replaced the receiver on its cradle as a mother would a sleeping baby. A kind of chill flashed up his back as he considered the implication of Michael's message. He would now have another book to write. And his future plans might have to wait.

As Joe sat back in his chair running his fingers through his plentiful, grayish-blond hair, he tried to remember what Michael had previously said about *Revelation*. He remembered weeping at hearing the truth behind the apocalyptic writing, then laughing at how it could have been so misunderstood. He remembered Michael telling him how a message had been given to the Apostle John to give to the seven churches so they might understand the error of their ways. In those days of the early Christian Church, the seven cities of Ephesus, Smyrna, Pergamum, Thyatira, Sardis, Philadelphia, and Laodicea were all located in Asia Minor. Each was more than a spiritual center; each was also a center of power, whether that was trade, learning, the arts, or suchlike. Because of the churches' failure to hear Heaven's message, there began the big lie that closed the door to most of God's children having a personal relationship with God. It had also stopped any further writings in the Bible, and institutional religion was born. The later mystification of *Revelation* by the churches had set into motion a fear-based spiritual concept demanding obedience.

Michael had revealed to Joe that *Revelation* was not meant for the future or the endtimes, but was meant for the early Christian churches of the first century, and not the people. Scholars had searched for the key to open the true meaning of *Revelation* and had fallen short. The later Churches had claimed there was no key, only the written word.

It was now time to bring before the world the true meaning of *Revelation*. This book of mystery, surrounded by great speculation, would soon be brought before the world by Joe and his newfound friend. That is, if Gary was willing to write the story. Joe remembered the first time Michael appeared to him. He remembered what Michael had said and how he, himself, had to make a choice similar to one that would face Gary. "This you must do or you will not be called upon again," Michael had said. "Teach

this which the Lord God has charged me to give you, for it is the Last Baptism of God's children. Have those you teach, in turn teach others, for they are well-meaning in their houses of God. You are not a Christ or even a prophet, but a servant of God (Who will put words in your mouth), and God's children will hear and understand."

It was not easy contacting the other six, as it turned out. Their lives had changed, and in some cases even their phone numbers. Deb had moved to Colorado to a new job. But after multiple attempts at leaving messages, all of the remaining six were eventually told what Michael had to say to each of them. Several days had passed since Gary and Joe had talked on the phone. Gary had made his decision. Something within told him he had to become a part of what Joe was attempting to do. Though he felt no closeness with the other six—and wasn't in much of a hurry to meet them—he finally decided he would allow himself to be considered "the seventh." It now seemed all that Michael had asked of Joe was in place.

Good Friday in California was not much different than any other day. Although some had the day off, Joe decided bills needed to be paid for materials used in a just-completed contract. As his hand scrawled his signature on one of the checks, he noticed sunlight on the wall in front of him. Looking up, he realized that the sun was shining in the wrong direction to be reflecting on his office wall. Not only was it on the wrong wall, it was also getting brighter and bigger. His eyes began to sparkle as he turned around to see Michael's familiar appearance. *He must be returning for another chat*, Joe thought as the brilliant light preceding Michael's form flooded the space before him.

The angel's presence emerged from the light as Joe chortled, "Well, Michael, quite an entrance this time."

The angel looked down at Joe's desk and spoke only one word: "Write."

"OK, you got it," Joe rejoined in an almost obedient manner. There was a serious tone in Michael's voice. "But give me a minute to get this thing set up." With nervous hands, Joe started up his Compaq computer and loaded his word processor. "Now, don't go too fast. You know what a lousy typist I am."

Michael said nothing as the software continued to load. "Done," Joe said. And as Michael spoke, Joseph typed.[1]

"Write what I say. Write not what you think I say, nor what you think you hear. Many have been called up to the highest to receive God's words, and upon returning have lost all meaning of God's truths. I will speak to you and you will write what I say. Add nothing and take away nothing, for I give you the words as given to me. Write them true, for God's scribe you will be in this.

"To the Whore of Babylon you will say:

You have been shown the truth of what was to come if you did not heed that which was shown to you. Did you change from the path you were leading my children down? Not one step did you take to lead them into the light. All that God gave you to alter your path was used to enslave my children to do your bidding. Had God been the angry, vengeful, and jealous God of which you speak, God's wrath would be now at your doors. The temples that you hold so holy would be laid to dust as would your Scriptures be in ashes. Count your blessings for it is a God of love that speaks to you.

The ransom that God's Son was said to pay was not to Satan or to any like being but was paid to the Churches. The ransom paid was his teachings, not his life. No treasure on earth is of more value than the words he spoke. This was paid to you for the freedom of my children, and you have twisted the words to bind them in greater numbers. Go to your flocks and say to them that when you were lame you did in God's name conspire against God's children. That you demanded their presence in your temples, you required their submission to Scriptures of your understanding, and if they did not obey, you threatened them with the loss

---

[1] Editor's note: Citations in brackets refer to corresponding passages found in *Revelation*, also known as *Apocalypse*.

of God's love and the pain of an everlasting hell. Say that you are no longer lame, and you now walk in the light of my love, and do these things no more. When this is done, if you wish to serve as a Church, you will serve God's children.

You have taken *Revelation* and added it to your Scriptures to make your words powerful and true—as if to set them in stone for all time—to judge and to damn by. I give you now, so all can read, that which was given to John. That you might see it has come to pass.

" 'Take this message to the seven churches,' was told to him [John].[2] He wrote to them what he thought it meant. The churches were trying to build a foundation that would stand through the ages. They built it out of the fears and desires of man. They had become like the Tower of Babylon, an object to stand upon to get to Paradise. Over and again you have said that this was the only way. To prove this, it was said that Scriptures could only be understood by the most righteous of my children, and all others were unworthy. Trusting not your brothers and sisters to find their own way to God, you conspired to lead them. God has shown you what would happen and you chose to ignore it.

"To the church of Ephesus, God said to teach divine love and grow in spirit, and they heard not.[3]

"To the church of Smyrna, God said to teach illumination of self through faith, and they heard not.

"To the church of Pergamum, God said to teach consciousness of natural knowing, and they heard not.

"To the church of Thyatira, God said to teach love as Jesus did, and they heard not.

"To the church of Sardis, God said to teach awareness and reason, and they heard not.[4]

---

2 [Rev. 1:4]
3 [Rev. 2]
4 [Rev. 3]

"To the church of Philadelphia, God said to open the gates to wisdom, and they heard not.

"To the church of Laodicea, God said to teach compassion and tolerance, and they heard not.

"When they received the messages, they made up stories of what God would do if they were not obeyed. What was shown to them was lost. Now, like an unpaid debt, it is time to be paid and the covenant fulfilled.

"He [John] was called up to the throne and, seated on it was the Love that God is.[5] The rainbow that was like an emerald is the Earth. The twenty-four Elders seated on the thrones are the hours of the day and night. The seven torches are the spirits of God that are given as gifts to mankind. The four beasts are the four natures of mankind. Mankind is mental, emotional, physical, and spiritual; and the spirit is of God and is in all things.

"It was then said, 'Who is worthy to open the scroll and break its seals?'[6] Not one of the churches was found to be worthy to open the scroll. Yet the scroll could be opened with the Christ Consciousness that was given to all of God's children. Murdered was God's Son for the truths he gave mankind. These truths will open the seals so that all will know the love that God has for them.

"Shown was the history of what had happened when the first seal was opened.[7] A white horse came forth, and its rider was armed with the bow of truth, and a crown of spiritual awareness was given to him that he could conquer all that lay in his path. In time he laid down his bow so that others could conquer for him. All the knowledge that was given to prosper, to heal, to live happily in a world of peace, was gone.

"The second seal was opened, and a horse of red came forth with a rider that was given a sword by man, that mankind might kill one another. Peace was no longer commonplace on the earth.

---

[5] [Rev. 4]
[6] [Rev. 5]
[7] [Rev. 6]

"The third seal was opened, and a black horse came forth with its rider holding a pair of scales. With these scales man must now pay to other men for the gifts that I have given to the world.

"When the fourth seal was opened, a pale horse came forth with its rider, and he brought death of all remembrance of the love God has for mankind.

"Then the fifth seal was opened, and he [John] saw all the enlightened ones that could not teach others of a loving God—they were killed for what they knew. They were given a place with God and told that more would come to receive their place, too, with God.

"When the sixth seal was opened, he saw that all the light had been taken or given away by man. All that they were left with was what the liars had told them. Empty were the words that were spoken. Mankind was in despair with nowhere to go, so they hid in the liars' temples out of fear.

"The four winds are the points of the compass that signify the mental north, emotional south, physical west, and the spiritual east.[8] Jesus brought these into balance that man could learn of God's love and compassion.

"The tribes of Israel were again given the enlightenment by God's Son. These were the twelve apostles that Jesus taught, and there was a great rejoicing for the gates were open to the love of God. More and more of God's children began to know of God's love. The ones that were dressed in white robes were the ones that heard the teachings.

"When the seventh seal was opened, there was a silence.[9] All who had heard the words of Christ need not hear more, for they were one with God. The seven angels that stood before God were again given the information to give to the churches. The message was again distorted, for man had not learned from the teachings of Jesus. Each angel's message was misused for the further spiritual enslavement of mankind. The bottomless pit of Ignorance and Superstition

---

[8] [Rev. 7]
[9] [Rev. 8]

was opened, and most of mankind fell into it. With this loss of spiritual enlightenment, the churches did battle with one another and the earth, and God's children all were to suffer at the hands of one another. Destruction was about the lands as war, famine, plagues, and the poisoning of the earth by mankind's actions.

"The four angels were released.[10] The mental nature was the first woe, and a third of mankind was seen as dead by the churches. The spiritual nature held fast with God. The seventh angel's trumpet was not to be sounded, for the time was not yet for all to hear. 'There would be no more delay,' was to announce that God's love for mankind was being fulfilled.[11] He went then to the angel of the Earth, who had an open scroll. He was given the scroll and told to eat it. God knew that what was in his mouth was sweet, but the digestion of the words would be bitter to him. Yet he was still to speak them to the world about peoples and nations and languages and kings.

"He was given a rod as a standard to measure what the churches said, but was told not to measure the enlightened outside the temple.[12]   For they will overcome the false teachings of the churches. The two witnesses will be given the authority to enlighten mankind and will come forth and teach. The sackcloth is the sign of mourning for the consciousness of mankind. They will speak of a God of love, and their words will be judged, and they will be dead in the eyes of the churches. In but a short time the two will be seen as the bringers of light, and the love of God will be seen. As the teachings of the churches are seen to be unfounded with the love of God.

"The emotional nature was the second woe, and another third of mankind will be seen as dead to the churches. The second woe had passed.[13] The physical nature was the third woe, which was soon to come.

---

10 [Rev. 9: 14-15]
11 [Rev. 10]
12 [Rev. 11]
13 [Rev. 11:14]

"The seventh angel blew his trumpet, and loud voices were heard, for God's love was now open to all as Jesus had said it was. This shook the last foundation of the churches.

"The female aspect of God appeared clothed with the sun, and the moon at her feet—both are symbols of light to the world.[14] The crown was that of the twelve powers of mankind. These are kindness, mercy, and contribution in the physical deeds of mankind. In the mental there is perception, understanding, and imagination. In the emotional are compassion, devotion and giving. In the spirit are faith, divine awareness, and consciousness. She is to give birth to a new state of being in mankind.

"The dragon that waits is the teachings of the seven churches, and would devour the child so it can keep its hold on mankind. This time divine intervention takes place, and the old teachings are denied the Child of Love. The woman had been sent into the churches to teach, that she would be safe, for it was prepared by God. The dragon would not easily find her there. The child that was to be born was the male aspect of God, and that is Love. The iron rod is a symbol of that unbreakable love.

"The dragon—being the old teachings of ignorance— and his followers, the seven churches, are cast out of God's authority to teach God's children. Then Michael and his angels did battle with the teachings by visiting mankind to spread the truth of God's love. In the enlightened of mankind, the awareness of salvation was proclaimed.

"With the old teachings having a short time, the dragon went after the woman. Trying to keep its hold on mankind, he spoke falsely of her. She was enlightened and rose above its words. The dragon, if it could not be accepted by all as the word of God, went to make it so.

"The beast that rose out of the sea was the new churches that rose out of the Age of Pisces, claiming to be aligned with the Christ.[15] It spoke of itself as the true word of God, and

---

[14] [Rev. 12]
[15] [Rev. 13]

many listened to it. **Those that spoke against it were killed or looked upon as dead. The God of love knew this and said that if you are taken captive, go into captivity and do not kill your captors.**

"**Then rose another beast like the first dragon and began to take authority over the earth.**[16] **As its legions grew, it deceived many, and it had the power over life and death. Anyone that did not have the sign of the beast could not buy or sell.**

"**Then were those that had the Father's and the Son's name written on them. No one could learn the new song but these. And they were those men that did not lay with women or women that did not lay with men.**[17] **They have been chosen as the first fruits and are the spiritual teachers. They are blameless and speak the truth of God's love.**

"**Fallen is Babylon the Great.**

"**Fallen, fallen is Babylon the Great.**

"**That which she has caused others to suffer will now be laid upon her. Those who had followed the beast and received the false teachings find it hard to accept the truth. Those that are enlightened are told to hold fast to the faith. Those that had left the old, false teachings were seen as dead. Those who now leave the false teachings die in the truth and will find peace in enlightenment.**

"**The false teachings, like grapes, were harvested and pressed to bring out any truth that they might contain. That which the teachings held was brought out into the light for all to see. The false teachings were thick with lies and were poured out on the ground because mankind could no longer consume them.**

"**The seven angels are called with their seven bowls and told to pour them out on the earth.**[18]

"**The first angel poured out his bowl onto the earth, and the physical began to heal itself.**

---

[16] [Rev. 13:11]
[17] [Rev. 14:4]
[18] [Rev. 16]

"The second angel poured his bowl into the sea, and emotion healed itself.

"The third angel poured his bowl into the rivers, and the mind became healed.

"The fourth angel poured his bowl on the sun, and the spirit came forth.

"The fifth angel poured his bowl on the throne of knowledge and changed it to divine knowing.

"The sixth angel poured his bowl on the great river of spiritual teachings, and they were seen to be untrue.

"One of the seven angels showed the downfall of all the teachings that were not of God.[19] Another angel came to bring enlightenment to the rest of mankind, and mankind saw what they had done.

"Then came a great awareness of what God has given to mankind, and great joy fell upon mankind. All of God's children were invited to share God's love. When they fell on their knees, they were told not to do that, for they were one with God.

"Heaven was open, and a white horse with a rider called Faithful and Truth came forth as the word of God, and was followed by another rider that spoke of God's love that all heard.[20] Then came an angel calling to the birds to feast on the false teachings. The spirit of mankind would no longer be harmed by these teachings. Then came another angel with a key to a pit and threw Ignorance and Want into the pit.[21]

"Then there was a throne, and on the throne were those that gave the truth a thousand years ago. Blessed were those that heard the first time, for they did not fall back into unenlightenment. Now that the thousand years has ended, the false teachings are to be cast out for all times.[22]

"The fire is the light in the darkness, and the sulfur is the love that heals. Then a great white throne appeared, and

---

19 [Rev. 17]
20 [Rev. 19:11]
21 [Rev. 20]
22 [Rev. 20:3]

it was again the Love of God upon it. All that is unknown or is of suppression is given Truth and is enlightened.

"Then there was a new Heaven and a new Earth, for all that was will pass.[23] The love of God will care for all according to their needs. Then one of the seven angels that had poured out his bowl took John to show him the Earth and all that will be.

"Then the angel showed the loving will of God for all mankind. He showed of a world without want, and nothing unloving can be found there. The sign of God will be on the foreheads of all. All that is written will be; blessed are those that can already know this.

"These words are as the light in the darkness—do not hide them away.[24] Let the unenlightened be unenlightened, and those that know the love of God know it. The loving God is bringing the rewards to all according to their works and will fill all that is needed.

"The last is a warning to those who would change the meaning of what is written.[25] The warning is of that which they denied themselves, of the gifts of God, but will be given in spite of what they do. The love of God is with everyone and everything, as God."

Anyone would have felt exhausted by such an intense effort of laying down exactly what had been dictated for such a long period of time. But Joe was aware how Michael's presence always filled him with energy. And this day was no different. Joe tried to comprehend what he could while taking Michael's dictation. Despite his efforts, he almost swooned with a sense of being overwhelmed by what lay before him.

"Michael, I am completely overcome by this once again," Joe said, remembering the first time Michael tried to tell him about *Revelation*. "I don't know where to start to ask you about all this. I am at a loss as to how people will hear this because I don't fully understand it myself. I know in my heart what you are saying, but in my mind it's a hard thing to explain to anyone. Some things are easily understood, but other parts are lost to me."

---

23 [Rev. 21]
24 [Rev. 22]
25 [Rev. 22:6]

The angel responded softly, "You have written things that are of the kingdom of God, not of the mind of mankind. I will teach you these things so mankind can understand. I tell you this now that you will know. Not all will be willing to hear. You will be scorned and called blasphemous names. To those, you will say that you were told to write this as a servant of God, and this you have done. You will not be alone, for one is with you that has known of God's works before."

"Are you talking about Gary or someone I don't know yet?'

"He knows who he is and has been, and the knowledge is but now coming back to him," Michael said.

"You're talking about when he lived during the time of Jesus, aren't you?" Gary had disclosed to Joe that he had been told by three separate adepts that he had walked with the Apostle Paul and other apostles.

"You still know things I have not told you." Which was Michael's way of saying, Yes, but why are you asking me something you've already been told? Joe had wanted verification of this information, and this was it.

"Does this mean I was someone big in the past?" Joe asked sincerely.

"In the past you were of no great importance to the teachings of the Master or the churches. It is not until this time have you chosen to do so."

"So what you are telling me is that I was a nothing and a nobody. Is that right?" There was that twinkle in Joe's eye again. He loved to poke fun at himself.

"All that you were in the past was to bring you and Donna to this point in your enlightenment. That is how it is for all. You are a part of God's plan, known for all times that were yet to come. We will speak of this with you and your Seven, and not now. I will return in seven days and we will speak again.

"Oh, Gary wants me to ask about some other things, too."

"In seven days we will speak again. Be at peace and teach only love." At that, Michael faded back into the surrounding whiteness of light, disappeared, leaving the office in a solemn quietude—as if out of reverence for what had just transpired.

THE CALL TO THE WHORE OF BABYLON

Something wonderful is going to happen," Michael had told Joe. The sound of Michael's voice, the feelings that emanated from his eyes had swept through Joe like an invisible crashing wave. *What could possibly warrant such a statement?* Joe wondered. Other than sounding like a quote from the movie *2010* Joe could only guess. As he reread the codex that Michael had dictated, his mind began to swim with questions. It was as if the decoding of *Revelation* was almost as mysterious as the original writing. How could he present such a document to people? How could anyone really understand it?

It was time to show this to Gary and see what he thought. And with the wonder of e-mail, the two men found themselves sending back and forth questions, and ideas, as well as possible answers. Joe's typing skills, or lack thereof, forced him to abandon any more e-mail. The next evening he called Gary. Like two kids who'd discovered a secret treasure, they chattered back and forth about the meaning of the latest information from Michael.

"Do you know what Michael meant by 'something wonderful'?" Gary wanted to know.

"He didn't elaborate. All I can tell you is we'll have to stay tuned to see how this will end." Annie's barking interrupted the conversation. "Scuze me, Annie is feeling ignored." Gary could hear the sound of her panting as Joe most likely was Dutch-rubbing her and talking at the same time. "But did you notice one passage in particular from the codex?"

"Well, I did notice that Michael kind of danced lightly on the matter of 666, perhaps too lightly. Whether Michael thinks so or not, this has been a major topic of theological and evangelical discussion for the last 1,500 years. You ought to ask Michael for more detail."

"No, that's not what I meant. Did you notice what he had to say about gays and lesbians?"

"Gays and lesbians? Are you sure?"

"You mean you missed it?"

"Gawd, I guess so. Can you read it to me? I have to tell you that I thought I read and reread that document thoroughly."

"Hang on. Let me find it." Joe's fingers tapped on the keyboard of his computer as Annie began woofing at something. Joe couldn't handle both the computer and her needs for affection at the same time. "Out!" he yelled with the voice of a drill sergeant. A short snort could be heard across the phone as the taps on the keyboard continued. "Here it is," he murmured. "You listening?"

"Yep."

" 'Then were those that had the Father's and the Son's name written on them. No one could learn the new song but these: And they were those men that did not lay with women or women that did not lay with men. They have been chosen as the first fruits and are the spiritual teachers. They are blameless and speak the truth of God's love.' Did you catch all that?"

"Yeah, I'm looking at it now. Joe, are you sure Michael was talking about gays? When I read that, I thought maybe he was talking about virgins, which is the classical interpretation, rather than gays and lesbians. I mean, those who choose a life of celibacy don't lie down with the opposite sex either."

"Hmmmm," Joe thought for a minute. "Nope, I don't think that was it. If Michael had meant virgins, I think he would have said virgins."

"Well, we really need to make sure, Joe. This has a profound impact on people like me. Spiritual first fruits? Jerry Falwell would have a cow. Certainly, I could see him calling us 'fruits.' But to be considered 'spiritual teachers' and 'blameless, speaking the truth of God's love'? Wow! That starts to fit in with my own ideas coming from the ancient notions of the indigenous societies. That gays and lesbians were seen as spiritually oriented rather than sexually oriented. Having an angel back that notion up could cause you a lot of trouble."

"Nonetheless," countered Joe, "I think I'm right on this. But I'll get more information from Michael when he shows up."

"Good. Be sure to also ask for more information on the 666 thing. If we do not address that in the book, no one, but no one, will take this information seriously."

"OK. I'll ask about it, but that doesn't mean Michael will answer. He tends to talk about what he thinks we need to talk about. You know what I mean?"

"I do. And if that happens, I'll respect it." The two chatted on until thoughts of bankruptcy over the phone bill caused the two of them to bid one another a good night.

As Joe hung up the phone, Annie ambled back into the office. She knew when she could and couldn't get away with asking for her needs to be met. "Oh, you want more loving, don't you? Well, what have you done for me lately? Have you done the dishes? No. Have you mowed the lawn? No." He sat there staring at the huge hound, drool dripping from her jowls. She stared back, answering with a "Woof," shaking her head excitedly, tossing missiles of white slobber across Joe's shirt. Rather than cringe, he grabbed for a drool towel like a father with a teething infant. "Come here, you sweet thing," he sighed tenderly, wiping the rest of the saliva from her drooping jowls, then the stickiness from his own shirt. Who could love such a creature more than Joseph?

After putting the towel down, Joe decided he needed some thinking time. It was just past 11:30 p.m., and what better way to think than getting lost in his favorite pastime—playing Tetris on his computer. Donna had recently reached top scorer, and Joe wasn't to be outdone. With the focus of a cougar in the hunt, he pursued

her hold on first place. After a few failures—or warming up, as he liked to call it—he climbed closer and closer to the tally. *One more level, and I should be able to beat her*, he snorted to himself. A light began spreading on the wall in front of the desk, but Joe was blinded by his great ambition: Tetris or bust. As the circle of light spread to a diameter of three feet, it caught his eye. The sound effects on the computer announced his defeat, but Joe heard nothing, saw nothing but the growing circle of light—now a full ten feet in diameter. The brightness blinded him as he barely made out the edges of the robe and the familiar platinum blond hair. Michael was back already.

Without even a *Hello, how are you*, he turned once again to his computer to load up the word processor. "Just a minute," he coached Michael, "Let me get things ready." As he loaded the manuscript of his past dialog with the angel on the screen, he set the typeface to blue and glanced at his heavenly companion. His eyes were like those of a thousand lovers melted into one. *A man could get lost in such love*, he thought to himself. But there was work to do.

"OK," Joe announced, clearing his throat. "Let's talk about this." He sounded more like a guy passing time with one of his buddies than a man sitting in the presence of a heavenly host. "I don't think what you have told me is any easier to understand than the original *Revelation*. Granted it does sound a lot more loving without the hellfire and brimstone. However, Michael, in order for people to hear this, it is going to have to be made simpler. When you speak it to me, I can see and understand, but afterwards, I just don't get it. If I can't, how in the world can anyone who has not talked to you understand? 'God's scribe you will be,' you said to me, and if I am that, then you need to help me write it in a way that anyone can read."

The loving eyes of the angel stared right into Joe's soul. "There is wisdom in what you say. Everything existing in the light of God is beyond the understanding of mankind. My name is in that light, and none of your words can say it. What has been shown is in the same light, is so awesome to behold that none can really see it. The words that are heard in that light are whispers in the minds

of mankind or as trumpets so loud you will hear it not. I will tell you in a way that all can hear."

"Great," Joe grinned with both hands in the air as if he were cheerleading. "Can we go over *Revelation*, like you gave it to me, step by step? If I don't understand it, or if I have some questions from the Seven, will you say it in a way that we will all understand?"

"I will give to you the words that will open understanding. Yet, some who read this will ask for more, and I have given what I have given."

Joe tapped his hand on the desk. "That means some people, no matter what we say, will want more information? I totally understand what you are saying. One more thing. Can you talk more like people, without sounding so much like an angel?"

"I will speak in a way that the truth is heard."

"OK, I guess. Let's start with the first ... "

Michael interrupted, "The Whore of Babylon is not a person or the Devil. A Church is not, in itself, the Whore of Babylon. The Whore is what you would call an institution, separate from God, of an idea or concept about God. Like a whore, it gives the illusion of love, and yet there is none. All that visit will need to return again, for they have been tricked into thinking that they have been filled. The words of the Whore are as a beast that will drag its victims back. Escape becomes impossible, for the victim has not the strength to do so and must return. Mankind has come to this, thinking the words are salvation."

Joe's fingers stopped their tapping. "So what you are saying, in other words, is that Churches are like that. They offer us a false sense of divine love that they do not have to give. In their teachings they leave us empty, with the need to come back for more, only to let us go, empty again."

"No," Michael responded. "A Church is something different than the entity. Or, what has been established as a church has taken the place of the true Church."

"Now I am really confused," Joe said. "You told me, before, that the Church has become more important than the people it is to serve. Now you tell me it ain't the Church. So why was John to take *Revelation* to the seven churches?"

The angel raised one of its hands, as if giving a blessing. "All will come to light as we go through *Revelation*. This a puzzle that has confounded your kind for ages. Be not too quick to understand just yet, for we are only at the beginning. Under each [passage] that I have given, you will write what has been made clear to you. So that your kind will understand, you and I will say it together."

"Let me see if I got this. You and I will go over everything you have told me? I can ask questions and you will tell me the answers?"

"You know most of the answers to your questions even now," said Michael. "You will put it in words for all to hear, and I will keep truth in what you write.

"One more question before we get started, though. Are you going to tell me who I am supposed to tell this 'Whore' thing to and how?"

"When the writing is done, the Whore will hear." Michael then began repeating the introduction to the codex, the message decoding *Revelation*. **"To the Whore of Babylon you will say: 'You have been shown the truth of what was to come if you did not heed that which was shown to you....'** " The angel continued until finishing the passage ending the direct address to the Whore: **" 'You have taken *Revelation* and added it to your Scriptures to make your words powerful and true—as if to set them in stone for all time, to judge and to damn by. I give you now, so all can read, that which was given to John. That you might see it has come to pass.' "**

As Michael paused, Joe peered at him with a quizzical look. "There are a number of things happening in your opening words. I will tell you what I think is being said, and you can tell me if I am correct.

(1) The Whore is a creation of man that has taken on a life of its own.

(2) A message was given to get it back on track.

(3) The message was misunderstood and used to coerce people into believing, out of fear.

(4) God sent Jesus with enlightenment as the ransom for the freedom of God's children.

(5) The ransom, or the enlightenment, was twisted and used against God's children.

(6) John was given *Revelation* to give to the churches, and it was used to frighten people into submission. What Churches must do is recognize their inaccuracies and teach only of God's love.

(7) You are giving the true message of *Revelation* so that we can really know about the love God has for us.

"Well said," the angel returned with a soft smile.

"That part isn't too hard to understand, but what comes after that is a mind-twister."

"Joe, what we are doing is untwisting the thinking so enlightenment will happen for all."

"Michael, you are speaking in a way that sounds more like we talk. I think this could work, so let's go on. Explain what is being said with the message to the seven churches."

With patience that would outlast stone, the angel continued going over the material from the codex. **" 'Take this message to the seven churches,' was told to [John]. He wrote to them what he thought it meant. The churches were trying to build a foundation that would stand through the ages. They built that foundation out of the fears and desires of man. They had become like the Tower of Babylon, an object to stand upon to get to Paradise. 'Over and again you have said that this was the only way.' To prove this, it was said that Scriptures could only be understood by the most righteous of God's children, and all others were unworthy. 'Trusting not your brothers and sisters to find their own way to God, you conspired to lead them. God has shown you what would happen, and you chose to ignore it.'**

"I will speak of the churches for what they are," the celestial continued, "so [all] will see the truth in what is said. A church is a gift from God to mankind to be used to help you through your time on Earth."

"You are going to need to get a lot simpler than that if you expect all of us to understand. Give me an example of what you mean as a church. You know, like something I can relate to."

With perseverance and understanding, Michael said, "Jesus was talking to his disciples and asked, 'Who do you say I am?' Each had their ideas of who Jesus was, but only Peter knew. Blessed was Peter, for he knew without being told, and it was on this rock that Jesus was to build his Church. Peter listened to his own knowing of truth and spoke with faith."

"So what does this have to do with the seven churches?" Joe asked with eyebrows raised.

"Churches are gifts that are given to mankind. The seven churches are those having each a gift to use in service to God's children. The messages to the seven churches were to tell each that they were misusing the gift. Four gifts are masculine: Philadelphia, Sardis, Pergamum, and Thyatira. The three feminine are Ephesus, Smyrna, and Laodicea."

"OK. I know what you are saying," said Joe, "but how do I say it so that others will understand?"

"Below each church write what I tell to you."[26]

To the church of Ephesus, God said to teach divine love and grow in spirit, and they heard not.[27]

"Ephesus is female in being and teaching. This church is as a mother's love, teaching her children of God's love. With knowledge of this divine love, her children will grow with a spiritual connection to God. John's message to this church was to put down its obedience to her new husband and return to her children lest they grow to be unknowing in spirit. Taken away will be gift to the church and its leaders if they do not—but they will eat the spiritual food of God if they listen."

To the church of Smyrna, God said to teach illumination of self through faith, and they heard not.

"Smyrna is female in the gift of life as a mother is. As in the beginning, before birth, a woman knows that there is life. Intuition

---

[26] Editor's note: All material in indented italic blocks reflects quotes from the codex (decoding of *Revelation*), found in chapter thirteen.

[27] [Rev. 2]

is the foundation that gives birth to faith. Listen to that which God is telling you and you will know not the fear of death. John's message to this church was to listen to the truth of God. False teachings will lead you away from your gift, and you will know it not. Those who claim to have authority of God have it not. Let them say what they will, for it is you who will have victory over the second death."

To the church of Laodicea, God said to teach compassion and tolerance, and they heard not.

"Laodicea is female with the gift to manage the home. As a woman runs the house, you will lead with understanding for those who know not. You will guide with mercy and tenderness in the words you speak as the woman of God's house. Know that you are loved and stand in the light of God, for true wealth is there. Speak of this love with authority and take your place to one side or the other. Give not your silence to those who would hear. Listen to your heart, for God speaks. Ignore it not."

To the church of Pergamum, God said to teach consciousness of natural knowing, and they heard not.

"Pergamum is male in spirit and knowing of God's love. You hold in your heart the truth, and knowing of God's love, you will not be moved. If the teaching of half-truths are told, you will only gain that which serves no one in spirit. If you gather that which does not nourish the spirit, your deeds will be made open for all to see. Hold true, for God will feed the spirit and forgive all that has been done."

To the church of Thyatira, God said to teach love as Jesus did, and they heard not.

"Thyatira is male in physical—the action of teaching of the love of God. You are doing the work that God has given you to do. Do not listen to the teachings that call you only to the physical world and of these things. All that was done will be undone when truth is returned. Guilt will be laid upon those who gathered material things only, and it will be laid on them by themselves. To those who kept balance, [they] will carry not [nor] lift upon themselves this burden called guilt. Hold fast and you will be known for loving as God does."

> *To the church of Sardis, God said to teach awareness and reason, and they heard not.*[28]

"Sardis is male in thinking—the mental understanding of the love of God. Clearheaded are those in truth, unlike those that seem to be awake but are yet asleep. Reason is not known to them, and all whom God has told of his love will pass them by. Those who would stay awake, God will give the authority to speak the truth, and the false teachings will shatter like clay pots."

> *To the church of Philadelphia, God said to open the gates to wisdom, and they heard not.*

"Philadelphia is male in the seat of passion and the gate of emotions. The key that you hold is that of outgoing love—the gift, the giving. Other emotions that you have would lead you astray if it were not for the love. Hold fast to the love and wisdom, for the other emotions will bow to you. For this you will be given an understanding of God and all that is of God."

As Michael paused, Joe summarized, "What I get from this is that each of the churches is more than just an actual building that housed a certain way of believing. Departed from the truth, their teachings were self-serving, to help them to grow in power, compromising what they knew to gain acceptance and be allowed to continue. Each church had a gift, like those given to mankind, and with it they would teach so we could understand. I also see that once they found something that looked like it was working, a foothold was made and most started to cater to the means and not

---

[28] [Rev. 3]

the message. John gave each a reminder of the gift they had been given, and told them to use it. Would you say that I have a pretty good understanding of what went on?"

"You say it well. Talk of it with Gary, for his words are of knowing in both worlds."

Which reminded Joe of the conversations, via e-mail and telephone, that the two friends had engaged in the last two nights. "Glad you brought it up," said Joe. "Listen. I've got a question about all of this. You told me that when God speaks, it is so that all can hear and know what is said. Well, given that statement, how is it possible that it got all screwed up? In case you haven't been keeping up on past and current events, most people don't have a clue what was said by John. Depending on whom you ask about *Revelation*, you will probably get as many answers as the number of people you ask. I guess what I want to know is what went wrong? If there was a wrong, that is."

"Had you been called up to God for this, you would see things that your kind are only now beginning to realize as possible. You are not ready to know of these in your mind. You would have stories of what you saw and heard that your mind cannot tell in true words. The way you receive these words, you have nothing to make up to describe it. I tell you what to write and if you do not understand, I tell you till you do."

"Would I be in error if I said our feeble minds are not capable of comprehending that much at this time?"

"Yes," said Michael, "and as Gary would say 'And that is being polite.' "

"Sorry I asked," Joe said with a knowing grin. "But I told you that you had the wrong guy for the job. Maybe I can impress you with what I know about the next part, given my limited awareness."

"Our time is done for now. Speak of this with Gary. After you do, we will speak again. Be at peace and teach only love." And with that, Michael stepped back into the light and vanished. Joe was getting used to the angel's abrupt departures at this point. There was little more to do than talk things over with Gary. Usually, when Michael departed, Joe felt exhilarated, wide awake with energy. But this time was different. Tiredness set in. And rather than give Gary another call or send e-mail, he decided to go to bed once the typing of all that had happened was finished and filed away.

The next day, Gary pored over the new e-mail. Each day seemed like Christmas, with a new present waiting for him online. Not only was the information from Michael spellbinding to Gary, but so were the conversations he was having with Joe. The two had grown quite close as friends. As he sped through the fresh text from Joe, he noticed that Michael had said nothing about the 666, nor had he addressed the question he and Joe had about whether gays and lesbians were, indeed, being addressed as "those that had the Father's and the Son's name written on them." It was time to call Joe.

As the two discussed the phenomenon of Michael and why he would talk about some things and not others, Gary asked Joe how the angel appeared to him. Was it like in a daydream or "for real"?

"I can tell you it ain't no daydream," Joe stated matter-of-factly. "He looks just as real as if you were standing in front of me. However, he has this kind of light around him that is unexplainable. If you've seen the movie, *Contact*, with Jodie Foster, where she ends up in the scene in space speaking with the alien who appears to her as her father, it's like that. The colors are like that. They're soft and almost iridescent. But very real. You could reach out and touch everything and feel it."

"Have you ever touched Michael?" Gary asked in the most polite way he knew how.

After pausing, Joe answered, "Ya know, I haven't, nor has Michael ever touched me."

"Do you feel you shouldn't touch him?"

"Well, yeah, kinda. I have this feeling that I don't want to be jolted across the room by touching him. You know what I mean?" The two men erupted into laughter.

"I think I do," chortled Gary. "In fact, I'd be thinking seriously if I should even be in the same room with him." There was a message of respect that flowed through Gary's words. It was one thing to hear people talk about angels. Joe was not the first person to talk to Gary about such matters. His own books relating to the realm of angels exposed him to many people who either had been touched by angels or had ventured into the world of the angelic.

But Joe was different. He was not starry-eyed, nor was he a fountain of what Gary called "angel-babble." Joe's feet were always planted on the ground. It was even easy to understand why Michael had called him for the work that was to be done. Joe saw the angel as a friend rather than a phenomenon. Michael was not some ticket into prestige. He was simply another loving friend. And Joe was a man who loved his friends.

Gary and Joe continued discussing what Michael might or might not talk about next. Each phone call brought a new list of questions to present to Michael. Oddly enough, Joe never asked one of those questions. He didn't need to. Michael seemed to be aware of them without their being asked. As the two hung up the phone, they both felt a sense of wonder about what was unfolding before them. Glimpses of Michael's early statement that something wonderful was going to happen began to appear between the lines of what was being given to Joe.

The next night, as Joe turned off the late show and headed down the hallway toward the bedroom, he noticed a light in the office. *Donna must've left the light on after working on the computer to finish her report for work,* Joe thought. The closer he got to the office door, the brighter the light emanated. Leaning his head forward through the doorway, it was what he suspected: Michael. "I was planning to go to bed," he told the angel in an almost kidding fashion. The truth of the matter was that he had been up until the wee hours the past three days typing out everything Michael had said to him.

"You have questions that I will answer," was all the angel said in response. It brought a smile to Joe's lips. He was tempted to ask Michael what happened to his sense of humor, but it was late, so why not get to the point?

"I do have a few questions that I would like cleared up," Joe said. "Gary and I were talking, and we got into what it meant about the seven churches. We talked about the meaning of the word "Church"—was it the religion or was it people or was it an institution? One other thing Gary pointed out was that, like the seven churches, the seven masters have things to work out in their lives. Do the seven masters represent the seven churches in this?"

Joe sauntered into the office to sit while Michael continued. "Gary is wise in seeing this. Yet to answer your question: All of the seven masters are as a church with a foundation to stand upon, to speak of God's love. Is it a mystery that each is of a different religion than the other? Each head of the seven churches was given a gift, as was each of your seven. Just as the ones that John wrote to and of, they were and are masters, yet they do not know this. This is your work—to teach them to know which church they are of."

"Why do you always do this to me?" Joe asked. "Why can't you just tell me, and I will tell them, and we can get on with it?"

"Should I tell you, and you them, they would believe it not. They will find which one they are of and will have victory over it. I am not here to talk of this now."

"I get it. We need to move on." Joe accepted with respect Michael's decision to get off this topic and move to another.

"This next part is pretty easy," Joe said, thinking about his next question. "After the seven churches got the message, they misunderstood and came up with what they thought the message was about. Now it's time to make things clear so God's plan can happen. Now this is were I get to impress you with what I figured out," he said with a knowing twinkle in his eye. "I was confused about the twenty-four Elders at first, but I think I got it now. Try this on for size. The Elders are the twelve apostles. I know there are twenty-four Elders, but with each there is day and night. The love of God is like the sun that shines on the earth of mankind. Sometimes there is light and sometimes there is darkness. The light is when we are enlightened, and the darkness is when we are in doubt. When we are in doubt, we have access to the seven torches to light our way. The four beasts are the four natures out of balance with one another."[29]

"Again you see the truth and speak it," Michael said.

"Thanks, but that's as far as I got. You will have to take it from here." Joe leaned back in his chair, wondering if he was going to have start typing away. Usually, when Michael wanted material dictated verbatim, he would say so.

---

[29] [Rev. 4:7]

When they received the messages, they made up stories of what God would do if they were not obeyed. What was shown to them was lost. Now, like an unpaid debt, it is time to be paid and the covenant fulfilled.

He [John] was called up to the throne and, seated on it, was the love that God is.[30] *The rainbow that was like an emerald is the Earth. The twenty-four Elders seated on the thrones are the hours of the day and night. The seven torches are the spirits of God that are given as gifts to mankind. The four beasts are the four natures of mankind. Mankind is mental, emotional, physical, and spiritual, and the spirit is of God and is in all things.*

It was then said, 'Who is worthy to open the scroll and break its seals?'[31] *Not one of the churches was found to be worthy to open the scroll. Yet the scroll could be opened with the Christ Consciousness that was given to all of God's children. Murdered was God's Son for the truths he gave mankind.*

Michael then said to Joe: **"Jesus was and is that Christ Consciousness. Jesus gave a message to the twelve and to the world. John saw what had taken place and what was yet to come."**

Shown was the history of what had happened when the first seal was opened.[32] *A white horse came forth, and its rider was armed with the bow of truth and a crown of spiritual awareness was given to him that he could conquer all that lay in his path. In time he laid down his bow so that others could conquer for him. All the knowledge that was given to prosper, to heal, to live happily in a world of peace, was gone.*

---

[30] [Rev. 4]
[31] [Rev. 5:2]
[32] [Rev. 6]

"The first seal was the white horse, and its rider was the corruption of that spiritual knowledge—the spiritual."[33]

The second seal was opened, and a horse of red came forth with a rider that was given a sword by man, that mankind might kill one another. Peace was no longer commonplace on the earth.[34]

"The second seal was the red horse, and its rider was given possession, and would destroy to keep them or to gather more—the physical."[35]

The third seal was opened, and a black horse came forth with its rider holding a pair of scales. With these scales man must now pay to other men for the gifts that I have given to the world.[36]

"The third seal was a black horse, and its rider was reason, and it judged all that was around—the mind."[37]

When the fourth seal was opened, a pale horse came forth with its rider, and he brought death of all remembrance of the love God has for mankind.[38]

"The fourth seal was a pale horse, and its rider was death, and it fed on anger, jealousy, and hate—the emotions."[39]

Then the fifth seal was opened, and he saw all the enlightened ones. That they could not teach others of a loving God—they were killed for what they knew. They were given a place with God and told that more would come to receive their place, too, with God.[40]

---

[33] [Rev. 6:2]
[34] [Rev. 6:3]
[35] [Rev. 6:4]
[36] [Rev. 6:5]
[37] [Rev. 6:6]
[38] [Rev. 6:7]
[39] [Rev. 6:8]
[40] [Rev. 6:9]

"The fifth seal was opened, and all that was enlightenment was destroyed."

When the sixth seal was opened, he saw that all the light had been taken or given away by man. All that they were left with was what the liars had told them.

Empty were the words that were spoken. Mankind was in despair with nowhere to go, so they hid in the liars' temples out of fear.[41]

"The sixth seal was opened, and, out of ignorance, God's love was gone. Insanity led mankind into temples to find their way to God's love. The four winds being held were the balancing of the directions of the four natures of mankind. When these four are in balance, no Religion is needed."

The tribes of Israel were again given the enlightenment by God's Son. These were the twelve apostles that Jesus taught, and there was a great rejoicing, for the gates were open to the love of God. More and more of God's children began to know of God's love.[42]

"The twelve tribes of Israel—which is *Ises*, *Ra,* and *El*— the three are female, male, and the child of love. The knowledge of this is the Oneness of God and is the completion of the number of mankind. When John speaks of a number in his writings, [it is] the vastness of God's love. When he speaks of white robes, he is speaking of those who are enlightened. When he speaks of blood, he is speaking of those who spend their lives in the service of God."[43]

The seven angels that stood before God were again given the information to give to the churches. The message was again

---

[41] [Rev. 6:12]
[42] [Rev. 7:4-9]
[43] [Rev. 7:14]

distorted, for man had not learned from the teachings of Jesus. Each angel's message was misused for the further spiritual enslavement of mankind. The bottomless pit of Ignorance and Superstition was opened, and most of mankind fell into it. With this loss of spiritual enlightenment, the churches did battle with one another, and the earth and God's children all were to suffer at the hands of one another. Destruction was about the lands as war, famine, plagues, and the poisoning of the earth by mankind's actions.[44]

The four angels were released.[45] The mental nature was the first woe, and a third of mankind was seen as dead by the churches. The spiritual nature held fast with God.

"The seven angels' trumpets that sounded were the messages of a warning of what mankind was to lay upon itself. The first four angels warned of misuse of Spiritual, Physical, Mental and Emotional. The fourth angel's trumpet sounded, and three woes would come out of this. Religious wars would come about. Famine, disease, and ignorance would grow out of this.[46] The first woe would pass, and two more would come.

The four winds are the points of the compass that signify the mental north, emotional south, physical west, and the spiritual east.[47] Jesus brought these into balance that man could learn of God's love and compassion.

"The sixth angel's trumpet sounded, and the four winds were released to enlighten humankind. Another third of humankind will be enlightened and seen as dead to religions. This is what is meant by 'All will be visited by the Holy Spirit and the Churches will fall away.'[48]

---

[44] [Rev. 8:1-5]
[45] [Rev. 9:14-15]
[46] [Rev. 8:12-13]
[47] [Rev. 7:1]
[48] [Rev. 9:12-15]

"The seventh angel sounded the seven thunders, but John was not to tell of them. It was not yet time for humankind to hear them. There would be no delay, for John was given enlightenment and told to give enlightenment to all nations. What he had received was the truth of God's total love for all. John knew that even if he was to speak it, not all would hear and believe. When John told of what he was given to tell, the people heard what they wanted."[49]

Michael stopped talking and stared at Joe to see if he had anything to say. "I know what you are saying about all this. But I am not sure that I am typing it in such a way that most people will understand it. My grammar isn't too good, and the way you talk, it is a little hard to get behind. Do I need not to change anything you say?"

"That which I have given you at first [the codex] is as it was given to me. Write it so," Michael insisted. "That which I tell you now, you tell in a way that others understand. You will not give it out until I tell you to. The message will not be lost or perverted again in a way so that it becomes lost."

"Does this mean Gary can fix things to say what you want it to say and be understood?"

"It does," was Michael's reply. "For that is why he is chosen. And if he strays, I will lead you back to the meaning. Our time is done for now. Teach only love."

Joe scooted his chair back to watch Michael fade into the light as he had done before. However, the angel did something he had never done before. Moving over to the sofa against the office wall where Poppy was sleeping, Michael looked down at her, snoring away as she normally did when Joe was at his desk. Michael bent over and placed his hand on her head. Her snoring ceased. As he stood back up and turned, he said to Joe, "You are truly blessed." Never had the angel touched anyone or anything in Joe's presence before. The gesture brought a broad smile to Joe's lips. Michael looked back at Joe, stepped back into the brilliance of light surrounding him, and vanished.

---

[49] [Rev. 10:3-11]

New Visions, New Understandings

*A*lmost a week had passed without Michael visiting. Frankly, Joe needed the rest. His maintenance business had suffered a bit from his late hours of typing while Michael spoke. Sometimes he wouldn't make it to bed before 6 a.m., while at other times he simply could not sleep from the charge of energy he had felt in the angel's presence. It was nice to get back to the routine of everyday living. However, it did not take long before Joe missed his celestial friend's company once again.

"Joe, rise and come with me." As Joe's eyes struggled to open, he could see a soft glow filling the dark bedroom. As he sat up, rubbing the sleep from his eyes, the angel's light brightened, eventually reaching the intensity of that first visit so long ago in this same bedroom.

With enthusiasm, Joe reached over to shake his wife. "Donna, you gotta see this," his gravelly voice urged loudly.

"She will not hear, nor will she awake," Michael said softly.

Joe looked down at his watch, reading it by the angelic light filling the room. It was two in the morning. He scratched at his haystack of hair, thinking that Michael was like some wrong number

in the middle of the night. Only, this night Joe wasn't going to roll over and surrender to sleep after hanging up. With a sense of inevitability, he mumbled, "Give me a minute to get some pants on."

"You need them not. Come with me," was Michael's retort. And without waiting for Joe to answer, he exited the bedroom and started down the hall.

Joe crawled out of bed and headed toward the office so he could write what Michael would tell him. But as he reached the doorway, he saw Michael continuing down the hallway toward the living room. *Where is he going?* Joe thought, deciding to follow him. Instead of going all the way down the hall, Michael turned right and went right through the wall.

"This is too cool" Joe chortled. Trying to follow the angel through the shortcut, he abruptly smacked his head against the wall with a thud. Shocked for a moment, Joe then shuffled on down the corridor, peering into the bathroom as he passed. He could see Michael's light coming in through the bathroom window. The angel had already exited to the outside and into the garden area. Joe quickened his footsteps through the dining room and out the patio door. Once outside, he felt the grass under his bare feet. But instead of coolness teasing the bottoms of his feet, he felt an unexpected warmth against his soles, as if a noonday sun had bathed the yard. For that matter, it should have been cold outside, but it wasn't. Joe was as warm as if he had stayed in bed. Michael was standing in the middle of the back yard with his back to Joe. Waiting there in his skivvies, Joe thought how comforting it was just to know that even Michael had a back. His hair lay on his shoulders and covered the neck of his robe. Michael's light shone against the night, reflecting off the fence, the neighbor's towering trees, the lawn, and all the surrounding plants. He stood there like a Christmas postcard staring toward the back fence. Joe walked up to his side and stood there, looking in the same direction. "What are we looking for?" he asked.

The angel looked down his shoulder at his companion and raised his arm, pointing with his finger in the direction of the back fence. Joe's eyes followed his arm to the end of his finger and past. As his gaze reached the fence, about head high, another light started

to overshadow Michael's. Joe didn't know what was going on, but he knew he didn't like it. Nervousness swept through him as he started thinking about being transported to a place he had never been—like maybe to see God—and he simply was not ready for anything like that.

"Hey, Michael, this whole thing is getting too scary for me. Where are you taking me?" Joe said with a voice that betrayed his fear.

"Fear not," was all Michael said. But Joe knew that when an angel tells you not to be afraid—well, that usually means there's a reason to be afraid. Something big was about to happen. Joe's mind was screaming at him to run away and save himself.

"I have come to show you, not to take you," Michael said comfortingly. This made whatever was about to happen easier, but Joe still didn't know if he was ready for it.

"Couldn't you just tell me, like before?" he implored.

"Behold the love of God!" Michael responded. And Joe stared point blank at exploding light opening before him. In the luminescence he saw what appeared to be a walking stick made of gold and surrounded by an aura of brilliance. The rod was encrusted with jewels along its side as if it were a rule for measuring. As Joe focused in on one of the segments to see how it worked to measure whatever it was it measured, he saw writing on it, formed by the jewels. But he couldn't read the inscription. Down at one end of the rod he saw what looked like a circular band or ring made out of diamond. The ring was about a quarter inch wide and about the same thickness. Although it encircled the rod, the ring didn't fit against it. It was more like a ring that's made too big for one's finger, but instead of falling off, it just hung there, sparkling like a diamond in sunlight. Little beams of light in all the colors of the rainbow shot off in all directions at once.[50]

It seemed odd to Joe that the ring rested at the bottom of the rule rather than the top. Why, he didn't know. His attention was drawn past the rod to what was appearing in the distance—something like a six-sided altar made of stones. The vision of the altar came into focus. The rod started to move towards the altar, and

---

[50] [Rev. 11:1]

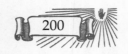

as it did so, the ring moved up to the top of the rule. The rod hovered above the altar for a moment, then eased down beside it as if to measure it. As soon as the rod touched the altar, the ring fell toward the lower end of the staff. When the ring reached a place on the rod apparently showing a measurement, a word sounding like thunder resounded from nowhere. Joe couldn't tell what point was being made, but clearly, a point was being made. Each time the rod moved away from the altar, the ring would slide to the top of the rod again. Each time the rod touched the altar, the ring fell about the same place, and another word thundered forth.

The rule measured each of the six sides of the altar. Then the staff and ring rose to just above where it had started before measuring. When it stopped rising, Joe heard what sounded like lightning start to crackle. The sound sizzled constantly without gaining or losing volume.

The rod pulled away from the altar towards Michael, and it then moved away as if to go somewhere else. Every time the rod arrived at something that looked like it was a religious object, it would measure it. Thunder erupted each time it measured, and then the crackling-of-lightning sound returned. Every time the rod moved, it went to what appeared before Joe like a statue or a grotto or an altar—some place of worship. Or a shrine or temple combining two or three sacred objects would appear before him and be measured. Most of the holy sites he didn't recognize, but he sensed that some kind of worship was held there. Then the rod started to move faster and faster from one place to the next. The space between one thundering word and the next became shorter and shorter. The crackling became a hiss, intensifying with each sacred place or object measured.

Joe then saw what looked like an Assyrian or Babylonian temple coming into view for measurement. Faster and faster and faster, from one to the next, ring and staff zipped like thoughts through one's mind. Some temples Joe recognized, and some he didn't. Each time the ring would move higher or lower on the shaft, and at no time did the ring go to the top. Then Joe saw the temple at Jerusalem in all its glory flash by, as did other temples, mosques, and churches. The Vatican, the Dome of the Rock, the Wailing Wall,

mighty cathedrals, even tents, and structures of every known religion were measured. The sound of the hissing crackle was now so loud Joe thought it would wake the neighborhood around him. He didn't know how much more of this maddening sound he could take without losing his sanity. He covered his ears to shut out the sound, but he could feel it vibrating in his head.

He yelled to Michael, "End this before I lose my mind!"

There was such an intense burst of all the released energy before him that Joe expected to be blown into fragments. Brighter than an atom bomb was the light, but there was no heat. The flash was the brightest thing he had ever witnessed. What he thought would be a forceful blast passed over him like a gentle breeze on a warm summer's day. A peacefulness engulfed him, filling him with a love he had never known. He felt ecstatic. There was nothing he needed or desired. He stood there bathed in a wash of love that he, in turn, felt for all of life. Turning to Michael, he asked, "Is this the reward for all of us from God?"

"No, Joe," Michael said with unequaled love, "What you feel is only the beginning. And like you say, 'You ain't seen nothing, yet.' Look." He pointed to the light again. Joseph turned to witness what he thought was impossible. He knew, without being told, it was the Christ, both in body and spirit, one a reflection of the other. The rod that had measured all the religions returned and measured the body, and the ring rose to the top of the rule. With each measurement the rod took, the ring stayed at the top. The sound it made was like music, and a gentle breeze carried forth the scent of flowers. The rod then went to the spirit and measured, and it was the same.[51]

"Why am I being shown this?" Joe asked.

"These things that I show to you are so that you may understand the work you are doing." Joseph looked back to the light and beheld the spirit and body once again. Then the two aspects of the Christ faded away.

He turned to Michael and asked, "What's this all about? First you tell me to write a book, and I do. Then you tell me to gather seven masters, and I do. Then you tell me to write about *Revelation,*

---

[51] [Rev. 11:3]

and before we are even done with it, you start me down another path, showing me this. Why?"

"Look at what you have learned from this. You now know what the rod was and how it was used. You know who the two witnesses are, and you know something else that you do not know you know." Joe remembered one of his conversations with Gary about the passage in *Revelation* regarding the two witnesses. Michael was answering this and other questions the two men had spent time pondering.

"This is like a puzzle," Joe said, "and you only give a piece of it at a time. Can't you give me the whole thing so I can figure it out?"

Michael responded, "This that you call a puzzle was given to John, and no one has been able to figure it out since then. If I tell you, you will believe it or you will not. If I take you through it, and *you* put it together, others will do the same through what you write with Gary."

"So then, you are still talking about *Revelation?*" Joe asked. "I need to go in and see where we left off last time, and maybe I will understand what you're saying." Joe turned to go back into the house and saw three of the dogs sitting in a row watching angel, man, and the light on the back fence. He looked around for the missing mastiff. "Where is the Bear?" he said out loud to himself.

"He guards the sleep of your wife and will not leave her side until your return," Michael answered.

Having had his question answered, Joe headed back to the house, the dogs following closely behind. As he shuffled through the door, he spotted the light he knew was Michael going down the hallway to the office. *I wish I could walk through walls*, he thought to himself. Rounding the corner, he joined the angel in the office. Michael stood in front of the desk. Poppy came into the room and walked around him to lie down at her usual place on the sofa. Joe could hear Annie climbing on the bed with Bear and Donna. Bogie had plopped himself in his favorite spot on the bathroom floor and had already begun his snoring sonata. Sitting down at his desk, Joe found where he and Gary had left off with the writing and started reading once more:

He was given a rod as a standard to measure what the churches said, but was told not to measure the enlightened outside the temple. For they will overcome the false teachings of the churches. The two witnesses will be given the authority to enlighten mankind and will come forth and teach. The sackcloth is the sign of mourning for the consciousness of mankind. They will speak of a God of love, and their words will be judged, and they will be dead in the eyes of the churches. In but a short time, the two will be seen as the bringers of light, and the love of God will be seen. As the teachings of the churches are seen to be unfounded with the love of God.[52]

"OK, I get most of this and what you showed me in the yard. Now it says that the two witnesses are given authority. I take this to mean that Jesus, the man, is one, and Christ, the spirit, is the other. John says that they will teach for three and a half years and then be killed. You said they will be seen as dead in the eyes of the churches." Joe went back and read again what Michael had said and saw what he meant. "Oh, I get it," he said. "Jesus, the man, was killed. When that happened, the spirit was gone, too. Three days pass, and resurrection. Both were called up to sit with God. Correct?"

The angel said nothing, so Joe guessed he was putting it together as it should be. "The sound of the seventh angel's trumpet was the announcement that the love of God is open to all freely. That shook the bases of all religions, given that they were not needed for us to have a connection with God."[53]

The seventh angel blew his trumpet, and loud voices were heard, for God's love was now open to all, as Jesus had said it was. This shook the last foundation of the churches.

"You see and hear that which is true," Michael verified. "Be at peace and teach only love. We will speak again soon."

Michael faded away into the light and was gone. Joe got up and headed off to bed.

---

[52] [Rev. 11:1-7]
[53] [Rev. 11:15-19]

The next day Gary was on the phone again after receiving an e-mail about what had transpired the previous night. "Joe, am I mistaken, or is Michael showing you what was shown to John before he wrote *Revelation?*"

"I believe that is exactly what is happening," said Joe. "And I'm not sure I care to see any more."

"Are you kidding?" Gary challenged, his voice filled with incredulity. "You get to see the visions of John, to witness the Christ, to hear the voice of God in thunder and music, and you don't like it?"

"It's not so much that I don't like it, it's that I am bothered by where this is going, where I might end up next. You didn't go through it. I actually thought I was going to go insane when that booming thunder went right through me. It was the loudest sound I ever came close to beholding. How would you feel having this going on around you?"

"Yeah, I see what you mean. Well, one thing is nice. And that is Michael is starting to give us the answers to the questions we've been coming up with. One can only wonder what else we're going to be told."

"Hang on to your shorts, Bubba, 'cuz I don't think this is over by a long shot."

The two discussed what each symbol meant and why Joe was allowed to see it. Their ideas only brought up more questions. Gary was beginning to understand Michael's comment about there never being enough words to tell everyone what the symbols meant. Like Jesus teaching his disciples with parables, the truth is in the story rather than the words. Each person hears as much meaning in the story as each is capable of understanding. It works like a hologram. For those who have little understanding, the story tells a little, but nonetheless contains the full truth. Not all truth is understood in the head. Indeed, it was becoming apparent that the greatest truth is understood by the heart.

The next day, Joe went outside to check the lily pond. Periodically it needed water added, especially during the oncoming

of summer. As he approached the Zen-like enclosure, he noticed a misty light forming just above the pond, and knew Michael was coming back. The closer he edged to the pond the clearer the angel became. Michael came into full view, then moved through the surrounding fence. He stopped and waited for Joe to approach.

Michael spoke: "Remove your shoes."

Joe realized that Michael was referring to this area being holy ground because of doing the Last Baptism there. Joe stepped out of his shoes as quickly as he could, commenting, "I guess this means we are going to do something?"

Michael was standing to the right side of the pond. Joe stood just outside the short fence, facing his heavenly companion. Michael raised his right arm up with his palm towards Joe, and, with a gesture, bid him to gaze at the pond. Joe noticed the papyrus plants had turned to gold. He moved up to the fence, and leaned on it with both hands. Peering down over the fence he noticed the rocks were also gold, as were the lilies in the water. The water had been changed to what seemed to be shining liquid silver. He thought to himself, *All this gold and silver must be worth a bazillion dollars*. He felt a little woeful, knowing Michael wouldn't leave it that way when he left. Light beams were shooting up and out from around the sides of the pond. "Impressed" would be an understatement for anyone who saw this spectacle.

"Behold, and write it," Michael instructed.

Immediately, an image started to form in the water, and it became clear to Joe that it was a woman. He thought, *This must be the woman that John spoke of. Yep, it has to be,* for she fit the description. She was standing on the moon and wrapped with sunlight. Her crown had twelve stars, like jewels, each a different color.[54] Joe didn't know how he knew, but he absolutely knew that the stars were the twelve powers given to humankind. They were placed on a crown because these were the highest of God's gifts to us. The child brought forth from her was to teach us about them and their use.

"Mary?" he asked.

"If it will help you understand," Michael returned.

---

[54] [Rev. 12]

That is when Joe felt that this wasn't a person as much as an aspect of the feminine. He saw the woman pregnant and crying out in the birth process, but not because the pain of birth was great. She was crying out because of the pain humankind was having spiritually. Through her would come the enlightenment. She was to end the spiritual suffering in the world.

> *The female aspect of God appeared clothed with the sun, and the moon at her feet—both are symbols of light to the world. The crown was that of the twelve powers of mankind. These are kindness, mercy, and contribution in the physical deeds of mankind. In the mental there is perception, understanding and imagination. In the emotional are compassion, devotion, and giving. In the spirit are faith, divine awareness and consciousness. She is to give birth to a new state of being in mankind.*[55]

Michael continued speaking as the visions appeared in the pond: **"The dragon is the ancient sign of spirituality. The color red is the symbol for the physical nature of mankind. The seven heads are the churches with seven headdresses that symbolize unenlightened thinking. The ten horns are the ten commandments on which the churches use to impale the minds of mankind."**[56]

Joe added, "The child is the Christ Consciousness that Jesus brought, and the iron rod is the unbreakable love that God is. What are the stars thrown to earth by the dragon's tail?"

"Whenever the darkness of unenlightenment stirs, it causes the light of true knowledge to fall upon the very darkness it is."[57]

"I think the woman in the wilderness symbolizes the women teaching in the early times, after Jesus was taken to God." Joe said. "The nature of woman fosters a birth of new enlightenment. She is honored as a teacher of light for about as long as Jesus is on Earth.

---

[55] [Rev. 12:1-5]
[56] [Rev. 12:3]
[57] [Rev. 12:4]

The war that broke out in Heaven was really the conflict between the false teachings and the truth. Since then, you and others have visited us to help us know of the love that God is. The dragon being thrown down is the false teachings being seen as false. The Devil is unenlightened thinking and all that comes out of it." Joe kept looking into the pond, watching this strange show of events, and realized what was being shown. Whenever any of it became unclear, Michael would speak to clear it up.

"The wings that are given to the woman are intuition and the ability to give birth to the innocence of truth. These things have allowed the light of the world to grow from time to time. The wrongful thinking is as the dragon, and it spews forth false words like a river. The earth opening its mouth and swallowing the river is the place where all lies will be tested. Truth will swallow up the muddy waters of the wettest of lies."[58]

The beast that rose out of the sea was the new Churches that rose out of the Age of Pisces, claiming to be aligned with the Christ. It spoke of itself as the true Word of God, and many listened to it. Those that spoke against it were killed or looked upon as dead.[59]

"The old teachings of old religions are losing the hold they had on mankind. Knowing this, a new beast rose out of the sea. That being the time of the Age of Pisces, it aligned itself with the signs of the age. The dragon had the same heads, headdresses, and horns as before. The blasphemous names were the names it called itself. With lies, it spoke of having authority given it by God. The dragon gave the beast all its teachings to tie the old with the new. One of the heads was claimed to be that of the teachings of Jesus who was slain. From this head, the beast had tied itself with the old covenant and the new. Mankind was enslaved to false religious systems that claimed authority from the old teachings of God. None could make war on the beast, for that would mean going

---

[58] [Rev. 12:14-16]
[59] [Rev. 13]

against the will of God. Anyone who was enlightened was only to believe what they were told and worship the teachings of the beast."[60]

Joe saw what looked like the waters that had been swallowed by the earth rise out of the earth again. This appeared to be a transformed image of the first beast, a greater likeness to the teachings of Jesus. He could not understand what this was all about, and Michael's words came to his aid.

"The second beast teaches that which is false. Look at its horns. They are like the male and female love of God, yet they are not. The mortal wound has been healed, it is said, and surely the path that is given is the true way to God. Humankind is now drawn into the big lie, saying that if you did not believe, you would be dead to God. The churches used an old ritual to bind humankind to the beast—this was the baptism on the forehead as a mark. A ring was placed on the right hand with a sign from one of the seven heads of the beast. Mankind was told they could not get or give enlightenment without this mark. God would recognize only those who had this mark, to be allowed into the love God is. This is the lie they told so often that it became as if it were true."[61]

Joe gasped as he finally realized what the last part concerning the number of the beast really was. "Michael," he said. "I know the number of the beast."

Michael just smiled back and said nothing, as if he was waiting for him to speak.

"When you came to me the other night," said Joe, "you showed me the number of the beast didn't you? It was all of the religions of the world, wasn't it? I bet if I had counted them all, they would have come to 666, wouldn't they?[62] That has been the lie we have been told over and over. *When we turn our relationship with God over to any system, we have taken the number of the beast.* That's why you are making me go through this a piece at a time, so I can find the light of truth from within." *I win the purple jelly bean*

---

60 [Rev. 13:1-10]
61 [Rev. 13:11-17]
62 [Rev. 13:18]

for this, Joe joked to himself. He understood the importance of his realization.

"Even better, Joe, you have taken the mark of God on your mind. Look again into the pool and see those that have the mark even now."[63]

Of all the things Michael had shown Joe, this was something he was not ready for. He burst into tears as he saw people he knew and had known standing with what looked like, what appeared to be, the Christ. He sobbed at the sight of his past gay friends who had died years ago. The joy was almost more than he could stand, knowing that they had made it. Heaven was theirs. Some of the people he saw were still alive today, and some were dead long ago. When he saw his old friend, Chico, who had died from AIDS, in the crowd, happy and healthy, he lost it. Joe's knees buckled under him, hitting the ground. Losing even his sense of balance, he fell, his back thumping against the fence. His emotions poured out of him.

"It's true," Joe choked through the tears, his nose running like rain on a window. "God is a God only of love, and God loves all of us." He then felt the warmth of a hand on the top of his head. Looking up he saw Michael leaning over him with his arm outstretched.

"Bless your heart," was all he said. The tears stopped and Joe regained his composure, but was still unable to stand.

Michael had never touched him before, and he had never tried to touch his heavenly friend. He didn't know why. As Joe's mind cleared, he thought, *Given the people I have just seen, and the fact that they were gay, does it mean I am too?*

"No," Michael said, knowing his thoughts. "You knew that these people were gay when I first gave you what to write. You and many others know things that you are not aware of yet. Be not surprised when you do. The song they sing has been learned, and is being learned, by the male and female in the male and female. These are the 'first fruits' spoken of in *Revelation*.[64] They are in touch with the male and female natures in all things. These are the ones who chose, and were chosen, to live life this way. The

---

63 [Rev. 14:1]
64 [Rev. 14:4]

religions of the world have cast them out as sinners and allowed them not the love of God. Blessed were they, for the love of God was all they had. They were set free to find the connection with that love.[65]   They feel the spiritual connection of both masculine and feminine."

> *Then were those that had the Father's and the Son's name written on them. No one could learn the new song but these. And they were those men that did not lay with women or women that did not lay with men. They have been chosen as the first fruits and are the spiritual teachers. They are blameless and speak the truth of God's love.*[66]

Joe responded, "Gary said this part could mean that they were celibates or virgins."

"Religion would tell you so," Michael said, "yet that does not make it so. When you abstain from sex, you abstain from nature, and are out of balance. Only when the four natures of humankind are in balance will you be one with God.

"The wisdom you have found will be found by others, and those that read this will see the truth in what is written. Much has been asked of you, and much have you given. I will not speak to you again until you have rested. Be about that which is before you. Be at peace and teach only love."

With that, Michael stepped back into the brilliance of light and disappeared. Joe sat there stunned by all he had seen, heard, and felt. The lilies were no longer made of gold nor the water silver. He stretched his hand over the fence to touch the pond, sending ripples across it, as if to remind himself and the life in the pond that they were still a part of the extraordinariness of ordinary life, though on sacred ground.

The next day, Gary devoured every syllable of Joe's e-mail. It was like reading a mystery, a love story, and letters from God, all wrapped into one. As his eyes widened toward the end of the message, gulping every word Michael revealed about gays and

---

[65] [Rev. 14:3]
[66] [Rev. 14:4-5]

lesbians, he dared not believe what he was seeing. Reading and rereading the passages could not satiate his desire for more truth. The fullness of the message grabbed his soul as if yanking it into a bonfire of light. Consumed with a growing blaze of feelings, he scooted his chair back burying his head in his hands. The weeping started softly as the realization that "those men that did not lay with women or women that did not lay with men" need not suffer any longer. Millennia of hatred, bigotry, retribution, and torture could now come to an end.

The weeping now became sobbing. Beneath the tears, Gary reviewed his own life in retrospect. So many wasted years living in fear, so many wounds uselessly inflicted, so much living in loneliness with dark secrets that could have been celebrated in the light. Michael's words echoed through his mind, his heart, reaching deep into his soul. He sat there reeling, seeing himself clearly for the first time. Amazement replaced grief. Could the world accept what he was reading? That all the separation, all the us-versus-them, all the hatred and violence were nothing more than waste and illusion? Nothing more than people choosing fear over love?

It would be so easy to rage against centuries of abuse fostered by the very religions that were supposed to inspire all of humanity to greater heights. But Gary found the angel's words were far too powerful for anger. The past was completed. It was time to look ahead to a new kind of world, a new way of living in the fullness of love. His soul now felt a healing balm in the truths Michael had shared. Heaven had delivered a gift. It was up to humanity to open that gift and delight in it. Like a sea moving to high tide, Gary was slowly flooded with a knowingness of what had to be done.

Automatically, his thoughts drifted back to what Joe had said about Mark. Had not Mark's own life been a harbinger of what was to come? Mark made no big deal out of the fact he was gay. In fact, he'd get just a little upset if people saw predominantly that in him. Mark had lived his life as a bridge builder, traversing many barriers that others had tried to beat down, blow up, or rage against. He had dealt not only with racial prejudices and religious prejudices, he had also dealt with being shamed for being severely dyslexic. And what

about Shari? She was not a woman looking for retribution. Her loving ways sought only truth, sought only peace. Her conversion to Buddhism was not a backlash response to the emotional injuries suffered at the hands of a Judeo-Christian culture. No. What she had asked from life was, simply, love and harmony. How trite such a notion might seem if applied to anyone else but this fortress of a woman. It was too plain to see—watching Shari snap a picture was an act of witnessing this woman of power capturing the most subtle beauties of life on film. Gary, Mark, and Shari all wanted the same end result: that they be acknowledged and accepted as a normal part of life. Michael was taking such acceptance one step further. Not only were these people a part of life, but an important part of life.

As Gary thought about what Mark stood for, his mind reflected on another Black man who had impacted his life in ways he could not have imagined. This gifted man was an African shaman-priest, Malidoma Somé by name. In American society, the closest description people could apply in describing him was "medicine-man," or "shaman." Not only was Malidoma no ordinary indigenous, he was no ordinary human, period. A learned scholar with two Ph.D. degrees and three master's degrees, Malidoma had divined for Gary things about himself he had told no one. It was Malidoma who had taught him about the "Gatekeepers," the spiritual ones. In his own tribal culture, there was no word for gay, because those who were gay were not seen as sexually-oriented. They were seen, treated, and revered as spiritually-oriented beings. They were a necessary and natural part of the village. These were the ones who could heal, could divine the future, could cross the dimensions between the natural and supernatural. These ancient tribal people knew why such transgendered beings existed. In the Otherworld, there was no male nor female. There was only the Oneness. And those who were blessed with the capacity of embracing both the masculine and the feminine were able to cross the boundaries of what Western civilization labeled "supernatural." To these people, there was no boundary between the natural and supernatural.

Had not Christian teachings carried a similar message buried within their own writings?: In Christ there is no male nor female.

Was this not also what Michael was referring to when he said, "You and many others know things that you are not yet aware of. Be not surprised when you do. The song they [gays] sing has been learned, and is being learned, by the male and female in the male and female. These are the 'first fruits' spoken of in *Revelation*. They are in touch with the male and female natures in all things. These are the ones that chose, and were chosen, to live life this way."

Had not humanity created war between the male and female? "East is east, and West is west [men are men, and women are women], and never the twain shall meet." Such separation was a war between the sexes, and such war was inevitably a war against the Self. In college, Gary had discovered (in his readings of psychologist Carl Jung) that in all of us are both male and female. This statement had led Gary on a search that never ceased. His first clue to the truth came in a course on history of the Bible. In the class, the instructor went back to the original Hebrew word for God. In Hebrew, the word is neither masculine nor feminine as it is in English. In fact, the Hebrew word for God is neuter. In English, neuter denotes neither masculine nor feminine, but in Hebrew neuter *includes* both masculine and feminine. God is not a he nor a she. God is a *we*. Once again, amazement filled him as he had experienced the full inclusiveness of God as described by Michael.

Gary knew that Michael's message foretold of a world of peace—not only physical peace, but mental and spiritual peace as well. His journeys with Malidoma had taught him that those who were gay had the capacity to own both their masculine and feminine in the most powerful of ways, living the Sacred Marriage of the Self. Even those who are not gay have the capacity of acknowledging and ultimately embracing their spiritual androgyny—their masculine and feminine balanced in harmony. All wars begin within individuals. All peace begins there as well.

Gary had to talk to Joe about all that was crashing in on him. *Imagine what Joe must be going through*, he pondered. *The visions of John are being relived and offered once again to all of us. Joe's mind must be in tatters, to say nothing of his heart.* That was it. He had to call Joe and bless his heart.

THE END OF ENDTIMES

*I*t had been several days since Michael's last visit, and Joe was not looking forward to the next. He had been overcome by the emotions and power of Michael's last two visitations. The sheer wonder and magnitude of the visions had taken his mind beyond its limits and his soul to its depths. Both Joe and Gary wondered what could be coming next. They joked about it on the phone.

"I hope that was Michael's peak performance this last time," Joe said half seriously, half hoping for a laugh. "Wouldn't it be nice if the rest of what Michael had to say was just warm and fuzzy stuff? You know, like everybody be happy, smile, peace will reign forever, and war will come to an end. That's not asking too much, is it?"

"Somehow, Joe, I don't think that's going to happen. There are still a few big questions that Michael hasn't addressed and a few small ones that are still on my list. Say, next time you see him, why don't you just kinda hint about leaving some of that silver and gold behind. I'm sure we could put it to good use."

The two men enjoyed a bit of irreverence mixed in with the awe that stared them in the face. "Kinda keeps things in balance," Joe would say. Gary had never met someone with the sense of

215

humor and sagacity that Joe possessed. It was as if vestiges of his Harley Davidson days, his long hair, too many cigarettes, and smelly leather, yearned to tease at the profundity enveloping his life from the angelic realm. Like giggling in church, this impish side wanted to do its own stirring up.

That night, as Joe played back in his mind the verbal fun and silliness the two men had exchanged over the phone, he could not escape a feeling of relief at not having heard from Michael in over a week. If the truth be known, Joe was even a little scared of seeing his angelic buddy again. There was no denying the changes that were coming over him at being the recipient of knowledge the world had long puzzled over. As the question, "Why me?" formed in his mind, out of the corner of his eye, Joe spied Poppy raising her head for no apparent reason. Automatically, he turned to see what she was looking at. "Well, here we go again," was all he said as he watched the familiar light overtaking the office space.

Trying to stall any show-and-tell stuff like he had witnessed during the last visit, Joe started talking even before Michael was fully present. This was Joe's counterpart to whistling in the graveyard. "Michael I have been reading the 'Babylon has fallen' part. That is another easy-to-understand part of what you have given me. Let me tell you what I think it means, and then you can tell me if I got it.

"The first angel brings a message of God's love to all people. He tells the religions of the world to return to teaching only of the love of God. The hour of judgment is to bring the truth of their teachings into the light.

"The second angel proclaims the fall of Babylon. What he is saying is the gathering of wealth by religion and governments is at an end.

"The third angel tells of torment that comes from their loss of all they have said to be true. To me it's like a man who has grown rich by taking advantage of others. He wakes up one morning to find all that he has is being taken away. He can't sleep, he can't eat, and worst of all, he has lost his ability to get it back.

"The inner voice of enlightenment says, Hold on to the truth. Blessed are those that are seen as dead by religions, for they live in the light of knowing.

"The Son of Man is the Christ Consciousness. The sickle is his teachings, and that is what brings all the enlightened together.

"The fourth angel that came out of the temple announced it was time to gather all the enlightened. The Christ Consciousness cleared the earth for spiritual knowledge of oneness with God.

"The fifth angel came out of the temple with a sickle that is the love of God. The sixth angel, from the altar, is the life that emanates from God. The seventh angel, with the fire, is the light of God.

"The grapes are the religious teachings that had grown over the years. They are pressed outside the city so everybody can see what was really in them—the city being all that was built on the foundation of these teachings. The blood that was pressed out are the lies that have been told for the last two thousand years. Given it takes two thousand years to go from one age to the next—which brings me to another point concerning the seven angels pouring seven bowls. If we are about to enter the Age of Aquarius, and that sign is a man pouring something, too, I don't think it is a coincidence."

Michael stared patiently as Joe finished his soliloquy. "It is not. For God has put the stars in the sky as a sign for all times, past and to come. You have done well with what you have seen."

Still stalling, Joe posited, "This brings up a couple of questions from Gary." The angel waited with patience. "Michael, Gary needs to know why you didn't answer me with some kind of response to what I said about the number 666? Also, what are you saying about religions being a gift from God?"

The heavenly guest answered, "One was not needed, for your words were true. Had you spoken of the sixty-six books of the Bible in the sixth century, I would have led you back to the path of truth. I will tell you when you are off the path."

Joe had to smile. For this answer indicated that Michael had been eavesdropping on the phone conversations that the two men were having. Joe had put forth the idea from information he had gleaned from a World Wide Web site which had postulated that 666 was in reference to 66 books existing in the Bible in the 6th century. Gary had disagreed, and believed the topic too important for conjecture. He had asked Joe to wait and see what Michael would say.

Joe tried to make his point one more time. "I want you to know that I trust you and what you say and don't say. However, if there is room for those to dispute it, they will. So all Gary wants to do is to make sure that it doesn't happen."

"I hear, and tell you this: Be not foolish in your thinking that mankind will not bend or deny what is written. I spoke not of religions being a gift from God, I spoke of the Church being a gift from God. Did not religions demand human sacrifice of children? Did they not do the same of women and men? Religions take from God's children, saying it is for the love of God. Did you not hear?" Michael asked point blank.

"Yes. I heard you," Joe said. "But most people seem to think of 'Religion' and 'Church' as one in the same."

Michael countered, "As they do money as wealth, sex as love, and dying as the end. A Church is a gift from God, that you may live in the knowledge of God's grace. A Church is the foundation on which the spirit stands. A Church is a wedding of like spirits to serve their brothers and sisters. They find their own Church. Religion [however] is a creation of mankind, to gather to itself, that it might grow and be powerful. Religion will make false claims to their kinship, God being the only kinship. Religion offers indebtedness to one another. A Church gives love freely to all of God's children."

"I feel like I am being scolded for not understanding a very basic concept. Michael, if you want people to understand, you'll just have to put up with these questions."

"Come," was all that the angel said.

Inside Joe rose an *Uh, oh*. "Can't you just tell me about whatever it is that we are going to see?"

"Come," Michael said again as he turned down the hall. Joe knew there was no getting out of this, so off he trundled, once again adorned only in his skivvies. Michael passed through the wall again while Joe raced through the patio door to the back yard. His eyes delighted in watching Michael move across the lawn with his light shining in the night as if he were a giant glow-stick trick-or-treating the neighborhood. The humor of the moment kept Joe's mind off of what might happen next. His celestial companion stood

in the middle of the yard like a fountain of light and pointed his finger at the top of the neighbor's pine trees. He then began to move his hand down with his finger still pointing as if tracing some outline against the night sky. As his finger moved down, the trees against the backyard fence began to glow with light. The tops of the trees turned to gold, as did the outside branches. As the trunks of the trees turned to gold, Joe realized, given the size, this was going to be something big. He swallowed hard, remembering the last time the angel displayed such wonder, although on a much smaller scale.

The fence and the pond were nothing compared to what was unfolding before his eyes. The trees were easily three stories high, and the space between them large enough to park an eighteen-wheeler. *Yes,* Joe thought to himself, *This could kill me.* A polished-silver water filled in all the space between the trees. A great tent of gold appeared, and it opened. As it did, Joe witnessed an angel looking a lot like Michael, but with red hair, emerge. Other angels now exited the tent, but they didn't look like Michael. One looked like he was Arab, the next looked Asian, another was African. The next looked like a Native American, followed by a Polynesian, and the last appeared to be Indian or Pakistani. Joe tried to make them out more clearly but couldn't quite get any of them in focus. Each was holding a golden bowl, and he heard a voice tell them to pour the contents onto the earth.[67]

The first angel came forward, and Joe couldn't help but notice his flaming red hair. *Irish,* he thought to himself. As the angel poured his bowl onto the earth, all that was unclean came to the surface of the land. What Joe could see was more than the earth itself. He saw what looked like flesh doing the same, appearing like pus from a festering wound. As the uncleanness came into the light, it was dissolved away.[68]

> *The first angel poured his bowl onto the earth, and the physical began to heal itself.*

[67] [Rev. 15:5-16:1]
[68] [Rev. 16:2]

The second angel came forth. He looked Polynesian, at least as far as Joe could make out. Or perhaps he was from some island nation. He poured his bowl into the sea, and it turned red as it rendered up anger and sorrow and hatred along with all the emotions that do not serve love. And they were dried up by the light.[69]

> *The second angel poured his bowl into the sea, and emotion healed itself.*

The third angel came forth and poured his bowl into the rivers. This was the Arab-looking angel. What he poured into the river attached itself to everything that was in the river and brought it to the surface. As all the substance surfaced, it turned to a blood-red color, very different from the sea. Joe felt a madness in mankind vanishing as the water cleared.[70]

> *The third angel poured his bowl into the rivers, and the mind became healed.*

The fourth, Indian-looking angel, poured his bowl onto the sun, and the sun became very bright. As the sun began to grow in size, Joe could feel a strange warmth, as if he were standing in front of a campfire. What seemed so strange was, instead soaking the warmth up from the outside into his body, it was just the opposite. There seemed to be a loving, warm glow beginning deep inside his body which then radiated outward. It was very clear to Joe that he was not his body.[71]

> *The fourth angel poured his bowl on the sun, and the spirit came forth.*

The fifth angel was African in appearance. And he poured his bowl on what looked like a throne. The throne was made of

---

[69] [Rev. 16:3]
[70] [Rev. 16:4-7]
[71] [Rev. 16:8-9]

books and scrolls that looked as if they were gold but were not. The throne started to fall apart and blow away like ashes in the wind. Joe saw people trying to catch the pieces that were blowing away. Frantically they attempted to put the throne back together. As the fake gold came off, Joe could see a throne of golden light taking the old throne's place.[72]

> *The fifth angel poured his bowl on the throne of knowledge and changed it to divine knowing.*

The sixth was the Asian angel, and he poured his bowl on a great shining river. Craters made of words came fourth as the river's light dried up. Joe saw people walking away from the false teachings. One by one, they walked away and became a light of their own. Some did not walk away but gathered together in numbers to have what has been, be again. Those not of light came down many roads to the place where the old throne had been. Some on the road became beings of light and walked away from those who were not of the light. Those remaining called after those of the light who were leaving. "Return to the flock and be saved. Go not, for if you do, you will perish and suffer forever," they cried out.[73]

> *The sixth angel poured his bowl on the great river of spiritual teachings, and they were seen to be untrue.*

The seventh angel, who appeared to be Native American, poured his bowl into the air. **"It is done,"** said a voice coming from the temple of the golden tent. Lightning flashed, and thunder sounded as the face of the earth changed. A great city of power was split into three parts. The first part of the city was that of religion, which was the emotional. The second part of the city was that of government, which was the mental. The last part was material things, and that was the physical. When these were split from one other, they could no longer hold power over the people. Small

---

[72] [Rev. 16:10-11]
[73] [Rev. 16:12-16]

groups, like islands of false teachings, disappeared, and great multitudes, like mountains of false beliefs, crumbled away. Like giant hailstones of light, enlightenment fell from the heavens as gifts to God's children. Those who had not yet received a gift cursed what was happening as the enlightened left the flocks.[74]

Then the angel with red hair said, **"Look! I will show you the truth of the Great Whore and of the nations drunk with ignorance."** Joe was shown what looked like a kindly mother caring for her children. She was adorned in what, at first, appeared to be fine silken robes, and she was covered with jewels, pearls, and gold. Looking closer, he could see the riches she wore were fake, dull like that of a copy, or paste. Her robes were made of rags, made to look as if they were silk. She had a cup of what looked to be gold filled with her own teachings. And she, too, was drunk with ignorance.

"Behold the truth of the woman and the beast and the one yet to come." Then Joe saw the seven churches that had strayed away from enlightenment. They held the chair of the woman, as a slave would, to do her bidding. Another church was about to come forth but was not visible yet. This church was to be the one that would claim to be the Christ returned to lead God's children back to God. The church would even appear to betray the Whore, but will be of her. The ten horns are the ten commandments that are falsely used to rule over God's children for a short time. Even as the Christ Consciousness dwells with the children of God, they will be told it is of Satan. Many will fear because they have not been enlightened yet. The Whore will appear to be overthrown and devoured by the beast and his followers. All this is done to pacify the emotional, physical, mental, and spiritual needs of humankind until the time when God's love is understood and received by all.[75]

One of the seven angels showed the downfall of all the teachings that were not of God.

The figures became unclear, and the light started to fade, until there was only darkness where the vision had been. The light

---

[74] [Rev. 17:1-2]

[75] [Rev. 17:3-17]

that came from Michael was all that was left in the night surrounding Joe's back yard. He was glad that the vision was over, sparing him from more tears. For the first time since this whole thing started, Joe was beginning to see real hope for everyone, who would now know that God loves everyone beyond measure. He turned to look at Michael and ask him a few more questions. But the divine guide started to talk, so Joe just listened.

"Write what you have seen here, for it has not yet all come to pass. That which you do not understand now, you will, as you see it happen. What Gary and you do together is blessed, and many are the bricks you make by your hands. Our time is over for now. Be at peace and teach only love. We will speak again."

Michael faded, leaving the darkness of the night to fill Joe's back yard once again. He stared up at the sky, soaking in the stars and thought, *What a wonderful time to be alive. I am so lucky to be able to be a part of all this, even if I don't know how it will all turn out*, he said to himself. Then it hit him, *I'm standing in the back yard with no shoes on, and it's dark. I hope I don't step in anything the dogs left behind.* He tip-toed his way back into the house, very carefully avoiding the doggie land mines.

The next day, Joe arose to reexamine the words he had typed in the wee hours of night before. Once again indescribable feelings rolled through him like the crescendo of a symphony playing at close range. The truth be told, Joe was a bit worn out from all that had transpired. He sat staring at the computer screen thinking to himself, *I can give myself a day off. After all, I am the boss of my own company. Who's going to fire me?* Besides, he had unfinished business with his publisher. Problems had developed over *The Book of Bricks*, and it was time to get it cleared up. Getting dressed, he thought about what needed to be said, asking Poppy what she thought about it. Her big brown eyes looked up as if to ask when the next hug was coming. Chuckling to himself, he rubbed her down, said goodbye to the other three darlings, and climbed into his truck. As he headed the truck toward the freeway, he waved to the front door, causing the furry quartet to shake the neighborhood with their harmonious barking.

Still composing dialog for the meeting with the publisher as he crossed the Bay, Joe piloted his low-flying truck over the bridge, unconsciously exiting off one of the Berkeley ramps. *Damn*, he thought, *This isn't the best way to get to where I want to go in Berkeley. Now I have to go through the Berkeley hills and down Ashby.* While charting the fastest route through the grid of streets, Joe started to think about a woman he once knew, named Holley, who had shown him a spot that overlooked San Francisco Bay. From there, one could scope out the panorama from Berkeley to San Francisco, as well as from San Jose to Marin County. It was one of his favorite places. *Why not?* he thought as he turned off the highway and headed up the road to the top of the hill. The higher up the hill he drove, the more he could see of the Bay. He searched for the spot where he and Holley had stood together some nine years ago, but everything looked so different. As the truck rounded a curve, Joe tried to keep his eyes on the road and still find the best view at which to stop. And there he was. Michael. Standing smack in the middle of the road.

The truck slowed to a crawl, Joe wondering what the angel would do if he just kept going. Would Michael disappear or would he pass right through the truck? An unmistakably impish grin stood out on his face as he imagined the newspaper headline: "Angel Run Over by Pick-up Truck." Thinking better of it, he pulled over to the side of the road, stopped, and eased himself out of the truck. By this time Michael was standing at the cliffside.

As Joe ambled over to his roadside companion, he opined, "Why do I get the feeling taking a wrong exit and getting the urge to come up here was no accident?" His head turned, checking out a car loaded with people drive by, gazing at the view. *They had to have seen us standing here*, Joe thought, *but just kept driving on past us.*

"No. They did not see me, nor did they see you," the angel stated.

"Too cool," Joe grinned. "I am invisible." *The invisible Joe*, he thought with a smile. *The fly on the wall.*

"You know what happens to flies, don't you?" Michael kidded, reading his thoughts.

"Just a thought," Joe said. "You're trying to be funny again, aren't you?"

Michael just smiled and said, "Take off your shoes."

Knowing no one could see him standing barefooted at the side of the road, Joe slipped off his footwear. *Besides, this is People's Republic of Berkeley I am in,* Joe mused, *and stranger things than these are seen every day.* Spotting different sizes of pebbles and stones on the ground, Joe started thinking about his tender feet. And the pavement was hot. That's when he noticed the sun was shining, yet it didn't feel hot outside. The wind was blowing through the trees but Joe couldn't feel so much as a breeze in the air. As he stood up, he noticed the ground felt like grass in that it was neither hot nor cool. *Something tells me I am not in Kansas any more,* Joe joked to himself. Looking back at Michael, he saw the angel gesture toward the Bay with his right arm. All of the land turned to gold and the water became silver as in the previous visions. The blue sky was gone, as was the sun. All he could see was an ocean of silver surrounded by gold that gave off a beautiful light. A sense of anxiousness flooded Joe, not knowing what Michael was going to show him this time. But given the size of this frame, he knew it was going to be big.

"What you see is the beginning. Those that speak of the Endtime speak of *their* end."

Joe looked and saw what appeared to be all the temples and places of worship he had seen measured in the earlier vision. All the places of worship were clumped together so, they looked like a big city. Idols and altars of stone were the foundation, shored up with crosses. Religious artifacts paved the narrow streets that ran from one temple to another. Joe began to understand that all this holy stuff was just so much junk that people believed in.

"The demons you see are the lies that have been told. The foul spirits are the nightmares to which the unenlightened have given life. The birds are the rumors of deceit spread to frighten all who search for truth. The beasts that prey the streets are the hate that each temple teaches of the other."[76]

As Michael talked, Joe could tell how religion after religion had taught hatred of other religions. This hatred of one another

---

[76] [Rev. 18:2-3]

bound them together like the weaving of a web made by a spider gone mad. Fear and mistrust of one another brought them together and made them the same.

"The nations that you see are the lands that give sanctuary to the false teachings, and the kings are those who gave power to those teachings. Buyers and sellers of goods paid tribute to the religions of the land. The voice you hear calling the children is the inner-knowing voice of God's love. You have heard this voice when you did not believe the lies you were told. Others hear it and walk away as you did. Look again to this Mother of Lies as she claims to be the Queen of God's Word. See how she has demanded tribute and said she will speak to God on their behalf. See how she has gorged herself with her own lies. Now look as those lies consume her."[77]

Light, as if it were a fire, fell upon the city—which was she and her lies—and it began to consume the city. Joe stared unblinkingly as altars and the idols that surrounded them crumbled to sand. Scrolls and books of her teachings and commandments melted into pools of a black liquid that burned everything it touched. Those who had not left were coming out of the city like a flood. Nations and their leaders, along with people of business, fled her like the plague to distance themselves from her.

"This is to be the fate that the Mother of Lies will bring upon herself. No evil thing can last in the light of God's love. All who did speak of a final judgment and punishment knew not of what they spoke. It is not God that will judge, for all God gives is love, and all else will wither in the presence of God's love. 'Fear not' was the message given over and over by God's messengers through the ages. 'Fear God' was the message given by religions over the ages."

Joe witnessed all that happened fade away leaving only the silver ocean in his sight. A rumble of a voice came from everywhere around him, drawing his focus into the silver ocean. He saw what looked like a ring of a sound, a wave go across the land announcing the love of God that is in all of us. The wave spread, and each

---

[77] [Rev. 18:4-19]

person it touched became connected to the others it had touched. *This must be the Oneness I have heard about,* he thought.[78]

"Michael, you have shown me many things, but are these the things that are to come, or things of the past, or the present?"

"That which you have seen is as it was and is to be," Michael said. "I have shown you what John was shown. I have shown you what John has done, and will do before we are done. Whether they have been or will be is of no importance. That which you must know, is that they are for you now to see."

Joe responded, "I have been able to follow what you have shown me in your last visits, pretty well. I see just about where we are in relationship to the writings of John in the Bible, but it is getting confusing. Where it talks about the marriage of the lamb, is that the acceptance of the Christ teachings? Along with those who were invited at the Last Supper, also invited was humankind to partake in the love of God that Christ taught?"

"You see most of it, yet not all. In what you call the Last Supper, Jesus gave each bread, as the body of his teachings, and wine, as the blood, being the love in his teachings. He then washed their feet to symbolize that they were no less loved by God then he was. When John fell to the feet of the angel, he was also told not to humble himself in such a way, for he was a child of God—as are you and all of humankind, held in that perfect love."[79]

> *Then came a great awareness of what God has given to mankind, and great joy fell upon mankind. All of God's children were invited to share God's love. When they fell on their knees, they were told not to do that, for they were one with God.*

"Look and see what has been and what will be."

A rider on a white horse appeared. And whoever he was, Joe knew he was no one to mess with. He said to Michael, "This is the Faithful-and-Truth guy, isn't it?"

"This is the true word of God given by Christ, and his armies are all of those who have heard the Word. For the first

---

78 [Rev. 19:6-8]
79 [Rev. 19:10]

thousand years, his words would be heard—and people lived and died for them. These new teachings would open the hearts of humankind, and some would hear and some would not. This is what you and John have seen as a battle between two armies. When in truth it is the battle that one has with their own body and soul."[80]

"I can see what you are saying," Joe said, "but you need to explain about the birds, the lake of fire, and those being killed by the sword. This writing has scared the hell out of people over the years. Besides, you know Gary is going to ask about it anyway.

"**Look and see the birds feed on the flesh, which is the substance that covers the truth. When it is picked away, all that will be left is the truth that is within everyone. You have done this, as have others when they question those that say they are righteous in the sight of God and have God's word. As the birds do, so do the enlightened. When you speak of the beast and of people being thrown into a lake of fire, the rest that you see are not being killed by a sword—as mankind has done. The sword is the Light of Truth that cuts through the lies that are being told. God does not kill. God brings life to the body and soul. This is when all their deeds and actions are brought into the light. The angel that comes with the key to the bottomless pit is a sign there is no ground to build on. The ones you see around the throne are all those who have been enlightened by the teachings of the Christ. We have spoken of the second death before, and that is what you see now, and that is why death has no power over them.**

"**The ignorance has been called 'Satan' by religions, and their teachings are trying to deceive humankind again. The lake of fire that you see is the light of God.**[81]

> *Heaven was open, and a white horse with a rider called Faithful and Truth came forth as the Word of God, and was followed by another rider that spoke of God's love that all heard. Then came an angel calling to the birds to feast on the*

---

80 [Rev. 19:11-16]
81 [Rev. 19:17-20:10]

false teachings. The spirit of mankind would no longer be harmed by these teachings. Then came another angel with a key to a pit and threw Ignorance and Want into the pit.

Then there was a throne, and on the throne were those that gave the truth a thousand years ago. Blessed were those that heard the first time, for they did not fall back into unenlightenment. Now that the thousand years has ended, the false teachings are to be cast out for all times.

The fire is the light in the darkness and the sulfur is the love that heals.

Then Joe was shown a great white throne, and he saw a being of perfect love and light seated on the throne. So great was the presence of the one sitting on the throne that neither the earth nor the heavens could be seen. He saw all the people of the world standing before the throne, and a great book was opened. Then another great book was opened, and he asked Michael what the two books were.

"The first book is the writings of all the religions and what they had to teach. The second book is the Book of Life. As each person that was seen as dead by religion comes forth, their name is found and their blessings, gifts, and deeds are recorded in the book. They are rewarded for these. And if they have fallen short, they are given all that was missing. The first book is used for those who have not been enlightened, so they will be. That which appears to be a judgment is a rewarding. That which is death and Hades is Ignorance and Want. Those found there are enlightened, and all who have been left wanting are filled. Ignorance and Want are cast into the lake of fire to be seen for what they are. All of God's children have been rewarded for their works and are enlightened."[82]

Not one person went into the lake of fire, but all the demons brought into being were cast in. For the first time, Joe was beginning to really see the love of God. All he had been told about God judging

---

[82] [Rev. 20:11-14]

the earth and its people was a lie. *The God that I see is a God of mercy and love for all things,* Joe said to himself. *The God that I am only beginning to know is in all of us. Whatever we have put in front of us to keep us separate will be removed by God's love for us.*

"Look again and see the love of God," Michael said.

This time Joe saw a new world that was clean and fresh with trees he had never seen before. And beautiful flowers. He saw all of the animals that had souls, because their blood was red, just as Michael had told him. He remembered why he had wept the day he was first told this while writing down the material in the scrolls of *The Book of Bricks.*[83]

"Won't that just be grand?" he said to Michael.

"It will only get better from here, Joe. That which I will show you next is the promise that God is. You must go now, but we will speak soon. Be at peace and teach only love."

Michael stepped off the cliff and floated out towards the middle of the Bay. He didn't shrink in size even though he got farther away from Joe. When he reached the middle of the silver ocean surrounded by the gold hills, he started to descend. The hill of gold returned to the way it had been with houses, buildings, and roads winding through them. It was as if everything was being pulled towards Michael. The Bay was starting to return to its watery essence, and Michael began to get smaller. Everything was back to normal, except a little dot of what was left of the vision, and Michael.

Joe was waiting to see it all vanish when he heard Michael ask, "How was that for an exit?"

"Show off," Joe called back. *Of course he could do that, he's an angel.* Joe turned and took a step forward to leave. "Ouch! That hurt!" he complained, stepping on gravel and hot pavement at the same time. *Next time I will put my shoes on before I start walking to my truck,* he promised himself. Whatever he had to talk to the publisher about could wait for another day. Jumping back into the truck, he drove home to write down all that Michael had shown and told him.

---

[83] [Rev. 21:1-4]

WHAT GOD HAS MADE

Word began to leak out to the rest of the Seven as to what was transpiring between Michael and Joe. It was not Joe's custom to act as if he had a special secret to which no one else was privy. If Steve wanted to ask what the latest was with Michael, then it was in Joe's nature to tell him. Kathleen, being the gregarious creature she was, talked with everyone, especially Steve and Joe. Almost all of the Seven had e-mail. It didn't take long for questions to start flying. Usually, when someone was ready to ask, it meant they were also ready to listen. When details were requested, Joe asked for patience, for he wanted to have the whole picture from Michael before giving the Seven the transcription of the new revelations the angel had imparted. Besides, Michael had asked that no one see the codex until "it was time."

In the meantime, Joe and Gary competed to see whose phone bill would be the most outrageous. Even though e-mail was cheap and immediate, Joe's typing skills made it too cumbersome to permit the exchange the two men were enjoying.

"Joe, you know, it seems to me that we are coming to the end of the *Revelation* material. Michael has pretty much answered

all the questions I have. And the ones he hasn't given the particulars to, I can either fill in the blanks or read between the lines. Did he say when he'd be back?"

"Nope. He said what he said. Since the time before last, when he said you'd have questions, he hasn't really asked me to do anything. It's mostly been show-and-tell time."

"No kiddin'. Are you doing OK with all this? I mean, if it were me, I'd be brain-warped by now."

"Actually, I'm doing all right. Those first visions really overwhelmed me, but I seem to have adjusted. Now that I know what John saw, I have an appreciation for what he must've gone through. However, I also feel he should've done what I did."

"What's that?"

"Ask questions. From what Michael has said in the past, John somehow lost his reference when he returned to ordinary reality. He lost the meaning of what was told him and ended having to just write about what he saw. That's happened with me once or twice. And I've had to ask Michael over again to give more clarity so that I could write it down. Some of this stuff is almost impossible to put into words."

"I know what you mean. And I think you've managed well. Part of me feels like I ought to have a thousand more questions to ask. But another part of me feels like I actually understand what's going on here. It's like the message itself is holographic. Not unlike what Jesus did with parables. Whenever Jesus would tell one of his stories, the apostles would bombard him with questions. Half the time he would ignore them, telling them the meaning would be found in their hearts. And the times he did go into explanation, he would only end up getting more questions. I feel this material is the same way. I need to look into my own heart for much of the meaning. I know it's there. There is as much truth in what Michael has given as there is room in each single heart for letting that truth in. Sometimes, I can sit for hours just thinking about one phrase he has handed us. For instance, scholars have been guessing for centuries what the mark of the beast placed on the forehead meant. When Michael revealed it was the misuse of Religions' sacramental baptism, where water is poured over the head, it really shocked me.

I spent a couple of days thinking about that one. And finally, I realized the truth of what Michael was saying. Who are we to say who goes to heaven and who doesn't? I remember when Catholics were taught by parish priests that Protestants couldn't get to heaven because their baptism wasn't legitimate. And I remember Protestant friends telling me that I couldn't get to heaven because Catholics weren't Christians. What a bunch of nonsense. Even though this kind of foolishness has gotten a lot better, the damage is still done. Instead of Protestants and Catholics, now it's Mormons and Buddhists who can't get to heaven, or who aren't Christian. I could sit and read this material forever trying to undo a lifetime of guilt and fear-mongering."

"Let's hope this manuscript from Michael will help," said Joe. The two then discussed their own roles and what more they could do to make sure people were able to read about the truth of *Revelation*. That reminded Joe he still had unfinished business with his old publisher. Wishing each other the best and blessing each other's hearts, the two friends went about their day with the knowledge that the boundary between Heaven and Earth was fading away. Every time Michael visited the line faded even more.

Donna had gone to a work-related training session leaving Joe to "bach" it for a couple of days. Frozen lasagna, ready-made soup, and sandwich fixin's had been spread out in the refrigerator. Even special little treats for the dogs had been left. Joe found himself immediately missing her bright personality, her tenderness for all she touched, and her unapologetic beauty. The sun had not yet set, and a cool breeze was blowing in from the open patio door. Joe began to smell what he thought was the odor of roses wafting in from the back yard. This seemed odd because there weren't any roses in the back yard. *What could the dogs have spilled to cause such a smell?* he wondered. "Better go see what they've gotten into," he mumbled to himself. Pushing the patio door aside, he stepped onto the concrete floor of the covered veranda. The corner of his eyes caught a figure over by the lily pond. With a jerk he recognized his angelic guest. His right hand pulled the patio door closed in slow motion. A sense of apprehension flowed through his whole body. Somehow, he knew this would be the last of the *Revelation*

teachings. What also worried him was that the visions had grown bigger and more overwhelming with each subsequent teaching. What was going to happen this time?

"Where to this time, Michael?" he called to the back of the yard, where Michael stood motionless.

"Come and see that which God has made for all."

Approaching the pond, Joe could already see it changing to gold and silver as it had done before. "Can you leave the gold this time?" he asked, watching the rocks match the luster of the papyrus. The lily pads turned gold and moved to the side of the pond giving way to the liquid silver that was replacing the water. Michael ignored the question. Joe remembered the last time he had kidded Michael about giving him the lottery numbers. "What could I give you that you have want for?" he had asked. "Do you not have everything you need?" It was true. Joe had a blessed life. Sure, a million dollars might be fun to play with: establishing charities, helping the homeless with outreach programs, maybe even getting a new house. But would he be the same Joe? Probably not. He smiled at the thought. He was happy with himself as he stood beside Michael, gazing into the liquid silver. A vision began to form, like a dissipating mist letting him see what had been hidden within its shroud. Although he was looking down into the pond, he felt as if he were looking up through a window.

This window was at the bottom of a valley opening out to the world. Joe saw trees bearing fruits of every kind and flowers so beautiful they took his breath away. Grains covered the lowlands in a field watered by streams and rivers flowing down from the mountains. The air smelled clean like it does after a rain. The water was so pure he could see to the bottom of the rivers and lakes scattered over the lands. All the deserts were gone as was rocky ground where nothing would grow. The world was full of life, a regular Garden of Eden. He then saw what looked like a city descending out of the heavens, not from above but more as if it were an airplane coming in to land.

Like John, he heard a loud voice from the throne saying, **"See, the home of God is with you, God's children. All that is not of love is passed away."** He then heard the voice say, **"See, I**

have made all things new. It is done. The love, I AM, is the beginning and the end. No one will thirst for this love ever again. All that has kept this knowledge from you is gone."[84]

Another of the seven angels with the bowls appeared in front of the two companions, angel and man. The viewpoint changed before them as if they had been moved to a higher vantage. From this vantage they now looked down upon the city.[85]

"Michael, is this the city that God has built for humankind to live in?"

"No, Joe, it is not as a city of buildings. It is a state of being that mankind has risen to."

"It looks like your run-of-the-mill city to me. Maybe cleaner and a lot more spectacular than anything I have ever seen, but it's still a city to me."

"When you were shown Babylon, it was as a city, yet it was not. The city you saw was like a magnet drawing everything into itself."

"I understand that, but for me to describe this to people, as was done in *Revelation*, will produce the same questions. You need to tell me what it all means, if it does mean anything."

"Look as I speak that you will know. This city's radiance is the enlightenment going outwards from within. It's high walls have twelve gates with twelve angels, and on the gates are the names of the twelve tribes. On the eastern three gates are written the names of the spiritual. On the northern three gates are written the names of the mental. On the southern three gates are written the names of the emotional. On the the western three gates are written the names of the physical.

"The walls of the city have twelve foundations, and the names of the apostles are written on these foundations. The walls are the masculine, and the foundations are the feminine of God. The angel holding the measuring rod of gold that you have seen measures the Spiritual, Emotional, Mental, and Physical to show complete balance. The twelve foundations

---

84 [Rev. 21:5-8]
85 [Rev. 21:9-10]

are covered with jewels that are the symbols for the powers of humankind represented by each element within the groupings of twelve. The twelve gates are each a single pearl as a symbol of God's perfect love. The gold streets are a symbol of all paths coming from and leading to God. There is no temple, for humankind is one with God, and that is all there is. No light shines down for enlightenment, for the enlightenment comes from within. All people are of this light and need no other teachings. The gates will always be open to show that, with God's love, none will need protection.[86]

"The angel then shows the River of Life from the love of God. You see both sides of the river. One side is male and the other is female. Each of the twelve trees bears a different fruit and so does each month. The leaves of the trees heal all the nations, and nothing accursed will be found there. The name written on the foreheads is the symbol of the knowledge of God's love.[87]

"You have been shown this as had John been shown. Blessed are the ones that know this, for God is coming soon to reward all of humankind. John fell down to worship at the angel's feet again and was told for the second time that he must not do that. Humankind is to be one with God. 'So why would your kind worship yourselves?' is the message he was given. John was told to let the people do as they do and religions do as they do, for none is beyond the love of God.[88]

" 'I am coming soon, with my rewards to repay all for their works. My love is the beginning and the end of all that is. It comes first and last.' Blessed are those whose robes are washed in truth. For all of God's children will have the right to the Tree of Life. Everything that was unenlightened will be away from God's children, so all will know of God's love. The Christ Consciousness calls out to the Spirit and the Bride, which are the male and female of humankind, to come. Let everyone who hears, come; and everyone who is thirsty,

86 [Rev. 21:10-27]
87 [Rev. 22:1-5]
88 [Rev. 22:6-11]

come. **Most important of all, let everyone that wishes take the Water of Life as a gift from God freely. These things you have seen are as it is, and what you have heard is as you heard."**[89]

The gold faded back to rocks, the silver returned to water, and the vision was gone. Joe turned to Michael and asked about the warning that John had given. "Won't I get a warning to give so these writings are left intact?"

"John set a warning with what he wrote to make sure what he had written was kept. What he saw and wrote held humankind for ransom by his words, and this will not happen again. What will be is no longer in the hands of humankind. That which has been promised by God will come to pass."

"I was expecting a bigger picture for this last part of *Revelation*," Joe kidded, "but I got what you gave me. Does this mean we are finished?"

"We are for now," Michael said. "Yet, you will see this is only the beginning of your work. Give what you have written to Gary for he will have questions. We will speak again soon. Be at peace and teach only love."

Michael faded into the light and was gone. *I have a lot to think about with all this information and the impact it will have. Maybe Gary will have something to ask. I am sure he will.*

---

[89] [Rev. 22:11-17]

THE GATHERING

*D*id Michael say anything yet about the small scroll that is eaten?"[90] Gary asked.

"Never came up," Joe replied blankly.

"Which means he probably said nothing about who the angel was clothed in a cloud with a rainbow over its head?"

"Not a word," admitted Joe.

"Ya know, Joe," Gary said, "Michael seems to have answered all my questions about *Revelation* except a consistent few. Those he never seems to speak of. Other than these remaining questions, I really don't have any new ones."

"It's interesting that you bring this up. We both know that Michael said he'd answer any questions we had. So why not these? Do we just wait?"

Gary sat silently, trying to make up his mind whether to tell Joe the real reason why he had e-mailed these unanswered questions in the first place. "No, I think the waiting is over. I have a sneaky suspicion that the time for questions and talk is over. Remember when Michael said that people would always have

---

[90] [Rev. 10:8-11]

questions? And not to concern yourself with the endlessness of people's doubts? Well, I think this is the reason the remaining questions will never be addressed, because something inside me tells me they have already been addressed, or we already know the answer. You, yourself, said that experiencing the visions gave you an unspeakable awareness of what John the Beloved had really seen some 2,000 years ago. Because of what Michael did with you, having you experience the visions, it seems to me you have become a walking library of actual experience. Maybe you haven't noticed it but I have. More and more you seem to know things before Michael speaks of them."

"I hadn't thought of that. But I don't have any recollection of a rainbowed angel."

Like a school kid holding his breath before diving off the school's high dive, Gary paused, wondering whether to jump into this issue or not. A hissing of breath escaped his lips. "Well, maybe this isn't one of the answers hidden inside you." He didn't want to say any more.

"Are you saying you know who the rainbow angel is?" Joe pressed.

"I don't know. Maybe. How can you tell with these things?" There was no way to kid Joe about this. The two had become such close friends that Joe knew Gary was hiding something. But rather than dig it out of him, Joe decided to let it go for a later time. The two men had shared together the wonders of truth from Michael's decipherings. It was not necessary they divulge their personal secrets as well. For Joe had a few of his own secrets. Something within told him that in the future there would arrive a time for revealing even these personal secrets.

Changing the subject, Joe commente, "So it seems neither of us has any new questions for the Big Guy."

"To be honest," confessed Gary, "I can't think of any question I need an answer to."

"Does that mean we are done with *Revelation?*

This seemed to be one of the clumsier conversations between the two men. Gary knew the angel had been generous in addressing his questions as well as his doubts. But he also knew that

the information from the angel had affected him in ways he could tell no one. It was as if ancient memories had awakened, memories he did not wish to share with anyone. At least not right now. And it was going to be that way regarding the rainbow angel. Now was not the time to tell Joe or anyone else that he had already met this angel. What had happened was deeply personal, life-changing. It was too important personally to share with anyone. "No, I don't think we are done," he countered begrudgingly. "I think there is much more coming, but in a different kind of way. I've been examining this information with a magnifying glass. And I've come to the conclusion that the heavens are giving the earth a second shot at the gifts which originally were bestowed on the seven churches spoken of in the new *Revelation*. It is my belief that these great gifts are being bestowed once again. If you look carefully at the messages Michael gave to each of the Seven and compare them against what the original seven churches were given—and misused—I think you will find that we represent the new symbol for the seven churches of *Apocalypse*."

"What?" interrupted Joe. "You mean the seven of you are a representation of the seven churches?"

"Bigger than that," continued Gary. "Remember that each of the Seven is to go forth and find seven more. I believe that each person in each of the sevens is an archetypal representation of what was intended 2,000 years ago. In other words, we may represent the new effort by Heaven to bring blessing to the Earth once again. In fact, I have matched up each of the seven churches with each in our Seven." As Gary listed the names of each person and the corresponding church, Joe wrote them down. He had to ask Michael about this.

It would be another three days before Michael appeared to Joe. Before he could open his mouth, Michael stated, "It is time for you to gather the Seven." All ears, Joe listened carefully to each word as angel and man discussed what the gathering would mean, what would happen, and how it should happen. *It's finally beginning*, thought Joe as he pondered the consequences of heavenly intervention in the ways of humanity. A shiver traveled through him as he remembered Michael's previous words: "Something wonderful is going to happen."

After Michael had finished his instructions for the gathering, Joe added, "Gary seems to think that each of the Seven represents one of the churches of *Revelation*." He watched as Michael's unblinking eyes looked deep into him. If an angel could ever be accused of smiling, Michael seemed to be doing it.

"Gary is correct," he said simply. "Each of the seven masters is one of the seven churches, as is everyone else. You were told which church each of the Seven belonged to. What you were told was lost to you for a reason, and some of what I have given you will return." It was not uncommon for Joe to forget some information while remembering other information in vivid detail. It was as if Michael somehow assisted his remembering process for some of the teachings while purposely letting his mind forget other parts. "This happened that you might find it with the Seven when you all meet. I will give you enough to get you started and you will find the rest together." What Michael implied was that oftentimes, the real truth is in the journey rather than the idea or the goal. As the angel began to speak about the churches, Joe took notes. He didn't want to forget again.

"Deb is as the church of Laodicea," Michael began. "This church is female in nature and as female it is a mother to all. People of this church have a natural sense of nurturing. This gift is given to both men and women as a path in life and in teachings. They are the ones that care for others as their children. They solve conflicts, understanding both sides with compassion—never making one or the other wrong. Tolerance is the teaching they easily share. People listen to them, learning to live and work together. They are merciful to those who have wronged them and do not seek revenge. The tenderness in their hearts lights the world.

"There is a trap that those of this church must look for in the work they do. So caring are these people that they will not teach, out of the fear they might hurt another's feelings. When this happens, they, themselves, think they are unworthy to give the gift they were given. They become silent and take no action one way or the other. They become poor in spirit and forget they are wrapped in God's love. They cannot see the gift they have been given and find no riches in what they do. The way to free themselves of this

is to give to themselves the gift they have been given. When this is done they will be a light to the world.

"Kathleen is as the church of Ephesus. This church is female in nature, and as female it is a mother to all. This church has been called the church of Mary. Like the mother of Jesus, the men and women of this church are people of divine love. Their gift is the uplifting of others. Their joy is giving of themselves for the happiness of others. They can see the divine light that shines in everyone and everything. They speak of it freely, wanting God's children to play and find the joy of life. They will support others in their work and will defend the greatness of those they love.

"There is a trap for them in their very nature that they must be watchful of. Their desire to lift everyone and everything up to its true magnificence is the nectar of life for them. They may find themselves as a butterfly fluttering from one flower to the next, being lost in the excitement of the flight. As an old bride to a new husband, the fire of the moment burns with passion and the children are forgotten. They forget the gifts they are and look to what they do to make themselves worthy. This church thinks it has need to suffer and do penance if all does not go well. The freedom of those of this church rests in the gifts they are, and only when they see this will they give to themselves. This gift to themselves opens their hearts to the divine love they hold.

"Shari is as the church of Smyrna. This church is female in nature, and as female it is intuitive. The people of this church have a gift for teaching others to see the truth in themselves. The faith they call forth in others opens the door to insight. They know things without being told and have faith in what they know. They lead others to a better place in life, from darkness to light. Where they go, others follow. With God's love for them and others, they are always being enlightened.

"Their trap is made by themselves. They will speak of themselves as unworthy. They will listen to the lies of others about them and believe it is so. They will lose union with their gift and sleep though they are awake. In this sleep, they are truly lost. For they can't lead and they will not follow. For them to awaken they must listen to what God is telling them and know the power they are.

"Mark is as the church of Thyatira. This church is male in nature. The gift of this church is that of a father holding his children in love. The male and female give teachings that are soft and gentle of words. They open their ears and hearts to what the children say. There is no judgment in what they hear. They have only love for those in turmoil, desiring only to help. As a father labors with his body to feed his children, so does this church. The church is the master of the song and dance, creating with its hands things of beauty through which lessons are learned.

"The trap that this church may fall into is that of material things. When they go searching in fulfillment of material and physical needs, they may lose union with the gift they are to give. Their desire for riches leaves them poor in spirit as well as gold. The song they sing is sour, the dance is that of the lame, and the creation of their hands is twisted and unkind to the eye. The escape from this trap is to give their gift back to themselves. God will supply all that is needed for the fatherly care of his children.

"Ben is as the church of Pergamum. This church is male in nature and seeks truth and knowledge to give to his children. Like a father who will find light to guide the way for his children in the darkness, this church is the one that makes the maps. Into uncharted areas, he will explore the best paths, lest his children should come to harm. Of all the churches, this church will find truth in the most cunning of lies. The sum of all wisdom is at their beck and call; and that which is true, they will find.

"The trap for those of this church is lack of faith in themselves. Their desire to be certain of what they say is true will be their undoing. They become internal, losing the reason for their work, and their gift is lost to them. They will give bits and pieces of the truth until not even they can put them together again so that it makes sense. The way out of this trap is for them to give themselves the gift of natural knowing. Connecting to their own consciousness and reason: That is their gift which will set them free.

"Steve is as the church of Sardis. This church is also male in nature, and those of this church are drawn to cure things. That which is bent, they will make straight. And that which is broken, they will mend. They are truly the healers of the churches in the

works they do. Their work consumes them and is nourishment for them.

"The trap they can fall into occurs if they begin to feed on the gift they have. They focus on themselves and are lost in the drunkenness of their own authority, only to find themselves empty and alone. The path out of this trap is to give out of nothing, save for the love of God. The power they have comes from God alone, and no other can fill it. This is the gift they have and must give to themselves.

"Gary is as the church of Philadelphia. This church is male in nature, with the gift of passionate wisdom. As a gift to all God's children, knowledge is the driving force of this church. Teaching is as the very air they breathe. These are the ones who hold the keys of wisdom that unlock the gates to let in the light. They are aware of body, mind, emotions, and spirit, and are in touch with both female and male aspects of themselves. They love all God's children equally, setting none higher or lower than the other.

"The trap for those of this church is the loss of any of the fourfold natures given to all humankind. When the balance is gone, the giver cannot give, and the teacher will not teach wisdom. The escape from this trap lies in the gift of the wisdom and love given back to themselves."

It was a typically gorgeous California summer day as Deb arrived at Kathleen's house. The trip from Colorado had gone smoothly; the rest of her family was enjoying their vacation with old friends not far away. It was August 1, 1997, the first day of the gathering. Deb looked through the open front door and yelled for Kathleen. "Anybody home?" she called out. No answer. How typical of Kathleen to be off and running at God-knows-what, leaving the front door wide open. Deb smiled as she eased herself into the living room. As she stared out the window overlooking the large deck that took up most of the back yard, she thought how this day had come about. The truth of the matter was that it almost had *not* come about. Joe had settled on the date shortly after Michael's last appearance, when Deb had called to tell him about coming out to California for a vacation the first week of August. Joe had taken it as a sign to plan the gathering around that date, since she and Ben lived the furthest away. But Ben was troubled with having to pay plane fare and pay substitutes to cover for him at his second job at temple. Then Shari had chimed in with concerns about a photo shoot she had to do this weekend. The closer the date for the gathering, the more the Seven seemed to find friction with one another or nit-pick about details that seemed to get in the way. At one point, it looked as if the event simply was not going to occur. Finally Joe had to put his foot down, stating in a message he e-mailed to everyone:

> It's not like these problems mean anything. This stream of questions and issues has no weight in what we are supposed to be about. Please pay attention to what's going on here. Whenever something important approaches in our lives, we get nervous. Whether it's a wedding or graduation or the birth of a child, we tend to get preoccupied with what's wrong in our lives, and it prohibits us from accomplishing those things that are really important to us. So either we let this moment slide by or we hang in there. The bottom line is that we have set a date for our gathering. Either you are going to make room in your lives for this, or you aren't. Hope to see you soon.
>
> Love,
> Joe

Like a house of cards swept away by a summer breeze, all objections had disappeared after that. Ben found a cheap flight, Shari rescheduled her shoot, and Deb had made arrangements with her family to let her spend this weekend with these special people, of whom her family knew little. And here she was, alone, in Kathleen's house, wondering where everybody was.

Not long afterwards, Steve arrived laden with groceries, water bottles, and picnic accouterments. "Hi, Deb. Where is everybody?"

"The place is empty. When I arrived, the front door was wide open. You don't think something has happened to Kathleen, do you?"

"Nahh," he said dropping bags on the kitchen counter. "She's probably out jogging. My guess is that she's nervous and needs to run off some steam." Deb smiled. She had heard from Joe that Steve was psychic, sometimes in an uncanny way. He would prove to be right about Kathleen. Ben, who had arrived the night before and, along with Steve, had stayed at Kathleen's house, hoisted a five-gallon water bottle through the door.

"Hi, I'm Ben."

"This is Deb," Steve offered. "Both of you have come a long distance. Deb used to live in the Bay Area." Introductions continued as each of the Seven arrived. Some were nervous, others delighted. Kathleen acted the perfect hostess after showering off the sweat from her run. It was about to begin. Steve was of the mind that Michael might make an appearance, in spite of cautions against such expectations from Joe. Others wanted to know what was supposed to happen. Steve and Ben had stopped by Joe's house the day before and passed on information they had heard from him. The truth be known, Joe wasn't sure *what* was supposed to happen. Michael had given him only so much information and no more. Apparently, it was up to them to make of it what they would. Gary had also stopped at Joe's the previous day, having driven down from Seattle, and had discussed some of the information from the angel with Joe. Everyone was abuzz with questions and excitement as they shared stories, waiting for the last two people to show up.

Joe arrived just as lunch was being prepared, and began setting up the living room the way Michael had instructed. All the furniture was taken out, and seven straight chairs were arranged in careful placement. In front of each chair, Joe place a colored mat, each a different color of the rainbow. Plants were moved to block off the front door entrance into the living room, leaving the dining room as the only access. Gary finally arrived. Everyone but Joe surrounded him and offered introductions along with drink and food. Gary stared at the large bottles of water. Steve seemed to read his mind and explained, "Joe said we'd be drinking lots of water. So we brought alot."

Joe emerged from the living room and hugged Gary like a long lost brother, even though they'd seen one another at Joe's house the day before. He searched Joe's face, finding emotion and seriousness camping out in every facial line. With a smile, he put his arm around the man who Michael had said would be "the servant" to the Seven at this event. "It'll be great, Joe. You'll see." It was time to begin.

In a loud voice, not unlike a town crier, Joe raised a hand to quell the chatter that had taken over the house. "Folks, we will start after lunch." Pointing to the large living room like some kind of tourist guide, he continued, "That room is now sacred space. Do not go in there with anything on your feet. And do not go in unless your feet are washed before entering. This is what Michael told me, and I now tell you. Once you enter, you won't be leaving until we are done. We won't have long sessions, so don't be concerned about holding your water. But take your potty breaks before you enter the living room. Once a session starts, you are to remain in your place until that session ends. I'll tell you more when we all enter the sacred space. Enjoy your lunch."

Everyone crowded around the entrance to the living room to see the curious formation the chairs were in. By this time, Ben and Steve had informed everyone about the two formations Michael had taught Joe, that he was to teach them. Excitement filled the air as the Seven got to know one another. The party atmosphere moved out onto the deck, everyone enjoying the beauty and privacy of Kathleen's back yard. She sat on one of the benches, not eating. Gary sat down beside her and asked if she was OK.

"I'm not feeling too good right now. What a time for this to start. Gawd, I hope I'm not going to miss any of this." Gary looked her over noticing how she wrung her hands like an old washer-woman, her skin fading to a waxy look. He could see she was starting to shiver. Searching his own heart whether he should do anything about this, he decided perhaps it was time to let the others know this other side of him. He looked over at Steve. "Hey, Steve, could you give me a hand here? I think Kathleen could use a little help." Almost dropping his sandwich, Steve quickly moved his large frame over to help Gary escort Kathleen back into the house. And

without saying a word, the two men laid her on the carpet, with Gary placing his hands on her forehead and right arm. "Kathleen, is it OK if we do some work on you? Would you mind?"

"Mind? Are you kidding?" her voice croaked. "I'll take any help I can get."

The two men looked at one another as if reading the other's mind. Steve seemed to know what Gary wanted to do. "Go ahead," he said, "I'll balance you."

As Gary looked across to Steve kneeling next to Kathleen, he silently began offering a prayer of assistance to the Highest. Closing his eyes while simultaneously adjusting his touch, he began to breathe in deep breaths, praying for Kathleen's highest good to come to her. Steve watched as his cohort moved into what he assumed to be a trance. And in turn his hands moved down the full length of Kathleen's body as if scanning for the cause of her discomfort. As his hands returned to the area of her liver, they locked into place, suspended for a while. Then in pirouette fashion, his hands seemed to dance in the air above her body, his fingers making motions hinting at the movement of energy. Steve's eyes stared into Kathleen as if he could see inside her, but what he was seeing was the *chi* or bio-force that surrounds the body. His hands were like shovels digging out blockages, trying to bring her body back into balance. He looked up at Gary once again as his cohort's breathing went from undulating breathing to large breaths that could be heard from across the room. It was as if he had finished running a race and was trying to catch his breath. The two men knelt in place, as one and then two of the Seven started to take notice.

"My goodness, your hands are getting hot," Kathleen volunteered. Steve had finished his hand dance and was now laying open palms on Kathleen's shoulder and left hand. For twenty minutes the three of them turned to statues, except for the soft weeping of Kathleen. Tears trickled down her face as a loving warmth swept through her in waves. She could feel the love as surely as if hugging her own sons. But this time she was receiving rather than giving. She thought about her two sons, both teenagers, who were away for the weekend with friends, almost laughing at the thought of what they'd say if they could see this. They wondered

about her as it was, the way she tried to dedicate herself to her health, the way she provided them with a roof, and the way she lovingly threw her motherhood into their lives while they protested like typical teenagers. Yes, if they saw this now, they'd surely think she'd lost it. A smile replaced the tears as her heart opened up to her boys. She missed them.

At that moment, Gary's breathing returned to normal. He opened his eyes and observed Steve as his large hands once again scanned Kathleen from head to foot. "I think that will do it for now," he concluded. "We can help you out again later if you need it. Just say the word." Steve knew that Kathleen's progress was one of baby steps. As a healer, he knew he could only assist Kathleen in her own healing process. With emphasis on the words "her own."

"You should drink a full glass of water," added Gary, groaning as his fifty-year-old legs protested having been folded under his body for so long. "I need to get grounded," he croaked as he stumbled off toward the kitchen faucet. Cold water poured over his hands as he offered a prayer of thanks.

Steve eased up alongside him as if his head hung in prayer. "That was truly great, my friend. I don't get to have an experience like that very often. The energy was wonderful."

"Sure, Steve, glad you could use your gift like that," was all he said as the coldness of the water ached through his hands. After taking a few more deep breaths, Gary fluttered his hands violently as if trying to flick off pain instead of water, turned off the faucet, and returned to finish his lunch. Steve picked up the remains of his meal and sat down beside his co-conspirator. A few minutes later, Kathleen stepped out onto the deck with water in one hand and a piece of fruit in the other. All eyes turned to her as she smiled at everyone.

"I feel great!" she sung out. "Can you believe this? What a weekend we're going to have." Little did she know how right she was. Eyes paired up in wonderment as if asking fellow gatherers what they had gotten themselves into. No one spoke a word for a few minutes. Kathleen joined Steve and Gary in conversation until Joe stuck his head out the patio door.

"We will begin as soon as everyone is ready."

While waiting for the Seven to finish up and join him at the living room entrance, Joe decided to carry out Michael's last instruction in preparing the sacred space. Walking into the center of the room he raised his hands and in a loud voice invoked, "Bless this room. All that I have not invited here depart away. All that is unholy in spirit or of spirit be gone." He took a deep breath, turned 180 degrees, and continued. "God's work is done here today, and God's children will not be interfered with. Go in peace. Go in love. Depart away in the light of God." There. It was done. It was time to begin the first session.

In bare feet, Joe exited the room and faced the starry-eyed Seven. "There are a few rules we need to go over before you start to enter this sacred space. First of all, you are only to enter this space bare-footed. The first time you enter, I will wash your feet as your servant and God's servant. After that, I will no longer wash your feet because you will wash one another's feet. If you have to leave the room, you must have your feet rewashed by one of the other masters before you re-enter. This is to remind you that you are both master and servant. Michael asked me to have you address each other as master followed by your first name. So Master Shari would address Mark as Master Mark if she wants to talk to him. You get the idea. There is a pitcher of water mixed with oil of myrrh as well as towels next to the entranceway. If you have any questions, save them for the next session. This first session will be short. I will seat you in your places as Michael instructed me. The formation of the chairs is one of two formations that Michael wanted me to teach you. I'm still not sure what they are for. Some of us have discussed what these formations might represent. We'll discuss that in the second session. OK? Let's begin."

Joe stepped inside the entranceway, seriousness taking his face hostage, yet filling him with a combination of mystery and awe. It wasn't the kind of seriousness that causes one to worry, it was the kind of seriousness that tells you not to laugh in church, or to automatically genuflect before the altar at Mass. He stood there waiting for the first bare-footed person to step forward. But no one moved. "Come on, come on," he exhorted, "someone's got to start. Deb and Steve stepped forward while the rest lined up behind them.

Deb looked down at her feet as Joe began pouring a mixture of water and myrrh, her face now matching his with seriousness, as a profound humility traveled up from her feet and into her heart. Softly, Joe chanted, "As I am a servant to you, so must you be a servant to others, ever mindful that I wash your feet to honor the master in you." As Joe reached for the towel, Deb's eyes grew moist with emotion. *How beautiful an idea*, she said to herself. She could feel every fiber of terry cloth on her skin sensitizing her to the fact that she was about to step onto holy ground. As Joe stood up, he leaned over and whispered into her ear, "Fold your arms across your heart and close your eyes." Like a caregiver leading a blind person, Joe escorted Deb to the north side of the room and gingerly sat her in her seat. "You can relax now," he said softly. She looked around the room at the remaining empty chairs and could not help but stare as Joe went to wash Steve's feet. As Steve was seated in the south, the rest began to feel emotion filling the air. No one knew what Joe was doing. The truth be known, Joe didn't know what Joe was doing. He was following Michael's instructions, hoping all this would explain itself.

Ben was placed in the northwest, Shari the southeast, and Mark the southwest. As Joe washed Kathleen's feet, her tears returned once again. She covered her face with her hands as he spoke the words and dried her feet. As she was seated in the northeast, a gladness came upon her while watching Gary take the last chair, in the west. Joe then sat on a short stool in the east, the place of the servant. Leaning over, he switched on the portable CD player. Gentle music mixed with the air as each of the Seven sat in silence. It was a silence the world had long waited for. The kind of silence that wakens the heart with a peace that passes understanding. Beauty fills the soul with such power that what we would call "calm" is more like a stealing of breath. Life teeters on the edge of ecstasy. The mind is deeply stilled, but the body fills with a verve that echoes its way into the heart like a thunderclap trapped within an empty canyon. All one can do is to decide whether to totally let go or fight for strings of consciousness that tie us to this world.

"Are there any questions?" Joe asked, shattering the peace-fulness with his words the way a lightning bolt splinters a giant oak.

No one could speak. Joe explained that he wanted everyone to have a brief experience sitting in the geometric formation to "kind of test things out." He went over some of the material found in Michael's *Revelation,* wanting everyone to understand why they were sitting where they were. He asked Gary to explain to the rest what he had explained to him the day before. Clearing his throat, unable to speak, Gary coughed to get his voice back. Reflecting on how he had felt the previous day, when Joe had shown him the new sacred geometry conveyed by the angel, a sense of ancient knowledge rose up again in him. Feeling almost embarrassed, he stuttered forth the explanation. "In my studies, I have read about certain formations that the Apostles were taught by Jeshua when he walked the earth." Gary's studies had included more than what can be found in books. "This information later became known as the secret teachings. I believe what Michael has given us is part of those secret teachings—what were called the triads. I believe we are sitting in one of the triad formations. Joe has received another geometric formation from Michael, which the angel called the Formation of Giving and Receiving. Like this formation, I believe it is one of the triads that were used for healing. But I'm not sure. Apparently, Michael wants us to figure these things out for ourselves rather than tell us outright."

Discussion filled the room after that. What were they to do? How did this relate to *Revelation?* What did it all mean? As a review, Joe had every person reread the message Michael had given to each, as well as read about the church they represented. Each person was to describe their gift and their trap. After all the questions had been answered, Joe ended the session, encouraging everyone to drink lots of water and use the bathroom during breaks.

The entire group stepped outside the room to chatter about the opening event. "Does anyone have any aspirin?" someone asked. "I've got a splitting headache."

"Me too," came another voice, and a third and a fourth. All but one person were suffering from sharp headaches. "I could really feel the energy in there," Steve reported, "but why do we all have headaches?"

Ben, true to his nature, joked, "Maybe we blew a circuit."

"Or maybe a fuse," Mark countered, "for those of us who live in the older section of the city."

"Wow. I wonder what's going on?" Deb asked in her sweet, gentle way. "Did someone say they had Motrin®, instead of aspirin?" A pharmacy of analgesics appeared as everyone tried to quiet their headaches. While all this was going on, Joe stepped outside for a breath of fresh air and a cigarette. Upon his return to the entrance-way into the sacred space, everyone kidded him about his habit and the heavy tobacco aroma following him.

Steve immediately took the position as the servant to wash Kathleen's feet. She in turn washed Shari's feet. All took turns washing one another's feet as Joe stood with arms crossed, realizing he would be out of a job as soon as the weekend ended. Returning to his short stool, he once again turned on a melodious CD and asked everyone to breathe in and out three times. Everyone was invited to meditate as the music continued. He waited patiently until the last person finished the meditation. Turning the music off, he sat in silence and just stared at everyone. For a good fifteen minutes, everyone sat there wondering what they were supposed to do.

"Does anyone have anything to say?" Joe finally asked. Again he waited as minutes ticked by. "Does anyone see anything?" Heads turned to see if anyone was going to speak. Finally, Steve volunteered. "I don't see anything, but I can definitely detect a presence. He pointed to the center of the formation. "It's right there in the middle."

"OK," Joe said, looking around at everyone. His eye caught Gary sitting across from him. It was obvious something was bothering him. "Gary?"

He said nothing. His face twisted as if he were trying to keep himself from burping.

"I ... I ... well ... yes. I do see something. It *is* in the middle of the formation." His face turned bright red with embarrassment. He had not wanted this to happen. But there it was. Just like the laughing angel he had seen months before, this new angel stood staring at him from the middle of the room. Unlike the laughing angel, it had no wings. "I'm not sure," he continued, "but I think it is Michael." *Oh shit!* he swore to himself, *What is everyone going to think of me? How in*

the hell do I even know this is Michael? Because of the difference in height, this angel being almost seven feet high, and because of the love that poured forth from it, something told him it had to be Michael. "I'm not seeing this the way you see Michael, Joe."

"That's OK," Joe encouraged. "Go on. Is it telling you anything?"

"Yes, it is. I'm not hearing it in my ears the way you do. I hear it speaking in my mind, telepathically."

This is exactly what Joe had hoped for. But getting Gary to reveal what he was seeing was like trying to get a knotted sock away from one of his dogs. "Don't worry about that. Just tell us what is happening."

"Well, the angel is pointing at Kathleen with one arm and me with the other."

"Ahhh," Kathleen bleated out. "No wonder I'm feeling this way. I feel like I've accidentally grabbed hold of a faulty wire and electricity is humming through my body. I thought I was going crazy!"

"The angel tells me to give you a message." At this point, Gary suddenly became aware of himself and what he was doing. Embarrassment flooded him. His mouth hung open like an empty mailbox. She could see he didn't like drawing attention to himself. But this was different. It had to do with her, and she wanted to know what was going on.

"Well, don't just sit there. What's he saying?"

"Uhhh, he says that you have gone through much, and there is still more you will have to face, but he tells me to tell you that your healing will be greatly accelerated. Be open to your own healing, for soon you shall be cured of your lupus." At that, the angel disappeared. Gary slumped in his chair as if trying to hide. But there was nothing to hide, in this place, with these people.

"Oh my God," Kathleen whimpered. "The buzzing is getting stronger. I'm starting to perspire. What's happening to me?" Panic seemed to be taking over as her body began to shake quietly at first, then uncontrollably. "What's happening to me?" she asked again, this time almost crying. Everyone in the room sat stunned, especially Gary. Joe looked over at him, and he back to Joe. *Something should be done*, he said to himself.

"Joe, perhaps we should move into the Formation of Giving and Receiving."

"I had exactly the same thought," said Joe. And without a word he started barking out orders. "Quick, move the chairs out of the way." Deb scurried over to Kathleen to lend support. As her hands touched Kathleen's, she could feel the heat rising off her. Kathleen's breathing was growing labored, but strong. Her eyes were beginning to take on a glassy look.

"What are you guys doing?" she whimpered again.

"Gary, you stand here," Joe ordered. "Steve on the opposite side. You two will be in the focus positions." As each of the Seven was put into the formation, Joe gave instructions as to what to do. He had discussed this with Gary, who somehow knew what this formation was for. As Gary stared at Steve and Steve at him, Gary's heart began to pound. *This seems so familiar,* a voice inside him said. *But why?*

"Kathleen, you stand here in the middle. You are the receiver." He helped Kathleen to stand up, her body still shaking. As Steve and Gary raised their hands on either side of Kathleen, the only thing in the room that could be heard was Kathleen's teeth starting to chatter. Immediately, a heat possessed Gary and grew steadily in intensity. His hands grew red with heat. Sweat began beading up on his head and arms.

"I'm so hot," Kathleen reported.

"You aren't the only one," Gary whispered under his breath. He stared across at Steve who was also turning bright red from the heat. Gary was now feeling so hot that he was starting to worry if something was going to happen to him. Gulping large amounts of air, he tried to funnel off some of the intense energy that was filling him by blowing the air out of his lungs to one side. Ben was standing behind him, and now Ben's hands were feeling like hot pokers. Kathleen's head went back as she started to mildly convulse. As she collapsed backwards, Joe's hands caught her.

"You guys put your hands together under her and lift her up," Joe ordered. Quickly the two men at the focus point responded, lifting Kathleen into the air with Joe holding up her head. She was on fire, and the fire was being felt by all seven participants. Gary felt he was standing in an inferno of light as sweat soaked through

his clothing. Watery beads flowed down his face, neck, and arms. He felt as if on the verge of bursting into flame. Just as he was about to collapse, it all stopped. As suddenly as it had begun, the buzz of electric energy slackened. Steve's eyes opened wide as if questioning whether Gary had felt it.

"OK," was all he could say.

Steve signaled Joe. "Let's get Kathleen into a chair, you guys." The formation broke as others carried Kathleen to a soft chair in the dining room. Gary stood in shock in the sacred space. He could hear Kathleen beginning to titter, then laugh, and eventually erupt into uncontrollable laughter. The other women tried to attend to her, starting, themselves, to laugh at her laughter. Her unstoppable laughter reminded him of charismatic religious gatherings where he had witnessed similar events. They had called it "holy laughter." Whatever it was, he must be the only person who didn't think it was funny. His body numbed against his gyrating emotions. The heat and the sweat were only slowly diminishing.

"I need to ground myself again," he mumbled, heading once again to the kitchen and the cold water of the faucet. As he placed his hands under its frigid stream, stronger and stronger emotions began to fill him—fill him to the point of making him dizzy. Placing his elbows on the edge of the sink to keep himself from falling to the floor, he fought for all he was worth to move the emotions out of his body, into the water, and down the sink. But Niagara Falls itself could not wash off the power of these emotions. Realizing he either had to pass out or quit trying to control the monumental flood of tenderness and love mixing with peaceful bliss, he began weeping. The leak in the dam turned into a flood as his weeping exploded into sobbing. He could not even sob quietly. It was as if all the gladness and the sadness of the entire world was trying to move through him. He shook with emotional weeping. His voice was that of Rachel weeping for her children—no, it was King David weeping with joy in his dance before the Lord. Mark and Steve were visibly alarmed by what they were hearing. Both men hurried over to see if Gary needed assistance. Ben completed the effort as the three men supported their friend as he wailed from the over-whelming emotions pouring out of him.

In the other room, Kathleen's laughter had changed to weeping, as well. Now, she, too, sobbed as if in a duet with Gary. Deb and Shari had no idea what to do except to hug her closely. The house was filled with contrasting silence of those embracing Kathleen and Gary whose voices cried out with unfathomable feelings. It was a minor miracle the neighbors did not call the police. Joe stood quietly by as all this unfolded. He was both delighted and shaken. *What was it that Michael was delivering to them?* he asked himself. What, indeed?

After waiting a half-hour for everyone to compose themselves, Joe called the group to gather again. Gary and Kathleen were the last to enter the sacred space. Neither was sure they wanted to see any more. If this was just the start of the first evening, what would the rest of the weekend be like? Each person in their own way needed to discover that. It was obvious to everyone. As Kathleen's and Gary's feet were washed, each felt the blessing and honor of the others as they entered on common ground. This was more than an individual experience, it was a group encounter with the heavenly. And like it or not, they all had said yes to heaven long before this day. Now was not the time to bail out.

That evening, Deb and Shari also entered into the Formation of Giving and Receiving. And like Kathleen, each had her own deep experience, though not as dramatic as had been witnessed with Kathleen. Each described to the group what she had heard, felt, and realized after the beauteous energy had coursed through, awakening her soul, stirring her with self-awareness. Each discovered a part of herself she had forgotten or never believed in. It was that part which shines with beauty, a kind of undeniable beauty which unleashes an inner light that can never be extinguished. Deb was aware the Navajo had a word for this kind of beauty: *hozro*. And she had felt *hozro* this night. It is the kind of light that touches all humanity when humanity is in harmony with Life.

It was close to eleven before Joe closed the first day of the gathering. After he headed home for a well-deserved night of rest, Deb felt the urge to approach Shari and Kathleen. After Shari had entered into the Formation of Giving and Receiving, Deb had felt a connection with both women she could not quite understand. She

knew that all three were in *hozro*, touched by the sacred bond of harmony. It was a triangle of light, a sacred triad, flowing between them. She wanted all three of the women to return to the center of the sacred space. Initially, her rational mind interfered, telling her it was late, everybody needed their rest. It had been a long and emotional day. But the feelings flooding her could not be dammed up, and finally she approached the other two women. Both Kathleen and Shari acknowledged feeling the same as Deb about the powerful force that seemed to connect them. At Deb's suggestion, the three washed one another's feet and returned to the center of the room where they all had been touched by the forces of heaven. All three huddled together with arms around one another. The light within them seemed to surge and propel their souls up from their bodies like swirling birds rising in flight. Each whispered about the sensation of looking down upon the triad, their spirits joining in oneness. For the longest time their bodies gently swayed in unison, words unspoken as tears trickled across their smiles. It was a night never to be forgotten, a night where the feminine moved into symbolic oneness as if foretelling a living prophecy to the world itself.

The women understood little of what they were sharing. It would be months later before the meaning of their celebration would speak to them. Each woman would inevitably realize the necessary role the feminine plays in the Divine Plan. In the future, the angelic realm would convey messages as to the role of the feminine in bringing healing to humanity and, ultimately, to the Earth. It was time for the world to recover from self-inflicted wounds propagated by a people blinded by their inability to recognize their own giftedness. What the three women commonly shared this night would be understood only in hindsight, as heaven would continue to reveal new teachings. They would come to realize how the blending of the masculine and the feminine, in *hozro*, is necessary in returning Eden to the Earth, borne on the wings of heaven.

While the women continued in their reverie, the men went their own ways, Gary sitting outside under a sumac tree hoping the night air might cool him down. His logical mind strained, trying to

figure out what had just transpired. Part of him sought to hide from his own embarrassment, while yet another part hummed with awe. Had some healing force caused this? Would Kathleen be cured of lupus? Or had the angels simply joined the Seven in a celebration of oneness, thereby unleashing both joy and profound emotion? Like the women, his questions would find answers months afterwards. All would face the inescapable confrontation either of discovering heavenly truths through earthly giftedness or of facing difficult lessons through their own individual traps.

As Gary continued in his thoughts, Ben and Steve compared ideas of what they thought was happening to the group. Mark enjoyed the starry night, his eyes serving as a testimonial of the coming together of Heaven and Earth this very night. No one felt like going to bed. Everyone felt giddy, as if something within each of them whispered, *This is the beginning. The great curtain between the natural and the supernatural has been rent. The realm of angels shall no longer be divided from humanity. All shall be One within the bosom of God.*

Joe arrived home sometime past midnight. He was drained, but could not sleep, even after trying to satisfy Donna's desire to hear what had happened. It was obvious by the look on his face that *something* had happened. As he sat in his office staring at the wall, light began to fill the space. It was Michael. Joe could only stare at the angel, unable to utter a word. Too much had affected him. His eyes said it all as they poured out thank-yous to his angel companion. "Joe, you have done well, as have the seven masters." Michael's praise could not make him feel any better than he was already feeling. He listened as the divine messenger bequeathed one more mystery to be taught to the Seven at the end of the gathering. Joe smiled, knowing the significance of the angel's trust. He and the seven master souls had learned more than heaven had assumed they would in this short amount of time. It was a good sign not only for them, but for all of humanity. Perhaps humankind was, indeed, ready to hear the teachings from the angel.

Joe finally felt able to sleep. While rearranging his pillow first one way then the other, he began to reminisce about all that had led up to this night. The next day he would discover an entire

new phenomenon as the men would enter into the Formation of Giving and Receiving. But that is another story for another day. Ben would be changed forever, his clever mind to be balanced by an open heart that would touch many. Steve would learn the lesson of his life, nearly sabotaging the entire purpose of his being called by heaven. Gary would be thunderstruck once more as Kathleen would bring healing to him in a completely different way than he had served as an instrument for her. Months from now, Kathleen's physicians would find no trace of her lupus—and no explanation as to its disappearance. She was cured, that was all they would be able to say. And Mark would continue to be Mark, ever the bridge-builder. Only later, his bridges would span more than cultural differences, they would span spiritual gulfs. These Seven would represent a never-ending story, given by Heaven to the people of the Earth.

Any who hear these words of the angel, who choose to enter into the Last Baptism, can drink from the cup of moonlight given to Joseph Crane. And as you drink from this cup, you may wonder as Joe did whether you are drinking of moonlight—or of moonshine that will steal your senses. Though others may wonder who filled this cup, it has become obvious to those who are filled by its light that this drink came from the hand of Heaven. That hand was given a name by Joseph Crane, and he called it "Michael."

Although the three mysteries given to the Seven cannot be put on this page, any may inherit these mysteries by crossing the path of one of the Sevens. For the seven men and women who shared this night with Joe Crane would be called to find seven more, and that seven, seven more. The mysteries are for anyone's ears, but for no one's pen. Look only for the light that shines in people, and you may have the chance to know what is meant for all of earth to know: We are not only masters of our destiny, we are masters of our souls. To fully know our souls is to find oneness with God. And in that Oneness lies the path back to Eden. Who of us would deny ourselves such an opportunity?

As sleep crowded around Joe, his mind played back the vision when he had heard the loud voice from the throne say:

 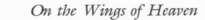
See, the home of God is with you, God's children. All that is not of love is passed away. See, I have made all things new. It is done. The love, I AM, is the beginning and the end. No one will thirst for this love ever again. All that has kept this knowledge from you is gone.

To be continued ...

Part V: The Seven Gateways:
The Angelic Book of Healing

Direct all correspondence, scheduling of interviews or speaking engagements with G.W.
Hardin to the following address:

DreamSpeaker Creations
P.O. Box 16134
Missoula - MT 59808

Hardin's interviews or speaking engagements
can be chosen from the following topics:
- The writing of *The Messengers*
- The writing of *On the Wings of Heaven*
- Angelic prophecies of a new world
- The role of gays and lesbians in the
  Divine Plan
- Indigenous societies and the spiritual
  orientation of gays and lesbians
- The new healing paradigm

Direct all correspondence, scheduling of interviews or speaking engagements with Joseph Crane to the following address:

Joseph Crane Spiritual Development
P.O. Box 700412
San Antonio - TX 78270

JCraneBook@aol.com

Joseph Crane's workshops can cover any of the following topics:
- Teachings from the angelic realm
- The writing of *On the Wings of Heaven*
- The angelic Book of Healing
  and the Gate of Grace
- The seven archetypal gifts and
  the Well of Souls
- Finding one's spiritual compass
- The Book of Bricks and how
  to build one's spiritual mansion
- Decoding the Book of Revelation—
  a promise beyond Eden